INNOVATIVE DUI TRIAL TOOLS

BY JONATHAN DICHTER

HIGHLIGHTS

With this update, new author *Jonathan Dichter* shares some of his most successful DUI trial strategies.

CHAPTER 1 PRE-TRIAL DISCOVERY AND MOTION PRACTICE
Three new motions to suppress FST evidence:
- Motion to Suppress FST Evidence—Lack of Relevance, §1:82
- Motion to Suppress FST Evidence—Lack of Strict Compliance with NHTSA Standardization, §1:83
- Motion to Suppress Refusal of FSTs, §1:84

(NEW) CHAPTER 2A JURY SELECTION: A STORYTELLER'S APPROACH
This method of "collaborative" jury selection offers a way to find the jurors who are on your side and inspire other jurors to move to your side, right from the start. With it, you can get jurors to:
- Internalize the presumption of innocence. §2A:21
- Agree to be unfair and partial. §2A:22
- Internalize proof beyond a reasonable doubt. §2A:23
- Understand the meaning of beyond a reasonable doubt. §2A:24
- Like you and willingly reveal their biases. §2A:25
- Understand why the Defendant is not testifying and not hold it against her. §2A:26
- Describe good driving so you can later connect their descriptions with your client's driving. §2A:27
- Doubt breath/blood testing accuracy. §2A:28

CHAPTER 4 CROSS-EXAMINATION
- "Baby stepping" a cop into saying your client is sober. Here's an outline with sample questions for tying an officer to the police report. The goal is to establish right away that if it happened, it's in the report. If it's not in there, it didn't happen. §4:04
- A strategy for winning refusal cases without the defendant's testimony. Common wisdom is that when your client refuses to provide a breath sample, the jury needs to hear from him. Instead, try this refusal strategy that has worked so well for the author that he has lost only two refusal trials in 10 years. §4:49

CHAPTER 7 CLOSING ARGUMENTS
- Seven slides for combining the "baby stepping" portion of the officer's cross examination with burden of proof arguments, §7:114
- Eleven slides on burden of proof and reasonable doubt. §7:01

CHAPTER 9 DRIVING UNDER THE INFLUENCE OF DRUGS
- Marijuana DUIs. Focusing on the pre-arrest investigation portions of a marijuana DUI, the author shows you how to use the NHSTA manuals and the lack of quality studies correlating marijuana consumption with driving impairment to challenge the prosecutor's case. §§9:60-9:64

AND MORE!

We Welcome Your Feedback

Our most useful source of improvements is feedback from our subscribers, so if you have any comments, we would be delighted to hear from you.

Revision Editor
James Publishing, Inc.
3505 Cadillac Ave., Suite P-101
Costa Mesa, CA 92626

Visit us on the Internet at www.jamespublishing.com.

How To Access Your Digital Forms

Included with your copy of this book is access to all its forms in digital format. So you can easily open and modify the forms, **we have replaced our jamesforms.com website and our old CDs with a convenient ZIP file of Word documents.**

Access is easy.
If you purchased this title on jamespublishing.com, a link to download the ZIP file should have already been delivered to your email inbox. Be sure to add customer-service@jamespublishing.com to your safe sender list so this message doesn't land in a spam folder. You can also access the download link at any time by **logging in at jamespublishing.com and clicking My Account** in the upper right-hand corner.

No account yet? No problem.
If you do not yet have a jamespublishing.com account, or you are having trouble, please contact customer support at **1-866-725-2637** or customer-service@jamespublishing.com. We will get you setup right away.

How to unzip the file:
Once you download the ZIP file, you need to extract the files onto your system. Typically, files are downloaded into your Downloads folder unless another directory was specified. Follow these steps to unzip:

1. **Double-click the ZIP file.** In Windows XP or newer and Mac OS X, you can double-click the ZIP file and it will open in a new window. You can then copy the contents to another folder. OS X will create a new folder next to the ZIP file when you double-click it, but may not open it automatically.

2. **Right-click the ZIP file.** In Windows you can right-click the ZIP file and select *Extract All…* or *Extract Here*. Extract All will allow you to set a path for the extracted folder to go, and Extract Here will decompress the folder and leave it in the same location as the ZIP file.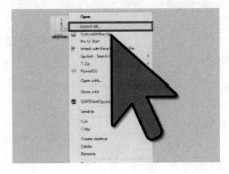

Can I share my digital forms with others?
No. Our forms are copyrighted, and they are licensed to a single individual book purchaser for his or her use only. It is unfair to our book authors if their forms are freely distributed, so please honor their hard work by not sharing their forms. Thank you for understanding.

(This page intentionally left blank.)

INNOVATIVE DUI TRIAL TOOLS

Jonathan Dichter

Bruce Kapsack

James Publishing

Contact us at (866) 72-JAMES or www.jamespublishing.com

Related Titles:
Attacking and Defending Drunk Driving Tests
California Drunk Driving Law
Criminal Defense Tools and Techniques
Relentless Criminal Cross-Examinations
Texas DWI Manual

Revision Editor
James Publishing, Inc.
3505 Cadillac Ave., Suite P
Costa Mesa, CA 92626

First Edition, October 2008
Revision 1, February 2010
Revision 2, June 2011
Revision 3, February 2014
Revision 4, June 2019

ABOUT THE AUTHORS

Jonathan Dichter is the managing attorney and founder of Dichter Law Office, PLLC, a small firm north of Seattle, Washington practicing exclusively in DUI defense. He received a Bachelor of Arts in the American Political System from the University of Akron, Ohio. He received his juris doctorate from the Seattle University School of Law cum laude. After graduation from law school, Jonathan was hired by a contract public defender's office to handle the public defense for a suburb of Seattle, where he handled hundreds of misdemeanors and gross misdemeanors solo and with part time support staff.

In 2009, after working as a private associate attorney for a few years, Jonathan opened Dichter Law Office, PLLC, which focused at the outset on low level criminal offenses, such as DUI and minor assaults. After a few years, Jonathan focused his practice exclusively on DUI defense and become a sought after resource and teacher for other attorneys and organizations. His skillset and background as a performer and storyteller bring a new and transformative spin into the courtroom during DUI trials, and the level of polish he applies to these cases in their presentation can rival the big budget week long felony trials you see on television. But he does it on a smaller scale, and in a day or two.

As a leader in the field of DUI defense, Jonathan has achieved many accolades. Jonathan is:

- A NHTSA qualified Instructor of Standardized Field Sobriety Tests (SFSTs) under the guidelines of the International Association of Chiefs of Police (IACP) and the National Highway Traffic Safety Administration.
- A NHTSA qualified graduate of both the basic SFSTs course and the Advanced Roadside Impaired Driving Enforcement (ARIDE) program.
- The author of "The DUI Survival Guide: For Good People Who Made Simple Mistakes."
- A frequent contributor to the Washington Association of Criminal Defense Lawyers (WACDL) DUI Newsletter.
- A lecturer and teacher to:
  - Defense lawyer organizations.
  - Public Defense Agencies.
  - County Bar Associations.
  - State Certified Treatment Agencies.
- Forensic Sobriety Assessment Certified.
- A contributor to the WACDL Defense magazine.
- The author of an article about client respect and care that is required reading in some public defense agencies in Washington.
- Frequently the highest rated speaker at conferences he teaches at.

When he is not defending clients or teaching attorneys how to more effectively advocate, Jonathan is an accomplished speaker, actor, improviser, comedian, singer, magician, author, and more. His passion and skills with storytelling led him to the personal revelation that dramatic presentation and thematic storytelling were not only possible in DUI (and indeed criminal) defense, but in fact, necessary to bring those skills to the next level. He's also the proudest Dad on Earth.

Bruce Steven Kapsack, author of the previous editions, was the senior partner of Kapsack & Bair, LLP, an AV rated firm practicing exclusively in DUI/ DWI defense. He received his Bachelor of Arts in Interdisciplinary Studies from Plymouth State College and his Juris Doctorate from American University. After graduation from law school, Mr. Kapsack was hired by the Bronx Public Defender where he rapidly rose to the position of Senior Trial Attorney. During the five years he was there, he became one of the top trial attorneys in that office.

After moving to California and opening his own practice, Mr. Kapsack became the Senior Attorney for the Office of Citizen Complaints, the San Francisco Police Department's Internal Affairs Office. His success there resulted in a Commendation from the Board of Supervisors upon his departure.

As a pioneer in the field of DUI/DWI defense, Mr. Kapsack has accomplished many firsts. He is:

- The first attorney in California to take and pass the American Bar Association's Board Certification exam for DUI Specialization.
- The first attorney in California to become an Instructor of Standardized Field Sobriety Tests (SFSTs) under the guidelines of the International Association of Chiefs of Police (IACP) and the National Highway Traffic Safety Administration.
- The first attorney in California to qualify as a DRE under Drug Ensic Systems.
- The first and only attorney in California to own and operate the Draeger 7410 and 7110 breath machines.
- The first attorney in California to own, operate and use in court an Intoxilyzer 5000 breath machine.
- The first and only attorney in California to depose Dr. Marceline Burns, the person responsible for the establishment of standardized field sobriety tests.
- One of the first attorneys to be trained as a user and maintenance technician of the Alco-Sensor IV hand-held roadside breath machine.

Mr. Kapsack has written extensively about DUI/DWI defense. He contributed to *California Drunk Driving Laws* by Ed Kuwatch (James Publishing) and wrote the yearly supplements from 2003 to 2007 for *California Drunk Driving Defense* by Lawrence Taylor (Thomson-West Publishing), the two seminal works in the field in California. He has written for DUI/DWI publications in other states including New York, Nebraska, Ohio and nationally for *The Champion* magazine.

EDITORIAL ADVISORY BOARD

Mark A. Foster
Foster & O'Daniel, LLP
Evansville, Indiana

Jeffrey B. Hayden
Attorney at Law
Redwood City, California

Douglas Hazelton
Attorney at Law
Bloomington, Minnesota

Evan M. Levow
Attorney at Law
Cherry Hill, New Jersey

Michael I. Littman
Attorney at Law
San Diego, California

Russell J. Matson
Attorney at Law
Braintree, Massachusetts

Andy Sotiropoulos
The Law Offices of
Andy Sotiropoulos & Associates, Inc.
Orland Hills, Illinois

EDITORIAL STAFF

Managing Editor:
Donna M. Cole, J.D.

Production:
Julie Anne Ines, J.D.
Alexandru Oprescu

ACKNOWLEDGEMENTS

Here, I'm supposed to talk about the people who've helped me make this happen and inspired me along the way personally and professionally. It's impossible to mention every single person whose influence and support helped create the perfect storm that allows me to share these strategies with you. But, since doing the impossible is what we do every day in defending drunk drivers, let's give it a shot.

First, I have to thank my mother and father. Neither of them were lawyers. Both of them were movie and theatre lovers. They created the landscape I grew up in and showed me how powerful the stories told by strangers can be. They sat with me as I cried when E.T. was fighting for his life, cheered when Inigo Montoya finally achieved his revenge, and found strength with me when Lt. Dan Caffey finally got Colonel Nathan R. Jessup to admit he ordered the code red.

My first supervisor as a legal intern, David Kirshenbaum, told me on my first day on the job: "All of us possess two characteristics in common—fragile egos and long memories. Remember that." I always have. Thanks Dave.

When I became a lawyer, I worked as a public defender for James Schlotzhauer. At our first holiday dinner in 2003, he had just seen me try one of my first cases for his office. He gave me a small handwritten slip of paper that to this day, wrinkled and battered, I still keep in my wallet. "Jonathan—Stay focused and motivated and you'll be unstoppable."

In 2009, I opened my own firm, and my DUI defense took a quantum leap forward through the guidance of two men: Mark Garka, an attorney who would also become my landlord and dear friend, and Thomas Missel, a private DUI investigator who showed me just how powerful knowing a NHTSA manual can be. Speaking of NHTSA, the next quantum leap came when I finally met and was taught by the incomparable Bob LaPier, who taught me SFSTs so thoroughly that I've taken three more courses from him and would never study under anyone else.

I'll specifically mention the inspiration and wisdom I've learned through the years from some select mentors like: Diego Vargas, Bill Kirk, Jon Fox, Francisco Duarte, George Bianchi, Mark Mestel, Anna Goyhkman, Virginia Landry and James Nesci to name just a few. There are literally hundreds of lawyers who I've known over 15 years in practice who I've learned from, chatted with, argued about, blissfully stolen content from, and more. There's no way to name, or indeed even remember them all. As often as possible, if I'm able to do so, I'll give credit to who I can—but even then, I can't promise I'm not just naming the person I stole an idea from and not the person who originally thought of it. That being said—these ideas and strategies are now fully yours for the stealing—so I'll just pay it forward by writing this book.

Finally—I have to recognize my families. Yes, I said families. First, the Dichter Law Office family—my associate Rachel, whose attention to detail makes her as formidable a negotiator and litigator as I've ever seen—and Andi, my law clerk, who never stops asking how she can help and what more she can do. Secondly, Alexandra and Elizabeth—my home, heart, and soul. I can't say the right things, so I'll just say thank you for existing.

DEDICATION

To Elizabeth—you inspire me to be a better dad.
To Alexandra—you have made me a better man.

To all my teachers and colleagues and clients and opponents and Troopers and Deputies and jurors and judges—I have learned something from each one of you.

I'll pass it all on to make us all better at our jobs.

Jonathan Dichter

TABLE OF CONTENTS

EXPANDED TABLE OF CONTENTS

CHAPTER 2A   JURY SELECTION: A STORYTELLER'S APPROACH

CHAPTER 4:   CROSS-EXAMINATION

APPENDIX A: THE DISTRICT ATTORNEY'S MANUAL

APPENDIX B: DEPOSITION OF MARCELLINE BURNS

APPENDIX C: ARREST VIDEO ANALYSIS FORM

CHAPTER 1

PRE-TRIAL DISCOVERY AND MOTION PRACTICE

I.   INTRODUCTION

The telling of your client's story is the most critical thing you must learn to do effectively in front of a jury. You can't tell a story unless you know the facts of that story. It's of particular importance to know the "high points"—the big moments—what, in theatre we might call the "beats" of a story. You already know most of these instinctively because you're in the practice of DUI defense. Your client was stopped—beat 1. Your client was contacted—beat 2. Your client was evaluated—beat 3. Your client was arrested—beat 4, and so on. Conceptualizing the case as a series of story beats allows you to easily and effectively separate your preparation into "chapters" and group your thoughts. It also allows you to know what facts just don't matter ultimately. Does it matter that your client drove a blue SUV and the officer noted it was black? If it does—then find a way to exploit that. If not, ignore it. You only have so much storytelling credibility and time from the start of your case to the finish, and if you waste it on things that don't matter, you're doing yourself, your story, and most importantly, your client, a disservice.

The following materials are presented with the hopes that they will encourage the readers to think outside the box. By no means are the included motions exhaustive. In fact, simpler motions, such as standard Motions to Suppress have been left out as they are fairly state-specific and readily available elsewhere.

This chapter consists of three parts: pre-trial discovery requests; discovery motions based on compulsory process; and motions in limine (both productive and prohibitive). Each part is preceded by a synopsis of legal principles upon which many of the included motions are based. Additionally, you will find many case quotes and citations that provide for the basic principles of obtaining information and presenting it in trial.

See **Appendix A,** *The District Attorney's Manual* for the prosecution's approach to pre-trial preparation and its strategies for responding to defense discovery motions.

II.   PRE-TRIAL DISCOVERY REQUESTS

A. General Points

§1:01   Legal Principles

Under the Due Process Clause of the Fourteenth Amendment, criminal prosecutions must comport with principles of fundamental fairness. The U.S. Supreme Court has long interpreted this standard of fairness to require that criminal defendants be afforded a meaningful opportunity to present a complete defense. To safeguard that right, the Court has developed "what might loosely be called the area of constitutionally guaranteed access to evidence." *United States v. Valenzuela-Bernal*, 458 U.S. 858, 867 (1982). These constitutional privileges require that the prosecution deliver exculpatory evidence into the hands of the accused, thereby protecting the innocent from erroneous conviction and ensuring the integrity of our criminal justice system. *California v. Trombetta*, 467 U.S. 479, 485 (1984).

A defendant has a constitutionally protected privilege to request and obtain from the prosecution evidence that is either material to the guilt of the defendant or relevant to the punishment to be imposed. *Brady v. Maryland*, 373 U.S. 83, 87 (1963). In *Brady*, the defendant was convicted of murder and sentenced to death. He claimed that, although he had participated in the crime, a companion had killed the victim. Before trial, his attorney had asked the prosecutor for statements made by the companion. The prosecution failed to disclose one statement in which the companion admitted to the murder. The *Brady* Court held that "the suppression by the prosecution of evidence favorable to an accused upon request violates due process where the evidence is material either to guilt or to punishment, irrespective of the good faith or bad faith of the prosecution." *Id.*

Even in the absence of a specific request, the prosecution has a constitutional duty to turn over exculpatory evidence that is material, *i.e.*, that would raise a reasonable doubt about the defendant's guilt. *United States v. Agurs*, 427 U.S. 97, 112 (1976). In *Agurs*, the defendant was convicted of stabbing her lover to death. She claimed self-defense. The defense did not ask the prosecution for the decedent's criminal record, and the prosecution did not voluntarily provide it. The decedent's criminal record revealed that he had one conviction for assault and two for illegally carrying knives. The Court concluded that this evidence did not meet the materiality standard.

In *California v. Trombetta*, 467 U.S. 479, 488-490 (1984), the defendant challenged his drunk driving conviction on the grounds the police had not preserved his breath sample so that it could be independently tested. The Court held that the state's duty to preserve evidence is limited to evidence that might be expected to play a significant role in the suspect's defense. To meet this standard of constitutional materiality, the evidence must both possess an exculpatory value that was apparent before the evidence was destroyed and be of such a nature that the defendant would be unable to obtain comparable evidence by other reasonably available means. Neither of these conditions was met. According to the Court, the evidence was unlikely to be exculpatory because the procedures followed in running the breath test rendered the results reliable. And the defendant had other means to demonstrate innocence. Under California law, DUI defendants have the opportunity to inspect the machine and its weekly calibration results and the breath samples used in the calibrations. These data could be used to impeach the machine's reliability.

§1:02   Use of Discovery Request

I cannot stress enough the importance of diligent use of discovery to obtain evidence that can be used to impeach the breath, blood, or urine test results. In the past couple of years experts and attorneys alike have found that prosecutors or state experts hide data regarding underlying software, faulty error messages and inaccurate test results. The labs in Missouri, Wisconsin, and the Los Angeles Sheriff's Department have done this. In Arizona, hundreds of cases were dismissed because of this type of hiding of evidence. *See State v. Meza*, 203 Ariz. 50, 50 P. 3d 407 (App. 2002); *see also State v. Chun*, Case No. A-96-06, N.J. Sup. Ct. (March 17, 2008).

During a scandal regarding the Washington State Toxicology Lab and its former head, King County Judges in Washington suppressed *all* chemical tests because defense discovery showed that the toxicology lab was so rife with issues that the evidence is not trustworthy. *See* "King Co. WA judges: State breath tests in DUI cases are no good," Gene Johnson, AP Legal Affairs Writer. (The lab has since renewed its accreditation and the court has reversed its decision.)

Attorneys representing DUI defendants in Florida have sought from the state the software that operates breath machines. The state has refused to turn it over because the manufacturer claims it is a trade secret. Judges in some Florida counties have suppressed test results from these machines finding that the manufacturer's refusal to turn the information over violates *Brady*.

B. Discovery Demand

Note: Your jurisdiction may have different rules and statutes, but as an example, I include my discovery demand in all DUI cases. It is worth noting that prosecutors do not always comply with all these requests.

It is important to know what you have asked for, what you have received, and what you are entitled to.

§1:03   Sample Discovery Demand: All DUI Cases (Washington State Example)

DISTRICT COURT OF _____
COUNTY OF _____, STATE OF WASHINGTON

Plaintiff, _____ vs. _____ Defendant.	Case No.:_____ NOTICE OF APPEARANCE DEMAND FOR DISCOVERY

TO: The Clerk of the Court; and

TO: The Prosecuting Attorney

PLEASE TAKE NOTICE that the Dichter Law Office, PLLC hereby enters its notice of appearance as attorney for the Defendant in this cause. Defendant demands a Jury Trial and objects to the arraignment date as untimely. Defendant requests a bill of particulars pursuant to CrRLJ 2.4(e) and 4.1(d) and further makes the following demands for discovery:

1. Copies of any and all police or investigative reports and statements of claimed experts made in connection with this particular case, including results of physical or mental examinations and scientific tests, experiments, or comparisons made in connection with the defendant's arrest;

2. Copies of any and all officer's notes regarding this incident, including but not limited to field notes, blue book notes and rough notes;

3. The names and addresses of any and all persons whom the plaintiff intends to call as witnesses at the hearing or trial, together with any and all written or recorded statements, and the substance of any oral statements of such witnesses, together with a summary of the expected testimony of any witness the plaintiff intends to call if the substance of the expected testimony is not contained in the materials otherwise provided.

Defendant requests the specific name of the BAC Technician and State Toxicologist who will testify in the above captioned matter. These requests are necessary to properly prepare the defendant's defense. We request that these names and all other relevant discoverable material be provided to the defense within 21 days of receipt of this request. This request is pursuant to CrRLJ 4.7(a)(1) and (2).

4. Copies of any and all forms read to or signed by the defendant containing information regarding his/her rights under CrRLJ 3.1(c)(1) and (2) and/or RCW 46.61.506 and 46.20.308, including information regarding the claimed basis for the arrest of the defendant and allegedly giving rise to the mandatory provisions of RCW 46.20.308;

5. Copies of any written or recorded statements and the substance of any oral statements made by the defendant or by any co-defendant if the trial is to be a joint one;

6. A list of, copies of, and access to any books, papers, documents, photographs, or tangible objects which the Prosecuting Attorney intends to use in the hearing or trial;

7. A list of all items or things which were obtained from or belonged to the defendant, regardless of whether the Prosecutor intends to introduce said items at hearing or trial;

8. A description of any other tangible evidence which the plaintiff intends to use at the hearing or trial which are not contained in the materials otherwise provide pursuant to these demands;

9. Copies of or access to any recordings or **video tapes** made of the defendant for viewing by the defendant and/or his attorney prior to trial;

10. Any record of prior criminal conviction known to the Prosecuting Attorney of the defendant and persons whom the Prosecuting Attorney intends to call as witnesses at the hearing or trial;

11. Any electronic surveillance, including wiretapping of the defendant's premises or conversations to which the defendant was a party and any record thereof;

12. Any information which the Prosecuting Attorney has indicating entrapment of the defendant;

13. Any material or information within the Prosecutor's knowledge which tends to negate the defendant's guilt as to the offense charged;

14. The specific names and contact information of any and all expert witnesses whom the Prosecuting Attorney will or may call at the hearing or trial, the complete subject of their testimony, and any reports they have submitted to the Prosecuting Attorney, any studies they intend to rely on at trial, or any other tangible documents to be used at trial; Defendant further demands that such expert witness be produced for testimony at trial;

15. List and describe all specific training and/or participation in group and individual experiments, seminars, workshops or any other instructional process from which <u>any</u> witness obtained information, sought to be introduced by the prosecution, regarding the effects of alcohol and/or drugs upon: (1) human motor responses; (2) the performance of divided attention tasks or field sobriety tests; and (3) the ability to operate a motor vehicle. This includes, but is not limited to: the dates of any NHTSA classes taken by any arresting officers, the dates of any manuals issued to those officers, and any syllabi for any additional classes taken by any officer or witness for the State. Further, the defense demands to know whether or not the prosecution will be offering any <u>expert</u> testimony as it relates to the requests in this paragraph;

16. A copy of the permit issued by the State Toxicologist to the operator who administered any tests of the defendant's breath, blood, or urine, or other bodily substance, the effective dates of that permit, together with a description of the training taken by that operator which qualified him/her for certification, along with the dates and places that training was completed, and a list of any/all documents or training manuals used in that training;

17. A copy of the breath testing device's maintenance and certification records, including any repairs, replacement of parts, unscheduled maintenance and reports of any malfunctions or difficulties made by any person whomsoever in the history of the instrument's use;

18. A copy of the results of all breath tests performed on the instrument used to test the defendant's breath in this case, i.e. database;

19. A copy of the results of all tests performed on the simulator solution used in the test of the defendant before and after the date of the test administered in this case, as well as preservation and access to the simulator solution used in the test of this defendant for reanalysis by gas chromatography;

20. Any information regarding the presence and/or use of radios at or near the location of the breath testing instrument at or about the time of the administration of the test concerned herein, together with any and all information, test results, studies, memoranda, or other material from the manufacturer and any other information from whatever source concerning the effects of radio frequency interference on the use of said instrument;

21. Preservation and access to any blood, breath, or urine samples taken from the defendant as a result of investigation of the charges pending herein;

22. A copy of the State Toxicologists written protocols and/or policies regarding certification, calibration, initial testing and installation of the DataMaster (or Draeger) in general and as applicable to the specific DataMaster (or Draeger) utilized in the instant case.

23. Copies of the maintenance and repair records, telephone complaint records, evaluation records, installation records and blood/ breath correlation results from studies or tests of the BAC Verifier DataMaster (or Draeger Alcotest) instrument used in conjunction with this defendant which are under the control of and/or maintained by the Washington State Patrol or other police agency or governmental authority;

24. A certified BAC Verifier DataMaster (or Draeger Alcotest) person(s) and/or technician(s) is hereby demanded at hearing or trial, along with a copy of his or her certification permit, together with the effective dates thereof. If the Prosecutor intends to offer said technician as an expert witness, defendant requests discovery of his or her education and training, both general and specific to the subject of his testimony, experience relative to the operation, maintenance and theory of the instrument used to test the defendant's blood, breath, or urine, and a description of the place, date, and subject matter of all training taken by the technician regarding the instrument in question and a full description of any experiments in which said technician has participated or about which he or she may testify;

25. We hereby demand at hearing or trial, the person(s) certified and responsible for the preparation of the simulator solutions (liquid or dry gas) used for certification of this particular BAC Verifier DataMaster (or Draeger Alcotest) and for the simulator solutions used in conjunction with this defendant's breath test, along with a copy of said person(s) permits, together with the effective dates thereof. Defendant further requests copies of any and all documents, to include but not limited to gas chromatograph charts and/or computer printouts associated with the preparation and/or checking of said simulator solutions. If the Prosecutor intends to offer said person(s) as an expert witness, defendant requests discovery of said person's education and training regarding the preparation of simulator solutions relative to the BAC Verifier DataMaster (or Draeger Alcotest). Further, defendant requests a full description of any experiments in which said person (s) has participated or about which he or she may testify, along with a copy of all policies and procedures for the preparation of simulator solutions and a copy of the standards established by the State Toxicologist for preparation and certification of the simulator solutions;

26. We hereby demand that at hearing or trial the individual who tested, calibrated, verified, and/or certified the mercury-in-glass (or any type of) thermometer used in the simulator associated with the DataMaster (or Draeger) used with this defendant be present and testify at trial. We further demand that any individual who tested, calibrated, verified, and/or certified digital reference thermometers associated with the testing, calibration, verification and/or certification of the mercury-in-glass thermometers, digital reference thermometers, or reference thermometers be present and testify at trial;

27. A copy of any tape recording of all radio broadcasts and transmissions occurring between the trooper and/ or officer who detained, arrested and/or transported the defendant on the date of the alleged incident herein, and any other agency, officer or station during the course of the detention, arrest, transportation, testing and booking or citation of the defendant, which relate to this defendant;

28. A copy of any tape recording of radio or telephone communications made over or through the "911" system and relating to the identity, detention, arrest and booking or citation of the defendant;

29. Timely inspection and an opportunity to photograph the breath analysis instrument used to test a sample of the defendant's breath herein;

30. A copy of the manufacturer's specifications and instructions for the initial calibration of the BAC Verifier DataMaster (or Draeger Alcotest) along with a copy of any manual or instructions issued by the State Toxicologist or Washington State Patrol regarding calibration, maintenance, or operation of said instruments;

31. Copies of the training manuals of the arresting agency for the detection, arrest and processing of individuals investigated/arrested for Driving While Intoxicated. This request is to include, but is not limited to, manuals and/or memoranda and/or documents and/or any other tangible things currently in the possession of the arresting agency as well as manuals and/or memoranda and/or documents and/or other tangible things which were/are used at the academy/ training facility for the arresting agency;

32. Please state whether plaintiff intends to offer testimony relating BAC DataMaster (or Draeger Alcotest) test results back to the time of driving, i.e. retrograde extrapolation, and/or Widmark formula. Further, please state whether the plaintiff intends to offer testimony to indicate that the defendant had present in his system at the time of driving a sufficient amount of alcohol to cause an accurate test of his breath administered within two hours of driving to register a measurement of 0.08 grams or more of alcohol per 210 liters of breath or more. If so, please provide qualifications of witnesses to so testify, and a summary of expected testimony, including predicate facts upon which any opinion will be rendered as well as a list of treatises/articles upon which any opinion will be rendered as well as a list of treatises/articles upon which said witness will rely for purposes of such testimony;

33. Any information regarding the presence and/or use of radios at or near the location of the radar instrument at or about the time of the administration of the test concerned herein, together with any and all information, test results, studies, memoranda, or other material from the manufacturer and any other information from whatever source concerning the effects of radio frequency interference on the use of said instrument;

34. A copy of any statements of policy and interpretations of policy, statute, and the Constitution which have been adopted by the Washington State Patrol, and/or the prosecuting authority in this case in relation to the use of radar to determine speed;

35. Copies of all administrative staff manuals or instructions to staff of the Washington State Patrol, and/or the prosecuting authority in this case in relation to the use of radar equipment;

36. Copies of all technical manuals, training manuals, operators manuals, and maintenance manuals and any other written materials relating to the radar instrument or device;

37. Copies of all planning policies and goals and interim and final planning decisions of the Washington State Patrol, and/or prosecuting authority in this case in relation to the approval and use of the radar device;

38. Copies of all factual staff reports and studies, factual consultants reports and studies, scientific reports and studies, and any other factual information derived from tests, studies, reports, or surveys, whether conducted by public employees or others, in the possession of or considered by the Washington State Patrol and/or prosecuting authority in this case relating to the use of radar devices or instruments;

39. Copies of correspondence and materials referred to therein by and with the agency relating to any regulatory, supervisory, or enforcement responsibilities of the agency, whereby the agency determines or opines upon, or is asked to determine or opine upon, the rights of the State, the public, a subdivision of state government, or any private party in the possession of or considered by the Washington State Patrol, and/or the prosecuting authority relating to the use of radar and/or the approval and/or use of this particular radar device;

40. Copies of all other facts, data, studies, research, or other information made available to the Washington State Patrol, the prosecuting authority herein, or any other state or private agency involved in the process of evaluation and/or approval of this radar device for use in the State of Washington, including but not limited to any such material gathered by the manufacturer, private research laboratory, or other state agencies or prosecuting authorities, or from any other source whatsoever which was considered in the process of testing and approving the use of this radar device;

41. Copies of all correspondence, documents, contract proposals, bid specifications, memoranda, and any other materials within the State's possession relevant to the bidding, purchase, and approval process involving this radar device by the Washington State Patrol, and other police or prosecuting authority or other governmental authority or private person or agency involved in the approval or purchasing process;

42. Copies of the maintenance, repair, and certification records of this radar instrument used in this case;

43. A speed measuring device expert is hereby demanded at hearing or trial, along with a copy of his or her certification permit, together with the effective dates thereof. If the Prosecutor intends to offer said person as an expert witness, Defendant requests discovery of his or her education and training, both general and specific to the subject of his testimony, experience relative to the operation, maintenance, and theory of the instrument used to establish speed by radar, and a description of the place, date and subject matter of all training taken by the person regarding the instrument in question and a full description of any experiments in which said person has participated or about which he or she may testify.

44. Timely inspection and an opportunity to photograph the radar instrument used to determine the speed of the vehicle;

45. A copy of the formula or formulae utilized in this radar device for determination of the speed of a vehicle;

46. Copies of all mathematical formulae utilized in this radar device by the Washington State Patrol in the evaluation, testing and certification process which was in any way related to the decision to purchase this radar device;

47. A copy of the manufacturer's specifications and instructions for the initial calibration of this radar instrument along with a copy of any manual or instructions issued by the Washington State Patrol modifying, amending, correcting, or otherwise changing the manufacturer's recommendations regarding calibration of said instruments. The names, addresses, and phone numbers of all persons the prosecutor intends to call as witnesses at the time of trial, together with any copies of any notes, written or recorded statements, and the substance of any oral statements made by any of those witnesses or by any third parties communicated to those witnesses bearing on any issue in this case;

48. A full copy of the entirety of any search warrant file maintained by the prosecutor's office and/or law enforcement for any search warrant executed herein regarding the defendant. This request is made pursuant to CrRLJ 2.3.

49. The full name and contact information of any technician, assistant, registered nurse, licensed practical nurse, physician, or other health care provider who took any part in the blood draw process—including but not limited to: basic demographic and medical questioning, preparation of the blood kit, drawing of the blood, transportation of the samples, preservation of the samples.

50. Any and all video/audio recordings of the room or location that the defendant's blood was drawn. This is a formal request to preserve that video/audio evidence for the entire duration of this case.

51. A full copy of any/all nursing log sheets and/or records maintained by the agency/hospital that drew the blood of the defendant.

52. A full copy of the specific instructions for any vacutainer, blood vial, or other apparatus used to draw blood from this defendant.

53. A full copy of any order reduced to writing by any registered nurse, health care professional, law enforcement officer or physician directing blood to be drawn on this defendant.

54. A full copy of any licenses or certifications in effect at the time of the blood draw possessed by any technician, assistant, registered nurse, licensed practical nurse, physician, or other health care provider who took any part in the blood draw process—including but not limited to: basic demographic and medical questioning, preparation of the blood kit, drawing of the blood, transportation of the samples, preservation of the samples.

55. A full copy of any training manuals, blood draw logs, or additional training logs kept or maintained by any technician, assistant, registered nurse, licensed practical nurse, physician, or other health care provider who took any part in the blood draw process—including but not limited to: basic demographic and medical questioning, preparation of the blood kit, drawing of the blood, transportation of the samples, preservation of the samples.

56. A full copy of any delegation of nursing task records kept or maintained by any technician, assistant, registered nurse, licensed practical nurse, physician, or other health care provider who took any part in the blood draw process—including but not limited to: basic demographic and medical questioning, preparation of the blood kit, drawing of the blood, transportation of the samples, preservation of the samples.

YOU ARE HEREBY NOTIFIED that failure to comply with the demands contained herein will result in the Defendant moving for appropriate relief at the time of motions or trial.

[§1:04 Reserved]

C. Independent Analysis of Blood Samples

§1:05   Considerations in Retesting

The prosecution team, either the lab or the arresting agency, is generally required to obtain, keep, and provide to the defense a sample of the defendant's blood or urine for re-testing. In some jurisdictions multiple samples are taken in separate vials; in other jurisdictions one sample of a larger portion is obtained. In either case, counsel may wish to have the blood analyzed by an independent lab.

There are some potential drawbacks to blood retesting. First as to alcohol level, if your results must be provided to the DA, then unless you strike gold (a completely different result or a slight decrease to get below a critical level (.08 or .15 or .20), the results may hurt your client. If you are not required to share the results, the prosecutor may still point out that you had the blood retested and the failure to share indicates that the independent result was not good for your client.

Next, as to preservative and/or contamination, some attorneys prefer to argue "It is up to the prosecution to show NO CONTAMINATION and proper preservative, not up to us to show improper levels or contamination." You must decide which is better in your case. Often this will be based on how far from your client's expected level the result of the original test is. If it is completely out of line with what your client tells you he drank, then a retest is probably warranted. Remember to always consider the context of the story you're telling to the jury when you are making these sorts of strategic decisions. Also remember that your story may not always come into sharp focus until you have all of the information. Tread carefully, but boldly.

If you decide to have the sample independently analyzed for alcohol level, preservative and contamination, the following form letters can be modified to your particular laboratories.

§1:06   Letter to Crime Lab Requesting Forwarding of Blood Sample to Private Lab

[Letterhead]

[Date]

[Crime Lab Name and Address]

Re: [Case name and number]

To Whom it May Concern:

Enclosed please find a check for $_____ to cover whatever costs are incurred performing the following request. Pursuant to [appropriate local rules], I am requesting your laboratory to furnish a sample of blood to a private laboratory for [specify type of testing, *e.g.*, BAC/preservative/contamination] testing. My client [Name], was arrested for suspicion of driving under the influence on [Date] (Crime Lab #_____). On that date, he submitted to a blood test. Please forward to the private laboratory a sufficient sample of the blood drawn that evening for a retest. The laboratory we wish to have retest the sample is:

[Name and address of private lab]

If you require any additional information please do not hesitate to contact my office at [phone number].

Thank you, in advance, for your assistance with this matter.

Very truly yours,

_____

§1:07   Letter to Private Lab re Blood Re-Testing

[Letterhead]

[Date]

[Private Lab Name and Address]

Re: [Case name and number]

To Whom it May Concern:

My client [Name] was arrested for suspicion of driving under the influence on [Date] (Crime Lab #_____). On that date, he submitted to a blood test. I have requested the Crime Laboratory for the County of [Name] to forward a blood sample drawn from my client to your lab to retest for [specify type of testing, *e.g.*, BAC/preservative/contamination]. Please send the invoice and the results of the retest to my office at:

[Name and address]

If you require additional information please do not hesitate to contact my office at [phone number].

Very truly yours,

_____

[§§1:08-1:09 Reserved]

D. Comprehensive Blood Discovery and the Reasons for It

By Justin J. McShane[1]

Author's Note: One of the most exciting aspects of criminal defense work in general, and DUI in particular, is meeting attorneys who see the world in a different way or who bring a different mindset to our field. Justin McShane is just that type of attorney. His scientific mind has taken the DUI defense world by storm. The following is his generous contribution when asked "Can you give me a little something on blood discovery?" I am very grateful that his idea of "little" is so large and I trust you will be as well.

Here is Justin's popular and successful list of items to request from the testing laboratory in a blood case, along with his insightful commentary on how to use the request.

1. General Points

§1:10   Need for Comprehensive Discovery Request

For many years, members of the defense community have rightfully noted that they cannot get the data from the testing laboratory that is necessary to verify the validity of the result offered into evidence against the accused. In motion to compel hearings, they wish that they could offer the court a single treatise to explain in plain English the historical setting of the request, and the theoretical need for the particular items (on an item-by-item basis). This division is written with that need in mind. It serves as that needed offer of proof.

Sections §§1:13-1:13.3 contain a list of items to request from the laboratory with comments explaining what each item is and why you should request it. See **Appendix D** at the end of this book, or in Digital Access for a version of this request with the comments omitted.

Many trial courts will not read all of this, although they should. Therefore, this material is intended for appellate courts and for post-conviction review.

CAUTION:

The comprehensive blood discovery request provided here is a formidable weapon to be used only by those skilled enough to appreciate it. In using the request, an untrained attorney, even a well-intentioned one, can make some truly bad law that many generations in the criminal defense community could be stuck with for a long time.

I have provided the form only for use in litigation and only by those who are prepared to prove it up. Please read §§1:11 and 1:11.1 before you consider using it. My goal is to provide well-trained attorneys the first opportunity to litigate these matters as they are the mostly likely to achieve success.

§1:10.1   Resistance of Forensic "Scientists" to Scientific Method

"The most exciting phrase to hear in science, the one that heralds
the most discoveries, is not 'Eureka!' [I found it!], but 'That's funny...'"

—Isaac Asimov (American author and
professor of biochemistry, 1920-1992)

---

[1] Justin J. McShane, Esquire is a Harrisburg, Pennsylvania based attorney who specializes in using forensic science for the benefit of citizens accused of crimes. He is a board certified trial attorney by the National Board of Trial Advocacy as well as board certified as a DUI Specialist by the National College for DUI Defense. He is a Fellow with the American Institute of Chemists (AIC). He is a member of numerous scientific organizations including the American Chemical Society (ACS), American Institute of Chemists (AIC), American Academy of Forensic Science (AAFS), American College of Forensic Examiners, Society for Analytical Chemists (SACP), National Fire Protection Association (NFPA), The Chromatography Forum of Delaware Valley, American Society for Testing and Materials (ASTM), American Association for Clinical Chemistry (AACC), National Conference of Standards Laboratories International (NCSLI International), Association of Analytical Communities (AOAC International), American Society for Mass Spectrometry (ASMS), Society for Applied Spectroscopy (SAS), and the American Society for Quality (ASQ). He is a published author. He is a frequently invited guest lecturer at national, state, and local seminars that are attended by lawyers, judges, scientists and policy-makers. He has twice been invited to lecture at the ACS National meeting and has been accepted to present AAFS. He is the Chairman/CEO of The McShane Firm, LLC, a six attorney criminal defense and DUI law firm. He maintains two blogs: www.TheTruthAboutForensicScience.com and www.PADUIBlog.com.

The idea of a testing laboratory trying to prevent criminal defense lawyers from obtaining the scientific data upon which their conclusions (which are really opinions) are based is wholly unscientific.

As a good friend and colleague, Attorney Kirby Riffel of Arkansas, once wrote:

A recent lecture pointed out that nearly 100% of scientific dogma in 1905 (when Einstein published the special theory of relativity) has been since falsified, amended, re-stated or has a major anomaly that is inconsistent with existing theory. That is the nature of true science, whose ethics demand a skeptical attitude and takes joy in falsification as the appointed path to greater knowledge. The corollary is that it is most likely that current dogma will not withstand the next 50 years.

Sadly, there is no such "joy in falsification" in forensic science. It makes us wonder if it is even science at all or simply a procedure. The inertia is so great and the anecdote so entrenched that even when there is accepted falsification of any hypothesis that is foundational to some discipline in forensic science, there is no joy. Instead the findings are dismissed with the constant refrain of anti-empiricists in their anthem of "this is the way we always did it." It is sad that, in general, forensic science is not like real science. Hopefully, this will change. It is up to us. One of the ways that we can do our part to change all of this is to perform an essential role of "external verification," otherwise known as auditing.

§1:10.2 Courts' Lack of Understanding of Significance of Testing Data

"What do you call an opinion with no data to support it? A guess..."

—Justin J. McShane, Esquire (a frequent opening and closing theme)

The reason that courts do not routinely order the production of the testing data is that jurists do not understand the significance of the data. The defense bar is clearly at fault for this. We do not know what we are doing.

In general, the discovery process is the exchange of information from the prosecuting agency to defendant's counsel or from third party vendors purporting to have relevant facts to counsel for the accused. There is the absolute requirement that prosecutors give over to defense counsel all exculpatory information, but generally, with some notable exceptions, prosecutors are not required to exchange inculpatory information with the defense.

What does this mean in a forensic science case?

§1:10.3 Scientific Evidence: Inculpatory or Exculpatory?

Where does scientific evidence fall in the inculpatory versus exculpatory scheme? In practice, it is an exceptionally tough question. Clearly, if all testing is performed 100% properly resulting in an outcome that is against the accused, then such evidence is inculpatory. However, if the testing is not performed properly, then such evidence is potentially or actually exculpatory.

What complicates this examination is the nature of the evidence. It is not like a police report or a witness statement that any layperson can look at and readily determine the exculpatory or inculpatory character of it. Testing and the data it generates are hyper-technical forms of information whose exculpatory or inculpatory nature may not be patent on their face. So again, it comes back to: what does this mean in a forensic science case?

Where is the line?

§1:10.4 The Scientific Method

I suggest that the best policy is the scientific one—the scientific method. The scientific method requires these steps:
1. Define a question.
2. Gather information and resources. (Make observations of the phenomenon.)
3. Form a falsifiable hypothesis that explains the observations,
4. Perform experiments and collect data attempting to falsify the hypothesis.
5. Verify the data.
6. Analyze the data.

7. Interpret the data and draw conclusions that serve as a starting point for new a hypothesis.
8. Publish the results.
9. Retest and repeat.

§1:10.5   Verification

It is the fifth step (verification) that holds the answer. A general definition of verification can be defined as "The ability to take all information provided and arrive at the same conclusions as the original analyst without the need to independently test."

If what is performed and presented in the courtroom is truly scientific testing based on sound scientific principles, then the proponent of the alleged scientific evidence must allow for a free and total examination of all of the uninterrupted raw data in order to fulfill the scientific requirement of verification. This is the way of science. Hiding and not being transparent is advocacy.

§1:10.6   Government's Response to Requests for Data

The government's response to the scientific community's call to for transparency does not meet reality. The records needed for verification exist [see §1:10.7]. They must be readily available to those in the laboratory and upon demand for auditing.

Defense attorneys regularly fail to educate the judiciary so that they can understand the requests. If the court did understand, then it would know that these items serve the essential role of external peer review and verification that is the hallmark of science.

The government's typical response to the call for transparency is that it would take too much time and too much effort. In other words, it would be a logistical nightmare and not practical. The heavens would fall, or so they claim.

But would they? Of course not!

§1:10.7   Availability of Data Needed for Verification of Blood Test Results

At first glance *any* request for material that could verify the testing seems voluminous to the uninitiated or the underexposed. However, in an accredited laboratory, these documents are required to not only exist, but they must be "readily available" and accessible and organized in a manner that allows easy retrieval upon demand of auditors or in-house technical reviewers, pursuant to the various published general standards.

All of the items requested in this chapter are needed to assess independently the validity of the conclusory opinion offered by the testing or calibration laboratory. In fact, the various organizations that produce the International Standards (IS) and other standards for accreditation have similar statements as to the need to provide sufficient documentation.

For example, ILAC-G19:2002 reads: "[I]n general, the records required to support conclusions should be such that in the absence of the analyst/examiner, another competent analyst/examiner could evaluate what had been performed and interpret the data."

The ASCLD/LAB standard reads: "The laboratory must create and maintain a unique case record for all administrative and examination documentation generated and/or received by the laboratory for each case involving the analysis of evidence."

In the corresponding "Discussion" section, the standard reads:

A laboratory case record consists of both examination documentation and administrative documentation which may be received or generated by the laboratory. The laboratory must maintain each case record . . . Administrative documentation includes laboratory reports, records of case-related conversations, evidence receipts, description of evidence packaging and seals, subpoenas, investigative reports and other pertinent information. Examination documentation is usually generated by the laboratory and includes references to procedures followed, tests conducted, standards and controls used, diagrams, printouts, photographs, documentation of observations, and results of examinations on evidence.

Its most recent standard, ASCLD/LAB International Supplemental Requirements-Testing: 2006, states clearly as follows: "Documentation to support conclusions shall be such that in the absence of the analyst, another competent analyst or supervisor could evaluate what was done and interpret the data."

Further, other standards producing bodies such as the Scientific Working Group for the Analysis of Seized Drugs (SWGDRUG) in its published standard writes: "Analysts shall…make and retain full, contemporaneous, clear and accurate records of all examinations and tests conducted, and the conclusions drawn, in sufficient detail to allow meaningful review and assessment of the conclusions by an independent person competent in the field."

2. Preparation and Knowledge Needed to Use Comprehensive Request

§1:11 Start With a Scaled Request

A discovery request is a powerful document. The discovery request provided in §§1:13-1:13.3 below is especially powerful. To a jurisdiction or a testing or calibration laboratory accustomed to producing nothing more than a conclusory report, such a document can be likened to a nuclear bomb.

There is no such thing as a limited nuclear war. You cannot go back once you push the nuclear button. Therefore, it is best to start out with a scaled request to the laboratory asking for the documents the laboratory is willing to provide without controversy. In some jurisdictions, it will be hard enough to get anything beyond the conclusory report.

Before making a comprehensive blood discovery request, you must win a public relations campaign in court. You must prove in successive cases the value of whatever information the laboratory is willing to give to you without a fight. You must first demonstrate that what you have uncovered with these simple documents matters. Then you can focus on widening the scope of your war against the laboratory that tests your client by advancing the nuclear option.

§1:11.1 Be Prepared to Meet Motion to Quash

If you threaten to use nuclear weapons, you should be prepared to actually use them. Likewise, if you decide to use the comprehensive blood discovery request, you have to be prepared to follow through in court to get the requested items when the laboratory inevitably resists.

Some lawyers advance discovery requests as a stalling tactic or a strategic move in hopes of noncompliance. If this is what you do, stop! This is unethical to its core.

"Action indeed is the sole medium of expression for ethics." -Jane Addams (1860-1935, first American woman to be awarded the Nobel Peace Prize).

If you are going to serve this discovery request, then you must be willing and able to prove it up in court in every single case. This is not a rote exercise of copy and paste. You should not simply use someone else's form from a book verbatim.

Every time you serve a comprehensive request, you must be prepared to meet the challenge of the motion to quash with experts (not just one). One hundred percent of the time you use this request, you will encounter a motion to quash. Do not even attempt to serve the nuclear option without having available to testify, at the very least, a PhD in analytical chemistry and preferably a certified laboratory auditor who performs ISO inspections. In every judge's mind, this request concerns "too much stuff."

You cannot be exposed as having made an empty threat. It must be a real threat that you can and will prove up with competent evidence of the value of all of the requested items.

Testing laboratories, just like any business owner, are terrified at the thought of anyone looking at "the books." The sad truth that any business owner knows in his heart of hearts is that there is always something wrong with the books. Well, a testing laboratory is no different. There is always something wrong. No laboratory is perfect. No quality assurance or quality control program is foolproof.

Accreditation costs many tens or hundreds of thousands of dollars to obtain and to maintain. If the testing was performed by an independent laboratory for profit, the accreditation is priceless and represents many millions upon millions of dollars. Besides that, every laboratory director is terrified of potential headlines like those of San Francisco, North Carolina, Colorado, Houston and the like.

If you are attempting to "look at the books," the laboratory officials will come at you with everything they have. I have had testing and calibration providers file grievances against me with the state disciplinary board. They will likely do the same to you.

You must be prepared. To that end, you too must be able to articulate the need for these items as undoubtedly the judge will call you (and not your experts) into chambers to "explain it all."

As noted Texas DUI attorney Troy McKinney says, "If you cannot explain what it is, then don't ask for it." If you are not yet at that stage in your scientific development, do not worry. Stick with it. You will "get it." Just remember, no good judicial decision ever begins with the litigating attorney saying "Well, I dabble in laboratory auditing issues…" or "I kinda understand ISO 17025…" There is always more training to be had. There are folks out there who are happy to assist who do understand it fully and will even help you litigate these matters.

3. Scope and Organization of Comprehensive Request

§1:12   Scope of Discovery Request

The scope of the discovery request in §§1:13-1:13.3 covers the testing or calibrating laboratory only. The requested items are documents and records that are in the care, custody, and control of the laboratory.

The items requested surround the actual analytical testing performed in the laboratory. They do not concern the matters that traditionally are outside of the laboratory. The most obvious examples of items that are not included in the listed items, but certainly may affect the validity and the trueness of the reported test result, are blood collection instructions and pre-analytical storage and transportation matters.

Although these listed items are defined and few in number, they do not represent all of the items that may be necessary to verify independently the validity and the trueness of the reported result of the analysis. Additional items may be necessary depending upon the testing method or the particular circumstances.

§1:12.1   Outline of Discovery Request

The general outline of the discovery request is simple. The items are grouped into four categories:
- General matters.
- Pre-analytical matters.
- Analytical matters.
- Reporting matters.

This data and information represents the bare minimum necessary to verify the validity of the reported test result.

Within those divisions appears:
(1) The exact language to be used in requesting the item,
(2) The simple English explanation of what it is, and
(3) The simple English explanation of why it matters.

Items one and two are addressed to the court as that is the intended audience.
This incarnation of the requested items list is purposed for both DUI and DUID cases.

See Appendix D at the end of this book and on Digital Access for a version of the request with the comments omitted.

4. Annotated List of Items to Request

CAUTION:

The comprehensive blood discovery request provided here is a formidable weapon to be used only by those skilled enough to appreciate it. In using the request, an untrained attorney, even a well-intentioned one, can make some truly bad law that many generations in the criminal defense community could be stuck with for a long time.

I have provided the form only for use in litigation and only by those who are prepared to prove it up. Please read §§1:11 and 1:11.1 before you consider using it. My goal is to provide well-trained attorneys the first opportunity to litigate these matters as they are the mostly likely to achieve success.

§1:13 General Matters

1. A copy of any accreditation certificates for the laboratory that were in effect at the time of the analysis.

Comment on item 1:

What is it? Many different accrediting bodies cover various aspects of a testing and calibration laboratory. Some of the common ones include ASLCD/LAB, FQS-I, A2LA, ABFT, NAME, COLA, CLIA and CAP. Also, there may be state specific accrediting bodies such as state Departments of Health.

Each certificate of accreditation should be dated noting when the accreditation was achieved and the length of the accreditation. Most importantly, most of the certificates will outline what the scope of the accreditation covers in terms of specific forensic science discipline or form of testing.

Why does it matter? While accreditation does not equate to automatic quality in results, it means that a laboratory adheres to some sort of external Quality Management System (QMS). How worthwhile that QMS is, versus what is necessary in the general scientific community to insure true results is debatable. Determining whether a laboratory is accredited and by whom is the very beginning of assessing the quality of the reported and alleged test result. These standards are minimum expressions of acceptable practices. A laboratory could and should decide to employ greater standards than the minimum to ensure quality of the results issued.

2. The laboratory's overall policies as to testing and calibration.

3. The laboratory's overall protocols as to testing and calibration.

4. The policies that apply to the section of the laboratory where this particular testing or calibration event occurred.

5. The procedures that apply to the section of the laboratory where this particular testing or calibration event occurred.

Comment on items 2, 3, 4, and 5:

What is it? Each laboratory should be divided into separate sections. A laboratory should have a written set of documents that outline the overall testing and calibration philosophy of the laboratory and/or the section.

Why is it important? These documents contain information such as the laboratory's and the section's statements about the need for its personnel to be well-trained, well-educated, and well-monitored. In addition, within these documents there should be language as to the need for every person in the laboratory to follow the laboratory's and the section's policies, procedures and instructions in order to achieve a valid and true (meaning actual) result. In addition, these documents should reveal the consequences for failure to follow the directions of the laboratory such as warning, suspension, retraining and firing.

§1:13.1 Pre-Analytical Matters

6. Validation studies (both internal and external) that prove the validation of the method and instructions used.

Comment on item 6:

What is it? Validation refers to documented proof that the process undertaken is suitable for its intended use and achieves the intended reported result correctly and is as free as possible from issues of imprecision (error).

Why is it important? Without using a validated method, any testing arrives at a non-validated result. This is to be distinguished from "invalid" which means that the method has been proven to be not valid. A nonvalidated result means that it may be valid or it may be invalid. This includes proof of achieving both unique qualitative results and then a unique quantitative result.

7. The policy that applies to the assay performed in this particular test or calibration event that covers the calibration or the achieving of a calibration curve.

8. The procedure that applies to the assay performed in this particular test or calibration event that covers the calibration or the achieving of a calibration curve.

9. The instructions that apply to the assay performed in this particular test or calibration event that covers the calibration or the achieving of a calibration curve.

Comment on items 7, 8, 9:

What is it? The act of calibration (and bias) is a procedure that imperfectly transforms the testing (the response from the analytical instrument) into a useful measure. Calibration and bias have to do with precision and accuracy respectively. The true issue surrounds analytical drift and other basics of metrology. Over time, all analytical devices lose their sensitivity, their precision, and their accuracy regardless of use (however, heavy throughput does exacerbate the problem, and so too does lack of use). A calibration curve is not a curve, despite its name.

Rather, if well preformed, it is a straight line as determined by various measures of linearity. The calibration curve is the analytical method that results in a plot of calibration data. It is a general method for determining the concentration of a substance in an unknown sample by comparing the unknown to a set of standard samples of known concentration.

Why is it is important? The consequence of failing to achieve acceptable calibration is that the quantization (how much do we have of what we measured) will always be wrong.

10. The calibration curves and all chromatograms generated on the batch on the machine on which the sample in this case was tested.

Comment on item 10:

What is it? For a discussion as to what a calibration curve is, please see the **Comment on item 7, 8, 9** above. A chromatogram is the written record of the testing event. Think of it as the receipt of the analysis. It can be likened to the breath test ticket that prints out at the end of an evidentiary breath test. This request asks the laboratory to produce proof that the policy, procedure and instructions outlined in requested item number 9 were actually conducted. This request includes all logs, reports, spreadsheets, control charts, and other documents, in whatever form, reflecting the calibration of all equipment used in the testing and the preparation of the sample at issue in this case as well as the preparation of all samples within the batch.

Why is it important? The consequence of failing to achieve acceptable calibration is that the quantitation (how much do we have of what we measured) will always be wrong.

11. The identification and source of all internal standards, standards, standard mixtures (separation matrix), verifiers, blanks, and controls that were run within the batch in which the sample in this case was run.

Comment on item 11:

What is it? An internal standard is a compound purposefully added to a sample in known concentration to facilitate the qualitative identification and/or quantitative determination of the unknown sample tested. "Controls" refers to the series of materials that are used for the assessment of the performance of an analytical procedure. They are standards.

Controls that appear before the unknowns are called calibrators. Controls that appear after the unknowns are known as verifiers. Certified Reference Materials are a type of extremely high quality controls used to check the quality and traceability of products.

This request includes all certificates of traceability for the standards, and controls used to analyze this sample. This request should include any quality control certificate provided by the supplier or manufacturer with, or applicable to, such solutions including reporting of uncertainty in them, control charts during their use and the raw data giving evidence of this. In addition, there should be documents reflecting the expiration date of all externally purchased solutions or reagents used in the batch in which the sample in this case was tested.

Why is it important? Part of the integrity of any testing of unknowns has to do with the veracity of the sources of knowns against which the unknowns are compared. For if we do not have certainty in the knowns and the references used, then there cannot be any confidence in our conclusions of the analysis of unknowns.

12. All records reflecting internal testing or quality control testing of all solutions, reagents, or standard mixtures used as, as part of, or in relation to internal standards, controls, standard mixtures, or standards in the batch in which the sample in this case was run.

Comment on item 12:

What is it? An important feature of achieving a true test result and one that is valid is not taking another's word for it. Simply relying upon a "trusted" manufacturer's or vendor's certification is insufficient.

Why is it important? Even the most "trusted" manufacturer or vendor can and will make mistakes in the manufacturing or packaging of its products that it allows into commerce. This is why it is essential for the receiving laboratory to verify independently that these items are what they are purported to be. Without performing this essential step, then the validity only is presumed and cannot be said to be proven even if all other aspects are correct.

13. All refrigeration logs, reports, or other documents in whatever form, for all refrigerated compartments in which this sample, other unknowns within the run, internal standards, controls, standard mixtures, standards, and reagents used in or in relation to the analysis in this case, were stored or kept at any time.

Comment on item 13:

What is it? All of the testing materials including the unknowns must be stored in the correct environment.

Why is it important? The failure to maintain the samples or the controls and other materials used in the testing within a narrow temperature range can lead to abhorrent results in the quantitative reporting. For example, in the case of testing those who are accused of a DUI where the accused's blood is collected, if the blood exceeds the normative temperature as prescribed by the manufacturer, and if *Candida Albicans* is present in the sample or the environment, then the neo-formation of EtOH can occur. In simpler words, if the blood sample is not refrigerated, then the blood can breakdown, resulting in a higher reported BAC that is not correct.

14. All proficiency testing results for the section of the laboratory testing the sample in this case as well as for the person who conducted the testing in this case—since the last date of accreditation inspection preceding the test, and for any such testing since the testing in this case. This specifically includes the summary report of expected results for the proficiency testing (and the manufacturer's information sheet) against which the proficiency test results are judged.

Comment on item 14:

What is it? Proficiency Testing (PT) is defined as a means of evaluating a laboratory's performance under controlled conditions relative to a given set of criteria through analysis of unknown samples provided. The best practice is for the PT testing to be "blind," where the analyst and the laboratory do not know they are being tested.

Why is it important? If the laboratory has no method to prove that its laboratory or its analysts can actually test the samples correctly, then the testing involving the accused is suspect. The records may show that the analyst is not testing perfectly.

15. Quarterly balance quality control records on any balance instrument related to the calibration of the EtOH standard solution or the preparation of knowns or unknowns used in the blood alcohol testing of the samples in this case. The records reflecting the calibration of weights on any balance or instrument related to this case as well as the control charts kept.

Comment on item 15:

What is it? If the laboratory performs any sort of independent verification of vendor provided material, or creates its own internal solutions from stock materials, or performs its own pipetting calibration, an analytical balance (otherwise known as a scale) is needed. Control charting is a graphical and empirical statistical tool used to detect excessive process variability to try to identify specific assignable causes that can be corrected.

Why is it important? The calibration of any analytical balance is only as tight as the items that are used to check and correct it. Control charting serves to determine whether a process is in a state of statistical control; that is, the extent of variation of the output of the process does not exceed that which is expected based on the natural statistical variability of the process. Control charting is a great way to identify the source of statistical outliers where a machine can be pulled, an environment checked or an inappropriate operator stopped or re-trained.

§1:13.2   Analytical Matters

16. The instructions that apply to the assay that was used in this particular testing or calibration event.

Comment on item 16:
What is it? This request covers that which was perhaps referred to as "Standard Operating Procedures."

Why is it important? Any deviation from a valid method, even a seemingly small one from the instructions, leads to a non-validated result. See the "**Comment on item 6**" above.

17. The employee training record, curriculum vitae, and resume for any person listed on chain of custody documents in this case or who performed the analysis.

Comment on item 17:
What is it? This request is self-explanatory.

Why is it important? An analyst is only as good as his or her training. A personnel file can outline work related deficiencies and lack of proficiencies.

18. Identify the make, model, and brand/manufacturer of the instruments and other supporting instruments (i.e. balance, pipette, etc.) used during the analysis and/or preparation of the samples in this case and the variables used in its installation and operation.

Comment on item 18:
What is it? This should identify the method of detection for the chromatographic method used in this particular testing (e.g., headspace injection versus direct injection; manual injection versus automated injection; split versus splitless injection port (in the case of Gas Chromatography); Wall Coated Open Tubular columns (capillary columns) versus packed columns; Electronic Pressure Control versus manual flow control; installation of a Mass Spectrometer versus a Flame Ionization Detector versus UV/Vis DAD system), as well as the conditions used (e.g. type of column and dimensions of the column; the length of the time of the run; the integration parameters; the carrier and makeup gas and its flow; inlet flow/pressure rate (split ratio); oven temperature; incubation time/ injector time; injector temperature; detector temperatures; equilibrium times).

Why is it important? All of this information is necessary to arrive at the quantitative result and the qualitative result. An analytical device can be likened to an automobile. Every automobile comes with various options that can either increase the performance of the automobile or make it not as good as the top of the line model. The same is true with analytical devices. Some are better than others.

Some have been upgraded to make them top of the line in terms of performance, while others are subpar. In addition, just as every automobile may be driven differently, each analytical instrument has variables as to its operation. Just as in the case of the automobile where one can control its use through its variables (for example, fuel efficiency by how one steps on the gas pedal), so can one change the fidelity of the result by changing the variables as to the analytical device used. This request focuses on how "good" the device itself is as well as how well it is being used according to its published method.

19. The policy concerning the sample selection criteria used in this particular case.

20. The procedure concerning the sample selection criteria used in this particular case.

21. The instructions concerning the sample selection criteria used in this particular case.

Comment on items 19, 20, and 21:

What is it? Generally across all of forensic science, only a remarkably small part of the whole, called an aliquot, is actually tested by any analytical device. This choice is referred to as "sample selection." A policy, procedure, and instructions should be in place to outline the sample selection process.

Why is it important? In essence, what happens in the laboratory when an aliquot is prepared involves a massive amount of truly subjective discretion by selecting a "pinch of this" or a "section of that" from the whole unknown sample submitted for examination. Sample selection is perhaps the single biggest area of potential uncertainty and error in obtaining true results. It remains one of the areas that is largely unexposed in the courtroom.

As a result of this testing method where only a part of the whole is examined, it is crucial for the laboratory to ensure homogeneity in the aliquot tested. This is a supreme challenge.

Even with a policy, procedure, and instruction in place, it is clear that by performing sample selection massive representation errors with respect to non-colloidal (nonhomogeneous) mixtures can occur. This is sometimes referred to as "random sampling error."

It is a very large potential source of error and, at worst, results in erroneous results. If the laboratory received more than one vial or container of blood or other substance, records reflecting which vial was selected for testing should exist based upon these policies, procedures, and instructions. Further, how the selection and preparation of the particular aliquot from the whole tube was arrived at should likewise be justified.

22. The source and type of all consumables used in collection, preparation, and analysis of the samples run in the batch.

Comment on item 22:

What is it? Just like an automobile, each analytical instrument has consumables. Instead, of air filters, lights, sparkplugs, windshield wipers, there are items such as inlet liners, septa, solvents, golden seals, tubing, vials, o-rings, ferrules and other items.

Why is it important? The failure to replace consumables can affect performance, just as the case with failing to replace worn out sparkplugs.

23. If a Gas or Liquid Chromatograph is used, the reporting of t0 time according to the method.

Comment on item 23:

What is it? t0 represents the time that it takes for the carrier gas to elute through the column.

Why is this important? t0 is the essential measure that enables an external auditor of the testing event to determine whether or not each test in a batch was performed properly and uniformly throughout the run. t0 is a means to verify retention time and relative retention time. Retention time is used to examine the validity of the qualitative measurement.

§1:13.3   Reporting Matters

24. The particular records for this testing or calibration event.

Comment on item 24:

What is it? This request calls for the production of all test specific information. It includes all laboratory notes, case files, case reports, or bench notes, by whatever name they are known, and in whatever form. It also includes all records contained in the testing folder specific to the test in this case. This includes a copy of the case or testing folder itself if it contains any notations or entries.

All data and notes including the chromatograms produced from all of the samples in this batch and run should be produced. This calls not simply for this one unknown sampled and tested that is attributed to the accused, but also for the records, such as the chromatograms, for all of the controls (calibrators, verifiers), standard mix (separation matrix), blanks, and other unknowns in the batch in which this sample in this case was run. It should include all chain of custody records specific to the specimen(s) in this case.

Why is it important? The need for these records should be self-evident.

25. The quality control policy and protocol for the laboratory, the section, and the assay performed.

26. The quality assurance policy and protocol for the laboratory, the section, and the assay performed.

Comment on items 25 and 26:

What is it? This refers to the written policy, procedure and instructions for the reporting of unexpected results as applies to this laboratory, this section and for this assay. This should include the information for the discarding or non-reporting of data or results (regardless of whether the data or results were or are made during the analysis or before or after the analysis).

Why is it important? Mistakes will happen in the laboratory. The question is what does the laboratory do when mistakes are caught before they are reported outside of the laboratory and what does the laboratory do when mistakes are caught after they are reported outside of the laboratory.

27. The full reporting and the underlying validation of the valuation of the uncertainty measurement (UM) in the ultimate reported result.

Comment on item 27:

What is it? A whole body of science is devoted to measurement. It is called metrology. A portion of metrology is uncertainty measurement (UM). UM answers the question of "how off is the test." Every testing event and every testing process has some inherent variability due to systemic and random factors over which there is no control and which cannot be eliminated economically.

Why is this important? As can be the case, a laboratory's stated but unproven error (often expressed as +/- x% or some fixed number) grossly understates reality. Without knowing the uncertainty of the measure, then the measure is not relevant.

28. If a Mass Spectrometer is used, then the following additional materials should be provided:
    28.1 If a spectral library is used to examine spectra and elucidate spectra, the source of the library spectra.
    28.2 The hit list, and the hit histogram for the testing.
    28.3 All "tune" reports ran within one year if a MS detector was used.

Comment on items contained in 28:

What is it? Mass spectrometry (MS) is a specific type of analysis. Mass spectrometry is the branch of science dealing with all aspects of mass spectroscopes and the results obtained with these instruments. It measures the mass-to-charge ratio of charged particles. It is used for determining masses of particles, for determining the elemental composition of a sample or molecule, and for elucidating the chemical structures of molecules. The MS principle consists of ionizing chemical compounds to generate charged molecules or molecule fragments and measurement of their mass-to-charge ratios. The result from the analysis of the unknown is compared against the known. In MS analysis, there is a library of knowns.

Why is it important? In mass spectrometry, the spectral library is crucial. It enables the analyst to compare the unknown to a known to arrive at an opinion that is often expressed as a conclusion. There are many different commercial sources for these libraries. Some are better than others. In fact, some systems allow the analyst to exercise his or her discretion in employing his or her own standards as opposed to the commercially available ones that are derived from CRMs.

Electron Ionization (EI) based Mass Spectrometry has been so fantastically removed from its base in science, that it has been simplified to accommodate the masses. In the modern crime laboratory, EI-based MS has been reduced to simple computer-assisted pattern recognition. Sadly, gone are the days of acid-based chemistry to elucidate mass spectral patterns. Instead, most analysts just let the computer do it. What the computer produces is a list of likely matches as compared against the library of reference spectra. This computer generated matching and evaluation produces match scores, probability scoring, and other grading methods. The analyst with this data then uses his or her own discretion based upon these lists, grading systems and scores to opine what the substance is.

[§§1:14-1:19 Reserved]

III.   MOTIONS BASED ON DEFENDANT'S RIGHT TO COMPULSORY PROCESS

§1:20   Legal Principles

In all criminal prosecutions, the accused shall enjoy the right to have compulsory process for obtaining witnesses in his favor. U.S. Const. Amend. VI. The Compulsory Process Clause, made applicable to state prosecutions by the Fourteenth Amendment, provides a basis for requesting the court to issue subpoenas for various documents and other evidence not available through other means.

It will be especially hard for the prosecution to argue against such subpoenas given the relatively limited amount of case law on the subject. As a matter of fact, the two most important cases on compulsory process both involve subpoenas directed to presidents of the United States, Thomas Jefferson and Richard Nixon. And, in both of those cases, the Court upheld the subpoenas. The Supreme Court discussed the relative lack of case law in this area in *Pennsylvania v. Ritchie*, 480 U.S. 39, 56-57 (1987), in which defendant Ritchie sought a new trial and access to confidential reports from the local child protection agency to aid in his defense on charges of child molestation:

> This Court has had little occasion to discuss the contours of the Compulsory Process Clause. The first and most celebrated analysis came from a Virginia federal court in 1807, during the treason and misdemeanor trials of Aaron Burr. Chief Justice Marshall, who presided as trial judge, ruled that Burr's compulsory process rights entitled him to serve a subpoena on President Jefferson, requesting the production of allegedly incriminating evidence. *United States v. Burr*, 25 F. Cas. 30, 35 (No. 14,692d) (CC Va. 1807). Despite the implications of the Burr decision for federal criminal procedure, the Compulsory Process Clause rarely was a factor in this Court's decisions during the next 160 years. More recently, however, the Court has articulated some of the specific rights secured by this part of the Sixth Amendment. Our cases establish, at a minimum, that criminal defendants have the right to the government's assistance in compelling the attendance of favorable witnesses at trial and the right to put before a jury evidence that might influence the determination of guilt.

> This Court has never squarely held that the Compulsory Process Clause guarantees the right to discover the identity of witnesses, or to require the government to produce exculpatory evidence. *But cf. United States v. Nixon*, 418 U.S. 683, 709, 711 (1974) (suggesting that the Clause may require the production of evidence). Instead, the Court traditionally has evaluated claims such as those raised by [the defendant] under the broader protections of the Due Process Clause of the Fourteenth Amendment. *See United States v. Bagley*, 473 U.S. 667 (1985); *Brady v. Maryland*, 373 U.S. 83 (1963). *See also Wardius v. Oregon*, 412 U.S. 470 (1973).

Ultimately the Court chose to adopt a due process analysis for purposes of the *Ritchie* case and deferred deciding whether and how the guarantees of the Compulsory Process Clause differ from those of the Fourteenth Amendment. 480 U.S. 39, 57. Under that analysis, the court decided that the defendant was entitled to have the file reviewed by the trial court to determine whether it contained information that probably would have changed the outcome of his trial.

Using these principles, you can issue, or have the court issue, depending on your local rules, a subpoena duces tecum for the officer's Field Sobriety Test Training Manual; operator, maintenance, and user manuals for the chemical tests (whether breath, blood or urine and whether for drugs or alcohol); 911 tapes and anything else you would like. Below is a sample of one such motion for the actual breath machine to be used as a template.

§1:21   Inspection of Breath Machine

The U.S. Supreme Court predicated its decision in *California v. Trombetta* [see §1:20], in major part, on the ability of the defense to get records and to see the machine and its environs. This is important to look for possible RFI sources, correct levels of electrical current, and other environmental factors (wet paint) which can affect the breath testing equipment.

§1:22   Motion for Subpoena Duces Tecum for Breath Machine

SUPERIOR COURT OF _____

COUNTY OF _____, _____ DISTRICT

)	Case No.:_____
)	
Plaintiff,)	
_____)	
)	
vs.)	
)	
_____)	
Defendant.)	

MOTION IN SUPPORT OF SUBPOENA DUCES TECUM FOR THE BREATH MACHINE USED IN THIS CASE

TO THE ABOVE ENTITLED COURT AND THE DISTRICT ATTORNEY OF RECORD:

COMES NOW, the defendant Dewey Drinkalot, by and through counsel of record, _____, and respectfully moves this court enter an order GRANTING the Issuance of a Subpoena Duces Tecum for the Intoxilyzer 5000 breath testing machine used in this matter.

This request is based on the attached Statement of Facts, Memorandum of Law, and supporting Declarations, as well as any evidence produced at the hearing.

Counsel further requests the right to submit additional Memoranda as necessitated by the evidence produced at the hearing.

Respectfully Submitted this ___ Day of _____, 20__.

_____
Attorney for Defendant

§1:23   Memorandum in Support of Motion for Subpoena Duces Tecum for Breath Machine

MEMORANDUM IN SUPPORT OF MOTION FOR SUBPOENA DUCES TECUM FOR THE BREATH MACHINE

In all criminal prosecutions, the accused shall enjoy the right to have compulsory process for obtaining witnesses in his favor. U.S. Const. Amend VI.

It is a long standing and well defined principle of Anglo-American jurisprudence that an accused is entitled to use the full power of the government to obtain evidence and compel testimony on his or her behalf. This principle, codified in the United States in the Sixth Amendment to the Constitution, has its history far deeper in time.

Lord Bacon recognized that all subjects must present their "knowledge and discovery," *Countess of Shrewsbury Case*, 2 How.St.Tr. 769, (1612), to the crown and the accused. This principle, which has roots at least as far back as 1562, was codified by 1742 when grand juries were recognized to have benefit of compulsory process based on the common law theory "the public has a right to every man's evidence." 12 T Hansard, Parliamentary History of England 675 (1812).

All of these sources were recognized as supporting the Sixth Amendment in *Kastigar v. U.S.* (1972) 406 U.S. 441. The Supreme Court went on to recognize that few limitations on this right can or should be recognized, and even certain other Constitutional rights must give way to this right.

One year later, the Supreme Court revisited the right to subpoena evidence in a landmark case. In *U.S. v. Nixon*, (1973) 418 U.S. 683, the president of the United States refused to honor a subpoena duces tecum. The Commander in Chief asserted that he was exempt from this process because of the nature of his office. This position was soundly rejected. Stating "the allowance of the privilege to withhold evidence that is demonstrably relevant in a criminal trial would cut deeply into the guarantee of due process of law and gravely impair the basic function of the courts," *Id*. At 712, the Court concluded that President Nixon could not ignore the subpoena.

The Court, noting many of the cases and histories cited above, held that even the president must produce evidence pursuant to a legitimate subpoena, unless he can show national security reasons for not doing so. (This must be reviewed by a court and shall not be taken at face value.) Furthermore, the Court noted that any privilege asserted to prevent compliance must be strictly reviewed as "Limitations are properly placed upon the operation of this general principle only to the very limited extent that permitting a refusal to testify or excluding relevant evidence has a public good transcending the normally predominant principle of utilizing all rational means for ascertaining the truth." *Id.* at 711.

In sum, the court noted, that "[t]he right to the production of all evidence at a criminal trial has constitutional dimensions" that "[i]t is the manifest duty of the courts to vindicate" requiring "all relevant and admissible evidence be produced." *Id.* at 711. *See also U.S. v. Nobles* (1974) 422 U.S. 225 ("To ensure that justice is done, it is imperative to the function of the courts that compulsory process be available for the production of evidence needed either by the prosecution or the defense.").

If the president of the greatest nation must honor a subpoena from the lowliest defendant, how can this court sanction the refusal to produce evidence necessary for the defense of this matter by a mere city attorney?

What the defense is hereby requesting is merely the right to defend. As was stated in *Washington v. State of Texas* (1967) 87 S.Ct. 1920, 1923:

> The right to offer the testimony of witnesses, and to compel their attendance, if necessary, is in plain terms the right to assert a defense, the right to present the defendant's version of the facts as well as the prosecution's to the jury so it may decide where the truth lies. . . . This right is a fundamental element of due process of law.

This right to compel witnesses and present evidence has been held so important, that it can override duly enacted state laws, *Id;* rules of evidence, *Chambers v. Mississippi*, (1973) 410 U.S. 284, or virtually any rule that prevents the presentation of a complete defense. *Crane v. Kentucky* (1986) 106 S.Ct. 2142.

The court should be mindful that it has been the prosecution that has been attempting to keep evidence away from the trier of fact. We made a discovery request to view the machine pursuant to *California v. Trombetta* (1989) 104 S.Ct. 2528. The prosecution failed to cooperate and so we brought this motion for a subpoena.

Respectfully Submitted this ___ Day of _____, 20__.

_____
Attorney for Defendant

§1:24   Statement of Facts in Support of Motion for Subpoena Duces Tecum for Breath Machine

STATEMENT OF FACTS

I, _____, attorney of record in the above entitled case, hereby state the following facts to be true and correct based upon information and belief:

1. I am the attorney of record in said case and as such am fully familiar with the facts of the case, including but not limited to, the police reports previously supplied by the district attorney's representative in this case.
2. Based upon these police reports, which have been submitted by the officers under penalty of perjury, Mr. Drinkalot was subjected to a breath test by way of an Intoxilyzer 5000. Specifically number 66-2486.
3. Attached hereto and incorporated herein by reference is the supplemental informal request for discovery issued by my office with regards to this machine (Attachment A).
4. Attached hereto is the response by the prosecution (Attachment B).
5. Counsel and, more importantly, Mr. Drinkalot's expert need to examine this machine prior to trial. (See Declaration of Ms. Knowitall attached to Attachment A).
6. Furthermore, counsel needs to use the machine as evidence in the above captioned trial.

Respectfully Submitted this ___ Day of _____, 20__.

_____
Attorney for Defendant

[§§1:25-1:29 Reserved]

IV.   DUE PROCESS AND MOTIONS IN LIMINE

A. General Points

§1:30   Legal Principles

Under the American system of jurisprudence, an individual who comes into contact with law enforcement and/or the criminal justice system has a number of well-defined rights. These rights can be found in the explicit language of the Bill of Rights (*e.g.*, the Fourth Amendment's prohibition against unreasonable search and seizures, the Fifth Amendment's protection against self-incrimination, and the Sixth Amendment's guarantee of counsel, the right to confront adverse witnesses, and the right to compulsory process). They may also be found in the case law interpreting and defining these rights. This concept of protection of the accused has been summed up in a number of decisions by the Supreme Court as fundamental due process.

Due process is applicable, not just to federal cases, but to state procedures and prosecutions as well, through the Fourteenth Amendment. These cases have established an accused has certain fundamental rights that he or she must be afforded prior to a loss of liberty imposed by the government. These fundamental rights of due process are so significant they supersede any other law that may interfere with their full enjoyment.

Perhaps the best outline of the basic requirements of due process exists in the often cited case of *In re Oliver*, 333 U.S. 257 (1948). This case, dealing with summary contempt proceedings, detailed much of the history of the rights of the accused. After reviewing in detail the right of the accused to a public hearing, the Court held:

> [F]ailure to afford the petitioner a reasonable opportunity to defend himself against the charge of false and evasive swearing was a denial of due process of law. A person's right to reasonable notice of a charge against him, and an opportunity to be heard in his defense-a right to his day in court-are basic in our system of jurisprudence; and these rights include, as a minimum, a right to examine the witnesses against him, to offer testimony, and to be represented by counsel.

Whether rooted directly in the Due Process Clause of the Fourteenth Amendment, *Chambers v. Mississippi*, 410 U.S. 284, 302 (1973), or in the Compulsory Process or Confrontation clauses of the Sixth Amendment, *Washington v. Texas*, 388 U.S. 14, 23 (1967); *Davis v. Alaska*, 415 U.S. 308 (1974), the Constitution guarantees criminal defendants "a meaningful opportunity to present a complete defense." *California v. Trombetta*, 467 U.S. at 485; *cf. Strickland v. Washington*, 466 U.S. 668, 684-685 (1984) ("The Constitution guarantees a fair trial through the Due Process Clauses, but it defines the basic elements of a fair trial largely through the several provisions of the Sixth Amendment").

An essential component of procedural fairness is an opportunity to be heard. *In re Oliver*, 333 U.S. 257, 273 (1948); *Grannis v. Ordean*, 234 U.S. 385, 394 (1914). This right is so fundamentally important, it has been used by the Supreme Court to overturn a variety of state laws. In considering whether state required discovery rules can be used to preclude presentation of defense witnesses in *Taylor v. Illinois*, 484 U.S. 400 (1988), the court stated:

> "[O]ur cases establish, at a minimum, that criminal defendants have the right to the government's assistance in compelling the attendance of favorable witnesses at trial and the right to put before a jury evidence that might influence the determination of guilt." *Pennsylvania v. Ritchie*, 480 U.S. 39, 56 (1987). Few rights are more fundamental than that of an accused to present witnesses in his own defense, *see, e. g., Chambers v. Mississippi*, 410 U.S. 284, 302 (1973). Indeed, this right is an essential attribute of the adversary system itself. [484 U.S. 400, 408] . . . . The right of the defendant to present evidence "stands on no lesser footing than the other Sixth Amendment rights that we have previously held applicable to the States." *Id.* at 18. We cannot accept the State's argument that this constitutional right may never be offended by the imposition of a discovery sanction that entirely excludes the testimony of a material defense witness." [484 U.S. 400, 410].

Few other rights are as important as the right for an accused to present his or her side of the story. In defending this right, even evidentiary rules have been struck down. *E.g., Webb v. Texas*, 409 U.S. 95 (1972) (trial court's extended admonition to petitioner's only witness to refrain from lying, coupled with threats of dire consequences if witness did lie, effectively discouraged the witness from testifying at all and deprived petitioner of due process by denying him the opportunity to present witnesses in his own defense); *Washington v. Texas*, 388 U.S. 14, 19 (1967) (state statutes that permitted co-participant in crime to testify for prosecution, but not for defense, denied defendant right to material testimony of a witness, and thus denied defendant right to compulsory process for obtaining witnesses in his favor); *Chambers v. Mississippi*, 410 U.S. 284 (1973) (murder defendant was denied due process by evidence rule that prohibited him from cross-examining his own witness who had confessed murder to third persons and by trial court's refusal to allow hearsay statements of third persons regarding witness' confession).

While states have the power to exclude evidence through evidentiary rules that serve the interests of fairness and reliability, limitations on evidence may exceed the bounds of due process where such limitations undermine a defendant's ability to present exculpatory evidence without serving a valid state justification. *Montana v. Egelhoff*, 518 U.S. 37, 63 (1996) (dissenting opinion).

As Justice O'Connor stated in her dissenting opinion in *Egelhoff*:

> Due process demands that a criminal defendant be afforded a fair opportunity to defend against the State's accusations. Meaningful adversarial testing of the State's case requires that the defendant not be prevented from raising an effective defense, which must include the right to present relevant, probative evidence. To be sure, the right to present evidence is not limitless; for example, it does not permit the defendant to introduce any and all evidence he believes might work in his favor, . . . , nor does it generally invalidate the operation of testimonial privileges, ... Nevertheless, "an essential component of procedural fairness is an opportunity to be heard. That opportunity would be an empty one if the State were permitted to exclude competent, reliable evidence" that is essential to the accused's defense. (Citations omitted.) *Id.* at 63, 64.

If we combine these foundational concepts, with dedication and mix in a little creativity we can come up with motions in limine that are effective in both getting our evidence admitted and keeping the prosecution's evidence out. In DUI cases, it can be argued that the defendant is merely seeking to defend himself by presenting easily obtainable, non-privileged, highly relevant evidence. On the other hand, the State is seeking to prevent it based not on any constitutional argument, or even any evidentiary objection, but merely on an argument of convenience. Therefore, given the constitutional rights involved, as specifically stated in the Bill of Rights and as interpreted by the wealth of United States Supreme Court Cases, the court can have little doubt that the evidence should be provided.

§1:31   Defendant's Motion in Limine (General Example)

In my jurisdiction, Motions in Limine are typically filed the morning of trial and are hurried through in about 30 minutes before selecting a jury. Their importance, however, cannot be overstated. These are the "rules of the game," so to speak. The court is essentially giving you the parameters through which you can tell your story effectively, or not. I will typically file several boilerplate motions in limine in every case, and have one section of my motions brief that is specific to the evidentiary issues in the case at bar. My motions are presented in short format with (usually brief) legal reasoning behind them. I have included examples of my motions in limine in addition to the extensive and well thought out memoranda from previous editions on specific issues.

DISTRICT COURT OF _____

COUNTY OF _____, _____ STATE OF WASHINGTON

	)	Case No.:_____
	)	
Plaintiff,	)	DEFENDANT'S PRETRIAL
_____	)	MOTIONS IN LIMINE
	)	AND ORDERS THEREON
vs.	)	
	)	
_____	)	
Defendant.	)	

DEFENDANT'S MOTION IN LIMINE

TO THE ABOVE ENTITLED COURT AND THE DISTRICT ATTORNEY OF SAID COUNTY:

COMES NOW, the defendant, by and through counsel of record, and respectfully moves this Court for an order in limine on the following issues:

I.1   The defense moves that the prosecution's **witnesses be excluded** from the courtroom during all trial proceedings. <u>Basis:</u> ER 615

Defense Motion is _____
(granted/denied/reserved)

I.2   The defense moves to preclude prosecution's witnesses, including police officers, from further **discussing their testimony with one another** or in the presence of the jurors until the close of proceedings. <u>Basis:</u> ER 615

Defense Motion is _____
(granted/denied/reserved)

I.3   The defense moves to **cross endorse all of the prosecution's witnesses** and requests they be directed by the Court and prosecutor to remain available and subject to recall by the defense.

Defense Motion is _____
(granted/denied/reserved)

I.4   The defense moves that the the parties be granted **60 minutes per side for jury selection**.
<u>Basis:</u> DUI is a complicated crime involving many moving parts. Many jurors have strong opinions regarding this crime. Often lively discussions regarding bias and burden of proof will become a crucial part of the voir dire process. Although not all may be needed, having a full 60 minutes of time with the panel ensures that all issues and discussions can be had in a full and fair manner without compromising the defendant's rights to an appropriate jury.

Defense Motion is _____
(granted/denied/reserved)

Respectfully Submitted this ___ Day of _____, 20__.

_____
Attorney for Defendant

[§§1:32-1:39 Reserved]

B. Partition Ratios

§1:40   Admissibility of Testimony Regarding Blood/Breath Partition Ratios

The partition ratio is the relationship of alcohol in the breath to alcohol in the blood. Evidence of individual variations in partition ratios is not admissible in all jurisdictions. Originally state per se statutes were phrased in terms of blood alcohol levels so breath machines had to convert the results to blood alcohol levels. They do that by multiplying the breath alcohol results by 2100 even though some individuals have lower (and higher) conversion ratios and an individual's partition ratio varies depending on food consumption and other factors. Thus, evidence of variation in partition ratios was admissible to show that breath tests do not accurately measure blood alcohol. Then many jurisdictions circumvented the need for partition ratios by amending their statutes to provide that driving with a specific level of breath alcohol was an offense. As a result, their courts refused to admit partition ratio evidence ruling that the evidence violated the legislative intent to create a specific breath limit. *See, e.g., People v. Bransford*, 884 P.2d 70 (Cal. 1995) (testimony of defendant's individual partition ratio was inadmissible, especially when the defendant exhibited clear signs of alcohol); *Burks v. State*, 394 S.E.2d 136, 137 (Ga. Ct. App. 1990) (testimony of a defendant's individual partition ratio of 1680:1 on day before trial was inadmissible when the defendant exhibited other visible signs of intoxication).

However, this concept is losing favor and can be overcome as outlined below. Admission of partition ratio evidence is important in borderline cases to build in a doubt as to the true blood alcohol level as opposed to the stated breath alcohol level. Additionally, it can be used to reduce a low breath result, say .09, to below .08, thereby eliminating any presumptions for the common law charge.

§1:41   Memorandum in Support of Defendant's Motion in Limine to Introduce Partition Ratio Evidence

MEMORANDUM IN SUPPORT OF DEFENDANT'S MOTION IN LIMINE TO INTRODUCE PARTITION RATIO EVIDENCE

TESTIMONY REGARDING SCIENTIFICALLY ACCEPTED VALUES FOR BLOOD BREATH PARTITION RATIOS IS ADMISSIBLE TO DEFEND AGAINST THE CHARGE THAT DEFENDANT WAS DRIVING WHILE IMPAIRED

Defendant requests permission to introduce general testimony regarding scientifically accepted values for blood breath partition ratios. For more than fifty years, the Supreme Court has clearly articulated the principle that in our justice system, a defendant has the fundamental right to present a defense and to present witnesses. In *In re Oliver*, Justice Black declared that a defendant's "right to his day in court" is "basic in our system of jurisprudence" and includes "as a minimum, a right to examine the witnesses against him, *to offer testimony*, and to be represented by counsel." 333 U.S. 257, 273 (1948) (emphasis added). Since then, the Supreme Court has again and again noted the "fundamental" or "essential" character of a defendant's right both to present a defense, *Crane v. Kentucky*, 476 U.S. 683, 687, 690 (1986); *California v. Trombetta*, 467 U.S. 479, 485 (1984); *Webb v. Texas*, 409 U.S. 95, 98 (1972); *Washington v. Texas*, 388 U.S. 14, 19 (1967), and to present witnesses as a part of that defense. *Taylor v. Illinois*, 484 U.S. 400, 408 (1988); *Rock v. Arkansas*, 483 U.S. 44, 55 (1987); *Chambers v. Mississippi*, 410 U.S. 284, 294, 302 (1973); *Webb*, 409 U.S. at 98; *Washington*, 388 at 19. The Court has repeatedly stated that a defendant's right to a defense and right to present witnesses and evidence emanates from the Sixth Amendment and the Due Process Clause of the Fourteenth Amendment. *Crane*, 476 U.S. at 294; *Strickland v. Washington*, 466 U.S. 668, 684-85 (1984); *Washington*, 388 U.S. at 17-18.

The Sixth Amendment source of these rights is the Compulsory Process Clause, which embraces "the right to have the witness' testimony heard by the trier of fact." *Taylor*, 484 U.S. at 409. *Washington* formally incorporated the Compulsory Process Clause into the Due Process Clause of the Fourteenth Amendment. 388 U.S. at 17-19. That case stated:

> The right to offer the testimony of witnesses, and to compel their attendance, if necessary, is in plain terms the right to present a defense, the right to present the defendant's version of the facts as well as the prosecution's to the jury so it may decide where the truth lies. Just as an accused has the right to confront the prosecution's witnesses for the purpose of challenging their testimony, he has the right to present his own witnesses to establish a defense. This right is a fundamental element of due process of law. *Id.* at 19.

The defendant in this case is seeking to bring forward evidence related to the section 23152(a) charge levied against him. Specifically, the defense seeks to introduce evidence concerning the variability of partition ratios. The State will likely argue that evidence on partition ratio variability is inadmissible under *People v. Bransford*, 8 Cal. 4th 885 (1994).

In *Bransford*, the court held that a defendant is not entitled to raise partition ratios to defend against a charge under California Vehicle Code section 23152(b) that he or she was driving with .08 percent or greater blood alcohol concentration. *Bransford* reasoned that, as amended, the statute defined the offense in terms of specific grams of alcohol per liter of breath, thereby rendering partition ratios comparing volume of blood to volume of breath irrelevant and therefore inadmissible. *Id.* at 893. Yet *Bransford* was silent on the relevance of partition ratio evidence to charges brought under California Vehicle Code section 23152(a).

People v. Acevedo, 113 Cal.Rptr.2d 437 (2001), interpreted *Bransford* to be self-limiting. *Acevedo* applied *Bransford* exclusively to section 23152(b), and to breath-alcohol, rather than blood-alcohol or urine-alcohol, test result challenges. *Id.* at 441-43. Accordingly, the *Acevedo* court found that *People v. Lepine*, 263 Cal.Rptr. 543 (1989), rather than *Bransford*, applies when urine-alcohol test results are at issue. Following the *Acevedo* court's reasoning, *Lepine* also controls when section 23152(a), rather than section 23152(b) charges are at issue. Under *Lepine*, a jury is allowed to consider that partition ratios may vary from time to time and from individual to individual.

State v. Hanks, 772 A.2d 1087 (Vt.1998), the only court to squarely address *Bransford's* application to partition ratios outside of section 23152(b) breath-alcohol test result challenges, also construes *Bransford* narrowly. At issue in *Hanks* was a Vermont statute that, like section 23152, distinguishes between so-called "generic" DUI violations that make it unlawful to drive while under the influence of intoxicating liquor, and "per se" DUI violations that make it unlawful to drive with a blood-alcohol concentration above a specified level. The *Hanks* court ruled that a defendant can introduce partition ratio evidence to defend against a "generic" statutory DUI charge. According to *Hanks*, *Bransford* only controls when "per se" statutory DUI charges are at issue. Hanks stated:

> Because defendant is charged with driving while under the influence rather than driving with an alcohol concentration exceeding the statutory limit, admitting scientifically accepted evidence concerning the variability of partition ratios will not negate a statutory offense or even an element of a statutory offense; rather, it will merely allow defendant to challenge the permissive inference and the State's charge that he was impaired.

Id. at 1092-93. We agree.

"The Sixth Amendment guarantees the right of an accused in a criminal prosecution to be confronted with the witnesses against him." *Alvarado v. Superior Court*, 23 Cal.4th 1121, 1137 (2000). The right of confrontation, "means more than being allowed to confront the witness physically." *Id.* Indeed, "[t]he main and essential purpose of confrontation is to secure for the opponent the opportunity of cross-examination." *Id.* The presumption of a person with a blood-alcohol content of .08 or greater being under the influence of intoxicating liquor is one affecting the burden of proof and requires the defendant to raise a reasonable doubt as to the existence of the presumed fact. Evidence of partition ratio variability has long been used in this state to rebut this presumption in the section 23152(a) context. *See People v. Campos*, 188 Cal.Rptr. 366 (1982). It is clear, under both *Acevedo* and *Hanks*, that *Bransford* does not render this evidence inadmissible to defend against section 23152(a) prosecutions.

Respectfully Submitted this ___ Day of _____, 20__.

_____
Attorney for Defendant

[§§1:42-1:49 Reserved]

C. Tolerance

§1:50   Precluding Evidence of Tolerance

More and more often we see the prosecution seeking to introduce evidence of tolerance through their expert. The evidence is often introduced through general testimony regarding what tolerance is and how it would come into play in a DUI case. Tolerance evidence is intended to explain discrepancies between the defendant's good performance on field sobriety tests or everyday activities and his or her high breath, blood, or urine test results (*i.e.*, that at a .20 the defendant should be falling down). The idea is to leave the jury with the thought that the discrepancy is because the defendant is a chronic drinker who can hold his or her booze and not because the chemical test results are wrong.

§1:51   Memorandum in Support of Defendant's Motion in Limine to Exclude Evidence of Tolerance

MEMORANDUM IN SUPPORT OF DEFENDANT'S MOTION IN LIMINE TO EXCLUDE EVIDENCE OF TOLERANCE

A.   Introduction

It is anticipated that the prosecution will attempt to argue "tolerance" and present "general" evidence of tolerance, that is, that some people can be "tolerant" to alcohol due to their history of drinking excessively on a regular basis.

B.   Evidence of Tolerance Is Inadmissible for Lack of Foundation Because the Prosecution Has No Proof That the Defendant Has a History of Drinking

The proponent of the proffered evidence has the burden of producing evidence as to the existence of the preliminary fact, and the proffered evidence is inadmissible unless the court finds that there is evidence sufficient to sustain a finding of the existence of the preliminary fact, when the relevance of the proffered evidence depends on the existence of the preliminary fact. Cal. Evid. Code §403(a).

There is no evidence that this defendant has a history of heavy alcohol consumption or that the defendant has any acquired tolerance to alcohol, or acquired the ability over time through practice to hide the effects of alcohol. Therefore, any evidence suggested by the prosecution of the defendant's prolonged and/or excessive drinking (*i.e.*, tolerance) is objected to on the grounds of foundation. The prosecution cannot demonstrate that such "possible" evidence relates to this defendant.

C.   Evidence of Tolerance Is Inadmissible "Profile" Evidence

In *People v. Robbie* (2001) 92 Cal. App. 4th 1075, the court held that the trial court abused discretion in admitting expert testimony constituting profile evidence. The prosecution, in a case alleging sexual crimes, called an "expert" from the Department of Justice "in the area of the behaviors and conducts of persons who commit sexual assaults." The expert had a great deal of expertise investigating sexual offenders. The testimony was that not all rapes involved violence or injury to the victim and described various kinds of conduct engaged in by rapists that were consistent with the facts of the prosecution's case, *e.g.*, the offender returned the victim to her neighborhood, engaged in small conversation, and other behaviors the expert testified were all consistent with sex offenders.

The Appellate Court noted that the admission of expert testimony will not be disturbed on appeal unless a manifest of abuse of discretion is shown (citation omitted) and that the expert's testimony constituted improper profile evidence. "Profiles" are a collection of conduct and characteristics commonly displayed by those who commit a certain crime. The court noted that "profile evidence is generally inadmissible to prove guilt." For example, drug courier profiles have been held to be "inherently prejudicial because of the potential they have for including innocent citizens as profile drug couriers...." Every defendant has a right to be tried based on the evidence against him, not on techniques utilized by law enforcement officials in investigating criminal activity. Drug court profile evidence is nothing more than the opinion of those officers conducting the investigations. *U.S. v. Beltran-Rios* (9th Cir. 1989) 878 F.2d 1208, 1210, quoting *United States v. Hernandez-Cuartas* (11th Cir.1983) 717 F.2d 552, 555.

In *People v. Martinez* (1992) 10 Cal. App. 4th 1001, the court rejected the use of profile evidence regarding driving a stolen truck. The trial court allowed police investigators to testify about the operation of auto theft rings which happened to match the defendant's circumstances (*e.g.*, the driver's denying knowledge that the vehicle was stolen), although the evidence was not characterized as a profile. *Id.* at 1006. The appellate court held that those issues are inappropriate for consideration on the issue of guilt or innocence because of the potential of including innocent people as well as the guilty.

Similarly, in *People v. Castaneda* (1997) 55 Cal. App. 4th 1067, testimony that the defendant "perfectly fit" the profile of a heroin dealer was inadmissible. The court held "every defendant has the right to be tried based on the evidence trying him to a specific crime charged, and not on general facts accumulated by law enforcement regarding a particular profile." *Id.* at 1072.

As stated by the *Robbie* court, "profile evidence is inherently prejudicial because it requires the jury to accept an erroneous starting point in its consideration of the evidence. The syllogism is that 'criminals act a certain way; the defendant acted that way; therefore, the defendant is a criminal.' Guilt flows from the major premise to the minor premise to the conclusion." The prosecution would argue that the defendant may have a high tolerance to alcohol (without evidence of that fact) and that is why he drove fairly well or to argue "possible" reasons for defendant's performance on the balance tests. The problem is that people who are not guilty of driving under the influence or having a BAC of .08% or higher also can drive fairly well, perform well on FSTs, and otherwise not show gross impairment.

D.   Evidence of Tolerance Is Inadmissible Because it Is More Prejudicial Than Probative

The court in its discretion may exclude evidence if its probative value is substantially outweighed by the probability that its admission will create substantial danger of undue prejudice, of confusing the issues, or of misleading the jury. Cal. Evid. Code §352. To allow the prosecution to introduce general evidence of "tolerance" without connecting it to the defendant would be to admit irrelevant, prejudicial, and speculative evidence. Such speculative evidence of tolerance, (*i.e.*, this defendant could be habitually drunk), is further objected to on the grounds of Evid. Code §352.

General evidence that the defendant might be a person who drinks excessively on a regular basis (thereby allowing an inference of conduct in conformity therewith) is highly prejudicial; especially when the prosecution has no evidence that the defendant drinks excessively on a regular basis. To allow the prosecution to present "general" evidence of tolerance, inferring that the defendant's conduct maybe in conformity therewith, would violate due process and the right to a fair trial.

The prosecution has no evidence that the defendant has a history of excessive and/or prolonged use of alcohol. Instead, the prosecution would inquire from its expert to extrapolate about the various possibilities that may exist in the world regarding the fact that some (other) people have acquired a tolerance to alcohol.

The prosecution expert would use a "blue print." Since some people are tolerant to alcohol, the defendant may be tolerant due to prolonged and excessive drinking. Because "criminal prosecutions cannot be blueprinted, but must be tailored to the charges and facts of each case in consideration of the individual rights of each defendant," such a method of imputing tolerance lacks any probative value and is impermissible. *See United States v. Vallejo*, 237 F.3d. 1008 (9th Cir. 2001).

The expert testimony would portray this productive citizen as a person who might possibly drink alcohol excessively on a regular basis without any evidence that those facts are true. Such evidence is improper expert testimony imputing facts to the defendant without any basis whatsoever and would constitute prejudicial error.

E.   Character Evidence of Prior and Prolonged Excessive Drinking Is Prohibited by Evidence Code §1101

California Evidence Code section 1101(a) provides that evidence of a person's character or a trait of his or her character (whether in the form of an opinion, evidence of reputation, or evidence of specific instances of his or her conduct) is inadmissible when offered to prove his or her conduct on a specific occasion. All the more does the exclusion apply when there is no opinion, reputation, or specific incidents. "Tolerance" is only another word for continued and excessive drinking over a long period of time, *i.e.*, character evidence. Even if the prosecution had evidence that the defendant drinks excessively on a regular basis, it would be excluded under Evidence Code section 1101 as inadmissible character evidence. The prosecution has no such evidence.

[Since some states follow the Federal Rules of Evidence, you may want to include the following.]

F.   "Propensity" Evidence Violates the Right to Due Process

The courts have held that propensity evidence violates an accused's right to due process. *Boyd v. United States* (1892) 142 U.S. 450; *Michelson v. United States* (1948) 355 U.S. 469; *Estelle v. McGuire* (1991) 502 U.S. 62; *McKinney v. Rees* (9th Cir. 1993) 993 F.2d 1378.

Federal Rule of Evidence 404(b) generally prohibits the introduction of evidence of other crimes, wrongs or acts to demonstrate the defendant's bad character, moral turpitude or criminal disposition to prove he acted in conformity with the prior acts or events. *United States v. Summer* 119 F.3d 658 (8th Cir. 1997); *United States v. Roberts* 88 F. 3d 872 (10th Cir. 1996).

G. Evidence of Prior Criminal Activity Is Inadmissible

Evidence of prior criminal activity is inadmissible to show defendant is a bad person or acted criminally on the occasion at issue. There is not a "conviction" for tolerance (or prior convictions for DUI). There is no proof of tolerance. To allow "tolerance" into evidence and somehow suggest that this defendant may have the acquired trait of tolerance due to the possibility of his excessive drinking would deny the defendant a fair trial.

H. Conclusion

There is no evidence that this defendant drinks excessively on a regular basis. If the court allows evidence of tolerance to alcohol, it would violate the policies that exclude reputation evidence and specific incidents of bad conduct. The admission of such prejudicial and speculative evidence would render the trial fundamentally unfair and deny defendant due process. This is all the more true when there is no evidence of regular excessive drinking by this defendant.

Respectfully Submitted this ___ Day of _____, 20__.

_____
Attorney for Defendant

[§§1:52-1:59 Reserved]

D. Retrograde Extrapolation

§1:60 Precluding Evidence of Retrograde Extrapolation

Retrograde extrapolation is a questionable process of looking at the chemical result at a specific time, say midnight, and predicting what the level it would have been earlier, say at 10:00 pm. This calculation is based on two major assumptions: first, that the person is eliminating alcohol (*i.e.*, his or her BAC is going down); and second, that the person is eliminating alcohol at a specific rate. The second assumption is based on the very limited range of elimination for all people. That range is roughly .015 to .02 per hour.

The first assumption is much more problematic. In order to know if the person is eliminating, one needs to know when the person started drinking, when the person finished drinking, the stomach contents and the person's metabolism, just to name a few factors. *See* Bartell et al., *Attacking and Defending Drunk Driving Tests* (James Publishing) for more details on this.

The prosecution likes to introduce retrograde extrapolation evidence because their expert will always opine that the defendant's blood alcohol was higher at the time of driving than the chemical test results. It makes your client look drunker.

§1:61 Memorandum in Support of Defendant's Motion in Limine to Preclude Evidence of Retrograde Extrapolation

**MEMORANDUM IN SUPPORT OF DEFENDANT'S MOTION
IN LIMINE TO PRECLUDE EVIDENCE OF RETROGRADE EXTRAPOLATION**

"It is a rebuttable presumption that the person had 0.08% or more, by weight, of alcohol in his or her blood at the time of driving the vehicle if the person had 0.08 percent, by weight, of alcohol in his or her blood at the time of performance of a chemical test within three hours after the driving." Cal. Vehicle Code section 23152(b). The defendant's blood draw occurred two hours and twenty minutes after the time of driving creating a rebuttable presumption. It is anticipated that the prosecution will ask the state's expert to perform a retrograde extrapolation from the defendant's blood test results to determine the defendant's blood alcohol at the time of driving. The extrapolation is not valid in the instant case. The reason is simple. The criminalist doing the "retrograde extrapolation" calculation must know, among other things, that the test subject is in the "eliminative" phase. Thus, a criminalist cannot do a valid "retrograde extrapolation" without a drinking and eating history.

The defense is unaware of any scientific literature or case law that supports a "retrograde extrapolation" when the expert or person performing the calculation does not have any of the following factors: (1) when the person began to drink; (2) when the person stopped drinking; (3) how much the person drank; (4) what the person drank; (5) how much the person weighs; and (6) if the person had a full or empty stomach. Given that such information, in whole or in part, is missing from this case, allowing testimony regarding retrograde extrapolation violates due process and scientific principles.

A preeminent forensic scientist, Dr. Kurt M. Dubowski, summarized the problems with "retrograde extrapolation" in his frequently cited article, "Absorption, Distribution and Elimination of Alcohol: Highway Safety Aspects," first published in the Journal of Studies of Alcohol (copy attached for the convenience of the Court and the parties. The quotation is found at pg. 106).32 Dr. Dubowski concluded "no forensically valid forward or backward extrapolation of blood or breath alcohol concentrations is ordinarily possible in a given subject and occasion solely on the basis of time and individual analysis results."

The Criminal Appeals Court of Texas in *Mata v. State*, 46 S.W.3d 902 (Text. Crim. App. 2001), addressed this issue and the scientific technique of "retrograde extrapolation" in excruciating detail. The *Mata* Court took judicial notice of scientific literature in the area and cited in its opinion numerous publications. The cited authority included that of Richard Watkins, Assistant Director of the Phoenix Crime Lab, and Eugene Adler, a toxicologist for the Arizona Department of Public Safety. *Id.* at 910; *see* "The Effect of Food on Alcohol Absorption and Elimination Patterns," 38 J. of Forensic Science 285-291 (1993). The *Mata* Court, citing from Watkins and Adler, stated that:

> The limitations and pitfalls associated with retrograde extrapolations are often not appreciated by lawmen and the courts. The authors [Watkins and Adler] conclude that "any attempt at retrograde extrapolations should be made with caution, and performed by a person able to assess and discuss the applicability of a retrograde extrapolation to a particular situation." *Id.* at 910.

The court noted that Watkins and Adler were cautious about the reliability of retrograde extrapolation. *Id.* The court relying on other experts in the field wrote the following:

> They [Watkins and Adler] write that retrograde extrapolation is a "dubious practice" and that expert testimony on the issue "requires careful consideration of the absorption kinetics of ethanol and the factors influencing this process." They explain that "the absorption profile of ethanol differs widely among individuals, and the peak [BAC] and the time of its occurrence depends on numerous factors. Among other factors, the drinking pattern, the type of beverage consumed, the fed or fasted state, the nature and composition of foodstuff in the stomach, the anatomy of the gastrointestinal canal, and the mental state of the subject are considered to play a role."

The *Mata* Court acknowledged that few jurisdictions have considered the reliability of "retrograde extrapolation" because many states have eliminated the need for "retrograde extrapolation" as a matter of law. *Id.* at 913. The statutes in these jurisdictions provide for a rebuttable presumption if the person's BAC is over the legal limit, "assuming the test was conducted within a specified or reasonable time from driving." *Id.*

The *Mata* Court was only able to find two courts in the entire nation that have touched upon issues of reliability of "retrograde extrapolation." *Id.* An Arizona appellate court made reference to the issue in a footnote stating that "the science of 'retrograde extrapolation' has achieved general acceptance in the scientific field." *Id.* citing *Ring v. Taylor*, 141 Ariz. 56, 59 fn 6. (Ariz. App. 1984).

The other court that discussed the issue of "retrograde extrapolation" was the Alabama Court of Appeals in *Smith v. Tuscaloosa*, 601 So. 2d 1136 (Ala. Crim. App. 1992). *Id.* at 913-914. The Alabama Court disagreed with the Arizona Court and found from studies that "retrograde extrapolation" is an unreliable method of determining a person's BAC. *Id.*

The inadequacies of retrograde extrapolation extend beyond mere technical inaccuracies to problems that are inherent in the basic premises and calculations of this technique. These inadequacies render retrograde extrapolation inherently untrustworthy and therefore inappropriate for use as evidence to convict drunk drivers. *Id.* at 914.

After complete and thorough study of retrograde extrapolation, the *Mata* Court concluded that, even those who advocate retrograde extrapolation as a reliable technique, use it only if certain factors are known, "such as the length of the drinking spree, the time of the last drink, and the person's weight." *Id.* at 915. The Texas Court further concluded:

The court evaluating the reliability of a retrograde extrapolation should also consider (a) the length of time between the offense and the tests administered; (b) the number of tests given and the length of time between each test; and (c) whether, and if so, to what extent, any individual characteristics of the defendant were known to the expert in providing the extrapolation. These characteristics and behaviors might include, but are not limited to, the person's weight and gender, the person's typical drinking pattern and tolerance for alcohol, how much the person had to drink on the day or night in question, what the person drank, the duration of the drinking spree, the time of the last drink, and how much and what the person had to eat either before, during, or after the drinking. *Id.* at 916.

Conclusion

Wherefore, the defense requests that the Court preclude the state from mentioning or eliciting any testimony regarding "retrograde extrapolation" as a result of the blood draw in this matter.

Respectfully Submitted this ___ Day of _____, 20__.

_____
Attorney for Defendant

[§§1:62-1:69 Reserved]

E. Prosecutorial Misconduct

§1:70   Precluding Prosecutorial Misconduct

When you read the following you probably will see things done to you that you either did not know were misconduct or did not have authority to use in objecting. If you did object and did have authority, the judge probably said it was done mistakenly and so only an admonition was necessary.

By filing this motion pre-trial, you are putting the prosecution on notice *not* to do any of these acts, and that if they do, it should result in a mistrial since they were on notice. In this regards it is a pre-emptive strike.

Special thanks to Ed Luss and Les Hulnick for this motion.

§1:71   Memorandum in Support of Defendant's Motion in Limine to Preclude Prosecutorial Misconduct

MEMORANDUM IN SUPPORT OF DEFENDANT'S MOTION IN LIMINE TO PRECLUDE PROSECUTORIAL MISCONDUCT

Counsel, by this motion, seeks to preclude the prosecution from engaging in conduct that many practitioners and courts heretofore have allowed due to ignorance of the illegal nature of such conduct. Post-comment curative instructions DO NOT adequately ensure a fair trial and so pre-comment rulings are necessary. Thus, the defendant requests the Court to preclude the prosecution from any of the following:

1. Any statement, remark, or insinuation that is intended to discredit defense counsel in front of the jury. *State v. Lundbom*, 96 Or. App. 458, 773 P.2d 11 (1989) (referring to defense counsel as "pimp" and "hired gun"); *Carter v. State*, 356 So. 2d 67 (Fla. App. 1978) (prosecutor referred to defense counsel as a "mouthpiece"); *Commonwealth v. Long*, 392 A.2d 810, 813 (Pa. Super. Ct. 1978) (prosecutor referred to defense counsel as a "not guilty machine"); *Commonwealth v. Sargent*, 385 A.2d 484 (Pa. Super. Ct. 1978) (reference to fact that defendant had a "paid attorney" hired to "acquit"); *People v. Weller*, 258 NE2d 806, 810 (Ill App Ct 1970) (stating that defense counsel "could... qualify as an SS Trooper").

2. Any statement that exalts the role of the prosecutor over that of the defender, *e.g.*, "I represent the people of the State of _____" etc. *Dykes v. State*, 325 S.W.2d 135 (Tex Crim App 1959) (prosecutor stated defense counsel is a mouthpiece for rapists and murderers, whereas counsel for the state is a public servant paid to represent the people of the community).

3. Any expression of the personal opinion of the prosecutor that the defendant is guilty, or that any particular witness is credible or not credible. *State v. Gairson*, 5 Or. App. 464, 469, 484 P.2d 854 (1971).

4. Reference to facts outside the record including comment or argument regarding matters pertaining to the societal risks posed by drunk drivers and other such irrelevant prattle. *See State v. Leon*, 1997 WL 598387 (Ariz. Sept. 30, 1997); and, any argument suggesting that the jury must protect society from drunk drivers with its guilty verdict. *State v. Hoppe*, 2002 WL 418379; *State v. Duncan*, 608 N.W.2d 551 (Minn. App. 2000).

5. Any statement implying that there are other facts available to the prosecution that are not brought into court. *Leon*, supra.

6. Any suggestion that the defendant has committed crimes other than those alleged in the information or indictment. *Leon*, supra; *State v. Blodgett*, 50 Or. 329, 343, 92 P. 820 (1907); *State v. Jones*, 279 Or. 55, 62, 566 P.2d 867 (1977) (rape prosecution; evidence adduced by prosecutor that witness said defendant had "done it" so many times before that he was going to the penitentiary).

7. Reference to matters going to prosecutorial discretion. *State v. Miller*, 1 Ore. App. 460, 465, 460 P.2d 874 (1970) ("The State is here. The State believes there is evidence . . .").

8. Reference to jurors or "fellow citizens" being, or having been, victims of crime. *State v. Bolt*, 108 Or. App. 746, 750, 817 P2d 1322 (1991).

9. Commenting on matters not in evidence. *Leon*, supra.

10. Incorrect interpretations of the law including, but not limited to, the suggestion or inference that drinking alcohol is a prima facie element of any crime presently charged. *State v. Molatore*, 3 Ore. App. 424, 428, 474 P.2d 7 (1970) (suggesting that defendant knew that jeopardy would bar prosecution on a related charge when, in fact, it would not).

11. Eliciting testimony that in the witness' opinion, the testimony of another witness is either true or false. *State v. Reimer*, 246 Ariz. Adv. Rep 53 (App. July 7, 1997); *State v. Isom*, 306 Ore. 587, 591-92, 761 P.2d 524 (1988) (On cross-examination, prosecutor suggested that contradictory witness was either mistaken or lying).

12. Suggesting that the defendant's exercise of the right to counsel implies that the defendant is guilty. *Hunter v. State*, 573 A.2d 85 (Md. App. 1990).

13. Any statement, comment, remark or insinuation whereby the government lawyer vouches for the credibility or integrity of state's witnesses. *State v. Leon*, supra; *United States v. DiLoretto*, 888 F.2d 996 (3d Cir. 1989) (prosecutorial vouching for credibility of witness is reversible error per se when based on facts outside the record); *United States v. Ludwig*, 508 F.2d 140 (10th Cir. 1974) (prosecutorial expression of view of the righteousness of his cause).

14. Reference to the defendant's off-the-witness stand behavior. *United States v. Pearson*, 746 F.2d 787 (11th Cir. 1984) (prosecutor improperly commented upon co-defendant Petracelli's nervous habit of jiggling his leg as bespeaking guilty fear); *United States v. Wright*, 489 F.2d 1181 (D.C. Cir. 1973) (prosecutorial comment on defendant's off-the-witness stand actions required reversal).

15. Any statement, comment or insinuation by the prosecutor characterizing the defendant's out of court statements as "lies" since that constitutes a comment on the defendant's demeanor and character when he has not testified or otherwise put character into issue. *Hughes v. State*, 437 A.2d 559 (Del. 1981).

16. Any statement or insinuation by the prosecutor that a person is not arrested unless he is guilty. *Hughes v. State*, 437 A.2d 559 (Del. 1981).

17. Any statements, remarks or insinuations that are in opprobrious language, invective, or from the making of any statement or inflections that have no place in argument, but are only calculated to cause prejudice. *Walker v. Penner*, 190 Ore. 542, 553, 227 P.2d 316 (1951).

18. Any statement that is calculated solely to evoke an emotional response from the jury. *Walker v. Penner*, 190 Ore. 542, 553, 227 P.2d 316 (1951).

19. Any statement, comment, insinuation or remark, be it emphatic or personalized, vouching for the integrity of the police. *United States v. Ludwig*, 508 F.2d 140, 143 (10th Cir. 1974); *see also United States v. Garza*, 608 F.2d 659 (5th Cir. 1979); *Gradsky v. United States*, 373 F.2d 706 (5th Cir. 1967).

20. Any statement, remark, comment or insinuation that the jury should "send a message" to the community that the defendant's alleged behavior will not be tolerated. *United States v. Solivan*, 937 F.2d 1146 (6th Cir. 1991).

21. Any statement, remark, or insinuation regarding the defendant's failure to testify, or intention to not testify. *State v. Halford*, 101 Or. App. 660, 792 P2d 467 (1990) (prosecutor reminded jurors that defender said in opening statement that the defendant would testify; defendant did not testify; conviction reversed and remanded

for determination as to whether retrial barred by jeopardy); *State v. Wederski*, 230 Ore. 57, 60, 368 P.2d 393 (1962) (such comments had a "presumably harmful effect").

22. Any statement, remark or insinuation that improperly places the burden of proof on the defendant. *State v. Walton*, 311 Ore. 223, 809 P.2d 81 (1991).

23. Any statement, remark, or insinuation regarding the defendant's contact of an attorney as evidence of a guilty mind. *Hunter v. State*, 573 A.2d 85 (Md. App. 1990).

24. Any statement, comment or insinuation that the defense attorney established a perjured defense. *State v. Pirouzkar*, 98 Ore. App. 741, 745, 780 P.2d 802 (1990).

25. Any statement, comment, or insinuation that the defense counsel made frivolous objections or tried to pull the wool over the jury's eyes or that the entire strategy of defense counsel was to keep was much evidence from the jury as possible. *Anderson v. State*, 525 S.W.2d 20 (Tex. Crim. App. 1975).

26. Any statement of fact within the prosecutor's own knowledge without first being sworn and taking the witness stand. *Tinker v. State*, 93 S.W.2d 441 (Tex. Crim. App. 1936); *Hemmerline v. State*, 314 S.W.2d 833 (Tex. Crim. App. 1958).

27. That the defendant has committed or may have committed some prior act of misconduct that is not in evidence. *Lookabaugh v. State*, 352 S.W.2d 279 (Tex. Crim. App 1961).

28. Suggestion that the defendant should be compared to an animal, coward, beast, sadist, maniac, or any other generic term designed to subject the defendant to personal abuse or to convey to the jury that he is in some manner "less than human." *Richardson v. State*, 257 S.W.2d 308 (Tex. Crim. App. 1953); 217 S.W.2d 1041 (Tex. Crim. App. 1949); *Marx v. State*, 150 S.W.2d 1041 (Tex. Crim. App. 1941).

29. Suggesting that defense counsel should be subject to criticism for making objections to the evidence. *Garza v. State*, 160 S.W. 2d 926 (Tex. Crim. App. 1942).

30. Raising the issue of the cost of crime generally and/or driving while intoxicated specifically. *Bridewell v. State*, 114 S.W.2d 259 (Tex. Crim. App. 1938) ("Our crime bill is mounting every year. It is costing you 15 billion dollars—every man and woman is paying $120.00 per year crime toll. Crime is on the increase.")

31. Any statement that the police would not "put their jobs on the line" by testifying untruthfully. *Clark v. State*, 632 So. 2d 88 (Fla. Dist. Ct. App. 4 1995).

32. Any assertion or suggestion of fact that there is any relationship between a subject's performance on so-called standardized field sobriety tests and that subject's ability to safely drive a motor vehicle. *State v. Meador*, 674 So. 2d 826, 21 Fla. L. Weekly D1152 (May 15, 1996)

33. Any attempt by the prosecutor to "load up" during rebuttal argument by arguing matters not raised by Defendant in his/her closing argument. *Hubbard v. Matlock*, 24 Ariz. App. 554, 540 P.2d 173 (1975) (It is the general rule that the scope of state's rebuttal is limited to matters discussed by the defendant during closing argument.)

34. Any attempt by the prosecutor to deny Defendant a fair trial by interposing spurious objections and gratuitous interruptions of defense counsel. *State v. Moore*, 108 Ariz. 215, 495 P.2d 445 (1972).

35. Any attempt by the prosecutor to shift the burden to the Defendant with arguments such as "The Defendant could have obtained an independent blood test" or "The Defendant could have independently analyzed the blood test kit," etc. *In re Winship*, 397 U.S. 358, 90 S.Ct. 1068, (1970); *State v. Jones*, 182 Ariz. 243, 895 P.2d 1006 (Ariz. App. Div. 1 1994).

Should the prosecutor violate any Order of this Court entered in response to this motion, the defense will seek dismissal of the instant charge(s) based upon a claim of jeopardy under the constitutions of the State of California and the United States and *Oregon v. Kennedy*, 102 S. Ct. 2083 (1982).

WHEREFORE, the Defendant respectfully requests that this Honorable Court enter its Order granting the relief herein requested with respect to all matters and, further, to instruct the state to prevent its witnesses from discussing matters herein precluded on the trial of this matter.

Respectfully Submitted this ___ Day of _____, 20__.

_____
Attorney for Defendant

[§§1:72-1:79 Reserved]

F. Field Sobriety Tests

§1:80   Precluding Field Sobriety Test Evidence

For years the judiciary and the public have been led to believe that field sobriety tests are a great magic invention. They are not. In fact, more and more scientists are writing peer-reviewed articles on just how bad the research and science behind them is. In order to create records, and hopefully eventually get judges to understand field sobriety tests are junk silence, the following motion lays out the bases on which hearings can be held. The first is the general, broad-based motion to get a hearing. The second is for specific performance criteria in allowing the tests into evidence.

It is worth noting that Washington caselaw [*State v. Mecham*, 186 Wash. 2d 128, 380 P.3d 414 (2016)] significantly confuses the issue of SFST admissibility as well as the admissibility of the refusal to perform SFSTs.

In *Mecham*, the court acknowledged that SFSTs are voluntary and a driver has no legal obligation to perform the tests. However, the court ruled that the SFSTs are a seizure but not a search so long as the driver is not already under arrest and the seizure is justified under *Terry*. The court further ruled that under those facts, the driver had no constitutional right to refuse the tests, and therefore, the refusal to perform the tests was admissible.

The court in *Mecham* did not address the question of how or why a refusal to perform SFSTs absent some explanation from the officer of a consequence of refusing would be **relevant** under the rules of evidence, leaving room for an additional motion in limine as suggested below.

Even in the wake of *Mecham*, some of my additional methods of attempting to suppress SFSTs are included in §§1:82-1:84.

§1:81   Memorandum in Support of Defendant's Motion in Limine to Preclude Field Sobriety Test Evidence

MEMORANDUM IN SUPPORT OF DEFENDANT'S MOTION TO PRECLUDE SFST EVIDENCE

I.   The Filed Sobriety Test Evidence in This Case Does Not Meet the *Kelly/ Fry/Daubert* Standards for Admissibility of Scientific Evidence

A.   Introduction

One of the most important functions of a trial court is to rule on the admissibility of evidence. This function is critical in ensuring only relevant and reliable evidence is received and used by the jury in determining a person's guilt or innocence. This role is so important, that motions in limine may be brought pre-trial to determine the admissibility of questionable evidence. *Charbonneau v. Superior Court* (1976) 42 Cal. App 3d 505.

By this motion in limine, counsel seeks to preclude any and all testimony from any and all witnesses regarding the defendant's performance and the evaluation of that performance on field sobriety tests. The field sobriety tests in this case are inadmissible under *People v. Kelly* (1976) 17 Cal.3d. 24, other relevant case law, and the California Rules of Evidence.

B.   Questions of Admissibility of Evidence Should Be Heard Pre-Trial and Outside the Presence of the Jury

In deciding the question of admissibility of evidence, the trial court is guided by a number of procedural rules. Pursuant to California Code of Evidence Section 402:

(A) When the existence of a preliminary fact is in dispute, its existence or nonexistence shall be determined as provided in this article.

(B) The court may hear and determine the question of the admissibility of evidence out of the presence or hearing of the jury; but in a criminal action, the court shall hear and determine the question of the admissibility of a confession or admission of the defendant out of the presence and hearing of the jury if any party so requests.

California Code of Evidence Section 400 defines a preliminary fact. As used in this article, "preliminary fact" means a fact upon the existence or nonexistence of which depends the admissibility or inadmissibility of evidence. The phrase 'the admissibility or inadmissibility of evidence' includes the qualification or disqualification of a person to be a witness and the existence or nonexistence of a privilege.

The admissibility of the proffered evidence regarding field sobriety tests in this case is based on the preliminary fact that the field sobriety tests constitute a scientifically valid way of measuring the defendant's sobriety. The defense disputes the existence of this preliminary fact as relates to the field sobriety tests used in this case, as argued below.

Since the prosecution is the proponent of this proffered evidence, they must bear the burden of production:

(a) The proponent of the proffered evidence has the burden of producing evidence as to the existence of the preliminary fact, and the proffered evidence is inadmissible unless the court finds that there is evidence sufficient to sustain a finding of the existence of the preliminary fact, when: (1) the relevance of the proffered evidence depends on the existence of the preliminary fact;

(b) Subject to Section 702, the court may admit conditionally the proffered evidence under this section, subject to evidence of the preliminary fact being supplied later in the courts of the trial;

(c) If the court admits the proffered evidence under this section, the court:

(1) May, and on request shall, instruct the jury to determine whether the preliminary fact exists and to disregard the proffered evidence unless the jury finds that the preliminary fact does exist;

(2) Shall instruct the jury to disregard the proffered evidence if the court subsequently determines that a jury could not reasonably find that the preliminary fact exists. Cal. Evid. Code Section 403.

As used in this article, "proffered evidence" means evidence, the admissibility or inadmissibility of which is dependent upon the existence or nonexistence of a preliminary fact. Cal. Evid. Code Section 401.

The testimony of the officer in this case, as relates to the defendant's performance on field sobriety tests, is "proffered evidence."

Based on the foregoing, any attempt by the prosecution to introduce testimony based in whole or in significant part on the performance of field sobriety tests must first pass a *Kelly* hearing outside the presence of the jury.

C. The Field Sobriety Tests Used in This Case Must Be Judged Under the Kelly Standard of Admissibility

1. The Current Rule of Expert Opinion Regarding Scientific Evidence as Defined by *Kelly/Frye/Daubert* in California Courts

In 1976, the California Supreme Court reached a unanimous decision regarding general principles of admissibility of expert testimony based on new scientific techniques. In that decision, *People v. Kelly* (1976) 17 Cal. 3d. 24, the court required a three-step approach for admissibility of evidence based on new scientific techniques: (1) expertly established reliability of the technique presented, (2) testimony on the subject by a properly qualified expert, and (3) adherence to the proper scientific procedures in the specific case. *Kelly*, at 30. The *Kelly* decision embodied the principles of *Frye v. United States* (D.C. Cir. 1923) 293 F. 1013 regarding scientific acceptance.

The United States Supreme Court took its own hard look at the *Frye* standard in *Daubert v. Merrell Dow Pharmaceuticals, Inc.* (1993) 509 U.S. 579. In that decision, the Court ruled the *Frye* standard had been superseded by the Federal Rules of Evidence and those rules were the standard for admitting or precluding expert testimony in federal trials.

The California Supreme Court was forced to reconcile these cases and this state's position on admissibility of expert opinion based on new scientific techniques in *People v. Leahy* (1994) 8 Cal 4th 587. After a detailed analysis of the above cases, the California Evidence Code, the legislative history of the California Code, and various authorities relating to the issue, the court concluded:

In sum, *Kelly* sets forth the various reasons why the more "conservative" *Frye* approach to determining the reliability of expert testimony regarding scientific techniques represents an appropriate one. *Daubert*, which avoided the issues of *Frye's* "merits," presents no justification for reconsidering that aspect of our holding in *Kelly*. Thus, we conclude that the *Kelly* formulation survived *Daubert* in this state, and that none of the above described authorities critical of that formulation persuade us to reconsider or modify it at this time. *People v. Leahy* at 597.

2. The *Kelly* Standard Is Applicable to Any Testimony Based in Whole or in Significant Part on Performance on Field Sobriety Tests

It is well established that the procedure set forth in *Kelly* is applicable only to "new scientific techniques." *See People v. Webb* (1993) 6 Cal. 4th. 494; *People v. Stoll* (1989) 49 Cal. 3d. 1136. Based on California Evidence Code Sections 802 and 803, and the persuasive holding in *Kumho Tire Co. Ltd. v. Carmichael* (1999) 526 U.S. 137, 119 S.Ct. 1167, the *Kelly* standard is also applicable to opinions expressed by police officers and other witnesses based in whole, or in significant part, on training and experience.

a. *Kelly* Is Applicable to Opinion Testimony Based on Training and Experience

Pursuant to California Code of Evidence Sections 802 and 803, a witness, whether lay or expert, may state an opinion and the reasons therefore unless the reasons or basis for the opinion is precluded by the court. Preclusion is warranted where the reasons or basis are improper. Such an evaluation of the admissibility of the opinion has been described as the "gatekeeping" function of the trial court. This entails a preliminary assessment of whether the reasoning or methodology underlying the testimony is scientifically valid and of whether that reasoning or methodology properly can be applied to the facts at issue. *Daubert v. Merrill Dow Pharmaceuticals, Inc.* (1993) 509 U.S. 579 (Inapplicable on other grounds in California [see above], but, principle of "gate keeping" survived); *People v. Leahy, supra; see also People v. Kelly* (1976) 17 Cal. 3d. 24; *Frye v. United States* (1923) 293 F. 1013; *Kumho Tire Co., Ltd. v. Carmichael* (1999) 526 U.S. 137, 119 S.Ct. 1167.

Although in *Kumho*, the United States Supreme Court was commenting specifically on the Federal Rules of Evidence as determined by *Daubert*, its analysis of the "gatekeeping" role under any standard, including the standard required pursuant to California Evidence Code Sections 802 and 803, is persuasive. The Court alluded to this position by stating that "the gatekeeping inquiry" of *Daubert* is applicable when "the relevant reliability concerns may focus upon personal knowledge or experience" of the witness. *Kumho Tire* at 1175. This is true because "some of *Daubert's* questions can help to evaluate the reliability even of experience based testimony" *Id.* at 1176.

In reaching this decision, the United States Supreme Court found it would be difficult, if not impossible, to hold the *Daubert* standard applicable only to "scientific" knowledge and not also include "technical" or other "specialized" knowledge. Stating "there is no clear line that divides one from the other," the court held:

> And whether the scientific expert testimony focuses upon specialized observations, the translation of those observations into theory, a specialized theory itself, or the application of such a theory in a particular case, the expert's testimony often will rest 'upon an experience confessedly foreign in kind to the jury's own.' *Kumho Tire* at 1174.

Based on this rationale, the standards of *Daubert* have been expanded and are not limited to traditional "experts" or "expertise." In fact, the *Kumho Tire* Court stated that "a trial court should use the specific factors identified in *Daubert* where they are reasonable measures of the reliability of expert testimony" *Id.* at 1176. This is necessary to make certain that a witness, "whether basing testimony upon professional studies or personal experience, employs the same level of intellectual rigor that characterizes the practice of an expert in a relevant field." *Id.* at 1176. It is important and relevant for the trial court to ask the witness how often he has produced erroneous results, whether his methodology is generally accepted, etc., even of a "witness whose expertise is based purely on experience." *Kumho Tire* at 1176.

b. Field Sobriety Tests Are a "New Technique"

While various types of field sobriety tests have existed almost as long as the automobile itself, time alone does not define "new" for the purposes of a *Kelly* analysis. In determining whether a scientific technique is "new" for *Kelly* purposes, longstanding use by police officers seems less significant a factor than repeated use, study, testing and confirmation by scientists or trained technicians. *People v. Leahy* (1994) 8 Cal. 4th 587 at 598.[2]

---

[2] The relevance of *People v. Leahy*, supra, to this entire discussion cannot be understated. *Leahy* is the seminal case regarding any aspect of field sobriety testing in California. In Leahy, the California Supreme Court was asked to look at the admissibility of Horizontal Gaze Nystagmus (HGN) as a field sobriety test. The court made an analysis similar to the one argued herein. In reaching their decision, the justices recognized several key points that are applicable to the case at bar: first, that despite longstanding use by officers, HGN is a "new scientific technique; second, that the applicable standard of evaluation is stated in *People v. Kelly*; third, that the proponent of HGN would have to provide "scientific" evidence of the reliability of HGN; and finally, that the above created questions must be answered at a properly held hearing. This is exactly the position being argued in these papers.

The only testing of field sobriety tests that meets this definition was conducted at the request of the National Highway Traffic Safety Administration (hereinafter NHTSA)[3]. Additionally, only the three standardized tests, and their standardized administration, adopted by NHTSA have been so evaluated.

In the case at bar, the officer did not use the three tests that have been made the subject of extensive research. The tests used by the officer are untested, unstudied and unsubstantiated as indicators of sobriety. While the proponent may argue that these tests have long been used by law enforcement in the performance of their duty:

> To hold that a scientific technique could become immune from *Kelly* scrutiny merely by reason of long standing and persistent use by law enforcement outside the laboratory or the courtroom seems unjustified. *Leahy* at 598.

Unless, and until, the proponent of the tests can establish their reliability, pursuant to *Kelly*, no testimony should be admitted regarding the performance by the defendant on those tests.

c.   Field Sobriety Tests Are a "Scientific Technique"

In *Stoll*, the court suggested trial courts define "scientific" for the purposes of a *Kelly* determination, by evaluating the purpose behind *Kelly*, *i.e.*, to protect the jury from techniques that convey a "misleading aura of certainty." *Stoll* at 1155. This same rationale was echoed by the United States Supreme Court's holding that *Daubert*, "applies not only to testimony based on "scientific" knowledge, but also to testimony based on "technical" and "other specialized" knowledge. *Kumho* at 1171.

In *People v. Leahy*, the court used just such an analysis of the Horizontal Gaze Nystagmus test. In determining that test was a scientific technique, the court noted that the name of the test, the manner in which it is given, and the testimony of the officer all tend to persuade the jury the test yields a "definitive truth."

The standard testimony with regards to other Field Sobriety Tests further fits the definition outlined in *Stoll* and *Leahy*. First, the name "Field Sobriety Test" implies a predetermined pass/fail or graded score. It is implied that someone, somewhere and at sometime, set forth a "key" for evaluating the performance. The formal sounding nature of each of the individual tests further enhances the perception that these tasks are definitive in their assessment of sobriety.

These factors are reinforced by the usual testimony of the officer as to the specific directions given the defendant prior to his or her performance of the tasks. In many cases this is further reinforced by the officer's demonstration of the events in court. Finally, the officer's use of pre-printed evaluation forms indicates to the jury that these tests have been studied and are reliable, when the evidence is clear such is not the case.

As stated in *Leahy*, "the aura of certainty emanating from the officers' description . . . was unmistakable. . . . A jury could be unduly and unjustifiably impressed by the confidence the testifying officers showed. . . ." *Leahy* at 599. This theory is based on the time honored perception that jurors can and do give undue weight to evidence that seems to be scientifically proven.

Therefore, in order to present testimony based in whole or in significant part on the defendant's performance on field sobriety tests, the prosecution must meet the burden set forth in *People v. Kelly*.

3.   The Field Sobriety Tests Used in This Case Do Not Satisfy the *Kelly* Standard

In 1975, NHTSA funded a research project run by the Southern California Research Institute. At that time, Dr. Marceline Burns was a founder and researcher at that organization. The project was to determine if there were, either individually or in combination, any roadside tests that could aid an officer in determining whether a person was under the influence of alcohol. *See* Statement Under Oath of Dr. Burns (hereinafter Burns Stmt.) attached hereto.

Pursuant to that contract, research was performed evaluating many of the commonly used roadside tests and narrowing the list to approximately 15 tests that were used nationwide and seemed to have some usefulness. From that group of 15 tests, only 6 were eventually believed to be valid and feasible at roadside. (Burns Stmt. at 10-15.)

These 6 tests were the n studied in controlled laboratory experiments to determine their accuracy. (Burns Stmt. at 22-24.) In the end, a combination of three tests was determined to be the best indication of impairment. These 3 tests, Horizontal Gaze Nystagmus, One-Leg Stand, and Walk-and-Turn, were adopted by NHTSA as the only tests to determine sobriety at roadside. (Burns Stmt. at 7-8.)

---

[3]   *See* "Driving Under the Influence Enforcement Manual" California Highway Patrol, 8-95, HPM 70.4 p. 2-8; "Driving Under the Influence & Under the Influence" San Francisco Police Department, 4-97, DM-3 p. 12.

To date, there has been no other scientific study correlating roadside exercises and sobriety. (Burns Stmt. at 38). (Relevant portion attached hereto and incorporated herein by reference. Available in entirety upon request.)

Additionally, as Dr. Burns has pointed out on many occasions, variance from the proscribed manner of administering, observing, and evaluating an individual's performance of the three standardized tests, deprives the tests of reliability and accuracy. "Therefore the scoring and the observations don't relate to any of the research data or any of the accumulated data over the years." (Burns Stmt. at page 30, line 4-7.)

This position, that only tests given in the "standardized" manner, have any validity is echoed in virtually every police manual regarding field sobriety tests[4]. (Relevant portion attached hereto and incorporated herein by reference. Available in entirety upon request.)

Furthermore, this position is the current trend in many other states. Most recently, the Ohio Supreme Court in *State v. Homan* (April 26, 2000) 89 Ohio St. 3d 421, 732 N.E. 2d 952, held that any variation in the use of the NHTSA Standardized Field Sobriety Tests makes the results completely unreliable as relates to probable cause, a lower standard than required for conviction[5]. The court found "it is well established that in field sobriety testing even minor deviations from the standardized procedures can severely bias the results." This is due in part , the court reasoned, to "[t]he small margins of error that characterize field sobriety tests making strict compliance critical" and "[w]hen field sobriety testing is conducted in a manner that departs from established methods and procedures, the results are inherently unreliable." *Id.*

Based on the foregoing rationale, the Ohio Supreme Court ruled "in order for the results of a field sobriety test to serve as evidence of probable cause to arrest, the police must have administered the test in strict compliance with standardized testing procedures." *Id.* at 4.

In the case at bar, the officer did not use the three standardized tests. The tests the officer did use have not been the subject of any review or study. Any tests that the officer did use from the three tests battery approved by NHTSA, were done inconsistently with the prescribed manner. As stated above, such variance from the standard effectively creates a new test. Based on the foregoing, those tests do not meet the *Kelly* test for admissibility. Furthermore, it is clear that the standard enunciated for admissibility in *Kelly* cannot be met by the prosecution.

D. Conclusion

The standard for admissibility of evidence based on new scientific techniques first propounded in *Kelly* and left unchanged by *Daubert* is applicable to field sobriety tests. Pursuant to the California Evidence Code and the decision of the United States Supreme Court in *Kumho Tire*, the *Kelly* standard is applicable to testimony based on training and experience, as well as more traditional "scientific" knowledge. Under that standard, field sobriety tests are inadmissible evidence until shown to be in conformance with *Kelly*. The tests used in this case do not and cannot be shown to meet this standard of reliability and should be precluded.

II. The Field Sobriety Test Evidence in This Case Is Irrelevant

Pursuant to California Evidence Code Section 350 "No evidence is admissible except relevant evidence." "Relevant evidence" is evidence that tends to prove or disprove any disputed fact of consequence to the underlying action. *See* Evidence Code Section 210. In the case at bar, the defendant is charged with violating two sections of the Vehicle Code, sections 23152(a) and 23152(b).

Vehicle Code section 23152(b) makes it illegal to drive with a blood alcohol content over .08. Vehicle Code section 23152(a) makes it illegal to operate a motor vehicle while impaired.

Evidence is relevant in this matter it proves or disproves either (1) a particular blood alcohol level, or (2) driving impairment.

Based on the analysis of virtually every state court decision, and hearing or reading from the foremost experts in the field of DUI/DWI investigation for both prosecution and defense, the United States District Court for the district of Maryland found "[t]he results of the SFSTs, either individually or collectively, are not admissible for the purpose of proving specific blood alcohol content ("BAC") of a driver charged with DWI/DUI." *U.S. v. Horn* (D. Md. 2002) 185 F.Supp.2 530. Therefore, evidence of performance on the SFSTs is not relevant to the charge of 23152(b).

---

[4]   *E.g.*, "To enjoy the full benefit of these tests in evaluating a DUI suspect, and the support of the correlation study in court, the officer must administer the tests as detailed below under 'test instructions' for each test." CHP Manual HPM 70.4

[5]   Ohio, like most other states, had previously determined, as argued herein, that only NHTSA Field Sobriety Tests have any evidential weight.

Dr. Marceline Burns, considered by most courts to be the foremost proponent of SFSTs (see, *e.g., Horn,* supra), has stated under oath "What you're asking is, are these tests of driving? They are not. . . . The officer is not charged with making a decision about driving skills at roadside. He couldn't. There's no way you can judge somebody in five minutes at roadside that you never saw before to make a decision about their driving skills." Statement of Marcelline Burns Under Oath, April 17, 1998.

Since these tests, according to their foremost proponent, cannot indicate driving ability, let alone impairment, they are not relevant to the charge of 23152(a).

Based on the foregoing, any testimony with regards to SFSTs is irrelevant and should be precluded.

Respectfully Submitted this ___ Day of _____, 20__.

_____
Attorney for Defendant

§1:82   Motion to Suppress FST Evidence—Lack of Relevance to Case in Chief

To suppress all evidence obtained in the course of "field sobriety" or other physical agility tests administered to the Defendant herein. ER 401, 403. *DWI Detection and Standardized Field Sobriety Testing,* NHTSA 2006.

Discussion: Every State Trooper is required by their academy training to go through a course designed by the National Highway Traffic Safety Administration. This course teaches them the Standardized Field Sobriety Testing battery. These tests were studied and vetted by NHTSA in a variety of studies, both lab and field. These tests are only validated for the purposes for which they were studied.

Early in the battery of DUI law, the Washington State Supreme Court acknowledged that "field sobriety tests are always used for the determination of sobriety." *Heinemann v. Whitman County of Wash., Dist. Court,* 105 Wash.2d 796, 718 P.2d 789 (1986). This statement is based on the misplaced belief that a "field sobriety test is designed to determine whether a person has the attention skills necessary for driving." *State v. Lovelace,* 77 Wash. App. 916, 895 P.2d 10 (Div. 1, 1995).

According to the NHTSA manual, developing tests to determine driver impairmentwas one of the original goals of the the researchers. However, it was quickly determined that: "[d]riving a motor vehicle is a very complex activity that involves a wide variety of tasks and operator capabilities. It is unlikely that complex human performance, such as that required to safely drive an automobile, can be measured at roadside...SFSTs **do not directly measure driving impairment**." (emphasis added) Marceline Burns et al., NHTSA, Validation of the Standardized Field Sobriety Test Battery at BACs Below 0.10 percent, p. 28 (1998) (Found in Chapter VIII of the SFST manual).

"[T]he intended purpose of the SFST battery is to establish probable cause for measuring the actual breath or blood alcohol concentration." Joseph Manno and Barbara Manno, Experimental Basis of Psychomotor Performance Impairment, in Medical-Legal Aspects of Alcohol, p. 310 (James Garriott ed., 4th ed. 2003).They "were never meant to be introduced as evidence in the prosecution's case." In fact, NHTSA "recommends that [the SFSTs] be used *solely* during the roadside stop to establish probable cause." Am. Jur. 3d Proof of Facts § 459.10 (2007).

Considering these facts, it is impossible for the State to provide any evidence of probative value or relevance to any material fact in issue in this case for the purposes of trial. Therefore, the SFSTs should be suppressed as irrelevant evidence for trial.

Motion is: Granted   _____
                     Denied   _____
                     Reserved   _____

§1:83   Motion to Suppress FST Evidence—
         Lack of Strict Compliance with NHTSA Standardization

To suppress all evidence obtained in the course of "field sobriety" or other physical agility tests administered to the Defendant herein. Washington Const. Art. I, § 7, U.S. Const. Amend. IV, ER 403, Frye v. United States, 293 F.2d 1013 (D.C. Cir. 1923); Seattle v. Peterson, 39 Wn. App. 524 (1985); State v. Cauthron, 120 Wn.2d 879 (1993); State v. Riker, 123 Wn.2d 351 (1994).

Discussion: In *State v. Homan*, 89 Ohio St.3d 421, 732 N.E.2d 952 (2000), the Ohio Supreme Court ruled that for the results of any field sobriety tests to serve as evidence of probable cause to arrest an individual for driving under the influence, the police must have administered the tests in **strict compliance** with the standardized test procedures by NHTSA. The Court went on to state that there must be strict compliance by the law enforcement officer with the NHTSA standards. (This is as opposed to substantial compliance.) The Ohio court determined in one respect the need for strict compliance was because:

> ... In the substantial-compliance cases, the minor procedural deviations that were at issue in no way affected the ultimate results. In contrast, it is well established that in field sobriety testing even minor deviations from the standardized procedures can severely bias the results. Moreover, our holdings in the substantial-compliance cases were grounded, at least in part, on the practical impossibility of strictly complying with the applicable administrative regulations. In contrast, we find that strict compliance with standardized field sobriety testing procedures is neither unrealistic nor humanly impossible in the great majority of vehicle stops in which the police choose to administer the tests.

Homan at 426.

Motion is: Granted   _____
                     Denied   _____
                     Reserved   _____

§1:84   Motion to Suppress Refusal of FSTs

To suppress any alleged refusal to perform any Field Sobriety Test pursuant to ER 401, ER 403 and *Seattle v. Salsbroten*, 138 Wn.2d 227 (1999) (see FN 2).

Discussion: The burden of proving the relevance of a refusal to take field sobriety tests rests solely with the prosecution. If the proper foundation cannot be laid, the testimony should be disallowed. Whether the refusal is testimonial or not, the court has refused to comment on whether or not they are relevant for any reason. *See Salsbroten, supra.* No statute allows for admissibility of the refusal to perform field tests.

It is without question that a person suspected of DUI is under no legal obligation to take a Field Sobriety Test. *Seattle v. Personeus*, 63 Wash. App 461, 465 (1991). The question of what should occur when a subject chooses not to take a Field Sobriety Test has been discussed at length by our Supreme Court in *City of Seattle v. Stalsbroten*, 138 Wash.2d 227 (1999). In *Stalsbroten*, the Court analyzed this issue in the context of the 5th Amendment, and whether the refusal of SFSTs fell under the protections afforded to a defendant with regards to self-incrimination. What the *Stalsbroten* Court failed to do, because the issue was not before it, was analyze this issue in the context of *relevance* under ER 403. In fact the *Stalsbroten* opinion specifically acknowledges this fact when it states, **"[w]e note, however, that the question of the *admissibility* and *relevance* of such evidence is not before us at this time."** Id., FN2, at 239 . (Emphasis added).

While the question of relevance in the context of refusing SFSTs appears to be an issue of first impression in Washington, the question of relevance with regards to refusing a **breath test** is addressed in *State v. Zwicker*, 105 Wash.2d 228 (1986). The Court in *Zwicker* held that it is inherently unfair, and in fact coercive, to grant a right to refuse a test without a corresponding warning of the consequences of exercising that right. *Id.* at 242. The Court goes on to state that, "there is no coercion in obtaining refusal evidence where the accused is fully informed of the consequences of exercising the statutory right of refusal." *Id.* at 243.

In the case at hand, Defendant was correctly advised that the decision of whether or not to perform Field Sobriety Tests was voluntary. He was not told that should he elect to forgo these voluntary tests, there would be a consequence to this decision; it would later be used as evidence of a guilty conscience. Under the *Zwicker* analysis, this evidence was unfairly coerced—in that he unwittingly provided the State with inculpatory evidence, never having been told that this would be the effect of his decision.

Moreover, given the limited nature of the opinion in *Stalsbroten*, Defendant's refusal to take what was described only as a "voluntary test" should certainly be considered within this context of relevance under an ER 403 analysis. ER 403, states that, "Although relevant, evidence may be excluded if its probative value is substantially outweighed by the danger of unfair prejudice, [or] confusion of the issues…" ER 403. Given the facts surrounding Defendant's refusal to take voluntary SFSTs, it is questionable whether this evidence is even relevant under ER 401; however assuming arguendo that it is relevant, the probative value is certainly in question.

Defendant, like most citizens, was likely aware of what taking SFSTs entails. We have all seen the television show COPS, and most of us have seen somebody on the side of the road engaged in the roadside gymnastics that are SFSTs. Given the choice between engaging in these awkward tests of agility in front of police officers under less than ideal conditions for performance, one must ask the question of why anyone would do them if the person believed that they could be refused with no consequence. Indeed, while the decision to forego these tests *may* touch on the issue of a guilty conscience, a refusal may just as likely be the result of somebody not wanting to do them because he is embarrassed, or scared, or uncoordinated, or all of the above. And it is without question that this evidence is prejudicial.

What would make this evidence **relevant** would be the exercise of this decision in light of a consequence; the defendant refused these tests, knowing full well that this decision would later be used as evidence of a guilty conscience. This fact would make it less likely that the decision to refuse was based upon something other than a guilty state of mind—which might outweigh the danger of unfair prejudice. As it stands, this evidence, at best, fails to satisfy ER 403, and at worst is coercive under Zwicker.

Motion is:	Granted	_____
	Denied	_____
	Reserved	_____

G. Averages

§1:85   Motion to Preclude Use of "Average" Evidence and Testimony

In every DUI trial I have ever conducted, read or heard about, the state produces some witness who discusses averages. Michael Fremont of San Diego did some research, and together we came up with the following Motion to preclude such testimony.

MOTION IN LIMINE TO EXCLUDE EXPERT OPINION AND SCIENTIFIC TEST RESULTS OR MEASUREMENTS THAT DO NOT INCLUDE A RANGE OF CONFIDENCE INTERVAL

The Defendant hereby requests the trial court to exclude any scientific evidence that either reports a value of measurement, or is based on or relies on values of measurement as the basis of opinion that does not include a confidence interval (uncertainty). Similarly, Defendant hereby requests the trial court to exclude any witness from testifying to any "results" that do not include a confidence interval (uncertainty). This evidence includes values reported for alcohol level from any testing device, whether breath, urine, or blood; or conversion of breath or urine to blood values. Also included is any testimony related to expected alcohol levels per volume of alcohol per weight, retrograde extrapolation, expected alcohol levels over time, absorption and elimination rates of alcohol, and any and all other testimony, the basis or conclusions of which are dependent all or in part on scientific testing or values.

This testimony is sought to be excluded under Evidence Code Sections 210, 352, 801 and 802 and Rules of Professional Responsibility 5-200.

[§§1:86-1:89 Reserved]

V.   CREATING YOUR OWN DATABASE

§1:90   How to Create

When I was a public defender in the Bronx, we started a database on undercover cops to see how unique their reports were. It turns out, not so much. I used this idea in DUI cases to start my own database. It led to finding one officer who did in fact cut and paste part of his report. Three cases were dismissed.

What you can find is not only cut and pasted reports, but you will find out just how accurate an officer is in FSTs. Suppose you find that the officer gave FSTs, arrested 10 people, but only 2 were actually over .08. Then this officer is only 20% accurate in FSTs.

Even if you have no computer literacy whatsoever, this database is so simple you will need less than an hour to set it up. The hard part is finding office staff to dig through your archived cases, read the relevant data and enter it. If your office is like mine, these files are in the dusty far reaches of the archived files, so suitable beverages for the retrieval are suggested.

Using Microsoft Excel, or your own favorite database, create a header row that includes the information you wish to compare. It was and is my belief that less is more in this particular endeavor. I wanted to receive a warning if any basic similarity between cases existed and to review the file in its entirety if such a correlation came to light.

With this in mind I set up the headers as follows:

OFFICER	MACHINE	PAS	LAB TECH	2nd OFFICER	CLIENT
Gogetem	68-0027	1355	Perfect	Sawnothing	Drinkalot

The most critical information is the location of the other files. It does you and your client little good if you cannot put your hands on the files involving the same officer, expert, technician or machine. I found the easiest way to reference my files was to use my client's name as the finder. This allows me to continue to maintain my archived files in simple alphabetical order. When I find an officer or other reference match, I pull the other client file and compare the notes.

Now that the database is created, you need to see to regular updates. My office routine requires that when a new client file is opened, the data is immediately entered into the system. Then a check is made of the players in the new case, and a note to the file is created listing all matches. (NOTE: Most computer operating systems will now allow you to add "tags" or the like to most individual files. If you scan your discovery into your system, you can simply tag the PDF of the discovery with the officer's name. Then you can do a search for the tag for Trooper Friendly, and find every PDF tagged with his name.)

§1:91   Using Your Information

There are a number of uses for the compiled information. Obviously, the cross-examination reference made at the outset is one such use. Experience, however has shown a few other uses. In California, for example, more and more courts are allowing the results of the Preliminary Breath Test (PAS) for evidentiary purposes. Some courts are allowing the results of the PAS in after a showing by the local police department of its reliability.

The testimony of the officer in charge of the PAS, in order to demonstrate its reliability, usually consists of a log sheet showing PAS results and the subsequent state-approved (blood, breath or urine) test. The officer then shows that the PAS is unerringly accurate. By maintaining our own database, which includes the PAS result and subsequent approved test, we have shown that the logs do not record every test. We have been able to show the officers have omitted PAS tests when the subsequent test is unaccountably different. This has helped persuade judges not to admit the PAS.

In another situation, our discovery, coupled with this database, has reaped a surprise bonus. During our routine discovery, which includes the monthly download of all tests run on the Intoxilyzer 5000, we discovered some officers whose arrests (presumably after FSTs, objective symptoms and the other "totality" factors) resulted in less than 50% accuracy. That is, in more than 50% of the arrests by these officers the breath test was less than .08!

Imagine that information at your fingertips. It has enabled us to request, and have the court order, the offending officer's reports for the prior year or longer. (District attorneys have routinely avoided turning over this information by dismissing or making great offers on the case.) Of course, even without the reports to test the officer's "experience," this information is deadly for cross.

A single firm's database is a good start; however, combining with several other law firms will multiply the benefits substantially. Try to get others to cooperate with you.

CHAPTER 2A

JURY SELECTION: A STORYTELLER'S APPROACH

A Note about the Two Jury Selection Chapters in this Book

Every attorney has a strategy and frame of mind from which to draw tactics. What works for some may not work for others and the best way to find your style is to learn and watch as many different styles as you can manage. You'll find different ways to conceptualize every part of a trial. Many attorneys see voir dire as their first chance to identify and eliminate bad jurors for their case. I think of this as the "elimination" model—and there is value in it. In fact, many people think of it as jury "de-selection". You are getting rid of the people you don't want. This is especially useful in jurisdictions where your entire panel may be predisposed against your client (knowing your jurisdiction is crucial).

As a storyteller, I have found great success with a different model of jury selection. One I think of as collaborative jury selection: a way to find the jurors who are on your side and perhaps even inspire more jurors to be on your side, right from the start. In this way you can begin to lay the foundation you need in order to have a jury who is open to hearing you tell your client's story—starting in jury selection. This method of jury selection has been so effective and well received that in two recent jury trials (both of which resulted in 'not guilty' verdicts for my clients) two separate judges indicated that in a collective 40+ years in practice, they'd never seen a voir dire as effective as this one. It was the best they'd ever seen.

This is not to say there is no value in the elimination model. On the contrary, there is great value in studying the tactics used by different trial lawyers to find what rings true for you. In fact, I'm quite sure that much of the material presented here includes questions, tactics and strategies I've gathered, adapted, and straight-up stolen from other attorneys over the years and cobbled together with my own style to create "my" approach. You need to create your approach. As such, Ch. 2 Jury Selection: the De-selection Approach by the previous author is retained in this edition as a supplement to this updated "Storyteller's Approach".

Jonathan Dichter

JURY SELECTION: STORYTELLER'S APPROACH

I.   INTRODUCTION

§2A:01   The Power of Voir Dire

A criminal trial can be won or lost during jury selection. Many prosecutors mechanically follow a script designed to find "defense jurors" and vastly misunderstand the power of the process. Defense attorneys can use this prosecution weakness to our advantage. The true power of the voir dire process is that it allows you to do several supremely important things that you cannot do at any other time during the trial. See the Defense's Goals in §2A:02.

§2A:02   Voir Dire Goals: State vs. Defense

As defense attorneys using a collaborative storytelling model for voir dire, we have different goals than prosecutors do.

The State's Goals. The State has two key goals during voir dire:
1. Find defense jurors and eliminate them.
2. Poison the other jurors as much as possible.

This is why prosecutors ask questions like "What does someone who's had too much to drink look like?" And then they elicit every single characteristic that your client showed upon exiting the car. This approach is designed to poison the well. The prosecutor wants jurors to hear the officer describe your client, remember their own descriptions of a drunk driver, and think "Oh right—that's what a drunk guy looks like."

The Defense's Goals. In contrast, the defense has these five goals during voir dire:
1. Figure out which jurors can vote not guilty.
2. Begin building a rapport with them.
3. Start being liked by the panel.
4. Lay the groundwork for telling your client's story.
5. Expose the fact that there is already reasonable doubt in every single juror's mind.

Notice—the prosecutor's goals are all about damaging your client and your case. Your goals are about bolstering your client's story—**not** attacking the State's case. You can do that in cross and closing—if you really want to, although buying into the State's framework instead of using your own may be counterproductive. Whenever you operate within the narrative of another story, what you are inherently doing is giving that story credibility. Even if you are using that framework to take it down piece-by-piece. As an illustration, if the State has three points and you have three of your own, you should make your three points, not counter theirs. If all you do is counter the opponent's story, you are telling the jury that their argument is strong enough that they should pay attention. Instead, tell your story, and if there are moments where you can contradict the State's story, do so—but within your own framework. It's a stronger storytelling position.

§2A:03   The State Starts Out Wrong

Voir dire is not about getting jurors to believe the State is wrong. It's about getting them to understand a fundamental truth that most of us have forgotten about the criminal justice system: the State **starts out wrong**.

Think about that a moment. The State starts out wrong. As the prosecutors sit there all smug in their seats with their cops and their witnesses and their complaints, they are wrong. Your client is innocent, presumptively. What does that mean to a juror? Nothing yet. The defense attorney has to get jurors to understand and believe it. That's a very important goal.

DUI cases are an anomaly in criminal law. In most cases, both sides have a story. The State puts on a case in which the victim and witnesses say x, y, and z happened. The defense puts on its witnesses who claim a, b, and c is what occurred. Then the jury decides which side they believe. There's always a story or an explanation on both sides.

In DUI cases often the State does not have a story or an explanation. Usually the witnesses for the State are the arresting officer, the breath or blood testing device, and a scientist or two. Who are your witnesses? Often nobody. Even though the defense does not put on a case, the defense must still tell an interesting story. The opportunity for telling that story begins with voir dire and continues through opening statement and closing argument.

[§§2A:04-2A:09 Reserved]

II.   HOW TO OUT PERFORM THE STATE DURING VOIR DIRE

§2A:10   Know the State's Mistakes

Before we get into what to do and what not to do—and most importantly—how to do it—there are some important points that require attention. Namely—what the State does that doesn't work at all. Many DUI prosecutors are relatively new, in some cases weeks or months new. They have a script. They tend to follow it. Knowing that script and its weaknesses allows you to use them to your advantage.

During voir dire, the state often makes these three mistakes:

- Most prosecutors miss the opportunity to frame issues and create a theme for their case. They forget (or never learned) that storytelling is the most critical tool in the trial lawyer's arsenal. They launch into "Good morning, ladies and gentlemen. I'm John Goodguy, and I represent the State and I want to talk to you about your qualifications as a juror." Boring. And useless air.
- They ask too many questions. They don't make enough statements.
- They are alone during voir dire. This is a distinct advantage you have over prosecutors. You don't have to go it alone. You have someone with you who cares about this case as much as (or even more than) you do! Your client.

§2A:11   Make an Impact and Be Memorable

In contrast with the prosecutor, the first thing you do should make an impact and be memorable. Don't waste time introducing yourself. The judge already did it. The prosecutor probably gestured to you and mentioned your name several times, too!

You can even use this moment to inject some drama into the process. Jurors expect (and even appreciate) a bit of theatricality and you can give it to them. But don't go over the top. Not every tactic works for every case, and not every lawyer can get away with the same things. What you do and say has to be genuine (which is distinct from 'seeming' genuine) to get jurors to like you. And remember, if they like you, they'll want to do something for you—and there's only one thing you want from them. A not guilty verdict.

One juror commented to me after a trial: "From the moment you started talking to us in jury selection, you owned every one of us. You owned every inch of the courtroom. When you moved in your seat, we sat up and paid attention to see what you were going to say or do next." That is **exactly** what you want. You want every word to be useful and not wasted breath. Get them to want to listen to you—and to enjoy hearing your arguments. And the only way to do it is to start right at the beginning.

§2A:12   Make Voir Dire a Mini Closing

Instead of taking up all your voir dire time with questions, you can make voir dire like a mini closing. You can educate jurors to your heart's content as long as you occasionally ask some questions and get some hands raised. You want the jurors talking, but you want to talk at least as much and get nods of understanding. Let's be clear—silence and understanding nods are not the same as silent patronizing nods.

§2A:13   Enlist Your Client's Help

Give your client a notepad and tell him or her to **watch the jurors** and ignore you. You don't matter. Instruct your client to watch for eye rolls, yawns, enthusiastic nodding—all the things you can't possibly see and take notes. When your client gets a strong feeling about a juror, good or bad, have the client make a note. And then, before you start your challenges, talk to your client. (This applies mostly to your peremptory challenges—challenges for cause are your domain and often have to be handled at the time they arise, so you may not have a chance to talk to your client—but that's okay).

You don't have to do what your client suggests, but listen to the client's reasons. Often he or she will have seen something you did not, and now you have an extra tool—an extra pair of eyes and ears—and an extra gut to check with.

Even if you disagree with your client, think of how engaged your client feels when you actively consult him or her about the case. It is part of client care that I discuss in Ch. 6 to make sure your client sees that you understand that it's about the client, not you.

§2A:14 Listen to Your Gut

Don't laugh about gut instincts. They can be very useful in voir dire. It's a first meeting of this entire panel and you might see one juror—just **see** them and instinctively think "she'd be a good person on this panel" for some reason. And guess what? More often than not—you are right. Listen to your gut instincts!

§2A:15 Tell a Story

Many attorneys will tell you to study great attorneys: Darrow, Spence, Lincoln, etc. Sure that's all fine and dandy. But I'll tell you to study one fictional film lawyer and one Hollywood legend.

> The lawyer—Vincent Laguardia Gambini, the protagonist of "My Cousin Vinny".
> The legend—Walter Elias Disney.

Both possessed the single greatest skill a trial attorney needs. They told **stories, memorable and moving** stories. And even better, no matter what their true personalities were, their public personas were downright lovable. You could not help liking them. And because you liked them, you were inclined to do what they wanted. In Vinny's case—root for the defense.

And in Uncle Walt's case—see his movies, go to his theme parks, and let him into your living rooms every weekend. Voir dire is where your storytelling starts.

Storytelling, as I've said before, and will say throughout this text, is the most crucial tool we have in our arsenal. When we sharpen it, we have a weapon that most prosecutors cannot contend with. Studying lawyers is fine—but studying storytellers is the next level.

STORYTELLERS TO STUDY—A Nonexhaustive List

If you are unfamiliar with any of these master storytellers, Google them. Trust me, you will learn a lot.

David Mamet	William Goldman	Martin Scorsese
Walt Disney	Stephen King	Christopher Nolan
Steven Spielberg	James Patterson	Alfred Hitchcock
James Cameron	Ernest Cline	Jim Henson
Ang Lee	Nora Ephron	Ron Howard
Joss Whedon	Albert Brooks	JK Rowling
JJ Abrams	Mel Brooks	Andy Weir
George Lucas	Cameron Crowe	Scott Meyer
The Coen Brothers	Aaron Sorkin	Isaac Asimov
Quentin Tarantino	Frank Darabont	Rod Serling
Francis Ford Coppola	Kevin Smith	John Grisham

[§§2A:16-2A:19 Reserved]

III.   HOW TO COLLABORATE WITH YOUR JURY PANEL: THE NUTS AND BOLTS

§2A:20   Ask for More Time

Time allowed for voir dire is limited—often to just 20 minutes. I always ask for at least 45 minutes. I typically will get about 30. But it is important to ask for more time. You do not want to rush, and some of the process takes jurors a few minutes to catch on to.

§2A:21   Get Jurors to Internalize the Presumption of Innocence

The first thing I do during voir dire is stand, plant my feet, put my hand on my client's shoulder, and ask: "Why is it in our system of justice, that innocent people (look at your client—or if you're more comfortable place your hand on the client's shoulder) get wrongfully convicted?"

Now wait. You will undoubtedly be met with silence. They weren't expecting questions like these. The prosecutor just asked them if they were excited for jury duty for goodness sake.

After a moment of silence, follow up with a smile. "Okay, how about an easier question. Who thinks that it never ever happens?" No hands will be raised.

"So we agree. Innocent people (look at your client) can be wrongfully convicted at a trial just like this one. So why does that happen?"

Now you'll start to get some answers. I will typically parrot the answer back to them and summarize it into two words. If they say "witnesses identify the wrong person," I simplify that to "bad identification." Usually you'll hear: bad evidence, bad ID, bad cops, bad jurors, etc. Sometimes you'll be given the gift of "bad lawyer." This is a great time to step back, smile sheepishly, and get a laugh from the whole panel. Laughter breeds friendship. And if you can get a laugh at **your** expense, not your client's, all the better to make the jurors friends with each other, and now friends with you. And frankly, if they don't give me bad lawyer, I give it to them. Why waste the moment of levity and friendship?

> **PRACTICE TIP:**
>
> If you have a paralegal or an intern available and a whiteboard, easel, or projector with a computer—feel free to have these answers written up for jurors to see as you go—two words at a time. I usually don't. I like a more conversational rapid style of chat.

> **PRACTICE TIP:**
>
> I rarely, if ever, prepare my client for what I'll ask or say during most of a trial. The more curious the client is, the more the client listens, the more invested the client seems, and the more the jury sees the client as taking the trial seriously. That being said, clients are often nervous, so to calm them down, I'll usually make them a small bet before the trial. I bet them that within two minutes of starting my jury selection the panel as a whole will laugh together with me, and then open up to me completely. It works nearly every time. In addition, your client thinks you're a genius.

Ask the panel what they can do as jurors to "guarantee that this is not a case where an innocent person is wrongfully convicted." What you're listening for now are jurors who are going to listen, stick to their guns, and try to be "fair." Fair is a great word. Listen for it. You'll be using it in a moment. Especially listen for "listen to both sides of the story." This is another gem. You're also looking for anyone who is willing to go out on a limb and say they're not willing to make that guarantee. You'll be back for them later, too. You're planting seeds right now to water and grow over the next 20 minutes.

Pick a juror you are okay "playing with" for a moment. Point her out to the jury. "You know, Ms. Jones, as it turns out, I was behind you in line this morning to get into the courthouse. And I saw you just throw a coffee cup on the ground. I was amazed—there was a garbage can right there. And you just littered." Hold on here a minute while she reacts to this and listen to the jury's emotional response. Try not to be aggressive at this juror. Make it seem playful and light. Then say as follows. "Now. Prove to the rest of the jury that you didn't litter."

The juror will likely give you a number of excuses. She doesn't drink coffee. She didn't have any this morning. She threw it away earlier. Juror #2 threw the cup away for her. After every single claim, simply ask the juror to "prove it." Be nice, but firm. Don't let her wiggle out of this.

You went to law school and you can Socratic method circles around this jury. Let the juror dangle for a moment or two until she realizes she literally cannot disprove your accusation.   This will begin a conversation about how difficult it is to prove something didn't happen. You can easily dovetail this conversation into a discussion of the presumption of innocence. It's impossible to prove a negative, so our system is designed so that you have to believe everyone is innocent unless the prosecutor brings the largest pile of proof required in our system.

PRACTICE TIP:

If jurors bring up "innocent until proven guilty," jump all over that phrase. I tell jurors it's my favorite expression because it's completely wrong. Even if the judge just said it, he or she was wrong. What "until proven guilty" means is that it's going to happen. You are just waiting for the prosecutor to do it. What the judge actually said (or should have said) was "unless" proven guilty. Ask them if that makes a difference. It does.

What you're trying to do here is get the jury to understand that it is not your job to prove your client did not do something; it is the State's job to prove he **did** something. I use a dinner party analogy in closing: the State invited you here for a dinner party, and it's their job to bring the meat.

PRACTICE TIP:

Here is a great place to insert a little self-deprecation but also remind people who you are and what your job is. Ask them straight up who doesn't trust you because you're a defense attorney. Ask what your job is. They should be starting to realize that maybe you're not the bad guy after all.

§2A:22   Get Every Juror to Agree to Be Unfair and Partial

It's time to go back to "fair" jurors. I usually ask this question:

"Who wants to be a fair and impartial juror?"

Everyone should raise their hands, but if not, challenge for cause to explore.

"What does fair and impartial mean?"

Likely you'll hear that it means not preferring one side to another. Now remind them of the presumption of innocence. "How can you square the fact that you have to presume someone is innocent unless the other side brings you a lot of evidence with the fact that you want to not prefer one side to the other? Doesn't the law seem to require you to prefer the defendant right from the start? In fact, doesn't the law require you to be a partial and unfair juror on the defendant's side?"

Now you'll get some stares. Remind them that the judge's job is to tell them the law, and that if what you were saying was untrue, the judge would have corrected you by now. You might draw an objection, but who cares? Nothing you have said is incorrect. While you go through these questions, you should not wait for answers. Just keep talking. They are questions, but this is one of those moments where you are sneaking a little story telling into voir dire. Questions come next.

"Okay—let's try to show this in a different way. Let's pretend the case is now over. You have all the information you're going to get at this point. You now have to vote. I'm going to ask each of you the same question starting with juror number one. I just want a single number from you. From a scale of 0 to 10, with 0 being completely not guilty and 10 being completely guilty, where are you right now about Mr. Defendant?"

Go person by person. Get every single number. You're doing two things here: you are preparing jurors to be educated about what presumption of innocence really is, and you are setting up challenges for cause of jurors who do not understand it.

Look for someone who said something around 4 or 5 and ask the juror why. The conversation might go something like this.

"Because there's no evidence. So I can't really vote either way."

"So if there's no evidence, what's your verdict?"

A few heads will nod. They are starting to get it. If they don't get it and stick to their original number, go to someone with a head nod.

"Not guilty." Push them now.

"So Zero?"

"Yes."

"Why?"

"Because there's no evidence."

"Same thing if there's not enough evidence?"

"Yes."

Now re-ask the question: "From a scale of 0 to 10, with 0 being completely not guilty and 10 being completely guilty, where are you right now about Mr. Defendant?" Tell them you are going to go back down the line and ask everyone for a number again—and do it rapid fire. Your goal is straight zeros from every single juror. If even ONE juror doesn't give you that answer, you have to push to get a zero from him, or challenge for cause because any number other than zero means a simple fact: that juror **cannot** presume innocence.

You've now conditioned your jury to be 100% on your client's side and to remain there throughout the trial unless the prosecutor brings them the largest amount of evidence the system requires. Get the jurors to promise you that they will do that. Get them to promise your client. Have them look at him or her.

"Look at Mr. Defendant, ladies and gentlemen. He's the defendant. He's the one that you've just agreed you must be 100% on the side of unless at the end of the trial the State overcomes the most massive burden of proof we have. Do you each promise him that you will remain 100% on his side—at that zero you just gave us—throughout the trial and throughout your deliberations unless the State does that?" Go juror by juror, and ask each by number to give you a single word answer. Yes or no. Prosecutors hate this. But it's what the law requires.

Often your client won't testify, you'll have no eye-witnesses, and sometimes no witnesses at all. Your case will rely on telling the jury "the State didn't prove it"—and unless they're preconditioned to understand how powerful an argument that is, it's going to be a sharp uphill battle. Trials can still be an uphill battle, but the collaborative approach to jury selection can help you ensure that the hill isn't quite as steep.

§2A:23   Get Jurors to Internalize Proof Beyond a Reasonable Doubt

Now you can discuss the burden of proof. Ask the jurors how much proof they'd want before they gave someone their money to invest. Then ask if they'd want **more** before allowing the State to take away their children claiming they were bad parents. Then explain that beyond a reasonable doubt is **more** evidence than that is. Let the gravity sink in.

This is a great place to re-address any jurors who said they would "Listen to both sides before making a decision." Remember them, the fair and impartial jurors? It's time to push them.

"Who said there'd be two sides? Does there have to be two sides?"

"If I don't put on a single witness, can I possibly win?" Now you're going to see blank stares again. They really weren't expecting this at all. If nobody knows the answer, suggest it.

"Suppose I don't put on a single witness, but the State's evidence doesn't actually prove my client did anything wrong with that mountain of evidence we talked about—then what?"

If you've primed them right, the two word answer is coming. "Not Guilty." If you don't have a single juror who answers this way, loop back and do the "vote now" section again. See §2A:22. Get every one of them on your side. This is imperative.

Press them.

"Do I need to prove anything?" Nope.

"Is the State on equal footing here with the defense, or are you already on the defense's side?" (Are you at a 0 or a 10?) One hundred percent with the defense is the answer you're looking for.

"So does there need to be two sides to this story?" Here's the best answer you'll ever get to this from a juror who **really** understands this. "I guess not—if they can't prove it, they can't prove it."

BINGO.

The other thing you're doing here is setting up your closing description of reasonable doubt. Your closing will all nicely flow together with the other parts of your trial presentation, like any good story should.

Consider the following statements, all of which are absolutely correct under law and all of which I use in my closing arguments.

- "You must be 100% free of reasonable doubt if you vote to convict."
- "If you have any single doubt, based in reason, you must vote not guilty."
- "If you have any appreciable degree of reasonable doubt, you must vote not guilty."
- "Beyond means past or to the exclusion of—meaning the State must prove their case beyond and to the exclusion of every single reasonable doubt. Not only do they have to prove their case, they must disprove reasonable doubt." (This is one of my favorites—especially since we just showed them disproving something is nearly impossible.)
- "Reasonable doubt exists already in your mind. By law, you are 100% on Mr. Jones's side right now. In fact, you begin your deliberations as follows—I doubt because. If you can finish that sentence, you have a reasonable doubt. And if all six of you can finish that sentence, your deliberations are over in less than 5 minutes. So start there."

As I mentioned previously, a story I use in closing is that the State has invited the jurors here. It's a dinner party at the State's request. If after dinner, jurors look at their plates, and they're still hungry, the State did not bring the meat to dinner. It was their job. If you are hungry, you vote not guilty. Here I lay the ground work here for that story. See Ch. 7 for closing arguments.

§2A:24 Get Jurors to Understand the Meaning of Beyond a Reasonable Doubt

Now it is time to get to every defense attorney's favorite phrase, beyond a reasonable doubt. Get jurors to define it for you in terms so simple that they will have to find a client not guilty by their own admissions and promises. Ask what a "doubt" is.

"A question." Not a bad answer. You're looking for something along those lines.

Now ask what the word "reasonable" means.

"Normal." The answer you're looking for here is normal or even better "non-crazy." If you need to press for more you can give examples. "Is it a reasonable explanation that I lost my keys when I got out of the car and they fell out of my pocket?" "Is it a reasonable explanation that I lost my keys when aliens took them from me?" The crazier the unreasonable example you give, the better. You're just setting the stage for your story later.

Now ask about "beyond." I use a drinking glass analogy. If it's filled with water right up to the brim, is it beyond full? Nope! Has to be spilling over. Right?

Combining this with the "fact" requirement from the last section, you can now check in with your jury panel again to make sure they are tracking you.

> "So would you all agree that in order to prove Mr. Defendant guilty, the State needs to bring you enough facts (not assumptions or statistics) to get beyond your normal non-crazy questions?" If they nod, you've got them. Go down the line again.

> "Will each of you promise that if the State does NOT present enough facts to get beyond your normal non crazy questions in this case, you'll find Mr. Defendant not guilty?" The whole panel should say now say yes. Again, the prosecutors hate this, but ah well, such is the presumption of innocence.

§2A:25 Get Jurors to Like You and Reveal Their Biases

Next share something about yourself by telling jurors that you might not be a great juror for a certain type of case. You're inviting them to kick themselves off the jury while humanizing yourself. Here's how this works:

"So you've heard that this is a DUI case. That's a really hot button topic. You know, I have the world's most adorable daughter. If this were a case about someone who did something bad to a little girl, the defendant would still be entitled to a good jury panel, and I'd want to presume innocence and be a good juror—but I know in my heart, I'd hold it against him. I'd see my daughter in my mind every minute. It would not be a good case for me. Now—as I mention this—you might be thinking to yourself—wow—DUI isn't really a great case for me, for whatever reason. You might have a knot in your stomach just thinking about it. You might think to yourself—this is the wrong case for me to sit on. And you know what? That's okay. It doesn't make you a bad juror or a bad person. It makes you human. But you can't sit on this jury as a result. It wouldn't be right. So—understanding that—if you're thinking there's something here that bothers me about this case already, raise your hand, please."

> "I'm so sorry you went through that. Nobody should ever go through that. Thank you so much for your honesty and sharing that with us. I'd imagine this is one of those experiences you carry with you every day isn't it?"

> "Yes."

> "It's one of those things that defines who you are as a person. There was you before, and you after, and you're not the same anymore?"

> "Yes."

> "I'd imagine it'd be hard to keep that out of your mind in the jury room. Almost impossible, wouldn't it? Like I said about my daughter."

> "Probably."

> "There's nothing I could really say that would make you forget that this happened, is there?"

> "No."

> "There's nothing the prosecutor could say?"

> "No."

> "I'd imagine there's probably nothing even the judge could say that would make you forget such a strong defining part of who you are."

> "No."

"I so much appreciate your honesty and candor. It's very brave to tell us these things. I'm going to ask the judge to excuse you so you don't have to sit through such a hard trial for you personally."

Be sympathetic. You're not striking jurors, nor are you stacking the jury. What you're doing is being a caring compassionate human who is letting people who are uncomfortable out of an uncomfortable situation. You are their hero. The rest of the jury sees you being a good person who isn't making that juror sit through something potentially traumatic or triggering.

Thank the jurors for their honesty. It's hard to open up in a room full of strangers and talk about your family member who was killed by alcoholism or a drunk driver. I've actually been moved to tears by jurors telling their stories to us during voir dire, and felt my heart break for their experience as the judge excused them from service at my request. You can be a human being **and** an effective advocate at the same time, and in fact, I'd say it's required of you to do the job at its pinnacle. Don't be afraid to say you're sorry they went through something, then wave goodbye and kick the prosecutor's butt because they're gone.

If they laugh, laugh with them. If they smile, smile with them. Be friendly. Be open. Be persuasive. They need to like you. And they need to do it fast.

§2A:26   Get Jurors to Understand Why the Defendant Is Not Testifying

It is rare that my clients testify in a DUI trial. Sure there are jury instructions about the client's decision not to testify and the prosecutor isn't allowed to argue about it, but I like to talk about it a little during voir dire if there's time. I go back to my juror from the littering game. See §2A:21.

"If you were accused of littering and you knew you didn't do it, why wouldn't you want to get on the witness stand in a trial and shout it to everyone?" Here's a mistake I've seen some attorneys make in this moment. I've seen our colleagues ask if you'd want to testify in your own defense, hoping that the fear of public speaking will win out. The problem is the age old adage that we always tout but often forget: never ask a question you don't know the answer to—which I'll here adapt to "never ask a question you have to hope for the right answer to."

The way I ask it, I'm essentially leading my juror. I'm suggesting to her that she already wouldn't want to. Now I'm asking her to justify it. Plenty of great suggestions and answers come from this discussion, but in the event nobody has any, feel free to go back to the old "tricky lawyer" well.

Now be careful here, because you can accidentally destroy your own credibility you've been working so hard to build by making yourself a spin doctor. But you can remind jurors that a skilled prosecutor, on the other hand, IS one.

"Juror #3, the prosecutor and I, we're lawyers. We use words for a living. Right?"

"Do you think with enough time, the prosecutor could confuse you with simple questions?"

"Do you think with enough time, the prosecutor could get you to admit to something you didn't mean to?"

"Do you think with enough time, the prosecutor could get you to admit to something that wasn't even true?"

Not only have you taught a jury why your client isn't touching the witness stand, but also planted the seeds that the prosecutor might just be the manipulator of facts they assumed defense lawyers were.

§2A:27   Get Jurors to Describe (Your Client's) Good Driving

Here is a reminder to use the prosecutor's tricks against him. If the prosecutor wants to describe drunk drivers by reminding the jury of all the characteristics they described that match your client, get the jury to describe other things your client did right. In the alternative, if you have a story that involves a different explanation for the driving, use that to get descriptive words.

"What does good driving look like?" Make note of everything a juror says in describing good driving that your client did because you know your client did 85% of it.

"Have you ever seen a driver you thought was falling asleep behind the wheel? What did their driving look like? Have you ever been falling asleep behind the wheel?"

"Have you ever seen someone driving while having a medical crisis like a diabetic episode? What did that look like?"

Remember to use what you have. The more you are able to get the jury to give you the details you need to tell your story now, the more familiar the story will seem to them when you tell it back to them later.

§2A:28 Get Jurors to Doubt Breath/Blood Testing Accuracy

Don't be afraid to take a risk on voir dire. Don't be afraid to make them smile and break that "serious" wall if there's a point to it, of course. For instance, one thing I will often do in a breath test case is begin setting the stage for challenging assumptions by officers or the "accuracy and reliability" of the breath testing machine. How? Not by talking about the officer or the machine, but by showing the jury that just because a person or machine says it—doesn't make it so—nor do expert witnesses make it so, especially if your common sense tells you something different.

"Suppose, ladies and gentlemen, that this was not a case about DUI, but rather a case where the prosecutor's office had to prove if it was raining outside right now (or sunny, if it is in fact raining). Suppose the State simply told you it was raining. Did they prove it?" Nope.

"Suppose the State brought in a witness who testified that it's usually raining on days like this. Did they prove it?" No, not yet.

"Suppose the State brought in an expert witness who studied an almanac and historical data for this very day and this very spot and that 85% of the time on this day on this spot, it's raining. Did they prove it?" Still no.

"Suppose the State could bring you an expert meteorologist who testifies that according to current weather trends and "accurate and reliable" scientific methods certified by the government, beyond a reasonable doubt it's raining outside. Have they proven it to you yet?" If you have any takers, ask why. If you need to set a juror against "yes" answers, ask why not.

"Suppose the State could bring you an expert meteorologist who testifies that according to an "accurate and reliable" scientific weather reading machine certified by the government, beyond a reasonable doubt it's raining outside. Now have they proven it?" Again—if anyone bites—ask why. Now you can ask why not. Why haven't they proven it? Answer: "Because they didn't just look outside."

Now we go further. "Can you ever prove something based on assumptions and statistics?" Nope. Great! "Will you each promise me that if the State's case relies on assumptions and statistics and not proof, you'll find my client not guilty?" Now go juror by juror and ask each one for a yes. Now you can remind them during closing (because truly all DUI cases are based on assumptions and statistics) what they promised you. Their work is done and they can vote not guilty and go home.

Technology is a constant companion in our lives now, and undoubtedly our jurors are all familiar with machines both electronic and medical. If you have a chemical test, it's important to start telling your story about it now, too. Jurors need to know these machines cannot be trusted the way the government uses them. They also need to know that generally, the government doesn't use them the way their doctor's office uses them. So ask these questions.

"Would you trust a medical test performed by a police officer less than one performed by a doctor?"

"Would you trust a blood test analyzed by a police agency less than one performed by a medical lab?"

"Would you trust a machine that hasn't been updated or maintained properly?"

And so on. These questions will be largely fact specific to your case, and there are numerous analogies to use. Or you can simply use the "raining" story and that might be all you need. Feel free to go further and develop more for your particular story. Ask about tech upgrades. Have the jurors hold up their phones. Find the newest iPhone in the room and ask the juror why he upgraded it. Talk about the benefits of new technology, knowing that the machine your client blew into is likely 5 to 10 years old already.

§2A:29   Get Jurors to Reveal Themselves with Two Final "Fun" Questions

I feel it's important after such heavy topics that we remind the jury that we are friends and lighten the mood with a couple of "fun" questions. These last three questions are a bit more whimsical and fun for me, and yet I often gain amazing information from them—sometimes more than I do from the rest of voir dire as a whole. Sure they can tell me they are at zero (see §2A:22) and they'll vote not guilty, but I've conditioned them to do that. Now I want to throw them a loop and make sure their actual brains and personalities are engaged. I want to see who I really do want and don't want.

Question 1: What sort of information would you expect to see in a DUI case? This question sets you up to show these jurors all the things the State did not bring with them in their arsenal—as long as it's reasonable to do so. DNA? Unreasonable in a run of the mill DUI. But if there's no dashcam in this day and age doesn't that say something about reasonable doubt in terms of the quality of evidence?

Question 2: Suppose you are going to stay for this trial, but you can't be a juror. You have to choose a new job. I'm going to ask you all to vote in a moment. You can either be a defense attorney, a prosecutor, the judge, or our clerk. Think a moment and then we'll vote.

Ask one juror who picked each job (assuming someone picked defense attorney—rarely do they) why they picked it. Jurors who pick prosecutor because they want to punish the bad guys are not great jurors for you. Feel out jurors who want to be the judge because they want to not favor either side and be fair and balanced. See where their interests are and what they've gotten from voir dire and if they're willing to play with you. If they laugh and smile and play along with you, they may just be on your side by now. The best answer I've ever gotten was from a rare person who chose 'defense lawyer.' I asked him why. "It's like you said earlier. You have the easier job. If the State doesn't do their thing, you don't have to do your thing." You'd better believe I re-used that phrase in closing when the State foolishly left him on my jury.

Question 3: Think of a person you admire—living or dead—but please make it a person we'd all know. We all admire a relative of some sort—like I adore my Dad—but that doesn't mean much to you. So if I said I admired Christopher Reeve because of how hard he fought after his horseback riding accident, that would ring true for some of you. So think of a person you admire. I'd like to know who they are.

Go juror by juror right down the line. You get lots of answers here but sometimes you get some really insightful ones. This question is a really benign way of prying into deeply kept values. Everyone will proudly tell you whom they admire. Generally, I find that anyone who names a Clinton, Obama, or liberal political figure is a good juror for the defense. Conversely, if they name a Bush, Trump, or conservative political (or religious) figure, they tend to be much more prosecution oriented. I also find that jurors who name military leaders are generally poor jurors for the defense, while those who mention civil rights activists or famous artists are generally good jurors for the defense.

I still can't figure out whether Oprah is a good or bad answer.

[§§2A:30-2A:39 Reserved]

IV.   A NON-EXHAUSTIVE OUTLINE OF POSSIBLE VOIR DIRE TOPICS

§2A:40   Using This Outline

Although in the preceding sections, I have given you a script, I don't work from a script during voir dire. I use an outline.

During voir dire, you should not be looking at paper. You should be looking at jurors, conversing with them, getting to know them, and vice versa. Your senses will pick up way more than your notepad can. You know when you're comfortable with someone and when you're not.

Also, you're building a knowledge base for jurors so they know what sort of lawyer you are later. You want to be able to tell them in closing—"Sure, the prosecutor gets a rebuttal, but you know me—you know what I'd say if I could. So you say it for me." And you want them to nod. "Yup. I know what you'd say!"

Let them see you-- the real you, not the "stuffy lawyer persona" you have. Leave that person in the parking lot. It's time to be real and talk to actual people. Make eye contact. It can be uncomfortable for everyone involved, including you. It's also how you connect. It's how you tell a story.

The sections below are an outline of some of my typical DUI voir dire topics. Although I know it well, I keep the outline with me just in case I miss something. I update it for each case. You should do the same. Don't use my outline verbatim. Alter it. Use the examples I give to create your own. The more of yourself that you put into it—the more of themselves jurors will give you.

Note: The questions about games and rules are designed to help you identify if you have mavericks on your jury panel. What you really want, if you set up your voir dire so that your jurors truly understand reasonable doubt and presumption of innocence, are jurors who will obey the rules of the game—even when they don't like them! ("Man, I hate drunk drivers, but the law says the State has to prove it so I guess I have to find him not guilty.")

§2A:41   DUI Voir Dire Outline

I.   **Presumption of Innocence**

A. Bad Evidence—Wrongful Conviction
- Why do innocent people get wrongly convicted of crimes?
- How can you, as a potential juror, guarantee that this is not going to be one of those cases?

B. Difficulty of Proving Something Didn't Happen
- I saw you litter—prove you didn't. (press the juror here—close up every single hole)
- CAN YOU PROVE INNOCENCE?
- Fair to both sides?
- Who said there'd be two sides?
- Does there need to be?
- How can you, as a potential juror, guarantee that you will hold the State to their enormous burden?
- Until vs. unless.

C. Role of Defense Attorney
- Who doesn't trust me?
- What's my job?

II.   **Unfair and Partial Jurors**

- I'm going to tell you something you already know: Client was arrested by a police officer, charged by the prosecutor with a crime, and here we are getting ready for trial: Based on that alone, on a scale of 0 to 10, with 0 completely guilty, and 10 completely innocent, how likely do you think it is that she is guilty?
- If you had to vote right now, how would you vote? Guilty or not guilty?
- Is it fair to Client that before you hear any evidence at all, some of you are ready to vote guilty?
- What are we going to do about that
- Should Client have to prove his innocence?

- The burden of proof is on the prosecution to prove all aspects of the case. The burden never shifts to Client to prove anything.
- Do you understand that Client is presumed innocent under the law? What does that mean?
- Unless v. Until?
- Does anyone have a problem with that?
- Who wants to be fair and impartial?
- Impartial means not preferring one side over another right?
- "Impartial" or 100% on Client's side—entirely?
- You start with "not guilty"—it's the State's job to try to change your mind.
- How many of you have children?
- Let's suppose that the government wants to take your children away from you, accusing you of being a bad parent. On a scale of 0 to 10, with 0 being no proof at all, and 10 being completely irrefutable certainty, how much evidence should the government have to have to take away your kids?
- How much should you have to convict someone of a crime?
- Does anyone know what the burden of proof is for a criminal case? And where does that fall on the scale of proof?
- Does anyone think that is too high?
- How can you, as a potential juror, guarantee that you will hold the State to their enormous burden?

III.   Beyond a Reasonable Doubt

- You all understand the State has to prove its case beyond a reasonable doubt.
- What does "prove" mean?
- How do I prove something to you?
- What is proof? What are facts?
- Are beliefs facts? Do we really know?
- What about assumptions—are assumptions facts?
- Why not?
- So if I have to prove it's raining and I say "Let's just assume it's raining"—have I proven it?
- Could I ever prove something to you relying on assumptions?
- Will you each agree that if the State's case relies on assumptions or statistics and not actual facts that you will find Client not guilty?
- What does beyond mean? (Past—foul ball on the line is still fair, right? Glass isn't past full until it's dripping)
- What does doubt mean? If you have a doubt what does that mean? (You still have questions—uncertainty)
- What does reasonable mean? (Not crazy.)
- Do you all agree?

IV.   Juror Bias

- We are looking for the right jurors for this case.
- You might be a great juror for another case, but not for this case.
- We all have biases. I have a little girl. I couldn't sit on a case where someone is accused of hurting a little girl.
- In this case, Client is accused of driving under the influence of alcohol. Has anyone had any life experience that they think would bother them to sit on a DUI case?
- Has anyone contributed time or money to MADD or a similar organization?
- On a scale of 0 to 10, is it OK to drive with a little alcohol in your system? 0 is no, not under any circumstances yes, as long as you aren't too impaired to drive safely.

V.   Why Defendant Does Not Testify

- Now, if somebody was accused of a crime that he didn't commit, do you think she would want to say so?
- Do you think some people lie to get themselves out of trouble?
- Would you think someone who didn't testify had something to hide?
- So if Client testifies some of you may think she is lying, but if she doesn't, some of you may think she is hiding something?
- Is it fair for Client to start in such a position? (circle back to presumption of innocence) What are we going to do about that?

- Can you think of any reasons why an innocent person might not want to testify?
  - Afraid of public speaking?
  - Afraid you would think he was lying?
  - Afraid of the prosecutor asking him tricky questions?
- Would it be bad lawyering on my part if I were to waste your time by calling extra witnesses, even Client, if I didn't believe the prosecutor had proven their case?

VI.   Driving Descriptions

- Good driving characteristics
- Medical crisis characteristics
- Drowsy driving
  - Night Owls?
  - Reports of tired or sleeping drivers?

VII.   Accuracy of Breath/Blood Tests

A. Proving Weather (rain example)
- Suppose the State simply told you it was raining.
- Suppose the State brought in a witness who testified that it's usually raining on days like this.
- Suppose the State brought in an expert witness who studied an almanac and historical data for this very day and this very spot and that 85% of the time on this day on this spot, it's raining.
- Suppose the State could bring you an expert meteorologist who testifies that according to current weather trends and "accurate and reliable" scientific methods certified by the government, beyond a reasonable doubt it's raining outside.
- Suppose the State could bring you an expert meteorologist who testifies that according to an "accurate and reliable" scientific weather reading machine certified by the government, beyond a reasonable doubt it's raining outside.
- Can you ever prove something based on assumptions and statistics?
- Will you each promise me that if the State's case relies on assumptions and statistics and not proof, you'll find my client not guilty?

B. Machines
- Would you trust a medical test performed by a police officer less than one performed by a doctor?"
- Would you trust a blood test analyzed by a police agency less than one performed by a medical lab?
- Would you trust a machine that hasn't been updated or maintained properly?
- Why upgrade your phone to the latest model?

C. Defendant Did Not Take Breath Test
- Can you imagine a circumstance where you wouldn't want to take a test of your breath?

VIII.   Games and Rules

- A trial is not a game, but it has some similarities to a game.
- How many of you have ever played a board game, like monopoly, etc.
- If you don't like a rule, do you change it, or do you play the game with the rules as they come on the box?
- Based on a scale of 0 to 10, how likely are you to change the rules of the game to something you like better, with 0 being you always strictly follow the rules exactly as they are on the box and 10 being you make up your own rules frequently.

IX.   Final Questions

- Types of evidence we would expect to see in a case like this?
- Job you will choose if you were not a juror: judge; prosecutor; defense attorney; clerk.
- Name of a person you admire living or dead.

CHAPTER 2

JURY SELECTION: THE JUROR ELIMINATION APPROACH

The author gratefully acknowledges the assistance of trial consultant Rich Matthews in the writing and updating of this chapter. Rich can be reached by email at Rich@Juryology.com. He writes a valuable and entertaining blog on jury persuasion at www.Juryology.com.

IV.   JURY QUESTIONNAIRES

V.   SLIDES AND SCORECARD TO USE WHEN VOIR DIRE IS LIMITED

VI.   REFRAMING

SPECIAL NOTE: *Becoming Part of the Jury*

I recently watched Marjorie Russell during a seminar by CACJ in Palm Springs. She stressed the "tribal" feeling of human interaction. One of the main points that struck me was her use of the first person plural pronouns "we" and "us." Using them, she argued—and I fully agree—creates a bond between you and the jury. I would encourage all attorneys to use first person plural pronouns, *especially* in jury selection and in opening/closing. Ask the prospective juror to explain a position "to us." When addressing the panel, tell the jurors, "We will." This creates fellowship between you and the jurors.

I. PURPOSE OF VOIR DIRE

§2:01   Exposing Juror Bias

One touchstone of a fair trial is an impartial trier of fact—"a jury capable and willing to decide the case solely on the evidence before it." *Smith v. Phillips,* 455 U.S. 209, 217, 102 S.Ct. 940, 946, 71 L.Ed.2d 78 (1982). *Voir dire* examination protects that right by exposing possible biases, both known and unknown, on the part of potential jurors. Demonstrated bias in the responses to questions on voir dire may result in a juror being excused for cause; hints of bias not sufficient to warrant challenge for cause may assist parties in exercising their peremptory challenges. If this process is to serve its purpose, the necessity of truthful answers by prospective jurors is obvious. *McDonough Power Equipment, Inc. v. Greenwood,* 464 U.S. 548 (1984).

Voir dire plays a critical function in assuring the criminal defendant that his Sixth Amendment right to an impartial jury will be honored. Without an adequate voir dire, the trial judge's responsibility to remove prospective jurors who will not be able to impartially to follow the court's instructions and evaluate the evidence cannot be fulfilled. *See Connors v. United States,* 158 U.S. 408, 413, 15 S.Ct. 951, 953, 39 L.Ed. 1033 (1895). Similarly, lack of adequate voir dire impairs the defendant's right to exercise peremptory challenges where provided by statute or rule, as they are in the federal courts. *Rosales-Lopez v. U.S.,* 451 U.S. 182 (1981).

The questioning should be conducted by counsel in such a way as to not only elicit information regarding possible bias, but also to assist the defense in creating a jury it feels appropriate to the case. "Voir dire examination serves the dual purposes of enabling the court to select an impartial jury and assisting counsel in exercising peremptory challenges." *Mu'Min v. Virginia,* 500 U.S. 415 (1991).

Let us be extremely clear here. Voir dire's primary purpose is to gather information so that counsel can intelligently exercise challenges, both for cause and peremptory. That means information that is actionable intelligence—that actually differentiates jurors into those more likely to side with the prosecution or with the defense. A very distant second purpose is to provide some of the case issues and themes. And somewhat behind that, the third purpose is to develop some level of rapport with the jurors who will remain when both sides have quit exercising challenges and accept the panel.

§2:01.1   Eliciting the Key Words

In order to ensure a challenge for cause for bias, you must show that the prospective juror has a firm opinion rather than a strong feeling about the facts or issues in the case. See *People v. Williams,* 199 Cal App 3d 469 (1988); *People v. Sanchez,* 208 Cal App 3d 721 (1989). The truth is that opinions and feelings are actually the same psychological phenomenon; they stem from a core belief system that is virtually impossible to supplant with legal and sometimes even emotional arguments. The key for the practitioner is to encourage and guide the juror to state this belief in such firm language as to support the challenge for cause. The following watchwords should be reframed to cement the challenge for cause:

- I feel.
- It seems to me.
- I believe.
- I see it.
- In my opinion.
- If you ask me.
- If it were up to me.
- I guess so.
- It sounds to me.

To move from feelings, which are not grounds for cause challenge, to solid opinions or core beliefs, which are grounds for such a challenge, try the following sequence to help the juror reframe the answer.

Q: Prospective Juror 2, you stated that you believe officers tell the truth. Is this just a quick opinion or is it based on your life experience?
A: Life experience, personal history, etc.
Q: Is this a relatively new belief or is it one you have had for a while?
A: For a while.
Q: So this is based not on emotion, but on reason?
A: Yes.
Q: While I am not asking for the reasons right now, you could give reasons to support this position?
A: Yes.
Q: And these are solid reasons in your mind that you have thought out?

Should a juror indicate that until you asked about the issue it was not on his or her mind, thereby creating the illusion for the judge that it is not a firm or solid belief but rather a spur of the moment response, you can turn to hot button social issues as examples of similar thought processes. In other words, until someone mentions abortion, gay marriage, taxes, etc., most people are not walking to Starbucks thinking about their position on those issues. However, no one would argue that a person's position when asked is just a quick gut response. These issues, while not in the forefront of our day-to-day thinking, are still core beliefs, well thought-out and based on life experience and reason. So too is the juror's position on the issue at hand.

Q: How many of us have watched a sporting event where the referee or umpire made a call that you thought was right, but then the instant replay showed the call was wrong?
Q: In other words, our eyes fooled us. Tell us about that experience.
Q: In this case we will hear the officer describe the events. The officer will describe them as he remembers them from his point of view. Then we will see the video tape. If they are not in agreement, which will you believe?

§2:01.2   Modern Sources to Reveal Bias

There was a time when asking people what television or radio they used regularly gave you an idea as to where they sat on the political and social spectrum. To some degree, Fox versus CNN does the same today, although more and more people watch those for pure entertainment rather than as a reflection on their own positions. However, the Internet locales such as blogs, Twitter, etc., to which a juror is either an active participant or a regular subscriber can show the juror's deeper bias.

Q: Does anyone regularly read, follow, or write blogs, Tweets, etc.?
Q: Which ones?

§2:02   Limits on Time and Scope

How often are we told that our voir dire is going to be limited in either time or scope? Is this right? Should we allow this to happen? Despite what many judges seem to think about voir dire, it is not only a critical aspect of jury trials, but also a part of the defendant's fundamental due process to engage in full probing voir dire.

Indeed, your jurisdiction's rules of jury selection might assist you in overcoming many judges' distaste for permitting counsel a full and wide opportunity to investigate bias and prejudice. For instance, California's Code of Civil Procedure (which governs jury selection for criminal trials as well) specifically says that "the trial judge should permit liberal and probing examination calculated to discover bias or prejudice with regard to the circumstances of the particular case. The fact that a topic has been included in the judge's examination should not preclude additional nonrepetitive or nonduplicative questioning in the same area by counsel" and goes on to say that "[s] pecific unreasonable or arbitrary time limits shall not be imposed in any case. The trial judge shall not establish a blanket policy of a time limit for voir dire." Cal. Code Civ. Proc. §222.5. It is hard to imagine a clearer statement from the legislature to permit a broad scope of topics and to forbid trial judges from imposing unreasonable and arbitrary time limits . . . but some judges still do.

As for limits on how long or how much questioning is allowable, while it is discretionary with the judge, there is authority for quite a lengthy process. "The voir dire in American trials tends to be extensive and probing, operating as a predicate for the exercise of peremptories. . . ." *Swain v. Alabama*, 380 U.S. 202 (1965).

With regard to the scope of voir dire, judges often believe that any attempt of counsel to ingratiate themselves with the jury is inappropriate. These judges feel that the questioning must and should be limited to challenges for cause, or as outlined above, to possible peremptory challenges only. They see no reason to allow counsel to explain his or her case, or to "soften" up the jury to counsel's position. However, there is authority to counter this position.

"Voir dire permits a party to establish a relation, if not a bond of trust, with the jurors. This relation continues throughout the entire trial and may in some cases extend to the sentencing as well." *Powers v. Ohio*, 499 U.S. 400 (1991).

"If conducted properly, voir dire can inform litigants about potential jurors, making reliance upon stereotypical and pejorative notions about a particular gender or race both unnecessary and unwise. Voir dire provides a means of discovering actual or implied bias and a firmer basis upon which the parties may exercise their peremptory challenges intelligently. *See, e.g., Nebraska Press Assn. v. Stuart*, 427 U.S. 539, 602, 96 S.Ct. 2791, 2823, 49 L.Ed.2d 683 (1976) (Brennan, J., concurring in judgment) (voir dire "facilitate[s] intelligent exercise of peremptory challenges and [helps] uncover factors that would dictate disqualification for cause"); *United States v. Whitt*, 718 F.2d 1494, 1497 (10th 1983) ("Without an adequate foundation [laid by voir dire], counsel cannot exercise sensitive and intelligent peremptory challenges")." *J.E.B. v. Alabama ex rel. T.B.*, 511 U.S. 127 (1994).

So it is clear that counsel should be given plenty of leeway in both time and scope of questioning in order to decide on how to pursue cause challenges, and if those fail or are not sought, then whom to strike from the potential panel.

§2:02.1   Whose 20 Minutes Is It?

As Allen Trapp stated in his review of this book, "not all of you can get away with all of what is presented"; this is one such idea. Try to have the judge agree that you are allowed "twenty minutes for questions" of the jurors. Keep meticulous notes of when you ask each question. When the judge seeks to stop you, explain in front of the jurors that your understanding was that *you* had 20 minutes and not that the jurors were limited by time in their answers. The point here is to show the judge and the jury that artificial time limitations get in the way of true voir dire as envisioned by the Supreme Court of the United States as presented above.

§2:02.2   Mini Opening Statement Before Questioning

Some jurisdictions permit the lawyers to make a brief opening statement before the oral questioning of prospective jurors. *See*, e.g., Cal. Code Civ. Proc. §222.5. If your jurisdiction permits this, you should do it.

The benefits of this for any lawyer are tremendous. Counsel can lay out the issues of the case in a coherent story, and not have to chop up the issues into little bits and sneak them into a dozen questions. The opportunity to give mini openings increases the quality of the information your questions will elicit because the venirepersons will be answering in the context of your case; their answers will be more relevant and useful to you because they understand the basic issues in the case.

If you are going to do a mini opening statement, keep it to about five to seven minutes. That is plenty of time to lay out the basic issues, the issues you want to keep in the spotlight for the whole trial. Merely piling more facts and data onto a person does not persuade. Less is often more. And in the case of mini openings, we are just trying to draw the prospective jurors' attention to the key moments in your story so that when they talk about what is acceptable or forgivable—or unacceptable or unforgivable—their answers will relate directly to your story without need for interpretation.

There is a tricky psychological trap that counsel must avoid with the mini opening, and it has to do with when it happens in the sequence of your trial: it happens *before* voir dire. Remember that the purpose of voir dire is to pull out *unfavorable* information from jurors, their attitudes and opinions that would be *bad* for your side. Yet, if you go in trying to "win" the mini opening, that might have the effect of making jurors less likely to reveal their views that are contrary to yours.

Therefore, the tone in a mini opening must be matter-of-fact, calm, informative, and neither argumentative nor intense. We do not want to arouse anyone's psychological resistance by pushing too hard too soon. It is also good to keep in mind that at this pre-questioning moment, we have built up literally no reservoir of good faith nor trustworthiness. Ideally, we will build some of that during voir dire, but that hasn't happened yet. It is worth keeping in mind that of all the parties except the actual defendant, the criminal defense attorney is the least trusted person in the room. Again, the idea is that you will turn that around. But it cannot happen before voir dire. Moral of the story: don't push it during mini opening.

§2:03   Uncovering Juror Personality Types and Finding Leaders

One aspect of jury selection is looking for the different personality types in the jury pool. It is obviously important to know who the leaders, followers, and lone wolves are. Using a peremptory challenge to remove someone who is bad for you on the issues but is so weak as to lack the capacity to influence others is not nearly as important as using it on the leader type who is borderline for you on the issues but who will run the jury. In other words, try to find the persons who are both bad for you on the issues and leaders.

The single most revealing fact is still what the prospective jurors do for a living, and what position they hold in that field. The 20-year employee who has never advanced beyond the basic levels is generally not a leader. The entrepreneurs, self-employed, small business owners or project managers are leader types. These people are used to setting up the parameters of a discussion and running the meeting to their ends.

Remember that what a person does for a living is not limited to traditional 9 to 5 employment. A stay-at-home parent who runs the mother's group, heads the PTA, or is in other positions of management has the same leadership traits as the head of eBay, or Google.

Here are some ideas as to how to uncover these people.

Q: Do any of you have a supervisory role, run projects, or in other ways have people who report to you as part of your day-to-day life, such as work, clubs, volunteering, etc.? Explain.

Q: Does anyone belong to a political, religious, civic or other such group where you served as an officer, on the board of directors/trustees, or something similar? Explain.

Q: Those of you who served our country, what was your final rank? Explain.

Q: Have any of you ever written an article, blog, or book? Explain.

Q: How about a letter to the editor, online review, e.g. movie or book review (like on a web page), or blog comment? Explain.

Q: How many and how often do any of you use Twitter, Facebook, MySpace, etc.? Explain.

Q: Who is a member of an online list serve? Topics and details.

NOTE TO THE COMPUTER LITERATE:

Assuming local rules allow, go on Facebook, MySpace, Twitter, or other social websites and look these people up. These postings are the real individual and not the voir dire-sensitive juror. Also, you would be surprised what witnesses, even police officers, have on their pages or on YouTube.

Lenny Stamm of Maryland came upon the work of Dr. Benziger and introduced it to us in 2010. Basically, the Doctor's work breaks people down to four personality types: Basal Left, Basal Right, Frontal Left, Frontal Right, as seen here (The Basal being the lower two):

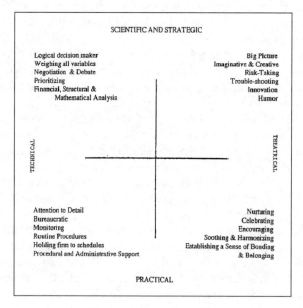

Figure 2-01 Personality Types

By listening to the answers given to you in voir dire, you MAY be able to make some assessments as to which of these four basic categories the potential juror falls. By doing so you can then TAILOR your closing arguments to each type. In other words, if you have several jurors who meet the frontal right definition, you might consider directing your humor and big picture ideas towards them. On the flip side, a Frontal Left person would be more receptive to the arguments of neglected duty, shortcuts and failure to follow the protocols.

§2:04   "Pre-rehabilitation"

Many attorneys fear a very detailed and full voir dire because they think it will reveal more challenges for cause against their side than for the other side. Even if true, you can make this problem irrelevant by "pre-habilitating" the juror who holds opinions favorable to your side. Simply put, you establish from the juror that while she has the beliefs or opinions you like and want, the juror will nevertheless keep that all-important "open mind." Once you are happy with the juror, try the following:

Q: Of course, Mr. M., you have not heard the facts and will not form any opinion until told to do so?
Q: You will keep an open mind?
Q: You will use your intelligence and common sense when evaluating this case?

Should a challenge for cause be raised, the answers to these questions are the rebuttal.

In many jurisdictions there are rebuttable presumptions regarding breath and chemical tests: first, the presumption that at a specific alcohol level the person is deemed impaired; second, that if the test is obtained within a specified time period, it is deemed the alcohol level at the time of driving. In order to deal with this in the case, attorneys need to address it in voir dire.

Q: If you are told that you may but are not required to conclude something from a certain fact, how would you go about deciding if you should do so?
Q: What kind of evidence would you need to combat this presumption?

[§§2:05-2:09 Reserved]

II.   WHAT KIND OF JUROR DO YOU WANT?

A. Ideal Juror Depends on Theory of Case

§2:10   Importance of Theory of Case

In some ways, it is self-defeating to think about what kind of juror you want for a case, because lawyers do not select jurors. It is jury *de*-selection; counsel can only seek to get rid of jurors he or she does not want. Therefore, our focus in voir dire is to identify those jurors least likely to be open to our story and our themes, and to draw out enough biased answers from them to support cause challenges, or failing that, to exercise our peremptory challenges most advantageously.

However, one place to start identifying the attitudes and experiences that we do not want is identifying those attitudes and experiences that would help us. So let us begin there.

The ideal juror is one who does in fact consume alcohol, who drives, and who seems open to whatever the theme of your case may be.

In order to decide what kind of juror you want for your case, you need to first decide on the theory of defense. It is often a losing proposition to approach a DUI trial, or perhaps any trial, with a "shotgun" defense. This kind of "throw it all up and see what sticks" is usually perceived as the desperate act of a losing defense. Find those one or two points that you have most strongly on your side and use them as the cornerstone of the case.

This is not to say that you should not bring up other issues if they exist. Instead, tailor those issues to the main theme of the case.

It is very important to know exactly what your theory will be. Determine whether you have medical or contamination issues, some kind of "disconnect," a refusal based on confusion or individual liberty issues, a bad test, or any of the dozens of defenses that exist. You can determine what kind of juror would be best for you only after you have decided what the main point of attack will be.

§2:11   Improperly Conducted Breath Test

Suppose your theme is that the breath test was improperly conducted due to no deprivation or observation period. This does not mean you do not bring up that the officer wrote the wrong make or color of the car in his report. What you do is show how the officer demonstrated sloppiness in his report, which is consistent with the sloppiness he showed in administering the breath test. Thus, the true theme within the "improperly conducted test" defense is sloppiness by the police officer, or carelessness of the police officer.

In this type of case, you would probably want a juror who believes in procedures. Former military or someone with a job that involves strict technical rules, such as engineering, accounting, or science, would be best. You want someone who would agree that procedures and safeguards need to be followed precisely. However, inasmuch as lawyers do not get to select jurors they like, defense counsel must look for the usual authoritarian personality types that all criminal defense attorneys must try to get rid of. These are the types who will forgive errors of the players they already like, namely law enforcement officers (and prosecutors).

§2:12   Disconnect Cases

If you are arguing disconnect, that is, when the chemical test results are inconsistent with the alleged drinking pattern and the performance on SFSTs, then you want skeptics. Look for people who agree that machines are imperfect and people who think that a parent knows when a child is sick despite what the doctor or thermometer may say.

Conversely, identify and try to eliminate authoritarians.

§2:13   Bad SFST Performance

To put it bluntly, get physically unfit people for cases in which the defendant performed poorly on SFSTs. Overweight, the elderly, and those who have complained of back problems will not be able to perform the tests and will have sympathy with your client on that issue.

However, you do want to stay away from people with obvious afflictions as they may consider their choice as a juror as an obvious attempt by you to exploit their issues.

§2:14   Rising Alcohol Cases

For a rising alcohol case, I always like to get people who are either "feeling sick" or just getting over a cold. They have two aspects that you can exploit: first, if they say they might be getting sick, you can query them as to whether they were sick yesterday, or, if they are feeling better, does it mean they are sick today compared to yesterday? In other words, liken the coming and goings of a cold with the up and down of alcohol's influence or effects.

§2:15   Refusal Cases

There are basically two kinds of refusal cases: confusion and libertarian. Medical refusals due to mental issues, physical disabilities or the like are in the first category. For the confusion case, you are looking for a juror with whom emotion and sympathy are major personality features—for instance, someone who could envision that at the scene of an accident, the driver may be overwhelmed by all the activity. A juror with less education and not a lot of life experience would also be good.

Stay away from someone who seems cold and mechanical. He or she will figure that if asked, the driver should have understood. Military people or law enforcement-oriented people should also be avoided.

As for someone who refused because of a correct or incorrect belief that he or she had that right, find jurors who believe in individual liberty, someone who has trouble with authority, or who believes that the government is too big and too much in our lives.

§2:16   Drug Cases

Drug cases present an interesting dilemma due to the nature of the charges. Currently, and for the foreseeable future, there is no per se limit for any drug above which a person is deemed to be under the influence because the research does not support such a finding. A DUI drug case is based more on perceptions and opinions of the officers and jurors than on the concentration of a drug in the defendant's bloodstream.

The first issue in selecting jurors for DUI drug cases is to find people who will not automatically accept what the officer says. You need jurors who will draw their own conclusion based on their independent evaluation of the events. DUI drug cases are usually circumstantial in nature; that is to say that there will obviously be proof of drugs, but only circumstantial proof of impairment. It is important to educate the jurors to the harm in jumping to conclusions.

In DUI drug cases, you may also have to confront the illegal use of the drugs. If the defendant has a prescription for the drug, this is not a problem, and the warning label may be the best or worse evidence in the case. But in a case of illegal drug use, counsel must first—and delicately—elicit the jurors' true feelings about the conjoined issues of drug use and then driving a car. Again, the primary purpose of voir dire is developing actionable intelligence for challenges. Adults tend not to change their opinions much just because they are told they are wrong.

Q: Mr. [Juror's Name], as you have already heard, this case involves accusations that someone used illegal drugs and then drove a car. Just knowing that much, how do you feel about that?

A: [Venireperson answers]

Q: And that's understandable—nobody is going to come in here and say it's great to do that. Let me ask you this, though: Are *part* of your feelings driven by the fact that my client is accused of using *illegal* drugs?

A: [Almost certainly "yes"]

Q: And we know that in cases like this, sometimes it is difficult for jurors not to think of that, not to think of the illegal drugs, and to just focus on whether the driver was impaired or not at the time of driving. How do you feel about that? Do you think that might be difficult for you, even if it's just a little bit?

A: [Probably a "no" or a "maybe"]

Q: [If "no"] Great; that's great to hear. What is it that would make that so easy for you? [Follow up with, "Could you tell us a little more about that?" "What's an example in your life where you had to separate out issues and ignore something that might be a little hard to forget?"]

Q: [If "maybe"] Hey, that's fine; like I said, that's hard for a lot of people. And as the judge has said, not every case is the right case for every juror. Sounds like this one might not be the right case for you, right?

Follow up on the answer to truly understand this juror.

Q: You understand that it is the prosecution that decided to bring just the DUI charges and not the drug charges?

Q: You understand there may be a number of reasons for this and none of that is relevant here?

Q: How do you feel about that?

[§§2:17-2:29 Reserved]

B. Jurors Usually Best to Avoid

§2:30   Prospective Jurors With Strong Anti-Alcohol Positions

It is probably obvious, but you want to stay away from people with strong anti-alcohol positions. These can be personal, as in the case of someone who has had bad experience around alcohol, to religious. Almost all of these individuals should be excused for cause. It is important to question them effectively. Start out by establishing that they are strong people, not subject to being intimidated by anyone. Then convince them that, should someone try to get them to change their point of view, they would consider it harassment. Finally, have them agree that they are firm in their non-alcohol position.

Q: Ms. Juror, you told the court you do not believe in drinking and driving at all?

Q: Now this is your position, and if you were a politician you would follow it?

Q: It does not matter what your neighbor believes on this?

Q: To you, if someone drinks and drives, that is it? Case closed; vote guilty?

Q: No one should tell you to accept what you feel is wrong, correct?

Q: In other words, no one can convince you that drinking and driving is acceptable?

Q: And any attempt to do so would be harassing and intimidating?

Under most state law any attempt to harass or intimidate a juror is misconduct. If this line of questioning has been followed, any attempt by the judge to sway the juror or to rehabilitate him or her is harassment and therefore misconduct. It will also alienate the judge and that juror since you will be objecting on his or her behalf.

This line of establishing that the juror has an unassailable position can be used for any aspect. It will also be critical if and when any notes regarding a deadlock are received. Should such a note come out of the deliberations, you will have grounds to argue that the judge cannot engage in any attempt to "force" a verdict.

§2:31   Prospective Jurors With Prior DUI Charges

Another juror who is generally not good for a DUI case is an individual who has had a prior DUI. These people: (1) tend to believe everyone is guilty because they were, (2) might resent your client for going to trial if they pleaded to an offense, or (3) may have a hidden thought that since a first offense is not so bad, this must be more than that. *However*, keep them if your questioning reveals that they went to trial or wanted to go to trial or in other ways feel they were not treated fairly.

§2:32   Truckers and Other High Mileage Drivers

Recent experience has taught us that people who do a lot of driving for a living, truckers especially, are not good for a DUI jury. They see too much and make too many assumptions with regards to this offense. Also, increasingly and nearly universal, truckers for commercial carriers are subject to extensive federal regulations regarding number of hours driving per number of hours of sleep, as well as GPS tracking devices on their trucks that create an alarm at the dispatch house if the truck deviates more than a few tenths of a mile from the specified route. With this kind of regulation and surveillance, truckers are less forgiving of breaking the rules.

§2:33   Avoid Uniforms

One of my friends and fellow DUI attorneys, Aaron Bortel, had the pleasure of sitting as a juror in a DUI drug case. I will let him tell the story of the entire process, but will share a note from that experience. *Never allow a uniform on the jury*. By "uniform" I mean any person who has worked as any type of law enforcement, firefighter, ambulance driver, paramedic, and so forth. What Mr. Bortel learned was that even when these people were confronted with blatant inconsistencies from the witness officer, the other uniforms still stood by the witness. The jury, I am told, spent much time pointing out the incorrectness of this position to no avail. If a jury with a defense lawyer in it cannot change a firefighter's opinion, then how will a regular jury do so?

[§§2:34-2:39 Reserved]

III.   SAMPLE VOIR DIRE QUESTIONS

§2:40   How to Use These Questions

While many of us deal with time or scope limitations on our voir dire, and how to handle that is dealt with elsewhere in this chapter [see §§2:80-2:81], sometimes a judge will give you more leeway. If you have the opportunity for extensive voir dire, then the following list of questions can be used. If time is limited, then look at this list for ideas and concentrate on those areas that fit in with your theory of defense.

Understand that abundant and conclusive social science research has proven that any questioning by the judge results in the worst quality information from jurors (aside from the standard set of demographic questions, such as their town, occupation, household status, previous jury service, and the like). This is because laypeople consciously or unconsciously want to please the judge, whereas they don't seek to please the attorneys nearly as much. However, in some jurisdictions some of the substantive voir dire is handled by the judge. If your jurisdiction's rules of procedure provide you the grounds to fight that, then fight it vigorously. If, however, your jurisdiction's rules call for judges to conduct the voir dire, then you can submit your selections from this list which fit your particular case.

Provide only those that fit your particular case. Judges are often receptive to work savings and time efficiencies; this list provides both.

To make it even more likely that the list will be used, provide the prosecution a copy in advance of the trial and ask for their input. If both sides find it acceptable, the judge is more likely to use the questions.

For the prosecution's perspective on voir dire and sample prosecution voir dire questions, *see* Appendix A *The District Attorney's Manual*.

§2:41 Questions Regarding Relationship to Defendant, Witnesses, Law Enforcement

Q: Does anyone know Mr._____?

Q: Does anyone know any of the witnesses?

Q: Have you or anyone close to you ever been employed by, or have a spouse or close friend who has ever been employed by, any of the following agencies:

    a. The District Attorney's Office.
    b. The U.S. Attorney's Office.
    c. The court system.
    d. Probation or parole.
    e. Police.
    f. Sheriff.
    g. Constable.
    h. Department of Public Safety.
    i. FBI.
    j. U.S. Customs.
    k. DEA.
    l. Military police.
    m. The military.
    n. A law office.
    o. Fire Department arson squad.
    p. Citizens' crime groups.

Q: Have you or has anyone close to you ever worked or served as, or had a spouse or close friend who has ever worked or served as:

    a. A security guard.
    b. A grand juror.
    c. A juror (civil and/or criminal).

§2:42 Questions Related to Police Officers

Q: Who here has ever wanted to be a law enforcement officer?
    a. Why?
    b. What happened?

Q: Who here has ever worked with police officers? When?

Q: Who here has had an uncomfortable or unpleasant experience with a police officer?

Q: Who here believes that police officers are more trustworthy than the average person?

Q: Who here believes that police officers are more truthful than the average person?

Q: Who here believes that police officers are more cynical or suspicious than the average person?

Q: If later on a police officer testifies that Mr._____ is guilty, and someone else testifies that he is innocent, who here would be a little quicker to believe the police officer than the other witness?

Q: Can you think of any reasons a police officer would testify as to one version of facts—and not be lying—but just be wrong?

Q: Who here believes a police officer cannot make mistakes?

Q: OK, then, who here believes that police officers make fewer mistakes in their jobs than other people do in their jobs? [If anyone raises a hand or even shifts position] Ah, Ms. _____, thank you. Tell us about that, please.

Q: Who here would be more likely to accept a police officer's opinion rather than your opinion where the officer and you have seen and heard the identical same things?

Q: Who here believes that the number of arrests a police officer makes would affect his chances for advancement?

Q: It could be said that any witness has a motive not to tell the truth, whichever side he or she is on. Can you think of any motives an officer might have not to tell the truth?

Q: Has anyone here ever had courses in police science, criminology, or investigation, or received any specialized training in police forensics or investigation?

Q: Would you agree that even the best individual in his or her own profession occasionally might make a mistake? Do chefs, road workers, government officials, and even teachers make mistakes?

Q: Do you think that for whatever reason, be it training, the nature of the job, or something else, police officers automatically have a lower rate of making mistakes?

To follow up with jurors who indicate a belief that police officers have lower rates of error (*see* Corresponding Slide in §2.81), try the following:

Q: So Juror 6, you come to this case assuming police officers are automatically more accurate in the performance of their jobs than other professionals are in the performance of their jobs?

Q: Therefore, the officer's testimony is more believable than other people's testimony?

Often attorneys try to dance around the straightforward question. We do so because we don't want to offend, or are trying to be nice, or for a number of other reasons; however, why not just ask the blunt question? After all, the answer will probably save you a lot of time.

Q: Who believes that in a DUI case, the testimony of the officer is more truthful, less truthful or as truthful as that of other witnesses?

Q: Who believes that in a DUI case, the testimony of the officer is more truthful, less truthful or as truthful as in other cases, such as rape or murder?

§2:43   Questions Related to Punishment

Q: Please describe your thoughts on the following theories of punishment:
  a.   Rehabilitation.
  b.   Deterrence.
  c.   Retribution.

Q: If Mr._____ is convicted by you of the DUI offense, the range of punishment will be from 72 hours in jail up to two years in jail, and that would be in addition to a fine ranging from $100 to $2000. What are your thoughts as to making a decision that might cause a person to be placed in jail and fined?

Q: Does anyone here know what "probation" is? Please tell us.

COMMENT:

Refusal Case Only: Our laws also provide that you the jury, upon conviction of Mr.____, can recommend to the court that his driver's license not be suspended, but rather, that it be probated for a year.

Q: What are your thoughts as to the proper punishment in a first-offender DUI case where there was no accident and the person arrested did not know he was legally intoxicated?

Q: Would the fact that Mr.____ has filed a motion for probation indicate to you that he is somehow guilty of the offense charged?

§2:44   Questions Related to Scientific Evidence

Q: Who here is familiar with the type of breath test machine now used by law enforcement in this state? It is called an Intoxilyzer.

Q: What do you know about it?

Q: Who here believes that machines are error-free?

Q: Who here has heard of mechanical and computer errors that have occurred in the past in our NASA Space Shuttle Program?

Q: Who here believes the quality of a machine has some bearing on its performance, accuracy, and reliability?

Q: Who here believes that simply because a machine has a computer inside it, it is somehow more reliable?

Q: Who here has had any experiences with sophisticated machine or computer-type machine malfunctions? [Raise your own hand; hold it up until many hands are up.] Who here has never ever had a malfunction with a machine or computer? [Drop your hand; pause for everyone's to drop.] Nobody, eh?

Q: Who here has ever had trouble with your automobile? Would the problem seem to come and go?

Q: Who here would accept the machine's proof automatically?

Q: Who here would require Mr._____ to disprove the machine before having a doubt or possibly disbelieving the machine?

Q: Who here believes the Intoxilyzer is incapable of making a mistake?

Q: Who here believes a machine would not make a mistake because the operating principles of the machine are based on science?

Q: Would you tell me what you think "science" is?

Q: Who here knows what the "scientific method" is?

Q: If the state were to introduce machine evidence, who here might find it a little bit hard or a little bit confusing to hold that evidence to the high standard of "proof beyond a reasonable doubt" in order to find someone guilty?

Q: Who here has had training, instruction, or experience in computer science?

Q: Has anyone here had an education in physics or electrical engineering?

Q: The Intoxilyzer, so the manufacturer tells us, operates on a principal known as infrared spectroscopy. Who here is familiar with infrared spectroscopy?

§2:45   Questions Related to Expert Opinion

Q: Who here feels like maybe an employee could be afraid to testify in a way that his or her bosses or co-workers wouldn't like? [Pause for answers.] For instance, who here thinks an employee on the law enforcement side might feel a little pressure to testify in a way that's good for the government even if the science raises some doubts about the evidence against Mr._____?

Q: Who here would automatically believe the opinion of an outside specialist who comes in and testifies? Explain.

Q: Who here would, after seeing the same set of facts as the outside specialist, automatically accept the opinion of that person?

Q: Who here would believe a specialist brought in by the prosecution more easily than one brought in by the defense?

§2:46   Questions Related to Blood Analysis

Q: Who here has ever had a blood test? What for?

Q: Who here has ever been misdiagnosed by a doctor or medical-related person? Explain.

Q: Who here has personally received an incorrect or mistaken laboratory result?

Q: Who here knows of someone else who has received an incorrect or mistaken laboratory result?

Q: Who here would automatically accept an alcohol blood test result as true because it had been offered as evidence by the state?

Q: How about a blood test result being untrue because it has been offered by Mr._____?

Q: Who here would automatically accept an alcohol blood test as true because it was a high alcohol reading rather than a low one?

Q: How about a blood test as untrue because it had a low reading?

§2:47   Questions Regarding Constitutional Issues

Q: Who here has a greater fear of letting a guilty person go than of convicting an innocent person?

Q: Who here might feel like punishing a person who accidentally committed a crime, i.e., had no intent to commit a crime?

Q: Who here thinks the law generally protects criminals too much?

Q: Who here thinks the right to assistance of an attorney after arrest is important? Why?

Q: Who here thinks it is important to have the right to consult with your attorney in private?

Q: If [Defendant's name] does not get on the stand and testify in this trial, what feelings or thoughts would you have about that? [Be prepared to follow up very nicely with "Sounds like you feel that pretty strongly, right?" ("Right.") "And it sounds like I could probably lecture you for 30 minutes and not change your mind or your feelings on that, right?" ("Right.") "Thank you, Mr./Ms. _____. A lot of people feel that way; it's totally fine, and I thank you for talking with us about it." Then challenge for cause as this person has a bias against the rights of your client, and you have established on the record that it is a strong and abiding feeling that is unlikely to change. If asked correctly and followed gently, but leadingly with these questions, this is perhaps the single most powerful question a criminal defense attorney can use to reshape the jury pool to be more favorable to your side.]

[§2:48 Reserved]

§2:49   Questions Related to Physical Characteristics of Intoxicated Persons

Q: Who here smokes a tobacco product?

Q: Has the smoke ever bothered your eyes?

Q: Who here would say that, after a prolonged period of time exposed to smoke, all persons' eyes would turn red? Why?

Q: Who here has ever worn contact lenses, either in the past or currently?

Q: Who here knows someone who wears contact lenses?

Q: Who here would say that wearing contact lenses contributes to bloodshot eyes?

Q: Would you agree that lack of sleep would cause a person's eyes to appear bloodshot? Why?

Q: Would you also agree that some persons may have naturally bloodshot looking eyes? Why?

Q: Would you agree that alcohol consumption might make a person's eyes red?

Q: Would you agree that a person who has bloodshot eyes is not automatically intoxicated?

Q: The same would be true even if they had been drinking?

Q: Would you agree that bloodshot eyes can be brought on by a combination of things like: alcohol consumption, smoke, lack of sleep, eye sensitivity and eyestrain?

§2:50   Questions Regarding Memory

Q: Who here thinks that a person's memory could change over time?

Q: Who here thinks that a person's memory could be affected by nervousness?

Q: Who here thinks memory is perfect, that everyone remembers the same things in the same way?

§2:51   Questions Regarding Odor of Alcohol

Q: Who here has smelled rubbing alcohol?

Q: What did it smell like?

Q: Who here has smelled beer, wine, or whiskey?

Q: Were you able to smell the alcohol in the substance or was it the solution that the alcohol was in that you smelled?

§2:52   Questions Regarding Nervousness

Q: Who here thinks that different people get nervous about different things?

Q: And who here thinks that different people show their nervousness in different ways?

Q: Who here has been stopped by a police officer while driving?

Q: Were you nervous?

Q: Would you say that you might have been more nervous if the officer had acted a little differently toward you?

Q: If you had just consumed a 12-oz beer, and you were not intoxicated, but realized there was an odor of alcoholic beverage on your mouth and the police pulled you over, might you be nervous? Why?

Q: If you had just come from a party and you were not drinking, but someone had spilled beer on your clothes and the odor was noticeable, and you were stopped by the police, would you be nervous? Why?

Q: Would you agree that "nervousness" does not equate to "intoxication"?

§2:53 Questions Regarding Intoxication

Q: Who here thinks that everyone's coordination is a little different?

Q: Who here thinks that sometimes these differences in coordination could be because of unfamiliarity with the exercise or differences in learning?

§2:54 Questions Related to Bodily Functions

Q: Who here has any formal education in anatomy?

Q: Who here believes that human beings are all identical in their bodily functions and physical characteristics, such as: height, weight, sight, hearing, coordination, digestion, natural learning ability, tolerance to alcohol?

Q: Who here believes that "normal" for one person may not be "normal" for another?

Q: Who here believes that "normal" for a specific person at one time in his or her life is the identical "normal" for that person at another time?

Q: Who here has spent any time studying the human respiratory system such as: the heart, blood, arteries, veins, capillaries, blood groups, lungs and exchange of gases?

Q: Who here has spent any time studying the human digestive system?

Q: Who here remembers the old warning that a person is not supposed to swim until waiting one hour after eating? What do you think is the reasoning behind that warning?

Q: Who here has taken an aspirin or some kind of pain killer and noticed that it does not work immediately?

Q: Who here has ever noticed that it takes prescription drugs time to affect either a virus or a bacterium that makes you feel ill?

Q: Who here has ever noticed that medicines are prescribed in different doses for different people because two persons may not be alike?

Q: Who here has any knowledge about human body temperature?

§2:55 Questions Related to Offense of DUI

Q: Who here has been a suspect in a DUI or public intoxication criminal prosecution?

Q: Who here has ever been a suspect in a DUI or public intoxication criminal prosecution, or had someone close to you who was?

Q: Who here has been a witness in a DUI prosecution or a witness or defendant in a civil case that involved alcohol consumption, or had someone close to you who was?

Q: Who here has been involved in an automobile accident in which one of the drivers had been allegedly consuming alcohol, or had someone close to you who was?

Q: Who here has heard of Mothers Against Drunk Drivers or Students Against Drunk Drivers or other similar groups? [To each person who recognizes MADD/SADD/etc.] What have you heard from them? How do you feel about what you have heard from them? Have you ever contributed money to them or supported them in any other way?

Q: What are your feelings on all DUI publicity in the media, newspapers, radio, television, etc.?

Q: Who here has had any formal or on-the-job training in the areas of alcohol research, medicine, nursing, or chemistry, or has someone close to you who has?

§2:56 Questions Related to Alcohol

Q: Who here has a job related to the alcohol business?

Q: Who here has never consumed alcohol in the past?

Q: Who here does not consume alcohol anymore?

Q: Who here has religious feelings against alcohol?

Q: Who here does not keep alcohol in the home?

Q: Tell me about your alcohol drinking. Would you call it occasional, social, moderate, or heavy?

Q: What kind of alcohol do you drink? Beer, wine, liquor?

Q: Who here knows the percent of alcohol in beer?

Q: Who here knows the percent of alcohol in wine?

Q: Who here knows the percent of alcohol in whiskey?

Q: Who here knows how many beers it would take to bring your own blood, breath, or urine alcohol concentration to .10?

Q: Who here knows how much wine it would take to bring your blood, breath, or urine alcohol concentration to a .10?

Q: Who here knows how much whiskey it would take to bring your blood, breath, or urine concentration to a .10?

Q: I know this is a really delicate question for lots of people, so I am really sorry that I have to ask it. Who here has a drinking or drug problem?

Q: Who here has a relative or close friend with a drinking problem or drug problem?

Q: Who here has ever been in an alcohol or drug rehabilitation program?

Q: Who here has a relative or close friend who was in the past or is now in an alcohol or drug rehab program?

Q: Who here has had some alcohol and then operated a motor vehicle within: three hours, two hours, one hour?

Q: Who here has a definition of "drunk"?

Q: Who here has a definition of "intoxicated"?

Q: Who here has a definition of "normal intoxication"?

§2:57   Staircase Metaphor

The staircase metaphor can be used in closing argument to explain to the jury the different levels of proof and the meaning of reasonable doubt. *See* Chapter 7. To prepare the jury for the closing argument, proceed along the following lines during voir dire.

"Ladies and Gentlemen, one of the most singular aspects of American criminal trials is proof beyond a reasonable doubt. It is so important that only the judge can discuss it with you; and yet, we expect you to be able to follow and understand it without discussing it here. But we can talk about other legal concepts and get your opinion on those."

"Juror number one, how much evidence would you expect there to be to allow an officer to stop you?"

[Listen to the answer, involve other jurors and try to elevate it to the highest opinion given by the jury panel.]

"Well, under the law, what you all just described is 'reasonable suspicion.'"

[Use Figure 7-01 Levels of Proof in Chapter 7 to illustrate or draw the bottom step of the staircase as shown in the figure yourself.]

"Now, juror number 2, given that we all agreed an officer needed (repeat from above) to stop you, how much more evidence would you want for that officer to be able to arrest and strip search your wife?"

[Follow up as before with the jury and then explain and use Figure 7-01 or draw probable cause to illustrate.]

"Juror number 3, given what we have so far, how much evidence would you want to be given to a jury in order to take you money?"

[Same follow up showing preponderance, the civil standard.]

"Given all this, juror 4, what should be required of the government in order to say that your children should take over your day-to-day decisions and run your life and money because you are no longer capable of doing so?"

"Or, juror number 5, [pick a woman with children] for the government to say you cannot raise your kids?"

[Same follow up showing clear and convincing.]

"Well folks, NONE OF THESE have risen to the level of beyond a reasonable doubt. That burden is higher than all we have discussed."

You now have the staircase, drawn by the jury, to use in closing. Be sure to incorporate their definitions.

In order to develop the staircase of proof concept, and then to use it in closing, use the following slides in the voir dire process, then use the second set (the ones with titles) in closing to show each juror where he or she has already fallen below the beyond a reasonable doubt standard. See Digital Access for this presentation in Power Point format.

USING THE STAIRCASE OF PROOF IN *VOIR DIRE*

How to set up the high level of Proof
Beyond a Reasonable Doubt through
a five-minute jury selection

Figure 2-02 Staircase of Proof in Voire Dire

Question 1

- Would you agree to vote guilty if at the close of the prosecution's case you were reasonably sure that the defendant was guilty?

Figure 2-03 Staircase of Proof – Question 1

Question 2

- Would you agree to vote guilty if at the close of the prosecution's case you were convinced that the defendant probably did it?

Figure 2-04 Staircase of Proof – Question 2

Question 3

- Would you agree to vote guilty if at the close of the prosecution's case you were convinced it was more likely than not that the defendant was guilty?

Figure 2-05 Staircase of Proof – Question 3

Question 4

- Would you agree to vote guilty if at the close of the prosecution's case you had clear and convincing evidence that the defendant was guilty?

Figure 2-06 Staircase of Proof – Question 4

Question 5

- Would you agree to vote guilty if at the close of the prosecution's case you only had a slight doubt that the defendant was guilty?

Figure 2-07 Staircase of Proof – Question 5

REASONABLE SUSPICION

- Would you agree to vote guilty if at the close of the prosecution's case you were reasonably sure that the defendant was guilty?

- This is the amount of evidence required merely to stop a citizen.

Figure 2-08 Staircase of Proof – Reasonable Suspicion

PROBABLE CAUSE

- Would you agree to vote guilty if at the close of the prosecution's case you were convinced that the defendant probably did it?

- This is the amount of evidence required for a judge to issue a warrant for arrest or to enter your home.

Figure 2-09 Staircase of Proof – Probable Cause

PREPONDERANCE OF THE EVIDENCE

- Would you agree to vote guilty if at the close of the prosecution's case you were convinced it was more likely than not that the defendant was guilty?

- Commonly referred to as the tipping of the scales, this is the burden used to award money in a civil case.

Figure 2-10 Staircase of Proof – Preponderance of Evidence

CLEAR AND CONVINCING

- Would you agree to vote guilty if at the close of the prosecution's case you had clear and convincing evidence that the defendant was guilty?

- The government needs this much evidence to take away children from parents or to allow children to decide their parents' fate late in life.

Figure 2-11 Staircase of Proof – Clear and Convincing

REASONABLE DOUBT

- Would you agree to vote guilty if at the close of the prosecution's case you only had a slight doubt that the defendant was guilty?

- If there is any doubt in a criminal case, the verdict is not guilty.

Figure 2-12 Staircase of Proof – Reasonable Doubt

[§§2:58-2:69 Reserved]

IV.   JUROR QUESTIONNAIRES

§2:70   The Benefits of the Supplemental Juror Questionnaire

It is a well-established feature of human psychology that people want to give answers that fit in with group norms. This is called the social acceptability bias. Another feature of oral questioning is the desire to please the questioner—though, as discussed, the layperson's desire to please the questioner is strongest when the judge is doing the questioning, which is why judge-conducted voir dire is not very valuable beyond demographic information. The supplemental juror questionnaire (SJQ) is the perfect tool for getting high-quality information that will differentiate jurors into groups that are more likely or less likely to be open to your story and your case.

While rules of procedure increasingly permit the use of the SJQ, judges have been a little slower to adopt them and, even rarer, freely suggest their use. Nevertheless, one of the benefits to the court is that SJQs can move the process along, and allow for more detailed and truthful answers. Moreover, the group dynamic of repeating previous answers is eliminated, which again leads to information that differentiates jurors from each other.

In addition to the actual data one collects from the SJQ, the attorneys or their trial consultants gain additional insights into personality and mentality by seeing venirepersons' written answers. For example, someone who prints neat capital letters with even spacing and punctuation is fundamentally different from someone with disorderly cursive writing. Scribbled out words, underlined emphasis, and social conformity (revealed by a unique and self-developed style of forming letters versus the perfect replication of the cursive letters formerly taught in elementary schools) give further insights that oral answers do not.

§2:71   Procedure for Using

First, know your jurisdiction's rules for SJQs. In nearly all jurisdictions, it is the judge who grants permission for them. As a practical matter, judges have a wide variety of attitudes toward SJQs. Many judges claim they have had bad experiences with them which predispose them against SJQs. Many judges simply have a knee-jerk bias against them, as they often have a reflexive dislike of any new methods. So it could very well require a bit of diplomacy and politeness combined with a tenacious grasp of the rules of procedure in your jurisdiction to get one approved.

Many judges have a default position to be more inclined to agree to the questionnaire if both sides have already agreed on the final version of the SJQ. Certainly, it is wise and advantageous to have already agreed on the final version of the questionnaire with the other side as discussed in a moment. However, if the other side does not agree or will not participate with you, don't give up. Remember that it is the court that grants the use of the SJQ, not the other side, and you should never permit either the other side or the judge to read into the rule an element that is not there: that both sides must agree. It is not true.

It is best to signal the trial judge as early as possible that you would like a SJQ to be given to prospective jurors. The best practice is to have already traded drafts with the other side and agreed on the final version if possible. This co-operation is in the best interests of both sides.

PRACTICE TIP: *Getting the Other Side to Agree While Keeping What You Want*

The best trial consultants suggest sending the other side the draft SJQ with the message that "While we think this adequately addresses all the issues from both sides, we will gladly add *anything* you want; and in exchange, we want what is in here already and we are not prepared to delete anything." That is, of course, a starting position, and there might well be improvements and edits that can be made through this process. Yet the main point remains: we are not getting rid of anything here, but will add whatever you want in order to make you comfortable with whatever we want.

Like oral questioning in voir dire, there is no reason to be afraid of anything the other side wants. We want more information from the venirepersons, more data, and more input, and it is our belief that we will do a better job refining that information into actionable intelligence than the other side will.

PRACTICE TIP: *Getting the Judge to Approve the SJQ*

When presenting your SJQ to the court, explain that it will cut down on oral questioning time, and explain that it will only take 10 minutes for the group to answer, as opposed to 10 minutes per juror if asked individually. Often, judges will agree to anything that will save significant amounts of court time. You may even offer to the judge that you would be willing to cut your time down if it is used.

It occasionally happens that the judge will remove some questions or suggest some changes before approving the SJQ. Usually, these changes do not improve the value or validity of the questionnaire as judges are not social scientists any more than social scientists have the education and experience to be a trial judge. Nonetheless, these suggestions are best taken.

Once approved by the judge, local customs vary as to who will do the photocopying of the questionnaires; in some places, the court does it and adds the cost to the jury trial fees, while in other places one of the parties takes responsibility for getting the copies immediately after approval and splitting the costs with the other side. In either case, enough photocopies for the initial panel of jurors summoned by the jury commissioner are delivered to the jury assembly room and distributed to those who were called for your trial.

They complete the questionnaire and leave for the day. The completed SJQs must then be copied for both sides and the judge; the originals generally stay as part of the case record. In a typical case, the SJQs are given to prospective jurors in the morning; they are completed by the noon lunch break; someone copies them (either court staff or one of the parties handles that); and each party gets their stack of SJQs in the early to mid-afternoon. Then counsel (and the trial consultant, if counsel engages one) has the rest of the day and the evening to read through them, highlight significant responses, and draft follow-up questions for the next day's oral voir dire.

§2:72   Analyzing the Results: Why a Shorter SJQ Is Better

This analysis is the key part of the use of the SJQ. The fact that you might have to go through 90 questionnaires in the span of nine hours—while taking notes, drafting follow-up questions, and creating some sort of simple spreadsheet to manage the significant data—means six minutes per questionnaire, not counting breaks for meals or other eve-of-trial work. This, of course, is happening the night before live jury selection and very possibly opening statements, thus counsel also needs a good night's sleep.

All this is to sensitize you to a crucial fact about questionnaires: Shorter is better. One of the inevitable facts about collecting data is that one then has to do something with it. Every additional question is another thing multiplied by 90 (or however many initial prospective jurors the commissioner provides the court for your trial). Asking something that could add 30 seconds of analysis time is an additional 45 minutes for you on that evening. Sometimes that is a worthwhile trade, but usually it is not. In the opinion of many trial consultants, your questionnaire should not exceed five or six pages. Beyond that, the returns for your efforts diminish quickly.

§2:73   SJQ Format

The questionnaire itself should include a cover page with a welcome to jurors and a brief and basic explanation of the jury selection process, along with instructions on filling out this questionnaire (they are under oath, please answer each question, do not write on the back because we must make photocopies, and so on). Make sure to keep your language simple and short. Do not use legal terms, and strike the tone of warm and helpful. The result will be better quality data.

This cover page need not have a space for their names, as these cover pages will be ripped off the top of each questionnaire after photocopying so that counsel can carry 90 fewer pages into court the next day. The real questionnaire begins on page two.

§2:74   Juror Spreadsheet

Ideally, the court will have already provided you with the randomized list of jurors; that is, the list of jurors in the order they will be called. That way, you can arrange the questionnaires into the order in which jurors will be called, and your simple spreadsheet will be arranged in the right order, too. This is crucial for the value of using the SJQ, as it allows counsel to see where the "good" and "bad" jurors are dispersed through the pool.

The spreadsheet for each questionnaire need not be very complicated. We suggest a column for juror number, name, city, occupation, a column each for some of the key questions, then a column for a leadership potential, and lastly a column for your grade of how they are for you on the issues. (People who are not great for your side but have low leadership potential might be preferable to someone who is a natural leader but only marginally better on the issues.)

§2:75   Sample Jury Questionnaire

This is not the format to use for your questionnaire, but it should include:

1. Name _____
2. City or town _____
3. Current occupation (if retired, previous job) _____
4. Current employer (if retired, last employer) _____
5. Do you or did you have experience managing other workers in your job or volunteer organization?
6. Highest level of education _____
7. Have you ever served in the armed forces? _____
8. If you have children, please write their names and ages, education, and employment. _____
   _____
   _____

9. Do you or anyone close to you work for any federal, state, or local law enforcement agency, personnel, or other government officers such as district attorneys or judges? _____
10. Have you or anyone close to you ever worked for or applied for a job with any federal, state, or local law enforcement agency? _____
11. Have you or anyone close to you ever wanted to go into law enforcement? _____
12. Have you or anyone close to you ever been stopped, arrested, accused, or convicted of committing any crime, including alleged driving under the influence? _____
13. Have you or anyone close to you been a victim of any crime? _____
14. Do you or any member of your family do any type of civic, club, organizational or other volunteer work?
    _____

15. If yes, please list. _____
    _____

16. Do you or any member of your family or close friends belong to any organization such as neighborhood crime watch, crime stoppers, victims for victims, or similar group? _____
17. What are your feelings about such organizations? _____
    _____

18. Are you presently or have you ever been a member of Mothers Against Drunk Drivers (MADD)?
    _____

19. Please tell us your opinion about groups such as MADD? _____
_____

20. Are you presently or have you ever been a member of AA, NA or any other similar group?
_____

21. Please tell us your opinion about groups such as AA. _____
_____

22. Have you or anyone close to you ever had a bad experience with a drunk driver?
_____

23. What have you heard, read, or seen on television about the law in California regarding driving under the influence? _____
_____

24. Have you ever had one or two alcoholic drinks and then driven a vehicle? _____
25. How many times per month do you have one or more alcoholic drinks? _____
26. Do you or does anyone close to you own or work for a business that sells alcohol or alcoholic drinks?
_____

27. Do you think club owners, club employees, or store employees should be legally responsible for determining if a person has had too much to drink? _____
28. Some people feel that it should be legal to have one or two alcoholic drinks and then drive a car or truck. Others feel that if you have any alcoholic drinks and then drive a vehicle it should be against the law. What is your opinion? _____
_____

29. If the state proved that the accused had been convicted of driving under the influence on two prior occasions, would that fact influence your decision of whether the accused was driving while intoxicated on this occasion? _____
_____

30. Have you or anyone close to you ever served on a jury for a case involving driving while intoxicated?
_____

31. Have you or anyone close to you ever been a witness in a case of driving while intoxicated?
_____

32. If the defendant does not testify in this trial, what feelings or thoughts might that raise for you?
_____

33. Do you drink alcohol? _____
34. Do you belong to a church or any other group that is against drinking alcohol?
_____

35. How do you feel about people who drink alcohol? _____
_____

36. Some people believe certain races have a more difficult time handling their liquor than others. What do you think about that? _____
_____

37. Have you ever been the object of a racist or prejudicial comment? _____
38. Have you ever been hit by a car that left the scene of the accident? _____
39. Have you ever seen a person after an accident? Describe how the person acted. _____
_____

40. What does "mentally impaired" mean to you? _____
_____

41. What are some characteristics of mental impairment? _____
_____

42. What does "physically impaired" mean to you? _____
_____

43. What are some characteristics of physical impairment? _____
_____

44. Do you think a person can drink one or two drinks and still have the normal use of his mental and physical faculties? _____
45. Have you ever had one or two drinks and then driven home? _____

46. Did you have the normal use of your physical and mental faculties? _____

47. Have you or anyone close to you ever been injured by a drunk driver? _____

48. What are your thoughts about street people? _____
_____

49. Do you think alcohol is a drug? _____

50. Do you think alcohol should be illegal? _____

51. Some medical studies say that a little alcohol is good for you. Do you agree or disagree?
_____

52. What do you consider too much to drink? _____
_____

53. What do you consider too much to drink and drive? _____
_____

54. How many drinks do you think it'd take for the average person to be tipsy?
_____

55. Do you think some people have a greater tolerance for alcohol? _____
_____

56. Have you ever driven and realized later that you probably had too much to drink?
_____

57. Have you ever stopped someone from driving because they had too much to drink? _____

58. Have you ever been stopped from driving by someone else who felt that you had too much to drink?
_____

59. Have you ever been driving and seen another car on the road whose driver appeared drunk?
_____

60. How do you feel about law enforcement's strategy of setting up road blocks to find drunk drivers?
_____

61. What difficulties might you have serving as a juror in this case, whether it is something physical, emotional, mental, religious, or other obligations?
_____
_____
_____
_____
_____

Tell us anything else about yourself that you think we should know.
_____
_____
_____
_____
_____

§2:76   Looping

As this book is not dedicated to voir dire or any other single aspect of trial work, but assumes the reader either has or will have such knowledge, I am not going to go in to great detail about the concept of looping. Suffice to say, it is the best tool for getting through to jurors since it involves their fellow jurors and not the court or attorneys.

In its simplest explanation, looping is when a juror, say number one, gives an answer and then another juror, perhaps number 12, gives the opposite answer. The lawyer should then go back to number one and ask what he or she thinks about number 12's answer. Basic human nature will then have number 12 wanting to give further explanation. Your job, as this escalates, is too look for the reaction of other jurors and pull them in. Here is an example:

Attorney: Juror number one, some people say that only someone who is guilty would refuse to testify at their own trial. Other people say that we have a right not to testify and it should be used. What do you think?

Juror 1: I agree. If you didn't do it, why not take the stand and tell us?

Attorney: Juror 3, I see you didn't agree with that – tell us your thoughts.

Juror 3: Well, maybe he just doesn't speak well or is nervous.

Juror 1: But he can tell us that he's nervous. Maybe he is nervous because he did it.

Attorney: Juror 4, I see you shaking your head.

Juror 4: I am nervous and I'm just a juror. We can't judge someone based on nervousness.

You can see how this dialogue can develop. What is most interesting is that when jurors speak to each other, they will let their true feelings come out. Furthermore, the deeper held beliefs of jurors will cause them to become more defensive or aggressive for their position. This then allows for the strongest argument to a challenge for cause.

Come back to the juror you do not want. Ask the juror to reaffirm his or her belief, e.g. people who do not testify are hiding something. Restate it. Then ask the juror if the juror feels it would be right for you to insist he or she change that opinion. Since we are generally the bad guys, the tendency is to tell you to drop dead. In other words, the potential juror will dig in even deeper. Then ask if it would be appropriate for anyone to tell this juror to disregard his belief. Once again, you will get a negative response and more entrenchment.

At this point you will not only have a challenge for cause, you will have safely prevented the Judge or prose-cutor from rehabilitation. One last piece to cement this puzzle would be to ask the potential juror, "Even the judge can't get you to drop this deeply held position?" "And we all agree it would be wrong for her honor or anyone else to try to force you to change that belief." The Judge is now stuck.

An Additional Bonus to This Tactic

In closing argument, you can remind the jurors of this event (and the Judge), not trying to force the issue. Then remind the jurors that just as it would have been wrong for the judge to change the potential juror's mind, it is equally wrong for the deliberating jury to try to force one or any group of the jurors to change their minds. Furthermore, you can explain that if any juror is the subject of such arguments or if any see it happening, they can and should report it to the judge as it is a violation of the deliberation rules.

This is one method of trying for the hung jury. Remember, it is not usually the guilty vote that is the last holdout, but the not guilty who needs reinforcement. Furthermore, in most jurisdictions retrials are rare on a misdemeanor and even more so if the jury vote stood primarily for not guilty. In other words, if this strategy enabled one or two guilty votes to hang the trial, and the prosecution or the court sees that, then the odds for a retrial are small. On the other hand, if the holdout(s) were for not guilty and a retrial is sought, you will learn (1) what the not guilty votes liked and (2) what the guilty votes did not like so that you can change the defense strategy to match.

I have yet to hear a defense attorney say that a second trial is not better for the defendant.

§2:77   How Did the Defendant Get Here?

I was in the middle of jury selection when a prospective juror stated, "Well, there must be good evidence against the accused to get this far." That's when it hit me – most jurors have no idea of what is required or what happens before the accused is brought to trial. During my follow up with this juror and others, I learned that most people believe that trials occur only after some type (they cannot articulate it) of intense scrutiny by someone. As defense practitioners, we all know this to be incorrect. The question becomes: how do we disabuse the jurors of this foundational concept? If they maintain this belief everything they hear will be colored by this frame (See Chapter 9).

Here is a synopsis of what I developed in that case, set forth in narrative form, which can be adapted as you see fit.

Ladies and gentlemen, the judge has informed you that anything the attorneys say is not the law. She is correct. What stems from that is that anything we say that is *not correct*, she will immediately correct. This is so that we do not mislead you. Having said that, let me ask the group if anyone knows what it takes to go from a citizen to a defendant? No one knows?

All it takes is an accusation. For example, if I told the police that juror number 3 hit me during the break and swore out a report, then juror number 3 would be arrested and become the defendant. If the injury was not severe, it would be a misdemeanor. So long as I did not recant my story, and juror number 3 maintained it did not happen, juror number 3 would become a defendant at trial. That's all it takes: one accuser.

Now you will notice that the judge has not corrected me. That means what I just said *is true*. So that even though your common sense may want you to believe that there is more to it, and that if someone is labeled defendant they must have done something, the truth is that being a defendant simply means someone said something against you.

After this little interaction no less than three jurors argued that this cannot be the law and that surely a judge or someone investigates the case. The judge was reluctantly forced to admit that only the <u>prosecutor</u> does an investigation. This then led 2 more potentials to indicate the system was wrong since up until this point the cops and prosecution worked hand in hand. We then entered in to a long conversation of how the true <u>independent</u> investigation was about to be commenced by the <u>jury</u>.

[§§2:78-2:79 Reserved]

V.   SLIDES AND SCORECARD TO USE WHEN VOIR DIRE IS LIMITED

§2:80   How to Use

With the increase of limited voir dire, it has become incumbent upon counsel to be prepared to ask quick, simple questions in order to pick a jury. While I do not favor allowing this trend to continue or expand (see the arguments in the beginning of this chapter) I am familiar with reality. The following power point slides were developed based on ideas from Robert Hischorn to deal with this problem.

These are not inclusive and should be a good starting point for your own adaptation and use. Add more specific questions that relate to the issues in your particular case.

Simply put one up on a screen or poster board and ask each juror to give his or her numerical position. After every three or four jurors, re-read the question aloud to stop an avalanche of following the answer given by the preceding person. Either you—or even better, your client—can input the score for each juror. The higher the score, the better the juror.

This can be done so quickly that the prosecutor is not able to keep up. And the prosecutor will not necessarily know that jurors with the low scores are the ones that he or she wants.

The beauty of this system is, by creating a simple score card to record the number of the answer chosen by each juror, you can tell who you do and do not like. Be sure to draft all your questions the same way so that the higher numbered answers reveal jurors with attitudes that are favorable to the defense. Thus, the higher the total score, the more favorable the juror. It will not help you if good jurors get ones on some questions and sixes on others.

SPECIAL NOTE ON SLIDE ORDER

Although wording the slides so that the lower number is bad for the defense and the higher number is good makes scoring easy, certain concepts cannot always be worded that way. In addition, smart prosecutors who have read this book can also keep score. Therefore, you may want to consider rewording the slides to mix it up. One easy way to do this is to make all your even numbered slides low number defense friendly and odd number slides low number prosecution friendly. While this pattern may become obvious, it is a start.

§2:81   **Sample Slides**

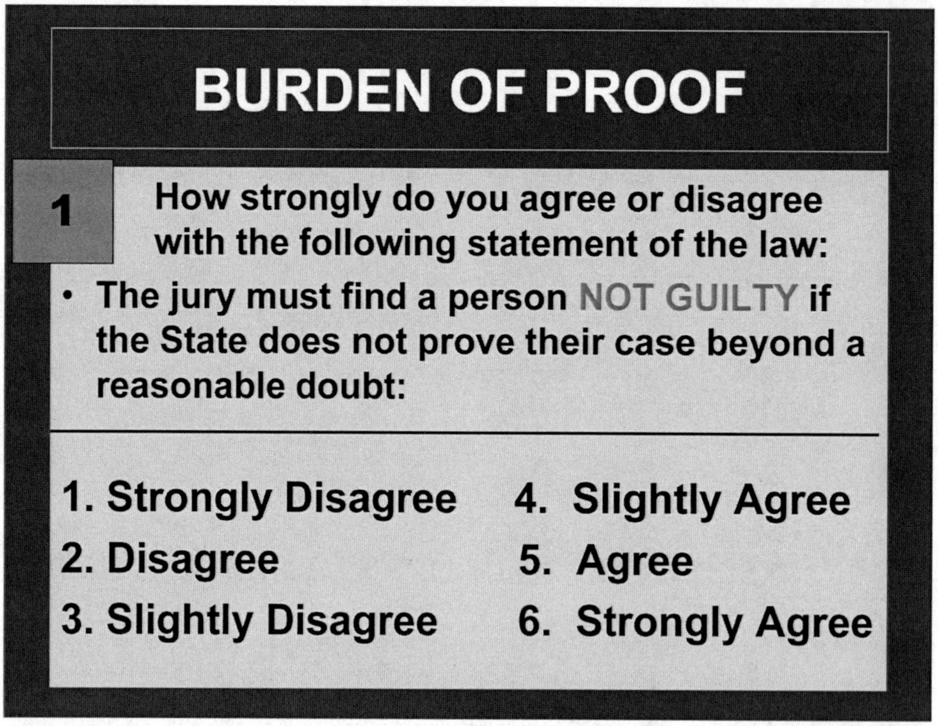

BURDEN OF PROOF

1 How strongly do you agree or disagree with the following statement of the law:

• The jury must find a person NOT GUILTY if the State does not prove their case beyond a reasonable doubt:

1. Strongly Disagree	4. Slightly Agree
2. Disagree	5. Agree
3. Slightly Disagree	6. Strongly Agree

Fig. 2-13 Burden of Proof

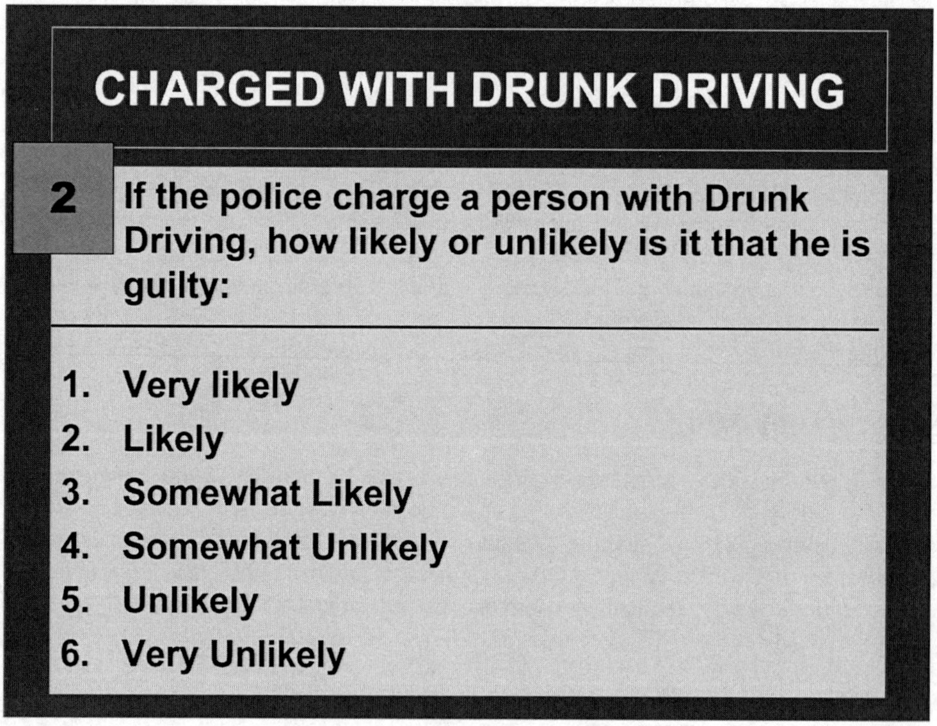

CHARGED WITH DRUNK DRIVING

2 If the police charge a person with Drunk Driving, how likely or unlikely is it that he is guilty:

1. Very likely
2. Likely
3. Somewhat Likely
4. Somewhat Unlikely
5. Unlikely
6. Very Unlikely

Fig. 2-14 Guilt Based on Being Charged

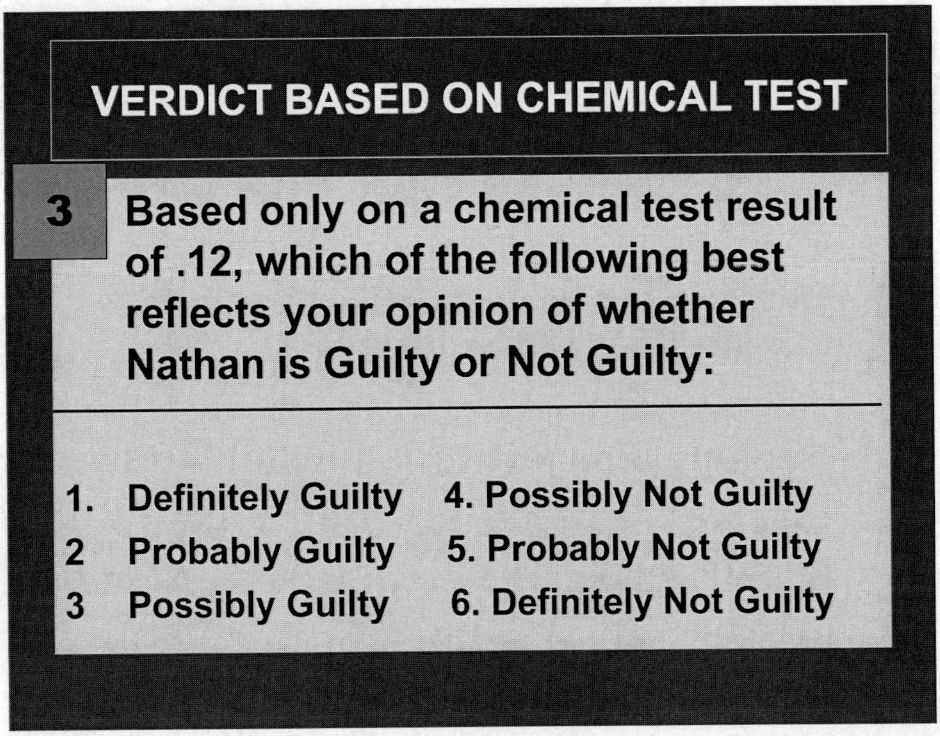

VERDICT BASED ON CHEMICAL TEST

3 Based only on a chemical test result of .12, which of the following best reflects your opinion of whether Nathan is Guilty or Not Guilty:

1. Definitely Guilty
2 Probably Guilty
3 Possibly Guilty

4. Possibly Not Guilty
5. Probably Not Guilty
6. Definitely Not Guilty

Fig. 2-15 Guilt Based on Chemical Tests

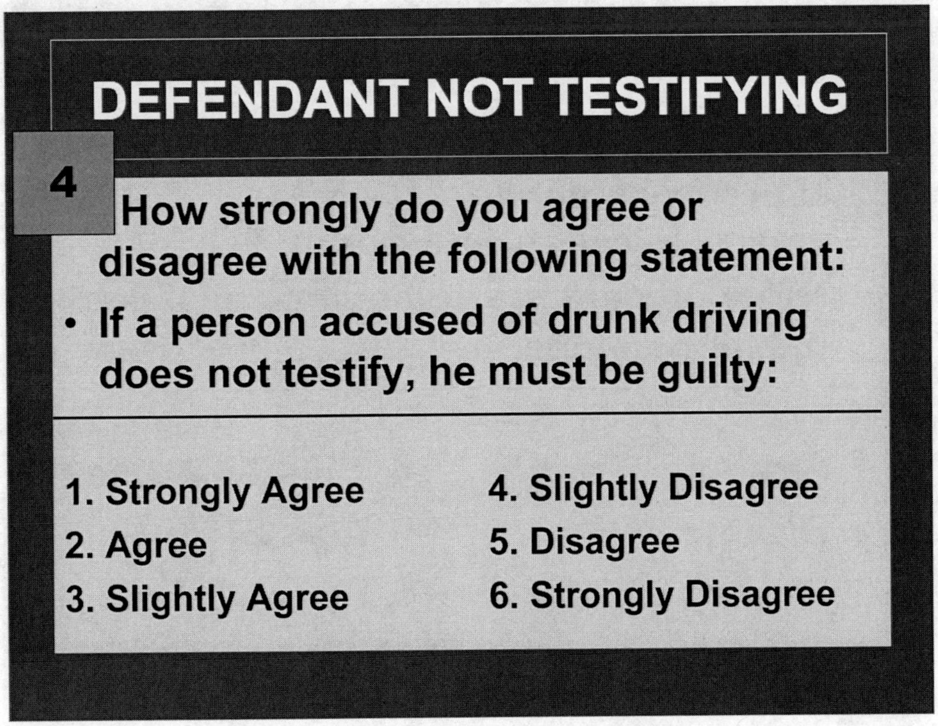

DEFENDANT NOT TESTIFYING

4 How strongly do you agree or disagree with the following statement:

• If a person accused of drunk driving does not testify, he must be guilty:

1. Strongly Agree
2. Agree
3. Slightly Agree

4. Slightly Disagree
5. Disagree
6. Strongly Disagree

Fig. 2-16 Guilt Based on Defendant's Not Testifying

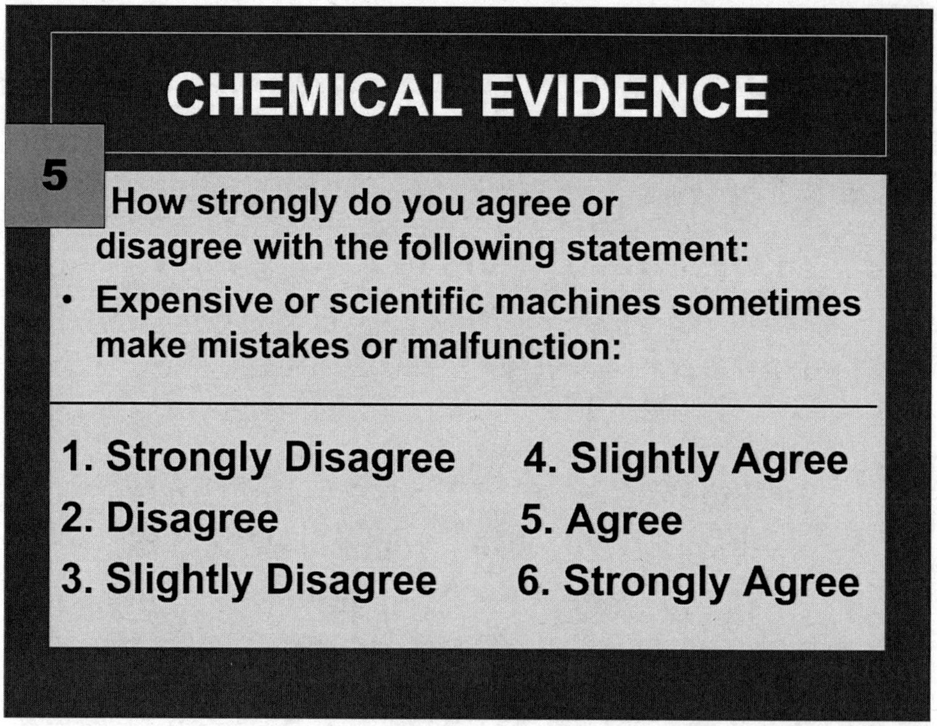

JURY SELECTION: JUROR ELIMINATION APPROACH

CHEMICAL EVIDENCE

5

How strongly do you agree or disagree with the following statement:

• **Expensive or scientific machines sometimes make mistakes or malfunction:**

1. **Strongly Disagree**   4. **Slightly Agree**
2. **Disagree**   5. **Agree**
3. **Slightly Disagree**   6. **Strongly Agree**

Fig. 2-17 Trustworthiness of Chemical Evidence

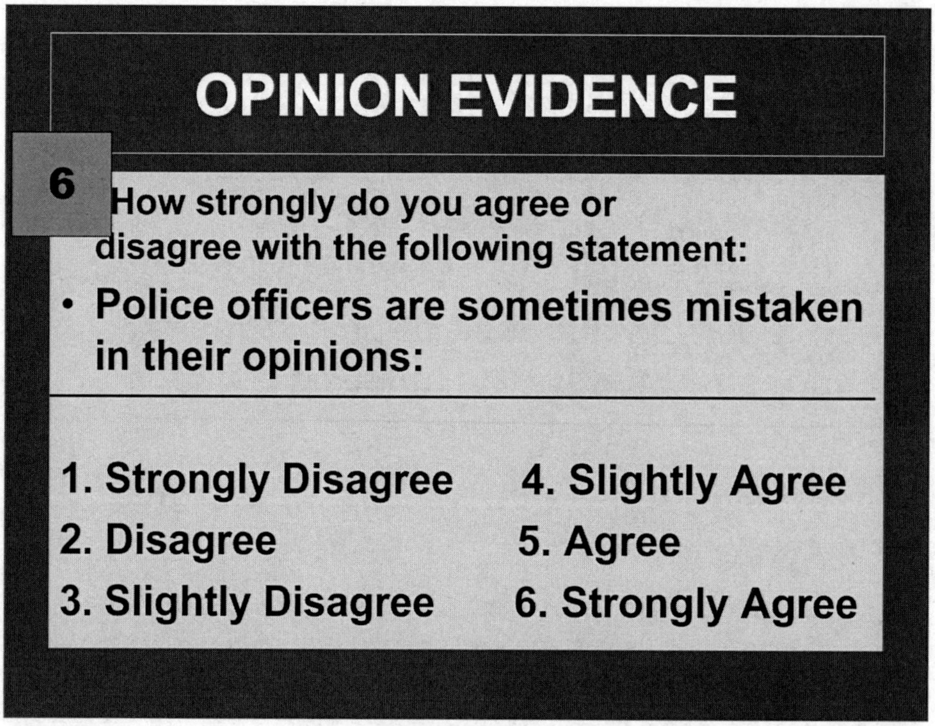

OPINION EVIDENCE

6

How strongly do you agree or disagree with the following statement:

• **Police officers are sometimes mistaken in their opinions:**

1. **Strongly Disagree**   4. **Slightly Agree**
2. **Disagree**   5. **Agree**
3. **Slightly Disagree**   6. **Strongly Agree**

Fig. 2-18 Trustworthiness of Officer's Opinion

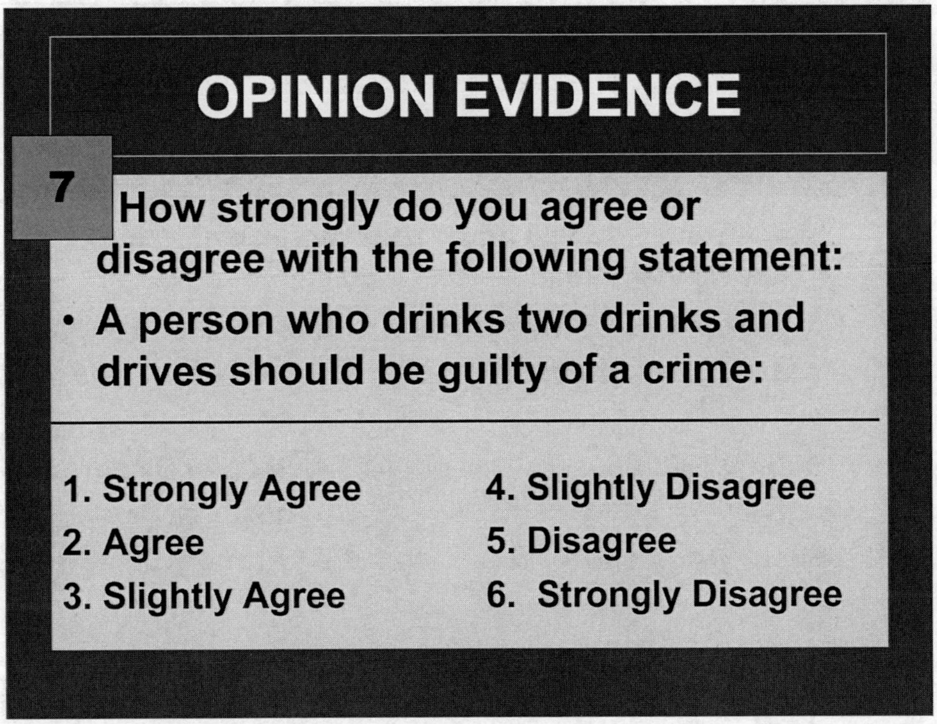

OPINION EVIDENCE

7 How strongly do you agree or disagree with the following statement:

- A person who drinks two drinks and drives should be guilty of a crime:

1. Strongly Agree
2. Agree
3. Slightly Agree

4. Slightly Disagree
5. Disagree
6. Strongly Disagree

Fig. 2-19 Guilt Based on Two Drinks

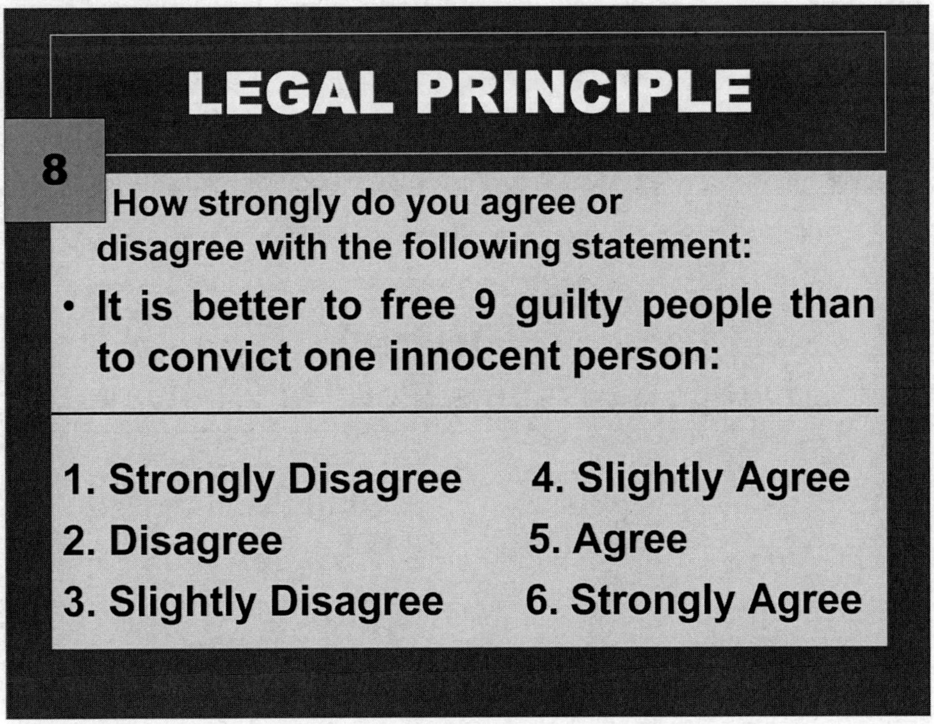

LEGAL PRINCIPLE

8 How strongly do you agree or disagree with the following statement:

- It is better to free 9 guilty people than to convict one innocent person:

1. Strongly Disagree
2. Disagree
3. Slightly Disagree

4. Slightly Agree
5. Agree
6. Strongly Agree

Fig. 2-20 Better to Free the Guilty Than Convict the Innocent

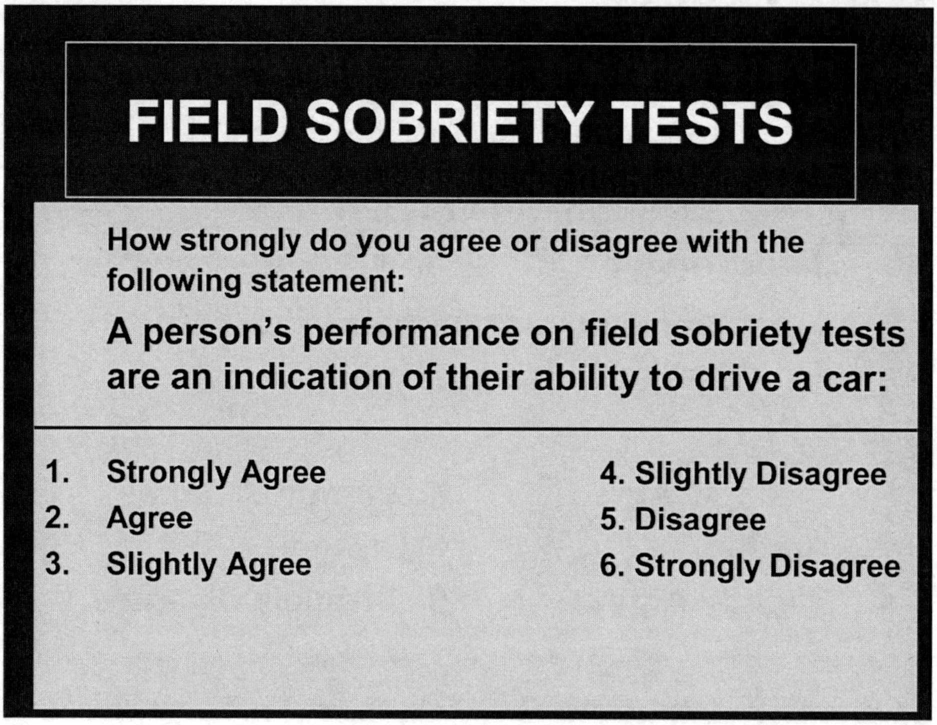

JURY SELECTION: JUROR
ELIMINATION APPROACH

FIELD SOBRIETY TESTS

How strongly do you agree or disagree with the following statement:

A person's performance on field sobriety tests are an indication of their ability to drive a car:

1. Strongly Agree
2. Agree
3. Slightly Agree

4. Slightly Disagree
5. Disagree
6. Strongly Disagree

Fig. 2-21 Field Sobriety Tests and Ability to Drive Car

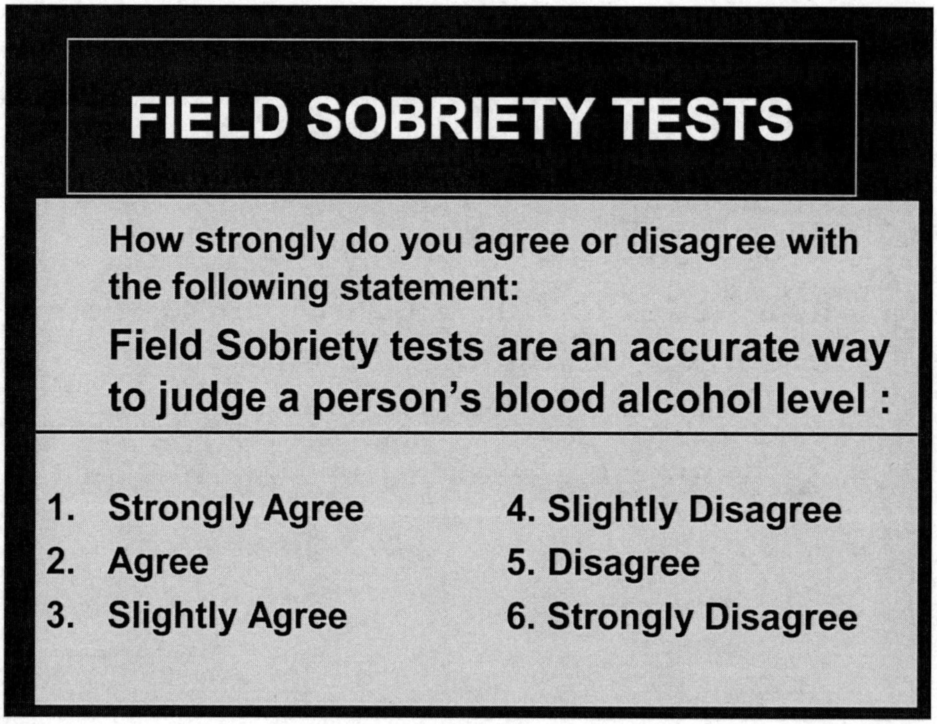

FIELD SOBRIETY TESTS

How strongly do you agree or disagree with the following statement:

Field Sobriety tests are an accurate way to judge a person's blood alcohol level :

1. Strongly Agree
2. Agree
3. Slightly Agree

4. Slightly Disagree
5. Disagree
6. Strongly Disagree

Fig. 2-22 Field Sobriety Tests and Ability to Judge Blood Alcohol Level

§2:82   More Sample Slides

Perhaps no aspect of the first edition of this book received more positive feedback than the voir dire slides. I have found that judges will actually approve many of them if shown early enough and will let most be adopted fairly simply to meet any concerns that may arise. With that in mind, here are some additional slides and usage notes to help guide you along.

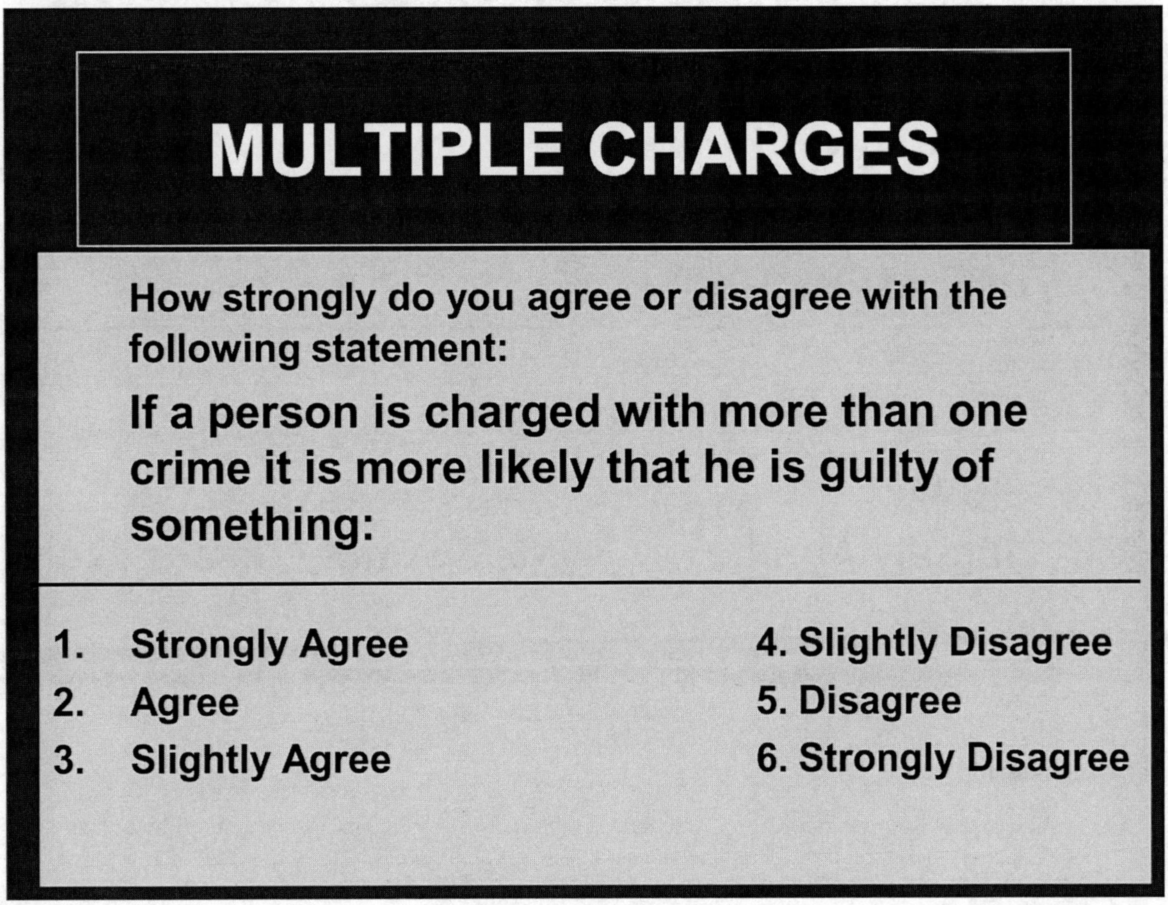

MULTIPLE CHARGES

How strongly do you agree or disagree with the following statement:

If a person is charged with more than one crime it is more likely that he is guilty of something:

1. Strongly Agree
2. Agree
3. Slightly Agree
4. Slightly Disagree
5. Disagree
6. Strongly Disagree

Fig. 2-23 Multiple Charges

Multiple Charges

There is a widespread phenomenon of negotiating a verdict among factions of jurors—some want to acquit on everything and some want to convict on everything, so they agree to convict on one charge and acquit on the other. One of the things that makes this psychologically palatable for the would-be "acquitters" is the nagging suspicion that the defendant might not be guilty beyond reasonable doubt on each charge, but if the two levels of guilt were somehow added together, they might add up to some sort of philosophical guilty verdict on one charge.

This slide is aimed at uncovering which potential jurors are already in the "where there's smoke, there's fire" camp. It may reveal which jurors are more skeptical or technical in their view of this process, properly seeing that each charge is individual and must stand or fall on its own proof.

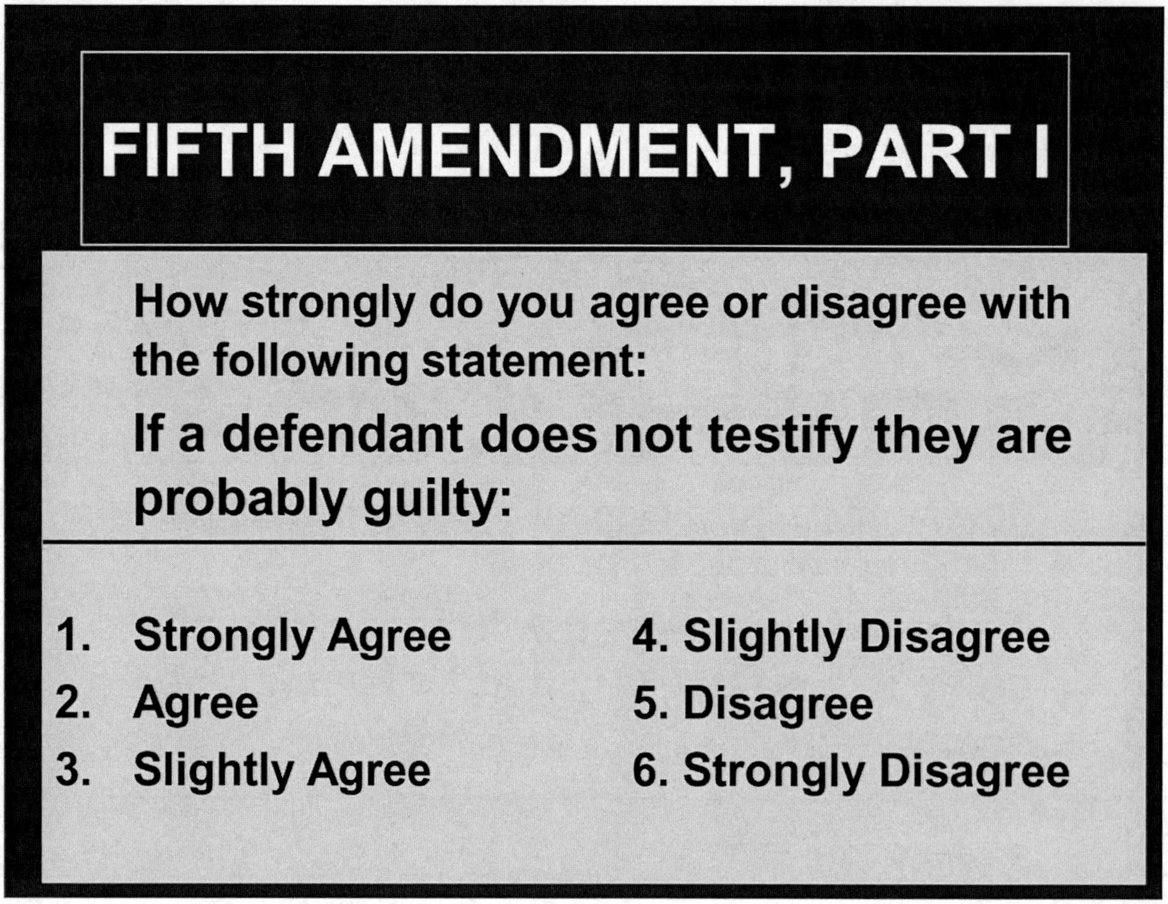

JURY SELECTION: JUROR ELIMINATION APPROACH

FIFTH AMENDMENT, PART I

How strongly do you agree or disagree with the following statement:

If a defendant does not testify they are probably guilty:

1. **Strongly Agree**
2. **Agree**
3. **Slightly Agree**

4. **Slightly Disagree**
5. **Disagree**
6. **Strongly Disagree**

Fig. 2-24 Fifth Amendment, Part I

Fifth Amendment, Part I

This slide is intended to surface the widely held notion that if a defendant has nothing to hide, then he or she "should" testify; therefore, if the defendant does not testify, the only reason for that is that there is something to hide. Note that this slide will be paired with the next one, "Fifth Amendment, Part II," and you will want to compare how each prospective juror scores on this one and the next one, and looking for conflicts and—perhaps more importantly—similarities.

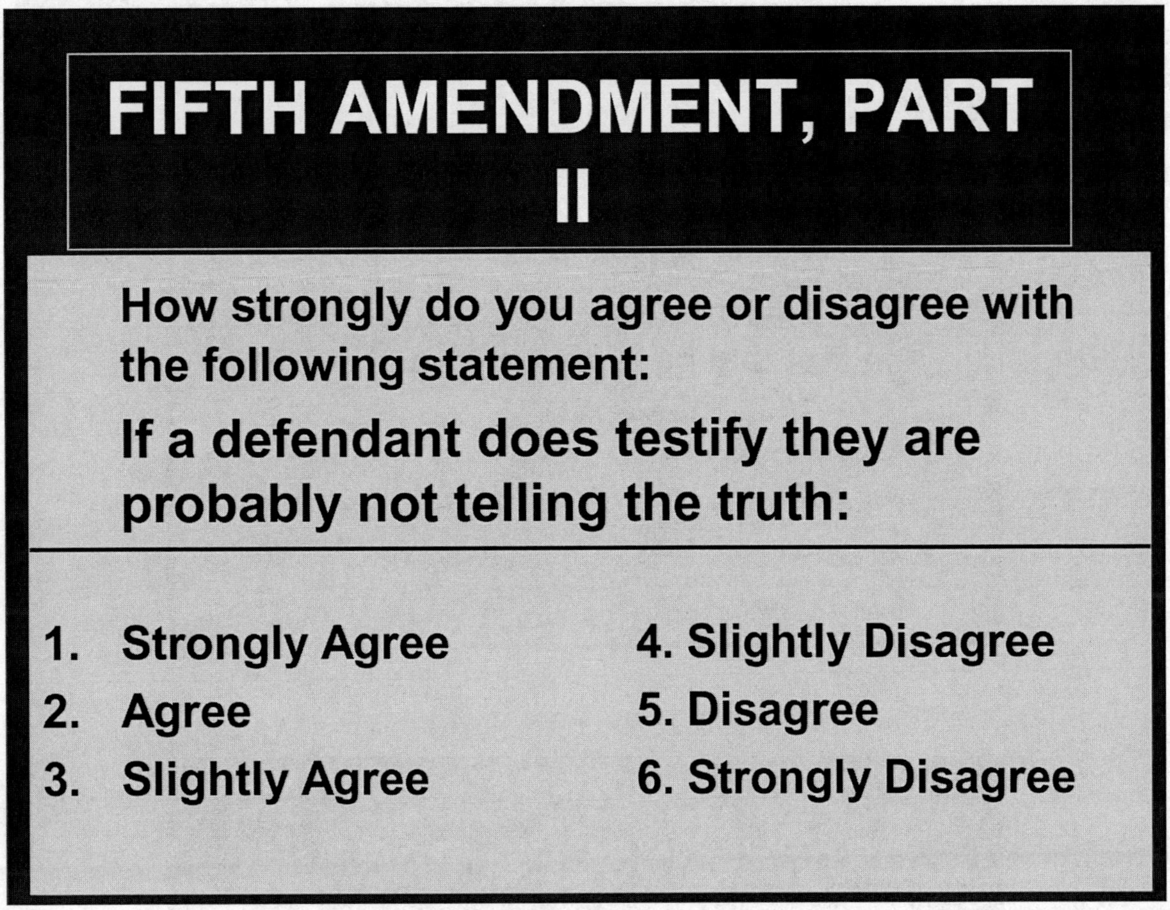

FIFTH AMENDMENT, PART II

How strongly do you agree or disagree with the following statement:

If a defendant does testify they are probably not telling the truth:

1. **Strongly Agree**
2. **Agree**
3. **Slightly Agree**

4. **Slightly Disagree**
5. **Disagree**
6. **Strongly Disagree**

Fig. 2-25 Fifth Amendment, Part II

Fifth Amendment, Part II

After scoring the responses to this, relate each score to the responses from the previous slide and see who rates high for "probably guilty if he doesn't testify" <u>and</u> "probably lying if he does testify." (Again, this is why having assistance at counsel's table to capture all the responses-probably two people to divide up the group-is absolutely critical.) Go back to these prospective jurors and ask with kindness and interest, "So, Number 17, it appears you have said that you feel pretty strongly that if someone doesn't testify, he's probably guilty, but <u>then</u> separately said that if he does testify, he's probably lying. So there's no way my client can win with you, is there?" Continue with an interested and kind exchange with this person.

Continue with anyone else who rated high for both "guilty if he doesn't testify" and "lying if he does."

Then identify prospective jurors who rated high for "guilty if he doesn't testify" and follow up with them, asking each person why he or she feels that way. Resist the typical lawyer's urge to jump in and educate them on their legal error after the first speaker. You want to get all such jurors on the record before you train them on the right answer to give.

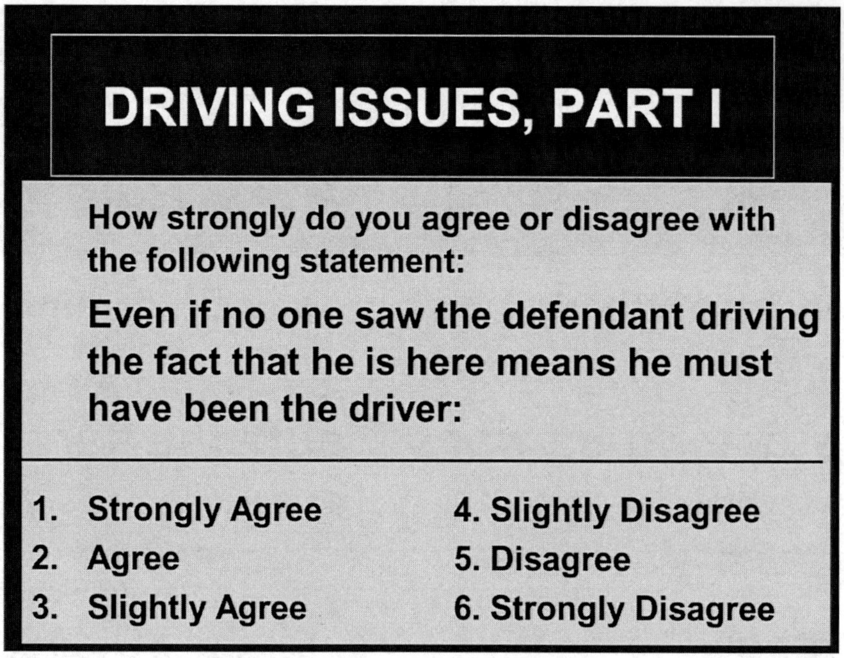

JURY SELECTION: JUROR
ELIMINATION APPROACH

DRIVING ISSUES, PART I

How strongly do you agree or disagree with the following statement:

Even if no one saw the defendant driving the fact that he is here means he must have been the driver:

1. Strongly Agree
2. Agree
3. Slightly Agree

4. Slightly Disagree
5. Disagree
6. Strongly Disagree

Fig. 2-26 Driving Issues, Part I

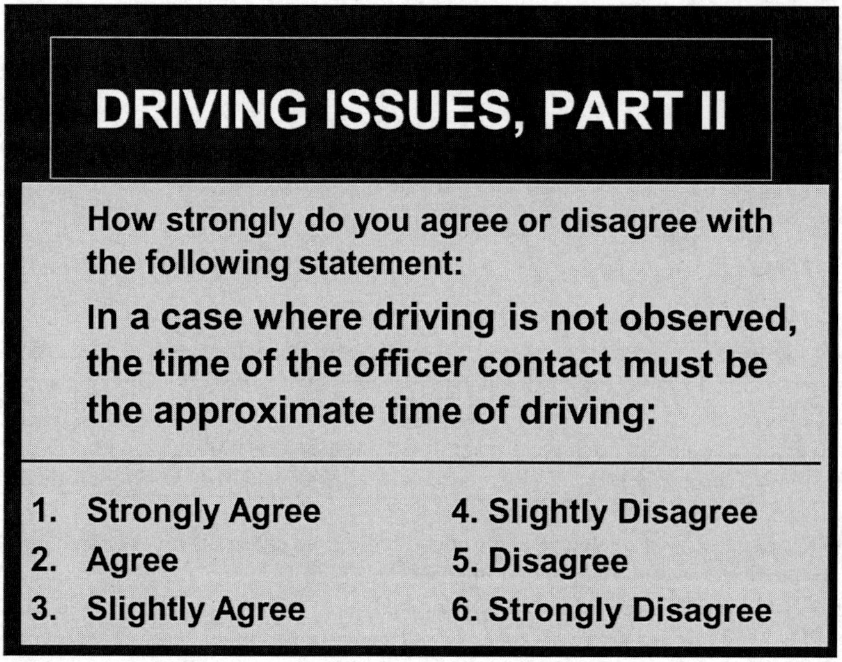

DRIVING ISSUES, PART II

How strongly do you agree or disagree with the following statement:

In a case where driving is not observed, the time of the officer contact must be the approximate time of driving:

1. Strongly Agree
2. Agree
3. Slightly Agree

4. Slightly Disagree
5. Disagree
6. Strongly Disagree

Fig. 2-27 Driving Issues, Part II

Driving Issues, Part I and Driving Issues, Part II

This pair of slides is aimed at uncovering two of the most vexing attitudes toward circumstantial evidence in cases in which the suspect was not driving the car at the moment he or she was first encountered by law enforcement. As with the pair of Fifth Amendment questions, look for venire members who score high on "defendant probably was the driver" and "probably driving close to the officer contact."

Needless to say, only use the first "Driving Issues" slide if the identity of the driver can reasonably be put at issue.

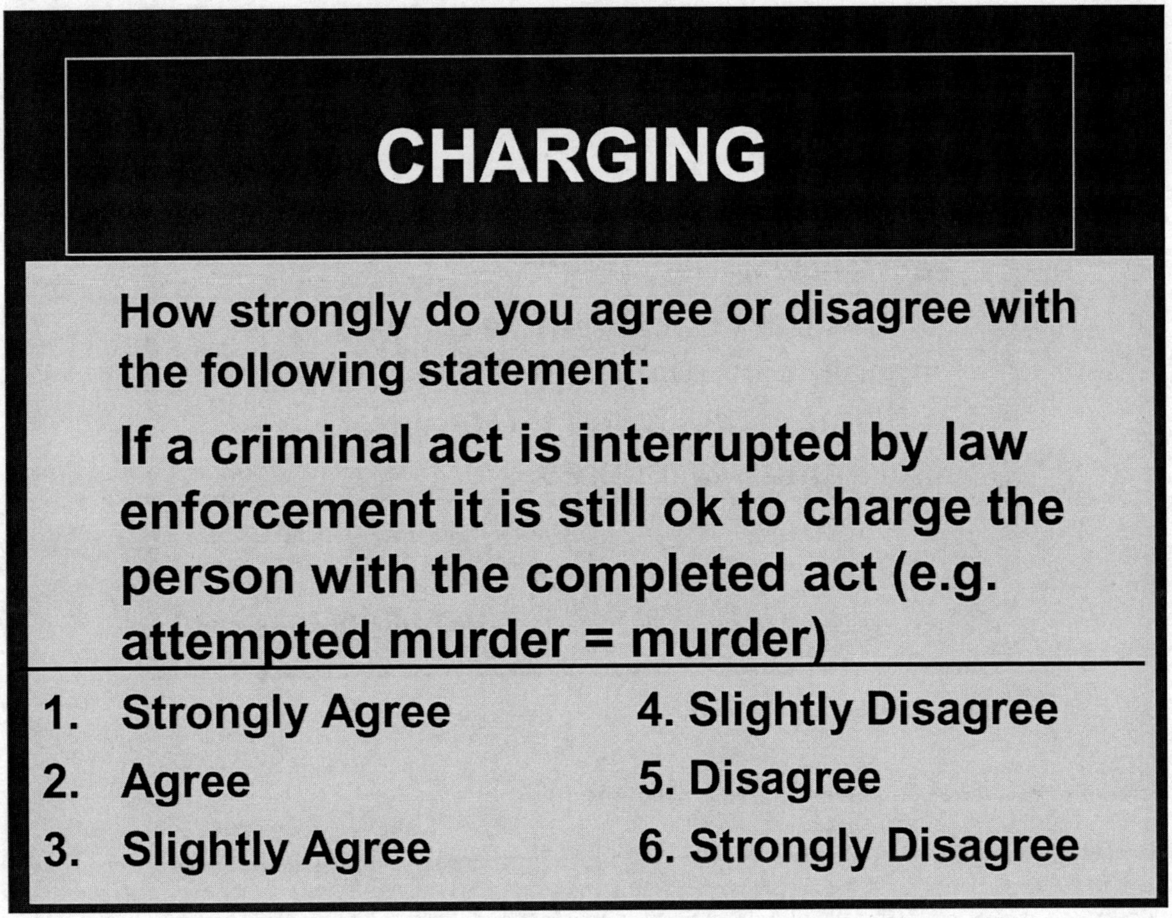

CHARGING

How strongly do you agree or disagree with the following statement:

If a criminal act is interrupted by law enforcement it is still ok to charge the person with the completed act (e.g. attempted murder = murder)

1. **Strongly Agree**
2. **Agree**
3. **Slightly Agree**

4. **Slightly Disagree**
5. **Disagree**
6. **Strongly Disagree**

Fig. 2-28 Charging

Charging

This question is the result of focus group research commissioned by a group of DUI defense attorneys that uncovered an interesting fact about jurors in so-called "rising cases." The research revealed that jurors are not persuaded by the argument that "the blood alcohol level was on the way up, but at the time of driving the defendant was under the legal limit and would have reached his or her destination still under the legal limit were it not for being detained by the police officer." To the contrary, they actually believe that a "rising" case is a crime in progress, and that the police officer was therefore stopping a crime in progress.

To surface this attitude, this slide asks whether a thwarted attempt at a crime should be charged the same as the completed crime—which is exactly what happens in a "rising" case. The answers to this will provide great jumping-off points for further drawing out of the prospective jurors.

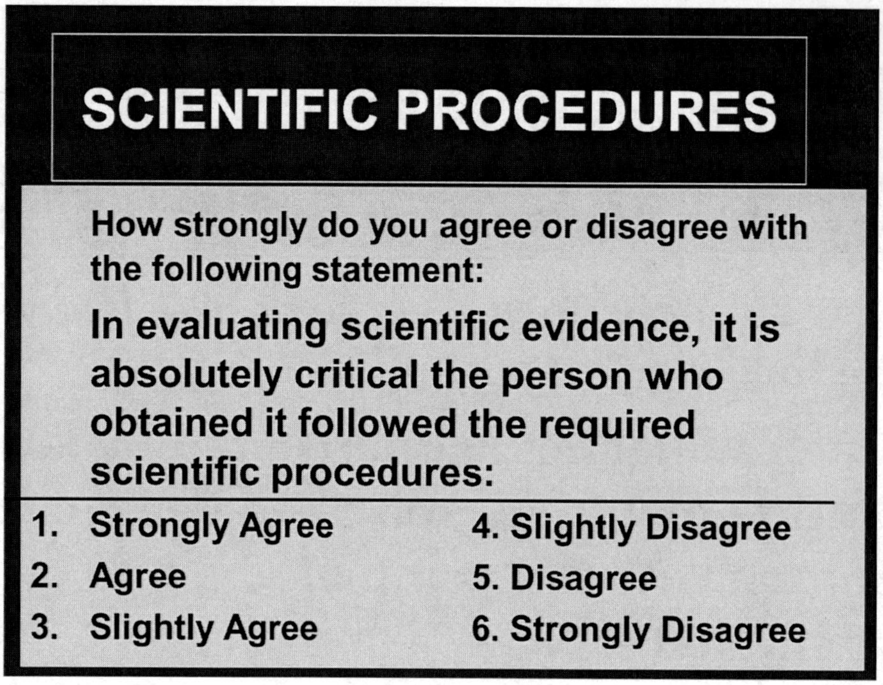

Fig. 2-29 Scientific Procedures

Scientific Procedures and Investigative Procedures

This pair of slides asks two separate but related questions aimed at drawing out prospective jurors on the "garbage in, garbage out" belief. Inquire further of people who rate low on believing that procedures must be strictly followed; they are not good for the defense, and if well developed, could be ripe for a cause challenge.

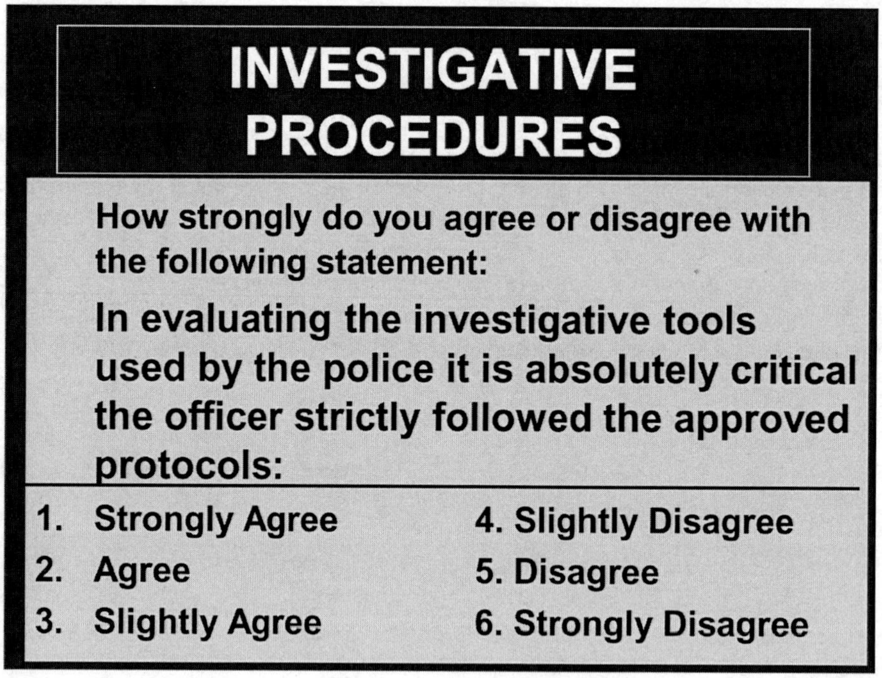

Fig. 2-30 Investigative Procedures

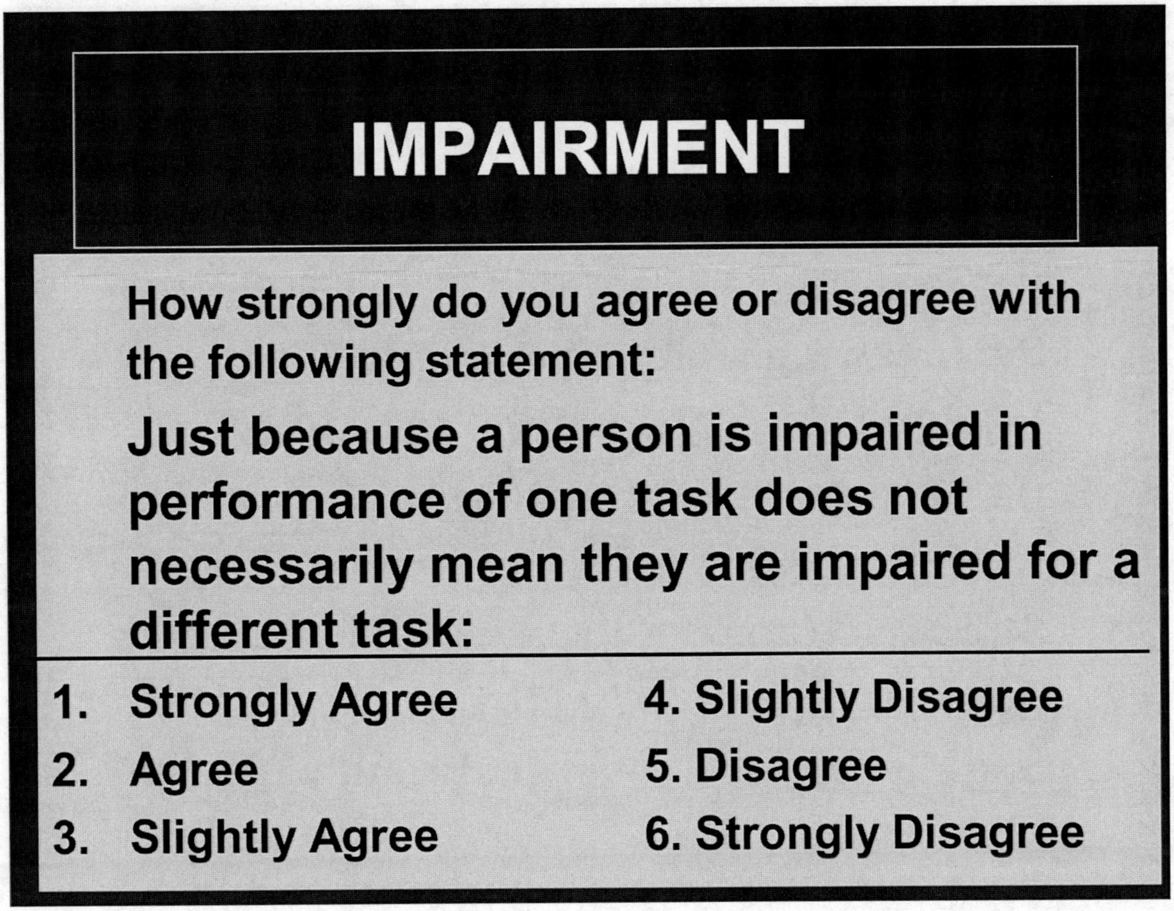

IMPAIRMENT

How strongly do you agree or disagree with the following statement:

Just because a person is impaired in performance of one task does not necessarily mean they are impaired for a different task:

1. Strongly Agree   4. Slightly Disagree

2. Agree   5. Disagree

3. Slightly Agree   6. Strongly Disagree

Fig. 2-31 Impairment

Impairment

In an appropriate case, this will help uncover attitudes for and against the idea that just because someone might slur a word or be unable to pass all the SFSTs, that person might still be perfectly able to do accounting, dig a fence post, or drive a car.

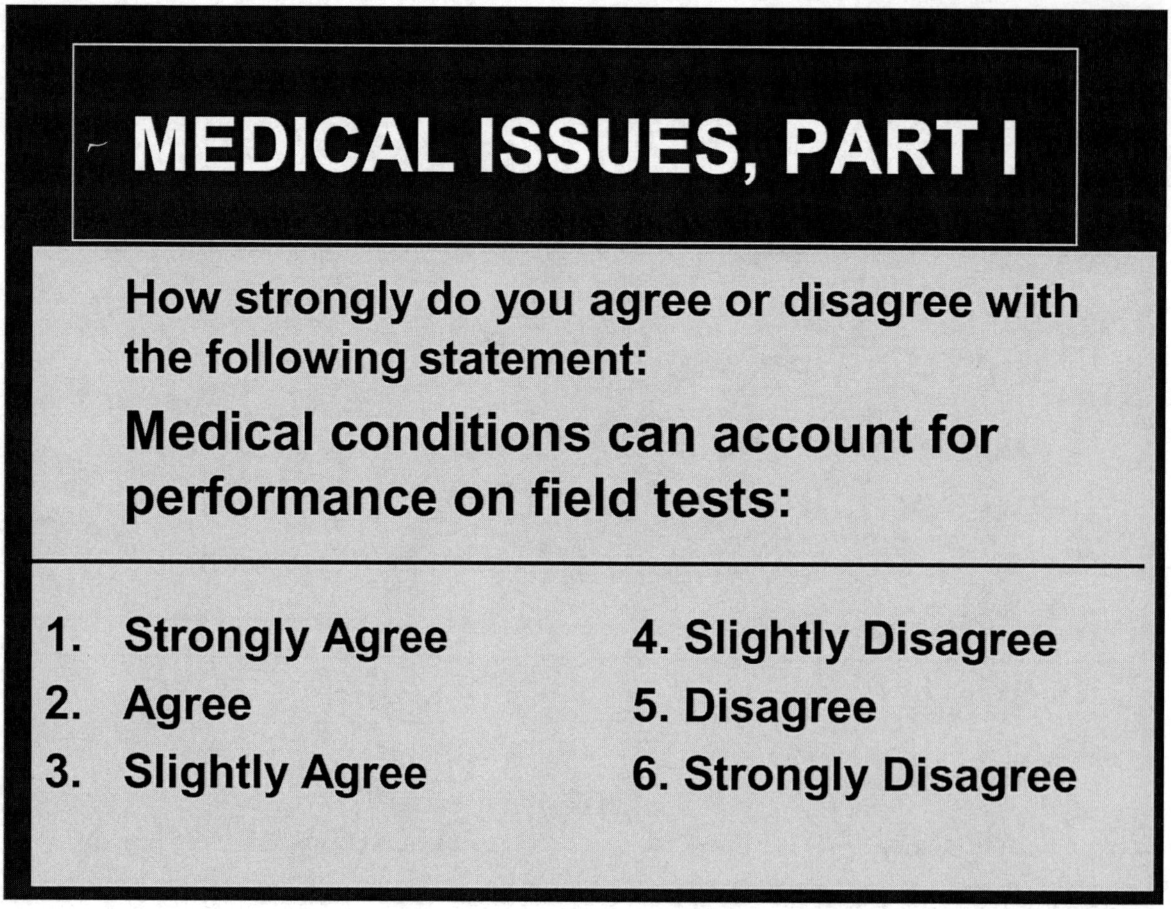

Fig. 2-32 Medical Issues, Part I

Medical Issues, Part I; Medical Issues, Part II; and Medical Issues, Part III

This trio of slides is to be used in a case in which a medical condition or a medication regimen is at play. The first slide is simply designed to find out the level of awareness in the panel and to uncover skepticism or openness to the idea that a medical condition might account for behavior that mimics impairment, or that might appear in a chemical test as consistent with impairment.

The second slide about "drug use" is deliberately broad and should be followed up with prospective jurors as to the very wide usage of prescription medications nowadays, including for depression, cholesterol, heart health, blood pressure, attention deficit, and so on.

MEDICAL ISSUES, PART II

How strongly do you agree or disagree with the following statement:

Medical conditions can account for chemical test reults:

1. Strongly Agree
2. Agree
3. Slightly Agree
4. Slightly Disagree
5. Disagree
6. Strongly Disagree

Fig. 2-33 Medical Issues, Part II

MEDICAL ISSUES

How strongly do you agree or disagree with the following statement:

Any drug use impairs driving:

1. Strongly Agree
2. Agree
3. Slightly Agree
4. Slightly Disagree
5. Disagree
6. Strongly Disagree

Fig. 2-34 Medical Issues, Part III

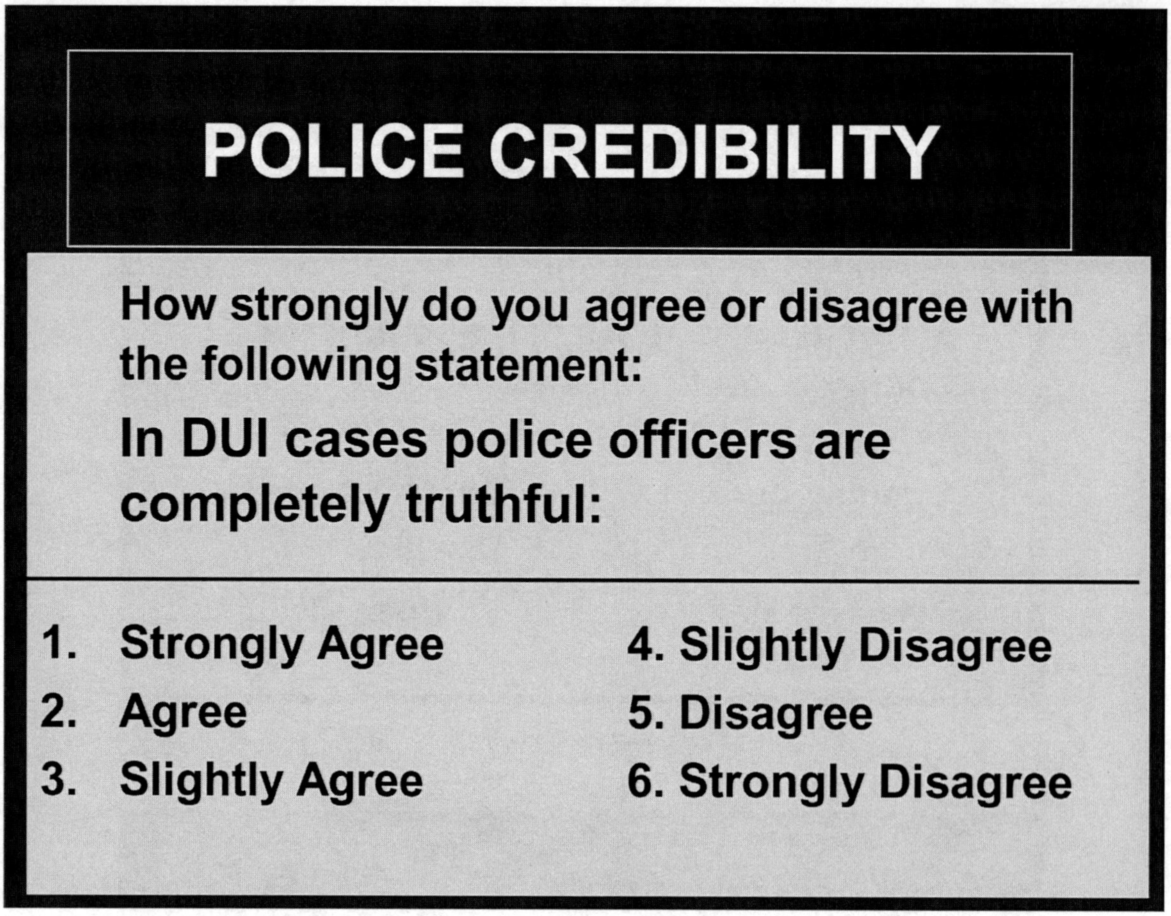

POLICE CREDIBILITY

How strongly do you agree or disagree with the following statement:

In DUI cases police officers are completely truthful:

1. **Strongly Agree**
2. **Agree**
3. **Slightly Agree**

4. **Slightly Disagree**
5. **Disagree**
6. **Strongly Disagree**

Fig. 2-35 Police Credibility

Police Credibility

This slide is to uncover the widespread attitude that police officers are more credible than others. This is absolutely essential to find out. Follow up with those who score high agreement that officers are completely truthful. Questions might include:

Q: Juror 14, I see you strongly agreed that officers are completely truthful. Do you think that of anyone doing any job? (Listen to answer.) Why is that? (Listen to answer.) I see. So what makes police officers different?

By the way, don't fear the phrase "completely truthful." It is not suggesting, endorsing, or confirming that officers are never incorrect. Rather, this wording is essential as a test question because it provides a firm extreme for respondents to push against—or not. And those people who score 1-2 on this one are definitely people you want to follow up with.

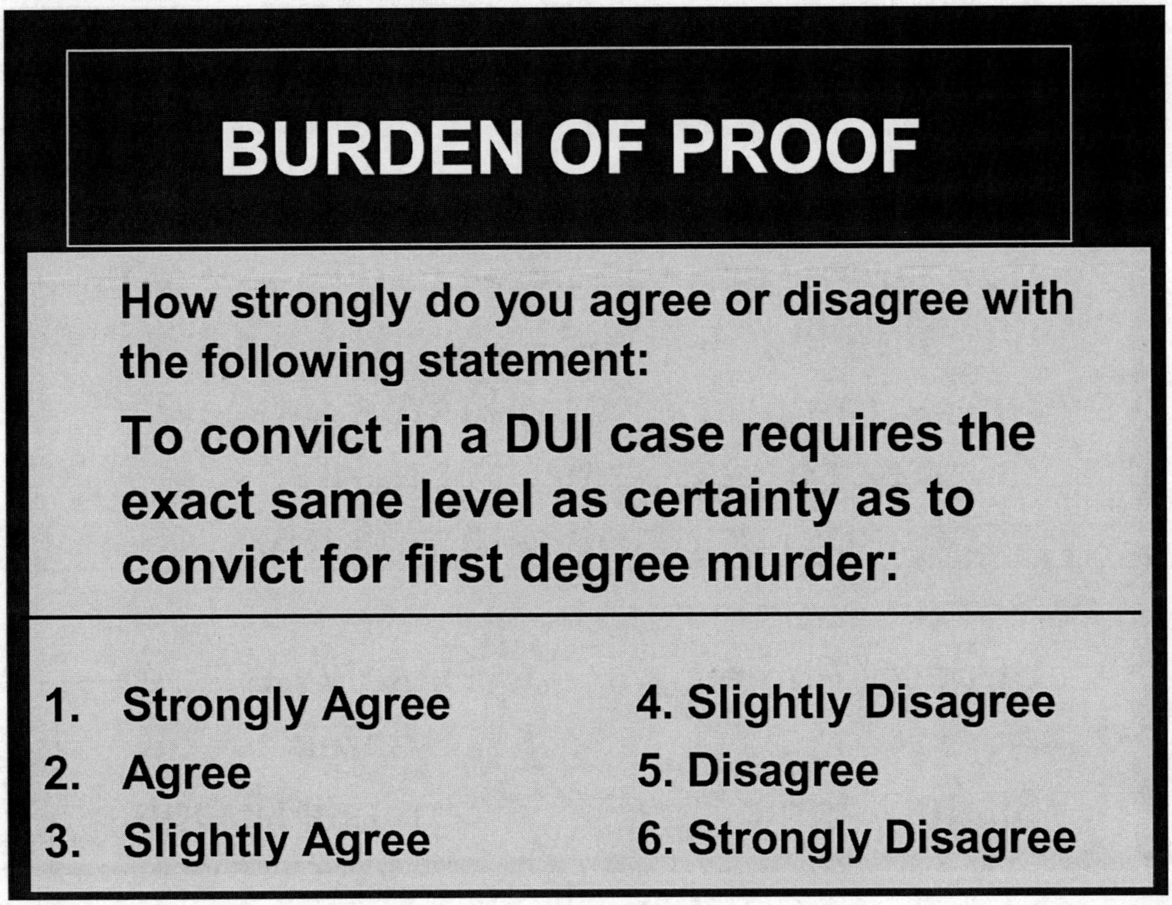

BURDEN OF PROOF

How strongly do you agree or disagree with the following statement:

To convict in a DUI case requires the exact same level as certainty as to convict for first degree murder:

1. **Strongly Agree**   4. **Slightly Disagree**
2. **Agree**   5. **Disagree**
3. **Slightly Agree**   6. **Strongly Disagree**

Fig. 2-36 Burden of Proof

Burden of Proof

Again, it is essential to understand who grasps and—more importantly—who fails to grasp this fundamental point of criminal justice. With prospective jurors who score 3 through 6, follow up and ask them why they think there is a difference. Get all the opinions out before you make the point that "beyond reasonable doubt" is the same no matter what the charge, that it is the highest level of certainty in the justice system, can be exercised only by groups of citizen jurors, and nobody before them in the whole chain of involvement in this case has had to meet that standard—then follow up again to see who has thoughts about that, who finds it odd or difficult, or even unfair.

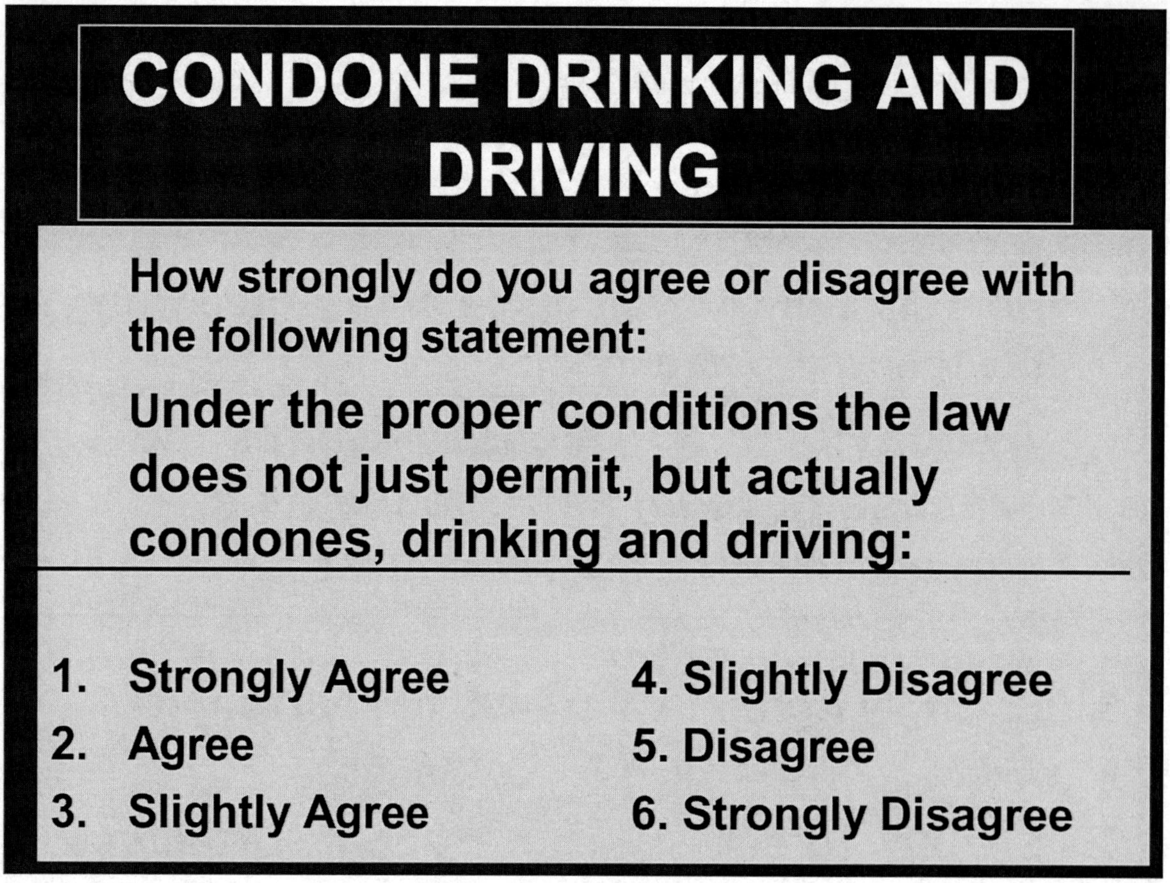

CONDONE DRINKING AND DRIVING

How strongly do you agree or disagree with the following statement:

Under the proper conditions the law does not just permit, but actually condones, drinking and driving:

1. **Strongly Agree**
2. **Agree**
3. **Slightly Agree**

4. **Slightly Disagree**
5. **Disagree**
6. **Strongly Disagree**

Fig. 2-37 Condone Drinking and Driving

Condone Drinking and Driving

This addresses a belief that is widely repeated as a mantra in our society but only superficially held: that nobody should "drink and drive." However, no state has a blood alcohol requirement of 0.0% in order to legally drive. It is absolutely true that in setting a BAC limit of 0.08% the law explicitly contemplates and condones drinking and driving. Not to excess, not to impairment, but to a degree higher than zero.

This question is aimed at uncovering how solid the view is that "nobody should drink and drive" in the face of the cold splash that the law would be 0.0% BAC if that were true, and that citizens do drink and drive quite regularly and safely.

§2:83   Slides Regarding Prior Convictions

While not all jurisdictions have allowed slides to be used in voir dire, many people have used the concept. Here are 4 more slides dealing with the concept of prior convictions. Obviously you would not use the ones that seem to indicate your client has a prior conviction unless the court is allowing such evidence to be put before the jury. On the other hand, I like the two slides dealing with no prior convictions as a way to sneak that thought into the jurors' minds.

The suggestion when there is no allegation or evidence of a prior would be to use this slide first:

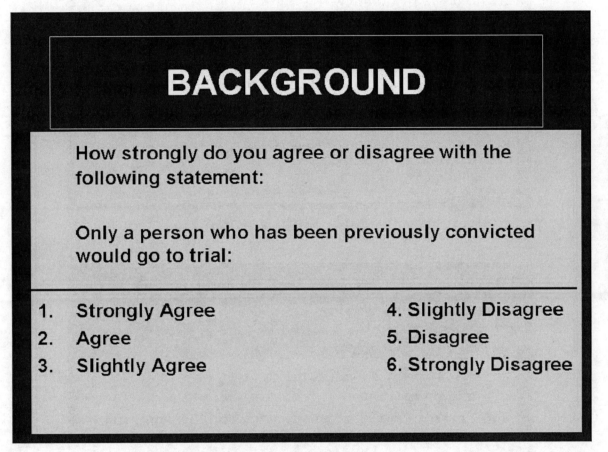

Fig. 2-38 Background

You can then follow up with one to three people, explaining how the statement is not necessarily true, that everyone has a right to go to trial and there may be a number of reasons why they would do so. This is an especially good place to 'loop' [see §2:76] with jurors who answered four to six.

Once you have made some points, or obtained answers that may lead to a challenge for cause, bring in the next slide.

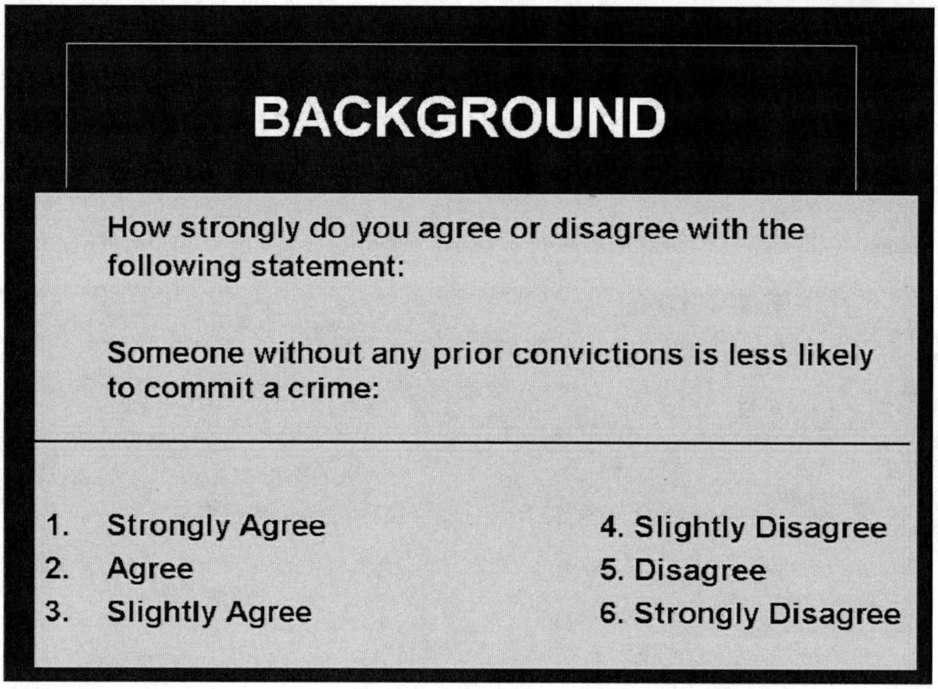

BACKGROUND

How strongly do you agree or disagree with the following statement:

Someone without any prior convictions is less likely to commit a crime:

1. Strongly Agree   4. Slightly Disagree
2. Agree   5. Disagree
3. Slightly Agree   6. Strongly Disagree

Fig. 2-39 Background

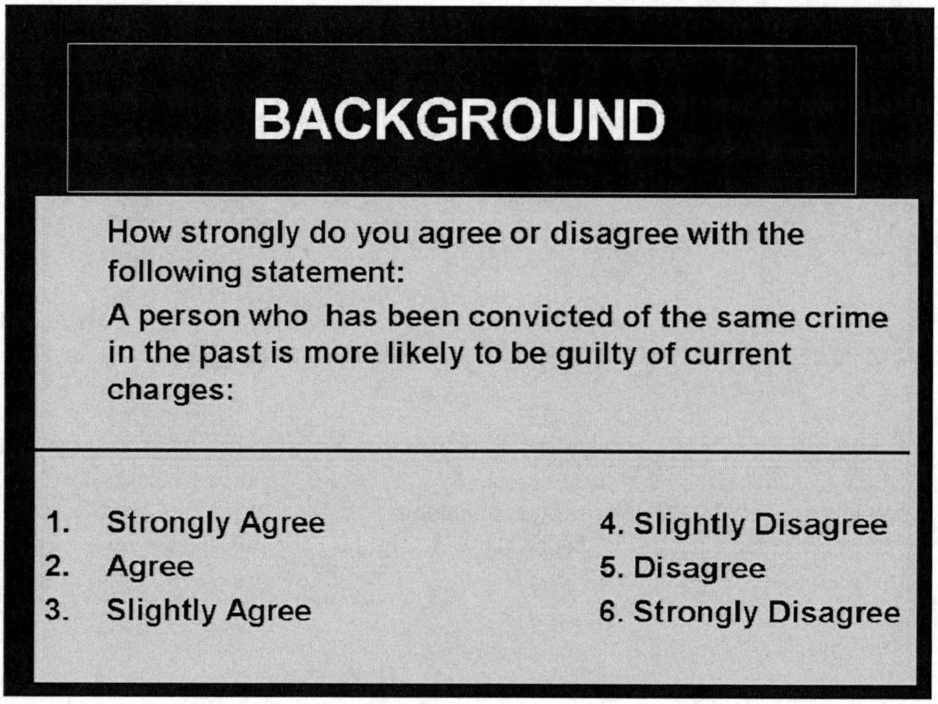

BACKGROUND

How strongly do you agree or disagree with the following statement:
A person who has been convicted of the same crime in the past is more likely to be guilty of current charges:

1. Strongly Agree   4. Slightly Disagree
2. Agree   5. Disagree
3. Slightly Agree   6. Strongly Disagree

Fig. 2-40 Background

This will naturally create the thought for the jurors that your client has not been here before. Personally, I do not believe for one second that such information does not sway a jury.

The other two slides, dealing with prior convictions, should be self-explanatory.

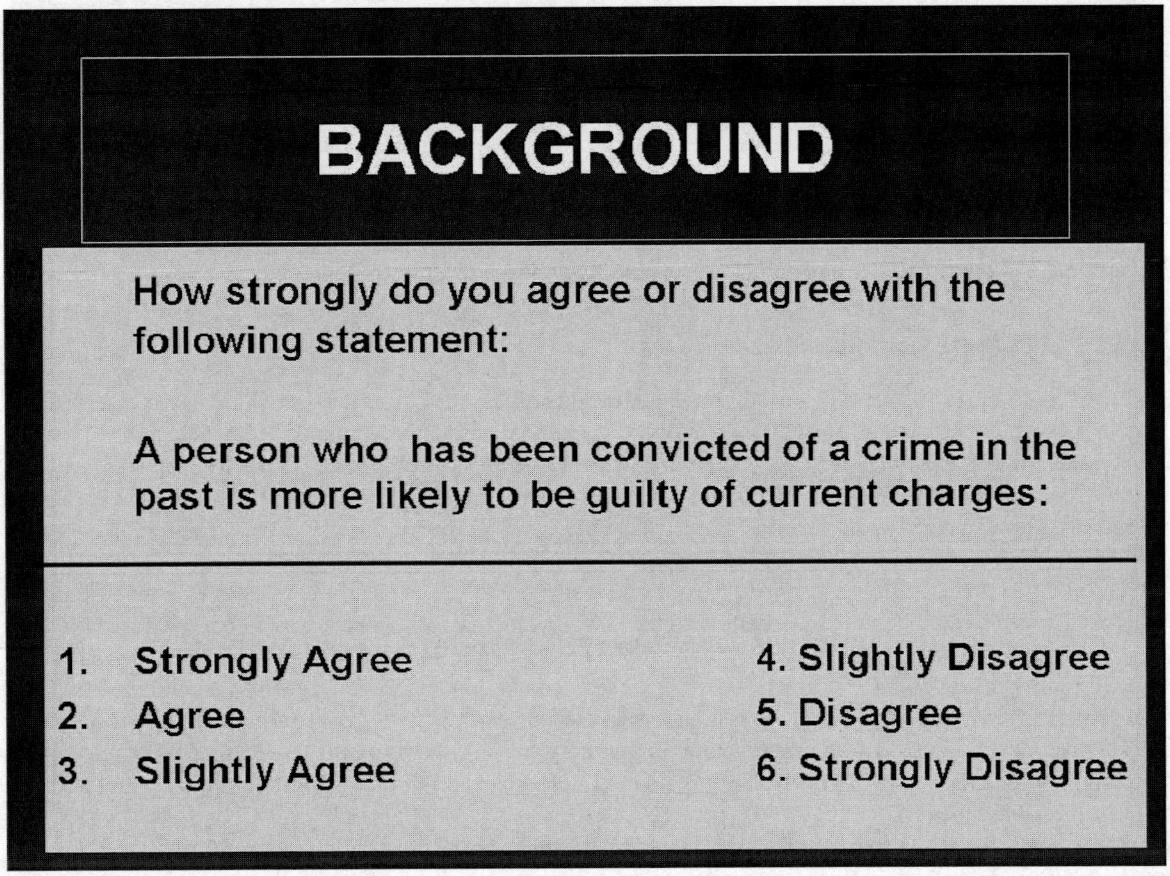

BACKGROUND

How strongly do you agree or disagree with the following statement:

A person who has been convicted of a crime in the past is more likely to be guilty of current charges:

1. Strongly Agree
2. Agree
3. Slightly Agree

4. Slightly Disagree
5. Disagree
6. Strongly Disagree

JURY SELECTION: JUROR
ELIMINATION APPROACH

Fig. 2-41 Background

[§§2:84-2:89 Reserved]

VI.   REFRAMING

§2:90   Background

For years, Cleve Johnson of Ohio has been pushing the concept of framing as the next great idea in criminal trials. He has based his work on the political writings of Karl Rove, George Lakoff, and others. (A summary of his work can be found in **Appendix E.**) Based on that work, I have developed certain themes which we need to reframe as part of our work. Although I have included them in this chapter on voir dire, these concepts can also be developed in opening or closing arguments depending on your own personal style.

§2:91   No More Common Sense

In every trial I have ever seen, the judge or the prosecutor argues that jurors need only use their common sense. This is a complete misstatement of the law. Proof in a criminal case is based on evidence: testimony, physical objects, and occasionally lay or expert opinions. This evidence must reach a level of proof beyond a reasonable doubt. Common sense, on the other hand, is a visceral interpretation of events. Here are some examples and an approach on how to develop the theme.

Rising sun. Common sense tells us, and for most of mankind's history we believed, that the sun revolved around the earth. Think about it. If you just went outside and watched the sun, it clearly goes from east to west around us. This also led to the belief that the Earth was the center of the universe. There was a doctrine based on these quasi-scientific observations, reinforced by the Catholic Church to the point that disagreement was seen as heresy.

It is only because of our scientific nature that we learned that in fact the earth revolves around the sun.

Flat Earth. Go outside, look around; it will seem that the earth is flat. That is what common sense tells us because we cannot of our own see the curvature. But we now know this to be untrue. We learned this by disregarding common sense and using logic. Specifically one example is the appearance of the top of the mast of a sailing ship before seeing the rest.

New Scientific Discoveries. When you are told by the judge or the prosecution to simply "use your common sense," they are in fact saying that you do not need scientific proof; you can just go with appearance. The fact that it is the government saying this to you may be akin to the Church's position regarding Galileo and his findings. But your job is not to follow such dictates; it is to be persuaded by science and facts.

And yet even science can change or get it wrong. Most if not all of us grew up in a solar system that had nine planets, the last being Pluto. We now know there are only 8. Did Pluto leave? No, it was simply demoted.

More recently, NASA scientist Felisa Wolfe-Simon discovered a new form of life unlike any other life form on earth—bacteria whose DNA uses arsenic instead of phosphorus. Wherein it was an axiom often repeated, always taught and rarely questioned up to today that:

All life on Earth is made of six components: Carbon, hydrogen, nitrogen, oxygen, phosphorus and sulfur.
Every being, from the smallest amoeba to the largest whale, shares the same life stream.
Our DNA blocks are all the same that is the condition called "life."
This axiom is no longer true. So science can be wrong.

Where does this leave us? Well, common sense tells us that if a person is on trial they must have done something. So if all we used was common sense, the verdict would be guilty. But that cannot be the case, because we do not convict based on common sense, but on scientific proof. So then what scientific proof has been presented to show guilt?

See §2:77 for discussion of the concept that "if the defendant is on trial, he must have done something."

§2:92   Silence Is the Only Choice

Judge: Does everyone understand the defendant has the right to remain silent?
JURY NODS IN UNISON
Judge: And do you all agree not to hold that against the defendant in any way?
JURY NODS IN UNISON
Judge: And none of you will allow it to influence your deliberation in any way?
JURY NODS IN UNISON
Defense Attorney post-conviction: So you figured his not testifying meant he was guilty?
JURY NODS IN UNISON

How do we avoid this? Jurors generally believe that if the defendant didn't do it, she is supposed to testify and if someone doesn't, then she is guilty. We have to reframe the point not as the right to remain silent, but that silence is the only reasonable option. As has been stated in many places in this book, the fundamental change required must come from within the jurors themselves. We can only guide them to it.

Once again, how you perform this task is up to you. It can be in voir dire through one on one questioning, or with the entire panel. Maybe you need to cover it in opening, or get to it during your closing argument. Whenever you do it is up to you, but here is the basic outline on how.

Start with the opposite position. Explore with the jury their thoughts on the veracity of a person who has something to gain from advocating a position. I like to use car salespeople, assuming none are on the jury, because most people do not believe all that car salespeople say. Get the jury to agree that the salesperson has a stake in the outcome, probably a commission. They will say this means they do not take all of his statements as totally true.

Now expand the criteria. What about kids accused of something at home? This is especially well-directed at parents in the jury pool. When the child claims innocence, doesn't the parent disbelieve her? Finish up with asking if the mere taking of an oath in court creates a cone of truthfulness. Most jurors will agree it does not. The salesperson might still puff her wares or the child continue the fanciful story.

So ask the jurors if this does not mean that your client will start off with tarnished credibility if he testifies. Clearly a defendant has a stake in the outcome so that the jurors will have a prejudice against him.

Remember at all times to be accepting to the jurors for this bias. They need to know that it is human nature to disbelieve the person who has something to lose.

Once that is established, switch the circumstance to not testifying. Go back to the parent, or pick another juror, and ask what a child's silence means when something is broken in the house and the child is questioned. You will get an instantaneous response of "The child did it" from the parent. Once again expand to the rest of the jurors. Use other examples such as politicians questioned about allegations who respond "no comment," celebrities in the news who won't talk, and whatever else you can think of.

Now I know you are thinking almost all of these examples are people who are guilty. Well, probably so, but the jurors are already thinking that if your client does not testify, she too is guilty. The goal here is to (1) ferret out the people who nodded their heads who really cannot put this concept aside, and (2) get the remainder to truly embrace the right at such a base level that it will be adhered to.

At this point you can look at the jurors and point out that they have proven the Catch 22; if your client testifies, he is not believed because it is his life at stake (and this is a good way to sneak in punishment theory), but if he does not testify he must be guilty.

Ask the jurors themselves for a solution. One of them will provide the answer—but if not, you do it—that the jury just has to ignore this issue altogether, that because our forefathers were persecuted and found to be guilty whether they protested their innocence or said nothing, they created this indestructible protection upon which we must necessarily rely in order to protect our citizens.

§2:93   Presumption of Innocence

Here again we run into that 'if he is here, he did it' common sense issue. Sure the jury will blindly nod heads to the judge's instruction of presumption, but do they really get it? We need to find a way to drive it home to them. Believe it or not, in the DUI context, this is easier than other cases. Start by asking the jurors what the opposite would be, a presumption of guilt. If we had such a position, then if a cop said you were drunk, then you would have to prove you weren't. How could you do so? There would not be a chemical test because the cop's accusation alone would be enough. So what would people do, try to get their own blood test if a cop arrests them?

Develop this theme with the jurors. How could any defendant win a case if the starting point was that they were guilty? What evidence would they possess and be able to present that would rebut this presumption. There is none. So lead the jurors themselves into saying that the presumption of innocence must exist or else there could not be a trial.

§2:94   Burden of Proof

Ask jurors what the burden is in a criminal case and they will probably be able to tell you it is beyond a reasonable doubt. Ask them to explain this and they probably cannot. Ask them if the flip side of the coin would help. In fact, use the coin analogy. "If I told you a coin landed heads up would you know what I meant? What if I told you it landed tails down?"

So proof beyond a reasonable doubt can be rephrased as disproving all reasonable doubts. In fact, isn't that an easier way to look at it? For example, ask jurors, "Would you agree with me that a reasonable doubt exists if the breath machine was broken? So then the prosecution must disprove this doubt, or in other words prove the machine was working fine."

I like to start there because, in most jurisdictions, the prosecution must in fact prove a working machine. Then you can continue as follows:

Would there be a reasonable doubt if the prosecution did not prove that my client is a suitable candidate to take SFST's, and does not have a physical ailment that would affect the results? If so, then it is up to the prosecution to prove my client IS a capable person. What about medical conditions for breath or blood testing?

In other words, any issues that you find reasonable, that cause a doubt, the prosecution must completely disprove. This then is when you reach proof beyond a reasonable doubt.

§2:95   Fair Trial

This is by far my favorite part of reframing. Time and time again we hear the judge or prosecution and even the defense say they want a *fair* trial. Wrong! Constitutionally the accused is entitled to an *unfair* trial.

First, let's look at the word fair. It means even. A criminal trial is *not* an even trial. The accused starts off *presumed innocent*. Or to put it another way, the accused starts off winning. That is not fair. Fair also denotes that a slight tipping to one side or the other means a win. We just discussed how that is not true. The burden is way higher than that.

Second, fair to most people means you hear from each side. In a criminal trial that is not the case. Only one side is *compelled* to speak. In what world is that fair? Also, in a fair debate, if one side doesn't answer a point, that point usually goes to the one who said it. Not so in a criminal trial. Merely raising a point does not make it so.

Third, fair means that if common sense helps you out you use it. As discussed above this is not the law.

To put it simply, a criminal trial is *unfair* in that the accused starts presumed to win, and can only lose if the other side disproves all other explanations, using science, without regard to action or inaction on the part of the accused.

CHAPTER 3

OPENING STATEMENTS

(This page intentionally left blank.)

I.   STRATEGIES AND TACTICS

§3:01   Stand and Deliver a Good Story

You have picked your jury, won and lost your pre-trial motions, and prepared your case. Now it is time to address the jury again. What will you do? It is my opinion that unless there is some compelling reason not to do so (some are discussed below), you should stand up and deliver a full-blown, story-driven, compelling opening statement.

If you do not open at the outset of your DUI case, the defendant's story will be told through the eyes of the prosecutor and the prosecution's witnesses. Jurors (despite your best efforts in voir dire) will use their imaginations to fill in any blanks that are left by the prosecution, and the way they fill in the blanks will be colored by the prosecution's presentation. You will not have a chance to erase the gruesome details.

Think it through. What's the State's story? The jurors are told that they will hear about some terrible driving done by your thoughtless client. They will picture the defendant as a perfectly healthy individual who was given absolutely perfect instructions by the officer on how to perform the SFSTs, which the defendant failed miserably for no apparent reason other than intoxication. Finally, they will be told of how the defendant's BAC was so high that he was a menace to society, a danger to life and limb, and a bad credit risk.

In many jurisdictions, some expert will come on and talk about the prodigious amount of alcohol your client must have consumed in order to be so drunk, and that your client was even more drunk when he or she was driving. *Why let that happen?*

To be clear, not every subsection here will be useful for every case. You need to pick and choose what you use and amend it for your own style and story.

For prosecution strategies for opening statements, *see* Appendix A *The District Attorney's Manual.*

§3:02   When to Reserve Opening Until After Prosecution's Case

Some cases may be ripe for reserving opening. These are limited to cases where you are not rebutting *any* of the prosecution's evidence but rather relying on some alternative defense theory, such as a medical defense.

Then it may be appropriate to not open until the prosecution ends its case. Such an opening would be along the following lines.

EXAMPLE:

We agree with all the prosecution has said. Bob was driving a car with an expired tag and then could not perform SFSTs and blew the .12. But what the prosecution left out is that Bob is a diabetic. Now you will hear from a trained medical professional as to how diabetes can mimic DUI in both outward physical signs and breath tests. And just so we are clear, we told this to the prosecution months ago so that they would not be surprised. If they had any doubts about it, they would have had their expert research this issue before we started.

§3:03   Set the Tone

You have picked your jury, made your motions, figured out your story, prepared your witnesses and readied your evidence. The judge has made his or her opening remarks and the race is on, or more appropriately, the story has begun. It is time for opening statements.

Rest assured that the prosecutor will deliver the standard monotonous (to us, not to the jury who has not sat through hundreds of these) dry opening recitation of the facts. You can even help your client feel more at ease by making this prediction. Tell your client to expect to hear a prosecutor's opening consisting of sentence after sentence beginning with "the evidence will show." Tell your client you will be different. This is your moment to shine.

A properly delivered opening statement sets the tone for the entire trial. Are you letting the jury know that you are on the defensive, meaning your client is guilty and just hoping for some miracle, or are you truly here to tell your client's story (or more often, simply show that the State's story isn't complete). Your opening will say it all.

§3:04   A Strong First Chapter, Not a Trial Road Map

"An opening statement is like a road map for the trial." Boring! Yet this is what virtually every jury hears from virtually every judge in virtually every trial. And more often than not, we defense attorneys fall into this trap. We give exactly that to the jury. Is it any wonder they pay little or no attention? Or worse yet, they pre-decide the case.

An opening statement should be a strong positive argument in your client's favor. "I know," you say, "but the judge won't let me make an argument." Well if you really think the judge is in charge, then find another line of work. A judge is no more in charge than a referee. The judge will call the obvious fouls, but a smart player can find ways to play around the edges of the rules. I am always reminded of the wisdom of an elder lawyer I heard speak early in my career. "You can do anything in court that you like—as long as nobody says 'objection!'" I tend to storytell my opening in a compelling and quick fire way, and am rarely (if ever) objected to. In fact, I am rarely (if ever) objected to in front of a jury, and I am pushing those boundaries every single moment of a trial. This comes in handy during closing argument when I will literally dare the prosecution to object—and they won't have the guts.

Back to storytelling your opening. You need to be compelling. They want to hear you. You haven't lost the jury yet. So make them interested.

In fact, you can think to yourself before you begin your opening "Once upon a time…" and then begin your story. If your story doesn't flow from that, you're doing it wrong.

Examine the following examples.

BAD EXAMPLE: *Bland, vague, and generic*

Bob was seen running a light and was stopped by the officer. When he was asked to perform SFSTs, he did so in accordance with guidelines, but not up to the officer's expectation.

Fairly standard by defense attorneys. Now try this.

GOOD EXAMPLE: *More detailed, positive, and personal—told like a story.*

The officer found what he wanted to find and saw what he wanted to see—and ignored any evidence to the contrary.

It must have been hard at that time of night for Bob to see the light had just changed from yellow to red. No one claims he was speeding; it was just a poor visibility situation. Something that can happen to any of us. We all do our best to follow the rules of the road when we drive, there will be no evidence that Bob did not. But despite our best efforts and well-meaning intentions, we can be suddenly confronted by an obstacle with no time to react. As soon as he realized what he had done, Bob slowed down and seconds later the police cruiser pulled him over. Bob knew right away he had made a mistake. In other words, he did everything right.

When he was first approached by the officer, he was cooperative and admitted to what he had done. With no problems or issues, he presented his ID, registration etc. In other words, he did everything right.

When asked to voluntarily step out of the car, he readily agreed to do so. Why not? He'd not done anything wrong. His normal behavior was normal and sober. When asked to perform these complicated roadside tests, he did so as best he could. The officer has practiced these for years. In fact, the officer has performed these tests over a thousand times, and they are not normal behavior.

So he did not do them perfectly. But who would?

This opening displays a positive attitude, an attitude that will stick in the jurors' minds throughout the trial. You've also begun laying the groundwork for repetition of some phrases and themes that you can come back to later.

§3:05 Grab Jurors' Attention

As mentioned throughout this book, start strong. No "my name is" or "we are here about" openings. We start with an active sentence, grabbing the jurors' attention and erasing the barely-scratched in image the DA has just portrayed.

EXAMPLES:

Three more minutes. If the officer had waited three more minutes we would not be here.

It was an investigation that was good enough for government work.

This is a drunk driving case without any drunk driving in it.

That's another point about opening statements—play the story card first. Let's face it, DUIs are emotional and hot buttons. DUI is the only political crime in the country. Name another criminal offense that can be prosecuted with no harm to property or person. There is none. The emotion/bias/prejudice card will be played; if you have a chance to seize the narrative and make it about the problems with the government's job here, you can seize the white hat and make your client the hero.

§3:06   Establish Rapport and Humanize Your Client

Another major point of opening is to establish a rapport with the jury. As more and more judges limit our voir dire to less and less time, and if you're not able to take advantage of the strategy outlined above, you risk losing that contact. Get it back in the opening. Take your time and give a mental/verbal handshake to each juror. This process is taught by communication specialists. Basically, it involves direct eye contact with a juror that you maintain until the juror recognizes you and signals the recognition. It is, just as it is described, like a handshake. The more time you take, the more interest the jurors will have in your client.

Involve your client. Walk to him, touch him, make the jury see a person, not the "defendant" the DA just discussed. (Always ask clients if they're comfortable being touched before doing it. Nothing is worse than a client recoiling from you in front of a jury.)

Try to have the jury relate to your client. Not only is your client an ordinary citizen just like them, they could be the one sitting in the defense seat. They, like your client, have busy lives and lots of things affect their days, moods, time management, and so forth. The prosecution will do the opposite. It is their hope to distance the jury from the defendant. He is a drunk; they of course would never break the law or drive drunk. This misguided assumption is what often causes the prosecution to lose. If you do your job correctly, the jurors will see themselves in your client.

EXAMPLE:

This is Robert Smith, ladies and gentlemen, not "the defendant." He is a hardworking man with family, friends and a busy life. But when the officer saw him, he expected to see a drunk and that is what he saw. When the prosecutor looks at him, all he sees is a defendant. But Robert and I want you to see him. A person, not a statistic. And when you do, you will see an innocent person.

§3:07   Fill in the Blanks With Positive Information

Your opening needs to paint a detailed positive picture of the defendant because, if it does not, the jury will form their impression of the defendant solely from the bad information presented by the prosecutor. This conclusion is based on simple human characteristics. We hate blanks. We do not like to leave gaps in our mind's eye. Ask a friend to picture a person. Do not give any more detail. Then ask the friend to describe the person. The friend will be able to give you a full description of the imagined "person." This is the fill in the blank theorem. Our minds cannot allow the gaps to exist so we fill them in. Jurors do this all the time.

Jurors will fill in, from their own experiences or their imaginations based on what they have heard so far, any detail that you do not fill in for them. Given that all they have heard from the prosecution is negative towards your client, the picture their minds will draw is not a positive one. You need to change all of that.

Better yet, you can simply point out that blanks exist in the State's case. You're "predicting" a lack of evidence—which is allowable—and shows the jury there's more than one way to look at it.

§3:08   Point Out Problems With the Prosecution's Case

Unless there is some extremely good strategy for doing so, let the jury know where you are going in this case. Explain exactly what your theory of the case will be. Point out those facts in the prosecution's theory of the case that support your theory or those facts that undermine the prosecution's. Closing argument is too late to let them in on what was missing from the prosecution's case. The one exception to this is if the missing fact or evidence is something big that you do not want the prosecutor to catch. Even then, be absolutely sure in your mind that the prosecutor does not know what is missing and will not anticipate the argument.

In fact, sometimes the opening can be used to bait the prosecution into answering you, which can then be turned on them. For example, assume that there is no documentation of a necessary fact in the reports provided during discovery. Assume this is the main defense in the case. You can either mention it in opening or not. If you do not and the prosecution suddenly produces this evidence in the middle of the trial, then you are limited to cross-examination on the evidence's late arrival, or to cry "foul" to the judge in some attempt at a mistrial.

But, if you throw it out to the jury in opening, and then the prosecutor covers that ground by producing the evidence you argued had been missing, you can argue "foul" and "I told you so." It will give you an opportunity to argue to the jury that the prosecution is just making it up as they go. By putting the missing evidence before the jury in opening, and having the prosecution 'miraculously' find it during the trial, you have a stronger closing argument that the government is either making it up as they go, or that they are being less than straight with the facts and jury.

EXAMPLE:

In one case the time of the events was critical. One witness placed the defendant on the scene at a specific time, but a second witness placed the defendant at the scene 10 minutes later. The prosecution was told about the discrepancy before trial and was ready. Here is what was said, in part, during the defense opening:

One factor the DA will not be able to change is recorded on the breath card in this case. The technician who administered the test put her time of observation as 2:00. The machine recorded its time of first test at 2:13. Any one of us can see that is NOT a fifteen minute observation as required by law. I can point this out before we even start the case because (1) these are set-in-stone facts that cannot be changed, and, (2) the prosecution cannot just make up facts to cover this glaring problem.

In his opening, the DA talked about how his grandmother always had him set his watch ten minutes fast so he would never be late. Sure enough, the witness who had the defendant on scene ten minutes later than the other witness testified that HER grandmother taught HER the same thing. The jury never bought it.

Had the defense attorney not called the jurors' attention to the discrepancy in the witnesses' stories in opening, many jurors would probably not have been skeptical about the witness' testimony about setting her watch ahead. But the jury, having been forewarned of the problem, heard the excuses as a made-up story.

The moral: don't hold back.

§3:09   Tell Jurors About Your Defense

I am assuming you have some defense to your case. Let the jurors know what it is. If your client has a medical condition that affected his or her performance on the SFSTs, tell them about it. Create the image of a person on death's door. This will then color the jury's interpretation of the evidence. How can the officer expect your client to stand on one leg when he had that terrible leg sprain?

Don't sell yourself or your case short. "They can't prove it" is, in fact, a hell of a defense. Bring that out, too. Tell them about all the things your client did right that the State forgot to mention in their opening. Tell them about all the things the Trooper could have investigated, but didn't. Tell them about all the proof that could exist in your case but doesn't for some reason.

§3:10   Boost the Officer and Prosecution Expert so You Can Knock Them Down on Cross-Examination

If you are attacking how tests were performed, emphasize and relate in detail all the training the officer or expert was given and how he or she ignored that training in administering or evaluating the results of the SFSTs. The more you boost the officer's or expert's credentials, the higher the jurors' expectation for that testimony. Then it is easier to destroy that image during cross-examination.

Think back to the Bush versus Gore debates in 2000. Everyone knew Al would kick George's butt in a debate. This was so well-known that the Bush camp at first refused to debate Gore at all. Finally, after too much public pressure was levied, a debate was set.

For weeks prior to the debate, the Bush press corps bemoaned how bad it would be. They created an image of Gore as an unassailable Socrates reincarnate. Bush, on the other hand, they described as a simple frat boy with no such skill. By the time the debate rolled around, most people felt if George got his name right, it would be a miracle.

We all know what happened at that debate. Bush did not look all that bad, given the lowered expectations, and Gore looked positively mortal given the heightened expectations for him.

Do this in your opening for your witnesses and for theirs. If you do not open, you will not be able to set the stage.

EXAMPLE:

Thousands of stops, hundreds of arrests, reams of police reports and who knows how many times in court. The officer will tell you that's what he has under his belt. At the academy, he was trained in how to perform SFSTs, how to document a case and how to testify. He will tell you that this is a major portion of his job. During his examination, he will be polished, sure, and all-knowing. This is his case and he knows he made no mistakes and he knows he is not wrong. This will be evident in the way he presents every detail of this case. Nothing went unnoticed by him, no fact was left out of his reports and no errors exist. And since he is a trained police officer, you should expect nothing less. None of us would want an officer to come in here less than fully-prepared or less than perfect. (You can adapt this for the state's expert(s) as well.)

Bob on the other hand has never been to court before. He is nervous as hell and will probably have a hard time talking from the stand. (This is good for a witness or the defendant.) Unlike the professional witnesses for the prosecution, he may have to have questions repeated, or give answers that seem unsure. We don't expect him to know what to say as we would the officer who has been through this dozens of times. In fact, if Bob makes it through this at all, I would be surprised. Think of how nervous you all were during the brief questioning we did in voir dire.

§3:11   Use Element of Surprise to Your Advantage

The beautiful thing about an opening statement is only you know the story you're going to tell. Until you address the jury, everyone is in the dark. This creates a natural anticipation from the jurors that you can use to your advantage. It also will be a surprise to the prosecution who should have little, if any, idea of what you will be doing in the case.

Unlike the prosecution, whose case is an open book if discovery was handled correctly, you need not show your hand. The prosecution must prep witnesses based on information contained in the police report, witness statements, and other information that you should have received prior to trial. (This is covered elsewhere in this book—make the prosecution do their work *before* trial. Not only are you legally entitled to discovery, the information in the reports and statements ties the prosecution's hands at trial.)

A prosecutor has no idea what the defendant's theory of the case is. Prosecutors can guess and surmise it, but typically do not even think about it because, after all, it is just a simple DUI case. There can be no defense; the cops and the machine do not lie. Let them think this way. Use it. Take their ignorance and show the jury, right out of the box, how wrong the prosecution is.

Another fear that all prosecutors have is uncertainty about whether the defendant will testify. I have addressed the issue of having your client testify in other chapters of this book, and while I rarely recommend it, don't let the prosecution know that the defendant will testify. Also, while you may be convinced the client will take the stand, if something arises and he or she does not, then you will look like you are hiding something. Prosecutors fear the unknown. If the DA thinks that your client will testify, he or she may prepare the case anticipating this testimony. Then, if the testimony does not occur, it looks like the prosecution has misled the jury and the jurors will be confused and feel as if the prosecution really did not know the facts very well. Conversely, when your client does testify, prosecutors are often unprepared for the testimony. Their routine DUI is no longer routine and there is no information in their DUI prosecution manual to rebut what your client has said. They are forced to think on their feet; their nice, simple DUI case is no longer so simple. No one likes to be surprised, especially when they have a preconceived notion of how things are going to go. So, as much as possible, limit any promise of defendant testimony in your opening statement.

§3:12   Go Out of Order if Called For

The people's case is often one of just setting out the facts, a simple straight forward series of questions of what happened next. This lulls the jurors to sleep. Wake them up. Depending on the type of jury you have picked, go out of order. Don't start with the first event in chronological order, "Bob ran the stop light." Maybe start with the last event. "After all his cooperation and explanation to the officer, Bob still ended up in jail for running the red light." Keep it interesting, make eye contact—besides voir dire, which is increasingly limited, this is your time to get the jurors to like you. Before the case even starts, you will have set the pattern. The jurors will know that they can rest while the prosecution presents their case, and perk up when you stand up.

§3:13 Wake Up the Jurors

Think outside of the box! Remember, people want to be engaged and feel as if they are involved. Use of eye contact, body language, voice levels, and "props" wakes them up and makes them feel as if they are important in the decision at hand. Defense counsel has worked hard and knows his/her case and wants all the facts to be conveyed so that the jurors can make an informed and intelligent decision. One prop I especially like is the missing element chart. Put a hand written chart of the elements in front of the jury, but leave out what you expect to be the missing fact. This could be who was actually driving, when the driving occurred, the time of the chemical test, the result of the test—whatever you will be focusing on.

[§§3:14-3:19 Reserved]

II.   SAMPLE OPENINGS

§3:20 Who Was Driving

Mike [the defendant] did a terrible thing. He lied to an officer. Now if you think about it, lying to a cop, and then coming here to admit it is way worse than drunk driving. So why would Mike do this? Why would he come in here to court and admit he lied to the officer? More importantly, why would his wife and best friend do so as well, unless there was something more at stake. Something like the truth.

You see, Mike wants all of you to know the truth. So he, and his wife and his friend will all testify that they did not tell the truth to the officer when the accident occurred. But more importantly they will tell you why they did so.

You see, they were scared. Not just afraid of a little DUI, but afraid of what might happen to David if the truth came out. Afraid it could result in terrible consequences for David.

David is from Africa. He is an amazing person who happens to be here on a Fulbright scholarship. You may have heard of that term before, Fulbright scholar, it is like hearing Rhodes Scholar. But how many of you know what it means? A Fulbright scholar is a foreign national whom the United States State Department thinks is so special, and will be of such potential help to our interests, that the State Department picks up the scholar's expenses for schooling, usually at a Masters or higher level. It is obviously quite an honor.

This is not something you lightly put in jeopardy. And since the recipient is usually from another country, like David, he may not understand all that is involved. But he does understand, as you would agree, it is not something you want to jeopardize. It is an opportunity that you treasure and protect. Sometimes wrongly.

David is such a scholar. He is from the Ivory Coast and was here studying for his Masters degree in international trade and economics. He hopes to go back to the Ivory Coast to help his people in boosting their trade with the United States. He was doing well until the events of October 25th got in the way.

You see, earlier that day David had joined Mike and his family at a barbeque. David had ridden there in Mike's wife's car and was having fun. As is his belief, he was not drinking but enjoying the company.

Mike, on the other hand was drinking. Mike, you will hear, owns a couple of companies. He used to be a vice president at Town Bank and is now a vice president at Sun Investments. This was a group of friends from Sun getting together for a family Saturday. As you would expect it was supposed to be fun only, but, as is typical, work crept in. Now Mike and his wife had an agreement, like many of us do. They had earlier decided who would drive home so that one of them could feel free to have a beer or two. Mike's wife was going to drive. That is why they took her smaller car rather than his bigger one.

So there it was, a beautiful Saturday afternoon—Mike was discussing work over a beer or two, David was meeting new friends in this beautiful country, and the rest of the family was having fun. The day wore on and it was time to go. But a problem arose. Mike's wife had developed a splitting headache. She did not want to drive.

They talked about it and decided Mike could not drive, but David could. He had a license, did not drink, and while he had only driven this car once before, he knew the way home with no problems.

A little side note here, you will find out that while Mike and David were not close friends prior to David coming to America, but they had since become friends. Picture yourself in a foreign country where you do not speak the language too well, customs are very different, and your family is not with you. Now suddenly, you meet a Californian—not just any Californian, but one who is in your line of work. Well, that was the story of Mike and David. While they are both from the Ivory Coast, they did not know each other, but work brought them together and they had become friends. In fact, David rented a room from Mike.

So it was no big deal to let David drive the car. They got into the car and home they went. David driving, Mike in the passenger seat and the kids and "Ms. Mike" in the back. About the kids. They were, as many youngsters are after a long day at a barbeque, tired. But the kind of tired that leads to crying and crankiness. That is what they were doing and it was all Mike's wife could do to keep them somewhat still. But the miracle of driving soon took over and they fell asleep. So did Mike's wife.

This is why she will tell you that when the accident did happen, she had no idea who was driving. She did see who was driving when they left. She saw who came out of what part of the car afterwards; but she cannot say who was driving since she was asleep.

Not that you will need to hear who was driving from her. The rest of the evidence from the prosecution will make it clear.

You will hear from the prosecution witnesses that they never saw a driver. Think on that. The prosecution will put its best case forward and not place Mike behind the wheel of the car. Instead they will allege that Mike admitted driving and THAT is their proof. And that is where Mike and David made a terrible mistake.

David was scared. He was afraid that this accident may cause him to lose his scholarship. He thought all his hard work would be down the drain and he would be sent back to the Ivory Coast. Mike thought so too. So, in a decidedly unintelligent move, they decided to have Mike say he was driving.

That's it. That is all the prosecution can bring to the table. Mike saying he drove. Now, all the witnesses will say that is not true. They will say that they (1) saw Mike exiting from the passenger side, (2) that David had been driving when they left the barbeque, and that (3) Mike and David made the story up.

But now, when truth is on the line and people are sworn, David and Mike will come in and tell the truth. The truth of who was driving.

§3:21   Refusals

Generally speaking, refusals fall into two categories: confusion or deliberate act. Each has a different focus and each should have a different opening. Both, however, can have a knockout punch added to the end, if it applies in your jurisdiction.

Confusion

According to the officer, based on his training, the purpose of asking for a person's driver's license and then asking some other question is to try to confuse the driver. The training manual talks about creating this confusion. During Jane's contact with the officer, she was asked more than 50 questions, had to perform numerous calisthenics, and was bombarded with information.

The officer will go into much detail about how he explained why she was pulled over, what he needed her to do, her rights and responsibilities, but some of these conflict with each other. For example, he will state that he told Jane that she did not have to supply a roadside breath test, that she did not have to talk to him per *Miranda*, and, if she did provide evidence, it may be used against her. Somewhere in the middle of all this, he told Jane she had to give a breath sample. But wait, didn't he also tell her she did not? When her confusion became clear, Jane asked for a lawyer, but was told she could not have one. But hadn't the officer told her that under *Miranda* she was entitled to one?

It seemed to Jane that everything she was told she had to do, she was also told she did not have to do. Is it any wonder that, given the lights, sirens, exercises and conflicting rules, she did not know what was or was not required?

Deliberate Refusal

Jimmy is a proud American. He thinks, as do many of us, that he understands his rights. Like many of you probably believe, he thinks that officers cannot just break down his door to his house unless they have a warrant. Well, suffice it to say, that is incorrect. You may think that your house or phone cannot be bugged, but it can. In fact, many of the rights you believe you have, you do not.

Well, Jimmy thought it was his right to not incriminate himself. He believed that it was the function of the government to obtain evidence to prosecute him. He thought that these were his rights as an American citizen. He was wrong.

Being wrong does not make you a drunk. It does not make you a menace to society. It is not proof of anything more than a common misconception of our rights as American citizens.

Knockout Punch

After taking Bob to the police station, Trooper Friendly read him some complicated legal paperwork. He listened and was told he had the right to refuse. Which he did.

But the story isn't over. Trooper Friendly could have proven this case to you. All he had to do was pick up the phone and get a search warrant. He knows how and has done it before. He could have strapped Bob to a table at a hospital and forcibly drawn his blood.

Then we'd all know how much alcohol—IF ANY—was active in Bob's system. But we don't. Trooper Friendly decided you didn't need it.

§3:22   FSTs

I believe in two approaches to FSTs: that the officer administered them incorrectly and the results don't matter, or the results are there, but "so what?"

Incorrect Administration

Take out a pen and paper and write your three times table. Remember that or something like it in school? What if I asked you to do that right now and then told you every one failed because I had meant the four times table. *Not fair*, you would say, and you'd be right. Well, FSTs are just like that.

The Federal Government, under the Department of Transportation, created an agency known as the National Highway Traffic Safety Administration, NHTSA for short. That organization spent millions of dollars in order to develop a tool for officers to use in helping to determine if a person was under the influence of alcohol. Years of research went into this project, the data was collected, computer algorithms were assigned, and the three-test battery was developed.

Then, in order to ensure reliability, more time, money and energy were expended in order to test the SFSTs in the field. After years of study, the results were in. *If* the officer uses the prescribed battery, and *if* the officer does it the required way, and *if* the officer scores the tests correctly, then they have some measure of reliability.

Well, you will hear that Officer Jones failed this administration. You will hear that in instructing Bob on the SFSTs, the officer misdirected Bob and miscounted so called clues. You will hear that the officer did not perform his tasks correctly. This violates not only common sense and good science, but the *specific language of the SFST manual.*

It is just like asking to name the capital of the U.S. when you really meant the capital of France, and then scoring the person wrong for saying Washington D.C.

So What?

SO WHAT? That is what you need to say to virtually every piece of evidence in this case. If a piece of evidence does not aid in your decision on the question of guilt or innocence, then it is irrelevant. This is the "so what" test. The sky was blue. So what? Unless that piece of knowledge is relevant, it adds nothing. That is the big, missing piece when it comes to SFSTs.

See, the officer will come in here and make a big production out of the SFSTs in this case. He will go into great detail about how he was trained in them, how he gave them to Joan, and how she did. My guess is that the testimony on this subject will take most of the officer's total time on the witness stand. But SO WHAT?

Unless someone can tell you a study that relates the performance of these tasks to the ability to drive a car, so what? AND I AM LAYING THIS OUT THERE NOW SO THE PROSECUTION IS ON NOTICE THAT YOU WILL DEMAND THIS. But they will not answer. Because they cannot.

Dr. Marcelline Burns is the woman who basically created these tasks. She has been asked time and again if the performance on these tasks can be related to either of the issues before you today: was Joan driving impaired, or was Joan over .08 at the time of her driving. EVERY TIME SHE HAS BEEN ASKED THIS QUESTION, THE ANSWER HAS BEEN THE SAME: NO.

SFSTs do not measure the ability to drive a car, and they do not predict a specific BAC. Rather, what they do and what they were intended to do, is aid an officer in his or her decision on whether to conduct a further investigation using some type of SCIENTIFIC measuring device.

So when you hear about these SFSTs, say "so what?"

§3:23   Rising Blood Alcohol

Rising blood alcohol is one of the best defenses in DUI cases. The simple concept is that a chemical test obtained some time after the driving does not reflect the actual BAC at the time of driving. The BAC at the time of the test may be higher than the BAC at the time of driving because alcohol takes time to be absorbed into the blood stream. Rising blood alcohol is a very simple concept which many people complicate. Use examples to the jury that they can understand.

It is not illegal to drink and drive, nor is it illegal to be over the legal limit. It is only illegal when the two acts are joined. In other words, to go out, get drunk, and come home to pass out on the couch is not illegal unless the driving was done when the BAC was illegal.

You will all hear that alcohol takes some time to get from our mouths, where we first drink it, to our blood, where it may become illegal. There is no set time for this to happen, and no way to predict it. Each person is different. But we can all picture it.

You have a cold. You take some medicine to clear your sinuses. Does it happen instantly? No. It takes time. How much time is different for every one here and may be different for you depending on what you've eaten, how you feel, etc. The same is true for alcohol.

Another example. You go out to eat at a really nice restaurant and order an appetizer, soup, salad, main course and dessert. When do you start to feel full? Not right way, but usually right when the dessert comes out. Many times you eat it anyway, but an hour later, THAT is when you feel over-stuffed.

Or if the food was too spicy, that is when you reach for the Tums.

The experts in this case will all agree to this simple concept. They will probably differ on timing. The State's expert will cling to a more specific time in order to show that Sue had to have been over the legal limit at the time she was driving. Our expert will admit that such a time is *possible*, but will tell you it is only *one possibility*.

Chances are, once we confront the State's witness, they will admit that our expert is correct, and that many variances exist that can change this pattern. Both experts will agree that in order to determine if Sue was over the legal limit at the time of the driving—which is the issue, not whether she was over the limit when at the police station—they need more information than a simple chemical test.

They need to know the entire drinking pattern; when she started, when she stopped, how she drank, what she drank, what she ate and more. Even then, they will admit, they are only giving a *theory* based on *averages*. We do not convict people on a theory of guilt based on an average.

§3:24   Keeping an Open Mind

When the Judge told you to keep an open mind, I was reminded of something that happened to me that I would like to tell you about. Something similar may have happened in your life as well. It is a quick example of how jumping to conclusions can lead to wrong results, much like how the officer in this case, expecting to see a drunk when he stopped Jody, looked only for the bad clues and ignored the good ones.

I received a phone call from school one day that there had been a fight between kids, and my daughter was at the principal's office. Just like the officer on receiving a dispatch about a possible drunk driver, I took off in my car expecting to see the worst: my daughter in trouble for fighting.

During the ride, I became angrier as I imagined grave consequences, just like the officer who geared himself up for the arrest he was going to be making.

Just as I had been told, the suspect was waiting. I looked at my daughter and noticed her flushed face, the scrapes, and her dirty hands. Similarly, the officer saw the eyes, the speech, and the gait of Jody, his suspect.

I asked my daughter what she had done, and received the same reply that Jody gave to the officer, "Nothing, I am fine." Both the officer and I *knew* this was a lie. We had been called because something was wrong.

The officer had Jody perform the roadside tests and noted all that was done wrong. Those done correctly, he ignored. I similarly ignored the other two people in the principal's office who were more upset than my daughter. In fact, my daughter was sitting there looking proud and smiling. *How inappropriate.* Just as inappropriate as the officer thought Jody's "innocent" behavior to be.

The principal then told me about a terrible playground fight, describing all the details of the scuffle. My pressure rose, compounded by the continued denial of wrongdoing told by my daughter's face. I can understand the officer's frustration as Jody made similar denials.

The officer ultimately arrested Jody and she is here today to explain that he made some bad conclusions. My daughter was luckier. Just as I was about to let loose, the principal remarked how great it was to have a child like her.

You see, she was the one who broke up the fight.

§3:25 It Wasn't My Client

I just had an embarrassing moment. On my way here I was in the elevator coming from the first floor up to the sixth floor. At two, a man entered who, let's just say he had some stomach issues. He left a reminder of this when he got off on the third floor. Well, as luck would have it, people got on at the fourth floor, and *instantly* gave me some nasty looks.

What could I do? Do you think they would believe me and my story of the missing man? I didn't think so either. Well, that is what happened in this case. No one believed my client didn't drive, even though no one saw him driving. Much like the elevator, it may stink, but that doesn't mean John did it.

§3:26 The Missing Element

Sometimes the defense in the case is very clear and straight forward, *e.g.*, a blown chemical test, missing evidence, and so forth. In these cases it may be best to come straight out and hit the jury with it. Throw down the gauntlet as it were. This will put pressure on the DA to answer your charge right from the beginning.

In order for the chemical test in this case to be relevant, in other words to actually matter to this case, the prosecution must prove that the test results were obtained within the statutory time period, that is three hours, of the driving. Well we know when the test was taken, it says so right here. BUT When did the accident occur? That is the one fact that the prosecution will not be able to prove. No one witnessed it and John can't remember. So, don't worry about taking notes or understanding all the irrelevant information the prosecution will throw at you. Just ask one question; how does this piece of evidence tell me *when* this all happened. If it does not answer that in some way, then it is not worth noting. In fact, you will see that I am going to agree to virtually everything the prosecutor brings. I may not even question some witnesses. I cannot put it simply enough; Mr. Prosecutor, just give us some evidence to prove when this happened. If not, then don't waste the jurors' time.

§3:27 You Cannot Believe the Officer

Be careful with the opening. It is usually not a good idea to ask the jury to disbelieve the officer. Despite what people say, we all want to believe that officers are truthful. We understand, however, they are human and not all of them are always truthful. If you have a case where you have *very solid evidence of untruthfulness*, especially a video, then you can try this.

No matter what tests are given, no matter what experience they have, no matter the line of work, sometimes people tell untruths. This does not make them bad people. It does not make them unworthy as individuals. It does, however, call into question their accuracy for not only that event, but other events closely related to that event.

In this case you will hear that Officer Kenny evaluated Mr. Arnold's performance on field sobriety tests. You will hear and see that Kenny also memorialized on video how he gave Mr. Arnold the tests. Unfortunately, you will also *see* what actually happened. You will see a video that clearly goes against how Kenny wrote that he gave the tests to Mr. Arnold and even more importantly how Mr. Arnold did on those tests.

Now, given what you will learn about Kenny's accuracy contained in the unimpeachable video record, you must ask yourself just how much you can believe him in the remainder of his positions. There was no video to record the alleged horrendous driving pattern, just Kenny's word. Does it have the same accuracy as his report on the field sobriety tests? If Mr. Arnold had a video, would it exonerate him just as it does on the tests? We will never know, but you will see that Kenny, in this case, was not at his best.

§3:28   Quick Ideas for Basic Issues

Here are the basic issues that arise in most DUI cases that you should address in opening and some quick ideas of how to do so.

The Crime

DUI is the only political and opinion crime we have in America. Think about that. In this case there is no victim. No one was hurt, no one had property lost or damaged. Instead, society has decided that this can be a crime based on POTENTIAL harm. Now while the concept of preventing crime is laudable, YOU are here to decide if Mr. Jones is guilty of an individual crime.

Similarly, this crime is based on opinion. The police will tell you that they FELT Mr. Jones was in violation of the law. They will not have any hard facts to support that. Well, opinion is fine in some contexts, but not in dealing with someone's life. You must be convinced beyond a reasonable doubt of the guilt, not just have an opinion about it.

The Burdens

You heard the judge mention the burden of proof, presumption of innocence and proof beyond a reasonable doubt; now is the time to apply those concepts to real facts. The DA has outlined all the facts he has in his case. Now you must listen to the ones I have. Applying those principles, if we both ended there, you would be required to find Jim not guilty since the burden has not been met and the presumption of innocence still applies. In fact, the presumption is like a broom. It constantly sweeps against the evidence the prosecution will offer, and only if the dirt is so overwhelming as to be inevitable, does it stop.

The Facts

Go into the specific facts, and deal with the field sobriety tests, driving pattern, chemical test or refusal or whatever else you need to deal with in your case.

The Law

If you will be resting any part of the defense on statutory violations, codes etc. be SURE to explain them to the jury in opening.

The law requires a 15 minute observation period. This is not something any of us can dispute. But you will hear that the 15 minute observation period in this case was not followed. The officer simply blew it. Now I am not sure how the prosecution will address this missing critical element, but I am here to tell you that they must somehow do so or the test results violate the law, the science, and—more importantly—Bob's rights.

Client Testimony

Ladies and Gentlemen, as we sit here right now I am not sure if Bob will or will not testify. That is because I am not sure what the prosecution will be able to prove. You see, if they were to stop right now, there would be no reason for Bob to say anything. On the other hand, Bob has told me that he wants you all to know his thoughts about what happened that day. Ultimately, however, it is *my* decision as to whether he will or will not talk to you and you must not worry about what might or might not have been.

How you present these topics has been discussed. More may be needed in some cases, less in others, but this is a general idea of what you should say.

A final note: the prosecution's opening is usually less than 10 minutes. While you can explain to the jury that you need more time to get them to see the details, in most cases going too long (more than about 20 minutes) will look like you are trying to bully the jury or hide some critical facts. If you go longer, best do it to show the jury what the State cannot and will not actually be able to prove.

CHAPTER 4

CROSS-EXAMINATION

CROSS-EXAMINATION

CROSS-EXAMINATION

I.   INTRODUCTION

§4:01   Cross-Examination Is Your Testimony

Cross-examination is testimony by the attorney for as long as necessary, broken into individual points that are consistently affirmed by the witness. This is the basic truism of cross-examination. Each sentence (and I do mean sentence, as cross should almost never be an actual question) should contain as few words as necessary to make the point. Only one point should be made in each sentence. The point should be phrased in the affirmative. After several points have been established, the thrust should be reiterated.

In order to become a master at cross-examination, one should read Posner and Dodd, *Cross-Examination: Science and Techniques*, Second Edition (Lexis Publishing 2004) and listen to Terry McCarthy's lectures scattered on the Internet from various seminars on the topic. Terry is especially insightful on small, quick statements for cross. His demonstration of one word questioning is simple, yet effective.

So here we go with a variety of cross-examination questions. Not every question is correct for every case, and not every possible question is delivered below. Instead, what we have is a group of questions that should provide 80% of what you need. Of course, case-specific questions will always be needed.

See Ch. 8, *Demonstrative Evidence*, for a variety of exhibits that can be used in conjunction with cross-examination of various witnesses. See Appendix A for the prosecution's approach to direct examination.

§4:02   A Kinder, Gentler Approach to the Officer

"Officer, isn't it true that everything you have just testified to on direct examination is a complete lie?" How many of us style our cross-examination on this model? It is the old tried and true method made famous in books and movies, but is it necessarily the best?

Sure, jurors expect us to cross-examine a witness, especially a police officer, aggressively. They may even look forward to some fireworks, but how often does this play to our ultimate benefit? How many times could we obtain the same answers without the possible backlash of juror sentiment? Benjamin Franklin was considered a master at the art of polite questioning which inevitably led to the conclusion he was after. Let's see if we can do the same.

When a defense counsel first rises to ask the witness a question, all is hushed. The officer is poised to respond as if a weapon were drawn upon him or her in the street. The DA is set to back-up the officer with objections and interruptions designed to shoot counsel in the back, or at least to wing 'em. Jurors, formerly asleep at the dull droning of direct examination, are now ready to see this new phase of the trial, and the judge is paying attention for the first time since he or she may actually have to issue a legal ruling.

The stage is set. All eyes are upon you and what you do. Nothing. Play it cool. Become the officer's friend and supporter. Set the trap and wait. Start by offering the most disarming array of questions you can: officer safety.

Q: What is the number one rule you are taught in the academy, and at every roll call, at every training and every day as an officer? Your safety is number one and all the number twos are way back.

The witness is totally unprepared for this. It is not only obviously true, it is solicitous. You are the enemy, yet you care; you know, you help. In one simple question you have disarmed the officer. How can he or she respond with "deadly force" when you have not shown any weapon?

Q: In keeping with rule #1, you are taught how to interact with people in all kinds of situations?

What can the officer say? "No, I was never taught how to deal with people," "I am unsure what that question means," "Maybe," "I don't know," "I can't remember"? Of course not. The officer will agree. Now develop this theme with the car stop.

Q: When you make a car stop, is that dangerous?
Q: In fact, aren't car stops the most dangerous time for officers to get hurt, or worse?
Q: You were taught that the first few moments of interaction are the most dangerous?
Q: You have no idea who, or how many, people may be in that car?
Q: And at night, like in this case, it is even worse?
Q: This makes you alert and ready—even nervous?

Now, without so much as one negative word, one bad question, you have set a stage where the guy with the gun is nervous and on-edge. Is it hard to understand why your client was equally, or probably even more, worried? This emotional response to the officer explains a lot of the initial "objective symptoms." Maybe it also explains the dropped wallet or fumbled license, but that is developed much later.

Q: Now for night time stops, there is a specific protocol on how to proceed?

Q: You call it in so that someone knows where you are?

Q: On a standard stop such as this one (NOTE: that will get an admission to be used later, that there was nothing out of the ordinary about this stop), you don't jump out of your car with your gun out? (By compounding the question, you force the negative answer creating the first admission.)

Q: You actually wait a second or two and see what the person does?

Q: Are they trying to hide anything, or grab anything that could be harmful?

Q: And my client did none of that?

We have not even had the officer exit the car and we have established your client was not a threat, not doing anything out of the ordinary and was understandably nervous. The jury is waiting for the shoe to drop, but is still paying attention because they are learning. Now we follow up with the learning aspect as we build your own expertise in proper police procedures.

Q: When conducting a car stop, you pull in behind the car and wait to be sure it is stopped and the driver is not trying to trick you?

Q: You do not pull up tight on the bumper, but leave room?

Q: In fact, you pull up off center on them, with your car slightly to the inside, away from traffic? Again for officer safety?

Q: This is done for two reasons: one, you have to get out of the car and do not want to get out into the actual road, and two, you want your headlight to be focused on the car's rearview mirror?

Q: You focus on the mirror so that the driver cannot get a clear view of you, just in case he or she is a threat or armed or dangerous?

Q: When you do this, it aims your passenger side headlight at the passenger side mirror of the stopped car so anyone in the stopped car could not use that mirror to see you either?

Q: If you have a spot light you may even use that?

Q: All in all, you are trying to (1) prevent the driver from seeing you, so you are protected, and (2) get as much light into the car as you can to see what the occupants may be doing?

This is a major point for any and all eye reactions for some time. Think about how you feel when you are driving at night on an unlit highway and then come into a tunnel or a well-lit town. It takes time for your eyes to adjust. Your pupils may even be dilated different from the norm.

So without one negative question we have set the stage. It is a dark night, our client is nervous, and the car has been unnaturally bathed in light. We have effectively neutralized the issues around nervousness and the eyes. Yet we have not fired one salvo.

See Appendix A *The District Attorney's Manual* for the prosecution's approach to direct examination of the arresting officer.

§4:03   Two Approaches to SFSTs

Knowing the Manuals—Befriending the Program

The SFSTs are standardized and scientifically validated. They have to be done the same way every time or else they are not useful. Garbage in—garbage out. Nearly every expert will tell you this. So it is critical that you know the tests and the protocols as well as, and better than, your officers.

Washington State Patrol, in an effort to be transparent for discovery purposes, has put every single NHTSA manual (basic, ARIDE, DRE, and more) up for FREE download on their website: breathtest.wsp.wa.gov—and if you haven't read them, download the student manual and start reading. Once you finish, the following discussion will make more sense.

Now that you have you facts and nomenclature together, you have to babystep the officer into this. You can use this manual to guide your officer step-by-step into every good thing your client did even before you get to the SFSTs.

Using the tactics outlined below, walk through these important points:

1) A DUI Investigation is a 3-step process
   a. Vehicle in Motion
   b. Personal Contact
   c. Pre-Arrest Screening
2) In each step of this process, the officer is given a host of tools that are statistically correlated to a likelihood that a driver is above .08.
3) Name every single thing your officer DIDN'T see your client do.
4) Walk through the SFSTs in Pre-Arrest Screening—talk about the clues. See if the officer actually knows them. Most likely the officer doesn't. Every mistake the officer makes triggers the invalidity of the test(s).

Using this manual and these tactics, you can literally walk your officer into being the best witness for your client. You walk the officer through every observation he made (or didn't make) one statement at a time, and watch the foundation of sobriety you can build. Below you will find a tactical article entitled "Babystepping a Cop into Saying your Client Is Sober" that I wrote in 2013 for an email listserv. I'm including it in full. Even though it repeats some of the material found elsewhere in this chapter, it consolidates the material into a useful "script" like approach. In essence, it shows you how to use a single witness (the officer) to tell the story to the jury that your client was sober.

A More Radical Approach

Let's look at this approach with the Standardized Field Sobriety Tests (SFSTs). There are as many ways to approach these as there are attorneys, but I suggest a rather radical approach: have the officer perform them. I know we are taught never to ask a question or conduct an experiment in court to which we do not know the answer or outcome. But I submit: you cannot lose by having the officer perform the SFSTs.

During direct examination, the officer has told the jury how he or she explained and demonstrated all the SFSTs to your client, who then failed them miserably. What assumption have the jurors made? They have decided the officer must have demonstrated them properly. In the juror's minds, the cop was perfect.

So, if you ask for an in court demonstration, what can happen: (1) the cop is perfect, which the jury expected, or (2) he isn't.

Let's step outside the trial for a minute. When do most arrests for DUI occur? During the night shift. What shift do most officers who make DUI arrests work? The night shift. What shift are most officers coming off of to testify? The night shift. When is the trial? During the day shift. This is the officer's normal sleep time. What is a major reason for poor performance on SFSTs, at least according to real scientists? Being tired.

This is a near perfect juxtaposition of events. A tired officer who has been working all night and sitting around all day waiting to testify is now asked, without warning, to perform the SFSTs just as he or she did before arresting your client.

Q: Officer, please explain the One-Leg Stand exactly as you did to my client that night.
Q: Officer, please demonstrate the One-Leg Stand exactly as you did to my client that night.

I always start with this test, as it is the easiest to explain while leaving the officer with little time to prepare. It is the hardest to do when you are tired, and the officer "cheat" is easy to spot. By "cheat" I mean that officers know if you bend the standing leg a tiny bit it is easier to hold position. Look for the officer to do this. If you catch it, actually push the leg into a locked position.

Yes, I know this will cause a commotion, but, if the jury sees the officer's leg snap back into a locked knee, then the anger is with the officer for cheating. This is the perfect place to unleash the killer defense attorney at the outrage and falsehood being attempted. But then come back to the nice guy. Let the jury know you were outraged for them.

If the officer, and almost all officers do, fails this test, do not attack. Remember we are kinder and gentler. Give the officer the excuse before he or she says it.

Q: I see you put your foot down early; have you worked a long shift?

A: Been up for a while, about 15 hours is how I count it.

Q: Hope you get overtime for this. (Gratuitous I admit, but it gets a laugh, keeps you on the 'good' side and is great for closing).

Q: Then you had to sit here waiting for us?

Q: Maybe got a little cramped up?

Q: My client told you he had worked the same number of hours you said you did?

Q: Bob told you he had been sitting in the car for the same amount of time you have been sitting?

Q: So Bob failed this test, just like you just did?

Do not ask why or leave any other opening for the officer to attribute your client's failure to alcohol and the officer's own failure to some other cause. It is a simple statement. Bob did not do it; he failed. The officer could not do it; he fails. It is blatantly unfair for the officer to attribute Bob's failure to alcohol and not fatigue if the officer's own failure, which mirrored Bob's, was due to fatigue.

It is up to you if you wish to go on. If you obtained the one failure, I would say stop. If not, go on to the next SFST. Again, you have nothing to lose. If you do move on to the other tests, change them. For example, change the feet on the Walk-and-Turn, but be sure to change the turn direction, unless the officer "wrong footed" your client.

If you change the feet position at the start, along with the turn direction, a tired officer will get it wrong. Some of them will be inexperienced or cocky enough to say it is because you gave the test differently than they give it.

Q: But officer, didn't you say part of these tests was the ability to follow simple directions?

Q: Does swapping left for right make the directions complex?

Q: You have done them your way a million times. It would be easy for you to do them that way, but not easy my way?

Q: That's because you have never done them that way before? (Do not ask if your client has performed these before as it may open the door to prior stops and/or convictions.)

In some jurisdictions, officers use a finger count test. This is particularly good for change. I have practiced both hands in both directions for so long, I could probably be the world champ. Officers always find one way they like and stick with it. When I changed up on one officer and told him he failed, he accused the test of being "subjective," his actual word. I sat down and said "Exactly."

See Appendix A *The District Attorney's Manual* for the prosecution's approach to direct examination of the arresting officer on FSTs.

§4:04   Article: Baby Stepping a Cop into Saying your Client Is Sober

By Jonathan Dichter

One of the most important concepts for our clients to understand is that the prosecutor's job is to **prove** they did it. Our job is to point at the prosecutor and say "they didn't prove it!" It's rare in a DUI case that we find ourselves with an alibi or a client who wasn't behind the wheel. Most often our arguments are:

1. Our client wasn't impaired.
2. The evidence doesn't show our client was impaired.
3. See #s 1 and 2.

And most often there's one primary witness - the officer in question. Leave the Tech and Tox to their machinery for now. The officer is the one who saw your client and is telling the jury he's convinced that the impairment was "obvious". But he's also leaving out a few points. Let's take a look at a standard DUI stop and arrest decision narrative. Here are the rough facts:

*   Defendant is speeding 10 miles over the limit.
*   Upon contact, the officer notes a strong odor of alcohol, bloodshot watery eyes, flushed face.
*   Defendant admits to a couple of beers.
*   Defendant agrees to SFSTs.
*   Defendant fails SFSTs.
*   Defendant blows a .11 on PBT.
*   Defendant is arrested because he's obviously impaired.

Sound familiar?

Here's the problem with this factual scenario. It leaves out a ton of information. And it's all good information for you. Imagine that—A cop only writing in his report the stuff that makes your client look guilty. So how do we get to the rest of that information? And what is it? Let's step through it moment by moment and task by task. There are some basic headers you're going to cross this officer about.

Tie Him to the Report

Tie Him to the Manual

Step through the Timeline

And it must be done in this order or you risk losing control of your witness and getting hammered.

Here's my rough outline of tying an officer to the report. The goal is to establish right away that if it happened, it's in there. If it's not in there, it didn't happen.

Q: You were trained at the academy to write police reports, yes?

Q: You write police reports in order to document the relevant facts to a case?

Q: You write police reports in order to refresh our memory later at trial?

Q: You're trained to be as complete as possible in writing a police report?

Q: You're trained to be accurate in writing a police report?

Q: You're trained to be precise in writing a police report?

Q: You're trained to be truthful in writing a police report?

Q: Generally you compile a police report as soon as possible after the incident, so it's as fresh as possible?

Q: You've reviewed the report today while testifying?

Q: You've reviewed the report prior to testifying to refresh your memory?

Q: Is it as complete as possible?

Q: Is it accurate?

Q: Is it precise?

Q: Is it truthful?

Q: Is there anything that you want to add to your complete, accurate, precise, and truthful police report?

Q: It's safe to say that if something relevant to a DUI arrest had happened, you'd have noted it in the report?

Q: So your report is the best record we have of your investigation and observations?

He can't leave that report now. If he does, he looks like an idiot. But we're not done setting the stage yet.

Q: You attended a NHTSA training course on DUI detection and SFSTs?

Q: You were trained in noting the cues of impaired driving?

Q: First observing the vehicle in motion?

Q: This helps you determine whether or not to make a traffic stop?

Q: Then observing the stop sequence?

Q: Making personal contact with the driver?

Q: This helps you determine whether or not to ask the driver out of the car?

Q: Observing the Exit sequence?

Q: And administering the pre-arrest screening of the SFSTs?

Q: This helps you determine whether or not to arrest a person on suspicion of DUI?

Now we need to establish that he was watching. We don't want "I didn't see anything"—we want "no, it didn't happen".

Q: Officer safety is rule number one, correct?

Q: You are told that every day?

Q: If there is a choice between your safety and getting a bad guy, your safety comes first?

Q: You were taught at the academy, and know from experience, that road stops are among the most dangerous aspects of an officer's career?

Q: Danger can come from the traffic around you and from the individual you stop?
Q: You have no idea who is in that vehicle, so you approach the car with the utmost care, and expect the worst case scenario?
Q: This is especially true at night?
Q: Your primary tool to keep yourself safe is your senses—sight, sound, etc.?
Q: So you're going to watch as closely as you can?
Q: Especially the subject's hands?

Now you're ready. His report is full, he's trained to watch, and he was in fact watching. Now let's go to the Manual. (NOTE: This isn't going to work with every stop;—you need to look at the cues. But if there's none, or only one or two—it'll work. Obviously you need to adapt to your case)

Q: NHTSA has identified 24 separate visual cues of impairment that you are trained to look for while observing a vehicle in motion?
Q: Each one is statistically correlated to a likelihood that a driver is impaired? Chapter V page 4
Q: Defendant showed not one single cue? (Note—speed isn't one of them)
Q: Not even to the slightest appreciable degree?
Q: NHTSA has also identified several cues of impairment that you can look for while observing the stopping sequence?
Q: Each one is statistically correlated to a likelihood that a driver is impaired? Chapter V page 10
Q: Defendant showed not one single cue?
Q: Not even to the slightest appreciable degree?

Now it's possible that the officer will fight you on these. If so - just open the manual to the section I've indicated and read each individual cue to the officer. (Was he weaving? No. Drifting? No. Etc.) If he says yes, and it's not in his report, impeach with his prior testimony about completeness. Now to the stop.

Q: Defendant recognized that you were a policeman pulling him over?
Q: He pulled to the right side of the road?
Q: He used his turn signal to pull over?
Q: He began pulling over immediately?
Q: He was showing complete mental clarity?
Q: Nothing appeared to be affecting his ability to think?
Q: Or drive?
Q: Not even to the slightest appreciable degree.

Don't forget your client had to identify himself at some point, right? How? Usually a license.

Q: You approached Defendant's car on the driver's side?
Q: You introduced yourself?
Q: Asked for license and registration?
Q: He seemed to understand all your requests?
Q: Never asked for one to be repeated?
Q: He produced his license from his wallet?
Q: Provided license—no dropping etc.?
Q: It was valid and in force?
Q: He produced his registration?
Q: Provided registration—no dropping etc.?
Q: No problems with his fine motor skills at this point?
Q: Not even to the slightest appreciable degree?

You can even go further with this line of questioning. You asked Defendant questions about his driving or drinking or whatnot. He understood. He seemed coherent, polite, and cooperative. Now let's get him out of the car and check his gross motor skills.

Q: You are trained by NHTSA to observe the exit sequence for cues of impairment?
Q: He exited the vehicle?
Q: He didn't react angrily?
Q: He didn't act confused?
Q: He followed your instructions?
Q: No problems opening the door?
Q: Didn't leave the car in gear?
Q: Didn't climb out of the vehicle?
Q: Didn't lean against the vehicle?
Q: Remembered to take off his seat belt?
Q: Didn't put his hands on the vehicle to hold his balance?
Q: Of the cues NHTSA trains you to watch for, he exhibited zero of them during the exit sequence?
Q: He showed no problems with his gross motor skills during the exit sequence?
Q: Not even to the slightest appreciable degree?

Every moment you're making him look more and more sober. And what you're doing is generating reasonable doubt for the jury. Because we all know what a "drunk guy" at .14 should look like right? And does your client look that way? Is your client falling down? Confused? Goofy? None of these things. You can use these same techniques to baby step through the SFSTs to show your client didn't do as badly as the officer says he did. And if he looks and acts sober NORMALLY—is it possible that the junky BAC machine might have gotten it wrong?

For slides for combining the "baby stepping" portion of the officer's cross examination with burden of proof arguments, see Ch. 7, §7:114.

[§§4:05-4:09 Reserved]

II.   THE POLICE REPORT

§4:10   Lock the Officer In

The first principal in cross-examination is to set boundaries. When dealing with an officer, expert, or any witness who has created a report, the boundaries have been set for you in the report. Your job is to establish those boundaries as unassailable before the chance to squirm through any hole exists. The following routine can be used for just about any witness who created a paper trail, but is especially useful for police officers.

Q: Officer, you went to the academy?
Q: Part of your training was in how to create the numerous police reports you would need in the future?
Q: It was stressed to you to be complete?
Q: Many cases do not get to trial for some time after your involvement?
Q: Therefore, the report must be complete so you can testify to all the relevant facts?
Q: You were also trained to be accurate in the report?
Q: Again, accuracy is necessary so you can give testimony at a later date and not have to rely purely on memory?
Q: It may seem obvious, but you were also trained to be truthful in the report?
Q: In this case did you make a report?
Q: Was it complete?
Q: Accurate?
Q: Truthful?
Q: Is there anything in your complete, accurate, truthful report that is not complete, accurate or truthful?
Q: Therefore we can assume it is a full report?

Now the officer cannot add in any facts that are not in the report (completeness); cannot change any misstatements (accurate); and cannot deny anything in the report you want to read to him (truthful).

Q: Officer, you are trained to record all important facts close in time to the event?

Q: You are taught to take notes?

Q: And to write a report based on those notes when the events are freshest in your mind?

Q: You reviewed your report before you signed and submitted it for review to your supervisor?

Q: You used your report that you made close in time to the events to refresh your recollection prior to coming here to court to testify?

Q: You have had many other cases since this one and obviously cannot remember ever fact of every case without using your report?

Q: In fact, one of the first things you did after you received your subpoena to testify was pull your report and review it?

See Appendix A *The District Attorney's Manual* for the prosecution's approach to the police reports and direct examination of the arresting officer.

§4:11   Establish Bias

A second aspect to bring out on cross-examination is the reason the police report was created in the first place. The following example is based on work by one of the top DUI defense attorneys I know, Timothy Huey of Ohio. He suggests the following to establish the report for just what it is, biased and slanted.

Throughout the trial the officer will be using his or her report in order to aid testimony. The report can be devastating in a trial since (1) it looks official and (2) the officer will use it to clear up any mistakes or inaccurate memories he or she has.

Q: Officer, do you remember when the prosecutor was asking you questions earlier and your memory of the facts was so insufficient that you needed to refer to your notes several times to find the answers he was looking for? Do you recall that?

A: I glanced over my report yes.

Q: Is that what you have there in front of you?

A: Yes.

Q: And at some point you gave a copy of that material or discussed some things in it with the prosecutor, correct?

A: Yes.

Q: She has a copy, right?

A: Uh yeah, I think so.

Q: You think so? Didn't you write that report primarily to provide it to the prosecutor?

A: (All possible answers to this are good. See below.)

Q: You do not mean you sent an improper ex parte communication directly to the court do you?

A: (If he says "yes"—and he might—then ask the court to take "Judicial Notice" that it would be improper. The judge will probably volunteer, "and it didn't happen, either."

Q: What you really mean is that you know the prosecutor can give it to the court (or read it to the court) for purposes of a plea and sentencing in cases where the defendant pleads guilty or no contest, correct?

Q: And usually you are not present in court for that, only your paperwork is, correct?

Q: Now, if the defendant pleads no contest—as long as you put enough incriminating evidence in the paperwork to appear to make it look like a good DUI charge—the court will find him guilty. If you don't put enough evidence in there, the court will find him not guilty or dismiss the case. That's what you learned in police school right?

A: I'm not sure what the court does, I just write down the facts.

Q: But you know that if your paperwork is not good enough, the court will dismiss the case, right? Or perhaps the prosecutor will not file one in the first place?

A: Yes. (Or, "I know that can happen, but it has never happened to me.")

Q: Wouldn't you agree that it would be kind of embarrassing to have a case dismissed when the defendant tries to give up, plead no contest and doesn't even challenge the case? That wouldn't be a high point in your career would it?

Q: You wouldn't want that to happen to you, would you?

Q: So you want to make your paperwork pretty strong, right?

Q: Now, the "paper allegations" might not be strong enough unless there are things in there like, "strong odor of alcohol about his person," "bloodshot eyes," and standard stuff like that. You've got to have a bit of that in there to make sure you don't suffer the dismissed case we just talked about, don't you?

Q: By the way "strong odor of alcohol about his person," is that different than "on his breath?"

A: It can be. (Come back to this later.)

Q: But a strong report needs more in it than bloodshot eyes and a strong odor, right?

Q: You have to allege the person walked or talked like a drunk. You also need to put in those standard signs, to avoid the dismissal, don't you?

Q: Now you said you wrote your report "for the court," but a strong report can have other purposes, true or false?

Q: In fact, the court does not see or hear your written allegations unless the accused person sees the handwriting on the wall, despairs, gives up, and just pleads guilty or no contest without any hearings, no trial, no testimony from you and no cross-examination challenging your story; no challenges whatsoever, correct?

Q: And you know an accused person might be encouraged to "give up" based in part upon a review of the unchallenged "evidence" in your report, isn't that true?

A: (He might have a decent answer for this, but so what?)

Q: So it never occurred to you that an accused might look at your paperwork and dispute some or most of the allegations, and could think you lied and be pretty upset by it—but decide to plead guilty or no contest because he or she knows, true or not, it's his or her word against yours? You're saying it's impossible someone could feel that way?

Q: In any event, you do know that an accused person who just throws in the towel and pleads guilty or no contest based on the "evidence" in your report will never be able to raise questions about or even attempt to disprove anything in your written account, correct?

Q: And lots of folks—heck, most folks—plead guilty or no contest without really putting your written account to the test, true?

Q: In fact, most of your reports pretty much go unchallenged, don't they?

Q: So really, whatever an officer wants a judge to believe, he can put in there without much fear of contradiction, right?

Q: If an officer gets a little sloppy, tells a few white lies, or exaggerates a little, no one is really the wiser, right?

Q: Those things could only come out if someone is strong enough to stand up and actually challenge the case, right?

Q: If that happens, you, or any officer, have to pretty much go with whatever is in the report; it would be a little too late to correct any misstatements then, right?

A: I submit the report to my supervisor.

Q: But he never does anything with it, does he?

A: He approves it.

Q: But you already filed charges before that, right?

A: Yes.

Q: Has your supervisor ever rejected your report in a DUI case and told you to immediately go and withdraw the charges?

A: No (or an even better answer, for us.)

Q: When the supervisor approves the report, he is making sure it meets his standards for such reports, right?

A: Yes.

Q: He is checking out and approving the way you wrote the report, right?

A: Pretty much.

Q: And if he sees something that needs to be corrected in an officer's report or has suggestions on how something could be better phrased, he will tell the reporting officer his thoughts. Again that is the point of the "review;" that's how you learn to write a good report, right?

A: Yes.

Q: And the officer will usually make any corrections his supervisor suggests. That's one of the points of the approval process; if it is not up to his standards you fix it, right?

A: That is part of the process, yes.

Q: And after the supervisor "signs off" on the report, then it goes to the prosecutor, right?

A: Back to me and then to the prosecutor.

Q: So finally, after the supervisor has made all the corrections and suggestions, that's when the prosecutor gets it, right?

A: Yes.

Q: So again, it is primarily written for the prosecutor's use, as I said earlier, right?

A: Yes.

Q: Thank you for answering that question the way you did. I didn't know this is a corrected and improved report.

A: My reports don't need correcting.

CROSS-EXAMINATION

Q: As far as we know, you mean. But we have no way of telling that from the report, right?

A: This report was not corrected.

Q: So you are saying you write darned good, bulletproof reports, right?

A: My reports are found to be satisfactory.

Q: I imagine they are, no matter what facts you actually viewed.

Q: All right, now this morning when you and the prosecutor were huddled in the back room for 45 minutes, I presume you discussed a few of the more important issues involved in this case, or were you discussing something else when I walked in and she asked me to leave? (Or "give us a few minutes.")

A: Well, we talked about a lot of things (Raise your eyebrows, etc.) and yeah, we quickly went over a couple things about this case.

Q: But your memory of the true facts of this case was a lot better before you and she talked, wasn't it?

A: No!

Q: The true facts of the case were not any fresher in your mind this morning when you woke up than they are now?

A: No.

Q: Well, were they clearer when you woke up or are they clearer now?

A: Well it's clearer now that I have reviewed it, in my own mind.

Q: And you were able to recall this case and discuss the specific details with the prosecutor, right?

A: Yes.

Q: And I presume you were able to remember the little details after you looked at your notes and got up to speed, right?

A: Well a little better, yes.

Q: And you did look it over before or while you and the prosecutor reviewed your testimony. You prepared at least a little before you came up to the stand, right?

A: I glanced over my report, yes.

Q: And you and the prosecutor did discuss matters that were in your report, correct?

A: A little.

Q: And Officer Fife was back there with you, right?

A: Yes.

Q: And you all also discussed some of his thoughts about the case, right?

A: A few.

Q: And he had written those down previously also, correct?

A: Yes.

Q: And the prosecutor has a copy of that too, right?

A: I think so, yes. (See, "you think so!?")

Q: And you did not suffer from sudden amnesia or loss of your mental abilities between the time you took the stand and your joint review of your and Officer Fife's prewritten testimony?

A: No!?

Q: But still, you needed to refresh your memory again while you testified, true?

A: Just a couple times.

Q: So since you got up this morning, you have glanced at or reviewed your notes a few times, correct?

A: Only the times I just talked about.

Q: Well, at this point—right now—do you have a pretty good grasp of your and Officer Fife's prewritten testimony or do you need to look it over again before I ask you about it and other things? (You could skip a lot of the above and just go to this question. But it is not nearly as much fun. And really does not expose the report for what it is.)

A: I don't need to review anything now.

Q: So you finally have it all memorized?

Q: Great. Your Honor, under [appropriate local evidence rule], I am entitled to review all written materials used to refresh this officer's recollection before or during testimony. May I do so now?

Court: Sure, If it gets you moving. But whatever you do, you'd better be done by lunch.

[Step forward and relieve the officer of the reports. As you read, them start questioning. Don't give them back until after you are done with him or the prosecutor or officer are dumb enough to try and get them back.]

Q: By the way, do you have any other written material relating to this case?

A: Well I have. . . .

Take all of it. (Go through above again if you have to.)

§4:12   The Supplemental Report

Jay Ruane from Connecticut is considered one of the masters of the business side of DUI work. Although he tends to fly below the radar in the trial work of DUI, once you see this idea of his, you will see why he wins.

When crossing the cop establish the following:

Officers write supplemental reports in some cases. It's not unusual to follow up when you find out new information or realize you left something out;

Then give the officer a chance to review his report in your case, and give the officer a pen and tell him to make any needed changes, alterations, deletions, etc. Nine hundred ninety nine times out of 1000, the officer will say "nothing to add or change."

Then break out a clean plain white sheet of paper and ask the cop to identify it as plain. Then say "Let's call this your "supplemental report" and by your testimony right now you said you have nothing to add, so let's write "supplemental report" on the top and you sign your name to it on the bottom for me."

Offer it as an exhibit. How can the state object to a plain piece of paper coming in?

Then begin substantive cross. Get the officer to admit all the things he didn't write in the report, like how your client got out of the car OK, didn't stumble, fall, didn't drop his registration, didn't lean against the car, etc.

Once he admits all these things on cross, get him to add them to his "supplement" since they are his true observations that night which didn't make it into his report, but he is testifying to them now. If the officer had observed any of these things he would have put them in. He has seen them in other cases, but didn't see them here. Wait until the end so he doesn't get wise to adding each item to the paper.

Build up all the good things that are consistent with innocence in the cross, then write them all on the blank piece of paper. Get him to admit that by not saying your client fell over while getting out of the car, it means "he got out of the car ok" in the supplement– which now, as a full exhibit, will go into the jury room with the jurors, to counterbalance the police report that they are getting.

I can even see getting the cop to say that even though his police report states that your client failed the HGN, he left out the part that his training didn't teach him anything about how the HGN impacts a person's ability to operate a car. So the line would read something like: "Based on my HGN testing of Mr. X, he failed, but I do not know anything about whether or not this shows his inability to operate a motor vehicle because it was not in my training."

[§§4:13-4:19 Reserved]

III.   THE INITIAL CONTACTING OFFICER

§4:20   Goals

The main point you need to make with this officer is to show either that:
- The client's driving was not indicative of DUI; or
- The indicative driving was not that bad.

If the stop was for a technical violation, it is pretty easy. If it is for run-of-the-mill violations, speeding, rolling stop, minor weaving, your work is to show that happens to all of us.

It is only when the driving pattern is particularly egregious that you may need to get into details of what was going on. With an accident case, which is what every juror fears from your client, you need to demonstrate that if the officer did not smell alcohol, he would not have made a determination as to fault. It was only his conviction of alcohol as a factor that led him to believe the accident was your client's fault.

This is where you will also start to build the lack of connection between the chemical test results and the client's behavior. In other words, the client does not have the manifestations of drunk driving.

The points to be made here are:
- The client's driving was not that bad.
- In fact, the driving pattern by itself is not proof of DUI.
- Driving in a safe, but illegal, manner is not proof of DUI.
- Your client's initial reaction to the officer's lights, siren or whatever the police used was consistent with sober driving.
- Your client's mental faculties were not affected.
- Your client behaved appropriately and as we all would have under the circumstances.

You can then go into the officer's approach to your client. Use the material below to set up how nervous both the client and the officer were. You can later use nervousness to explain any bad behavior or actions by your client. The client was obviously startled by the passenger side approach. The client's eyes were obviously blinded by the lights.

Again, you build your client's mental acuteness by his or her ability to respond to the officer's directives—by his or her ability to provide the necessary information to the officer.

The points to be made here are:

- Intentional off balance questioning and contact by the officer created much of the symptomology.
- The officer is trained to put suspects in a bad position.
- Too much light flooded the client's car for his or her pupils to adjust.
- The client was scared.
- The officer intentionally tricked the client.
- Your client responded appropriately.

See Appendix A *The District Attorney's Manual* for the prosecution's approach to direct examination of the arresting officer.

§4:21   Technical Stop (for Burned Out Lights, Expired Registration etc.)

Q: The first time you saw my client there was nothing unusual in his driving?
Q: You state he was stopped for the bad tail light?
Q: Anyone can have a burned out tail light?
Q: In fact, usually such an offense results in a "fix it" ticket?
Q: So nothing about the tail light contributes to a determination of guilt?
Q: Would you agree that the overwhelming majority of people you have stopped for such an offense were not involved in DUI?
Q: So then the odds are that such a person is not DUI?

§4:22   Driving Violation: Speeding

Q: My client was speeding?
Q: You pull over hundreds of individuals for speeding?
Q: Most of them get a warning or a ticket and are let go?
Q: Speeding, according to NHTSA is *not* an indicator of DUI?
Q: In fact, speeding requires *more* attention to details, as road events happen much more quickly?

§4:23   Driving Violation: Illegal Turn

Q: You observed the moving violation, an illegal u-turn?
Q: Did John cut anyone off?
Q: Did he hit anything?
Q: Did anyone have to avoid John?
Q: In other words, aside from the illegality of the u-turn, there was no danger or other safety issues?
Q: Had John made this turn under the same conditions and in the same manner at a different location, one in which the u-turn was not illegal, then it would have been fine?
Q: So his driving, while technically illegal, was not reckless?

§4:24   Accident

Q: You did not witness the accident?
Q: Your job in an accident investigation, with no alleged DUI, would be to take statements, make a report, and clear the scene?
Q: In such a case, you do not make a definitive decision as to who was at fault, since you were not there?
Q: That is left up to the parties, which sometimes means a civil suit?
Q: In such a lawsuit, you would only testify as to what you *actually saw*?
Q: In this case, however, you have testified to your opinion as to fault even though you were not there?

Q: You based this on the allegation that John was DUI?

Q: If John had not been allegedly DUI, you would not have had an opinion?

Q: John and the other person gave differing stories about the accident?

Q: In this case, again because of the alleged alcohol use, you believed the other person over John?

Q: Do you always disbelieve someone who has consumed alcohol?

Q: Is every accident the fault of one who has consumed alcohol?

Q: So if I asked you if a person sitting at a red light was rear ended by another driver, and the victim said the light was red, but he had been drinking, you would still say it was his fault?

Q: Are you allowed to issue a ticket for a violation of traffic codes you do not see?

Q: This is because if you did not see what happened, it is not your job to decide fault?

Q: But in this case, you did decide fault merely because John had consumed some alcohol?

Q: Therefore, if you are the officer, regardless of the facts, if there is an accident and someone had alcohol, it is that person's fault?

Q: John never had a chance with you?

§4:25 NHTSA Criteria

Rather than go into every aspect of the NHTSA criteria, I would suggest you read the NHTSA SFST Training guide and question from there about every type of driving behavior that can be observed but was not seen by this officer. See above.

§4:26 The Stop

Q: Once you observed the (fill in reason for stop), you activated your overhead lights?

Q: John reacted immediately and appropriately?

Q: John did not come to a screeching halt, but rather slowed down and pulled over?

Q: John did not stop in the middle of the street?

Q: He did not drive up on the sidewalk?

Q: John did not keep driving?

Q: In all your years of experience in DUI stops, have you seen people stop in the middle of the road?

Q: Seen them hit the curb or other cars?

Q: Drive up on the sidewalk?

Q: Keep driving?

Q: Do a variety of other totally out of the expected driving patterns?

Q: But John did none of this?

Q: He showed appropriate mental ability by an appropriate reaction to your signal?

Q: Once he pulled over, did he remain in the car as required/instructed?

Q: Did he put the car in park, or otherwise secure it?

Q: You must have seen people who jump out of their car?

Q: People who are so intoxicated they leave the car in gear?

Q: People who have the car roll because of not securing it?

Q: John did not exhibit any of these signs of mental impairment?

§4:27 Stop Set-Up

Q: At the academy you are taught that officer safety is rule number one?

Q: You are told that every day?

Q: If there is a choice between your safety and getting a bad guy, your safety comes first?

Q: You were also taught at the academy, and know from experience, that road stops are among the most dangerous aspects of an officer's career?

Q: From both the concept of the traffic around you, and from the individual(s) stopped?

Q: You have no idea who is in that vehicle, so you approach the car with the utmost care, and expect the worst case scenario?

Q: In so doing, there is a specific way you park your vehicle behind the car in order to (1) maximize your safety, and (2) minimize risks?

Q: This is especially true at night?
Q: One of the 'weapons' at your disposal for this is your vehicle?
Q: It is not only big and metal, it has a lot of lights on it?
Q: You have been trained how to use those lights to increase your safety?
Q: The lights can be focused in such a way as to illuminate the entire inside of the car so you can see what is going on in there?
Q: And also, you can use the lights to limit, if not prevent, the occupant of the car from seeing you?
Q: To do this you pull your car slightly *inside* the other car?
Q: In other words, you line up off center to the inner part of the road?
Q: This is also safer for you to exit your vehicle since you will be exiting on the traffic side?
Q: This then places your passenger headlight in the passenger mirror of the stopped vehicle?
Q: Your driver's lights are aimed at the rearview mirror of the car?
Q: Did you have a side spotlight?
Q: Did you use it?
Q: That is aimed at the driver's side mirror?
Q: In other words, all of your lights are used to try and prevent the occupant(s) from using their mirrors to see you?
Q: This also places a large amount of light inside the car's passenger compartment?
Q: You can see what (if anything) the people do?
Q: Now you make your approach?

§4:28   Approach

Q: Do you use a driver's side or passenger side approach?
Q: When approaching from the passenger side, you do not walk in between the lights of your vehicle and the suspect's car?
Q: You walk behind your car, and then up the passenger side of the two cars?
Q: You then make yourself known at the passenger window?
Q: You would agree that most people who have been stopped would be looking for you on the driver's side?
Q: Suddenly becoming aware of your presence at the passenger side would be startling?
Q: In fact, that is part of your safety mechanism, to startle someone in case they did mean you harm?
Q: When you approach the driver's side, you do not walk right alongside the vehicle?
Q: You approach at an angle in order to see what is going on in the car?
Q: You do so in order to be safe?
Q: It affords you the best view of the entire car, and hopefully prevents bad guys from getting a good view at you?
Q: You then make yourself known quickly in order to stay safe?

(Both of these will explain any "nervousness" on the part of your client in the first few minutes of contact.)

§4:29   Pre-Exit Interview

Q: Once you establish contact with the driver, you do a quick look in the vehicle for your own safety?
Q: You "scout it out?"
Q: Then, you ask for a driver's license and car registration and proof of insurance?
Q: While an individual is getting these, you ask some other question, such as why they think you stopped them?
Q: This is a taught technique to try and see if the individual can do two things at once?
Q: You are taught this trick in the DUI training?
Q: Ever been to a wedding?
Q: Ever seen the bride and groom have trouble with the vows and rings at the ceremony?
Q: In other words, while placing the ring on a finger and saying whatever is being said, ever seen the person be nervous, drop the ring, misspeak?
Q: Now, presumably they were not drunk?
Q: And you did this to John?
Q: You have made hundreds of traffic stops?
Q: You usually ask what the person thinks he did wrong?

Q: I am sure you could make all of us laugh with some of the answers you have received?

Q: Would you admit that many people have not been honest with you?

Q: Have people told you they had no idea how fast they were going, then admit they did?

Q: People ever deny running a stop sign?

Q: Anyone ever tell you the light was still yellow?

Q: Now giving false information to a police officer is a crime?

Q: But none of these people were arrested for what they said?

Q: In fact, it is part of the routine to have people be less than forthcoming when pulled over?

Q: Anyone ever tell you they had no idea their license, registration, insurance was expired?

Q: So it is fair to say you get lots of less than true answers during a traffic stop?

Q: None of them mean the person is DUI?

Q: It is just a fact of life?

Q: John did tell you why he was stopped?

Q: He was honest with you?

Q: He did show good awareness of his situation?

Q: Where was John's license?

Q: Registration?

Q: Insurance?

Q: John did not have any problem getting those for you?

Q: You said he fumbled for his license, was it in his back pocket?

Q: Did you give him a chance to stand up to make it easier to retrieve?

Q: Did you let him undo his seat belt?

Q: How big was John's wallet?

Q: You said he could not immediately find his insurance/registration?

Q: Was it in his glove box?

Q: Was his glove box like most of ours, a complete mess?

Q: Did he eventually find the right one?

Q: In order to do so, didn't he have to read a lot of other papers?

Q: So he was able to discern the right papers from the wrong ones?

Q: Officer, ever been given a completely incorrect response to the license registration question?

Q: Ever get a credit card?

Q: Library card?

Q: Were all those people DUI?

Q: Could it have been nervousness?

Q: Yet John gave you the right papers at the right time?

Q: And when you asked him where he was going, or whatever you did in an attempt to distract him, as per your training, he answered appropriately?

If the officer reported that the client had slurred speech, ask the following questions. The idea is to establish that any "slurred speech" issue is not supported by the officer's actual conversation.

Q: During this process, was there anything you did not understand?

Q: Tell me, what words or conversation was slurred?

[§§4:30-4:39 Reserved]

IV.   THE ARRESTING OFFICER

§4:40   Goals

As this is a nationwide book, we will act as if each player is unique. This is true in some jurisdictions, whereas in others, the first officer does it all. Regardless of how it is done in your locale, the points to be made are the same. I have just broken them into the individual components in order to lend some structure.

The main focus of the arresting officer, or questions related to the next phase of the investigation, is to continue to build the premise that your client had no lack of mental capabilities. You should also deflate or defuse any admission of drinking or change in that respect to number of drinks. Finally, the arresting officer is the person who gave your client the roadside maneuvers known as SFSTs. These need to be attacked at this point.

There are a number of ways to attack SFSTs. I have included the most common showing them to be biased, unfair, and irrelevant. If you wish, you may also attack their validity, but that is generally not a question for the jury.

Points to be made:

- Your client still showed no sign of mental impairment.
- It is not uncommon to deny wrongdoing.
- SFSTs showed physical but not mental problems.
- None of the results of the field tests really matter.

See Appendix A *The District Attorney's Manual* for the prosecution's approach to direct examination of the arresting officer.

§4:41   General Questioning

One major defense in DUI cases is to show a lack of mental impairment. This is important because *every* expert in the world will admit that alcohol causes mental impairment before it causes physical impairment. This means, if there is no sign of mental impairment, then any physical signs must not be due to alcohol.

Q: During your encounter with John you asked quite a few questions?

Q: You spoke quite a lot? (If the officer denies this, any comments about slurred speech would be unsubstantiated. How can the officer know of slurred speech if there were only a couple of one word answers?)

Q: Without deciding whether John was telling the truth in the answers he gave, were his answers appropriate to the question?

Q: In other words, you asked if he was under the care of a doctor or dentist?

Q: What did he say? (If the DA objects as calling for hearsay, indicate the answer is not being introduced to its truth but for the appropriateness of the response, *i.e.*, that he had no mental breakdown. Also, the answer can be introduced to show lack of slurred speech. In either case, much of your defense can be elicited from the officer this way.)

Q: You asked him where he was coming from and where he was going to?

Q: What did he say? (You can get the long work shift out this way, or the almost home rising alcohol defense.)

Q: In other words, he was able to articulate (argues against slurring) an appropriate answer to all your questions?

Q: Jumping ahead, did you get a chance to verify any of this information, such as John's correct address?

Q: So his answers, as far as you could verify, were also true?

§4:42   Admission of Drinking

Q: At this point you asked John if he had been drinking?

Q: He denied it?

Q: You already told the jury that many people you stop deny the reason for the stop, such as saying the light was yellow?

Q: So this is not uncommon?

Q: This is not someone trying to make up a story?

Q: It is just sort of a natural reaction?

Q: Officer, are you married?

Q: Ever come home late?

Q: Did you always tell your spouse the real reason you were late?

You can substitute curfew as a kid, gambling loss versus wins, or a host of other ideas. The point is to show even this person has made stuff up.

Q: Eventually my client admitted to drinking?

Q: He even told you how much?

Q: Was this before or after you informed him of his *Miranda* rights?

Q: Now *Miranda* indicates that what a person says to you may be used in court?
Q: Yet you never told him of this prior to these questions?
Q: And here you are telling it to the jury?
Q: So at this point, Officer, did you arrest my client?
Q: But you did have him exit his vehicle?

§4:43   The Exit

Q: You instructed John to exit the vehicle?
Q: He did so?
Q: Did he take off his seat belt first?
Q: Ever see someone who did not?
Q: Ever see it on the NHTSA training video, known as "The Business Man"?
Q: Not taking it off would show a lack of mental ability?
Q: Did he have car in park/brake on?
Q: That is appropriate?
Q: Not doing so would be a sign of mental impairment?
Q: Did you conduct your further investigation there?
Q: You told him to move to another location?
Q: He did so?
Q: Followed your instructions?
Q: Went to the new location?
Q: Waited for you?
Q: He did not run?
Q: He did not fight?
Q: He did everything you asked?
Q: These were all fairly regular tasks?
Q: Everyday kind of things, get out, walk, wait etc.?
Q: John did them all with no problem?
Q: You then talked with him for a minute or two?
Q: Did you tell him what was going on?

(If the answer is no, then argue to the jury later that it was a total set up. If the answer is yes, continue.)

Q: So John knew that his freedom was at risk at this point.
Q: He knew it was time to face what came next or he could go to jail.
Q: That would make a person nervous, wouldn't it?
Q: So you commenced your investigation using SFSTs at this point.
Q: But you told us during direct that your "investigation" was based on all the circumstances?
Q: That no one factor counted more than any other?
Q: To this point you have seen some minor bad driving (or none if technical stop), no lack of mental ability, ability to follow instructions, and appropriate reaction or responses to a situation?
Q: To this point there is not enough to arrest John?
Q: So you set up some tasks to see if you can get enough to do so?

§4:44   SFSTs

Q: You first gave the NHTSA HGN SFST?
Q: Then you gave the One-Leg Stand?
Q: Then the Walk-and-Turn?
Q: Okay, please stand here and demonstrate the One-Leg Stand exactly as you did that night.
Q: Did John appear to understand your instructions? (The officer must say yes. If not, then the results are not relevant since a failure to understand the instructions means the scoring is irrelevant. Officers will always say yes to this.)

Q: He stood where you asked?

Q: He listened?

Q: He told you he understood?

Q: When told to do so, he lifted a foot?

Q: He stopped when you said or when he felt he could not do any more?

Q: You found this to be wrong?

Q: You told us that John did not perform as instructed?

Q: Okay, was the failure to perform as instructed due to alcohol or is John a clumsy person?

Q: Officer, step down here please?

Q: When I tell you so, I would like you to lift either leg approximately six inches off the ground and hold it that way for 30 seconds. Keep your hands down at your sides and if you put your foot down, please lift it back up. Oh, lift the leg behind you.

Q: Can't do it?

Q: Is that because you are drunk here today?

Q: Is it because you don't understand?

Q: Is it because you cannot follow directions?

Q: Is it because it is not something you normally do?

Q: Is it because you are tired?

Q: Not very balanced?

Q: Getting back to John, while he could not do the balancing act, he did try as best he could and did so in the manner you asked?

Q: So John failed because he is not athletic. I bet you won all the ribbons in summer camp, Officer?

Q: You gave him instructions on the Walk-and-Turn as well?

Q: He listened?

Q: Seemed to understand?

Q: Then tried it?

Q: Again you indicated he did not perform it to your satisfaction?

Q: Oh, by the way, where is the video for these tests?

Q: Wouldn't you agree that a video would be better proof of how John did than your explanation?

Q: You were trained with video?

Q: So, it is more important to have video to train an officer than it is to judge a person in court?

Q: Can you please explain and demonstrate the Walk-and-Turn just as you did that night?

It is too cumbersome to go into every detail to look for on this test. In fact, the previous example is only a base of what can be done in the OLS test. In order to be able to fully exploit the NHTSA SFSTs, a DUI defense attorney should, at the least, attend the Administrator course, if not the Instructor course as well. (Both the Student and Instructor Standardized Field Sobriety Test classes are offered by a number of organizations. Be sure that you enroll in the National Highway Traffic Safety Administration/International Association of Chiefs of Police approved curriculum. One such source is Robert La Pier of La Pier Consulting.)

Q: Was there a line?

Q: You asked my client to imagine a line?

Q: I would like you to walk my imaginary line.

Q: First, what color is it?

Q: What size?

Q: Heck, where are these lines anyway?

Q: So if you do not know the size, color, shape, or direction of the line my client was walking, how can you say he stepped off it?

Q: Let's get back to the facts though. John did in fact attempt to walk heel to toe up an imaginary straight line, turn and come back?

Q: He appeared to understand what you wanted?

Q: But he could not do it as you asked?

Q: If I asked you to walk down a 4 x 4 beam on the ground, you could do that?

Q: If I took that same beam, and lifted it 50 stories in the air, that would be a challenge?

CROSS-EXAMINATION

Q: This is a phenomenon we are all familiar with?
Q: The board does not change?
Q: You do not change?
Q: But the gravity of the situation changes, thereby making you nervous?
Q: You told us John was aware of the gravity of his situation?
Q: So he had that same nervousness affecting him?
Q: Now you also gave the HGN test?
Q: Did John understand the instructions?
Q: Did he attempt to follow them?
Q: He stood still?
Q: Kept his head still?
Q: Followed the pen with his eyes and his eyes only?
Q: No problems?
Q: So he could follow these directions?
Q: You observed the onset of nystagmus prior to 45 degrees?
Q: Are you familiar with all the other causes of HGN?
Q: You were trained that HGN can be caused by brain injury?
Q: It can occur naturally?
Q: It can be optokinetic?

Keep going in this vein from whatever DUI manual you would like to be able to use. Once the officer indicates an "I don't know" ask to refresh his memory. Use your book to do so. Do this several times, each time using less of an identification of your book. This will allow for future reference to the book without the officer being able to deny its veracity.

Q: Officer, you are familiar with caloric nystagmus?
A: No.
Q: Do you recall being told of it in training?
A: I don't recall.
Q: Let me show you the Department of Transportation, National Highway Safety Administration Standardized Field Sobriety Test Administration Manual to see if that refreshes your recollection.
A: Okay.
Q: Does that refresh your memory?
A: Yes.
Q: Caloric nystagmus is [read the definition from your manual].
A: Right.
Q: What are PAN I and PAN II Nystagmus?
A: I don't recall.
Q: If I show you the NHTSA Manual, will that refresh your recollection?
A: Yes.
Q: Exactly how long should a NHTSA HGN test take?
A: I would have to add it up.
Q: If I showed you the manual, would that help? [Bingo, the manual is now evidence.]
Q: Okay, so to sum up to this point, you have asked John to perform a number of tasks, all of which he appeared to understand?
Q: John was unable to perform them to your level of satisfaction?
Q: His failures were purely physical?
Q: He did not fail to comprehend what was going on?
Q: You learned about these tests at the academy?
Q: In fact, you took several hours of training on them?
Q: You had to pass a test at the end in how to administer the tests?
Q: I assume you passed?
Q: Were you able to give the instructions and demonstrations exactly right the very first time you heard of them?
Q: No, you had to practice?

Q: Especially how to move a stimulus for the HGN?

Q: It is difficult?

Q: But eventually, you passed?

Q: Now how many times did you give John to practice?

Q: How many attempts did John get?

Q: How many hours did John have to study?

Q: In other words, with no warning, no practice, no experience, John was given these tests in the field knowing his freedom was at stake, and he was not given a chance to explain, retry, or practice?

Q: Officer, you have a driver's license?

Q: Did you take driver's education?

Q: Did you practice before your road test?

Q: Do you think you would have passed without all of that?

Q: Well officer, before we go much further, I would like the jurors to see what the scene looked like, so can you do this for me:

Q: With the black marker, please draw the roadway and all crossing streets, plus the lane configuration, including a north arrow. Then, draw my client's car in blue, using an arrow to show which way it was facing. Then, put all police vehicles in red, also with a red arrow indicating which way the cars were facing. Finally, use the green pen to draw the location of the field tests, including use of arrows in green to show where and how the field tests were oriented. Mark all street names in red, and draw and label for the jury any adjacent businesses or residences in blue.

(This example is courtesy of William "Bubba" Head of Atlanta, Georgia, who has allowed me and others in the DUI community to paraphrase his original example. It contains almost the exact number of words and tasks as the Walk-and-Turn test. Use it that way. In other words, give the officer this "SFST.")

§4:45   Preliminary Breath Tests

More and more jurisdictions are using some kind of roadside breath test. The best use from the defense point of view for this test is to attack the previous investigation. If you can show that the cop had no clue what to do up to this point, then what use is the previous investigation? If the officer will let your client go upon showing a 0.00, then the previous SFST exercise was one of futility.

Q: Did you use a preliminary breath test?

Q: Are you in charge of maintaining this device?

Q: John blew into it?

Q: You had him do so because you still had not made up your mind if John was under the influence?

Q: If the result was 0.00, then your thoughts to this point would have been wrong?

Q: John was not under the influence?

Q: That would mean that John's performance on the SFSTs was not satisfactory just because John is not coordinated enough for you?

Q: But the results did show alcohol?

Q: Just as John had told you?

Q: So John had been honest with you?

§4:46   The Arrest

There is still some room here for development of the "no mental impairment" theme. Show how your client knew what was going on and made intelligent choices.

Q: Now, you finally decided to arrest John?

Q: You told him so?

Q: Was his reaction appropriate?

Q: He knew what this meant?

Q: He showed no sign of non-comprehension?

Q: You have a choice at this point with regards to John's vehicle.

Q: You can have it towed, leave it there if it is safe and legal, or have it moved by yourself or someone else, if John says it is okay to do so?

Q: Did you talk to John about this?

Q: Did he understand?

Q: Did he make a decision that was appropriate?

Q: You also told John that at this point he was required by law to submit to a further testing of his blood, breath or urine?

Q: Did he understand?

Q: Did he make an appropriate choice?

Q: So you then transported him for that test?

§4:47   Drinking Pattern

Perhaps no other area is important as the drinking pattern. If the prosecution cannot establish a solid drinking pattern, then any resultant chemical test is subject to interpretation. In some jurisdictions, the drinking pattern may be subject to irrelevancy objections since there is a presumption of applicability of the breath test to the alcohol level at the time of driving that cannot be countered. In other words, some jurisdictions state that the test result is the driving BAC regardless of elapsed time and science. While officers often ask a little of the drinking pattern, like "When did you start drinking?" and "When did you stop drinking?" they never get into the type of detail that is necessary to disestablish a rising alcohol defense.

If you can couple the lack of mental impairment to the rising alcohol defense, the not guilty verdict is practically in your hands. By setting up the lack of information from the officer, any hypothetical to the state's expert regarding rising, falling or other alcohol level later can be disregarded, or possibly not even allowed.

Q: Did you ask John when he started drinking?

Q: Did you ask when he finished?

Q: Did you ask what he had to eat?

Q: Did you ask when he ate?

Q: Did you ask what he was drinking?

Q: Did you ask the size of the drink?

Q: Did you ask how much John currently weighs?

Q: You got his weight from his license.

Q: If guilt or innocence were based on the weight on a person's driver's license compared to the person's actual weight, how many men would be "innocent?"

Q: How many women?

Q: Did you ask what John's drinking pattern was like?

Q: Ever play softball or basketball in the summer?

Q: Have a couple of beers afterwards?

Q: Ever go to a barbecue and drink some beer?

Q: Ever go to a fancy dinner and drink some wine?

Q: What about a wedding?

Q: How about a college party?

Q: Would you agree that you drank differently in each of those situations?

Q: Sometimes you drink more in the beginning of the event and less later on.

Q: Other times it is the other way around.

Q: How was John drinking that night?

§4:48   Transportation and Observation

More and more courts are holding that the 15 minute observation period, the time that an officer is required to watch your client in order to ensure a proper breath test, which all experts agree is critical, can be satisfied in a pro forma method. This means that instead of the face-to-face observation to ensure no burping, regurgitation, ingestion etc., which can foul a breath test, merely being present is good enough. Sometimes, it can even be a client in the back of the squad car while the officer is driving. One has to wonder how can an officer ensure no hiccup under such a scenario, but the courts have found that officers have such ability. However, state experts do not always go along with this program. Try to set up gaps and mistakes in this protocol to be used against the breath expert later.

Q: You took John to the breath test facility?
Q: While you were driving, you were communicating with dispatch?
Q: Told them who you were, who you had, and what was happening?
Q: John was in the back?
Q: How fast did you drive?
Q: Was there other radio traffic?
Q: Were you driving carefully?
Q: So your attention was divided?
Q: You kept your eyes on the road?
Q: Your ears open for your call letters/names on the radio?
Q: Watched for other bad traffic violations?
Q: In other words, you kept doing your job on the road? (Then how could he have performed a proper observation period of John?)
Q: When you arrived at the breath test facility, you exited the car?
Q: Walked to open the door for John?
Q: So for that few seconds, John was not within your hearing, or smelling, and was only within your limited sight?
Q: Do you have to secure your gun? (If so, set up more gaps in observations).
Q: Did you help John out of car?
Q: He was handcuffed?
Q: Behind his back?
Q: Got out with no problems, or at least the same as others who are so encumbered?
Q: Did he understand where he was?
Q: Did he follow your directions?
Q: Was he aware of what was happening?
Q: You took him for the breath test?

§4:49   Strategy for Winning Refusal Cases without Defendant's Testimony

Common wisdom is that when your client refuses to provide a breath sample, the jury wants to hear from him. Jurors want to know why. I have never had a client testify in a refusal trial—because it's not our job to prove why our clients did something. We have spent hours now proving this to a jury.

Instead, I have developed a refusal strategy that works so well in my jurisdiction that since stumbling onto over it over 10 years ago, I've only lost two refusal trials.

I'll go a step further and admit to something shocking. Even if there's a really strong legal argument to do so, I rarely move to suppress refusals pretrial. I like them admissible against my clients.

Now there are instances where I will move to suppress refusals—just rarely. Also—I will always explain to my clients the risk this entails, including higher penalties if they lose (but in my professional opinion, a better chance of winning)—and give the client the option. I explain it in writing with a "trial risk form" I've generated and have the client sign. The form includes the penalties if the client loses at a trial without a refusal as well as with a refusal in evidence. It also explains the legal issues that could result in suppression of the refusal. Finally, it explains that as a trial lawyer, I believe the client's case is stronger with the refusal admissible than without. I discuss with the client the risk/reward calculation the client has to go through and then let the client make an informed decision.

So how and why do I think the case is stronger with refusals admissible? It's something I learned from the late, great Pat Morita.

In "The Karate Kid" Daniel Larruso sees his mentor Mr. Miyagi performing a kick on a stump at a beach. When he asks him about it, Miyagi tells him:

"It's called Crane Technique."
Daniel asks if it works.
"If do right, no can defense."

This is how I feel about my refusal argument. If it's done properly, I don't see a valid counter argument for a prosecutor to make. I've had juries find not guilty after head on collisions because of this argument.

In voir dire, if you're using the strategy I outlined for you (see Ch. 2A), you're priming the jury to presume innocence. You are also getting them to acknowledge the burden of proof. You want them saying that it's absolutely the State's job to prove guilt. You don't have to prove anything. The entire burden lies with the State. The State will likely "gladly accept" this mantle. That's exactly what you want.

If you're really lucky, you'll even have a prosecutor say something in Opening like "some bad driving and symptoms of alcohol consumption might be enough for you and me, but not for Trooper Friendly. The State Patrol wants more proof." Usually this goes into the SFSTs. But make a note of it. You'll come back for it later.

Now—go through your normal cross with the officer. At the conclusion, you add a few simple questions. But BEWARE here. Do not go too far. You do not need to underline your point. You just need to make it. Trust me—the prosecutor will do the rest for you.

Here's the script for cross-examining the officer:

Q: When you offered my client a breath test, he declined to give one?
A: Yes.
Q: Now when someone declines a breath test, you have the ability to get a warrant at that point?
A. Yes.
Q: All you have to do is call a judge and request one?
A. Yes.
Q: And assuming the judge grants one, you can take that person to the hospital?
A. Yes.
Q: And you can forcibly draw the person's blood?
A. Yes.
Q: Whether the person likes it or not?
A. Yes.
Q: And have it analyzed for alcohol content?
A. Yes.
Q: And we'd all know today what my client's blood alcohol content was on that day?
A. Yes.

Now - resist the urge. Don't you dare ask that next question. Do the right thing, shut up, and SIT DOWN. I'll say it again—TRUST ME—the prosecutor will do the rest.

On redirect, the prosecutor will likely ask a question like this: "Trooper, do you always get warrants for blood? Or this "Trooper, do you actually have the authority from your agency to get a warrant for blood?" Or even this: "Trooper, why didn't you get a warrant for blood in this case?"

You don't care what the answer is. The truth is that many troopers would have to call their supervisor for approval, and would then be told no because on "routine" DUIs they just don't request blood. In addition, sometimes you will get the even more fun answer of "I didn't need one; he was smashed," which if you're paying attention is essentially the officer saying "trust my assumption."

Now wait for closing. When you get to the point where you're going to talk about the refusal, here's how you can turn that simple admission into one of the most powerful arguments you can make.

Remind the jury that it's the State's job to prove this case—not suggest it—not assume it—not infer it. Prove it. And they could have. But they chose not to do so.

Let that sink in and say it again. The State (the trooper, WSP, whomever you can lay blame at the feet of) chose not to prove this case.

And why? (This is the first part of the one-two punch.) Because this case wasn't important enough to investigate fully. (Hey – the State assumes stuff about your client all the time—we might as well assume their motives, too.)

Ladies and Gentlemen, the six of you, weren't important enough to demand real proof.

Now push this as often as you think you can without seeming like a jerk. Then when you sum up at the end—hit part two of the one-two punch. It's not just that the State didn't prove the case to you; in fact, they actively avoided proving the case to you.

Remind the jury that they were not important enough for real proof, but rather only for guess work. Remind them that they promised you in voir dire to hold the State to their immense burden (which the State welcomed)—and if you're lucky—remind them that the police wanted better evidence than guess work (see above)—and if that's what they wanted, shouldn't we hold them to it?

Then wait for the prosecutor's rebuttal. Every time I've made this argument, prosecutors simply ignore it in rebuttal. And why wouldn't they? How on earth do they justify an incomplete investigation when there's no good reason not to do one?

Answer: they can't.

Because there is no justification. There is no excuse for trying our citizens without proof when they have the ability and authority to get it. Whether a simple .08 first offense or a vehicular homicide, we should require our government to prove cases. And this argument calls that to the forefront.

About a year ago I got a phone call out of the blue from a DUI attorney in Kansas. I'd never met the gentleman before, but he called me. He'd been going into a felony refusal trial a few days prior and had no idea how he was going to get through it. His client was facing years in prison. He did a search of listserv we're members of and found a write-up I did of this argument.

"I literally found it the night before trial. I had no time to even adapt it. I printed it and read it verbatim from the page. The jury found my client not guilty in 20 minutes. I'm crediting you with this win."

I'm not saying this will work in every trial, but I am saying if you have not thought of encapsulating the burden the State has this way, you're missing a huge story to tell.

[§§4:50-4:59 Reserved]

V.   THE BREATH TEST OPERATOR

§4:60   Goals

If this is a handoff jurisdiction, meaning the officer who made the arrest is not the officer conducting the chemical test, then the prior aspect of bad observational activities needs to be highlighted. If it is not, then follow up with the other problems in breath testing. Some of these include temperature issues with your client, partition ratio, bad machines, estimations, inaccuracies, etc.

You can also use this as a time to show the jury that the machine is only half tested, if that. Show them that no one ever really put this device through its paces. Finally, get the state's witness to admit that when all is said and done, the best we get is a number, floating in space, which may or may not reflect the blood alcohol of your client.

See Appendix A *The District Attorney's Manual* for the prosecution's approach to direct examination of the breath machine operator.

§4:61   Observation

Q: You have been trained on breath testing?
Q: The most important aspect is to have a good sample?
Q: This requires a 15 minute observation period?
Q: You did not do one in this case?
Q: So you cannot say what belching, if any, John did prior to getting to you?
Q: You do not know how much chaw he had in his mouth?
Q: You do not know when he last hiccupped?
Q: When he last threw up?
Q: Or anything else prior to your meeting John?
Q: If the sample is contaminated, the results are no good?
Q: So based on what you know, the results in this case are still open to question?

§4:62   Accuracy

Q: What is a simulator?
Q: Is temperature of the simulator solution critical?
Q: In other words, in order to be assured of the machine's working capability, we test it on a known sample of alcohol.

Q: That known is based on a temperature of the simulator.

Q: 34 degrees Celsius to be exact, plus or minus .2 degrees Celsius?

Q: If the temperature is off more than that, then the results are not accurate?

Q: Every degree of temperature above that number creates a 6% increase in reported breath alcohol content?

Q: A breath machine does not measure the alcohol concentration in the blood, does it?

Q: It measures the alcohol concentration breath?

Q: We then, or more accurately, the machine then converts the breath concentration to a blood equivalent.

Q: What is the software that does this?

Q: Do you know how it works?

Q: The formula makes a number of assumptions?

Q: First, it has to assume a ratio of alcohol in the breath to alcohol in the blood?

Q: That is because breath and blood do not exist in equal proportions in our body?

Q: We have way more blood than breath?

Q: So if we want a blood alcohol number, and we use breath to get it, we have to multiply the breath by some number to get the blood equivalent?

Q: What is that number?

Q: Where did it come from?

Q: Does it represent everyone in the world?

Q: So that a 250 pound male has the same ratio of breath to blood as a 100 pound female? (By framing the question in the negative, an affirmative answer seems more ridiculous to the jury).

Q: What you really mean is that there is an assumed average used for the conversion?

Q: Let's talk about numbers for a few minutes. We all know what average is, you add the numbers up, then divide the answer by the number of numbers you added up.

Q: What is range?

Q: What is median?

Q: What is mean?

Q: So the "average" you used before is really the mean of the range?

Q: Let's look at this jury. If we took their weights and added them up and then divided by 12, we would get the average weight of the jurors?

Q: That does not mean everyone is that weight?

Q: Same with their height?

Q: If we took their height average and their weight average, we could then go get a suit from Macy's. This suit would not fit all of the jurors?

Q: In fact, chances are it would not really fit any of them?

Q: If, on the other hand we used the median weight or height, and bought the suit to fit that one measurement, the number that is in the data for which an equal number are above and below, then one person would fit the suit and the others would not?

Q: This 2100 to 1 is an average?

Q: So you cannot say that ratio is correct for everyone?

Q: In fact, it is more likely that the ratio is not correct for a particular person?

Q: If a person's ratio of blood alcohol to breath alcohol is lower than average, then the person's true blood alcohol would be lower than reported by the breath machine. And that is because the breath machine multiplies the alcohol in the breath by the average ratio to get the alcohol in the blood?

Q: Conversely, to be fair, if a person's ratio for the relationship between blood alcohol and breath alcohol were higher than average, the report from the breath machine would be lower than the person's actual blood alcohol?

Q: So all we know is that the reported breath result in this case may be an accurate reflection of blood alcohol?

Q: Getting back to the temperature, was it checked on the machine?

Q: When?

Q: How often?

Q: Was it accurate?

Q: Is this important?

Q: It is in fact so important, it is a regular part of the maintenance of the machine?

Q: It is written in the manufacturer's manual and in the laws regarding breath testing themselves?

Q: So you are positive that temperature had no effect on the breath machine?

Q: What about my client?

Q: He is a "machine?"

Q: John has a temperature that would also affect the breath results?

Q: John's temperature would have the exact same effect on temperature as would the temperature in the simulator.

Q: Then if John were running warm, the breath results would overstate his blood alcohol content?

Q: So again, the breath results in this case are not the true blood alcohol level, just an educated guess?

Q: Putting aside these fluctuations which may affect the true levels, the results only indicate what John had in his breath at the time of the testing?

Q: In other words, none of this tells us what John's blood alcohol was when he drove?

Q: You did not observe John's driving?

Q: You did not observe John's performance on any roadside tests?

Q: You did not take John's temperature?

Q: You did not check John's partition ratio?

Q: All you can tell us is that he blew a number?

Q: Not whether it accurately reflects his blood alcohol at the time?

Q: Not whether it accurately reflects his breath alcohol at the time of driving?

Q: And surely not if it accurately reflects his blood alcohol at the time of driving, the critical issue in the case?

Evidence of individual variations in partition ratios is not admissible in all jurisdictions to refute a charge that the defendant was over the legal limit. Many jurisdictions have circumvented the need for partition ratios by amending their statutes to provide that driving with a specific level of breath alcohol is an offense. As a result, their courts have refused to admit partition ratio evidence. *See, e.g., People v. Bransford*, 884 P.2d 70 (Cal. 1995) (testimony of defendant's individual partition ratio was inadmissible, especially when the defendant exhibited clear signs of alcohol); *Burks v. State*, 394 S.E.2d 136, 137 (Ga. Ct. App. 1990) (testimony of a defendant's individual partition ratio of 1680:1 on day before trial was inadmissible when the defendant exhibited other visible signs of intoxication). See Chapter 1 for a motion to allow the admission of partition ratio evidence in certain circumstances.

§4:63   Maintenance

Q: You are in charge of maintaining this machine.

Q: When was the last time it was calibrated?

Q: So it needed a correction?

Q: These machines can be inaccurate?

Q: That is why you check them?

Q: How often?

Q: Now do you do it, by phone or in person?

Q: What do you check?

Q: So it is fair to say that the basic check of this machine is to ask it to tell you if it is okay on the inside, which you do not physically check, then run a simulator through it to see if it guessed correctly?

Q: This is the latest, greatest breath machine on the market? (If the witness answers no, then ask why not).

Q: It has a number of safeguards?

Q: It checks to see if RFI (radio frequency interferants) are present?

Q: RFI is why we have to turn off electronic devices prior to take off and landing on a plane?

Q: RFI is the emission of electric signals by all electric devices outside of their "shell?"

Q: RFI has been an admitted concern in breath testing?

Q: If RFI is present and not picked up, it can interfere with the breath testing?

Q: This would cause bad results?

Q: The machine also checks for ambient air failure?

Q: This means alcohol in the room?

Q: Possibly from clothing?

Q: Or if the last person tested really reeked?

Q: Almost anything that is creating alcohol vapors in the room would do this?

Q: The device also checks for mouth alcohol?

Q: That is residual alcohol from recent consumption, or burping and the like, which will skew the results?

Q: There are also filters and such to be sure the results are alcohol and not a similar compound?
Q: In point of fact, this machine does not check for "alcohol" as we define it?
Q: Instead it checks for certain chemical bonds in the ethyl group of molecules?
Q: This group is also found in other substances, especially in the paint thinner, varnish field?
Q: Now during the regular maintenance of the device, it told you it was okay on all these areas?
Q: No one physically checked to see if the RFI detector was working?
Q: No one checked to see if the machine knew the difference between alcohol and turpentine?
Q: No one blew into the machine in a smelly room?
Q: No one tried to fool the slope detector?
Q: So all you know is that under pristine conditions, *i.e.*, via the phone to an empty room on a Monday morning with a non-human subject, the machine got it right one time?

[§§4:64-4:69 Reserved]

VI. THE STATE'S EXPERT

§4:70 Goals

Not every state brings in an expert to tie it all together. Some states have an independent person for this; other states leave it all up to the arresting officer. In either case, the key to a compelling cross-examination of a state's expert is your own preparation.

You must be in possession of, and have read, every article upon which your defense is based. You must know all the ups and down of the science. If you are discussing rising alcohol, be aware of the negative articles against you. Be sure to be armed with copies of the positive articles to support your position and know how to get them into evidence or at least be allowed to cross-examine the state's expert on his or her positions.

At the end of the book is a list of must-read articles and books for a serious DUI defense attorney (*see* Appendix F). Much of what will be discussed in the next section requires intimate knowledge of the science behind DUI.

Points to be made:
• This is not Joe Average on trial.
• No one can say what the client's blood alcohol level was at the time of driving.
• There is no dispute that mental capacities are affected before physical ones if alcohol is the cause.
• Any presumption of continual alcohol level is a farce.
• SFSTs cannot show a specific blood alcohol level.
• SFSTs cannot show driving impairment.
• Garbage in garbage out.

See Appendix A *The District Attorney's Manual* for the prosecution's approach to direct examination of its alcohol expert.

§4:71 Voir Dire

Do not automatically accept the witness as an expert. During your discovery, get the witness' CV and check it out. I have actually caught experts who lied in the CV. Further, since I fully believe you do not plow with another man's mule, meaning you always have your own expert, it can be critical to establish the ratings early on.

Q: Dr. State Witness—
A: I am not a Dr.
Q: Oh, sorry, our expert is… So what exactly is your Master's degree in?
A: I only have a Bachelor's.
Q: Can you explain peer-reviewed articles?
Q: Do you have any published papers at all?
Q: What is a correlation study?
Q: How many have you run, not participated in, but run?

Q: Okay, so would it be fair to say most, if not all, of your theoretical knowledge comes from reading rather than hands on studies, such as absorption rates?

Q: And how many articles have you read?

Q: Name some of the authors.

§4:72   Articles

Q: So you are familiar with Dubowski? Jones, etc.?

Q: Well, based on your reading, and not any personal studies, what is your position as to time to peak alcohol absorption?

Q: Can you please draw a standard alcohol curve for us?

Q: Would you agree that all of your testimony is based on the original work by Widmark?

Q: He is the one who figured out how much alcohol a man or a woman needs to drink to get to a particular blood alcohol level?

Q: From that you can figure out what a level would be based on consumption, or what consumption is needed to get to a level?

Q: Please write the formula on the board for us? (None of them can.)

Q: So, with only a BS degree, no personal experience, and you cannot even write the basic formula for all other opinions, you believe you are qualified to testify?

Q: Based just on what you have read?

Q: So I guess I'm an astronaut since I read *Apollo 13*?

§4:73   Science

Q: All of your answers today have been based on certain assumptions?

Q: You assumed a certain absorption time?

Q: You assumed certain drink sizes?

Q: You assumed certain alcohol percentages?

Q: You assumed certain partition ratios?

Q: You assumed certain temperatures?

Q: You made a ton of assumptions, none of which are known by you to be true?

Q: And if any of those assumptions were not true, the answer you gave would be wrong?

Q: Let's take an example. You indicated that John's statement that he had three beers was a lie.

Q: That is because you said three beers could not equal a .12 breath alcohol. If I show you and the jury it could, would you admit you were wrong in calling him a liar?

Q: Would you further admit that your testimony is tainted?

Q: Okay. First, what size beer did you assume?

Q: How do you know it was a 12 oz.?

Q: So since you do not, if it was a 22 oz. airport beer, then three of those would be a .12 or so, wouldn't it?

Q: So you were wrong and he did not lie? Tell the jury.

Q: Okay, maybe that was a bit unfair. What percentage alcohol was in the beer?

Q: Who told you it was about 5%?

Q: So if it was a stronger microbrew, the results would change?

Q: So if it were three 12 oz. 7 percent beers, it would be a .12.

Q: So tell the jury you were wrong.

Q: Okay, how about this, the Widmark formula is for blood alcohol, not breath?

Q: In order to use the formula for breath, you must convert from blood to breath?

Q: In doing so you use the 2100 to 1 conversion?

Q: How do we know if John is 2100 to 1?

Q: So you lied to the jury?

Q: In fact, with the three examples I have given, size, potency or John's own body, if they are changed to numbers, which are well within the range of normal, John told the truth and you condemned him anyway?

Q: Let's talk about ranges. Dubowski, who you said is a virtual god in the field, indicates peak absorption can be from 15 to 165 minutes?

Q: Jones, in his study on GERD confirmed peak absorption as about 70 minutes?

Q: Yet you use 30 minutes?

Q: Those studies were peer-reviewed?

Q: Your position has never been evaluated by your peers?

Q: So, these great doctors, in peer-reviewed studies, indicate a realistic time of about an hour to peak absorption, and you with your BS and no review claim to know better that it is a half hour?

Q: And that was based on your study of how many people? None, since you never did an independent study?

Q: Okay. Would you at least agree with all the other experts in the world that there is no mathematical formula for alcohol absorption?

Q: In other words, we cannot say at what rate a person goes up?

Q: On the other hand, we can state a fairly specific range for burning off or eliminating alcohol?

Q: That rate is about .02 percent per hour?

Q: The low being about .015 and a high of about .025?

COMMENT:

The numbers don't matter. Just the expert admitting there is a range, and we don't know the client's specific burn off rate.

Q: Again, though, such numbers cannot be placed on the absorption phase?

Q: So it is possible to go from zero to whatever the peak would be, based on how much was consumed, in one hour?

Q: And there is no way to graph this without continuous blood draws?

Q: So that based on the one reading in this case, you cannot say whether John was going up, coming down or at the peak when the chemical test was given?

Q: You would agree that blood alcohol levels change over time?

Q: In fact, you drew that for us?

Q: If I were to tell you to assume a blood alcohol level is constant over three hours, would you accept that as scientific?

Q: You would agree that blood or breath alcohol goes up shortly after we start drinking, peaks after we stop, and then goes down as we eliminate alcohol?

Q: So that saying you can presume a blood alcohol at 9:00 based on a test at 12:00 is absurd?

Q: In fact, without knowing the exact drinking pattern, you cannot say if the person's blood alcohol is rising or falling?

Q: In this case we asked the officer if he asked John his specific drinking pattern and it turns out he did not, so it would not be possible based on a single set of results to say which way his blood alcohol was heading?

Q: Let's switch gears. You are familiar with SFSTs?

Q: Name the study or studies that show SFSTs can be correlated to a specific blood alcohol level?

Q: Name the study or studies that show they can be directly correlated to impaired driving?

Q: Neither can be done?

Q: In fact, you know who Dr. Burns is?

Q: She "invented" SFSTs?

Q: Have you heard her position on them?

Q: Let me show you. (Introduce *U.S. v. Horn*, 185 F. Supp. 2d 530 (D. Md. 2002); *State v. Meador*, 674 So. 2d 826 (1996) and the deposition transcript of Dr. Marceline Burns. (See Appendix B.))

Q: She has said that SFSTs cannot be correlated to a specific BAC?

Q: Nor can they be tests of driving?

Q: So SFSTs are just a tool to aid in the arrest decision?

§4:74   Henry's Law

Q: You understand Henry's Law?

Q: According to Henry's Law, if water containing a particular concentration of alcohol is placed in a simulator and heated to a particular temperature, the concentration of alcohol in the vapor above the water will be a specific percentage of the concentration of the alcohol in the water based on that temperature. Isn't that correct?

Q: For alcohol in water at 34 degrees Celsius the vapor created will contain 82.7 percent of the level of the alcohol in the water?

Q: So that if a .10 percent solution of alcohol in water is placed in the simulator and is heated to 34 degrees, and the simulator is inserted in the breath machine the measurement of the alcohol in the vapor should read .086.

Q: If it reads .10, then the breath machine is clearly out of range.

Q: So if I showed you the PAS logs in this case, where the solution is listed as .10 and the temp is listed as 34 and the result is listed as .10, that would be fatal.

Q: Out of calibration?

Q: No good?

Q: Well, look at the exhibit [logs of the breath machine]. It shows a solution of .10 percent alcohol?

Q: That was heated to 34 degrees Celsius?

Q: The vapor of which was introduced into the breath machine?

Q: Which then read the vapor?

Q: And reported the *vapor* as .10?

Q: But we know, based on Henry's Law, the result *must* be .086 to be correct?

Q: So the machine was inaccurate?

Q: Now in this case, Henry's Law would apply to John as well.

Q: If his core body temperature were higher than the 98.6 norm, then the ratio of alcohol in the blood to alcohol in the breath would be off using Henry's Law.

Q: In fact, the reported breath alcohol result would be 6% higher for each degree John's temperature was above the 98.6 assumed norm.?

Q: In other words if John was running hot, the breath results would not be his true blood alcohol level.

[§§4:75-4:79 Reserved]

VII.   BLOOD CASES

A.   Background Information on Blood Testing

§4:80   In General

For many of us, cross-examination is our favorite part of trial. The concept of going one-on-one with the witness has a special thrill. We spend much time in training and lectures to learn as much as the officers about field sobriety tests in order to show them up during cross.

At the same time, unless we wish to go to medical or scientific training, we are less equipped to combat the blood expert. Even were we to be so trained and skilled, it is much more difficult to get a judge or jury to understand the issues in blood testing than in breath. Yet, as we run into more "drugged" driving cases, more jurisdictions that allow for officers to choose the test, and more people opting for blood, the blood test is becoming more prevalent.

The next few pages will be an attempt to help you develop some knowledge and skill in order to take on a blood test. Let's start with an outline of how blood is obtained for chemical testing and a look at the various procedures for testing. With this knowledge we will then explore some areas which are ripe for cross-examination.

§4:81   Taking a Blood Sample

Anyone with a little training, and the guide sitting right next to the machine, can take a breath sample. Push the button, wait for the tone, and have the person blow until the machine says stop. Simple. Blood is not so easy. Each state has its own procedures, but many of the general principles are the same. First, the blood must be obtained from a venous puncture. This is mostly for safety purposes, but also because venous blood reflects the alcohol that is currently passing into the system. The blood must be obtained using medically acceptable methods, *i.e.*, clean needle, vac-u-tubes etc., *but*, unlike most procedures using a needle, the skin must be cleaned with a non-alcoholic swab.

The sample needs to be obtained using a vacuum-sealed tube with an airtight stopper. In most states, both a preservative and an anti-coagulant must also be in the tube. All of this is usually done by some type of trained professional other than the police officer. Many states require that two tubes be obtained in order to allow for duplicate testing. The amount received is state-dependant (one tube or two) but is significant.

In order to prevent any fermentation in the sample, some preservative is necessary. The most common preservative is sodium fluoride. A specific amount of the preservative is necessary depending on the amount of blood being drawn. In other words, the specific amount of sodium fluoride in the tube is dependant on the volume of blood in order to achieve a set percentage. If the state has deemed it necessary to have a final outcome of 1% sodium fluoride, based on 5 ml of blood, then taking less blood would increase the percentage, as more blood would decrease the percentage.

See Appendix A *The District Attorney's Manual* for the prosecution's approach to direct examination of the phlebotomist.

§4:82   Transporting and Storing a Blood Sample

We will forget detailing chain of custody, as it is expected that practitioners understand this line of cross-examination. Once the blood has been drawn, the mixture of chemicals and blood must be integrated. Generally, integration is accomplished by inverting the tube several times. This is to ensure a good mixing without causing destruction of the blood cells.

The now-mixed solution must make its way from the locale of the draw to the site of the test. During this time period, the blood should, but does not have to be, refrigerated. The longer the delay, the more important refrigeration becomes. Documentation of custody and transportation is critical to ensure a chain of custody and should be obtained using the standard discovery practice for your jurisdiction.

Once the blood arrives at the lab, it is generally logged in, stored in some common refrigerator and not bothered with until the testing.

§4:83   Testing of the Blood Sample

There are several ways in which blood can be tested. The most common is gas chromatography. Two others, enzymatic and dichromate can also be used, but are not generally available. In order to fully understand the chemical aspects of blood testing, refer to Bartell et al., *Attacking and Defending Drunk Driving Tests* (James Publishing).

§4:84   Plasma vs. Whole Blood

In hospital settings, and some other jurisdictions, blood testing may be done after the separation of whole blood into its component parts. Then, only the plasma is tested. How and why this is done is unimportant; what is important to note is that any reported result from such a test must be re-calibrated to the whole blood value. Failure to do so can result in an overstatement of the true blood alcohol content by as much as 59% [*Relation Between Serum and Whole Blood Ethanol Concentrations* Rainey, 39 (11) Clinical Chemistry 2288 (1993)], this being the percentage of plasma versus the whole blood in the person's whole blood.

With that general description of the process, let's look at how to cross-examine the state's expert on some of the issues raised.

[§§4:85-4:89 Reserved]

B. Cross-Examination of Specific Witnesses

§4:90   The Witnesses

While we may generally think of the expert as the individual who provides the final testimony, *i.e.*, the blood alcohol concentration, blood draw cases usually have several people to examine. In the setting of the chemical aspects, there is the phlebotomist (the person who draws the blood), the analyst, the individual who takes the blood tubes and sets them up for the testing run in the machine the lab uses, and finally the in-court witness, who may be the analyst or may be a supervisor. Additionally, there are chain of custody witnesses, the officer or messenger service or whomever transports the blood, the receiving individual at the lab, and any people who have touched the sample along the way.

All of these should be at the trial. I would like to say *must* be at the trial, and indeed the *Crawford* case [see §4:130] would seem to so require, but many judges do not see it that way and will allow for presentation of some of this evidence through hearsay or declarations. This can actually work to your benefit, as it leaves many of the questions that follow unanswerable except by speculation.

§4:91   The Phlebotomist

We all know a blood test is a more accurate measurement of someone's blood alcohol content than a breath test. But the collection of blood is much more difficult the collection of breath. Additionally, due to budgetary concerns, blood draws are now often in the hands of virtually untrained police officers or technicians who have little concept of what they are doing—they can be easily attacked.

Points to be made:

- The witness has no knowledge of presence or level of preservatives in the vials in which the blood was collected.
- The witness has no knowledge of presence or level of the anti-coagulants in the vials in which the blood was collected.
- The witness took the blood from an artery instead of a vein.
- How and why the chain of custody has not been established.
- That there may be hearsay problems with the testimony about collection. See §§4:130-4:132.

Unlike a breath case, where you are often looking for specific answers (usually wrong ones) to your questions, most blood cross-examination will elicit a non-response. *This is good.* How can a trier of fact decide that the case is proven beyond a reasonable doubt if the witnesses answered a majority of the questions with "I don't know"? For example:

Q: Phlebotomist, of your own personal knowledge, how much preservative was in the tube at the time of the draw?
A: I don't know.

It is *critical* that the question be phrased in such a way as to relate *only* to the witness' personal knowledge. Otherwise, the witness may opine that it is "usually" or "supposed to be" or some other save-all. Second, you must prevent the prosecution from eliciting similar answers during re-direct. Such a question is improper as it is (1) hearsay if the witness is relying on what he or she read on the tube, and/or (2) speculation that it is actually in the tube.

Should you be lucky enough to be in a jurisdiction where the phlebotomist is not testifying, then the same query can be put to the witness on the stand with even more expectation of lack of knowledge.

Continuing on, we end up with a cross-examination, purely on the taking of the blood sample, where the majority of the answers, from the witness' own personal knowledge, is "I don't know."

Q: What was the name of the swab you used?
Q: When did you measure the amount of blood in the tube?
Q: What was the expiration date of the tube?

COMMENT:

This is important for one true reason and one speculative. If the tube is past its "shelf life," the vacuum may be compromised; that is the main reason for the date. An argument may also be made, although it is generally thought to not matter, that the chemicals, anti-coagulant and preservative, also may have a shelf life that has expired.

Q: What was the amount of preservative in the tube?
Q: What was the amount of anti-coagulant in the tube?
Q: What was the final percentage of each chemical to the sample?
Q: Did you use a clean vial?
Q: You used a wipe on my client when taking blood from the artery?
Q: How do you know it was non-alcohol?

COMMENT:

You may have objected during direct on hearsay grounds when she was asked what type of wipe she used. If your objection was overruled, renew it and ask the court to strike her answer since now it will be clear to all that she just read the label on the packaging and has no independent knowledge that the wipe contained no alcohol.

Q: Which arm did you get the arterial draw from, left or right?

Q: You never saw any driving?
Q: Never saw any roadside testing?
Q: Never asked about drinking?
Q: You told John where to sit?
Q: Told him how to hold his arm?
Q: Told him to make a fist?
Q: He did all this?
Q: He had no problems understanding you?
Q: You had no difficulty understanding him?
Q: In fact, John was very cooperative?
Q: You did not drop the vials?
Q: Did not alter them?
Q: Did not add anything to them?
Q: Take anything out?
Q: Who took control of the sample when you were done?
Q: Where was it stored?
Q: How was it stored?
Q: What about the second tube?
Q: You finished and handed the tubes carefully back to the officer?
Q: You watched as he did nothing to them and put them in the envelope?
Q: You were done?

Many of the questions in this line of inquiry should receive no real answer at all. Armed with these 10 "I don't knows," you can argue in closing that the complete lack of specificity in the obtaining of the blood sample compromises the entire operation. Moreover, you have now set the stage for total destruction of the blood test results by the lab tech or whoever reports the results. There is no proof of preservative or anti-coagulant, as she indicated a "clean vial." There is evidence of an arterial rather than a venous blood draw. There is no non-hearsay evidence that she used a non-alcoholic swab. And finally, there is no proof of vial inversion as required mixing the sample. No one in their right mind would trust such a sample.

To further bolster your argument that the blood results are not reliable, you can ask if the results are entirely dependent upon a properly obtained sample. The analyst must admit that if he or she is given a sample that has been compromised, then the resulting analysis is suspect. "Ladies and gentlemen, if I were to give you ice cream, milk, and syrup and told you to make a milk shake, in order to be sure it tasted right you are relying on me not to give you sour milk."

As previously mentioned, if the phlebotomist is not there, then the same line of questioning should be posed to the witness along with a few others.

Q: Of your own personal knowledge, was the swab non-alcoholic?
Q: Was the blood obtained from a vein or an artery?
Q: Was a new and clean syringe used?

The point here is to establish the old adage of "garbage in, garbage out." Without knowing these important details of the initial capture of the blood sample, the integrity of the entire process is questionable.

If the phlebotomist did not testify on direct examination that the sample was mixed, we have an area for some fun. Do not cross the witness on this. Instead, ensure the witness leaves mixing out and ends with handing the sample over to the officer.

Q: Officer, once you got the sample you were careful with it?
Q: You didn't sit there and shake it all up?
Q: You never tossed it around?

Keep going along these lines and like a colleague, you can get the officer to explain to the jury that he or she handled the tube(s) as if they contained nitroglycerin. Then in closing argument, you can read the instructions from the blood kit which *demand* inversion five to seven times.

Speaking of the blood kit, you should try to obtain one used in your jurisdiction. It will have the complete instructions inside. As any of you are surely capable, you can read these and turn the instructions into further cross-examination.

Before you let the phlebotomist go, be sure to establish that once the blood was given to the officer, the phlebotomist has no clue where it went or what happened to it.

See Appendix A *The District Attorney's Manual* for the prosecution's approach to direct examination of the phlebotomist.

§4:92   The Officer With Custody of the Blood Before Pick-Up and Delivery

Well, somehow the blood got from your client to court. Lots can happen along the way, just ask any FedEx package. Find out what went on. Every time someone new handled the blood, you can be sure a record was created. Be extensive in your blood discovery in order to find out what happened with your sample.

Q: Officer, after you deposited the blood in the lock box, what happened to it?

Maybe he knows, but probably not. This means you can drive a wedge into the integrity of the sample. Make sure to drive the following points home:
- What time the blood sample was taken.
- What time it was picked up.
- What time it arrived at the lab.
- How much time elapsed from the time the blood was drawn until it arrived at the lab.
- How it was transported.
- If it was transported by car, where in the car it was placed (in the hot trunk, for example).
- It was not refrigerated.
- The pick-up and delivery person is not here in court.
- What the delivery person did with it (one case showed the person took blood home with him).
- What happened along the way.
- Who was the delivery person anyway.
- Who the sample was delivered to at the lab.

Now an interesting controversy can be created between the police and the transportation access. The officer who took custody of the blood will want to insist he placed it in a secure location that no one has access to. The delivery person will obviously need to have access to pick up the blood. The officer who had possession of the sample before it was picked up will usually testify that he or she placed it in a secure location. Run rough shod over the officer about how unsecure this secure location may be. The first reaction of an officer to a defense question is to disagree, then to entrench on that disagreement.

Q: Officer, now this lock box, anyone can get to it.
A: No, it's secure.
Q: But it's in the middle of the station?
A: Only officers can get there.
Q: Is it locked?
A: Always.
Q: But you opened it.
A: No, there is a one way slot.
Q: Well, what if you mislabel it, can someone open it?
A: No one except the sergeant.
Q: So it can be opened?
A: Only by the sergeant.

§4:93   The Pick-Up and Delivery Person

To highlight the importance of the pick-up and delivery procedure, here is a quick true story. For years the area around Colusa, California, north of Sacramento, was serviced by Valley Toxicology, a private independent lab. Blood from local police stations was picked up, stored and then transported to the lab. No one ever questioned how this was done. Noting a lack of paperwork, I inquired of the officer if he knew. Turns out the lab hired a high school student to swing by the local police stations once a week to pick up the blood and deliver it. No paperwork, no logs, nothing. We were able to show that the kid not only had no idea how to handle the stuff, but he made pickups off schedule and fudged, and kept the sample a day or two if the weather was too bad to get it to the lab.

   Anyway, you see the idea. Now ask the delivery boy how he gets the blood.

Q: You make regular pick-ups?
A: Yes.
Q: You go through the sergeant?
A: No, I just go to the box.
Q: You use the police's key?
A: No, I have my own.
Q: Ever get sick?
A: Yes.
Q: Have a replacement?
A: Yes.
Q: He or she made the pick-up?
A: Yes.
Q: Used your key?
A: Yes. (Whether the answer is yes or no does not matter. A no is impossible based on his previous testimony. A yes contradicts the officer's testimony about "secure" lock box.)
Q: So, jurors, anyone who says she is from the lab can walk in, use a key, and get the blood. Not nearly as secure as the officer made it out to be.

   I am not saying this will be the Grail in your case. I am pointing out that the integrity of the sample has many problems. The question is whether or not a juror would trust this sample in deciding to undergo chemotherapy.

   Be sure to check your local law as to how quickly a sample needs to be tested. Can it sit around forever, or must any testing be done within 10 days?

§4:94   Login at the Lab

   Our happy little vials of blood have arrived in the lab. You can be darn sure there is a login procedure here. Someone is signing for all that blood. Find out who signs for the blood and what he or she does with it. Some labs store the newly-received blood in the "front" refrigerator where lunch is also kept.

   Cross-examine the person who logs in the blood as you would the transportation individual. Continue to show that this sample, supposedly kept intact and unavailable except for the analyst, is there for the taking for anyone who wants it.

§4:95   The Analyst

   Next is the analyst. Some person, the "analyst," usually newer in the lab, will come in and set up a run of blood and sometimes urine samples. A "run" is the actual use of the machine to test samples. A run is done when there are enough samples to be economical to run the machine. Included among the samples should be controls, internal standards, calibrations, and blanks. Be sure to review the documentation on these as well as your client's sample. See Bartell et al., *Attacking and Defending Drunk Driving Tests* (James Publishing) for details on these terms and processes.

   The analyst will take a small amount of blood from your client's vial. This will be put into two new vials for use in the GC (Gas Chromatograph). The internal standard is added, the vials are heated and so forth.

   There is a lot of room for error and inquiry here. What follows is just the tip of the iceberg. Hopefully, this outline will enable you to take on a blood expert and do so without fear.

Q: How much blood was removed from the original vial?
Q: How was that measured?

CROSS-EXAMINATION

Q:　How was the testing vial sealed?
Q:　How was documentation performed?
Q:　How is the transfer from the test vial to the sample port performed?

COMMENT:

There are two methods here, automatic whereby the GC does it all, or by hand. Clearly if it done by hand, there is more room for error.

Q:　When was the last time this method was checked for accuracy?
Q:　How is the internal syringe cleaned?
Q:　How did you clean your pipette?
Q:　When was the pipette last calibrated?
Q:　What is used as the internal standard?
Q:　(If headspace GC is used) What is the salting out agent?
Q:　Who mixed the internal standard?
Q:　When was it last checked?
Q:　When was the salting out procedure last verified?
Q:　When was the last time the internal syringe was calibrated?
Q:　What carrier gas is used?
Q:　When was the carrier gas regulator last calibrated/checked?
Q:　Who made the calibration standards?
Q:　How were they made?
Q:　How were they checked?
Q:　Are they water based?
Q:　Who labels the samples?
Q:　How are they labeled?
Q:　How are the results printed out?
Q:　Are the reports here in court the originals?
Q:　Is the final report a synopsis of other reports?
Q:　Who corrects any calibration errors?
Q:　When was that last accomplished?
Q:　Where were you during the run?

As you can see, the main problem with the final analysis of blood centers on measurements, calibration, and sterility. Use your imagination to explore all of these with the expert. The goal here is not traditional embarrassment of the expert, rather it is to create uncertainty with the jurors.

Q:　You would agree that if we are attempting to determine John's blood alcohol level, blood is more accurate than any other source?
Q:　In order to have a good blood result you need a good sample?
Q:　You were not present when the sample was obtained?
Q:　In order to have a scientifically valid sample, you need it from the vein?
Q:　Obtained with a non-alcoholic swab?
Q:　Placed into a container with preservative?
Q:　And anti-coagulant?
Q:　Mixed thoroughly?
Q:　Refrigerated until tested?
Q:　Then tested in an approved lab?
Q:　Now, you are from the lab and can attest to the procedure used once the sample got there?
Q:　Where did it (the blood or urine sample) come from?
Q:　If you do not know, do you know if it was refrigerated?
Q:　The phlebotomist told us the vial was clean and empty. This means no preservative was added. This means an invalid sample?
Q:　She told us it was an arterial draw?

Q: Again, an invalid sample?

Q: She told us she did not shake the vial?

Q: But since there was no preservative, shaking would not have helped anyway?

Q: So, while you can attest to the correct procedure, the sample given to you was not up to scientific standards?

[§§4:96-4:99 Reserved]

VIII.   DOCTORS

§4:100   Reluctance to Disagree With Other Doctors and Peer-Reviewed Articles

Once upon a time, doctors, lawyers, teachers, and police had the honor of holding esteem throughout society. Today, police are mistrusted, teachers are set upon from all sides, and lawyers are considered one of the least liked professionals around. Only doctors have held on to their position of respect and awe. Perhaps this is due to the reluctance of doctors to bad mouth each other. Indeed, it is rare to find a doctor willing to second guess another doctor's position on any medical call. Just ask your local medical malpractice attorney.

This creates both a disadvantage and an advantage for cross-examination in DUI cases. While the doctors will usually have very strong opinions about DUI, they will be very reluctant to deny the position of other doctors. In fact, most doctors who will testify in court are very used to couching their testimony in terms of likely and not likely, as opposed to the definitive terms used by officers.

Additionally, you will find that most doctors have limited, if any, personal familiarity with the DUI world. Instead, they will base their opinions on general knowledge, often learned years ago, and the current statements by the American Medical Association. It is therefore necessary to conduct full discovery prior to any confrontation. It is equally helpful to provide the witness with any and all publications that will support your point. This is one area in which opposing doctors are good for the defense. They will readily admit to the tenor, if not the actual findings, of virtually any peer-reviewed information.

§4:101   Some Words About the AMA

The American Medical Association is no different than the American Bar Association. It has no "authority" over its members as such. It is a voluntary group created mostly for political purposes. While it does take a position on a number of issues, that position is not binding on any one, nor is it necessarily a fact. Positions are created by various committees, then brought before the entire group and voted upon. Doctors are not required to belong to the AMA, and some of its positions are the position by a one vote majority.

The AMA defines "impairment" as *any* deviation from the norm. The deviation can be caused by any factor, external or internal. Hence the outcry recently over 'sleep-impaired driving.' You must be sure to elicit this information from the professional doctor witness. It goes a long way to undermining the prosecution's case.

§4:102   Sample Cross-Examination

Q: Dr. Smith, when did you graduate medical school?

Q: Have you done any studies of alcohol and its effects?

Q: Ever run a breath machine?

Q: Ever take a blood sample for alcohol determination?

Q: Ever run a GC or immunoassay?

Q: So, it is safe to say your testimony here is based on reading and training?

Q: You were not present during any of the events we are discussing?

Q: You never met my client?

Q: Never examined him?

Q: Never even asked to discuss what he says happened?

Q: Would you ever diagnose a patient that you never met, never spoke to, and never received the patient's version of how he feels?

Q: If I came to you and described my wife's symptoms, and showed you the results of a test and you knew nothing about its reliability, would your malpractice insurance allow you to make a life or death decision regarding her condition or treatment?

Q: I thought not.

Q: You belong to the AMA?

Q: You indicated the AMA's position is that no one should drive at a .08.

Q: The AMA also takes the position that a person under 21 should not have any alcohol and drive?

Q: Can you tell me what physiological change occurs at midnight between a 20-year-and-364-day-old and a 21-year old that causes the difference in this assumption of impairment?

Q: There is none?

Q: Now the AMA has a definition of impairment, correct?

Q: It is any deviation from the norm?

Q: If it is related to drinking, then the AMA adds "caused by alcohol."

Q: BUT, under the AMA definition, any time foreign substance is introduced into the person's body, he may be impaired, if the norm is affected?

Q: First, what is John's norm?

Q: You would not treat a patient based on averages, would you?

Q: It would not be a good medical decision to give a 250 pound male the same strength prescription as a 100 pound female.

Q: You need to adjust for the person's own uniqueness?

Q: Getting back to impairment, if I were to drink a couple of cups of coffee, that may make me more awake?

Q: In fact, isn't that why many of us drink coffee?

Q: Now, if I had previously been tired, drank a couple of cups, and woke up, I would be off my norm?

Q: Therefore, I would be impaired?

Q: Can internal factors lead to impairment?

Q: So, if I were very tired and driving, that would be impaired?

Q: If I were very distracted, I would be impaired?

Q: What if I had a killer headache?

Q: So, according to the AMA, all of this would be impairment?

Q: Therefore, any time we drive in a less than perfect state, we may be impaired?

Q: Now, you obviously get paid a lot for your time to come here and give these opinions.

Q: In order to render an opinion, medical or otherwise, you depend on the accuracy of the tests performed?

Q: If I showed you the results of a blood culture, for example, you are relying on the concept the blood was properly obtained, and the culture properly run?

Q: If the culture were contaminated, then your opinion may be flawed?

Q: In fact, if you saw something in the culture and prescribed a course of treatment, that treatment could be completely off base if there were contamination?

Q: You also rely on others to provide you with certain baseline information?

Q: Such as pulse, blood pressure, temperature, etc.?

Q: This means you place a lot of faith in your support staff?

Q: If they give you bad information, then the decisions you make may be faulty?

Q: Of course, you do have the ability and time to discuss the entirety with the patient?

Q: You received our letter inviting you to discuss the case with John and myself?

Q: We wanted to tell you why he had trouble balancing.

Q: We asked if you wanted to check John's eyes to confirm that he has natural nystagmus?

Q: We asked if you wanted to discuss his symptoms?

Q: We asked if you wanted to discuss his drinking pattern?

Q: Yet you did none of this?

Q: What do you think the AMA would say of a doctor who diagnosed a patient without conducting an exam, speaking to him, or checking his history?

Q: Yet you are doing so here?

Q: You are familiar with how alcohol affects an individual.

Q: You would agree that mental impairment must occur prior to physical impairment?

Q: If there is no sign of mental impairment, then any physical impairment must be non-alcohol related?

CROSS-EXAMINATION

Q: In this case, the officer admitted to no sign of mental impairment on John?

Q: No mental impairment means there must be something other than alcohol at work?

Q: This procedure, looking at symptoms and evaluating and eliminating possible causes, is similar to how you would conduct an examination of a patient.

Q: You see the symptoms, then run tests to rule out possible causes?

Q: For example, a sore throat, trouble swallowing, redness etc. are signs that most likely point to strep throat.

Q: You take a culture to confirm this?

Q: Possibly start treatment?

Q: If the culture comes back not being strep throat, you then look to something else?

Q: Because while you can have all the symptoms of strep, if the culture is negative, it is something else?

Q: One could say, the bacteria comes first, physical symptoms second. So, that if there are physical symptoms, but no bacteria, it is something else?

Q: You read the material I sent you?

Q: You would agree that there is absolutely no research that allows SFSTs to be correlated to a particular BAC?

Q: You would also agree that SFSTs are not designed as driving tests?

Q: You must agree that we all process alcohol, food, or anything else we put in our bodies at different rates?

Q: In order to determine how fast or slow any of us metabolizes anything we ingest, you need to perform a specific case study on that person?

Q: This is like how people react to medicine. Some people react well to some drugs, others have side effects or may need a slightly different drug?

Q: How fast does John absorb alcohol?

Q: Without knowing that fact, can you say if his blood alcohol was rising or falling, even if you had his drinking pattern?

Q: Such an opinion would only be an educated guess?

Q: You have testified in civil cases before?

Q: In a civil case the burden is preponderance, 51 percent to 49 percent. When asked an opinion in a civil case, you make it in terms of "to a reasonable degree of scientific certainty?"

Q: So can you say in this case, to a reasonable degree of scientific certainty, that John was *not* under .08 at the time of driving?

Q: In other words, you cannot rule it out under the preponderance standard?

Q: So you cannot rule it out even at 51 to 49?

[§§4:103-4:109 Reserved]

IX. LAY WITNESSES

§4:110 Goals

Perhaps no more damning witness exists than the lay witness. Generally they have no axe to grind, nothing to gain, no interest. They will be completely unaware of studies. They will have no knowledge of field sobriety tests. They will be well received by the jury. On the other hand, they will not be experienced in court. They cannot testify to a specific blood alcohol level. They have no experience in the field of DUI investigation.

All things considered, it is my opinion that a lay witness, unless some other facts come out, be treated respectfully and quickly. Show what they do not know and get them out of there.

Unlike other witnesses, the lay witness will be open and available to you for pre-trial interviews. Use this opportunity, interview them, speak to them, get them to trust you and, more importantly, know what they know. This witness can totally surprise you without adequate communication and preparation. Much of what you may want to ask from below is premised on knowing the answers.

§4:111 Sample Cross-Examination

Q: Ms. Jones, you called the police?

Q: You were concerned?

Q: You saw some bad driving?

Q: Have you ever received a ticket?

Q: Any one in your family?

Q: So there has been some bad driving there?

Q: Were they or you drunk when that happened?

Q: Have you ever seen or been part of an accident?

Q: No alcohol there?

Q: So you understand that bad driving does not necessarily mean DUI?

Q: You have no idea what the actual blood alcohol level was in this case?

Q: If the officer had told you that the bad driving you saw was because John spilled his coffee, that would be a plausible and adequate explanation?

Q: If it had been someone on a cell phone, you may have understood the driving?

Q: Or maybe, someone was driving erratically because there were children in the back that were acting up and requiring attention?

Q: In other words, all you know is that the driving was bad enough to make you call someone, then you heard from the officer or the DA that alcohol was involved?

Q: Did the officer tell you that?

Q: Was it at the scene?

Q: If the officer had said no alcohol, you would have believed him?

Q: But since they said it was alcohol, you believed them?

Q: So what the officer told you made up your mind for you?

You can run the same line with the DA or whomever it was that told this witness about alcohol. The bottom line is to show the witness had no *independent* position or opinion.

Q: Did you ever speak to John?

Q: Did you ask what happened?

Q: So you made no independent investigation?

Q: In summary then, all you know is you saw some bad driving, which may or may not have been due to alcohol, and called the police?

[§§4:112-4:119 Reserved]

X.   CROSS-EXAMINATION ETHICS

§4:120   Ethical Limitations of Cross-Examination

There is an old story that when Richard the Lionhearted arrived in the Middle East during the Crusades, he met with his Islamic counterpart. In order to demonstrate the might of the Christian armies, he had a stump brought to the pavilion and with his broad sword, he cut the stump in two. In response, the Suleiman had a piece of the finest silk dropped from high up and merely held his scimitar beneath it, demonstrating the keen edge of his weapon and his men. Whether your own approach to cross-examination is to pound away with a broad sword, or to make fine, delicate cuts with a scimitar, one axiom remains constant: cross-examination must be conducted in an ethical manner.

Before continuing, I must point out that there is a difference between morals and ethics. Morals, it is submitted, are personal values to which we subscribe individually, or occasionally, in groups. Ethics, on the other hand, are rules that apply to all in a particular endeavor. While it may not be moral to attempt to impeach a witness who is clearly telling the truth, it is ethical to do so. Many authors have argued that this separation should be discarded and that the rules of ethics should be ones of morals. *See, e.g.,* George Wright, *"Cross-Examining Legal Ethics: The Roles of Intentions, Outcomes, and Character"* 83 Kentucky Law Journal 801 (1994-1995). In fact, lawyers of all persuasions may engage in conduct of questionable morals, which are nonetheless ethically sound. *See, e.g.,* Abbe Smith & William Montross, *"The Calling of Criminal Defense,"* 50 Mercer Law Review 443 (1999).

In order to discuss the ethical restrictions of cross-examination in a criminal context, we will look to three sources: The ABA Model Rules of Professional Conduct, traditional Supreme Court cases, and modern Confrontation Clause case opinions by Justice Scalia.

CROSS-EXAMINATION

§4:121   The American Bar Association Model Rules of Professional Conduct

The first comment on a lawyer's rules for cross-examination can be found in the preamble. "As advocate, a lawyer zealously asserts the client's position under the rules of the adversary system." As currently designed, cross-examination is an integral part of the adversary system. *See Davis v. Alaska*, 415 US 308 (1974) and cases cited therein. "Zealous" is defined as ardent, passionate or fervent. This then sets the stage for a lawyer's rigorous cross-examination. Clearly then, as far as the tenor of the cross-examination few (if any) ethical boundaries apply.

However, the preamble also sets the first restrictions on the use of cross. By declaring that the lawyers' use of legal procedures should be "only for legitimate purposes and not to harass or intimidate others," the Model Rules encode what case law has recognized for years. *See Alford v. United States*, 282 U.S. 687 (1931). Cross-examination for no purpose other than to harass or annoy does overstep ethical boundaries. Balancing these two aspects, it is clear that regardless of the tenor of the questioning, so long as it is being conducted for legitimate purposes and not to harass or intimidate the witness, cross-examination should remain unfettered by the court.

While not dealing directly with the topic of cross-examination, Rules 3.1 and 3.3 can be cited as support for limits on cross-examination. Rule 3.1 provides that a lawyer shall not bring or defend a proceeding, or assert or controvert an issue therein, unless there is a basis for doing so that is not frivolous, which includes a good faith argument for an extension, modification or reversal of existing law. Rule 3.3 states that a lawyer shall not knowingly make a false statement of material fact or law to a tribunal, or offer evidence that the lawyer knows to be false.

Fortunately, a closer look at Rule 3.1 destroys such a position because it further states that a lawyer for the defendant in a criminal proceeding may nevertheless so defend the proceeding as to require that every element of the case be established. Clearly this allows the intense, but not harassing, questioning of every witness brought forward by the prosecution regardless of the lawyer's personal knowledge of the facts or thoughts of the witness' credibility.

As for Rule 3.3, as every trial lawyer has heard in every case in which there has been live testimony, "Statements made by attorneys during the trial are not evidence. . . . A question is not evidence and may be considered only as it enables you to understand the answer." CALJIC 1.02. Therefore, Rule 3.3, as it is limited to evidence, is not valid authority to ethically limit the cross-examination.

This, the art of cross-examination, is one of those areas where morals and ethics split paths. While misleading a witness during an examination may be morally wrong, it is ethically acceptable. *See Wright*, supra. However, such a position of being morally wrong but ethically acceptable fails to account for an even deeper underlying value of many if not most criminal defense attorneys: that upholding the adversary system is of utmost importance since the system protects all of society, rather than any one individual. Under such a theory, that upholding the system is the utmost value, the occasional wounding of a witness' pride is a small price to pay for the freedoms we enjoy. For more on this topic, see Monroe H. Freedman, *"Professional Responsibility of the Criminal Defense Lawyer: The Three Hardest Questions"* 64 Michigan Law Review 1469 (1966).

Rule 3.4 of the Model Rules states unequivocally lawyers should not "counsel or assist a witness to testify falsely." Although this rule obviously applies to direct examination, it also raises the question, "doesn't an attorney have the right to zealously cross-examine a witness to ensure that false evidence has not been admitted?" Cross-examination is the perfect, indeed the only, tool to pick apart the true from the false.

Either alone, or in combination, the Model Rules do not place any limit on the ability to cross-examine a witness, regardless of the attorney's knowledge of the witness' truthfulness or lack thereof. So long as some legitimate goal is served by the questioning, it must be allowed. This position is further supported by the American Bar Association's Standards for Criminal Justice Prosecution Function and Defense Function (1991). Standard 4-7.6(b) starkly reads "Defense counsel's belief or knowledge that the witness is telling the truth does not preclude cross-examination." What clearer dictate can we require?

§4:122   Traditional Supreme Court Cases on Cross-Examination

While cross-examination is not mentioned in either the Constitution or the Bill of Rights, it has been held, time and time again, that cross-examination is such an integral part of the Sixth Amendment's right of confrontation that limitations on its use will be evaluated under strict conditions. In *Douglass v. Alabama*, 380 U.S. 415 (1968) the Court stated "Our cases construing the [confrontation] clause hold that a primary interest secured by it is the right of cross-examination." This statement was echoed in *Davis v. Alaska*, 415 U.S. 308 (1974) where the Court not only supported the idea of virtually unfettered cross-examination, but held that the right of cross-examination

CROSS-EXAMINATION

supersedes the rights enacted by states to protect their citizens. In so doing, the Supreme Court cited, with favor, Professor Wigmore's Treatise on Evidence:

> "The main and essential purpose of confrontation is to secure for the opponent the opportunity of cross-examination. The opponent demands confrontation, not for the idle purpose of gazing upon the witness, or of being gazed upon by him, but for the purpose of cross-examination, which cannot be had except by the direct and personal putting of questions and obtaining immediate answers." 5 J. Wigmore Evidence 1395 (1940).

The Court went on to say "A more particular attack on the witness' credibility is effected by means of cross-examination." The *Davis* case merely summarized decades of decisions on cross-examination; that the right of confrontation encompasses the right of zealous cross-examination. *See e.g., Alford v. United States,* 282 U.S. 687 (1931); *Pointer v. Texas,* 380 U.S. 400 (1965); *Greene v. McElroy,* 360 U.S. 474 (1959); *Smith v. Illinois,* 390 U.S. 129 (1968); *Brookhart v. Janis,* 384 U.S. 1 (1966). In sum, these decisions hold that only upon a showing of "harassment, humiliation or annoyance" can any curtailment of zealous cross-examination stand up to constitutional scrutiny.

"It cannot seriously be doubted at this late date that the right of cross-examination is included in [the Sixth Amendment]" and that denial or curtailment of this right "would be constitutional error of the first magnitude." *Pointer v. Texas,* 380 U.S. at 404; *Brookhart v. Janis,* 384 U.S. at 3. Aside from the admonition not to use cross-examination to harass or annoy, there appears to be no limits on how far counsel may ethically go, although one's own personal morals may dictate limits. Perhaps we can be best guided by the concurring opinion of Mr. Justice White in *United States v. Wade,* 388 U.S. 218, 256-257 (1967):

> But defense counsel has no comparable obligation to ascertain or present the truth. Our system assigns him a different mission. He must be and is interested in preventing the conviction of the innocent, but, absent a voluntary plea of guilty, we also insist that he defend his client whether he is innocent or guilty. The State has the obligation to present evidence. Defense counsel need present nothing, even if he knows what the truth is. He need not furnish any witness to the police or reveal any confidences of his client, or furnish any other information to help the prosecution's case. If he can confuse a witness, even a truthful one, or make him appear at a disadvantage, unsure or indecisive, that will be his normal course. Our interest in not convicting the innocent permits counsel to put the State to its proof, to put the State's case in the worst possible light, regardless of what he thinks or knows to be the truth. Undoubtedly there are some limits which defense counsel must observe but more often than not, defense counsel will cross-examine a prosecution witness, and impeach him if he can, even if he thinks the witness is telling the truth, just as he will attempt to destroy a witness who he thinks is lying. In this respect, as part of our modified adversary system and as part of the duty imposed on the most honorable defense counsel, we countenance or require conduct which in many instances has little, if any, relation to the search for the truth.

[§§4:123-4:129 Reserved]

XI. CROSS-EXAMINATION, HEARSAY, AND THE CONFRONTATION CLAUSE

§4:130 Crawford and the Right to Confront

Every once in a while, the U.S. Supreme Court gets it right as it did in *Crawford v. Washington,* 541 U.S. 36 (2004), perhaps the most important case on cross-examination to date. *Crawford* holds that the Confrontation Clause prohibits the admission against a defendant of testimonial hearsay from an absent declarant unless the declarant is unavailable and the defendant had an opportunity to cross-examine the declarant when the statement was made.

While *Crawford,* like many Supreme Court decisions, answers the question that brought it to the court, it leaves many more issues unanswered. In fact, the Court admits that the question of what is meant by the term "testimonial" is being left for another day. Of course, this very issue is critical to practitioners. Or as one court put it "The Crawford decision is rich in detail about the law of England in the 16th, 17th and 18th centuries, but—as the Chief Justice points out—it fails to give urgently needed guidance as to how to apply the Sixth Amendment right now, in the 21st century." *People v. Moscat,* 2004 NY Slip Op 24090.

CROSS-EXAMINATION

§4:131   What Is Testimonial

The definition of "testimonial" put forth by the Court, albeit admittedly not comprehensive, is as follows: (1) "ex parte in-court testimony or its functional equivalent—that is, material such as affidavits, custodial examinations, prior testimony that the defendant was unable to cross-examine, or similar pre-trial statements that declarants would reasonably expect to be used prosecutorially" or (2) "statements that were made under circumstances which would lead an objective witness reasonably to believe that the statements would be available for use at a later trial." 541 U.S. at 1364.

The first category is rather simple in scope. Any statement inculpating the accused, orally or in writing, made to any government official is inadmissible, no matter how reliable it may be, if the declarant is absent from court and the accused was not given the opportunity to cross-examine the declarant at the time the statement was made. Such statements may include those made before a grand jury, or during a coroner's investigation, preliminary hearing, or even police interrogation.

The second definition is the troubling one. Under the old rule in *Ohio v. Roberts*, 448 U.S. 56 (1980), the admission of a hearsay statement of an unavailable declarant in a criminal prosecution did not violate the Confrontation Clause if it fell within a "firmly rooted" hearsay exception or had "particularized guarantees of trustworthiness." Under *Roberts*, Confrontation Clause analysis and hearsay analysis became almost identical. This is no longer true. "Admitting statements deemed reliable by a judge is fundamentally at odds with the right of confrontation." See *Crawford*, 541 U.S. at 61.

§4:132   Application to DUI Cases

Perhaps the easiest way to apply *Crawford* is to use the old law school evidence class approach: consider what is being offered and who is offering it. If the evidence being offered is a fact that is critical to proof of the alleged offense, then it is testimonial. If the declarant is not present in court, and the accused has not had the right to cross-examine the declarant, then confrontation is being denied. For example, if the evidence is the results of a blood test performed by Dr. Jones, then Dr. Jones must be available for cross-examination or the results may not be admissible under the *Crawford* rationale.

Now, looking at this issue purely from a hearsay point of view, should Mr. Smith come in and state that he is the custodian of records, that the lab report was made by Dr. Jones at or near the time pursuant to both an official and business duty, as the crime lab is county run, and it appears to be trustworthy, then the results would be admissible over the hearsay objection as either a business or official governmental record. However, *Crawford* demands a higher standard. "It is not enough to point out that most of the usual safeguards of the adversary process attend the statement, when the single most important safeguard missing is the one the Confrontation Clause demands." While everyday business records may not be covered by *Crawford*, and by every day I am thinking of inventory, accounting etc., a report of a chemical test that encompasses not just the numerical value but that also attests to procedures, methods, training, etc. is a different type of business record.

In other words, allowing the test record of a blood test result into evidence without a chance to cross-examine the individual deprives the defendant the right to question how the test was performed. The defendant cannot point out the inexperience of the analyst, the problems with the machine or any other aspect going to the underlying reliability of the result. It comes down to "it is printed here so it must not only be true, it must be perfect." This is a clear denial of confrontation.

We can obviously see what this means in the above example or similar forensic test results, but let's go further. For years we have been attempting to obtain the inner workings of the various breath machines; that is the internal codes, procedures and assumption upon which the machines rely, but which no defense attorney has ever had access. Since the eventual result of the chemical test is to be used in court, and is produced through this unknown formula, there may be an argument that the underlying concept of confrontation has been violated. We have been denied at every step. Now, under *Crawford*, we have a new tool.

The machine and its results are clearly testimonial. In fact, it is *the* piece of testimony necessary, and indeed often the only one needed, to prove a per se charge. That being said, aren't the inner workings of the machine necessarily testimonial? Let's look at it in the manner we first suggested, the evidence approach.

The print out of the machine is in court; it is *saying* "here is the BAC of Mr. Defendant." If this were a live person, we would ask, "How did you arrive at this number?" We would clearly be allowed to ask, "What science did you use? Where is your math? What are your procedures?" Yet because it is a machine, we are denied this confrontation.

CROSS-EXAMINATION

The machine printout is precisely the type of evidence about which the Framers were concerned. Involvement of government officers in the production of testimony with an eye toward trial presents unique potential for prosecutorial abuse—a fact borne out time and again throughout a history with which the Framers were keenly familiar. This consideration does not evaporate when testimony happens to fall within some broad, modern hearsay exception, even if that exception might be justifiable in other circumstances.

CROSS-EXAMINATION

CHAPTER 5

PREPARATION OF DEFENSE WITNESSES AND DIRECT EXAMINATION

PREPARATION OF DEFENSE WITNESSES AND DIRECT EXAMINATION

I.   INTRODUCTION

§5:01   Types of Witnesses

There are basically four kinds of witnesses for the defense in a DUI case:
- Percipient witnesses. See §§5:10-5:15.
- Field test experts. See §§5:20-5:26.
- Alcohol experts (*i.e.*, experts on breath testing, blood testing, and alcohol metabolism). See §§5:40-5:69.
- Medical experts. See §5:80-5:82.

Each one has a unique perspective and each one needs to be handled in a special way. The open-ended questions you can lob at your expert are probably not appropriate for your client's buddies. A bartender can more easily discuss the night in question than the doctor who has been treating your client for years. However, don't overlook that many of these people may be able to get more than just the facts out before the jury.

See Appendix A *The District Attorney's Manual* for the prosecution's approach to cross-examination of defense witnesses and common chemical test defenses.

§5:02   Direct Examination of Experts: The Correct Approach

Richard Mathews is a jury consultant in San Francisco. His research shows that jurors don't like the word "expert." Juries have not even formed a trust relationship with the attorney and yet the attorney is telling the jury to take his or her word that the witness is an expert. Turns out this backfires. Instead, Rich argues, use the word "expert" against the state, but refer to your witness as a "specialist," "top person in the field," "recognized chemist," "outsider," "top teacher," or "author."

For many of us, direct examination of an expert is an opportunity to show off. We can demonstrate to the jury just how well we know the science and how much we have learned about all the other evidence in a DUI case. We have spent hour upon hour in classes and at seminars costing us thousands of dollars. Now is the time for us to make all of that pay off by lining up our witnesses and letting fly.

THIS IS THE WRONG APPROACH.

Jurors did not "pay" to see you. They do not want you to give a long-winded recitation of theories. They want to hear from those who were there or from those who have initials after their names that indicate some type of advanced knowledge.

This is not to say that you should not get the training. Rather, it is important to have that training in order to intelligently discuss the various defenses with your client and expert and to know what to present to the jury. It is just a question of who presents the information.

§5:03   Some Tips From Our Experts

Tom Workman is one of the more knowledgeable experts out there. Experts like Tom spend great time, money, and energy doing research, prepping cases and teaching us lawyers how to defend cases. What we forget is that what is one case to us, may be a career to them. Here are some suggestions that Tom made when asked what we should know in using experts in court:

1.   Never stipulate to your expert's credentials. If you do, the jury will not hear the credentials of the defense expert, and consequently it will go with the government's expert.

2.   The prosecution may move to exclude your expert and ask for the substance of the testimony, at a hearing. If you don't object, the ADA will get a dry run at the testimony, and newer judges tend to "split the baby" and only allow half of the evidence in. You must explain to the judge that so long as your expert is qualified, and the testimony is relevant, it is for the jury to decide what if any weight the testimony should be given. If the judge insists on knowing more, then ask for in camera ex parte showing. Explain to the judge that to have a full-blown hearing with the prosecution is equivalent to a deposition of your witness, which the prosecution is not allowed. Further, the role of the judge in such a motion is not to weigh the evidential value, but merely to see to it that the testimony will be relevant. This evaluation does not require cross-examination.

3.   When an attorney retains an expert, the attorney holds that expert's future in her hands. If the government attacks the expert and an appeal should be taken, the attorney should not simply say: "Too bad, you,

Mr. Expert, are screwed," knowing that the expert has no standing to take an appeal, and is stuck with a possible career-ending decision. You should consider filing the appeal regardless of the client's ability to pay. A few hours of your time in performing the appealing may not only get the reversal your client would like, but also save the expert's reputation, or in some cases, the very type of defense you argued.

4. When working with an expert for the first time, you must ask the expert what attacks on their credibility to expect, and not be afraid to resurrect the expert on re-direct.

5. When an expert is not qualified in a court, it does significant damage to that expert's future career. In my reflection, it is usually the fault of the attorney, not the expert. What attorneys must do is to provide more than the basic information to have an expert so qualified. One great way to do this is to write a chart of the qualifications of the states expert on one half of a poster paper and then put your experts next to it.

Example:

STATES EXPERT	DEFENSE EXPERT
Bachelor Degree	Masters Degree
12 years state lab	20 years state lab, 3 years independent
No correlation studies	7 Studies
No peer reviewed articles	2 peer reviewed articles
No independent work	5 years independent work

Here are a few other issues that arise in conjunction with expert witnesses that we need to be aware of and perhaps file a Motion in Limine to prevent:

1. Attacking the expert on the names of the seminars or the specific topics they have given. Be sure that the judge and jury know that those names are chosen by the people putting on the lecture and are a way to get people to pay to attend the lecture.

2. Using the Internet to get alleged "dirt" on the expert from someone else's web site. Many of us like to say such and such expert is affiliated with our firm. This may make you look impressive but it hurts the expert. Again, this information is *not* within the expert's control.

3. Claiming that the expert has no direct knowledge of the specific issue in the case, e.g. never did a study on Celiac disease and blood testing. Be sure to point out that 99% of the state's experts have not done studies. In fact, the overwhelming number of studies have been performed by a select group of individuals. One need not do the specific test to understand the conclusion.

If we don't protect our experts, then we will lose them.

[§§5:04-5:09 Reserved]

II.   PERCIPIENT WITNESSES

§5:10   Preparation

More than any other witness, except possibly your client, the percipient witness needs to be prepared. The witness has probably never testified in court and will be extremely nervous about doing so. That said, a properly coached percipient witness can win the case for you.

The key is the cross-examination preparation. The DA will ask a series of questions designed to show that this witness is not being honest. Prepare the witness for questions about getting in the car with an obvious drunk. Be sure the witness understands the need to vouch for his or her own sobriety.

In preparing a percipient witness or the client, you should engage a fellow attorney to act as prosecutor. Rehearse until the witness knows that he or she will be able to handle any question the prosecutor might possibly pose. That is the key to testifying: you must know that what you say is the truth and is relevant no matter what the other side tries to spin.

Be sure to instruct percipient witnesses on the basics of testifying:

- Look at counsel for the question.
- Pause.
- Answer the question to the jury.
- Answer only the question asked.
- Don't guess at the question if it is not clear.

Your witness needs to know that "I do not understand your question" or "I don't know" is a good answer.

Of course, your evaluation of the witness under the examination of a partner will ultimately determine if this witness can be put up. If the witness is not going to stand up to pressure, consider using someone else.

§5:11　　Purpose and Goals

Assuming you are comfortable with your percipient witnesses after going through the preparation process outlined above, the next issue is what these witnesses can bring to your case. Generally, a percipient witness can provide testimony as to:

- The client's drinking pattern, *i.e.*, the times of drinking, the amount and type of drinks, and other relevant information (receipts from the bar or restaurant are especially helpful in this regard).
- Your client's driving pattern, *i.e.*, where the client started from and where he or she was going (good for rising alcohol cases), or the actual driving issues (useful in motions to dismiss or in trial). This assumes the witness was a passenger or observed the driving.
- The client's state of sobriety, including the alleged objective symptoms of slurred speech, bloodshot eyes, and so forth.
- Mechanical issues with the car or physical issues of the client or environmental issues with the entire events of the day in question.
- The client's character. If the DA has opened the door to character evidence (and raising the issue of your client's tolerance for alcohol may do so) then feel free to introduce all of your client's friends merely to show the character trait of sobriety to counter the DA's character evidence. Consult your local rules of evidence.
- Any other aspect of the case that you want to get in front of the jury without putting your client on the stand. For example, I had a client who was African-American. The officer claimed the client admitted to drinking at a specific bar, which was known as less than open to people like my client. We actually had regulars testify that they would clearly remember if a person of my client's race had been in the bar and they most emphatically stated he had not. This severely undercut the officer's credibility.

§5:12　　Establish Witness' Lack of Personal Interest and Attempts to Talk to Prosecution

At the beginning of your direct examination of a percipient witness, be sure to establish that the witness has a lack of personal interest in the case. Let the witness explain that he or she would not lie just because of a pre-existing relationship with your client, and he or she is not testifying out of friendship or guilt. Often, it is good to have the witness explain that he or she tried to tell the officers or the DA what the witness is about to tell the jury, but was ignored.

§5:13　　Sample Direct Examination of "Drinking Buddy"

Q: Mr. Friend, have you ever been in court as a witness before?

Q: Are you nervous?

Q: Are you prepared to tell us everything you remember?

Q: Did you write out a report like the police did in this case?

Q: Let me tell you, they had some mistakes, and they had a report, so if you make any mistakes, let us know. In fact, if you have any questions, go ahead and ask them, okay?

Q: What we want is your version of the events, not words the lawyers put in your mouth, so if any of us misstate what you said, let us know, okay?

Q: Now, how long have you known John?

Q: Are you close friends?
Q: And you were with him when he was arrested?
Q: What did you see?
Q: Did you try to tell the officers this information?
Q: What did they say?
Q: Did you try to tell the DA prior to today?
Q: And he refused to meet with you?
Q: Did you tell him you wanted him to know the truth?
Q: How do you think the officers treated John?
Q: What makes you say that?

You get the picture. Continue in this vein to make all your points.

See Appendix A *The District Attorney's Manual* for the prosecution's approach to cross-examination of the defendant's drinking buddy.

§5:14   Introduction of Receipts Through Percipient Witness

Percipient witnesses, whether drinking buddies or the bartender, are a great way to indirectly introduce receipts from the night's drinking. While you will probably not be allowed to introduce the actual receipt, a clever direct exam will slip it in as a past recollection refreshed.

Q: Bobby, do you remember exactly who had what to drink?
Q: Well, if I showed you the receipt from that night would it refresh your memory?
Q: So, after looking at the receipt, do you now remember what you and James had to drink?
A: Yes, I had two white Russians and he had two Coronas.

You can do the same with the bartender.

§5:15   Sample Direct Examination of Bartender

On the topic of bartenders, assuming you have a cooperative one, try the following line of questioning to contradict the officer's observations of your client's allegedly intoxicated behavior.

Q: Bartender Peggy, part of your responsibility is to not serve people who are drunk?
Q: You could get in a lot of trouble if you did?
Q: Did Jimmy ever seem drunk to you?
Q: Was Jimmy slamming down drinks?
Q: Did Jimmy appear to you to be sober?
Q: Could he walk okay?
Q: Was his speech slurred?
Q: Did he stumble around?

Go through as many of the "objective" symptoms as you want to contradict the officer.

See Appendix A *The District Attorney's Manual* for the prosecution's approach to cross-examination of the bartender.

[§§5:16-5:19 Reserved]

III.   FIELD TEST EXPERTS

§5:20   Selection and Preparation

In selecting an expert on field tests, two considerations need to be addressed: the expertise of the witness and the comfort level between the attorney and witness and between the witness and the case. The witness you use must be someone who has the requisite knowledge in the field along with comfort in working with you, the facts of the particular case, and in courtroom testimony. There are many people who have great knowledge on a given subject but do not present well in a courtroom setting. Conversely, some witnesses have a great ability to communicate and connect with a jury but do not have a whole lot to say.

Most FST experts are former law enforcement personnel. That experience provides them with virtually unassailable expertise and probably a fair amount of trial experience. These people usually make great witnesses for the defense. In fact, it is not unusual for prominent DUI attorneys to keep an eye out for DUI cops who are nearing retirement in order to foster a relationship for possible use as a defense expert. While these types of experts have good courtroom presence and "on the job" experience, they sometimes lack the ability to understand whose side they are now on.

The second type of FST expert is the scientific witness. Usually, these are people with experience in other aspects of DUI defense work, such as breath or blood testing, who have obtained additional training and studied FSTs in order to testify as experts in this arena. Their scientific training will allow them to wax poetic on the correlation, or lack thereof, of FSTs to DUI, and will add a certain luster to theoretical or statistical aspects. However, they will be attacked on their lack of "hands on" experience. Prosecutors will be ready with the simple question of "How many DUI arrests have you made?" in order to undercut their testimony. But as one of my favorite experts once said, "I have never shot a suspect, but I know when it is right to do so and when it is wrong."

Finally, some attorneys feel comfortable using in house investigators or friendly lawyers who are trained in FSTs as their experts. This usually limits the witness to factual testimony as to how FSTs are supposed to be administered correctly versus how the officer in the case at bar administered the FSTs. This is clearly not the best witness but may be the only person around, especially in pro bono or public defender cases.

While not typical, I have occasionally used an independent police evaluation expert as a witness. Many jurisdictions have independent police review agencies, a type of civilian internal affairs or oversight. The investigators in these agencies, while not officers themselves, have been trained and make their living rendering opinions, or even decisions, on the correctness of police conduct in all manner of situations from dress codes to shootings. One of these can be used, not on the DUI aspect of FSTs, but in a pure "Did the officer follow the applicable rules?" manner. It is devastating to the prosecution to hear the witness say that, if the case were before him, the officer would be sent for re-training based on the mistakes made.

§5:21   Purpose and Goals

Once you have selected your expert, or more likely in conjunction with the selection, you need to decide your avenue of attack on FSTs. There are basically four avenues you can explore:
1) The officer did not administer the tests correctly.
2) The officer did not interpret the results correctly.
3) The tests have no scientific value.
4) "So What?"

Let's look at each of these in turn. But remember, this may be the one time where a shotgun is the weapon of choice over the laser. You can argue that the tests were given incorrectly *and* interpreted incorrectly and mean nothing—or that they were given correctly but mean nothing.

For exhibits that can be used when examining witnesses about SFSTs, see Ch. 8, *Demonstrative Evidence*.

§5:22   Administration of SFSTs

Probably the most common starting point of direct examination of an FST expert is that the officer in your case did not give the FSTs as required. Depending on your jurisdiction, this may lead to preclusion, such as in Ohio, or just go to weight, as in California. In any case, the starting point for this discussion will be not just your expert, but the training material of the officer. The NHTSA manuals, and most local training guides as well, have cautionary language that failure to follow the *exact procedures* in administration renders the results invalid. Get this in front of the jury.

Upon completion of the testimony as to the specifics of *how* to give a particular test, analogize it to the jury. The simplest query is:

Q: "So if an officer asks a person to take twelve steps instead of nine on the Walk-and-Turn, he asked for too much, and the test is no longer valid?"
A: Yes.

For more on this, see the various studies on SFSTs and statements of Dr. Burns (Appendix B). Simply put, changing the number of steps makes fatigue, rather than alcohol, the triggering event.

§5:23   Interpretation of SFSTs

Working hand-in-hand with proper administration is proper interpretation. The three Standardized Field Sobriety Tests were allegedly designed to be objectively given and scored. That is, any officer viewing any performance, with or without viewing the instructions, would be able to grade the performance. Of course, history and real world studies have proven this theory absurd. Officers go off on individual tangent instructions, and the officer's interpretation is in the eyes of the beholder, but since this is the government's game, we can make them play by their written rules.

The scoring criteria for SFSTs, and for most non-standardized field tests, are written in local training material or the NHTSA SFST Manual. Your expert can use these to grade the grader. In fact, the NHTSA slides in Chapter 8 can be used to point this out to the jury, as it is the criteria an Instructor (the one who has been trained to teach officers to administer SFSTs) uses to test officers upon completion of SFST administration testing. (There are several levels of SFST qualification. An officer is trained as an Administrator. This is approximately a 20-hour class. It is taught by an Instructor who has had not only Administrator training, but also approximately 40 hours of additional training as an Instructor. The Instructor class is taught by a Master. There are only a handful of Masters in the United States, most of whom were trained by Dr. Burns herself.)

Your witness can use Power Point to show the correct interpretation criteria and the faults made by the administrator in your case. One of the most common mistakes is faulty counting in the One-Leg Stand. This is not a recognized 'clue' by the standardized procedures, so it should not be counted.

§5:24   Reliability and Meaning of SFSTs

The next two aspects of SFSTs are more scientific: that SFSTs have no acceptable scientific reliability, and that they mean nothing.

First, more and more articles, many of them peer-reviewed, have been published showing a complete lack of scientific reliability to SFSTs. If properly qualified, your expert may be able to show that the SFSTs are a pack of "magic beans" sold to the courts with no scientific basis.

The second aspect is easy to understand. There is no study, case law, or other resource that relates SFST performance, in whole, part or any combination, with either a specific BAC or the ability to drive a car. This has been said on numerous occasions by Dr. Marceline Burns herself.

The former (scientific reliability) is of more use before a judge in trying to exclude the tests, whereas the latter (FST performance and BAC or driving ability) is for a jury.

With those ideas in mind, and clearly the list has not been exhausted, let's look at how we can use our expert.

§5:25   Direct Examination of SFST Expert: Version 1

The following direct examination is based upon conversations I had with Robert La Pier, a well-known SFST expert. It reflects his opinions on how he would like to be examined. It started with this tidbit Bob imparted before a trial:

By not asking me each little detail on how the officer administered the standardized field sobriety tests it will make us look good. By not belaboring the tests (other than we flat cannot trust them) we will not look like we are flailing away. Let the prosecutor ask about the details. My experience is that the prosecutor will ask the witness for those details and it's a double edge sword for her. By asking for the specifics of what was done wrong she is admitting there may be mistakes and that they matter. When she asks I'll drive it home in closing.

Like many former law enforcement individuals, Robert La Pier actually believes in SFSTs, provided they are given and evaluated correctly. I would not use an expert who takes that position in a case where the attack is on the science underlying the tests.

Bob believes the expert's direct testimony is most effective if it focuses only just three points:

- That SFSTs are unreliable unless the officer administers them in accordance with strict standards;
- That the officer failed to adhere to these standards; and
- Therefore, the results in this case are unreliable.

He believes that it is best to leave the details about how the tests should have been performed to the prosecutor who usually will bring them out on cross.

Given my experience with Bob, I like this approach. Based on the level of comfort we have (over ten years of trials and of running SFST trainings), I can basically wind him up and let him go. Here is an example of this type of direct.

Q: Would you state your name and spell your last name, and your address for the record?
Q: What is your occupation?
A: I am a DUI and drug recognition expert consultant and trainer.
Q: What is your background that allows you to do your present occupation?
A: [He reviews his CV.]
Q: You have a great deal of experience in DUI enforcement, and training in that field, as well as breath testing training?
A: Yes, I do. Like I said, over 21 years of experience.
Q: You were in the courtroom and heard Officer Snodgrass testify, didn't you?
A: I was.
Q: Now in regards to the standardized field sobriety tests, would you explain to the court/jury how these tests were developed?
A: [He describes in detail how the tests were developed and stresses that the results are invalid unless the tests are administered in the prescribed standardized fashion.]
Q: As you stated earlier you were in the courtroom and heard Officer Snodgrass testify?
A: I was.
Q: And you heard him explain how he administered the standardized field sobriety tests?
A: I did.
Q: Let's talk about the Horizontal Gaze Nystagmus test. Did Officer Snodgrass administer this test in the prescribed standardized fashion?
A: No, he did not.
Q: What did the officer do wrong?

COMMENT:

Allow the expert to give the details and leave follow up for the DA.

Q: Since he did not administer the HGN in the prescribed manner, what does that do to the reliability of the test?
A: If any one of the standardized field sobriety test elements is changed, the validity is compromised. You cannot trust the results.
Q: Okay, let's talk about the next test, the Walk-and-Turn. Did Officer Snodgrass administer this test in the prescribed standardized fashion?
A: No, he did not.
Q: What did the officer do wrong?
Q: Since he did not administer the Walk-and-Turn test in the prescribed manner, what does that do to the reliability of the test?
A: If any one of the standardized field sobriety test elements is changed, the validity is compromised. You cannot trust the results.
Q: Okay, let's talk about the last test, the One-Leg Stand. Did Officer Snodgrass administer this test in the prescribed standardized fashion?
A: No he did not.

Q: What did the officer do wrong?

Q: Since he did not administer the One-Leg Stand in the prescribed manner, what does that do to the reliability of the test?

A: If any one of the standardized field sobriety test elements is changed, the validity is compromised. You cannot trust the results.

Q: Can a person have difficulty with the Walk-and-Turn and One-Leg Stand tests, even though he or she has consumed little or even no alcohol?

A: Yes, some people have difficulty with balance even when sober. Original research indicated the Walk-and-Turn and One-Leg Stand tests were not necessarily valid for persons with injuries to their legs, or persons with inner ear disorders.

Q: Let's talk about the balance test. Is the balance test a standardized field sobriety test validated by scientific research?

A: No, it is not.

Q: So because the balance test is not validated by any scientific research, the officer can judge a person's balance anyway he wants?

A: Yes.

Q: How about the estimating 30 seconds test? Is it a standardized field sobriety test validated by scientific research?

A: No, it is not.

Q: So because the estimating 30 seconds test is not validated by any scientific research, the officer can use any means he wants in having a person estimate 30 seconds?

A: Yes, he can.

Q: And finally the finger to nose test. Is this test a standardized field sobriety test validated by scientific research?

A: No, it is not.

Q: So like the other tests we have been talking about for the last couple minutes, the officer can administer the finger to nose test anyway he see fits?

A: Yes, he can.

Q: Okay. Let's talk about the third test, the alphabet test. Did Officer Snodgrass administer the alphabet test in the prescribed standardized fashion?

A: Well, first of all, the alphabet test is not a standardized test, as are the previous tests we have talked about. However, we all learned to recite the alphabet one way, and that was A through Z.

Q: Was Mr. Defendant instructed to recite the alphabet in the way we all learned to recite it?

A: No, he was not. He was instructed to recite it from D through X.

Q: What does that mean if anything?

A: Well, it is not the normal way to recite the alphabet as we all learned to do.

Q: So it is misleading?

A: I would say it wasn't fair.

Fairness is a concept jurors can relate to. A good point to make throughout a trial is that your client was never treated fairly. Jurors want to be fair, the officer said he was fair, although through cross you will show he left out all the good and only included the bad, so how fair is that? Let your witness tell the jury it was not fair.

§5:26　　Direct Examination of SFST Expert: Version 2

Suppose you are using a less authoritative or less experienced expert or have a judge who requires you to maintain tight control of witnesses. Here is a step-by-step approach to field sobriety tests that can be customized to meet your fact pattern. This approach will get into all the details of the test.

I find it rather long-winded for a jury, and it may put them to sleep. On the other hand, if the point you want to make is that the quick explanation given by the officer during his testimony was rather misleading in its apparent simplicity, it works. Officers can explain and demonstrate the One-Leg Stand in seconds to a jury and then spend minutes detailing the mistakes. This approach allows you to detail the intricacies so the mistakes seem less out of proportion.

Another use for such a detailed examination is punishment of the court. Let's face it, we all try cases for no other reason than to stand up to a judge, DA or sometimes entire benches. If you want to take a "routine DUI trial" and turn it into something more, this approach will help.

Finally, remember expert witnesses, because of their deemed knowledge, can be led by either side in trial. Leading questions are useful if the witness is knowledgeable but has little courtroom presence as compared to the attorney. By using leading questions, you may be able to get the jury to attach your personality to the witness' answers and combine you both into one entity in their minds.

After eliciting the witness' name and credentials, proceed as follows:

Q: Are all field tests standardized?

A: No, three are and the rest are not.

Q: Which tests are standardized?

A: Walk-and-Turn, Horizontal Gaze Nystagmus, and One-Leg Stand.

Q: What are standardized tests?

A: Tests that are given and evaluated the same way by every person based on some correlation studies.

Q: When you say standardized, those are the three you are talking about?

A: Yes.

Q: Where did this research and standardization come from?

A: The Southern California Research Institute.

Q: If you recall, what are the names of the authors or people who are at the Southern California Research Institute?

A: The primary people were Dr. Moscowitz and Dr. Burns.

Q: Do you have any relationship, formal or informal, with Dr. Marceline Burns?

Q: Dr. Marceline Burns is the one who did the studies, validated these tests, and that's who trained you?

Q: And now you train others?

A: Yes.

Q: So you were trained by the people who developed these tests?

A: Yes.

Q: Have you maintained your training?

A: Yes.

Q: And is there any significant difference in how these tests are given today as compared to when you were trained?

A: No, that is what is meant by standardized. They are always given and evaluated in the same way, in every situation.

Q: What, if anything, does the training material indicate if an officer does not administer a standardized test correctly?

A: The validity of the results is compromised.

Q: Then let's look at each test.

One-Leg Stand Test

Q: Could you tell us whether the One-Leg Stand is standardized?

Q: What instructions should the officer give to the person who is taking the test?

A: The subject is told to stand with his feet together hands down at his sides and not to start until the officer tells him to begin. He is told that when the officer tells him to begin, he is to lift one leg, either leg of his choice, approximately six inches off the ground. He is to keep the toe pointed out, look down at his foot, and count out as follows "One thousand one, one thousand two, one thousand three," until the officer tells him to stop. He should keep his hands at his sides and not put his foot down. After providing these instructions, the officer should ask the subject if he understands them, take a safe position to view the performance, and tell the subject to begin. After 30 seconds, the test is over.

Q: Are there certain aspects of the individual's performance on the One-Leg Stand that count more than others or that the officer should take note of?

A: There are four recognized clues: swaying, hopping, putting the foot down, or raising the arms more than six inches.

Q: Those would be the standardized clues, correct?

A: Yes.

Q: Are there non-standardized clues?

A: No.

Q: What if the subject slurs words or does not reach 30 in 30 seconds?

A: These have no bearing on the test performance and have not been correlated to any aspect of DUI.

Q: The pass/fail, or "decision criteria" on this test is two?

A: Yes.

Q: When you stated the instructions you said that the person taking the test is supposed to count one thousand one, one thousand two, and so forth, correct?

Q: Is the way that the individual counts recognized as a clue under this standardization?

A: No.

Q: With regards to the instructions, you said the person being tested is supposed to lift his foot approximately six inches off the ground, is that correct?

A: Yes.

Q: Is an instruction to lift your foot approximately 15 inches off the ground in compliance with the standardization?

A: No.

Q: If an officer had someone lift his foot 15 inches off the ground, would you have an opinion as to the validity of the test?

A: Yes, validity would be compromised.

Q: Therefore, since the officer in this case had the person lift his foot 15 inches, the validity of this test for the arrest/no arrest decision is compromised?

A: Yes.

Q: And so this test has no relevancy to the case?

A: Correct.

Heel to Toe or Walk-and-Turn Test

Q: Now with regards to the Heel to Toe Test or Walk-and-Turn test, you are familiar with that one correct?

Q: That's a standardized test as well?

Q: Could you tell us what the standardized instruction for that test would be?

A: The Walk-and-Turn test has two aspects: the instructional phase and the performance phase. During the instructional phase, the subject is told to place her left foot on a line and then put her right foot in front of the left, touching heel to toe. She is to remain like that, with arms at her sides until told to begin. She is asked if she understands. When instructed to begin, she is to take nine steps down the line walking heel to toe. When she reaches the ninth step, she is to leave that foot on the line and take a series of small steps around it to face back down the line. She then is to walk back nine steps heel to toe. Once she begins, she is to look at her feet and count out loud. She should not stop or use her arms for balance.

Q: With regard to the Walk-and-Turn test, since it's standardized, are there standardized clues that the officer is supposed to look for?

A: Yes, two during the instructional phase and six during performance. In the instructional phase, we look for breaking the stance or starting too soon. In the performance phase, we look for missing heel to toe by more than two inches, stepping off the line, an improper turn, using the arms to balance, and not taking the correct number of steps.

Q: The pass/fail, or "decision criteria," is two on this test as well?

Q: What exactly does a person need to do during the instruction phase to indicate a loss of balance?

A: The subject must *completely* break her stance.

Q: So using arms here is not a clue?

A: No it is not.

Q: It must be a complete break of stance?

Q: With regard to a gap between the heel and toe, does each gap count as a separate point, or is it simply a gap/no gap single pointer?

A: One point is assessed for any gap of more than two inches regardless of how many gaps there are.

Q: What about stepping off of the line?

A: Same thing, it is worth one point no matter how many violations.

Q: Not counting out loud?

A: This is not a scoring criterion.

Q: Using the arms to balance?

A: During the instructional phase, it is not relevant and during performance, if it is observed, it is one point.

Q: So, for instance, if I had my arms out from my side for the entire nine steps up and nine steps back, I don't get negative 18?

A: Correct, you get one.

COMMENT:

Once again, go to the officer's exact instructions and scoring and re-hit the compromised validity section.

HGN

Q: How does one correctly perform the Horizontal Gaze Nystagmus?

A: The subject is told to stand feet together arms at his side. A stimulus is held 12 to 15 inches from the subject's eyes and he is told to follow the stimulus with his eyes and only his eyes. The stimulus is then moved at a slow and steady pace to the subject's left extreme, at slightly above eye level. Then the stimulus is moved to the right extremity. Each aspect of the test, there are four, is done twice on each eye. The officer first checks for equal tracking in each eye; do the eyes work. If not, the test is stopped as this may indicate brain abnormalities. Then using a pace of about four seconds from nose to extremity, each eye is checked for smooth pursuit. Next each eye is checked for distance and sustained nystagmus at maximum deviation, holding the stimulus there for a four second minimum. Finally, using a slower pace, the officer checks for angle of onset, using the same four-second rule.

Q: Must each eye be checked twice?

A: Yes.

Q: Why?

A: To ensure the officer's observations were correct and to ensure the result was not officer-induced.

Q: What do you mean by officer-induced?

A: An officer's actions can create nystagmus in some circumstances. For example, a rapid movement to the extreme can create what is known as "rebound" nystagmus.

Q: Is there a set amount of time you need to hold the stimulus at maximum deviation?

A: Yes, four seconds.

Q: Why?

A: Because less than that is not sustained and therefore not in conformity with the studies and instructions.

Q: Is there a set time to hold for angle of onset?

A: Yes, four seconds.

Q: Why?

A: To be sure it is nystagmus and not something else.

Q: Can environmental factors have an impact on this test?

A: Yes.

Q: Like what?

A: The lights on the patrol car or passing traffic can distract the eye and cause it to bounce as if nystagmus is present.

Q: Does an officer have to remove these factors?

A: The officer should do so to ensure a fair and uncompromised test.

Q: How precise must you be in the 12 to 15 inches?

A: The officer must be within those numbers or the test is invalidated.

Q: What about the angle of onset prior to 45 degrees?

COMMENT:

Now bring in the officer's performance as above.

Non-Standardized Tests

Q: Previously you mentioned there are non-standardized tests?

A: Yes.

Q: What does this mean?

A: These are tests that have not been studied that we know little or nothing about.

Q: Are they useful?

A: Not really, we do not know if they relate to alcohol ingestion, let alone impairment. And we certainly do not know if they relate to driving a car.

Q: So they relate about as much as juggling?

A: Truthfully, I can't say if they relate more or less than juggling to a DUI investigation.

COMMENT:

Next you can use the officer's training material on non-standardized tests following the same approach as was done above with standardized ones.

All Factors to Consider in Decision to Arrest

Q: You would agree with the officer that you put all the information you have together and you don't base your decision on any one thing, correct?

A: Correct.

Q: But, you cannot use information that was gathered improperly?

A: Correct.

Q: So tests that have had their validity compromised must be disregarded?

A: Correct.

Q: Why?

A: It is not fair to base a decision on data that the officer might have created himself.

Q: Can you give me an example in this case?

A: Several. The officer indicated the client failed HGN because of nystagmus at maximum deviation. But the stimulus was moved too fast and not held long enough therefore indicating rebound nystagmus and not alcohol nystagmus. So those results are not reliable. Same with the One-Leg Stand and the Walk-and-Turn as we discussed.

Q: In other words, you do not use the results of tests done wrong.

A: Exactly, and that leaves us with nothing to rely on in this case.

Q: With regard to the physical performance on all of these tests, standardized, non-standardized, how would you characterize Mr. Client's performance?

A: Again, we cannot fault Mr. Client for inadequate performance based on officer mistakes. That would be like holding the DA responsible for the officer mistakes. So based on that, I would say the officer's conclusions were incorrect.

Q: Now, an officer in the field would have other factors besides just the field sobriety tests, correct?

A: Yes.

Q: The officer would have a driving pattern?

Q: The officer would have what are commonly referred to as objectivity symptoms, correct?

Q: The officer would have anything else brought to his attention during the investigation?

A: Yes.

Q: Have you ever testified in court in the past with regards to your opinion as to the correctness of an arrest decision using all of that information?

A: Yes, both in my own cases and in evaluating other people's cases

Q: What would your opinion be in this case?

A: The officer's decision was not proper in this case.

Obviously there are a million deviations on these themes. The bottom line is to get the trier of fact to understand that for the test results to be valid, the testing apparatus must be correct. Put the officer on trial for his or her failure to give the test correctly and hold that up as a yardstick to your client's performance.

Final Questions

If you get really lucky, you may be able to produce a witness who can also answer these final questions to drive it all home.

Q: Are you are familiar with all the data behind SFSTs?

Q: Putting aside any statistical anomalies, what did Southern California Research Institute indicate the reliability factor for these tests would be in their original research?

Q: Seventy-seven percent, meaning that if the standardized field sobriety tests were administered to this jury, they would inexcusably condemn three of them despite their innocence?

Q: Assuming again that the tests are given correctly, what do they tell us about the person's ability to drive?

Q: Then why are they even used at all, if they cannot measure driving ability?

[§§5:27-5:39 Reserved]

IV.   BREATH EXPERTS

§5:40   Selection and Preparation

Much like FST experts, comfort and quality are important. However, there are added factors to be considered. Is there some physiological aspect of the case that may require a breath expert who also has some medical training? Does the expert need to know about GERD, dentures, Atkins dieting, or long-term exposure to chemicals which may cause false readings? Be sure that your expert is knowledgeable about breath testing in general and the facts of your case in particular.

While jurors are told that in evaluating experts they should not rely just on credentials, we know this is bunk. A Ph.D. outranks a B.S. every day of the week. Go for the best you can. Remind your client, he or she is the owner of a professional team. The client hired you, a great quarterback/coach, but if you do not have receivers to throw to, you will never score a touchdown.

§5:41   Purpose and Goals

I am assuming that the reader has some basic understanding of both infrared and electrochemical breath testing as well as physiology. If not, you need to obtain that training. See Bartell et al., *Attacking and Defending Drunk Driving Tests* (James Publishing). And after you have obtained the training, you still need to be able to get some of the basics to the jury so they can understand what you and the witness will be discussing. Here is a basic outline of just such a direct examination.

Once again I caution that a shotgun approach is not a good weapon for trial; jurors will see it as reaching for straws. A laser missile is much more effective. Pick one or two aspects of the testing that you can attack and go with those. In other words, don't use all the topics below, just the ones that fit your case.

Checklist: Attacking Breath Testing

While not exhaustive, here is a list of some of the more common areas of attack on breath testing.

- Machine Issues
    - Maintenance
    - Accuracy
    - Temperature
    - Margin of Error
    - Specificity/Interferants
    - Calibration/Henry's Law
- Testing Issues
    - RFI
    - Observation period
    - 2 Samples
    - Slope Detector
    - .02 Agreement
- Subject Issues
    - Temperature
    - Diabetes/Hypoglycemia
    - Mouth Alcohol
    - GERD
    - Solvents

I owe a great deal to Charles and Jeff Sifers of Oklahoma for this section, and for much more. Jeff Sifers has testified in just such a fashion for years for his father in DUI cases. Without them, this section would be much less understandable.

For exhibits that can be used when examining breath experts, see Ch. 8, *Demonstrative Evidence*. See Appendix A *The District Attorney's Manual* for the prosecution's approach to cross-examination of defense breath experts and common breath test defenses.

§5:42   Basic Operation of the IR Machine

Q: In layman's terms, will you please explain how breath testing works?

A: Breath is introduced, through a hose, to a sample chamber. The basic aspect of this chamber is that light is shown through it at one end and measured at the other. The light used is at a specific wavelength and certain chemicals, like alcohol, will absorb some of the light. The lessening of the light is measured and is converted into an alcohol reading.

Q: Alcohol in the breath does not impair a person, does it?

A: No.

Q: Alcohol in the blood does impair a person though? How?

A: [Explanation of alcohol impairment]

Q: Do breath alcohol measuring machines measure the amount of alcohol in a person's blood?

A: No.

Q: You know that there is a breath alcohol test result in this case of ____%.

Q: What did this machine measure if not my client's blood?

A: His breath.

Q: How does alcohol get from the blood so as to be measured through the breath?

A: [Explanation of physiological process]

See Ch. 8, *Demonstrative Evidence*, for diagrams illustrating the operation of the breath machine and photographs of the machine that can be used in conjunction with these questions.

§5:43   Blood/Breath (Partition) Ratio

Evidence of individual variations in partition ratios (the number that breath machines automatically multiply breath alcohol results by to convert them to blood alcohol) is not admissible in all jurisdictions. Originally state per se statutes were phrased in terms of blood alcohol levels only so breath machines had to convert the results to blood alcohol levels. They do that by multiplying the breath alcohol results by 2100 even though some individuals have lower (and higher) conversion ratios. Thus evidence of variation in partition ratios was admissible to show that breath tests do not accurately measure blood alcohol. Then many jurisdictions circumvented the need for partition ratios by amending their statutes to provide that driving with a specific level of breath alcohol was an offense. As a result their courts refused to admit partition ratio evidence. *See, e.g., People v. Bransford*, 884 P.2d 70 (Cal. 1995) (testimony of defendant's individual partition ratio was inadmissible, especially when the defendant exhibited clear signs of alcohol); *Burks v. State*, 394 S.E.2d 136, 137 (Ga. Ct. App. 1990) (testimony of a defendant's individual partition ratio of 1680:1 on day before trial was inadmissible when the defendant exhibited other visible signs of intoxication).

Even if partition ratio evidence is inadmissible in your jurisdiction to refute a charge of driving over the legal limit, it may still be admissible to refute a charge of driving while impaired. See Chapter 1 for a sample motion in limine.

Q: How does the machine convert the measurement of the amount of alcohol in a person's breath into the amount of alcohol in a person's blood?

A: The machine assumes a blood to breath ratio of 2100 to 1.

Q: What do you mean by blood/breath ratio?

A: It is the ratio of total blood in a human to the total capacity of their lungs.

Q: Is this the same for everyone?

A: No, much like shoe size, it varies greatly from person to person.

Q: What is the acceptable range of this ratio?

A: 900 to 1 through 2700 to 1.

Q: Can this be important?.

A: Yes, if you are at the low end, breath results will significantly overstate the true blood alcohol level and if you are at the top end, the results will understate the true level.

Q: Can you give us a concrete example?

A: Sure. Let's just go with simple numbers. Assume a person has one part alcohol in the blood. If his blood/breath ratio is 2100 to 1, and he takes a breath test, the machine result would be 1. But if that person's personal blood/breath ratio is only 900 to 1, the machine would report that same one part as nearly 2.4, a 240 percent overstatement. To put it another way, a reported .08 alcohol of someone who is at the lower end of the ratio, and let's just use 1050 (half the 2100) to 1, would actually be a .04 *true* alcohol level in the blood.

Q: So this person would be well below the legal limit and yet the machine would convict him.
A: If we let the machine do that, yes.
Q: Is this blood/breath ratio constant, say like a person's height?
A: No, it varies.
Q: How and why would it or could it vary?
A: One important factor is consumption of food. After a meal, the ratio goes way down since blood is being used for digestion. It is one reason we get sleepy after we eat a lot, less oxygen.
Q: And all breath machines assume all people are 2100 to 1?
A: Yes.
Q: Why?
A: Because years ago this was what the machine manufacturers decided to use.
Q: What if my client is not average?
A: The truth is few people are "average." Remember average is taking all the data, adding it together, then dividing by the total number of people. It does not mean anyone actually has that number. It would be like adding the ages of all the jurors, dividing by twelve and saying all the jurors should act the resulting age. Some jurors may like that, but others would be very upset.
Q: Can a person's blood/breath ratio vary during a single drinking episode?
A: Yes.
Q: Would you explain how?
A: [Allow expert to explain.]
Q: Is there any way to comfortably predict what any person's ratio might be during any evening of drinking?
A: The only way to know a blood breath partition ratio is to simultaneously draw blood and measure breath, so no.

§5:44   Absorption Phase Testing

Q: Can you explain the three phases of alcohol ingestion?
A: Yes, absorption, equilibrium, and elimination. It looks like this (witness draws the curve). As we consume alcohol, the curve goes up, this is absorption. We continue to absorb even after we finish drinking because of digestive delay. Then as our bodies' elimination catches up to the absorption, we reach equilibrium. After that the body gets rid of the alcohol, elimination.

COMMENT:
For an alcohol curve, see Ch. 8 Demonstrative Evidence.

Q: If a person is still absorbing alcohol, will the test result be accurate?
A: No, it will be higher in the breath than the true blood alcohol level
Q: Why would it be higher?
A: During the absorption phase the alcohol concentration in the arteries is higher than in the veins because the alcohol goes from the GI tract into the arteries first. And the alcohol in the veins is what should determine a person's blood alcohol. But the breath machine indirectly measures that alcohol in the arteries because the alcohol in the breath comes from the alcohol in arteries running through the lungs.
Q: Well, the test was done about an hour after my client was arrested. Wouldn't he have been absorbing alcohol at the time of the test and therefore would have had a result that was *higher* than his actual blood alcohol level at the time of driving?
Q: If so, wouldn't his actual blood level—and the degree of impairment—have been lower than the test suggests?
A: Yes.
Q: Why?
A: As I stated earlier, the arterial blood, which is reflected in the breath test, has not yet brought alcohol to the brain. Therefore, impairment has not yet begun. If the result of the breath test is 200% too high, as suggested by various studies, then what appeared to be a .10 is truly a .05, a level presumed to be unimpaired.

§5:45   Temperature Issues

Q: Can the temperature of the person's breath affect the test results?
A: Yes.
Q: Why does temperature matter?
A: Because of Henry's Law.
Q: What is Henry's Law?
A: Henry's Law states that in a closed system, such as a human body, the amount of a volatile substance contained in a gas in contact with a liquid is directly related to the volume of the substance dissolved in the liquid and temperature.
Q: Can you explain this a little better for the jury?
A: Yes. Let's look at the simulator used in breath testing. The simulator is a jar partially filled with alcohol and water. When we heat the liquid, both water and alcohol evaporate into the air in the jar above the liquid. If we know the amount of alcohol in the liquid, let's say .10 percent, and we know the temperature, let's say 34 degrees Celsius, then we know that there will be .0827 percent alcohol in the air in the jar. In fact, that is exactly how the machine was calibrated in this case.
Q: So does this work with people as well?
A: Yes, if we increase the heat in our human "simulator," then we will increase the breath results over the true blood alcohol level.
Q: How much?
A: For every one degree Celsius we would see a 6% falsely high reading.
Q: Does this machine account for this important factor in breath testing?
A: Not this one.
Q: Can anything be done to account for it?
A: Yes. We can measure the breath temperature of the person as he provides a sample.
Q: What machines do account for this important factor?
A: The Draeger can do it, and in Alabama they do.
Q: But, although it is possible to eliminate this problem from the reliability quotient in this machine, this machine does not do that?
A: No it did not.

Here is another approach for either direct or cross-examination.

Q: Did you test this machine for accuracy using a "simulator"?
A: Yes.
Q: What is a simulator?
A: [See explanation above.]
Q: Why is it of paramount importance that this container be at a known temperature when it simulates a person breathing into this machine?
A: In order to know how much alcohol will evaporate into the headspace gas (that is the gas above the liquid) we need to know the temperature to apply Henry's Law.
Q: What does a simulator simulate?
A: It is a reservoir with a heater to hold the controlled solution and allow the air to pass through it for testing by the instrument itself.
Q: Okay. Would it be appropriate to say that it simulates a human breathing?
A: Yes, I believe so.
Q: How does the simulator work?
A: It sends the headspace gas into the machine so the machine reads a known quantity. If the machine guesses right, it is considered accurate.
Q: Because these machines don't test blood, they test gas?
A: Yes.
Q: You connected the simulator to the machine and heated the solution?
A: Right.
Q: Did you wait until it was at the right temperature before you tested the solution with the machine?
A: Yes.

Q: The right temperature is 34° C plus or minus two-tenths of a degree?
A: That is correct.
Q: If that simulator is not at the proper temperature, then the test is invalid, isn't it?
A: Yes, sir.
Q: That means if the temperature in the tested container is outside those parameters, the test is invalid?
A: Yes.
Q: So the temperature of the container in which there may be alcohol is of paramount importance. You must know what it is to know whether the test is valid and accurate?
A: Right.
Q: Because the higher the temperature of the liquid, the higher the alcohol in the gas that is tested from the container?
A: Right.
Q: Can you tell us what the temperature of this container [standing behind and pointing at defendant] was when he was tested by the machine?
A: No, sir. I cannot.
Q: So, what does that tell you about the validity of the test of this "container" [the client]?
A: I don't know.
Q: Then, without knowing what my client's temperature was when he blew into this same machine, can it be known with any degree of certainty that the numbers given were correct?

§5:46   Two Samples

Q: Why is it important—according to Dubowski's earlier referenced article—that two or more samples of a person's breath be taken?
A: Well there are several reasons. One is steepling; the other is accuracy. We all know the old saying: measure twice, cut once.
Q: What do you mean by "steepling"?
A: [Allow witness to explain.]
Q: Does that have any bearing on the issue of trying to calculate a person's alcohol level at the time of the arrest as opposed to the time of the test?
A: Yes, if the test is a single blow, and we do not know if it is a true reading or a steepled reading, then we have no basis for any guess as to true alcohol level.

§5:47   Steepling Example

Q: The officer has testified that the defendant was arrested at 1:50am and tested at 2:25am with a result of .10 percent, thirty five minutes after the stop. The officer testified that my client did not drink anything after he was arrested. Apparently, my client told him that he had had four beers at a bar just a few blocks from the stop and all within about an hour of the officer's arrest.
A: Okay.
Q: Do you know how long it takes a person to absorb a single beer?
A: It varies, anywhere from 30 minutes to an hour and a half.
Q: Generally though, all the alcohol would be in a person's blood within an hour and a half after he finished drinking the beer, right?
A: Yes.
Q: If my client had drunk one beer just before he drove, the test at 2:25 would show a higher blood alcohol than what was in his system at 1:50, the time when he was stopped?
A: That's possible.
Q: It would likely still be rising though 35 minutes after the last drink?
A: Possibly, yes.
Q: If a person was drinking a beer or just finished one at, say, 1:50am, his alcohol level at, say, 2:30am, would not have peaked, right?
A: Maybe, and in fact probably not. How fast he drank it, whether food was in the stomach, etc. can all affect the speed of alcohol rise.

Q: Well, in this scenario, with the level still possibly rising, and at a rate we don't know, there's no way to know what his level was at 1:50am, correct?

A: Without more information, I would agree.

Q: Knowing only a test result at a specific time, without more, cannot give you sufficient information to determine the level of that person at a specific time earlier, right?

A: Yes, that's right.

Q: It might well have been below .10 percent just as likely as not, right?

A: Counsel, with only the information you have given me, it would be impossible to pinpoint.

Q: There has been testimony by the prosecution that with my client's test result of .14 percent, that he would have had a level of .15 percent to .16 percent at the time of arrest a little over an hour earlier?

A: That's one *possibility*, but it assumes that your client was eliminating. Since he had nothing to drink during the time of arrest to test, under that theory, he would have been going down. The average is .015 percent to .02 percent, an hour. Therefore, he was very likely at about .15 percent or .16 percent at arrest. But that is not the only possibility.

Q: What other possibility is there?

A: That he was not finished absorbing and therefore was still rising from 1:50 to a peak at 2:30.

Q: Are you familiar with Kurt Dubowski from Oklahoma?

A: Yes.

Q: He is an authority in the field?

A: Yes, perhaps the pre-eminent authority in the field of alcohol and testing.

Q: Are you familiar with his 1985 article Absorption, Distribution and Elimination of Alcohol?

A: Yes, I have been for years and reviewed it again after you sent me a copy.

Q: Do you look to him for guidance?

A: I don't know if I'd use the word "guidance" but, his theories and articles are extremely influential in the field.

Q: On page 106 of that article, didn't this pre-eminent authority state that "no forensically valid forward *or* backward extrapolation of blood or breath alcohol concentration is ordinarily possible in a given subject solely on the basis of time and individual analysis results."

A: Yes.

Q: So, my client could have been below that .14 percent at the time of arrest, and judging from these graphics, it could have been a lot, right?

A: Possibly.

Q: No one can really tell us what my client's alcohol level was at arrest can they?

A: Not with any certainty.

§5:48   Two Breath Samples With .02 Agreement

Q: Are you familiar with the fact that most states require two breath samples with results that are within a plus or minus .02% or each other?

Q: Is this to accommodate any specific concern?

A: Yes.

Q: What is that concern?

A: Well, first is machine accuracy, but more importantly is mouth alcohol. It is felt that a .02 agreement eliminates the concern of mouth alcohol.

Q: You said earlier that Dubowski served as the head of Oklahoma's testing program for many years.

Q: Are you aware that he required a ±. 03% variance?

Q: So, two samples—one of .07% and .09% (or .10% in Dubowski's home state)—are acceptable?

Q: Which one is correct?

Q: Is either one correct?

Q: Then, the state would have this jury consider a test accurate and reliable if the results varied as much as 20 to 30 percent?

Q: What would you do with your thermometer if *it* varied that much between readings of your son's temperature within just a couple of minutes?

§5:49   Example of .02 Agreement

The following is just a sample of how you can use the above information with your own or the state's witness. Depending on your own personality and the witness's, it can be more or less comical.

Q: Sir, you are familiar with alcohol elimination rates in persons, aren't you?

A: Yes.

Q: Generally, it is .015% to .020% of the peak per hour, right?

A: Yes.

Q: State's exhibit 3 is a printout of my client's test?

A: Yes.

Q: The results of a .12% on this first blow at 1:32 a.m. and a 10% on his second blow at 1:35 a.m.

A: Yes.

Q: That's an elimination rate of what?

A: I don't understand your question.

Q: He eliminated .02% of his alcohol in three minutes which would be an elimination rate of .40% an hour, wouldn't it? That's double the average?

A: Well, that's not right.

Q: That's not possible, is it?

A: No.

Q: Are you aware that there has been testimony from the officer that my client was arrested at 1:50 a.m.?

A: Okay.

Q: If he was eliminating alcohol at the rate of .02% for every three minutes, that would mean that he was at about .50% or so seventeen minutes earlier at the time of arrest, huh?

A: Not likely.

Q: It's not very likely though since death occurs at about .50%, right? He obviously wasn't dead, huh? He's sitting right there.

A: It is not likely, no.

Q: You agree that it is scientifically, at best, improbable that a person's level of alcohol in his body would vary .02% in three minutes, wouldn't you?

A: Yes.

Q: If this machine measures alcohol in his body, you would further agree that one of these results isn't accurate?

A: That's right.

Q: Which test result is inaccurate?

A: I don't know.

Q: Which one is accurate, then?

A: I don't know.

Q: Can you really give any opinion within any reasonable degree of scientific certainty that either one is the accurate level of my client's blood alcohol level at the time of testing?

A: No one can.

Q: If this machine measures alcohol in his body, you would further agree that one of these results isn't accurate?

A: That's right

Q: Even though the results varied by almost 20 percent, are you comfortable that the results are accurate?

A: Absolutely not.

Q: Have you flown recently?

A: Yes.

Q: Would you have had a similar degree of "discomfort" if you had known that the altimeter of that plane had been off 20 percent?

§5:50   Machine Specificity and Interferants

The first few questions need not be asked if they have been asked previously. If this is the opening salvo in your defense then be sure your expert answers these questions to get the jury up to speed.

Q: What is infrared spectroscopy?

Q: How and why is it considered reliable in measuring chemicals in breath?

Q: Is this system ethanol specific?

A: No.

Q: Tell us how this machine uses energy variances to predict the amount of alcohol in a test sample?

A: Infrared energy is sent through the chamber where the breath is analyzed. The IR is set at a variety of wavelengths which can be absorbed by substances including alcohol.

Q: What do you mean by "interferants"?

A: Other compounds that also absorb energy at the same frequency as alcohol as illustrated here.

Q: Can these add to an alcohol reading on this machine?

A: Yes.

Q: Does this machine account for this?

A: Some do and some do not.

Q: How?

A: By separately measuring these other substances at still different frequencies and subtracting any result out of the alleged alcohol result.

Q: Will you please explain these "filters" and how they work to safe-guard against a test result that is inaccurate?

Q: Does the diagnostic system check to see if these are working?

A: No, they need to be independently checked.

Q: How many different chemicals can absorb IR around the range that alcohol does?

A: Hundreds.

Q: Is it normal for people to have any of these in their system?

A: Some of them can be found in the human breath, especially among industrial workers.

Q: What are toluene and acetone?

Q: When are these present in a person's system?

A: When the person works with solvents, paints and other toxic substances.

Q: How do they affect a test on this machine?

A: They both will absorb energy at the same frequencies as alcohol.

See Ch. 8, *Demonstrative Evidence*, for graphs and charts illustrating interference that can be used in conjunction with these questions.

§5:51   Acetaldehyde

Q: Isn't true the first by product of alcohol metabolism is acetaldehyde?

A: Yes.

Q: The faster the initial breakdown, the higher the level of this chemical that builds up in the body and blood?

A: It can build up. Usually, if it does, it can make the drinker very sick.

Q: Like my client when he vomited in the breath test room?

A: That is a possible outcome.

Q: Many things can increase this breakdown like sugars, and so forth?

A: Yes.

Q: Are you familiar with the way the Intoxilyzer 5000 works as an infrared spectroscopy device?

A: Of course.

Q: You know that the 5000 will read interferants as alcohol if they aren't filtered out?

A: Yes, it is supposed to take them out. The instrument has filters to remove acetone from contributing to the alcohol reading.

Q: Why did CMI put that into the machine?

A: It was discovered that acetone could be misread as alcohol.

Q: So the reason CMI put that filter in the machine was to avoid a false reading or result?

A: Right.

Q: Does this machine used in my client's test have this filter?

A: Yep.

Q: So we know that any acetone did not add any false reading to my client's test result, right?

A: Yes.

Q: Because this machine had one of those filters to take acetone out?

A: Correct.

Q: CMI wouldn't put that filter in the machine if acetone didn't give false readings, would they?

A: That a reasonable assumption.

Q: In fact, this 5000 has three filters, one for alcohol, one to remove acetone, and one that creates a baseline, right?

A: Generally, yes.

Q: You are aware that the newer 5000s have five filters now?

A: Yes.

Q: You are aware that one of the two additional filters is to filter out acetaldehyde and the other for toluene?

A: Yes.

Q: The one used for my client's test doesn't have these filters, does it?

A: No, it doesn't.

Q: You agree that when the company that makes these machines discovered that acetone gave false readings as alcohol, they put a filter in the machine to take it out? Since they have now put a filter in it to take out acetaldehyde, doesn't that mean this substance also gives false readings?

A: I can't speak for CMI.

Q: Well, CMI wouldn't have put those filters in there if those substances weren't giving false readings, would they?

A: That is a reasonable conclusion

Q: Is there any way to tell how much of my client's test result was a false positive from the natural breakdown of alcohol? From acetaldehyde?

A: There is no evidence that there was any.

Q: You can't say, though, since we didn't have it filtered out, that there was no contribution by this by product to the result that the machine reported, can you?

A: No, I would say that there is no way of knowing

§5:52   Airblank Fallacy

As most of you probably know, breath machines perform an air blank between tests. This is where the machine purges the sample chamber by bringing in air from the room through the breath hose, and pushing it through the sample chamber to "clean" it out. In order to prove this worked, the machine then allegedly measures the sample chamber and prints a result of "0.00" to show no alcohol. Sounds great.

We learned that it was all a lie. The machine was not in fact cleaning out the chamber and ensuring no alcohol remained. Instead, it was measuring what alcohol was left, and resetting itself to consider that residual a zero. Supposedly the software then deducted this number from the next result. Of course, since the manufacturers hid this from everyone, no one ever had the chance to test to see if the math was actually being carried out.

Q: This machine ran an "air blank" before and after my client's two tests.

A: Yes.

Q: Tell us what that is and why that is important?

A: Supposedly the air blank is used to purge the sample chamber of all alcohol. Then the machine measures the chamber to ensure it is alcohol-free.

Q: Is this what really happens?

A: No, turns out the machine does not ensure an alcohol-free chamber. It merely resets itself to zero based on what is left behind.

Q: So, if there is any alcohol in the chamber when my client is tested, it is added to his result?

A: Yes, both residual and new alcohol would be measured, but the machine is "supposed" to account for this.

Q: Has whether the machine accounts for this ever been tested?

A: No.

Q: Does it ignore these interferants during this air blank, too?

A: It would treat them the same.

§5:53   Slope Detector/Mouth Alcohol

Q: What is mouth alcohol?

A: Mouth alcohol is alcohol still in the oral cavity due to recent ingestion, dental issues, such as a cavity trapping alcohol, or any other way alcohol is still in the mouth.

Q: How does that affect a breath test?

A: Well, it would be blown into the machine with the lung air and measured as if it were lung air.

Q: So what?

A: Well, since this is undigested, uncirculated, unpartitioned alcohol, in other words "pure," it would be in a 1 to 1 ratio, and it would be multiplied by the 2100 we previously talked about.

Q: How do we ensure that we are not getting a mouth alcohol reading?

A: By an observation period, .02 agreement, and a slope detector.

Q: What is an observation period?

A: It is a period of time, not less than 15 minutes, where the subject is observed to ensure he does not ingest alcohol and that alcohol from the stomach is not reintroduced into the oral cavity by belching, regurgitation, or the like. The subject's mouth should also be empty of gum, chaw, or any other foreign substances.

Q: So, this deprivation or observation period is *crucial* to eliminating this concern for a false positive on a test reading?

A: Yes.

Q: Can you explain the importance of this?

A: [Allow expert to explain.]

Q: If a person belches or burps during this period, will it or can it affect the accuracy and reliability of a breath test?

A: Yes.

Q: Does the machine have any built-in protections to assist against this problem?

A: The slope detector is supposed to account for this.

Q: What is meant by a "slope detector"?

A: A slope detector checks for a rapid fall off in the breath alcohol readings. If the breath alcohol rises rapidly and falls off, it is a sign of mouth alcohol.

Q: Can you explain how it works in a breath test machine?

A: [Allow explanation.]

Q: If this feature is present on all 5000's, why do a deprivation period?

A: Because it is not foolproof. It is like a new car. It has an airbag, but you still wear a seatbelt.

Q: Explain how the slope detector may not work properly.

A: The slope detector is triggered by a rapid drop off from the readings, but if the person *does* have alcohol in his system, the drop off will not be that major as the initial reading from the mouth is slowly replaced or supported by alcohol from the lungs.

Q: You can show us? Please do.

A: [Witness will draw a slope detector model.]

Q: Can the machine check to see if this feature is working on it?

A: Not on its own.

Q: It's self-diagnostic does not check it?

A: No.

Q: Can it be tested?

A: Yes, but most labs do not correctly do so.

Q: Please explain?

A: As I said, if the machine sees a rise and a dramatic drop off, the detector is triggered. Most labs have a subject put a drop of alcohol on the tongue and blow. The machine shoots up to .2 and then instantly falls to 0. Well that's no test. A true test is if a person is a .06 and he swishes and rinses his mouth with alcohol, like a burp or hiccup would do, and then blows. Now we would see a rise to about .10 and a leveling soon thereafter as mouth and lung alcohol mix. The machine would then report the .09 or whatever when the true level is much lower.

§5:54   Diabetes, Hypoglycemia, Dieting

The argument you are making in diabetes, hypoglycemia, and diet cases is that the machine reads some other substance in the individual's breath as alcohol. These defenses are based on chemistry. In all of these conditions, the individual may not be burning the proper fuel in his or her body for energy. This then creates a process of ketosis that causes the release of ketones in the individual's breath. These ketones will absorb the same infrared light as alcohol and will contribute to the final reading.

Q: Ms. Expert, are you familiar with ketosis?
Q: When would a person be likely to be in such a state?
Q: What would a person in ketosis look like?
Q: So they appear as a drunk would?
Q: Would this also affect their balance?
Q: How about mental faculties?
Q: Could this condition create the "objective symptoms" of alcohol consumption?
Q: So the person would look, smell, sound, and act drunk?
Q: Would the person also test positive on a breath machine as a drunk?
Q: Why is that?
Q: So these ketones that the body is producing have the same fingerprint as does alcohol?
Q: Are you saying the breath machine does not test for alcohol?
Q: What does it test for?
Q: And these molecular bonds are found in the ketones as well as alcohol?
Q: Where else can they be found?
Q: What other types of alcohol can there be?
Q: Is methanol usually found in a person?
Q: So a person could have methanol in his or her breath if the person used certain cough drops or cigarettes?
Q: What about isopropyl alcohol?
Q: So some people produce isopropyl alcohol during the process of ketosis?
Q: In other words, a diabetic, hypoglycemic, or protein dieter is self-producing two substances that look like alcohol to these machines?
Q: A case of mistaken identity, as it were?

§5:55   GERD Cases

GERD is one of the most popular defenses in breath testing. Be forewarned, the prosecution will come after your client to be sure his condition was not suddenly discovered post-arrest. Therefore, you must ensure that your client can document his or her condition with medical reports.

Q: You have read my client's medical reports?
Q: You are not a medical doctor, but you do understand the condition reflected in those reports?
Q: You discussed his condition with my client's treating physician?
Q: Does anything about my client's health cause you to question the breath results in this case?
Q: What?
Q: What is GERD?
Q: How can it affect breath testing?
Q: So the upper valve in the stomach does not close, allowing gas to escape?
Q: This then gets tested by the breath machine?
Q: Won't it set off the slope detector?
Q: Why not?
Q: Doesn't the 15 minute observation period eliminate this problem?
Q: The officer indicated he told my client to blow hard and long; what does that do?
Q: Does this compression of the diaphragm make the GERD issue worse?
Q: Why?
Q: Wouldn't my client have to bring up a large amount of stomach gas to significantly increase the reading?
Q: So what if the gas is pure?
Q: What is the blood/breath ratio?
Q: That is for breath in the lungs, correct?
Q: What is the ratio for stomach gas?
Q: Why?
Q: So, if I understand correctly, the stomach alcohol gas is direct 1 to 1 ratio, not a diluted 2100 to 1.
Q: So, much less alcohol causes much higher readings?

[§§5:56-5:59 Reserved]

V. ALCOHOL EXPERT AND RISING ALCOHOL

§5:60 Selection and Preparation

Rising alcohol is a favorite defense for many attorneys, probably because it is a truthful one. It is not unusual for people to finish their last drink as they are leaving a restaurant or bar. Given that it takes some 30 minutes, at least, for this drink to affect a person, and that many people are within that amount of driving time of their final destination, the drink would not reach a critical level until they get home. That is, until the police interrupt these plans.

The most important factor in presenting this defense is cohesiveness between the police report, the objectively ascertainable facts, and the science. If the facts show a drinking pattern that ended six hours ago, do not try to get your expert to opine the alcohol level was still rising. While it is possible, it is not believable to a jury. Instead look for a case where the client has witnesses and statements to the police that show drinking just before contact and an end point near where they were stopped.

Virtually any qualified expert can establish this defense, so look for one who is comfortable with your client and the facts he or she will need to support.

§5:61 Purpose and Goals

In order to successfully bring a rising alcohol defense, you must do three things:
* Explain the basic physiological aspects of alcohol.
* Destroy any presumptions in your jurisdiction. These may be presumptive alcohol levels, or time of driving/time of testing presumptions.
* Create a question in the minds of the jurors as to the client's exact blood alcohol content at the time of driving.

This last step is greatly aided by the disconnect theory. The disconnect theory is the concept that any outward manifestations showing a lack of impairment, such as good field sobriety test performance, do not agree with subsequent alcohol levels. In other words, if the guy looks sober, how can he be so drunk? The disconnect theory requires either good performance on SFSTs, refusal to submit to SFSTs, or explainable failure on SFSTs, and relatively few or explainable "objective symptoms." For more on these concepts see the subdivision below.

See Appendix A *The District Attorney's Manual* for the prosecution's approach to cross-examination of defense alcohol experts and common chemical test defenses.

§5:62 Physiology of Alcohol

Q: Ms. Expert, can you tell me the three basic phases of alcohol dynamics in a person?
A: [Absorption, distribution and elimination. See explanation above.]
Q: Give us some idea of what occurs during absorption.
A: [See above.]
Q: What happens during distribution?
Q: And elimination?
Q: Now, based on this, would I be accurate in describing the process as a dynamic, rather than static, one?
Q: In fact, the state's expert agreed with that position?
Q: So, you are in agreement with the state's expert to this point?

§5:63 Destruction of Presumptions

Q: Now, based upon what you just said, would you find it scientifically acceptable to presume a person's alcohol level would remain the same for a period of two (use your own state's presumption) hours?
A: No.
Q: Why not?
A: Because the digestion of alcohol is not static. When we drink, alcohol levels go up, plateau, and then fall.
Q: So if we had a person's BAC at say midnight, we would be wrong to presume it to have been that level at 10:00 p.m.?
A: It would be wrong to presume that. Now, it could be that the level is the same, indicating a peak in between. But it is just as likely, or even more likely that the level was lower or higher at the earlier time. And given the times you have listed, I would guess it would be lower.

Q: Or, equally wrong to presume it would stay at that level at 2:00 a.m.?
A: If all I know is the result at midnight, then I can also not say what the result at 2:00 a.m. would be. It could be the same or lower or higher. It all depends on the drinking pattern, specifically when the person had the last drink, the person's own metabolism and stomach content.
Q: Again, the state's expert felt the same way?
A: If you say so.
Q: Would you agree with an instruction that tells the members of the jury that they should presume a person's BAC at the time he was tested is the same as it was at the time of driving?
A: Well that would not be scientifically accurate.
Q: This is because of what you have previously told us?
A: Yes.
Q: Again, why is this?
Q: You have spent a lot of time studying alcohol and its effects on people, haven't you?
Q: Have you ever read, heard or otherwise been made aware of anyone in the scientific community who would hold such a concept, that BAC is static?
A: No one does.
Q: The fact that a group of lawmakers got together and set this concept up, does that make it true?
A: Lawmakers cannot regulate science.
Q: Can anyone legislate science?
A: No.
Q: Wasn't that why Galileo was imprisoned?
A: Actually, it was.
Q: Given what we have discussed, would you agree with the state's expert that it is impossible to say that a BAC at the time of testing is a true and accurate reflection of the BAC at the time of driving?
A: Yes.
Q: Why?
A: Because, as we discussed, we don't not know if the alcohol level is rising or falling, unless you give me a lot more information.

§5:64   Creating Doubt

Q: Well then, Dr. Expert, given all we discussed, can you tell me what my client's BAC was at the time of driving?
A: No I cannot
Q: Can you give me a range of possibilities?
A: I can, but it would be a very large range.
Q: So, the BAC could be higher, lower, or the same?
A: Those are the only three possibilities.
Q: Is there any way we could know for sure?
A: If we took a sample at the time the person was driving we would know. Absent that, we can only theorize what it might be, and then only after more information and a number of assumptions.
Q: What information would you need?
A: I would need to know age, sex, and weight to start. Then I would need to know when the person started drinking, what he was drinking, what the drinking pattern was, and if the person had anything to eat and what. Even then, it would be only be a range of possibilities based on some scientific averages.
Q: Well, since we do not have all that information, can you hazard a guess?
A: A guess? Sure, but it has no basis in fact.
Q: But the state expert did say his opinion was our client's BAC was higher at the time of driving then it was at the time of the test.
A: As I said, that is one possibility.
Q: So it is possible, but not definitive.
A: Correct.
Q: Would you say it is reasonable to so assume?
A: No, I would not.
Q: Would you say it is beyond a reasonable doubt to so assume?

A: Definitely not.

Q: Why not?

A: Because the state's expert is assuming the person is eliminating alcohol when the facts do not indicate he was. In fact, the facts seem to indicate that the alcohol level was rising.

§5:65   Disconnect Theory

Q: Since we cannot tell what my client's BAC was at the time of driving, based upon this later test, is there any other information that may aid us in deciding if the level is rising or falling?

A: If there are no other chemical tests, no specifically known drinking pattern, then we may be able to gain some information from field tests, but this would be speculative as well.

Q: What would that be?

A: If we see horrendous performance on FSTs, then it may be further evidence of a high alcohol level. Of course it could be poor performance based on a variety of other factors as well, so it would not be definitive. On the other hand, if we see strong performance on FSTs, that is a good indicator that the alcohol is not yet influencing the person so the level must be on the rise.

Q: So if we see performance on the field sobriety tests that does not correspond to the predicted BAC, it would aid us in our determination?

A: Yes, especially if the physical manifestations are opposite the chemical results.

Q: In this case, have you evaluated John's performance the FSTs?

A: Yes I did.

Q: Is it consistent with a true BAC at the time of driving, which is represented by the BAC in the chemical test?

A: No it is not.

Q: Why not?

A: Assuming the BAC of .10 is correct, and further using the state's position that an hour earlier he was a .12, we would expect to see fairly poor performance on the FSTs. But we do not. In fact, we see very good performance on the FSTs. This indicates little or no alcohol impairment, so the alcohol level at the time of driving must be lower than that at the time of the test. Or simply put, lower than the .10.

Q: Are there other factors that you would look at to support or deny this rising alcohol conclusion?

A: Drinking pattern, amount of alcohol and so forth.

Q: So if we put it all together, knowing all you know, what is your ultimate opinion as to my client's BAC at the time of driving?

A: It must have been below the .10 and in all likelihood, well below .08.

§5:66   Tolerance

Q: We heard the prosecution witnesses talk about tolerance. They indicated there are two types of tolerance. One is a learned tolerance. That is where a person repeats a task so often that it becomes second nature. The other is individual tolerance. That is where the person has built up a pseudoimmunity to the interfering factor, in this case alcohol. Are you comfortable with these definitions?

A: They will do.

Q: With regards to the "learned" tolerance, can that be true of SFSTs?

A: No. Learned tolerance, if there is such a thing, would be development of the ability to perform a task under adverse conditions through repetition. For example, if I asked you to walk all day with a ten pound weight on your back, you would tire more quickly than normal. But, if you always walk with such a weight, then doing so at my request would not be bothersome. In order to have learned tolerance for alcohol and SFST performance, the person would have to get drunk all the time and practice FSTs when drunk.

Q: But the person would (1) have to perform these on a very regular basis?

A: Yes.

Q: And (2) perform them regularly while intoxicated?

A: Exactly.

Q: Yet there is no evidence of this type of tolerance in this case, is there?

A: None whatsoever.

Q: As for immunity-type tolerance, we are talking about an alcoholic, are we not?

A: Yes.

Q: Is there any evidence of alcoholism in this case?

A: None.

Q: So the basic assumption behind the prosecution's theory of tolerance is that Jim is a chronic alcoholic who practices FSTs on a regular basis?

A: That seems to be what they are getting at. But there is one other issue. There are studies that show that even chronic alcoholics do not have tolerance when it comes to SFSTs. They may be able to mask signs of alcohol in day-to-day tasks but not for SFSTs.

Q: The contrary theory is that he was not drunk at the time of performing the FSTs and that his good performance is consistent with not being under the influence, correct?

A: Yes, and that is the simpler explanation in keeping with Occam's Razor.

§5:67   Consistency Theory

Q: Let's talk about consistency theory.

A: I am not sure what you mean.

Q: The state's witness made a big deal of labeling all the symptoms as "consistent" with alcohol. Does "consistent with" mean proof beyond a reasonable doubt?

A: No, it merely means that a given symptom is not contraindicative of what you are theorizing.

Q: Let's look at some examples. If a woman came to you and said she missed her period, that would be consistent with pregnancy, wouldn't it?

A: Consistent, but not proof.

Q: Add in sore breasts and we have more consistency?

A: Yes, but still not proof.

Q: Morning sickness?

A: Yes.

Q: Swelling?

A: Yes.

Q: A recent sexual experience?

A: Yes.

Q: But, would any self-respecting scientist say she is pregnant just based on this?

A: No.

Q: They would want more?

A: Yes.

Q: You wait for a definitive blood test, correct?

A: Yes.

Q: Because a consistent symptom merely establishes a possibility, it does not dictate a certainty, does it?

A: Correct.

§5:68   Blood Tests

Q: Let's stick with this pregnant woman. Would you agree that the objective symptoms and roadside tests are like the factors we listed above?

A: Yes

Q: Does it mean the woman is pregnant?

A: No.

Q: Does it mean that John is guilty?

A: No.

Q: Why not?

A: Well, for the woman, it could be menopause, a missed cycle or other issues. For John, it could be fatigue, sickness, or he just found out his wife is pregnant again. That would explain the bloodshot eyes and disorientation, especially at his age.

Q: Okay, so all these "consistent" symptoms and tests do not answer the query of pregnancy or of DUI. But they would be a reason to go get a blood test?

A: Exactly.

Q: Now, the first thing we want to be sure of with the blood test is that we don't contaminate the results. How do we do this?

A: Well, we start with a non-alcoholic swab, a clean vial, and a trained phlebotomist. We need a special vacutainer tube with anticoagulant and a preservative. Once the sample is taken, it needs to be kept refrigerated and properly tested.

Q: So we ensure the integrity in obtaining the sample. Do we stop there?

Q: What are the necessary ingredients in the vacu-tube?

Q: What is sodium fluoride, and why does it matter?

Q: What is potassium occulate and what does it do?

Q: Looking at the vials and exhibits in this case, were those substances there and were they in the correct amounts?

Q: Is this specific for alcohol testing?

A: Some of it is, but anytime you take blood for any reason, you need to be sure it is clean, preserved, and correctly tested.

Q: So, right off the bat, we may be telling this woman she is pregnant and we have a bad sample.

A: Possibly.

Q: This will cause her heartbreak later on.

A: Yes.

Q: But nothing like what would happen to my client if this jury convicts him on such flimsy evidence.

A: Depends on who you ask, but I get your point.

Q: Getting back to the sample, a good draw and a good vial are all we need?

A: No.

Q: What else?

Q: What is this chain of custody?

Q: So we need to be sure that the results of the test, be it for pregnancy or for alcohol, are Brenda's and we don't assign them to Bill?

A: Yes.

Q: Although that would be a heck of a story?

Q: Once the blood sample gets to the lab are we done?

A: No.

Q: What can happen if the blood is not properly stored?

A: It can generate alcohol on its own.

Q: So we could get a spontaneous positive result without it being true.

A: Probably not with the pregnancy, but definitely with the alcohol.

Q: How does that work?

Q: What studies do you use to have that opinion?

Q: Is there any way we can check for contamination?

A: Yes, by culturing the blood.

Q: Are talking about a culture like for strep throat?

Q: Just like our possibly pregnant woman, our possibly drunk client or a possible strep throat has a number of "consistent" symptoms, but only a culture will tell for sure if they are pregnant, drunk, or sick. Correct?

Q: But, the difference is that with strep throat, we give a mild drug as a precaution?

Q: One that will not have any lifelong negative effect if we were wrong?

Q: Was any culture done in this case to be sure that we are not drugging Bill for no reason?

Q: So we do not know if this blood sample is good?

Q: Bill may be poisoned by the opinions rendered in this case based on error?

Q: Let's assume the sample is not contaminated. Are we done yet?

A: No, we still need to check the lab testing for calibration and accuracy.

Q: What are calibration and accuracy?

§5:69 Henry's Law

Q: We previously heard from the officer that he took a .10 solution Heated it to 34 degrees centigrade and tested the corresponding vapor, obtaining a .10. Is this good?

A: No.

Q: Why not?

A: At 34 degrees a .10 solution should read as a .08 vapor.

Q: Let's take it a step at a time. What do all breath machines check, whether in calibration mode or evidential testing?

A: Some type of air.

Q: The air they check, where does it come from?

A: Either a person, in testing mode, or a simulator in calibration mode.

Q: For an evidential check, it is from a person, for a calibration or accuracy check, it is from the simulator.

A: Yes.

Q: The simulator, can you describe it?

A: It is a jar, like a pickle jar, attached by a hose to the back of the breath machine. It contains liquid—water and alcohol—about three quarters full.

Q: So this pickle jar sits on the back or next to the breath machine and pumps a vapor into the machine?

A: Yes.

Q: Where does it get this vapor?

A: The simulator is heated to a set temperature, usually 34 degrees Celsius, creating a gas above the liquid.

Q: Okay, the jar is partially filled with liquid, where does this liquid come from?

A: Either it is made in lab or purchased from another lab.

Q: If it is made up in the lab how is it checked?

A: By titration and a secondary method such as specific gravity or GC.

Q: Would it be proper to check the final result on the same machine you are calibrating?

A: No, that would be like using your bathroom scale to measure out 10 pounds of grapes, then putting that same bag of grapes on the scale to see if the scale says it weighs ten pounds. If the scale was wrong initially, it would still be wrong.

Q: If it is purchased, how do we vouch for its accuracy?

A: By tracing the product back to the lab and its methods. Usually these go back to NIST (National Institute of Standards and Testing), the federal government official weights and measures bureau.

Q: Let's assume it is what it is said to be, the simulator heats the liquid up and a vapor is formed, correct?

A: Yes.

Q: What is this vapor called?

A: Headspace gas.

Q: So the breath machine then "inhales" the headspace gas. How do we know what the alcohol level in the headspace should be?

A: Using Henry's Law.

Q: So it is dependant on the percentage in the liquid and temperature?

A: Yes. Henry's Law states that at any given temperature, the amount of a volatile substance contained in water will create a vapor of a specific proportion.

Q: Does it equate to a one to one ratio, if we are talking about alcohol?

A: No, at 34 degrees the ratio is 82.7 percent.

Q: So at 34 degrees, the content of the vapor of a .10 solution, would be .0827?

A: Yes.

Q: And this is Henry's Law?

A: That it is.

Q: Therefore, when the officer explained, as we stated before, that he used a .10 solution, heated it to 34 degrees and obtained a .10, this would be a major problem?

A: Most major.

Q: Mr. Expert, how do you properly handcuff a suspect?

A: I don't know.

Q: You don't know. Is it fair to say the science should be left to those with scientific training and the police work to left those with that training to avoid these mistakes?

[§§5:70-5:79 Reserved]

VI. MEDICAL EXPERTS

§5:80   Treating Physician

I know, your client cannot afford a doctor as an expert. Are you sure? You would be surprised how many ordinary doctors would like to testify in court. Speak to your client's treating physician to see if he or she can come into talk about injuries (for SFSTs), medical conditions (for diabetes or GERD) or whatever else you may need.

§5:81   Validity of Test

DA's are trained to not take on the medical expert or the conditions directly. Instead, they will get the doctor to admit that (1) alcohol is bad, (2) if your client's alcohol level was what the machine indicated, your client was impaired, and (3) the doctor would not get into a car with someone who was impaired. Knowing this, try the following approach.

I am leaving out the medical direct as I am sure you can draft it yourself.

Q: Doctor, you agree that someone who is impaired by alcohol is not safe to drive?
Q: You would also agree that if the chemical test in this case is correct, then Bobby was impaired?
Q: So, the question for you, and for everyone else, is whether this test result is accurate?
Q: You are familiar with the phrase "reasonable degree of medical certainty"?
Q: This is the level to be safe in your diagnosis?
Q: It is not a guess?
Q: But it is also not beyond reasonable doubt?
Q: So, can you say to any degree of scientific certainty that the chemical test in this case was valid?
Q: Why not?

Let the doctor talk. Allow him or her to fully explain what conditions your client has that prevent reliance on the test. Your job at this point is to watch the jury. Interrupt only when necessary to have the doctor explain parts the jurors seem to miss. Have the doctor repeat the critical issue in the case.

§5:82   Cross-Examination

Now the DA will come back with questions pertaining to that night. The DA will attempt to show that the doctor has no knowledge of whether or not the condition was "active" at the time in question to compromise the test. This is a gold mine waiting to be tapped.

Prepare your expert to answer as follows:

DA: Well, you do not know if the defendant was having a GERD/Diabetes/whatever attack at the time of the chemical test, do you?
A: My understanding is that you, Mr. Prosecutor, need to show he wasn't, given that no one was there to test him for it.

It is that simple. Jurors will pick this up.

Try not to cover too much in redirect of the medical doctor; it looks like you are covering for him. Understand that a doctor still enjoys a large amount of respect from the jury and that unless the prosecutor made some huge points, the jury will allow you to argue on the expert's word alone.

[§§5:83-5:89 Reserved]

VII. COUNTERING THE PROSECUTION'S "THE DEFENSE EXPERT WAS NOT AT THE SCENE" STRATEGY

§5:90   You Must Show the Jury That Independent Review Is More Reliable

We have all been there when the prosecution asks our expert this series of questions: "You weren't present when the officer witnessed the driving?" "You weren't there when the officer saw the objective signs of intoxication?" "You weren't there when the officer administered the SFST's?" And so forth. The jury hangs on every "no" your expert states and then uses it to find him or her not believable.

This is very misleading in that an *independent* evaluation of the facts is the scientific method. One person makes the observations, publishes the results, and makes available the underlying data so that others can evaluate the conclusion.

Do judges require such scientific methodology in our cases? Heck no. They let anything go. Therefore, it is our responsibility to show the jury that the independent review is not only appropriate, it is more reliable.

First, you need to lay the groundwork in voir dire or opening statement, or both. Then you need to follow it up in cross-examination and direct examination. Then finally drive it home in closing.

§5:91   Opening or Voir Dire

Ladies and Gentlemen of the jury (or potential juror number 5 if in voir dire), assume you go to a doctor with some symptoms, whatever they may be. The doctor runs three or four tests on you and concludes you have a serious situation and must be sent for a long treatment in isolation. However, before you agree, you ask for an independent evaluation by an equally, or even better trained, professional. This professional is paid by you since your insurance company already paid for the first opinion. (If in voir dire, ask if people are ok with this or if they feel the second opinion would be biased.)

Now the first professional gives you all of the information he gathered. You turn it over to your professional, who looks at how the data was gathered, how it was interpreted, and the final conclusion. Since this data is objective, would it matter if the second professional were there when your pulse was measured? When your temperature was taken? When your X-ray was taken? Of course it wouldn't; data is data. (Put this in the form of a question if this is in voir dire.)

The point is that there is no need for the specialized professional to have been present when the information was obtained if it was obtained according to protocol, and was honestly reported.

§5:92   Cross-Examination of the Arresting Officer

Now let's see how we can use these concepts during the cross of the cop. (This assumes you are familiar with the three phases of Standardized Field Sobriety Test Investigation, and pinpoint cross-examination.)

Q: You were trained to obtain information for the DUI investigation?
A: Yes.
Q: That includes driving pattern?
A: Yes.
Q: Initial contact?
A: Yes.
Q: And then SFST performance?
A: Yes.
Q: The driving pattern is objective?
A: Yes.
Q: You say what you saw?
A: Yes.
Q: The initial contact is objective?
A: Yes.

Q: You say what you smelled?
A: Yes.
Q: Heard?
A: Yes.
Q: Saw?
A: Yes.
Q: Your report answers these questions?
A: Yes.
Q: All without embellishment?
A: Yes.
Q: Just the facts?
A: Yes.
Q: Then you report the SFST's?
A: Yes.
Q: Objectively?
A: Yes.
Q: For example, he put his foot down twice on One Leg Stand?
A: Yes.
Q: You also report how you explained the test?
A: Yes.
Q: And how you demonstrated the test?
A: Yes.
Q: At some point you record all of this?
A: Yes.
Q: And you report it factually?
A: Yes.
Q: Without bias?
A: Yes.
Q: Without subjectivity?
A: Yes.
Q: Just as it happened?
A: Yes.
Q: Your report gets reviewed?
A: Yes.
Q: If there were issues, they would be brought to your attention?
A: I assume so.
Q: That didn't happen?
A: No.
Q: So the report was considered an objective compilation of the relevant factors for the arrest?
A: Yes.
Q: Anyone can look at the facts and rely on them?
A: Yes.
Q: Because they are objective?
A: Yes.
Q: If I gave you someone else's objective report, you could review it as well?

This is a no win for the officer. If he says no, then one can ask what the report is good for. If he says yes, which he will, then you have tied the officer in to agreeing that review is possible regardless of presence.

§5:93   Direct Examination of Your Expert

Having laid this ground work with the officer, use it with your own expert.

Q: You reviewed the report and the testimony by the arresting officer in this case?

A: Yes, I did.

Q: Is that typical?

A: Yes, since the observations in the three phases of a DUI investigation are objective, then anyone who is properly trained can review the decision. It is similar to a medical second opinion. If there is an X-ray and the first doctor who took it says no problem, but you bring it to a second professional with more experience who sees a fracture, it doesn't matter the second professional wasn't there when the X-ray was taken. He, and I, can rely on the data gathered by the first one on the scene.

Q: But doesn't the one who is there have more information to go on?

A: There shouldn't be anything more. If there is more, then the reporting person is not being objective. He is subjectively modifying the information, which then renders his own diagnosis suspect. In other words, when one is making a decision based on objective data, then one records and reports that data in order for the conclusion to be supported or refuted later. That is the scientific method.

§5:94   Closing

Now the prosecution made some point of arguing that Mr. Defense Expert was not present during the investigation of Bob. However, ask yourself if it really matters. You heard first from the government's own data collection expert, the arresting officer, that he/she did a full objective evaluation of Bob, which was then honestly recorded without bias and finally relayed to you here in court. You then heard from L.P., a SFST instructor, that he evaluated all the data in an objective manner. L.P. showed you in his testimony that there are rules to follow in data gathering which were broken (e.g., wrong instruction on the walk and turn), that certain data was included that is irrelevant (the manner of counting in the one leg stand) and that factors which negate the test (unequal tracking) were ignored. He then told you that based upon this, the resulting conclusion was not supported based on the objective criteria. It doesn't matter that L.P. wasn't there, just as it wouldn't matter if your doctor did the X-ray, so long as he had a chance to see it and evaluate it for himself.

(This page intentionally left blank.)

CHAPTER 6

THE CLIENT'S TESTIMONY

PROLOGUE

I WILL STAND WITH YOU: Remembering what our clients really need.

Before we begin negotiations with the prosecutor—before we draft motions to suppress—before voir dire—before closing arguments—before everything we consider to be at the core of our job, we have a truly core task: caring for our clients. Now, I know what you're thinking. We all know that we represent clients. We know our obligations under the ethics rules. We know that clients are how we get paid. But we often forget some basic truths about clients that will help us be better at our job.

What is our job? It's not to win. We can't control the outcome of our cases. Even the best of us lose. Even a lousy case sometimes turns into a winner. Our job is to **help** our clients **through the process**. And make sure they do not feel like they are going through it alone.

Look—we all have lives. We have spouses, children, mortgages, parents. We have good days; we have bad days. But we have to remember our clients through it all. A client once told me that a former attorney was angry with him because he'd reoffended. This made almost no sense to me. This client sat and cried in my office because he'd angered someone he viewed as a trusted advisor. I know that clients struggle—and it's not my job to judge or be upset. If a client comes to me for help, it's my job to be there for the client and continue helping him or her. My job is to make sure the client is **not alone**.

Let's consider how we **could** be viewing a first offense client.

My first offense clients are typically in their late 20s or early 30s. They have jobs. Often they have a child or two. And most of them (whether they'll admit it or not) are **terrified** to have to call me in the first place. They are about to embark on a journey that will cost them days of work and (in some cases) thousands of dollars they may not currently have. It will cause marital strife. It will cause their children to ask questions ("What's that you're blowing into daddy?"). And even if they are able to get a great result (reduced charge or whatnot), the impact will follow them for years. And they need to know this.

Many clients ask their lawyers **after court**: "Wait…what happened?" Remember, the average DUI client does not know what a continuance is—much less a suppression hearing. Imagine if instead of business as usual, we took an extra five minutes before a court date to explain to the client what was going to happen, and more importantly **why** it was going to happen.

Imagine if, during our initial consultation, we listened more than we talked and were able to connect with the client on a **human** level. Imagine we used this connection to explain to the client that what he or she was about to go through was going to be very hard—but that we would be by the client's side every step of the way. Not just fighting **for the client**—but fighting **along with him** or her. Think about being that scared client and realizing that you have such a committed defender and supporter with you. Regardless of the outcome, you will be a happier client.

Now, your first offense clients may not look like mine. They may be younger, older, or different in every other possible way. But no matter what, you can always control the attitude that you have towards and about your clients.

Here's another important truth that many of us forget. Yes, this is a professional business. Yes, we have higher education than most of our clients. And yes, most often we know what's best for them. But at its heart, this is a **customer service industry**. If we do not provide good customer service, we do not get clients. We do not get referrals. We do not thrive and prosper. And frankly, we don't deserve to.

We—the DUI defense bar—take up the mantle of defending one of the most vilified of all defendants, the drunk driver. We dedicate our lives to standing with them and defending their rights. We ensure the police and prosecutors follow the rules and treat our clients like the human beings they are. But our foremost responsibility is to **remember** that they are human, and simply to treat them that way. To help them through the forest, guide them, talk to them, and when necessary, hold their hands while we do it.

Look, we can't always win. But we can always win our clients' respect and give them ours. And that's what they deserve—our very best. Every day. Every time. Because they have **way** more at stake than we do.

I.   HOW TO EVALUATE WHETHER THE CLIENT SHOULD TESTIFY

A. In General

§6:00   Focus on the State's Failure and You Won't Need the Defendant's Testimony

As storytellers, we need to know who the protagonists and antagonists in our stories are. If we have set up the jury with the understanding that the State's job is to prove their case and that the defense lawyer's job is to point out that their case isn't proven, we have set up an interesting dichotomy that flies in the face of everything we have been told juries believe and know.

The antagonist in our story (the bad guy) is the State Prosecutor. The protagonist (the good guy) is the defense lawyer.

Our clients and the officers are just characters in the stories. But, believe it or not, they are not the main characters in the story we are telling to the jury. Why? Because the story we are telling the jury is:

- The State has a job,
- The State has invited the jury in to watch them do their job.
- It's the defense lawyer's to point out why the State didn't do their job.

That's the story summed up in three bullets and it includes nothing about witnesses.

At it's heart (although we'll explain it to our juries a bit differently), our story is about defense versus prosecution, rather than client versus cop. This gives us a very valuable axiom that I have used in my practice successfully for over a decade.

It is (almost) never a good idea for a client to testify in a DUI case.

We've just spent time establishing to a jury that your client doesn't have to testify, and in fact, shouldn't have to testify. You have placed the burden squarely in the State's lap and are ready to hold their feet to the fire in ways they can not anticipate or respond to. There is one thing that can screw it all up for you—and that's your client. Leave her sitting next to you at counsel table beaming confidence to the jury in the fact that she knows the jury will reach the only proper verdict—not because she "didn't do it"—but because nobody can **prove she did**.

There are obvious exceptions to this rule, but they are much fewer and farther between than you might think. In over 15 years of DUI practice and well over 100 cases tried to a jury, I can think of two instances where I've advised my clients to take the stand in a DUI case.

Many of the exceptions are discussed below in the words of the previous author, all of which are valid and may lend themselves to your practice style. I simply present this alternative approach as a cohesive storytellers toolkit that has worked well because at the end of the day—I'm a better storyteller than my clients are.

§6:01   To Testify or Not to Testify, That Is the Question

Ask any group of criminal defense attorneys about having their client testify and you will get the entire range of answers:

"I lost because of what he said."

"She won the case for me."

"The jury couldn't understand why he didn't testify."

"The jury wondered why she took the stand."

Personally, I will never forget the case in which the jurors were out for two days. After the not guilty verdict, they told me the prosecution had not made out guilt beyond a reasonable doubt. However, my client's testimony during the defense case had brought the jury close to a guilty verdict. For the two days they discussed what to make of his testimony. Finally, one juror remembered the court's instruction that the burden was on the prosecution and that the case should be looked at from what they proved.

This led me to form the following rule: If you are considering having your client testify, ask for a break to discuss it with the client. If you are still convinced, ask fellow attorneys. If you are still convinced, go in and tell the court "The defense rests." I have followed this rule religiously, except when I have violated it.

So, how do you know when to have your client testify? You don't. But, there are certain factors you should evaluate in order to come to the decision.

§6:02   Jurors Expect Innocent Clients to Testify

Despite what we say and do, most jurors nowadays do want to hear from the defendant. The media, both legitimate news and fictional shows, have convinced the population that only someone with something to hide would not take the stand. I cannot think of one courtroom portrayal, in movie or television, where an *innocent* defendant did not take the stand. Every script indicates that the defendant does not testify because he knows the truth and wants to hide it.

Of course, in DUI defense we have a slight advantage. Very rarely are our clients hiding the facts. Since most of our cases do not involve hiding the driver's identity, nor are they based on a theory that the victim deserved it, the absence of our clients' testimony is more easily understood. Why put the client on to repeat the drinking pattern he or she told the officer? There is no need to put the client on to explain a medical condition (diabetes, GERD, etc.).

On the other hand, if the case is a refusal, many DUI lawyers feel that some explanation needs to be given about why the client did not take the test. But see Ch. 4, §4:49 for a winning strategy for refusal cases that does not require the client's testimony and focuses on cross-examination of the arresting officer and closing argument.

§6:03   Memorandum in Support of Defendant's Motion in Limine to Limit the Scope of Defendant's Cross-Examination

For other defense motions in limine, see Chapter 1.

MEMORANDUM IN SUPPORT OF DEFENDANT'S MOTION IN LIMINE TO LIMIT THE SCOPE OF DEFENDANT'S CROSS-EXAMINATION

I.   THE PRIVILEGE AGAINST SELF-INCRIMINATION LIMITS THE SCOPE OF CROSS-EXAMINATION TO THE EXTENT OF MATTERS MADE RELEVANT BY DEFENDANT'S TESTIMONY BECAUSE DEFENDANT'S DECISION TO TESTIFY IS ONLY A LIMITED WAIVER OF THE PRIVILEGE

The constitutional privilege against self-incrimination, U.S. Const., 5th Amend; Cal. Const., art. I, §13, mandates that the scope of cross-examination of a defendant be limited to that which the defendant testified to on direct, or that which tends to impeach the defendant's credibility. This long-standing proposition is embraced both by the United States Supreme Court, *see U.S. v. Havens* (1980) 446 U.S. 620, 100 S. Ct. 1912; *Brown v. U.S.* (1958) 356 U.S. 148, 78 S. Ct. 622, and the California Supreme Court, *see People v. Boyette* (2002) 29 Cal. 4th 381, 58 P.3d 391; *People v. Schader* (1969) 71 Cal. 2d 761, 457 P.2d 841. It has consistently been reiterated by the federal and California intermediate appellate courts. *See U.S. v. Black* (9th Cir. 1985) 767 F.2d 1334; *U.S. v. Hearst* (9th Cir. 1977) 563 F.2d 1331; *People v. Foss* (2007) 155 Cal. App.4th 113; *Nienhouse v. Superior Court* (1996) 42 Cal. App.4th 83; *People v. Johnson* (1989) 211 Cal. App. 3d 392; *People v. Alfaro* (1976) 61 Cal. App. 3d 414; *People v. Matola* (1968) 259 Cal. App. 2d 686.

A defendant who testifies at trial waives his Fifth Amendment privilege and may be cross-examined on matters made relevant by his direct testimony. The scope of the defendant's waiver is coextensive with the scope of relevant cross-examination. *Brown*, 356 U.S. at 154-6, 78 S. Ct. 626-27.

The witness himself, certainly if he is a party determines the area of disclosure and therefore of inquiry. Such a witness has the choice, after weighing the advantage of the privilege against self-incrimination against the advantage of putting forward his version of the facts and his reliability as a witness, not to testify at all. He cannot reasonably claim that the Fifth Amendment gives him not only this choice but, if he elects to testify, an immunity from cross-examination on the matters he has himself put in dispute." *Id.*

The focus is on whether the government's questions are "reasonably related" to the subjects covered by the defendant's testimony. *Hearst*, 563 F.2d at 1340

In *Schader*, 71 Cal. 2d at 770, the California Supreme court recognized the constitutional necessity of limiting cross-examination to the scope of direct.

Even when a defendant chooses to offer testimony on his own behalf, the privilege against self-incrimination serves "to prevent the prosecution from questioning the defendant upon the case generally, and in effect making him its own witness." (citations omitted) Such general compelled cross-examination would not only post the same "cruel trilemma of self-accusation, perjury or contempt" recognized in *Murphy v. Waterfront Com., supra*, 378 U.S. 52, 55; it would also penalize and thereby deter a defendant's assertion of his right to take the witness stand to explain or contradict a particular aspect of the case against him.

II.　THE PRIVILEGE AGAINST SELF-INCRIMINATION LIMITS IMPEACHMENT OF A DEFENDANT BY THE GOVERNMENT TO THE SCOPE OF RELEVANT CROSS-EXAMINATION AND CREDIBILITY

A defendant's statements made in response to proper cross-examination reasonably suggested by the defendant's direct examination are subject to otherwise proper impeachment by the government. *Havens*, 446 U.S. at 627, 100 S. Ct. at 1917. When a defendant takes the witness stand, "his credibility may be impeached and his testimony assailed like that of any other witness, and the breadth of this waiver is determined by the scope of relevant cross-examination." *Hearst*, 563 F.2d 1331 at 1340, quoting *Brown*.

III.　CALIFORNIA EVIDENCE CODE LIMITS CROSS-EXAMINATION TO THE SCOPE OF DIRECT

California Evidence Code Section 761 states that cross-examination is "[examination] of a witness by a party other than the direct examiner upon a matter that is within the scope of the direct examination." Evidence Code Section 773(a) discusses the appropriate subject matter of cross-examination, stating that "[a] witness examined by one party may be cross-examined upon any matter within the scope of the direct examination by each other party to the action in such order as the court directs." As the plain language of the Evidence Code suggests and the courts' interpretation of this language concludes, the scope of cross-examination is specifically limited by the subject matters covered in direct. *Foss* at 127. The California Supreme Court has characterized Section 773(a) as "an indispensable ally of the federal and state constitutional rights guaranteeing that 'a person shall not be compelled in any criminal case to be a witness against himself.'" *Schrader* at 769 (interpreting former Penal Code §1323 now Evid. Code §773(a)).

Respectfully Submitted this ___ Day of _____, 20__.

_____
Attorney for Defendant

[§§6:04-6:09 Reserved]

B.　Cases That May Call for Client's Testimony

§6:10　　Client's Testimony Is Only Source of Evidence

There may be no other way to get the information to the jurors. If the officer did not obtain a good drinking pattern from the client, and you are using a disconnect theory, it may be necessary to have your client testify. (Disconnect theory relies on a showing of symptoms that are completely inconsistent with the alleged blood alcohol level. In other words, when the client indicates little or no alcohol, has good performance on field tests, does not need a restroom, and yet has a particularly high blood alcohol level. The manifestations and admission are inconsistent with the chemical test and so they are disconnected. The lawyer must then show that the results should not be trusted by attacking the test.)

PRACTICE TIP:

　　If you are trying one of these types of cases, here is a suggestion. Send the DA and the State's expert a letter indicating what your defense will be and asking for an appointment at which they can interview your client.

In other words, "Dear prosecution team, our defense of Joe is premised upon his having consumed just two glasses (approximately 6 oz each) of wine between 10pm and 11pm. This would create a maximum BAC of only

.06. This BAC is in keeping with his excellent performance on the field sobriety tests, but in disagreement with the breath results of .10. Therefore, the breath results must be wrong based on some machine error. In order to expedite this trial, we are asking you to contact us to set up an interview of Joe to aid in direct and cross-examination of all the witnesses."

You can then pose a hypothetical question based on these facts to the state's expert.

EXAMPLE:

Mr. State's expert, as we indicated in our letter to you regarding the facts of this case, assuming a person of my client's age, sex, weight, and so forth, and assuming the following drinking pattern (just as you put in the letter) wouldn't you agree the blood alcohol level should be .06?

When the objection comes, be it for facts not in evidence, improper hypothetical or whatever the prosecution dreams up, and such an objection will come, pull out the letter and ask if the prosecution reviewed it and why they did not take you up on it. The content of the letter is hearsay, but the failure to follow up is proof of bias, and ultimately those facts can provide a legitimate hypothetical to be asked. The objection then becomes irrelevant since the facts can be considered a hypothetical. However, the jury will be likely to concede those facts must be true since you had previously disclosed them. Additionally, you can then argue, in closing, that the failure to meet and consider the drinking pattern spelled out in the letter demonstrates a bias on the part of the state's expert and a refusal to objectively investigate the facts.

Now, the prosecution will *never* take you up on this offer. You then get the information contained in the letter and used in the hypothetical and present it to your expert during his or her opinion testimony. This plays very well in front of the jury and explains away your client's lack of testimony. It creates the illusion that your client was and is willing to tell his or her version of the events, and in fact he or she has done so to everyone including the prosecution but they ignore it. You then follow up on this in closing by telling the jury "You heard from my client through the state and our experts. You heard he was willing to meet with them to go over this. There was nothing more for him to say that he had not already said that you have not already heard."

§6:11   Client Has Physical Problem That Interfered With SFSTs

Some clients need to show the jury the physical problems that interfered with their performance on SFSTs. Jose was a client of mine years ago. He was an older gentleman who had grown up without access to the most modern medical care. As a young child, he had been involved in a terrible motorcycle accident. His right leg was full of old fashioned hardware, which was visible through the skin. His leg also had no muscular development. Naturally his FSTs were poor, but the officer had "taken this into account."

We put Jose on the stand and asked him to remove his pants for the jury. Of course he was prepared and had worn shorts under his slacks. The obvious embarrassment of Jose was not lost on the jurors. Then, when his leg was revealed, and counsel had to verbally document all the aspects to the jury, the mood was palpably sympathetic. The officer lost all connection with the jury and the prosecutor, when trying to keep it light, annoyed the jury by commenting on Jose's alleged foot odor (Contempt was held the next morning).

This is an example of how a physical demonstration can sway the jurors. Whether the client actually testifies during this is another story. Remember, physical demonstrations are non-testimonial. The client is not subject to cross-examination merely by showing part of his or her body to the jury.

§6:12   Client's Testimony Will Evoke Sympathy

Some clients need to play the sympathy card for the jury. This is especially true of painters, auto mechanics and any one else who works around highly toxic materials. As you should know, many solvents, paints, lacquers etc. contain organic compounds which will show as alcohol in many breath machines. Individuals who work around these substances on a regular basis will become saturated with the volatile substances. Later breath testing can be skewed by the exposure.

All of this can be brought out by your expert. They will be able to explain and demonstrate the effects for the jury. But, you will need to have your client testify for two reasons: first, to show the actual exposure; second, to get the jurors sympathy. Ask your client to bring in the OSHA documentation for the chemicals to which he or she has been exposed. At the bottom of each of these documents, there will be a warning that the exposure is (1) deadly because of cancer, and (2) kills brain cells.

Jurors will immediately feel sympathy for the client and will be willing to let them off in order to 'make up' for the prosecution's putting your client through this, since the jurors have all bought or used the products or services produced by your client.

§6:13 Client Has Sufficient Physical Evidence to Make Up for Slips

You may want your client to testify when your client possesses enough physical evidence to (1) support his or her testimony, and (2) the physical evidence can make up for any slips the client may have during the testimony. The best example of this is a rising alcohol case in which you have receipts for the client's purchase of the alcohol.

Any time a client presents you with what appears to be a rising alcohol defense, immediately start the search for supporting evidence. Fortunately a computer log is kept in virtually every establishment that sells alcohol beverages. Although the purpose of log is to prevent any give away policy by the servers, the log can be used for the client's benefit.

Have your client or your investigator return to the establishment and obtain not just the receipt for payment of the tab, but the full print out of the client's activity. This will usually include the time the check was opened, the name of the server, the type of drinks, the amount that was consumed, and so forth, as individually rung up, and the time of the closing of the tab. This is virtually untouchable evidence.

With this in hand, your client can be allowed to testify provided he or she is reminded to stick to the script. If the client runs into any problems, the paper trail is there to refresh or correct memory.

§6:14 Client Has Medical Condition That Interfered With Breath or Blood Tests

Your client may need to testify if he or she has a medical condition that affects his or her results on the breath or blood test or the physical performances on field sobriety tests. However, if at all possible, limit the testimony to the medical condition and do not let the client testify to the facts of the incident that led to the DUI charge.

In order to limit the cross-examination, you will probably want to file a motion in limine asking the court to rule that should your client testify, any cross will be limited to the direct testimony. While we all know that this is the rule for cross-examination, some judges and prosecutors will try to elicit testimony about the specific event rather than about the general condition. This is especially true in cases with GERD.

The district attorney will attempt to go into whether or not the GERD was acting up before the incident. The prosecution may also go into the concept that GERD and alcohol do not mix. In fact, people with GERD are usually told to stay away from alcohol as part of their diet.

To counter this tactic, point out to the jury in closing or even through questioning of the client or other witnesses from either the prosecution or the defense, that we are all told to stay away from certain things, and yet we all engage in them, cigarettes, speeding, and coffee just to name a few.

In order to determine how much the judge will allow, file the motion. If you feel that the cross will get out of hand, then look for another witness. If not, then prepare your client to testify taking special precautions against "opening the door" during direct.

People with diabetes or hypoglycemia can usually testify without fear of cross since these conditions are permanent and the events of the day have little to no effect. But beware, a smart prosecutor may be able to crack the door and then obtain a ruling from the judge to drive the truck through that crack.

The good news, once again, is with the jury. Jurors are very sympathetic to a person who has physical conditions that may affect the test results. You must be sure to start and finish your questioning with these topics.

§6:15 Client Has Necessity Defense

I know, many of you are wondering how can there be a necessity case in a DUI. One answer is domestic violence (or almost any other violence situation). A second is a real emergency.

Years ago a man was sitting in his house drinking when he heard a horrendous screech and crash. Looking out his window he saw his six year old neighbor had been hit by a car and she was in bad shape. Somehow though drunk (and we admitted he was), he knew that the little girl would not survive if he waited for an ambulance. So, without consideration for his position, he put her in the car and rushed her to the hospital.

The entire emergency room staff testified that he had been correct. They were just barely able to save the little girl's life. The ambulance arrival and return time would have been too long and she probably would not have survived.

The prosecution knew this was a tough case. They knew that the drive to the hospital would be allowed by the jury; in fact the judge had basically indicated the facts would not let the case go to the jury. The prosecution thanked the client for his heroics and instead prosecuted him on his return home.

Knowing this, the defense put the client on the stand to detail the events, the drive to the hospital with the crying and literally dying little girl. We then asked why he drove home. His answer was simple, he was done and that was where he needed to go. The jury nearly spit on the prosecutor on the way out after delivering the not guilty verdict.

The moral of this story is that, given the right set of facts, the jury will excuse otherwise illegal behavior, if they hear from your client. The client *must* admit that what he or she did was wrong, and that he or she would not have done it except for the extreme nature of the circumstances.

In a recent case, we argued to the jury that threats from the client's very large drunk boyfriend to her nieces at the party led the client to fear for all their safety. She was able to testify to the jury that she was so scared and the threat so real, that driving under the influence was the lesser of the evils.

In both of these types of cases, your client cannot try to waffle on his or her own culpability. This is an all or nothing approach. The jury is not going to feel sympathy for the client if the client argues both that he or she had to drive under the circumstances and that he or she was not really intoxicated. To a jury this sounds like a straw grasp. Instead, the client must step up, admit wrongdoing, and then explain the reason for it.

§6:16   Client Has SODDI a Defense

SODDI, "some other dude did it," is one of the most commonly used defenses in criminal law. It is, however, rare in the DUI arena. Most DUI cases are premised on the simple fact that an officer saw your client drive. In some cases though, such as accidents, hit and run, and citizen reports, the client is not behind the wheel when the officer confronts him or her. In such a case, the failure to put your client on the stand looks quite bad to the jury.

This is one of those situations in which the jurors will ask themselves why your client did not testify. After all, if your client wasn't driving, what does he or she have to hide? Now, sometimes this SODDI defense can be presented by the actual other driver. But more often than not, your client will be necessary as well.

The good news on the SODDI case is a lack of confrontational evidence. Since no one actually observed your client driving, your job will be to explain the (1) circumstantial evidence and (2) any alleged admission.

The key here for your client is deny, deny, deny. The client cannot, in any way, shape, or form, indicate that he or she may have been driving. The client must stick to the concept that someone else drove. The client can let the prosecutor have a field day with cross-examination on how drunk the client was, how poorly the client performed on SFSTs, and so forth. The only fact the client needs to repeat is "I was not driving."

It will be up to you to destroy the other witnesses during your cross. You may also have to confront any alleged admission of driving that your client allegedly made. The easiest way to do this is to show the difference between the witness' admission and your client's admission. The following example of questioning of the officer should demonstrate what I mean. Notice how we *intentionally* use statement and admission to develop our point.

EXAMPLE:

Q: Officer, you obtained an admission from the independent witness?

A: I took a statement.

Q: Did you have the witness read and sign this admission?

A: The witness read and signed the statement.

Q: When did you let my client read and sign his statement?

A: I took down your client's admission.

Q: So, if you write it down, it's an admission; if someone else writes it, it is a statement? Well here is John's written statement that he was not driving. Could you please attach it to your report?

[§§6:17-6:29 Reserved]

II.   SAMPLE TRIAL EXAMINATION QUESTIONS FOR CLIENT

A. Preliminary Questions

§6:30   Introduction and Setting Client at Ease

Q: John, please state your name for the jury.

Q: How old are you?

Q: Where do you live? (Be careful if your client is from out of town and that will upset the jury.)

Q: Why were you visiting here? (Have client highlight some local attraction.)

Q: Now John, are you nervous?

Q: How come?

Q: So you have never testified before?

Q: Remember during voir dire I told the jurors to relax?

Q: Some of them still had a hard time speaking to us. We let them take their time to settle down.

Q: So you can do the same, okay?

Q: I am going to try to ask you simple questions, but sometimes they can be confusing. If that happens let me know.

§6:31   Why Client Has Decided to Testify

Q: When I am done, if I have left anything out, the prosecutor will also question you. He may be a bit more confusing because he has not taken the time to get to know you, but answer him if you can, okay?

Q: In fact, we sent a letter to the prosecutor indicating you wanted to talk to him?

Q: They never called you?

Q: Never took the time to listen to what you had to say?

Q: Jumping ahead, did the officer ever sit you down and ask for your side of the story?

Q: No, they just followed their script?

Q: Asked you the questions we heard during the trial?

Q: Well, we will get into all of that now, okay?

Q: You decided to talk to the jury even though you heard the judge tell them you did not have to?

Q: Why is that?

Q: How important is it to you that the jury hears your side of the facts?

§6:32   Stress on Client on Day of Incident

Q: So let's talk about the events of [date on which DUI arrest occurred].

Q: Were you at work?

Q: How long have you worked at IBM?

Q: What kind of work do you do there?

Q: Sounds like a responsible position.

Q: So the company you work for figures you to be a responsible person?

Q: One of good judgment?

Q: Do you supervise others?

Q: How many?

Q: On this day, was there anything special happening at work? (There is almost always some extra stress at work or at home. This is good to get in front of the jury as it lends a human aspect to the case.)

Q: How big a project was this?

Q: Had you been working a lot of extra hours?

Q: What time did you get to work?

Q: What time did you leave?

Continue on in this vein until you have fully painted the picture for the jury of the stress of the day. The same approach can be used if the client had been at home.

[§§6:33-6:39 Reserved]

B. FSTs

§6:40   Direct Examination

Q: John, you heard the officer testify here?

Q: Do you disagree with any of the testimony?

A: I wouldn't say I disagree. I just have a different take on it. My own perspective.

Q: Can you explain that?

A: Well like the tests.

Q: You mean the Field Sobriety Tests?

A: Yes, he said I failed them. I did not think so.

Q: How is that, are you saying the officer is lying or making this up?

A: NO. He never told me what he was grading so I thought I did okay.

At this point pick one SFST where your client did part correctly and part incorrectly. Preferably choose one where what the client did correctly is *not* important and what the client did incorrectly is.

Q: Let's take the One-Leg Stand. The officer indicated you put your foot down several times. Did you?

A: Yes, but he had told me if I put my foot down to pick it up and continue counting. That is what I did.

Q: In fact, the officer told us that. So I am confused by what you mean.

A: Well the officer told you I put my foot down, but he never told me it was putting the foot down that was wrong. I thought it was the counting.

Q: I see, what you are saying. He told you to lift your foot and count, and you concentrated on the counting, not the foot.

A: Exactly.

Q: So you felt, at the time, that you had passed since you counted correctly, as the officer told us here in court?

A: Right.

Q: But, now you know it was the foot part and not the counting part?

A: Yes, I know that now.

Q: So do you think it was fair in the field to not tell you what did or did not count?

A: No.

Q: But, do you still think you passed this test?

A: Not now that I know what the rules are.

Use this template for as many of the FSTs as you can. Prosecutors are taught to attack the defendant on FSTs by trying to get them to conflict with the officer. You need to set up the client's testimony to explain that there is no conflict per se, rather a misunderstanding created by a lack of honesty with the officer.

§6:41   Cross-Examination

Q: Okay, Mr. Smith, you say you felt you did fine on the FSTs?

A: Not now that I know the rules.

Q: Well the officer told you what to do, didn't he?

A: But not what counted.

Q: So you are saying the officer lied here in court when he told the jury he explained and demonstrated the test for you?

A: No, I am saying he never told me what did or did not count.

Q: Well he told us he takes it all into consideration. So it all counts.

A: But apparently some things count more than others.

Q: Well do you still think you passed?

A: It depends on how you grade it. I can see why the officer said I failed.

Q: You admit you failed.

A: I admit I did not perform the part the officer was checking the way he wanted me to.

This is the key. Prepare your client to deflect rather than confront the prosecutor on these questions.

Q: Well, John, getting back to where we were, you feel that officer was wrong in arresting you based on your FST performance?

A: Not really, I think that I did fine, given what I was trying to do. Since I did not know the rules and he did, his arrest seems to be okay.

Q: So it is a matter of perception based on limited knowledge?

A: Correct.

[§§6:42-6:49 Reserved]

C. Physical Limitations

§6:50   Direct Examination

Q: John, you heard me tell the jury during opening that you have physical limitations that made your performance on the FSTs difficult if not impossible. Can you please tell these to the jury?

Q: Can you give us some more specifics?

Q: Okay, but didn't the officer ask you if you were under the care of a doctor or dentist?

A: Yes.

Q: Did you bring any of this up?

A: No.

Q: Why not?

A: When someone asks if I am under the care of a doctor or dentist, I take it to mean regular everyday care. Like a cancer treatment patient.

Q: So, how often do you see a doctor about your condition?

A: Not often at all. I go when it acts up or for my occasional physical.

Q: Why so little?

A: Two reasons, first, it's life, we all have pains and aches we have to deal with. Second, I don't know about you, but I cannot afford to go to the doctor every time my back acts up.

Q: Well, wouldn't it have been important to tell the officer that you had this condition so that he could use it in evaluating you?

A: The officer never told me *why* he wanted to know this. I had no clue as to what he was looking for.

Q: How about after the tests? Didn't you know then?

A: After the tests, they arrested me. There was nothing else to say.

§6:51   Cross-Examination

Q: So you have a bad back?

A: Like many other people.

Q: But you did not mention it to the officer?

A: I did not know the importance. I bet a few jurors also have a bad back, and none of them told the judge during the questioning.

Q: I am not asking about the jurors. I am asking if you told the officer you had a condition that would affect your performance on the FSTs?

A: I didn't tell the officer *because* he never asked the question like you just did. He asked if I had any physical limitations. Not if anything would affect the FSTs.

Q: So, is it your testimony the officer lied when he testified he did ask you those questions?

A: No, I do not think the officer ever lied here in court. I am saying he did not make it as clear as you are as to why he was asking me. So I was not as clear in my answers.

Q: Then it is the officer's fault?

A: No, it is no one's fault. Just a lack of understanding.

[§§6:52-6:59 Reserved]

D. Refusal

§6:60   Due to Confusion

Q: John, you heard the officer indicate you refused to take any chemical test?
A: Yes.
Q: Was there any particular reason why you refused?
A: I was confused.
Q: How were you confused?
A: The officer told me at the scene that I did not have to take the breath test, and then he told me I did have to take one.
Q: Hold on. When did the officer tell you that you did not have to take a breath test?
A: When he arrested me.
Q: Before or after the arrest?
A: When he arrested me.
Q: Okay, let's take this one step at a time because it is confusing me. The officer testified that he had you perform FSTs and asked for a roadside breath test, do you remember that?
A: Yes.
Q: Then he arrested you and read the admonition about a chemical test.
A: I don't know.
Q: What do you mean?
A: After he told me I needed to take a breath test, he told me it was voluntary, so I said no. Then he arrested me and told me I had to take a test, and I said no, just like I had said. I did not realize they were different tests.
Q: So, let me see if I can understand you. You did the FSTs?
A: Yes.
Q: Then the officer read or told you the PAS admonition?
A: Yes.
Q: Which is voluntary?
A: Yes.
Q: Which you declined as is your right?
A: Yes.
Q: Then, the officer told you that you had to give a test?
A: Yes.
Q: And that confused you since he had just said you had the right to refuse the test?
A: Exactly.
Q: About how much time went by between the time of the PAS request and the second request?
A: Less than 30 seconds. It was "I would like you to take this test, but you do not have to" followed by you are under arrest, then "you are required to give me the test."
Q: So it was one right after the other?
A: Yes.

§6:61   Due to Belief in Right to an Attorney

Q: Is there any reason you refused to give a chemical test?
A: Yes
Q: What is that?
A: I thought we all had a constitutional right to an attorney before we gave evidence.
Q: Did the officer tell you that you did?
A: No, he said I did not.
Q: So why didn't you believe the officer and give him a sample?
A: I did not believe him. I have always been told we can have a lawyer with us. I thought he was trying to trick me.
Q: Why would you think the officer would mislead you?
A: Well that is what they do on TV and in the movies, and he had already told me I failed the FSTs when I thought I had passed them. I just did not think the officer was on my side.

Q: Anything else?

A: Yes. I always was taught that it was a lawyer who would tell you and the officer what was correct or not. I have never been in this position so I felt it was my right to ask someone else what to do. That someone else would be a lawyer.

Q: So it was because of what you have read, seen or been taught that made you believe that a citizen had the right to an attorney?

A: Yes.

Q: It was not to try and hide evidence?

A: No, just the opposite.

Q: What do you mean by that?

A: If I had given the test, it would have shown I was not over .08 so I would not be here. If I could do it again, I would take the test to show my innocence.

§6:62   Due to Belief Officer Had No Right to Demand Compliance

Q: You admit that you refused the chemical test?

A: That's right.

Q: Any particular reason why?

A: Yes. This is America. The government is not allowed to force us to give evidence against ourselves.

Q: So are you saying that the chemical test would be evidence against you?

A: No. I am saying that the government has no right to force me to do anything.

Q: But the request would show you were innocent?

A: It doesn't matter. The government has no right to come into my house or into my body.

Q: So even though the test would have helped you out of this predicament, you refused?

A: Wrong is wrong. It is the obligation of the government to prove my guilt. I do not have to prove my innocence and I do not have to give the government the evidence to do so. That's what this country is based on, or so I thought.

[§§6:63-6:69 Reserved]

E.   Rising Alcohol Defense

§6:70   Direct Examination

Q: When was your first alcoholic drink?

A: At eight o'clock.

Q: How can you be sure?

A: We arrived at the restaurant at 7:30 and we were seated about ten minutes later. The waitress came by, asked for our drink order and then brought me my glass of wine.

Q: Who paid for dinner?

A: I did.

Q: Did you pay with cash or credit card?

A: [The answer is unimportant.]

Q: Do you recall how much the total was?

A: No.

Q: If I showed you the receipt from that night would that refresh your recollection?

A: Yes.

Q: Look at this receipt, and see if it refreshes your recollection?

A: It does. The total was $125.

At this point counsel should try to move the receipt into evidence. I know it will not be received. The concept here is to show the jury that there is evidence that will detail exactly what happened and the prosecution is keeping it from them.

Q: Does the receipt show what the party had to drink that night?

A: Yes it does.

Try to move it in again with the same result and reason. Keep trying to get the receipt in front of the jury.

Q: Okay, John, let's move on, how much did you have to drink?
A: As I told the officer, I had three glasses of wine from when I arrived to when I left.
Q: What time was the last glass?
A: I am not sure.
Q: Would looking at the receipt help you out?
A: Yes.
Q: So what time was it?
A: Well as I said before, my last glass was just as we left, so it would have been nine o'clock.
Q: And what time did the officer say he stopped you?
A: Well I remember it being about 9:15 and he said it was 9:19 in his report.
Q: So, you had just finished the last drink within 20 minutes of leaving?
A: Yes.
Q: Any reason why you had one more so close to the end?
A: It was a glass of dessert wine. You only have that at the end.

§6:71   Cross-Examination

The prosecutor will try to intimate that your client pounded his or her last drink and that such behavior is unbelievable and not realistic. Prepare your client to indicate that the last drink was a dessert wine or other after dinner drink that everyone knows is consumed at the end of a meal, or perhaps a little leftover wine.

If the client's last drink was leftover wine, do not be afraid of showing your client to be a bit miserly. Almost all of us have had the occasion of getting ready to leave, and seeing half a glass or so of the wine we had ordered during dinner. Given the prices we pay, most of us decide not to waste the wine and take the last bit as one final gulp.

Such "thriftiness" by your client will not bother the jury. *But* prepare your client to admit it. The admission may seem harmful, but you can spin it into a showing of honesty and typical human nature during your closing argument.

[§§6:72-6:79 Reserved]

F.   Medical Condition

§6:80   Direct Examination

Q: John, you indicated you have a medical condition?
A: Yes.
Q: What is it?
A: Diabetes.
Q: For those of us not familiar with that condition, can you tell the jury what it means, as least as far as you understand it?
A: My body doesn't produce enough insulin to correctly metabolize foods.
Q: Now you told the officer you had this?
A: No.
Q: You did not tell the officer about this?
A: No I did not.
Q: Why not?
A: I did not know at the time that diabetes could affect breath tests. It wasn't until I saw the numbers and did some research that I learned about the interplay between my condition and breath testing.
Q: Are there any side effects to diabetes?
A: Yes.
Q: Like what?
A: Well it affects my weight, my balance, and my bone structure.
Q: Can you tell us more?

A: Yes, as a diabetic my ankles are degenerating. This makes it harder for me to maintain my balance and to walk in a manner you would consider normal.

Q: What about your weight?

A: Diabetes is a contributing factor to my weight problem.

Q: What happens when you are not in a good state of blood sugar?

A: I become light headed, dizzy, and sort of out of it. My eyes become red, my face is flushed, and people say it smells like I have been drinking.

Q: So you look, smell and act like a drunk?

A: A very intoxicated person, yes.

Q: Has this ever caused you problems in the past?

A: Yes, several times people have mistaken my condition for being drunk. It usually happens under stressful situations.

Q: So whether you have had alcohol or not, you can look and smell like you have been drinking, all because of this disease?

A: Yes.

At this point counsel may wish to elaborate on the problems associated with the medical condition, ask how it affects the client's day to day routine or anything else to illicit jury sympathy. The major aspect of a medical defense will come out through the expert.

[§§6:81-6:89 Reserved]

G. Environmental Exposure

§6:90   Direct Examination

Q: John, what kind of work do you do?

A: I am a furniture stripper.

Q: What does that entail?

A: I use solvents to remove old paint, stain, varnish etc. from chairs or whatever and then refinish them.

Q: How do you remove the finish?

A: We use highly potent chemicals.

Q: Do you have a list of those chemicals with you?

A: Yes.

Q: Do you need to refer to the list to tell us about them?

A: It depends. I know what we call them, but if you want to know the chemical name, or what they are made of, I would have to refresh my memory by looking at them.

Q: Okay, if you need to do so then tell us?

A: Sure.

Q: What is the most basic substance you use?

Now have the client go through each and every substance he uses in his work. Start with the name he uses for the product. Have the client then give the actual chemical name. Finally, ask the client to explain what it is made from and what it does.

Either through judicial notice or through admissions, have the judge acknowledge the lethal nature of the substances. Since the documents are from the state OSHA equivalent, they are subject to both judicial notice and to party admissions.

Q: John, you have spent the last half an hour explaining to us that you are routinely around some very toxic chemicals.

A: I am.

Q: And you told us that they are all slowly killing you.

A: Well I don't look at it that way, but I guess you are correct.

Q: Why do you do this?

A: I love my work. I have always loved repairing old furniture.

Q: What safety precautions are supposed to be used?
A: We are supposed to use full breathing apparatus.
Q: Do you?
A: No.

§6:91 Cross-Examination

The prosecution will jump on your client's failure to take proper safety precautions. They will try to make your client look like he or she is lying about the failure to take full precautions, or that the client's condition is his or her own damn fault. The latter will not fly with a jury. It is easy to address in further examination or in closing. The former is a bit more serious.

Prepare your client to explain to the jury that life is just not as simple as the DA would have them believe. We all know what we are supposed to do to be safe, and yet many of us take shortcuts. How many of us regularly download the updates for our computers?

Q: John, the DA pointed out that the simple cloth mask you wear is not sufficient, is that true?
A: Yes.
Q: Why don't you wear the correct equipment?
A: Well it is a matter of time and money. If I was to put on and take off all that gear every time I did a job, I would only get one or two done a day. I would not be able to make a living that way. So, I take my chances on the safety gear.
Q: Is that smart?
A: Obviously not, but it is what we have to do to make ends meet.

This same approach can be used for auto workers, painters, and so forth. The key is to get the jurors to feel for the worker.

§6:92 Alcohol to Feel Better

That's right. People who work with toxic chemicals will often consume alcohol to feel better. While this may sound absurd, it is true and medically correct. During the breakdown of the toxic chemicals used by these workers, a large amount of isopropyl alcohol is created. This is because toluenes and acetones are very toxic, but can be broken down into isopropyl alcohol and other less toxic byproducts.

Now, isopropyl is still toxic to humans, just less so than the others. The first course of treatment for isopropyl poisoning is ethyl alcohol. The ethyl alcohol helps the body break down the isopropyl alcohol. Any emergency room doctor can testify to this.

So you can have your client testify that drinking a couple of beers makes the client feel better after a long day's work.

Q: John, you told us you had two beers after you got off work?
A: Everyday.
Q: And you told the officer you did so to make you feel better?
A: Yes.
Q: Now, just like the DA, the jurors and the judge, the officer was skeptical of this practice?
A: Skeptical is putting it nicely.
Q: Well where did you learn to do this?
A: It is just known around the job. We all get a headache or nauseous feeling at the end of the day and a couple of beers make that go away.
Q: Well John, I bet you, and everyone else, would be surprised to learn that medically you are right?
A: Excuse me?
Q: If I told you that the chemicals you have been exposed to are broken down into other compounds, and one of them is isopropyl alcohol, and that large amounts of isopropyl alcohol cause those feelings and further, that medical doctors use ethyl alcohol to combat isopropyl poisoning, then you would understand you were actually following a medical protocol?

DA: Objection.

Defense: Judge, I will link all that up through my expert.

Point made!

[§§6:93-6:99 Reserved]

III.   CLIENT HANDOUT

If you intend on having your client testify, then send the following Ten Rules for testifying to him or her. These rules have been borrowed with permission from my good friend Gary Trichter of Texas.

§6:100   Ten Rules Every DUI Defense Witness Should Know Before Testifying at Trial: The Nickel and Dime Mnemonic

Let's face it; our clients are not professional witnesses and sometimes not the brightest of individuals. They will be nervous and make mistakes when testifying. In order to help them remember HOW to testify, give them the NICKEL and DIME rules.

Nervousness is acceptable. The jury will understand if you act nervous, so admit it to them.

Intense listening is critical. Be sure to listen to the exact question asked of you by the lawyers from either side.

Count to three before you give an answer. It gives you time to think about what was asked, as mentioned above, and it gives your attorney a chance to object.

KISS, the old adage of "keep it simple, stupid" applies here. Provide short specific answers to the exact question. Do not elaborate.

Exact answers to each question. If the question is wrongly asked, don't try to give the answer you know they want. The prosecutor is the pro; let him or her act like one in framing questions.

Look up at the jury when giving the answer. People who look down in their laps look like they are hiding something.

Demonstrate when appropriate. Jurors love to watch things so if you can, SHOW them.

IDon't Know is a perfectly acceptable answer when true. We can't remember what we had for dinner last night, never mind three months ago. Tell the jury if you cannot remember or do not know.

Make eye contact with individual jurors. Find a friendly face in the crowd. They will help you later in deliberations.

Emote. If you were angry or upset when you were arrested, it is okay to let the jury see it in court.

CHAPTER 7

CLOSING ARGUMENTS

I.   INTRODUCTION

§7:01 · Goals—Reasonable Doubt In All Cases

I typically start trial preparation by preparing my closing argument. Then I go back to jury selection and then to opening. Proceeding in this way lets you do something storytellers need to do—define the end of your story first. Then go back and figure out where you start. Once that's done, getting through the middle is just about putting down the plot points that will connect the dots.

In almost every closing, I start with a theme of my story. I have a few stock ideas I use time and again but there are literally hundreds. I mentioned several in the opening statement chapter. But, before I get to the specifics of this case, I always begin by reincorporating the discussion we had during voir dire about presumption of innocence and burden of proof. See Ch. 2A.

I use Powerpoint for every closing, and have frequently been told it creates one of the most polished presentations possible. I'm including some screenshots of slides for my reasonable doubt section. I would be remiss if I didn't mention the amazing James Nesci of Arizona here. Jim's lectures on cramming reasonable doubt down a prosecutor's throat and "bad breath" are some of the best I've ever seen—and Jim is the person who inspired me to create my own powerpoint presentations. I'll freely admit that I built mine on the bones of what I learned from Jim—so now you're learning from us both!

Remember as you begin your closing that it's your last chance to tell your story—and your most powerful chance. That being said, all the work is already done. You've laid the groundwork and it's just about reincorporating the story for the jury and pulling it all together. What's the goal?

Not to convince the jury that your client is not guilty—but rather to explain why they already know that their verdict **must** be not guilty. It's a subtlety but it is important, and you'll see why as we discuss reasonable doubt with our jury and ramp up to the facts of your individual case with the jury right along with you.

Memory researchers have taught us the concepts of primacy and recency; what we hear first and what we hear last sticks. This being so, closing argument is vital. It is the last chance for a jury to hear you. Therefore, you must make it count. In some jurisdictions the prosecution will get both the first and the last word during closing argument. In others they merely go last. In either case, your voice will not be the last the jurors hear, but it is the voice you want to be ringing in their ears.

Fig. 7-00A State Has Invited You to Dinner

I use this analogy to conceptualize burden of proof and remind the jury why they're here—at the State's invitation.

The Different
Levels of Proof
BEYOND A
REASONABLE DOUBT
Not Guilty
Reasonable
Doubt
Not Guilty
Clear and
Convincing
Not Guilty
Preponderance
Not Guilty
Probable Cause
Not Guilty
Reasonable Articulable Suspicion
Not Guilty
Scintilla of Evidence

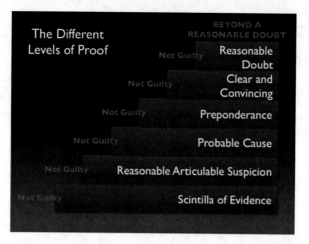

Fig. 7-00B Different Levels of Proof

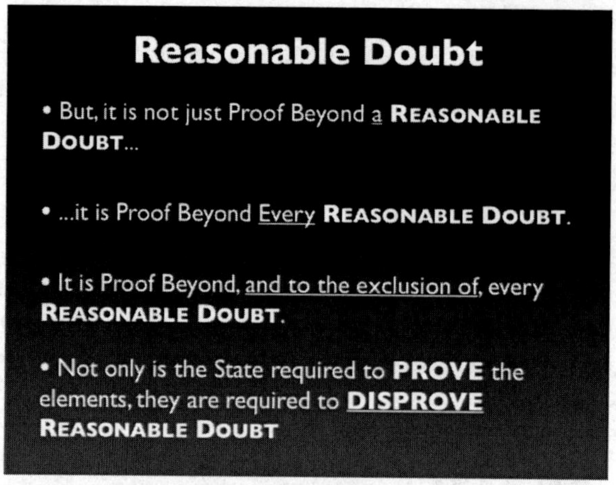

Reasonable Doubt
• But, it is not just Proof Beyond a REASONABLE DOUBT...
• ...it is Proof Beyond Every REASONABLE DOUBT.
• It is Proof Beyond, and to the exclusion of, every REASONABLE DOUBT.
• Not only is the State required to PROVE the elements, they are required to DISPROVE REASONABLE DOUBT

Fig. 7-00C Reasonable Doubt, slide #1

You can start to see the connective tissue between the jury selection questions and exercise and what I'm doing here.

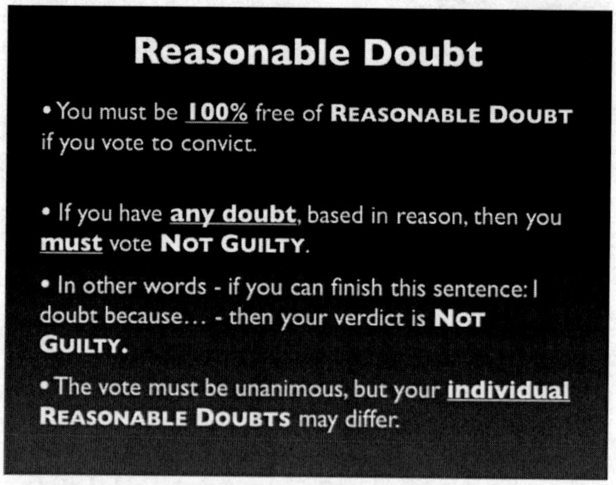

Reasonable Doubt
• You must be 100% free of REASONABLE DOUBT if you vote to convict.
• If you have any doubt, based in reason, then you must vote NOT GUILTY.
• In other words - if you can finish this sentence: I doubt because... - then your verdict is NOT GUILTY.
• The vote must be unanimous, but your individual REASONABLE DOUBTS may differ.

Fig. 7-00D Reasonable Doubt, slide #2

Here I like to point out the possible individual reasonable doubts and offer them to jurors by gesturing to them: "Your reasonable doubt might be that there was no video; your reasonable doubt might be that the field tests were done wrong; and your reasonable doubt might be that the officer didn't fully investigate this offense. You all have different reasonable doubts—but your verdict is the same."

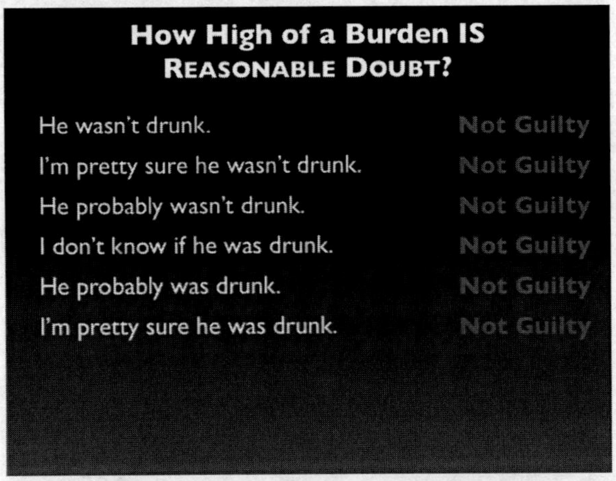

How High of a Burden IS REASONABLE DOUBT?

He wasn't drunk.	Not Guilty
I'm pretty sure he wasn't drunk.	Not Guilty
He probably wasn't drunk.	Not Guilty
I don't know if he was drunk.	Not Guilty
He probably was drunk.	Not Guilty
I'm pretty sure he was drunk.	Not Guilty

Fig. 7-00E How High a Burden, slide #1

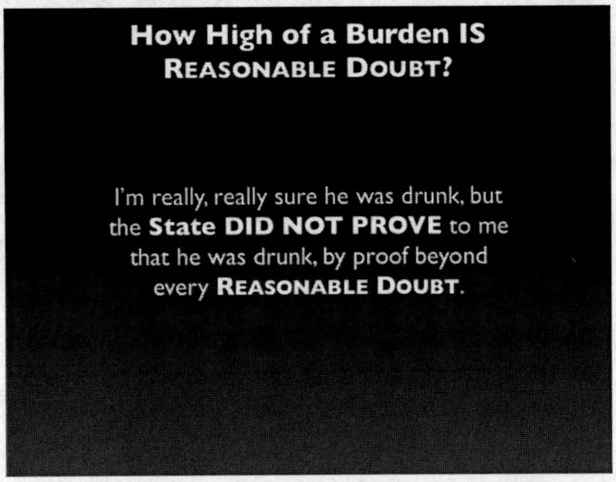

How High of a Burden IS REASONABLE DOUBT?

I'm really, really sure he was drunk, but the **State DID NOT PROVE** to me that he was drunk, by proof beyond every **REASONABLE DOUBT**.

Fig. 7-00F How High a Burden, slide #2

How High of a Burden IS REASONABLE DOUBT?

NOT GUILTY

Fig. 7-00G How High a Burden, slide #3

CLOSING ARGUMENTS

Fig. 7-00H How High a Burden, slide #4

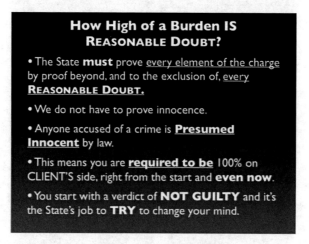

Fig. 7-00I How High a Burden, slide #5

At this point, I do something that could be classified as ballsy. Often the jury is starting to get skeptical of me, and during voir dire we talked about the skills attorneys have with words. So I call them out on it, and then invite the State to challenge me. They never have.

"Okay, now let's hold on a moment. I see the faces and looks I'm getting. Some of you are thinking to yourself, 'That Mr. Dichter. He's doing that sneaky defense lawyer thing. He's using all the words and saying them fast and twisting them around to make this seem way bigger than it really is.' I understand your skepticism.

But, a few moments ago, you heard the judge give you your jury instructions. You heard that at times, we as attorneys, have the right and in some cases the duty to object when we make mistakes. You've seen that happen, and you've heard the judge correct our mistakes.

If anything I just told you wasn't true, someone would have stopped me by now."

Now I just stand there and wait for a few seconds—no more than three or four. Silence and stillness are power. Besides, every second that that room is silent is the judge and prosecutor telling the jury that you're absolutely right. And even if they do object, the judge will undoubtedly overrule the objection—because nothing you've said is improper.

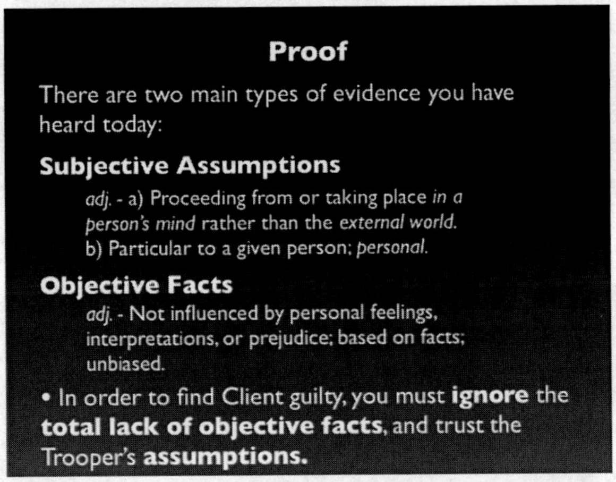

Proof

There are two main types of evidence you have heard today:

Subjective Assumptions

adj. - a) Proceeding from or taking place *in a person's mind* rather than the *external world.* b) Particular to a given person; *personal.*

Objective Facts

adj. - Not influenced by personal feelings, interpretations, or prejudice; based on facts; unbiased.

• In order to find Client guilty, you must **ignore** the **total lack of objective facts**, and trust the Trooper's **assumptions.**

Fig. 7-00J Proof, slide #1

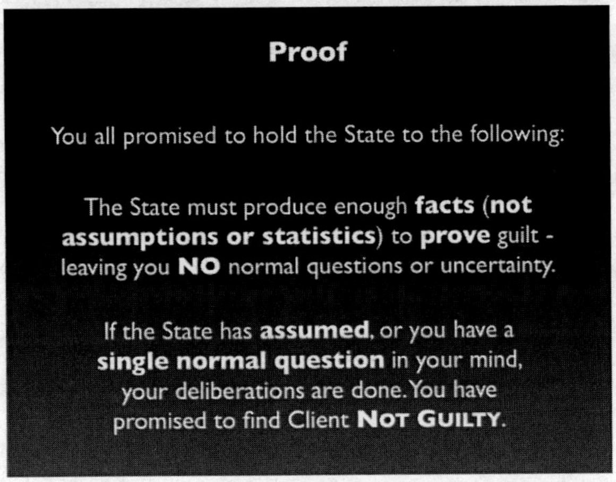

Proof

You all promised to hold the State to the following:

The State must produce enough **facts (not assumptions or statistics)** to **prove** guilt - leaving you **NO** normal questions or uncertainty.

If the State has **assumed**, or you have a **single normal question** in your mind, your deliberations are done. You have promised to find Client **NOT GUILTY.**

Fig. 7-00K Proof, slide #2

I like to remind them of their duty here. It's not that they get to find your client not guilty. It's not that I'm suggesting they should find your client not guilty. I'm not even saying it's likely your client is not guilty. I'm saying that it's their job. It's what they promised to do.

For additional slides on burden of proof, see §§7:80, 7:90, and 7:91.

§7:02 Neutralizing Prosecutor's Closing: Solutions to Not Having the Last Word

Jurors subscribe to the ideal of fair play. Numerous books, articles and research papers have been written on this. They want to do what is right. Use this.

Let the jury know that if given the chance you would have more to say. Be sure they understand that constraints of time, judicial authority, and going first or in the middle make it difficult to answer every question that may arise. Let them know that the prosecution very well may come up with a surprise or two, but if they follow the advice you give them, they will see that these are not really surprises, just minor facts that do not matter and that you did not get around to, or did not anticipate. This is especially true when the prosecutor gives a perfunctory closing, regardless of how long his or her argument is. Let the jury know the prosecutor did nothing more than recite his or her opening statement with support. Tell the jury that given the chance, you would be happy to point out all the flaws in the prosecution's theory. But under the rules of *this* court, you cannot. Tell them that custom dictates the prosecution gets the last word because it is their job to carry the burden.

How do you do this? I have found the following to be simple and direct approach.

In a few moments, I'm going to say thank you, look at each of you, and sit down. At that point, my job is over. I've done everything I know how to do in order to help my client. I don't get to say anything else. But the State does. They get a rebuttal, because of their immense burden of proof..

But that doesn't mean my case is done. You get to take it into the jury room and argue it. In fact, you're supposed to. You've been with me for a few days, and you've heard my arguments. You know what I'd say if I could. So say it for me. Say it for my client.

Answer each and every one of the prosecutor's points for me, and if something they say isn't an actual fact, or they ask you to assume something, you can completely ignore it, because it's not proof.

Remember you start from "I doubt because…" and if you can finish that sentence, you're done and we can all go home.

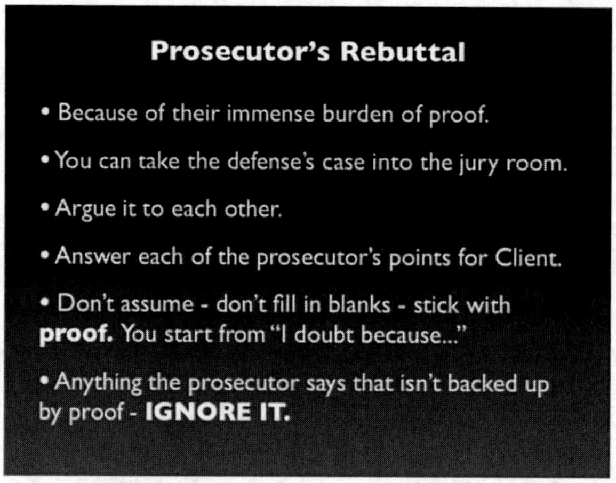

Prosecutor's Rebuttal

- Because of their immense burden of proof.

- You can take the defense's case into the jury room.

- Argue it to each other.

- Answer each of the prosecutor's points for Client.

- Don't assume - don't fill in blanks - stick with **proof.** You start from "I doubt because…"

- Anything the prosecutor says that isn't backed up by proof - **IGNORE IT.**

Fig. 7-00L Prosecutor's Rebuttal

See Appendix A *The District Attorney's Manual* for the prosecution's approach to closing arguments and typical responses to common defense arguments.

§7:03   Capturing the Jurors' Hearts and Minds

You have begun your closing argument. The jury understands why you are here, what you will do, and you have read them a caution regarding the last word aspect discussed above, now it is time to get to work.

To consistently win DUI cases, you need to capture both the hearts and the minds of the jurors. Although jurors make their decisions based on both, the mind is actually the simpler to persuade. You capture the jurors' minds through your cross-examination, if the defense is one of prosecutorial problems (*e.g.*, bad machine, bad procedures), or through your witnesses if the defense is something else (*e.g.*, GERD, necessity).

The heart is more difficult. To persuade the heart, you need to give the juror a simple answer to the question posed by family and friends "How come you let the drunk go?" You need to make the jurors *want* to let the client go. The simplest way to do this is with the storytelling approach we've been developing through this book. Remind them that you are the good guy—and so are they. That they're on the side of innocence, and only if the State proves the case with the most evidence they can possibly bring, do the bad guys (the State) win. If you can seize the framing of the case and make it about innocence and not guilt, you can get them to want to let your client go.

§7:04   Developing Your Own Voice

The number of books dealing with closing argument is legion. From Bailey to Spence, it seems everyone has something to say on the topic. If you are truly a dedicated trial attorney, you have read, are reading, or should be planning to read as many of these as possible. Start by examining the arguments of the best advocates to help shape your own voice.

And having your own voice is critical. Flem Whited, an extremely accomplished DUI attorney from Florida, once remarked, "You need to be yourself. If that isn't working, change who you are. If that still does not work, then be someone else." Juries, much like young kids, dogs, and student loan collectors, have a strange ability to sense when an attorney is not being honest with them.

§7:05   Handling the Defense Stigma

We all know that we are not well-liked. Attorneys in general are not respected, criminal defense lawyers even less (unless people find they need one) and DUI defense least of all. We are seen as using tricks and traps to mislead to get drunks off. Okay, so we need to deal with that. Remind the jurors of the oath they took. Explain that you are under a similar oath, as is the Judge and prosecutor. Simply put, all of you are there to do your job to the best of your ability, based on *what was given to you*. Explain to them that the prosecution did their job as best they could but *lacked the evidence*. All you did was to point that out to the jury. The Judge did his or her job by letting the jurors see what was or was not found in the case. Now it is their job, *no matter how they feel about it*, to acquit your client.

Provide the jurors with some relief by describing the functioning of the system as more important than any one decision. They need to know that as long as the verdict is *based on the evidence*, or lack thereof, then *justice* was served in that a true verdict had been returned. It is critical to be sure the jurors feel comfort with this.

[§§7:06-7:09 Reserved]

II.   TYPES OF CLOSING ARGUMENTS

§7:10   Basic Categories of Closings

Over the years, I have distilled closing arguments into three basic categories: The Story, The Rules, and the I Cannot Believe This Piece of Junk Made it This Far. It is rare that a particular case will fit completely into one of these categories, and in fact the best closings have some element of each. These general names help to guide us to where we want to be.

[§§7:11-7:19 Reserved]

A. The Story Closing

§7:20   Effective Storytelling

There is nothing like weaving the facts brought out in trial into a campfire story. Stories, when used appropriately, teach morals, explain the cosmos, and illustrate how we live our lives. They grab the heart.

One of the greatest benefits to a "story" close is that it constrains the prosecution's ability to interrupt. Sure, the DA can object, but no one likes to have a story interrupted. Who cares if the teller is getting some fact wrong or is enlarging some parts and omitting other facts? Our human nature wants to hear the entire story uninterrupted. If the DA does object, chances are the judge will comment that defense counsel's interpretation of the evidence is reasonable or that it is up to the jury to decide if that was the testimony or the judge will simply make some other non-intrusive ruling.

Should the DA object repeatedly, a gentle reminder of how much commercials interrupt our favorite shows may be in order.

> Ladies and Gentleman the prosecutor is within his rights to make objections. It is his/her job. Just like commercials during television. And just like those commercials, I ask that you listen to what I am saying and not what he is trying to hawk.

§7:21   **Example: Bloodshot Eyes**

When summing up a DUI case, tell a story. Tell the jurors all about your client. Tell them where your client came from, where your client was going, and why your client needed to do what he or she did. Explain to the jury why the allegedly "bad" facts are nothing more than everyday occurrences, which, when viewed in the light of the pre-judgment the arresting officer had, appeared to be bad.

For example, here's a suggestion for dealing with bloodshot eyes. The officer will have testified that your client had red, watery bloodshot eyes and that such a symptom is consistent with impairment. The DA will list this in his or her closing argument as further proof of your client's guilt. During your close you should speak on this.

Don't simply reiterate what you obtained from the officer or experts during cross or direct exam that "blood-shot eyes can be caused by…" Tell the story. Remind the jury that your client told the officer he or she woke up at around 5:00 that morning and worked all day, had dinner, and was on the way home for a few hours of shut eye before doing it all again. Try something like this:

> We all know Bob is a hard worker. Bob told the officer (even though he didn't have to, but that's just the kind of cooperative guy Bob is) as the officer noted in his report, that he had worked since 5:00 am that day. We all heard that Bob, like too many of us, spends too many hours in front of that curse of modern life, the computer, staring at the ever more blurry screen as he tries to do the work of two people in this time of economic trouble. He barely had time to take a lunch, and not nearly enough time to stretch his cramping legs or expand his vision beyond the 12 inches from desk to desktop. When he finally did get a chance to open his eyes, it was well past a normal knock-off of 5 or 6. He did not leave work until almost 7 that night. Driving the short distance to Cheers in twilight further impacted already tired eyes. Is it any wonder that when he met the officer four hours later his eyes showed signs of fatigue, overuse and stress?

What have we accomplished here? Not only did we diffuse the "objective eye symptom," we also brought Bob to the jury. We made him sympathetic. After that kind of day, who wouldn't want to join Norm and Cliff for a tall one?

You will be able to judge the success of your story by the DA's response. If the DA gets up and starts to answer your story, then he or she is giving it credibility. The DA is saying, "yeah, I agree with all that, but…." You have the jurors hearts. Hopefully during the trial you gave them something for their heads.

§7:22   **Chronological Order Is Best**

When telling the story, it is best to tell it in the chronological order of the events of the day. Start by simply writing out the story, or if your memory is good enough, just tell it aloud, and see if you covered all the basics. Then, go back and fill in the nuggets, good or bad, that were brought out during the trial testimony.

An easy way to do this is to list all the good and all the bad facts, evidence, testimony and opinions from the trial. See where they best fit into the general framework of the chronological story, which may not be where they came out in the trial. The example above of the eyes is illustrative. Chances are the jurors heard about Bob's eyes halfway through the officer's direct testimony. You could address Bob's eyes when commenting on the officer's testimony, but it seems a bit defensive. Instead, talk about them in the very beginning.

REMEMBER: this is *your* arena. *You* set the rules; *you* set the framework. Do not answer the DA; make the DA answer *you*. And trust me, the DA will and the jury will notice it.

§7:23   **Tell Story in "Here and Now'**

When you tell a story, do it in the "here and now." Make yourself the players. Obviously you need to set the stage, but once you get the jury back to the time of the event, *stay there*. Capture the jury right out of the gate. Compare the following two examples:

On May 5th 2001 Bob was driving home. At about 8:00 he stopped for a couple of beers at the Hideaway. You heard from the bartender he was there for half an hour. She told you he then left. Officer Smith watched as he pulled out.

Bob decided to stop at the Hideaway for a couple of minutes on his way home. It was early May, the 5th to be exact, a weekday, so Bob was only there a short time. Cheryl remembered serving Bob a couple of beers in the half hour he was there. As Bob was leaving he noticed Officer Smith behind him.

§7:24   Emphasize Theme

If you have a catch phrase or single word theme of the case, use it. In the example I gave to start the oral presentation, my theme was "responsibility." It was the *first* word out of my mouth and the last word on my lips. Find that word, phrase, or theme for your case and hit it hard.

If you have no such easily pronounced theme, then try for an emotional grab or the "you're already in the middle of the cliffhanger" approach. "Bob was pissed. Another 12 hour day without recognition or thanks. He just wanted to get home to see his kids, who were already asleep, and go to bed." That grabs the jury. It sets the stage. You do not need to fill in dates or times. The jury is with you.

§7:25   The Moral

When you have finished telling your story, be sure to tell the jury the moral, which should be that Bob is not guilty. Don't worry about reminding them of reasonable doubt or any other legal jargon. They have heard it, they know it, and they will follow or ignore any or all of it to reach the verdict they want.

[§§7:26-7:29 Reserved]

B. The Rules Closing

§7:30   What Is a "Rules" Closing?

The "Rules" closing, also called the list closing, is a point-by-point evaluation of virtually every action by the prosecution witnesses in the case. It should be done in a strict format that leaves little room for rebuttal. It is simpler, more direct and in many ways easier to deliver. It is just as effective, in the right case, as "The Story," and is generally more effective for technical cases—that is, cases in which the defense is concentrated more on machine or officer error, calibration problems or other specific mistakes.

§7:31   Rules Closing Must Be Accurate

One of the biggest pitfalls to the Rules closing is inaccuracy. When telling a story, people will grant the storyteller literary license, even in court. However, when you are acting as the "inspector," your information better be precisely accurate or you will lose the jury. If you can deliver a Rules closing without any wiggle room, then any response by the DA will be perceived by the jury as an attempt to change the facts.

§7:32   Use Outline, Rather Than Chronological Organization

A Rules closing should be presented (and written) in outline form. This allows you to be sure to cover every point, and it allows the jury to follow along. Use charts if at all possible. [See §7:35.] Nothing more effectively assists the triers of fact in following you, evaluating your point, and agreeing with you, than seeing it laid out in writing before their eyes.

In a Rules closing, the need to be chronological is diminished. Since the point is to show all the mistakes, the timing of the mistakes is relatively unimportant. Instead, use the concepts of primacy and recency. We tend to remember the first thing we hear and the last thing we hear and forget the stuff in the middle. Put your best bits up front and at the end.

§7:33   Repeat "Reasonable Doubt"

When using the Rules approach, it is best to repeatedly use the phrase *reasonable doubt*. The point you are usually making in listing the mistakes by the officer is that individually, and most certainly in combination, these omissions lead to reasonable doubt. Every so often remind the jury of that point.

It may be that the best time to do this is between each subsection of the list. In other words, after listing the three or four mistakes in any one Standardized Field Sobriety Test (SFST) or listing the three or four mistakes in the SFST in total, then explain that this created reasonable doubt. This allows you a natural break to move to the next topic.

§7:34   Tailor Trial Examination to Closing

As we all know, or should know, the closing argument is where you start the case. In other words, write your closing argument first, then tailor your trial examination to fit the closing. It is much like any other project in life: You figure out what you want, and then how to get it. If you are planning on a Rules closing, tailor your examination for it.

This means not just the questions, but the entire procedure. Use charts, graphs, and other physical tools to help. It is impossible to argue with a closing argument based on writings that were either created or admitted to during the trial and then re-published in the closing.

§7:35   Use Charts

Let's take field sobriety tests as an example. You have discerned from the police report that the officer did not administer the tests correctly. You could just go through the incorrect procedures that the officer used during cross and then repeat his testimony to the jury in closing. Boring! Instead, create a chart based on the officer's report, testimony, and the standards. Here is an easy example:

OFFICER'S INSTRUCTION	CORRECT PROCEDURE	PROBLEMS CREATED	FOLLOWED
10 steps out 8 steps back	9 steps each direction	Wrong footed turn	
Pen 8 inches on HGN	12 to 15 inches	Bad angle, bad focus	
Count to 30	30 seconds	Too long	

You can create the headers and even fill in the "Correct Procedures" column ahead of time. Then, during your closing, you mark off a big NO in the "FOLLOWED" column. Leave the chart up for the prosecutor's close. The prosecution will not be able to argue against the truth of what is contained in the chart. Instead, you will force the prosecution to explain it away. Be sure the jury understands that when a prosecutor does this, he or she is admitting to reasonable doubt.

This same approach can be used, and will become more prevalent, in cases involving chemical testing. More and more states are allowing chemical tests in evidence even when they are not performed in compliance with local rules or general scientific principles, holding that it is up to the jury to decide how much those violations matter. Charts can effectively point out these mistakes.

§7:36   Use Demonstrations

Another way to bring home a Rules closing is by a demonstration. My partner, Hudson Bair, represented a client where the main issue was lack of a 15-minute observation period. Records established the wait was 13 minutes long. To demonstrate (1) that the wait had occurred, and (2) that two minutes would not mean anything to the officer but meant everything to the case, Hudson stood in front of the jury for 120 seconds without saying a thing. He then pointed out that that simple rule meant the difference between a trustworthy test and an unreliable one.

§7:37   Combine With Story Close

It is often effective to have a "List Hook" in a Story close. This is the one aspect that the jurors use to let your client go when explaining their decision to the crestfallen DA. In other words, find some technical aspect for acquitting your client, as outlined above, and combine it with the heart wrenching story. The combination of the two provides both the rationale and the reason for letting your client go. Examples are partition ratio, absorption periods, elimination curves, body temperature, medical or dental issues, etc. Providing this "hook" to the jury, coupled with an engaging story, gets both the heart and the head of your juror.

Ladies and Gentlemen, you heard about how Tommy was not feeling well when he left work. He told you he came down with a terrible flu over the next few days. He stopped at the bar for a glass of wine to clear his head so he could go to sleep. Well we all know how hot we run when we have a flu. Now you also learned how a slight elevation in body temperature will lead to a falsely high breath alcohol reading. Is it any wonder why the BrAC was so high in this case? Not really considering all that we know now.

[§§7:38-7:49 Reserved]

C. The "I Cannot Believe This Piece of Junk Made It This Far" Closing

§7:50   When to Use

This is both the last-ditch closing and the "it is so obvious" closing. It should only be used when you have no other defense or when it is so obvious that the prosecution is missing key evidence that anyone would acquit.

An appropriate case for this closing is a case where facts are missing, such as the non-observed driving case. Whether this is the accident, the parked car with the guy sleeping in it, or the hit-and-run found later, the attorney can look at the jury and point out that the most basic factor—when/who drove—is missing.

§7:51   How It Works

Keying in on this one factor, as if the whole world recognizes the futility of having gone forward without the evidence, can be a very effective tool. One can do this in a variety of methods. Bob Chestney of Georgia starts this closing with the simple statement: "That's it? Didn't you think they would have more?" He then goes on to show that none of the testimony of the prosecution's witnesses matters or that it all is just speculation. In other words, it is the cop's opinion.

Here are a few other approaches:
- "I cannot believe the DA brought this to you knowing he did not have ANY evidence to establish my client as the driver. I guess the DA was just hoping something new would spring up to make up for the missing information.
- "I understand how tough it is for the DA to dismiss a DUI when he is facing re-election and how much easier it is to put it off on you."
- "That is why we have juries in these cases to protect each and every one of us from a DA who is (1) overzealous, (2) hopeful, or (3) political." Remind jurors that they stand between common citizens and the government.

§7:52   Two Cautions

Avoid Unrelated Aspects of Case. If you are using this closing in a case where you focus in on one completely missing element, *do not engage against unrelated aspects of the case.* If you say that your client was not the driver, do not talk about SFSTs, chemical tests, etc. Only someone who is conceding the issue would talk about that. In fact, highlight how the prosecutor, who knew the problem with the case, spent so much time on how drunk your client was, a point you are not contesting, and no time placing him behind the wheel of the car. The same would be true in a time-of-driving defense.

Keep It Short. If you are using this closing because you have nothing else, don't belabor the point. Get in and get out fast. Let the jury know, by your attitude, that if they spend any time at all on this case, they are thinking too much.

Perhaps the best example is in the rare case of the obviously lying officer—the officer who testifies to events that are not physically possible or that are clearly not documented, such as on a videotape. Once you establish that the officer is not to be believed, then leave everything else alone and fall back on how the DA, sworn to uphold the law and elected by us to do so, could allow this cop to testify.

§7:53   Sample Closing Argument

SO WHAT? That is my main point here ladies and gentlemen. SO WHAT? The District Attorney has just asked you to condemn my client and given you a list of reasons why. But for each of these reasons I say "SO WHAT?"

Because unless the DA has some rational relationship to the fact they present causing you to find my client guilty BEYOND A REASONABLE DOUBT, that fact earns a big SO WHAT.

Here is an example of what I mean. In the 30s and 40s beards were not that common and, in fact, having one caused eyebrows to be raised. Why? Because Lenin had a beard. Nothing more, nothing less; it was a sign of the times. There was no relationship between being bearded and being communist. But people were made to believe there was.

The DA is trying to do the same thing. He told you my client had bloodshot eyes. So what? Do bloodshot eyes mean you are over the legal limit? Nope, no such evidence was presented.

My client's voice appeared "thick" or "slurred." Again, so what? No evidence linked that to a particular blood alcohol level.

And trust me ladies and gentlemen, if such studies existed the prosecution would have brought them forward. None were mentioned because they just do not relate.

Of course no one is foolish enough to say that bloodshot eyes means you cannot drive. If they did so every cold or allergy sufferer in the world would be guilty.

So what? Unless and until those facts can be made to relate to the charges, then they deserve a big "so what." They do not add to the concept of proof beyond a reasonable doubt.

What of these specialized "tests," the SFSTs? Did anyone tell you they measure a person's ability to drive a vehicle? No; in fact, our expert told you the creator of the darn things specifically said **they do not**. So what?

Finally we have the breath test. A test obtained 1.5 hours later. So what? What does this number mean as far as my client's condition at the time of driving? Because unless someone tells you what it means, I say "so what?"

[§§7:54-7:59 Reserved]

III.   ANALOGIES, ANECDOTES, AND STORIES

§7:60   Introduction

Solomon was approached by one of the many nay-sayers and rumor-mongers of his time. This particular individual spent many a day crafting ways in which he could prove Solomon was not so wise. On this particular day, the conspirator figured he had a fool proof plan.

In his hand he held a small bird. He would ask the wise king if the bird was dead or alive. Should Solomon answer dead, the scoundrel would open his hand and allow the bird to fly away, proving Solomon wrong. However, if the king guessed correctly, that the bird was alive, then the mean one would crack the bird's neck, killing it, again showing Solomon to be incorrect.

When the nefarious ill-doer reached the throne, he posed the question to the great king, was the bird dead or alive. Solomon, realizing the trap, returned the burden to the man. "The choice is yours."

So too, is the choice in this case, for you see, the state has asked for a guilty finding on either .08 or driving under the influence. Either way the state is happy because they kill the bird with either choice. But you have the power to let the bird go free.

This kind of an analogy works well with jurors because it forces them to visualize what is an otherwise hard concept to understand: the idea that the state will play one hand against the other to obtain its conviction even to the point of contradiction.

Individuals in a variety of professions (*e.g.*, law, teaching, sales) have learned through experience that people process information and make decisions using both the left and right portions of their brains. To arouse a juror's empathy for our client, we must engage both the creative/imaginative side as well as the logical/mathematical side of the juror's brain. For years, attorneys have concentrated on the latter rather than the former in trial work. However, as the science presented in DUI trials becomes more complicated, the need for easily recognized and understood examples becomes greater. The following is a list of ideas, some original, many adapted, of useful analogies and anecdotes.

Please feel free to use them as you will, make them your own, or attribute them to someone else. I hope these help you in some small way to convey to the jury what we all know: that people's lives are in their hands; convictions need to be based on solid substantial evidence; a criminal conviction should only be handed down when the jury has a moral conviction that the defendant is guilty. As mentioned in my acknowledgment, many ideas in this book come from friends and associates. The following is the best example of this. I cannot say which of the following are completely mine, partially mine, or just reused. If they come from one of you, thanks.

§7:61   Witness Testi mony

Ever notice how perfect the state's witnesses are during direct examination? No question from the prosecutor seems to throw them, nor does it generally require much thought. As attorneys we know why this is. The questions are designed to lead the witness through his or her report to get out the bad facts. At no time is it truly a search for the truth. Maybe it is due in part to the fact that the officer and DA got together to rehearse this testimony before we got here.

Then comes cross-examination. Suddenly the witness answers more slowly, has some "I don't knows" or "I don't recalls." We remark on this to the jury, but do they listen or do they just assume it is part and parcel of the trial show? Here is a way to show them what it really means.

I used to play softball in a bar league. I was lead-off hitter batting up near .600, with good speed. I had great coverage in the outfield and a fair arm. When I played, I could wait on pitches and pretty much put the ball in play anywhere I wanted. It was a piece of cake.

One year, I switched to a more competitive league. I saw my first underhanded fastball. To this day I have no idea how fast it was. I would say 150 mph. Needless to say, I never laid a bat on it. Within weeks, I was riding the pines.

Well, here, the officer was a lot like me. When the DA was pitching, the softballs went out of the park. But once we got up, and started heating things, the officer started to miss. He fouled them off, and never quite recovered. This is how you need to look at his batting average. Not just on when his team threw him the ball, but more importantly how he did under real game pressure.

Another twist on this has to do with the All Star Homerun Rally. Relate how the pitcher to the sultans of swat during this fan fest is always the batter's friend/coach. It is easier to hit them out of the park when they are being pitched *exactly* where you want them.

§7:62   Minor Problems

Ladies and gentleman, you heard from the witnesses as to certain inconsistencies, deviations and problems with the maintenance and calibration of the Intoxilyzer administered in this case. Now the prosecutor tells you that they are small issues raised by the defense as a smokescreen. That a bad test or two, in the entire logs of the Intoxilyzer, do not matter.

This reminds me of when my wife and I were shopping for our first house. We knew that it was a huge investment so we were taking our time. Finally we found what appeared to be the perfect house for us. A beautiful Victorian with lots of detail and plenty of room to expand as our family would.

CLOSING ARGUMENTS

During the final walk through, I noticed a couple of termites in the corner. Upon pointing this out to the agent of the owner, he squished them, turned to me and said problem solved.

Needless to say we did not buy that house. Those two termites were just the easiest to see examples of some fundamental problems. Just as with the house, the examples of problems on the Intoxilyzer used in this case are only the tip of the iceberg. Clearly there is a major problem with the machine and with the prosecution's case. Ask yourself if this is a house you would buy.

Here is another quickie but goodie.

You are not feeling very well so you visit your doctor. The nurse comes in and takes your temperature. It is a little high. Then she notices your pulse is rapid, and blood pressure is up. The doctor comes in, looks at all this and says, "you are fine." Satisfied? Hopefully not. You would want a second opinion, or at least to discuss the symptoms. But not here—here the 'expert' says he knows best and you should just go home.

But will they be answerable when in the morning you cannot get out of bed? No way, José. You see it is not their fault if they are wrong. They just relied on the information and took their best guess.

§7:63   Acceptable Machine Errors

No place in a DUI trial has more easy to adapt analogies than the math of the machine. Here are just a few of my favorites.

- Ladies and Gentleman, this is your pilot. Our flight today should be smooth as silk and ahead of schedule. Due to some overstocking of champagne, everyone can have free drinks. The movie is a classic and we have plenty of extra seats for you to spread out. The one bad note is that my altimeter, the device that tells me how high I am flying, is not 100% accurate. You see it is set within plus or minus 10%. We should have no problem getting over the mountains and hitting the landing field. (10% margin of error on calibration)
- Ma'am, I have taken your child's temperature twice now. Once it read 107 degrees and once it read 90 degrees. So we are going to send you home now as no problem detected. This is the same as a machine that tests a known sample of .10 at .09 to .11. Just as we have here.
- Well, the state has agreed that there is a 10% margin of error in their case. They say that is good enough for them and should be good enough for you. I say, okay then, when you have your next headache, use this bottle of aspirin. It contains 100 pills. 90 of them are in fact aspirin. However, 10 of them are poison. It is the same 10%, but will you take that pill?

§7:64   Machine vs. People

You have heard from both my client and his friends. They all say Bob was not so impaired as to be violating the law. In fact, they said he did not have enough to drink to be over the legal limit or to reach the .12 the machine pegged him at. The state wants you to trust the machine and not trust the people. This reminds me of a lesson I learned long ago.

I grew up in New York—Queens, specifically. In that neighborhood we still had an old fashioned soda counter at one of the drug stores. We also had some new soda machines in the brand new stores. Like many people of his generation, my grandfather was a walker. Rather than taking the bus, he relied on his own two feet to get most places. As a young boy, I would complain that the walk to the stores was too far.

One day, as we were running some errands, I decided I was thirsty and could not wait until we arrived at the fountain. I had some change from my allowance (actually change was the allowance in those days) and I told my grandfather I wanted to get a soda. He told me we would once we got to the drugstore, but I insisted on buying one from the vending machine.

After I put my money in and pressed the button nothing happened. I yelled, screamed and carried on as you would expect. My grandfather asked me what happened and I told him. He asked me what I learned and I said that the machine was broken. No, I was told, you learned more than that. What you really learned was that no matter how fancy and new a machine may be it is never perfect, and that while you can place your money in one, NEVER place your faith in a machine. Faith, life or liberty, is to be placed in people and religion only. And even then, only after long thought and evaluation.

Once we arrived at the soda fountain, Grandpa bought me a soda from the counter. It arrived just as promised, served by someone who we could see, evaluate and trust.

Well, the state wants you all to put Bob's fate, life and liberty into the trust of this machine. They want you to believe this machine over people. I know how grandpa would decide.

§7:65 Rising Alcohol

About a month or so ago, Charles Sifers from Oklahoma sent me the following quote, "An argument is an exchange of ignorance." And asked what I thought. My initial reaction was that it had the ring of truth, but I could not fathom why. Then I watched the spinmeisters after the presidential debates. I saw why this statement rang true. If the facts are known, then there can be no disagreement. Only opinions are open to debate. Opinions are the one thing all of us are entitled to form and to form in any way we wish. Therefore, to argue about them is to show our ignorance.

Well, in this case, and most other cases I have ever seen, there is little debate as to some basic facts. Jim was driving. He took a blood test. It showed a .13. The disagreement comes down to whether or not he was over .08 at the time he was driving.

The fact that both sides are arguing this opinion shows our ignorance. We are both ignorant of the true BAC Jim had. Now, if this were a presidential debate, you would have to decide which of the two of us seemed more persuasive. But it is not. It is a criminal trial. This means the state must convince you it is not ignorant of the actual BAC in order for you to convict. And it must do so beyond a reasonable doubt.

§7:66 Circumstantial Evidence

You must pre-condition or explore the idea of corporal punishment with your jury prior to using this example. Ask jurors during voir dire if they feel it is acceptable to spank a child for extreme behavior. Those who say no are probably good jurors overall, but bad for this analogy, and vice versa.

I came home one day in a terrible mood. During dinner my eldest son was particularly obnoxious and talked back more than I could stand. I sent him to bed. Like many 8-year-olds he stomped up the stairs in defiance. I ran over to the stairs to let him know in no uncertain terms that his attitude had best change. I also warned him not to slam his door, as is his usual action.

Just as I sat back down—wham—the door was slammed. I bolted out of my chair, stormed upstairs and flung open the door. As I grabbed him screaming at his disrespect, he told me that he did not do it. This obvious falsehood sent me over the edge. I sat down on the desk chair, pulled him on to my lap, and struck a blow across his bottom.

Just then, a breeze went through the room, and wham, the door slammed.

To this day, I do not know if he or the wind slammed the door. All I do know is I can never undo that terrible blow. In this case, the prosecutor is asking you to strike a similar blow on my client, with the same type of evidence.

§7:67 The Note Pad

No one is sure who started this idea, but I heard it from Gus Hawkins although I have heard George Stein take credit. Be that as it may, I did expand on the idea.

Ladies and Gentlemen. When you go back to deliberate about this case, the first thing I would like you to do is to take a piece of paper and write on it all the issues you have with this case. All the doubts, reasonable of course, that are in your mind. These may be doubts I explain to you during the remainder of my time; or, they may doubts you have figured out for yourself.

Whatever they are, please write them down. After you all have done that, turn the pages over. Unless every page is blank, you have reached a verdict. If any one of you has written a doubt which you find to be reasonable on your paper, then you are not convinced by the evidence, beyond a reasonable doubt. At this point it would be wrong for you to change your mind based upon the pressure of any other juror.

It would be even more wrong for a juror to try to force this person to change his or her mind. In fact, as you stated during voir dire, you would report such pressure to the court. The verdict, if only one or two of you have a doubt, is "We are hung."

Well, not quite. You see, it is wrong to dissuade a juror from changing a not guilty to a guilty, since that would be interfering with their thoughts; but if any of the rest of you look at the reason or reasons they have written down, and you agree with them, then it would be appropriate to change your mind and vote not guilty. That's how it works.

A defendant is PRESUMED innocent until and unless the contrary is proven beyond a reasonable doubt. When one of you writes down a reasonable doubt, unless the others agree and a verdict of not guilty is returned, then no verdict of guilty can be returned unless the juror(s) who had reasons were forced to change their minds. Doing that would violate all of your oaths.

So here now are some of the reasons to put on that piece of paper.

At this point you go into whatever may be the major issues in your case. The next argument tailors well with the note pad.

§7:68   The Tripod

Many times important facts are based on preliminary facts that must be proven to the jury. In some jurisdictions the underlying facts must be proved beyond a reasonable doubt, not so in others. Regardless of the level of proof needed, the following segment can be added into your closing argument. This argument will also work as to the ultimate question of DUI so long as the prosecution was missing an element, such as in the example, time of driving.

Ladies and gentlemen, the prosecution has asked that you find Jim guilty beyond a reasonable doubt. In order to do so, you must have an abiding conviction of the truth of the facts alleged. That means you must be willing to stand, or in this case, sit, on your decision with no hesitation. This means you must be convinced of 3 facts: that Jim was the driver, that he had a chemical test over .08 (or he was impaired), and that the test (or impairment) existed at the time of the driving.

Three legs to a conviction, just like there are three legs on this stool. [Pull out a stool or tripod.] Now, if all three legs are solid then you can sit on the stool with no fear of falling. But, if the chair has wobbly legs, or even worse, one leg is missing, then you would not sit on it. You would not have that abiding conviction in the strength of the chair, just like you could not have an abiding conviction in the strength of the guilt of Jim.

Remember in the beginning of this case I told you to keep your ears open for a missing element? Remember when I said it might be who was driving? Well I am sorry to say I misled you. See, I knew they would probably be able to prove that Jim was the driver. But what they could not and did not prove, was when was Jim driving. And, without knowing exactly when Jim was driving, there is no proof he fits within the three hour requirement [or other applicable law] so that he could be considered under the influence based on the chemical test.

[Start to remove a leg or fold one down.]

In other words, Ladies and Gentlemen, one leg of the stool is missing. Not only can you not put your abiding conviction in that stool, you would not even think about putting any weight at all on it.

As I said, this can be used with SFSTs, by substituting proper administration or proper scoring as the bad third leg; breath testing, by using any of the missing administrative or maintenance issues; or virtually any other aspect of the trial.

§7:69   The Reveal: No Observed Driving Case

This closing relies on misdirection. In your opening, you will bring out a chart that lists the offense with your alleged ace card; no one knows who was driving. It will look like this:

> THE PROSECUTION WILL
> **NOT**
> BE ABLE TO PROVE
> **BEYOND A REASONABLE DOUBT:**
>
> MR. SMITH DROVE A MOTOR VEHICLE

Keep this chart up throughout the case so that the jurors remember it. Ask every witness just one question; "When was the first time you saw Mr. Smith driving?" Of course, they will answer "I never saw Mr. Smith driving." The prosecution will spend the entire time in closing arguing the circumstantial evidence of Mr. Smith's driving: his car, his admission, his seat adjustment and anything else they can throw in. You then get up and admit to the jury that you were not completely accurate in your opening. But explain to the jury that you did so to highlight what everyone, *even the prosecutor*, knew was the *real* issue in the case. Tell them that the real issue in the case turned on the *time* of driving. Then write "WHEN" on the chart.

At this point, tell the jury that you are done and the prosecutor gets a chance to rebut your argument. Remind them you have only *one* argument; no one was able to say *when* Mr. Smith drove. Therefore the chemical test is not correlated to the time of driving and there can be no presumption of being under the influence based on it or based on field tests or objective symptoms. All of those pieces of evidence point to being under the influence at the time of contact, *not* at time of driving.

Now, turn to the prosecutor and issue a challenge; "You have the floor to present argument, based on evidence received at this trial, to rebut the lack of time of driving."

Once the prosecutor starts, you have two choices; to object to everything said that is not rebutting this lack of evidence, which could lead to a lot of objections, or, and I think this is the better approach, wait until the prosecutor finishes and then move to strike the entire argument as non-rebuttal.

§7:70   Three Verdicts: The Hung Jury

Most people, even judges and lawyers, believe there are only two verdicts possible in a criminal case; this is *wrong*. There are three possible outcomes; guilty, not guilty, and hung. A hang is a defense attorney's second best friend. Often prosecutors will not retry a hang but if they do, it is usually at a major disadvantage to the defense. Here is one way to get the hang.

Remember when we were in voir dire? All of you promised me two things; (1) that you would reach an independent decision, based on deliberations, and (2) that you would not surrender that position merely from peer pressure. Well the pressure cooker is about to start. In a few minutes you will leave to deliberate and I trust you all to do so. But not at the expense of another's, or your own, view.

In fact, if someone is putting pressure on anyone to change their view, that is misconduct. If that happens to you, or you see it happening to anyone else, you must tell the judge. It is perfectly okay for all of you not to agree. If there is no unanimity, that is fine. Just let us know. People often can and do see things differently, and to force a person to surrender his or her view point violates the concept of a jury trial.

§7:71   Lack of Rebuttal

One trick I have started using as of late is to keep the State's expert in court during my expert's testimony. Rarely does the State call the expert up. Nail them with this in closing.

One final note with regards to the defense case. You saw that I asked Mr. Toxicologist to remain in the court so that he could hear what Dr. Gengo had to say. Well we know that if there were any way for the toxicologist to show Dr. Gengo was incorrect he would have. He did not. The only rational conclusion to draw from that is that the toxicologist agreed with Dr. Gengo's position.

§7:72   Urine Testing: Hawaiian Punch Demonstration

With the increased number of DUI drugs we are seeing, the number of urine tests is increasing. The problem with a urine test is that urine is only a guideline to past events; it is not an indicator of a current situation. This becomes relevant whether your jurisdiction uses voiding or not.

Voiding is when the procedure for urine testing requires a person to urinate to empty the bladder and then urinate a second time to provide a sample for testing. If there is no void, then the argument would be that the urine does not represent any current level of drugs in the body. If, on the other hand, there is a void, then you use Hawaiian Punch.

Ladies and gentlemen, the prosecution in this case is based on a urine test. The government has argued that since Bill emptied his bladder and it filled back up, it must have filled with NEW waste. Then they ask you to believe that it was this new waste that contained the drugs fresh from the blood. But this is just not true.

As was admitted by the state's witness, no one can fully void his or her bladder. Well, as Billy Crystal said in *Princess Bride*, mostly dead means partly alive. A bladder that is not fully voided is a bladder that has remnants in it. The problem is that without knowing how much was left, we cannot tell what effect it had on what came in.

Here is an easy way to picture it. Let's assume this is the drugs (pour packet of red punch into pitcher of water) being added to a clean system. It turns the water red. This symbolizes the urine pre-void. So we void (pour out the percentage equal to what the expert has said can be voided) and now the current situation is added (pour in clean water).

Notice that the urine is still contaminated even though no new drugs were added. This shows the flaw in the prosecution theory. The remaining contaminant looks like current influence even if it is not. The critical and unknown factor here is how strong the punch was when the void occurred. No one knows.

Does this mean Bill took a lot of the drug? No. As you can imagine and as you may remember from childhood, the strength of the punch depends on how much water you add when you make it. Likewise, the amount of drugs in the urine depended on how hydrated Bill was.

And don't forget, the drugs alleged to be used in this case are only illegal here. There are many places where taking such drugs is not illegal. Here is another quick example: suppose your doctor gave you a three-day prescription for a drug. After the final dose, you are arrested and it is found in your urine. Was the use illegal? No.

§7:73   Keep it Fair

Larry Denny of Ohio gave this one at the annual Ohio Association of Criminal Defense DUI Seminar in 2010. It is not a complete closing argument, but is a nice piece that can be inserted when talking about field sobriety tests or partition ratio. The basic thrust is that one size does not fit all, and if we want to be fair we need to take in to consideration, age, sex, and size.

I come from a big family. Every year we have an annual picnic where the whole clan gets together. We swap stories, catch up on new additions, mourn passings, and just celebrate life in every way. As you can imagine, there is lots of great food, good laughs and it all ends with a softball game. Now we played a tight game of softball, but fair. Each person gets the usual 3 strikes or 4 balls. My dad was the pitcher, and while he was really accurate, problems would arise.

You see, Cousin Eddy, he was a big old boy, 6 foot 6 or so. That meant he had a huge strike zone and my dad, being accurate as I said, could toss the ball way up high in the zone or down low in the zone. This meant Eddy struck out a lot or just barely got a piece of the ball. On the other hand, my sister was a little thing, all of 105 pounds at best, and just about 5 foot tall. So you can imagine how hard it was to get her struck out. She would draw more walks than anyone. But, fair is fair and rules are rules on the softball field.

But that's not right when it comes to breath testing. You see, this machine is set for the average person. It is not set for my sister or for Eddy. What may be a strike for the average person, who has normal lungs, would not be a strike for my client who has asthma (or whatever the defense may be).

§7:74   The Flight Attendant Analogy

JUDICIAL NOTICE
For SFST's and a whole lot more (studies etc.):

Have you ever noticed that when you are on a plane, even when the plane is on the ground, the flight attendants always walk down the aisles with their hands above their heads sliding along the overhead storage? Did you really think that this procedure was necessary for the perfect operation of the flight? Probably not. We all know that the reason they do this is based on the training they received to ensure that the darn bins don't fly open and bonk someone on the head with roll aboard luggage. Even though this is not critical to the smooth operation of the flight they do it. Every time. Without exception. Why? Because that is how they were trained and that ensures safety for all of us.

Well, in this case, you heard the officer was trained to perform (fill in the task) in a specific way *every time*. But you also heard that in this particular situation he didn't do it. Has our safety been compromised? Is the case about to crash? Yes. You see, the flight attendants aren't doing that hand above their heads exercise for fun. They know that if something falls out, then it could hurt a passenger or worse yet break something on the plane that really matters. The same is true in this case. You are not trained professionals in the (fill in task). You do not know if the omission by the officer won't cause injury to Bob or cause this case to crash.

As a juror, it is not your job to figure this out. As a juror it is your job to tell the government to be sure they keep their hands above their heads so that nothing falls out of the sky and hurts a citizen or worse yet causes the entire plane to crash.

Understand that the evil caused by either omission is horrendous. Hundreds may be injured in a plane crash, but the entire justice system is destroyed when the government is allowed to forego the rules. You may have heard this before; it is often summarized as "Better nine guilty men go free than an innocent be convicted." What is left out is the remainder of the phrase "for once innocent men are convicted by the government, the state no longer has the support of the innocent as they cannot trust in that state." In other words, if you can be sent to jail even if you did nothing, why would you support that government?

§7:75   Lack of Observation Period Covered by Technology

Maybe this is a California thing, but I bet it will come to a state near you. An officer fails to perform the 15-minute observation period, or performs it inadequately. This period is of course necessary to rule out mouth alcohol. In comes the states expert to save the day, and opines that the 15-minute observation period is from the time when the slope detector was not around or was not that good. The prosecutor then calmly tells the jury that while the observation period is a codified procedure, it is rendered obsolete by the slope detector.

I heard the prosecutor make that argument and I was shocked. The idea that once a secondary safeguard is put into place, the government is relieved of the requirement of using the primary safeguard, especially one set forth by statute, is absurd. If this was so, then why do we still need seatbelts? After all, airbags will do the job. And why is that rule still on the books if the new technology is so good? Could you imagine fighting a seatbelt ticket by saying, "Judge, I don't need that seatbelt anymore and I am free to disregard the rules, because my car has an airbag."

§7:76   Thermometer Analogy

(Hold up rectal thermometer)

I know only a few of you will recognize this, but it may be one of the most important medical devices used. It is an old-fashioned rectal thermometer. It is the state of the art and way more reliable than under the tongue, arm infrared etc. It is also very easy to use. You merely make sure it is brought to zero, usually by merely shaking, then you insert it for the required time. Read the results and you are done.

In order to trust this device, you only need to follow three rules. First, trust the manufacturer; second, reset the device; and third, wait the required time.

Well, the breath test in this case is much the same. If the prosecution proves the manufacturer is trustworthy, the device was properly reset and the time taken, you can trust the results.

But what do we know? First, we know that the manufacturer won't tell us how they set it up. The thermometer manufacturer will tell you exactly how they use scientific standards to measure every thermometer they make. It's called quality control.

Second, you heard this machine was not truly reset. Instead it engaged in subtraction based on an unknown formula. How many of you would use a thermometer that has instructions "This one is reading thirteen percent too high, so just subtract that at the end?"

Finally, and most significantly, the time lines were not followed. Suppose your child is sick and you are trying to see if there is a fever. The instructions say, "wait three minutes," yet you only waited two, and look, the thermometer only got to 98.6. Is this really the temperature? No, it is only what you got by cutting the test short.

But think about this. What if you were at the doctor and the temperature was the deciding factor on an operation? You see the doctor go get the thermometer, and it has been leaning against a light bulb. He doesn't shake it down, only waits one minute out of three, and gets a reading of 105. Do you say OK or do you say "Do it again?"

§7:77   Averages

See §1:85 for a motion to preclude average testimony.

A police officer is monitoring a particularly dangerous highway where people are known to travel way above the speed limit, 65 MPH, and this has caused horrific accidents. As she is sitting with her radar gun, she takes three readings: 105, 75 and 55. She looks up in time to see all three vehicles hit their breaks and slow to 50. She flips on her lights and pulls all three cars over. Once she gets the three drivers out of their cars, they all insist they were not speeding. She tells them that since their average speed was over 78 mph, they will each get a ticket.

This is obviously unfair. We all realize that if these people were to go to traffic court, their convictions could not stand since the officer cannot say that any *one* of these drivers was in fact speeding. Yet this exact logic, which could not support a traffic ticket, is being used here to get a *criminal conviction*.

The evidence has shown to you that the average person has (here is where you can bring in the issue you have, e.g., estimate 30 seconds, walk and turn or any other field evidence, or an issue with human physiology like partition ratio, hematacrit etc.) a body temperature of 98.6. The evidence has also shown that for every one degree increase in temperature, the reported breath alcohol is 6% higher than the true blood alcohol. You also heard that Fred had the flu and had an elevated temperature. Is it fair to convict Fred by using the breath alcohol result of a person with an average temperature? Isn't that just like giving a ticket to each of the three people that the radar gun captured?

[§§7:78-7:79 Reserved]

IV.   BURDENS OF PROOF

A. The Staircase

§7:80   Introduction

The Staircase metaphor cannot be used in a vacuum. It must be set up during voir dire. See Ch. 2 *Jury Selection*. Assuming you have properly set up the staircase now is the time to unleash it.

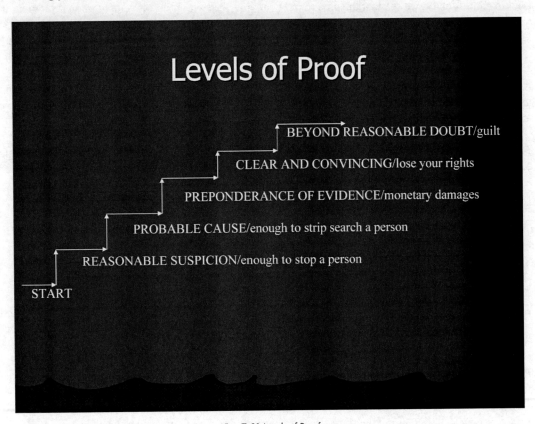

Fig. 7-01 Levels of Proof

Figure 7-01 shows the Levels of Proof in our society as a staircase. Generally, I prefer to unveil each step one at a time. This allows you to discuss what each one means. By watching the jury you can discover if they are with you or not. Like climbing any set of stairs, some people will climb faster than others. The job of a successful trial attorney is to see to it that no one gets left behind, and that all the jurors end up at the top stair. Or in the case of the actual trial, one step shy of the pinnacle.

We start with a 'hunch.' It is a guess, with no rhyme or reason attached to it. In the context or criminal law, a hunch can be used for nothing. It is as valid as trying to predict a coin toss.

§7:81   Reasonable Suspicion

The first important level of proof for the criminal courts is Reasonable Suspicion. As lawyers we all know what that means. It is specific and articulable facts that give rise to a reliable suspicion. What we need to explain to a jury is this amount of proof, which existed in the first contact between the officer and our clients, allows for nothing more than the power to stop.

Here is the first place you can pause for the jury. Highlight some examples of reasonable suspicion. I personally like to use the facts of *Terry v. Ohio* because most judges and prosecutors do not know the facts. I have actually had one or two objections over the years that the facts I recited would actually be *more* than reasonable suspicion.

There is an added benefit to *Terry*: the facts are racist. We all know that the jurors during voir dire talked about how they can be fair. We also know that prejudice exists. By giving an example of prejudice to the jurors, you are challenging them to say that it is not fair. A careful recitation of *Terry* can lead the jury to feel that *Terry* is a wrongfully decided case. This then *raises* the issue for you. If a juror feels that *Terry* was based on race, then they will go out of their way to find that *stronger* evidence is needed as we go up the stairs.

Once you have explained the facts, let the jury know what power is then given the officer. Let them know it in the starkest terms. Remember the goal here is to convince the jury that (1) the facts do not reach the BRD standard, and (2) the awesome responsibility that BRD conveys.

Looking at this chart, we see that the government can interfere with your movement upon a showing of reasonable suspicion. Now reasonable suspicion has been defined as specific articulable facts that would lead a neutral objective person to believe some criminal activity is afoot. What does that mean, well here is an example.

A sergeant of over 25 years' experience in the same neighborhood sees some people who do not belong there. They happen to be black, but that is not important; they could be white in a black area or Chinese in a Mexican part of town, whatever. He just knows he has never seen them here before.

So this cop sets himself up to watch them. What he notices is that 2 or 3 of them walk up and down the same block and look into the same store window. Are they looking for a friend? Waiting on a shopping spouse? He does not know. Instead, after several up and down trips, he approaches them and demands they stop.

That's it. Citizens walking and looking get stopped by this officer because of his (1) "experience," (2) their walking behavior, and (3) they don't belong there.

Now, what does this allow the officer to do? He can stop them; talk to them, and **for his own safety** check to see if they have any weapons. Nothing more. If they wanted to leave they could.

Well in our case, the officer has much less experience, observed much less of a behavior pattern, and had no clue as to where my client "belonged." Yet he stopped my client and conducted an investigation.

The importance of this, Ladies and Gentlemen of the jury, is that all the evidence you have been told by the DA to this point allowed nothing more than the stop. It is not even close to the ultimate standard of beyond a reasonable doubt that the prosecutor must produce. But let's move on.

You have now started to climb the stairs. Watch your jurors to see if any of them need help.

§7:82   Probable Cause

Next we have probable cause as a standard. Again, the legal definition is unimportant. What we need is for the jurors to understand how much evidence is necessary. This time, however, we are going to approach it backwards. That is, from the outcome rather than the start.

During voir dire you must have established with one juror, hopefully still present, that a lot of evidence should be needed in order to arrest someone. Bring that example up now. Add in the fact that an arrest allows for strip searches. Exactly how much evidence is needed for the cops to take you in and make you disrobe until you are naked? What about your wife?

Show the second level and ask, rhetorically of course, how much evidence would you need in order to tell someone to take off their clothes?

By law, we call it probable cause; that is, that it is more likely than not that a crime has been or is being committed. In other words, someone did, or is about to do something. Not a suspicion, or a hunch or even reasonable cause. We need more. We need to know something is afoot.

In our particular case when was probable cause established? When the officer first saw my client? No. When Bob admitted to drinking? No. When Bob fell over on the field exercises? No. It was not until Bob did all of that and provided a PBT sample that the officer had probable cause. And that was all he had. The officer admitted during cross-examination he was not convinced to arrest Bob until then. Well if he was not convinced, and there is no way he could have been, how can you be? You cannot.

§7:83   Preponderance

In our society we next come to the preponderance of evidence standard. Preponderance is the easiest standard to convey to a jury. It is the slightest weight over 50-50 to either side. It means if you have the slightest inkling for one side over another, then that side wins. Explain that preponderance is the standard used to award millions of dollars in civil cases; based on this slightest of feelings. It is the amount of evidence needed to force any one of us to pay the bills of someone who said we did them wrong. Put it in the jurors' heads that their money would be up for grabs. Once they believe they have a personal stake in it, see how hard they would hold on to the money. In other words, how much evidence would you want someone to put forward to take YOUR (the jurors) money.

During voir dire see if any members of the jury have been sued. Focus on them with this standard in mind. If they lost at a trial, they will probably feel like there was not enough evidence to support the finding. You can focus in on them as to how much more evidence must be needed now.

Drive home with the jury that if they were not prepared to bankrupt their own mothers over the facts in this case, then they are not even close to a finding of guilt. If at all possible, talk to them about recent high profile cases.

§7:84   Clear and Convincing

Now we get to some serious levels of proof, starting with clear and convincing evidence. As noted in Chapter 2, this is started in voir dire. Follow up with the concept of how much evidence is needed to take a child from his or her mother. What should the state have to prove in order to force someone into a mental hospital, drug them and appoint a stranger to run their affairs?

Explain to the jurors that this level does not have a number attached to it, but that it lies between preponderance and beyond a reasonable doubt. Jump ahead and explain that no doubt is 100%. You have now set up a division between 51% (preponderance) and 100% (certainty) into which both clear and convincing evidence and beyond a reasonable doubt must fit.

Follow up on this by returning to the example of children.

Madam Juror, would you want a judge to take your child away from you if he was 75% convinced you were unfit? Sir, would you want your family to be able to commit you if they convinced a judge 80% of the way? No. Any and all of you would want the person deciding your fate to be surer than that. You would want them to be clear and convinced, not "pretty sure," or "reasonably certain."

§7:85   Beyond a Reasonable Doubt

With any luck, you have now put Beyond a Reasonable Doubt into the 90% range. It is time to bring it over the top. Be sure to explain to the jury that this decision is one they must live with for the rest of their lives. For example:

> Beyond a reasonable doubt has been likened to an abiding conviction of the truth of the charges. I like that, an abiding conviction. It means that when you leave here, you must feel the same way as when you cast your vote. When you wake up tomorrow and think about what has happened to John, you must not have any question in your mind. A month from now if someone asks how was your service here today; you must be able to say without hesitation, that you made the right decision. In a year, as you think of this day a smile should appear on your face knowing your decision is still correct. But most importantly, in your final hour, you must be able to face what comes next knowing you will not be second guessed.

If you happen to live in one of those few jurisdictions that still allow moral certainty as an explanation of BRD, then go to the story of Cain and Abel. Point out that when Cain was asked what became of Abel, and lied, there was a moral certainty of his guilt.

§7:86   Prosecution's Rebuttal

Last but not least is covering the prosecution's usual rebuttal: "The defense wants you to picture an imaginary doubt" or some such argument. Find one aspect of the case to which there is no disagreement that inures to your benefit. Point out that this is not "imaginary," that it is a real problem. Explain that other problems exist in the case but are not as easy to point out because the prosecution has all the evidence. Remind the jury that the reason why the burden is on the prosecution to prove the case is the impossibility of your proving the negative.

> Ladies and Gentlemen, the prosecution may very well stand up here and say that machine error is just a possible or imaginary doubt, but that is not the issue. What matters is whether or not the prosecution has disproved the error. There is a very simple explanation for this; they have the machine. How could any person prove an error in an item they do not have access to? Suppose I were to say to you that you broke my car when you borrowed it. How could you prove it is not in fact broken unless I let you examine it? You cannot. So the law, recognizing this, places the burden on the prosecution to prove the machine is not broken, just as I would have to prove my car was. They must come in here and prove to you, beyond a reasonable doubt, that the machine was working properly at the time of my client's test. If not, then they have not met the burden and the "imaginary doubt" that is in their custody and ability to disprove has not been. One may even ask one's self; why would they not disprove this issue unless they cannot?

No matter what you argue to the jury, always end with some highlight of this burden. Do not leave open the possibility of the prosecution coming at you with some form of "if there is a problem why didn't the defense show it." You will always lose this, but it should never arise if you handle it pro-actively.

[§§7:87-7:89 Reserved]

B. Closing Argument Aids

§7:90   Burden of Proof Building Blocks

The burden of proof staircase [*see* §§7:80-7:86] used earlier in this book has been a mainstay for many of us for years. The Santa Clara Public Defender's office has created a couple of variations on that theme and graciously shared them with me to pass along. The first slide is merely an overview and can be used by itself.

The next group of slides is meant to be used one after the other as you develop the concept of reasonable doubt. Unlike the staircase, which is keyed mostly to legal standards, this presentation is tied into the thought process of the jurors.

Presumption of Innocence
Reasonable Doubt
Burden of Proof

Guilty	-	Proven Beyond a Reasonable Doubt
Not Guilty	-	Probably Guilty
	-	Possibly Guilty
	-	Maybe Guilty
	-	Likely Guilty
	-	Unlikely Guilty
	-	Not Guilty

Figure 7-02 Burden of Proof Building Blocks #1

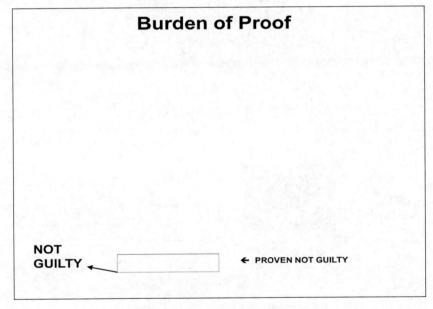

Figure 7-03 Burden of Proof Building Blocks #2

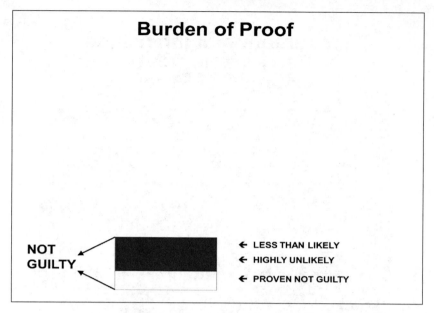

Figure 7-04 Burden of Proof Building Blocks #3

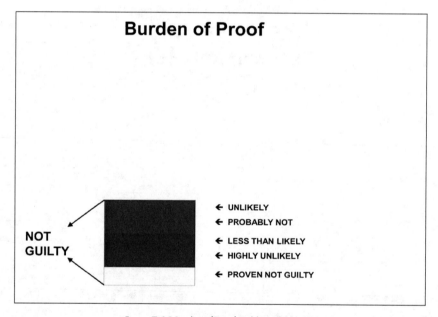

Figure 7-05 Burden of Proof Building Blocks #4

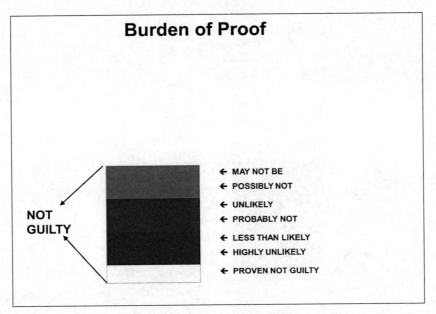

Figure 7-06 Burden of Proof Building Blocks #5

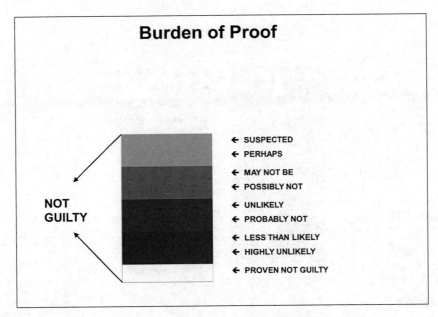

Figure 7-07 Burden of Proof Building Blocks #6

CLOSING ARGUMENTS

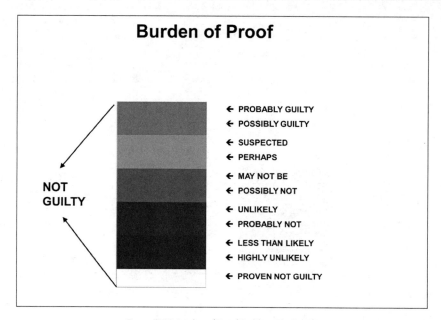

Figure 7-08 Burden of Proof Building Blocks #7

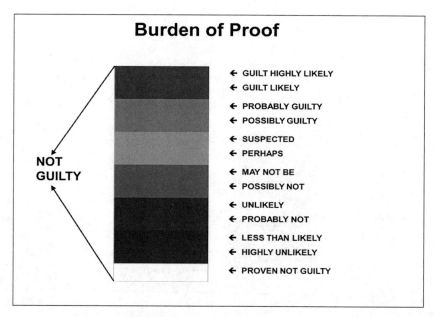

Figure 7-09 Burden of Proof Building Blocks #8

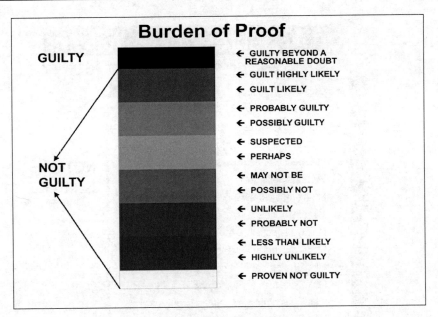

Figure 7-10 Burden of Proof Building Blocks #9

§7:91   Degrees of Guilt

The next two slides allow you to either hand-draw the differing levels as you speak, or to present them side by side.

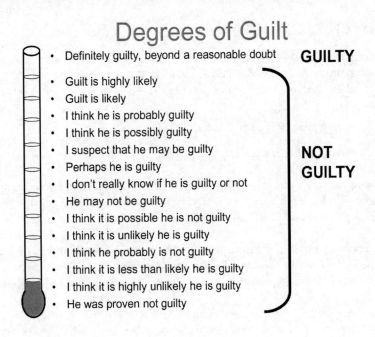

Figure 7-11 Degrees of Guilt #1

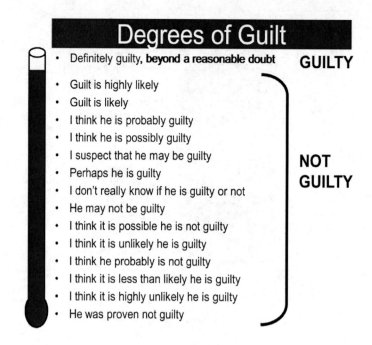

Figure 7-12 Degrees of Guilt #2

[§§7:92-7:99 Reserved]

V.   COMPLETE CLOSINGS

Here are examples of nearly complete closing arguments. I am neither intending nor am I expecting you to recite them verbatim. Instead take some of the radical ideas that are conveyed and use them as you can. They are somewhat overbroad and "in your face" so that you can see the tenor and tone it down as you need.

§7:100   The Interrogator (Refusal Cases)

Thanks to Peter Carini of Medford, Oregon.

Imagine that you are an interrogator in the Army. You have been highly trained and schooled. No lesson has been more instilled in your training than this: the ultimate decision on whether to torture or not is yours. No one else can order you to do that, and no one else will have to answer for any mistake.

You have been given a special assignment today. The General has told of you of a terrible menace. This particular enemy is one who kills with neither rhyme nor reason. Men, women, children are all targets. The enemy cares not for innocence or guilt, involvement or disenchantment. It kills at random.

The General tells you that a Lieutenant has captured this enemy, and now an intelligence officer is confirming this. Your orders are clear. Go to the location, make the decision, and if justified, carry out your deadly task.

Upon arrival, you meet the intelligence officer. He tells you what the Lieutenant has found. They show you the room they have set up with the prisoner and tell you to use all those techniques of torture you have to break this person.

You slide up to the window and look into the room. For some reason you hesitate, and immediately the intelligence officer and the Lieutenant tell you to do it. "This is my decision" you tell them, knowing that you, and you alone, are responsible for what happens.

During training you were told that above all, friendlies and innocents must never be tortured. To do so would undermine all faith in this system. Should an innocent ever be made to suffer, everyone would figure that this program was wrong. That the system of checks and balances, of which you are an integral part, does not work. What you see through the window reminds you of this responsibility.

But the image is not clear; it is just a vague outline. Neither you, nor anyone else, can be sure exactly who is at the other end. It is impossible to be sure that the person you are targeting is or is not the enemy.

Both the Lieutenant and the intelligence officer tell you they are sure. But still, you know it is your decision, not theirs to make. They offer to help you. They tell you to look again and see it how they saw it. You do so, but the details are fuzzy.

Just then, the Lieutenant and the intelligence officer slide up next to you describing what they see.

"Officer do you see what the target is wearing?"

"Yes, sir, he is wearing military style boots."

"That's consistent with what the enemy wears?"

"Yes sir it is."

But our men wear boots, and so do innocents, you say. You cannot make a decision based just on this.

"Well was the suspect walking back and forth like he was patrolling?"

"Yes sir he was."

"Doesn't the enemy walk patrols?"

"Yes sir they do."

But lots of people pace—friendlies, innocents, even our own troops. It is not an uncommon event. Your decision cannot be based on such flimsy evidence.

"Can you hear what the target was saying?"

"Not exactly sir, but it sounded foreign to me."

"The enemy speaks a foreign tongue, doesn't he?"

"Yes sir he does"

But so do the innocent people around here. So do interpreters, translators, aid workers and many others. In fact, you are not sure the Lieutenant and the intelligence officer could even hear the prisoner speak from where they were. Even if they could, they never met this person before, so how do they know what he normally sounds like. How can you perform the ultimate act based on something so common?

"Officer, could you see the way the target's eyes looked? He was squinting, wasn't he?"

"That's exactly what I saw sir."

"Does the enemy squint."

"All the time sir, it is a leading sign."

But it's the middle of the day. Everyone is squinting. Even you, the Lieutenant, and the intelligence officer are squinting in the sun. This is what happens in this bright land. Still you cannot be sure.

The intelligence man and the Lieutenant try one more tactic.

"Officer, did you get a smell from this person?"

"Yes sir I did. He smelled like the enemy."

But after being here everyone starts to smell like this. You just remarked on that fact the other night to some others. It is not who you are that creates such odors, it's where you are. It is like smelling like smoke after being in a smoky room even if you never touch tobacco. This is not enough for you.

"But look where he was, only the enemy would be out there at that hour."

Wait, many people are out at that hour. Does that make them the enemy? No. This is still not enough for you to torture someone.

You have made up your mind. Just because someone looks and walks and talks a particular way, and has certain odors is not enough for you to decide his fate. You need more. After all, there is no going back if you are wrong. No one can second guess your decision, right or wrong. You tell this to the other two men. They cannot believe you need to know more, but they try to convince you.

Another officer is called in. Like the Lieutenant, he has years of experience. He has been trained to spot the enemy. He comes to you and says he knows it is the enemy. You ask him how he knows. He then repeats everything you already saw and evaluated. Well, he says, two of us say so, therefore it must be true.

You shake your head. Conjecture and speculation are not the evidence you need to make a decision of this nature. You want some hard facts.

Finally, the intelligence officer tells you there is one more piece of evidence to prove this is the enemy. You sigh as you wait to hear this in order to be at ease with your decision.

"We asked him if he were the enemy and he did not answer. When we asked him to be tested to see if he were the enemy he refused. Only the enemy would refuse to submit to our testing without question."

Now this is important. After all, given the chance to prove yourself, who would refuse?

"Yep, right after we captured him, subdued him, and dragged him to the prison; we told him he could prove us wrong."

Well wait, hadn't he said you were wrong all along, you ask. You told me that when you first met him he said he was not the enemy. He told you he did not do what you said he was doing. I thought you told me that he told you that he looked and acted the way you described because he was tired, cold, old, etc.

"Sure he told us that, but we know the enemy lies. Just because all those things may be true, doesn't mean they are true. They still might be lies."

You shake your head in confusion. A person tells the truth, and what he says makes sense, but it is believed to be a lie? What kind of Orwellian world is this? You remember your training; that is why you are here, because the officers and intelligence people round up anyone they think is suspicious and leave it to you to decide the truth. The General even told you this. In order to bring a prisoner in for you to execute, the field operatives only need a probability. That's all. Not proof, just cause. Your job is to see if the case has been made.

So back to this test. As you ask, you find out the prisoner was told that the test was optional. That he did not have to submit. He was told that if he did not do so it would be used by people to decide his fate. Still he refused. When he asked how reliable the test was, he was given no answer. He was never told how the test works, or if he could get other tests.

Of course, this was after he repeatedly declared he was not the enemy to the officer and was laughed at. It was after he did all the calisthenics the officer required, and correctly. In fact, from his point of view, this person did all he could to show he was not the enemy and was constantly berated for it. No one believed him. Why would he put his faith in a machine that no one explained to him and that was run by the very people calling him a liar? No, he knew that sooner or later a person, you, one of independence and integrity would come to evaluate the situation. He put his faith in you, rather than a machine.

Well, it is now that time. You have to decide. Is it the end or do you say you are not sure? You marshal the evidence. You have walking, talking, looking, and sounding like the enemy, but also like anyone else in the same situation. In fact, none of those factors are unique to the enemy. That's not enough.

You have the refusal to submit to a test, but the test is optional. Given the circumstances, many people would not take the test. Still not enough.

Finally, you have the fear. And the fear may be the most important aspect of all. In fact, the intelligence officer has been pushing the fear factor all along. Actually, when you get right down to it that is what they have hinged their entire case on; your fears. Fears for your family, yourself, society. They constantly mention or hint at the idea that if you are wrong, this person will wreak havoc. But no evidence of that has been presented. If this is the enemy, they admit he might never come back; if it is not, he should never have been here.

As you reflect on this you remember your training. The words come freshly back to you. Do not make a decision based on fear, prejudice, or worry. It is the facts, and only the facts, which count.

Well ladies and gentlemen; this is what you have before you. Bobby has been held prisoner by these people since he was first stopped. Bobby constantly and consistently said he did nothing wrong. He was cooperative, performed all their tests and answered all their questions. And, according to the officer, did so truthfully. Yet here he sits; about to be executed by your decision. But the fact is Bobby looked, talked, acted, and responded like anyone would in the same situation. The only thing Bobby did wrong was he did not take a test.

Well, do we condemn people for not kowtowing to the government? No. This is still America; we still have the right not to submit to every order of the police.

In the final analysis, just like the official before, it is you who get to decide. But unlike the officers, your level of proof is not a probability, it is not a preponderance, nor is it clarity. It is proof beyond a reasonable doubt: the highest level of proof known to general society. The level of which has been equated to a moral certainty.

Once you reach your decision, there is no going back. It is final. You must be able to live with it from now until forever. If you have any thought or doubt leading to hesitation, then you must not torture the prisoner.

§7:101   The Inspector (Breath Test Cases)

Thanks to Felipe Plascencia of La Habra, California.

In life we make many important decisions. No decision you have ever made, unless you have served on a criminal jury before, is even close to the one you make today. Without trying to sound facetious, let's look at the biggest decisions we have made in our lives.

Let us start with what many consider the number one decision, marriage. I am not going to get into the idea of divorce. I will avoid the political and religious concepts. Instead I want to tell you what the courts have said in likening a marriage decision to your decision here today; they do not compare.

That is correct. I am not the one who is saying this, but the judges we have all elected, these scholars who have shown their wisdom over the years. When a trial judge, just like the one sitting here, once likened the decision in a criminal case as similar to the one for marriage, he was rebuked. The more learned judges said he was wrong. They told us that the decision here is far more consequential.

Like it or not, it does make some sense. I apologize to those of you of strong religious beliefs, but it is a reality of today that marriage is not necessarily forever. And if any of you mention this to my wife, we will have a problem, because I do believe in one lifetime marriage. But we all know that divorce is not uncommon. The difference is that you cannot 'divorce' a criminal conviction.

Now what I just said is not entirely true. For the last 15 or so years we have heard of the Innocence Project. That group of lawyers who have used DNA evidence in heinous rape, murder or other crimes to show people were wrongly convicted. So I guess you can 'divorce' a criminal conviction. But not until you sit in jail for 10, 15, 20 years.

Well, in this particular case, DNA evidence will not save the day. So let's look at other decisions.

My good friend Felipe once said, a criminal case is like buying a house. You have the seller (the police officer); the District Attorney as the agent, and you, ladies and gentlemen, are the buyers. You see, the officer has a house he believes you should buy. He has decided to work with the DA to convince you to buy the house. Before you do so, you must have absolutely no questions as to the soundness of this property.

What is my job, you ask? I am the inspector. I will take you up and down in and out of this house to show you why this house is NOT worth buying. There is no way you would want to spend the rest of your life in this house.

So let's look at this house the DA is trying to sell you. Like any house we start with the foundation. In the context of a DUI case, the foundation is the basic rules of how tests are conducted and evaluated. It is the machinery on which any test is performed. We all know, without a strong foundation, the prettiest of houses will eventually crumble.

The foundation of a breath test is Title 17. In order to have a good foundation for your house, you want poured concrete, not river rock or brick. You want the concrete to be poured to the correct thickness, with appropriate rebar. In a breath test, you want a modern machine, used properly, within the working parameters.

We do not have those aspects in this case. The officer admitted that the observation period was compromised. He watched for 5 minutes, then was interrupted, albeit briefly, and resumed for 10 minutes. This composes, and compromises, his observation period. Well, just like concrete needs a certain time to set, a breath test needs certain time to be acceptable.

If you need to see to it that your slab has 15 days to 'cure' with no rain, it is not okay to say I was there days one to five, left on days six and seven to return on days eight to eighteen. But that is exactly what the DA is trying to sell you here. He says the officer did a pretty good observation period, and the missing couple of minutes does not matter.

Well, just as the builder cannot tell you what happened in those missing days to compromise the integrity of the slab, the officer and the DA cannot tell you what happened to compromise the validity of the test results here. Don't buy this house.

When you build a house, you need to be sure that the parts are all within the appropriate variance. For example, if a wall is not quite straight, say an inch off center at one end from the other, then the next wall will not meet it. You end up with a gap. So too in breath testing. The machine must be within a given range of operation or else the resulting test is not worthwhile. We heard evidence in this case that the breath machine is allowed to be off by .01. Upon my careful inspection, and make no mistake, that is what I get paid for, we find out the machine was off by more than that.

Now, as a good agent, the DA is trying to tell you the officer's house is still a good bargain. And if you had the time, money and experience to buy this house as a 'fixer,' it may be worthwhile. But you don't. This is a buy it and live with it deal. No work. No going back. You buy, you are done. So does this margin of error matter? Of course it does.

When walls do not match up, then spaces exist. Wind comes in. Rain starts leaks. Roofs collapse and the house becomes a nightmare. Well if machines are inaccurate then people get wrongly convicted. A leaky roof is nothing compared to a wrongful conviction.

Finally, as relates to the breath test foundation, we have applicability. We all know, the foundation necessary in California is very different than needed in Maine. Our earth moves on a fairly regular basis, theirs does not. While they may be able to get away with a 2 inch slab, we need pylons. That is the same in breath testing. Not everyone is the same. You heard the experts admit that some people need longer to absorb alcohol than others. Some people can get to a higher or lower BAC than others with the same number of drinks.

Just as different parts of the country require different building materials and specifications, different people require adjustments for their unique characteristics. But the house here is a "one size fits all" model. The owner and his agent are not worrying if the house will work where you need it. They are using it for themselves and you should just accept that. But you can't. You have to live with the house forever.

So we say a compromised foundation, that is not fit for the place the house resides. Let's move upstairs and look at the floor plan.

First, this house is designed for the "average" family. It has three bedrooms and two baths for the 2 kid, one dog typical family. But you told me you are a bachelor, or a large family, or grandparents; this house is not your size. Well the testing done here is not my client's size.

You see Bob here is not "average." He absorbs, distributes, and eliminates alcohol uniquely. When we asked, all the witnesses said they cannot tell us how fast or slow he does these things. Yet they want him to live in this house. It does not fit him, nor does it fit you.

They told you that you can presume his numbers to reflect his BAC at the time he was driving. That would be like presuming you can live in this 3 bedroom house without knowing the size of your family. How presumptuous. Suppose we told you that because you are looking at a house, our statistics say that this size is right for you as an "average" family. But you have 5 children and your mother-in-law lives with you. Do you want to spend the rest of your life forced to live like this? Not if you can help it.

Well Bob does not want to live with this either. It is within your power to not buy this house so that both you and Bob can find one more suitable to you.

We also know that some additions were done on this house. Of course, the officer told you he has done those additions before, that they only make the house better, and that you should trust him, he knows what he is doing. No thank you. We have permits and inspectors to be sure that when someone makes any additions to the house they do so following the codes. Sure that extra light in the kitchen makes cooking easier, but did you know it overloads the circuits which will lead to a fire?

What about the shortcuts the owner told you he took on the windows. When it rains will they come mop the floors? The standardized field sobriety tests are set up not to leak or overload the system. They are the only tests that count. The other tests the officer gave are untested and uninspected. No one knows what they will do to the house, but we do know they are not approved.

Even those standardized tests the officer used, he performed incorrectly. That is like putting the windows in backwards. It is not something you would want. So looking at these "additions," we see they are untested, done wrong, and unreliable.

Is this the house for you? It is not a house I would want.

Finally we come to the roof. The covering of the entire house. Does it leak? How old is it? Well, as we look at the overall covering of this house we see that it is all based on the agent's representations. The agent says he likes this house. He has spoken with the owner and he would live here. He has no problems with this roof.

But that is his job. He is supposed to tell you the house is fine; he does not get paid unless he makes this sale. Well it is not all fine. We cannot go up on the roof, or visit the scene, because the receipts for the roof repair were never kept. Just like no video or other evidence of the night in question was made. Nothing remains for us to look at objectively.

With its faulty foundation, illegal additions and uninspectable roof, this house is a money pit. You can buy it if you want, but remember, you have to live with it just as it is today forever. You can never change any aspect of your decision.

Now the seller's agent is going to stand up here and gloss over all these problems. He will tell you how they really do not exist. He will highlight the curb appeal of the house, you know, how when the seller first attracted you in it was with color, sight and smell.

Curb appeal does not decide the issue. Fresh coats of paint, the smell of new carpet and sound of soft music is just staging. So too are red eyes, slurred speech or alcohol odors; just staging. You do not buy a house on such flimsy stuff.

So listen to the agent and ask yourself this: If the house were so great, why would they spend so much time dressing it up?

§7:102 Disconnect Cases (High BAC)

So here we are at the end of the case. You have heard all that the prosecution had to give you. They have no more evidence, no more witnesses, no more opinions. They gave it all, and yet it was not enough. I say this to you because the evidence they presented does not match up. If you look at each piece of evidence, it doesn't make sense.

The reason why Bill was stopped was a technical violation. He had a busted taillight. Now ask yourselves, how does a broken light indicate drunk driving? It doesn't. Such a violation is no more an indication of DUI then a light out in the home is indication of a drug user.

Next, we have the field tests. Both the officer and the experts agree that Bill's performance on these tasks, while not perfect, was relatively good. Bill had good mental ability and understood the complex tasks he was supposed to do. His only issue was in the physical performance.

Well, what do we know about alcohol and its effects on people? We know, from every witness in this case, that alcohol has a very specific chronology of effect, and it starts with the brain. Evidence of mental impairment MUST appear before there will be evidence of physical impairment. This means the converse is true; physical impairment without evidence of mental impairment cannot be a result of alcohol. Such results, physical problems, without mental issues, indicate a lack of coordination, physical disability or the like. So Bill's performance indicates a LACK of mental impairment and therefore is NOT alcohol related.

So, ladies and gentlemen, we have a person who exhibited no bad driving, does not appear to be under the effects of alcohol, and yet the DA is urging a conviction. What does the DA ask you to use in this decision? A chemical test. But not just any chemical test, one with a result that everyone agrees should make a person hammered.

The test result in this case is a .16. The experts all told you that such a number indicates consumption of about 9 or 10 beers. The person should be falling down drunk. Yet Bill is not even close to that. Can we trust this test?

Here is another factor in deciding that all important question, BILL NEVER HAD TO USE THE BATH-ROOM. Think about that. In the three hours he was with the officers, with ten beers in his body, Bill never has to pee. Does that make sense? Is that believable? I don't think any of you would be able to do that, because no one can.

Where does this leave us? Bill has no bad driving, no mental impairment, does not have to use the bathroom and yet is alleged to have 10 beers on board. This defies logic so the prosecution forwards two unsubstantiated theories; that Bill is tolerant to alcohol, and that he has a huge bladder. We on the other hand merely forward the Sesame Street/Occam's Razor scenario.

Occam's Razor is a scientific principle that holds that, all things being equal, the simplest explanation is usually the truth. Apply that here. The simplest explanation, that of the defense, is that there is a problem with the chemical test. Since none of us were there, it is impossible for us to definitively show this, but it also impossible for the prosecution to definitively DISPROVE this. Since the burden is on the prosecution, and they have not met it, then the defendant is entitled to this in his benefit. That is, that you can assume the machine was not properly working and the results are not trustworthy.

On the other hand, the prosecution, as mentioned before, forwards two complex theories. First that Bill has somehow developed the ability to mask huge amounts of alcohol from both his mental and physical performance. Second that he has trained his bladder. This is ridiculous.

I mentioned Sesame Street. How many of you remember the "One of these things is not like the other"? That was where the performer put up a board with four squares. Each square had one object in it. Three of the objects were obviously the same and one was not. The children had to figure it out. Well, ladies and gentlemen, let's do that here.

No bad driving	Good SFST
Says 2 beers	.16

Fig. 7-13 Disconnect Defense Chart

It is as easy as Sesame Street to see which one of these things does not belong. Just as it is as easy to find Bill not guilty.

§7:103   Circumstantial Evidence Case (No Test or Other Guy Drove)

No one knows what Jan's alcohol level was when she drove. Yet the prosecution wants you to convict her of drunk driving. They say it is based on the circumstances surrounding her arrest. They say that these allegations are sufficient to call Jan a criminal and destroy her life. To make her a convict. To convince you beyond a reasonable doubt. I disagree.

You see, I have been the victim of a rush to judgment based on circumstantial evidence. Years ago I had a friend who had a very traditional New York Italian mother. They had the traditional split level ranch house with a formal living room. This formal room had the white furniture, white rug, and the protective plastic on the couch. No one was allowed into the room.

As we grew up, all of us knew that to even THINK of going into that room would get a whack upside the head by Paul's mom. While we used to razz Paul about it, like teenagers would do to anyone about anything, we knew that the room was off limits. Well one day we had played our usual game of fall football. In New York this was particularly fun because it was usually a mud ball game. Lots of slipping and sliding and no one gets hurt.

So we finish the game and decide to go to Paul's house since his mom made the best snacks. Some of the guys went home first but John and I went straight over. John was a new kid in our neighborhood. He had never been to Paul's house before and he had never known about the "white room." There we are walking into Paul's house covered in mud, and you guessed it, John walked right into the white room. I screamed at him, explained the rules and he panicked and ran out of the house. Of course Paul's mom heard the noise, ran up and saw the muddy prints all over the place.

I am sure you can guess what happened next. Despite my protestations, which included the fact that I KNEW BETTER, I was the guilty party. Now Paul's mom didn't hit me since I was not her kid. Instead, she told me he would arrange for me to clean the carpet which would take hours. I went to John and told him to fess up. Do you think he did? Nope. I was stuck doing his dirty work even though I was not guilty.

Well, that is what the DA is trying to do here. It was not fair to me and it is not fair to Jan.

§7:104   GERD

I have dealt elsewhere in this book with the medical defense of GERD. Many prosecutors try to attack this defense by arguing that the slope detector would be triggered and a valid breath sample would not be obtained. (This assumes the breath test was not performed on a hand-held device since they do not have slope detectors.) They also argue that the 15-minute observation period would eliminate GERD since they liken it to mouth alcohol; this is the fallacy that needs to be corrected.

Here is one of the problems/issues with GERD. The prosecution thinks and is trying to convince you that GERD is like a volcano: it has eruptions that cause huge plumes, but then dissipate. That's just not true.

Most people with GERD have a completely incompetent upper sphincter. This means the gases are constantly flowing freely up the esophagus. Instead of an eruption, it is a constant smoking.

Have you ever made homemade spaghetti sauce? If you are not careful and have the heat too high during the simmering phase, PPLOFFPP! You get that huge eruption and sauce all over the floor. That is a regurgitation for which the cop is on the lookout.

But if you are a good cook, you keep that heat low so the sauce barely bubbles. From across the room you don't see the action, but boy do you smell it. Well, my client's GERD is like the simmering sauce; there is no messy explosion, just a constant simmer.

That is why the slope detector does not catch it and that is why the two results can be the same. Until we eat all the sauce, or until my client empties his stomach, we will have the aroma. And sometimes even after that.

[§§7:105-7:109 Reserved]

VI. CONSTRUCTING A POWER POINT CLOSING ARGUMENT

§7:110 Introduction

If you have little or no experience with Power Point, the following simple closing argument can be used for almost any DUI case provided you set the stage during the trial. I have set forth the basic points you will want to elicit from various witnesses prior to the relevant slides. Below that, I am including several slides from a DUI investigation portion of a closing showing you how you can use the "babystepping" portion of the cross examination to combine with your burden of proof arguments.

To create the slides, just use the pre-set basic presentation and insert your facts as you see fit. The idea here is not to overwhelm the jury with your presentation skills, but rather to use the 'television-like' imagery of power point in order to focus the jurors on the relevant testimony.

For additional Power Point presentations and exhibits that can be used during closing argument, see Ch. 8, *Demonstrative Evidence*.

§7:111 The Evidence

In this case the testimony of all the prosecution witnesses was rather vanilla. The officers saw a drunk, the drunk didn't do well on FSTs, the drunk admitted to drinking, the drunk blew over the limit and the expert opined he was drunk. During cross-examination the officers admitted that FSTs do not equate to a particular alcohol level, the FSTs do not measure the ability to drive, and that they are a tool for probable cause. The expert admitted that alcohol levels go up then down and that given the test, without a known drinking pattern, there is no way to know if the defendant was rising or falling.

§7:112 Essential Points to Be Made on Cross-Examination

During trial you need to have the officer admit that:
- FSTs are used since they are the "best tool" in making an in field investigation; and
- The officer uses the "totality of the circumstances" in reaching his decision, which is probable cause to arrest.

Point out through cross-exam that probable cause means more likely than not under the law.

During cross of the expert, present hypothetical questions that demonstrate that the alcohol level could have been rising or falling depending on the drinking pattern. This then creates the possibility that the client was drunker than the test level or well below the legal limit at the time of the driving.

In either a blood or breath case have the witness admit that since no one checked the FILL IN THE BLANK (and here you need to find some element of the testing procedure which was not up to snuff, such as not checking the blood for preservative), then all the jurors can say is it was *supposed* to happen. There is no proof that it actually was done.

Finally get the witness to admit that they are assuming the alcohol was fully absorbed prior to the stop without *any factual basis* to do so. At the same time, present them with the concept that ALL of their testimony is based not on the client, but on the 'average' person. With that, introduce literature in the field that expands 'average' to the full possible range.

§7:113 The Presentation

As with any good closing argument, first start with an overview of the theme.

The Doctor and Mrs. Smith's Son

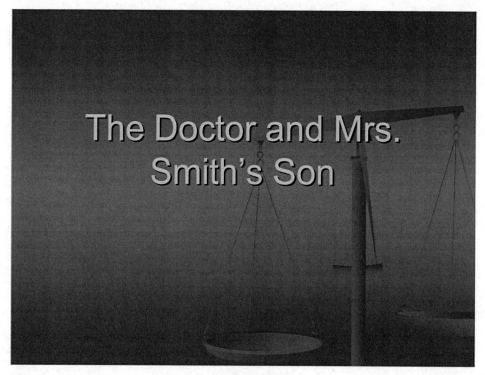

Fig. 7-14 The Doctor and Mrs. Smith's Son

"Ladies and gentlemen, this is the case of a concerned mother and her very sick son. When they visited the Doctor they were told the following…"

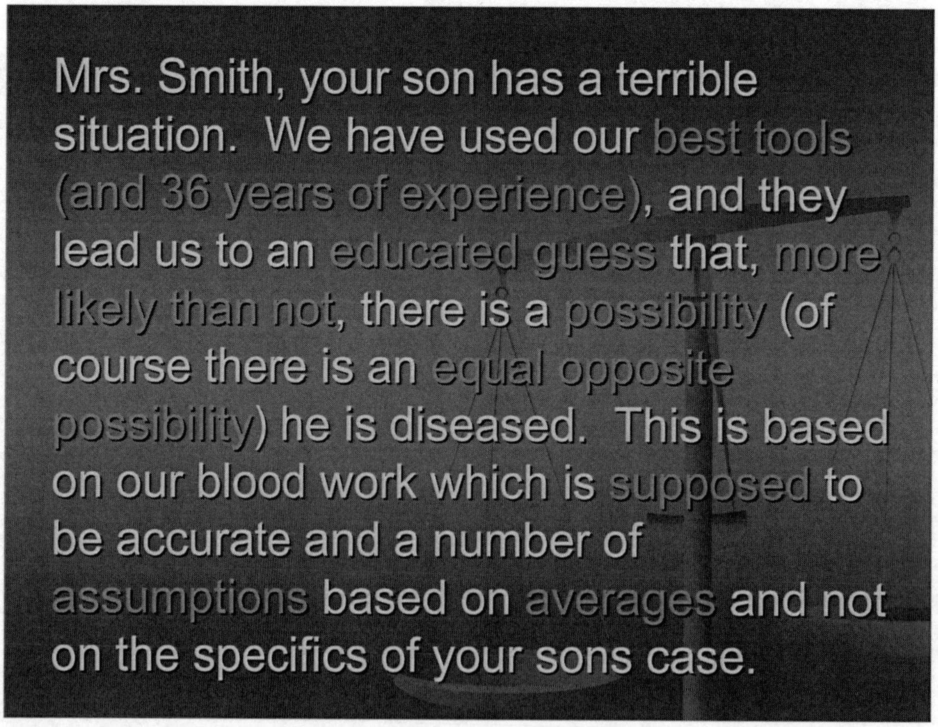
Mrs. Smith, your son has a terrible situation. We have used our best tools (and 36 years of experience), and they lead us to an educated guess that, more likely than not, there is a possibility (of course there is an equal opposite possibility) he is diseased. This is based on our blood work which is supposed to be accurate and a number of assumptions based on averages and not on the specifics of your sons case.

Fig. 7-15 The Doctor's Diagnosis

"Now, how do you think the mom felt? Not very confident and certainly not convinced beyond a reasonable doubt to allow the doctor to operate. Well, this is EXACTLY what has been given to you in this case."

Now you use the following slide to explain where you obtained each red phrase.

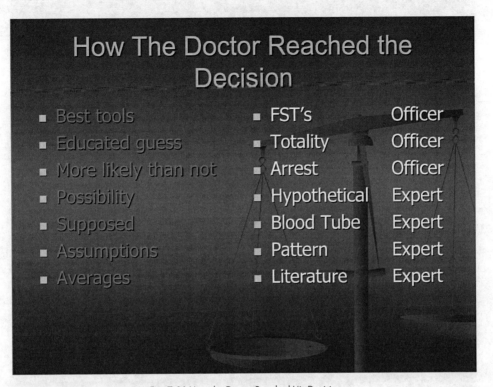

Fig. 7-16 How the Doctor Reached His Decision

The following slides further break down each of these elements. They are the specific points you need to present during your examination of the witnesses as just mentioned.

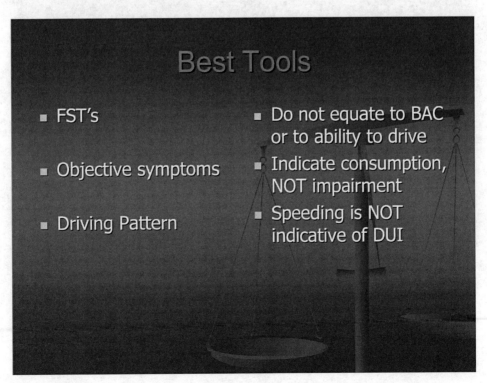

Fig. 7-17 Best Tools

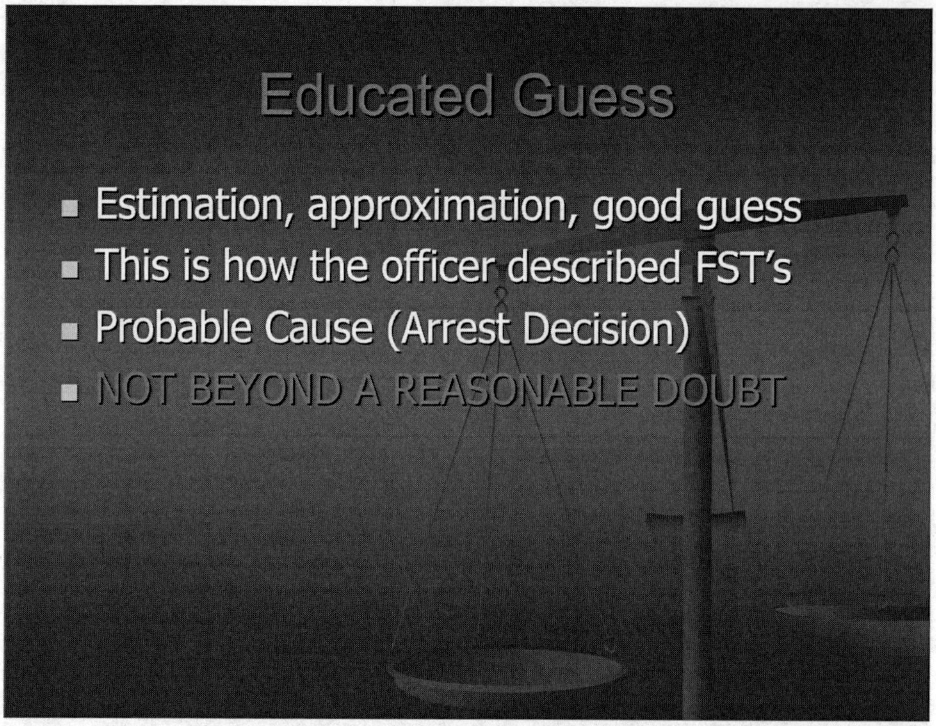

Fig. 7-18 Educated Guess

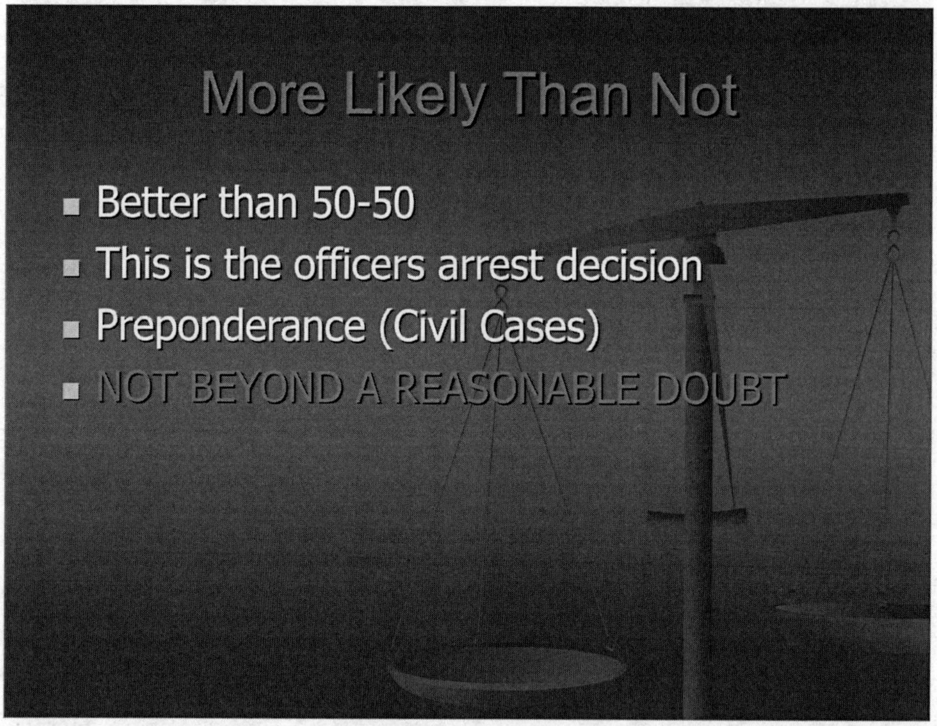

Fig. 7-19 More Likely Than Not

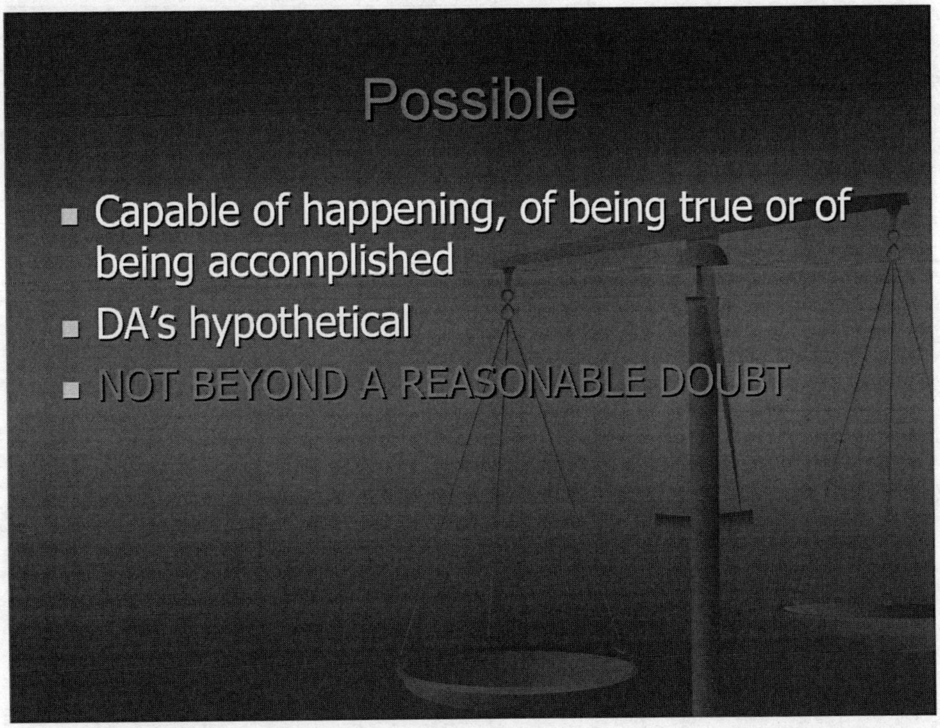

Fig. 7-20 Possible

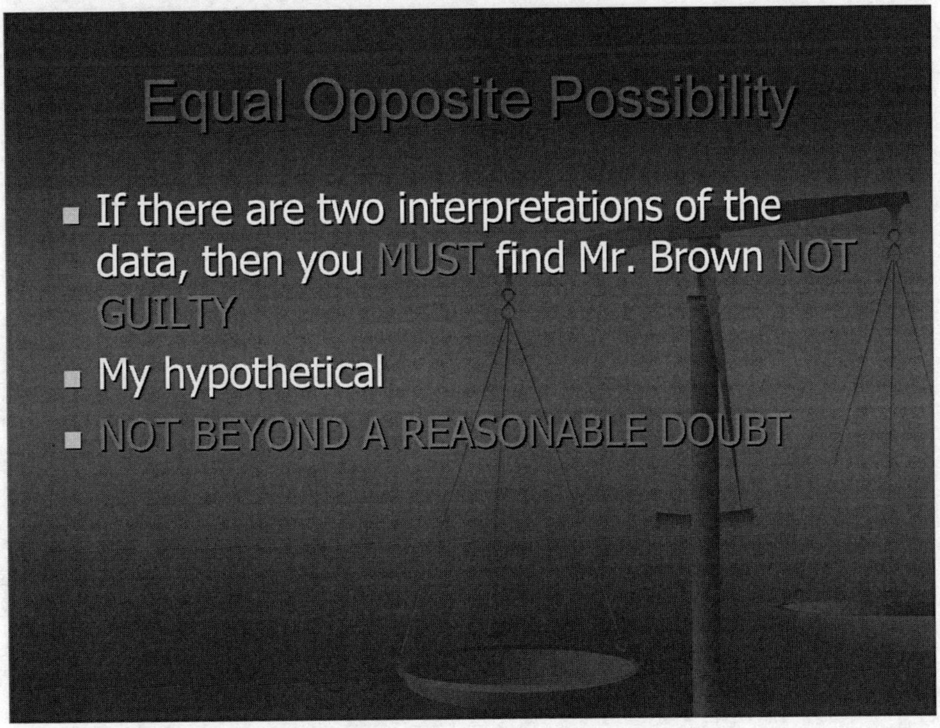

Fig. 7-21 Equal Opposite Possibility

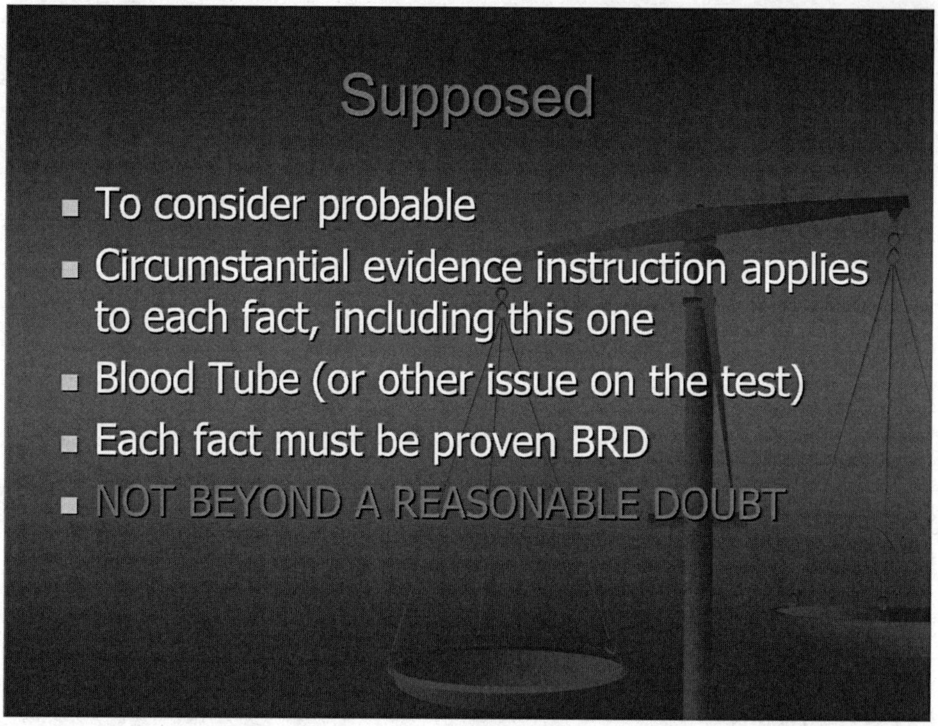

Fig. 7-22 Supposed

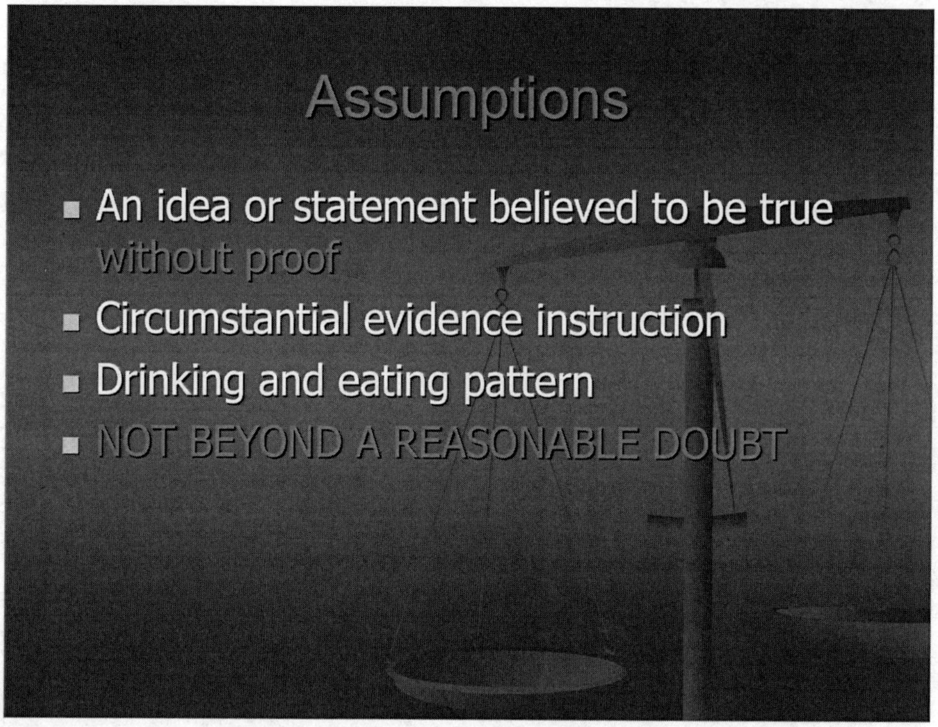

Fig. 7-23 Assumptions

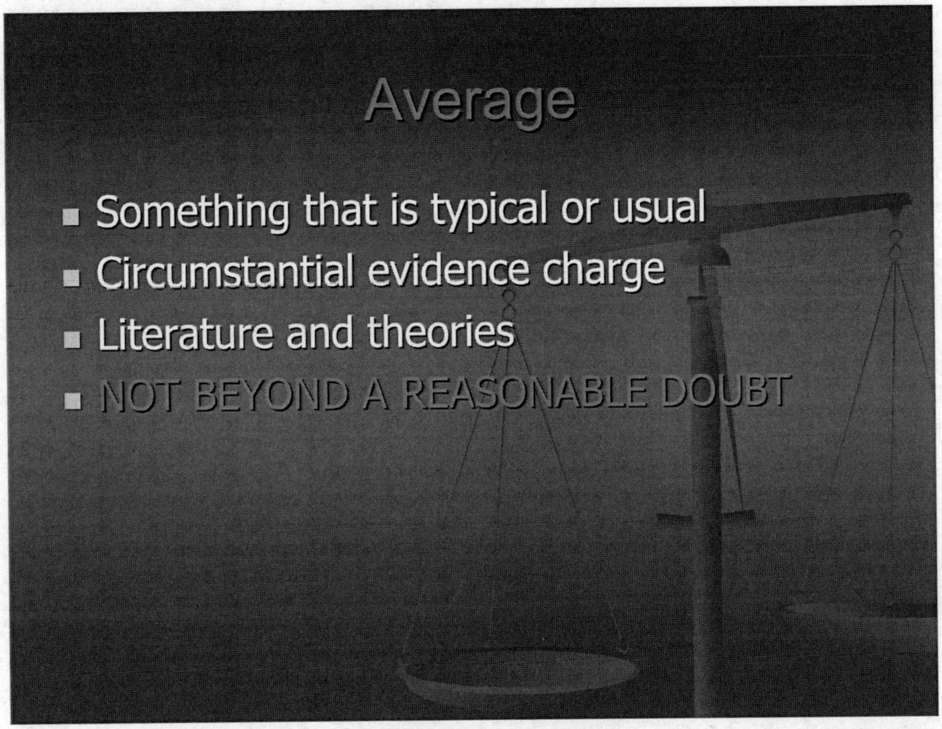

Fig. 7-24 Average

So we re-combine what was said by the witnesses with our original statement and put forward the following.

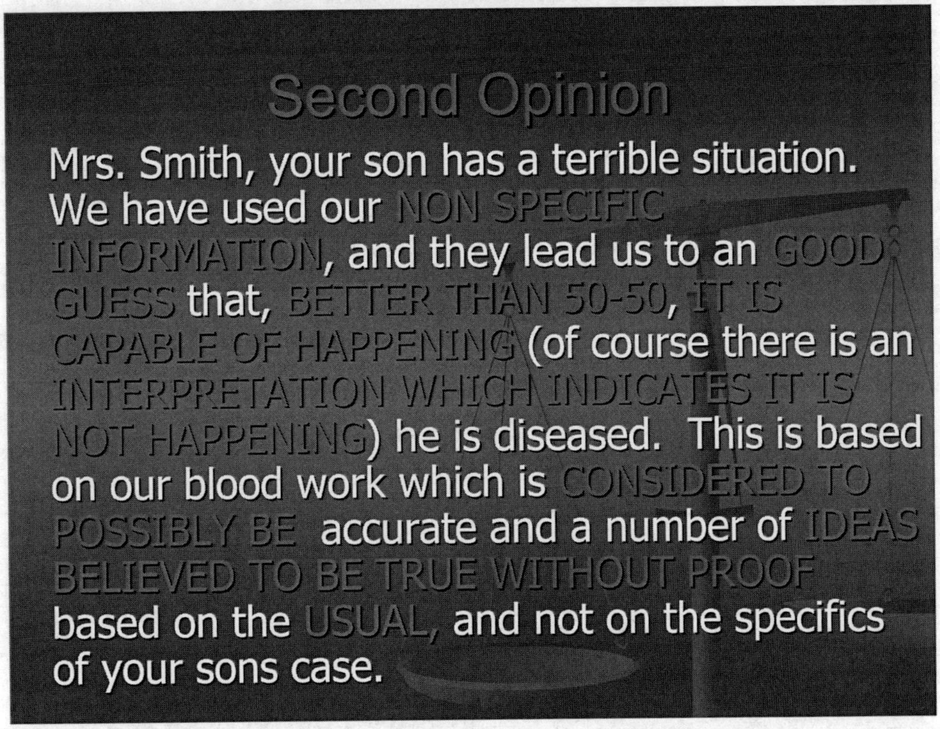

Fig. 7-25 Second Opinion

Then end with the ultimate question:

DO WE OPERATE or DO WE
WANT A BETTER OPINION?

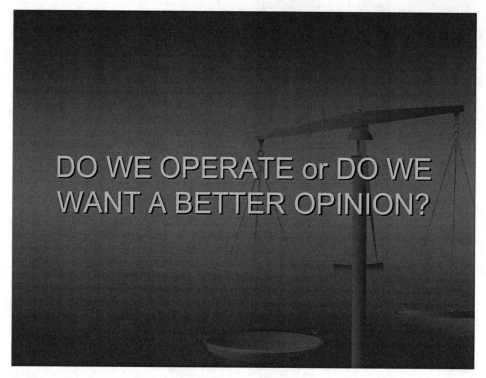

Fig. 7-26 Do We Operate

§7:114 Slides for Combining the "Babystepping" Portion of the Officer's Cross Examination with Burden of Proof Arguments

See Ch. 4, §4:04 for how to babystep a cop into saying your client was sober.

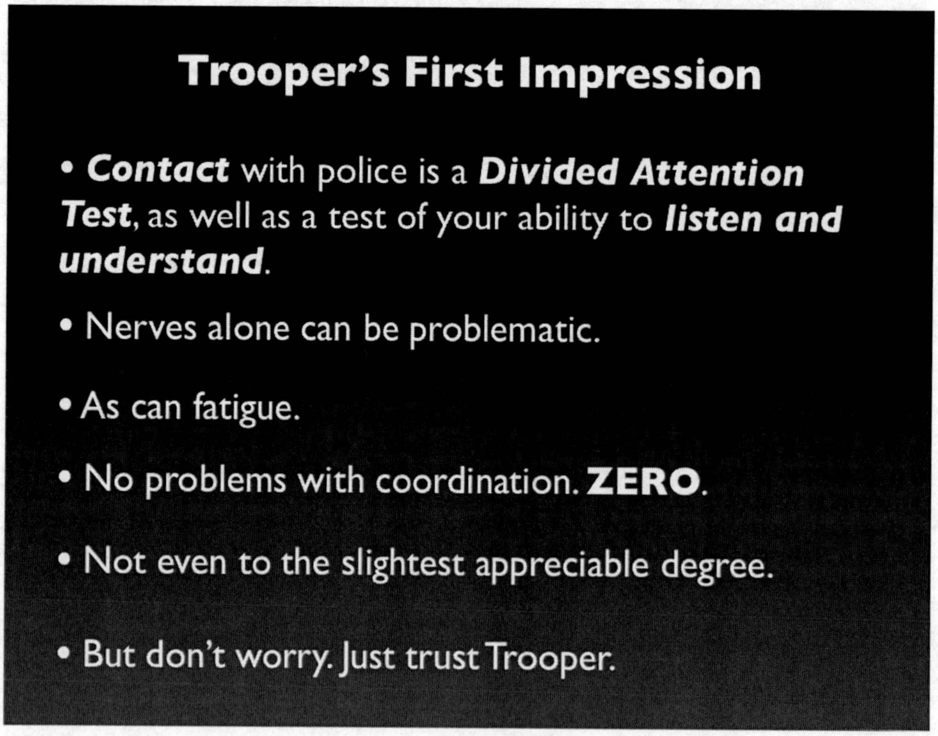

Trooper's First Impression
• Contact with police is a Divided Attention Test, as well as a test of your ability to listen and understand.
• Nerves alone can be problematic.
• As can fatigue.
• No problems with coordination. ZERO.
• Not even to the slightest appreciable degree.
• But don't worry. Just trust Trooper.

Fig. 7-27 Trooper's First Impression, slide #1

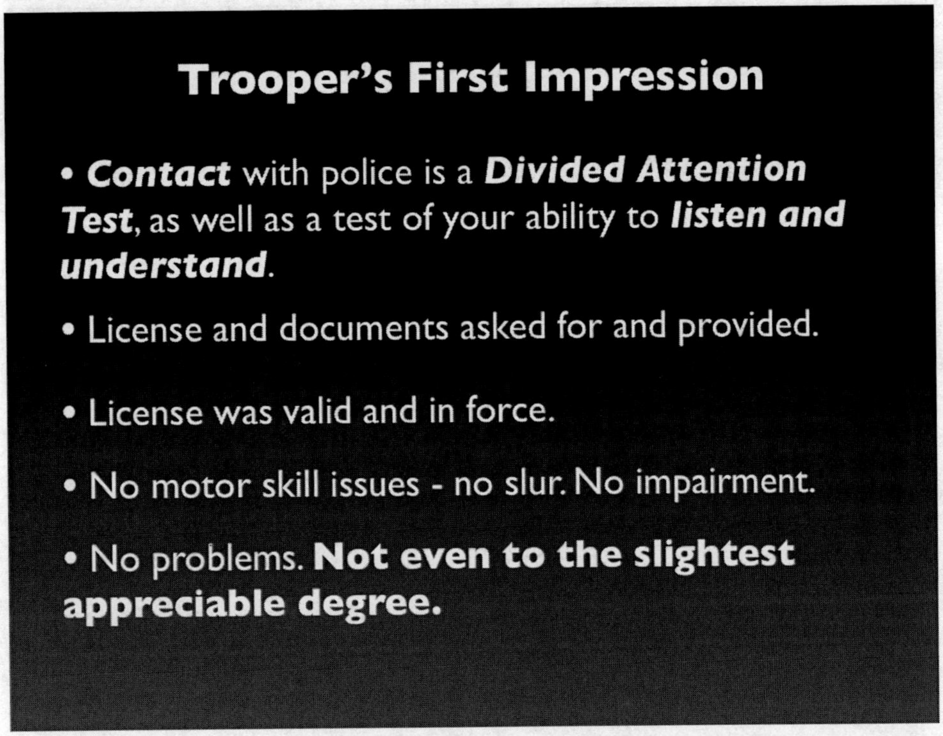

Trooper's First Impression

• **Contact** with police is a **Divided Attention Test**, as well as a test of your ability to **listen and understand**.

• License and documents asked for and provided.

• License was valid and in force.

• No motor skill issues - no slur. No impairment.

• No problems. **Not even to the slightest appreciable degree.**

Fig. 7-28 Trooper's First Impression, slide #2

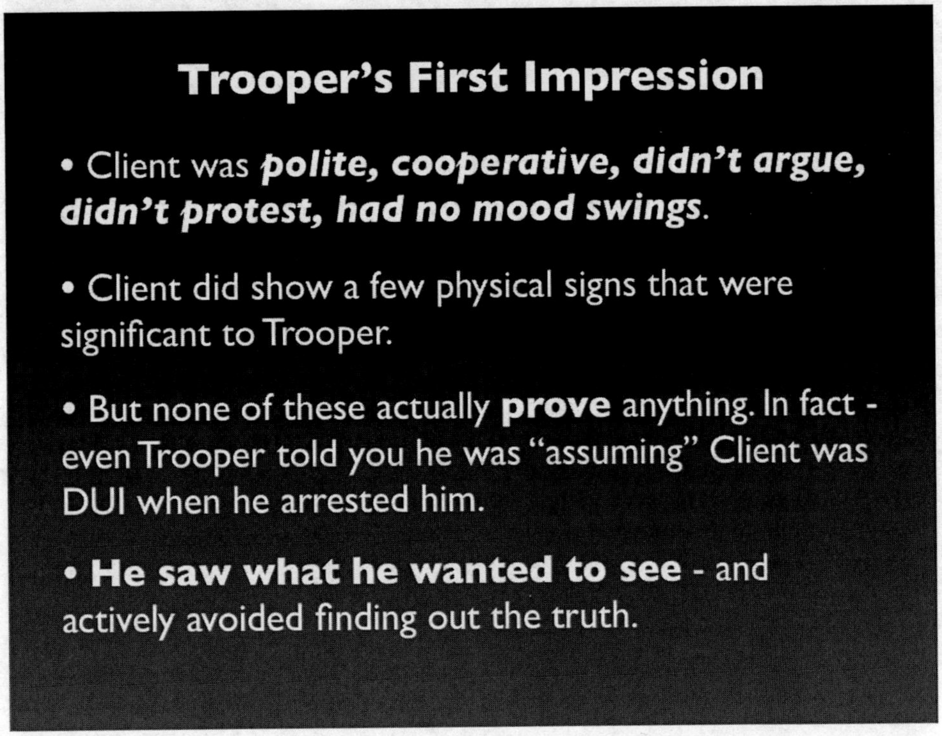

Trooper's First Impression

• Client was **polite, cooperative, didn't argue, didn't protest, had no mood swings**.

• Client did show a few physical signs that were significant to Trooper.

• But none of these actually **prove** anything. In fact - even Trooper told you he was "assuming" Client was DUI when he arrested him.

• **He saw what he wanted to see** - and actively avoided finding out the truth.

Fig. 7-29 Trooper's First Impression, slide #3

CLOSING ARGUMENTS

Exiting the Car

• Exiting the car is a ***Divided Attention Test***, as well as a test of your ***balance and coordination***.

• Client exited on command from the officer.

• Client remembered to take off his seat belt.

• Client did not use the door of the car for support.

• Client did not use the roof of the car for support.

• Client did not use the frame of the car for support.

• Client did not stumble out, stagger out, or fall out.

• Client walked around normally. **SOBERLY.**

Fig. 7-30 Exiting the Car

Walking from the Car

• Normal behavior indicative of normal coordination.

• Client did not use the car for support.

• Client did not trip.

• Client did not stumble.

• Client did not stagger.

• Client did not sway.

• Client did not fall.

• Client's behavior was picture perfect. **SOBER.**

Fig. 7-31 Walking from the Car

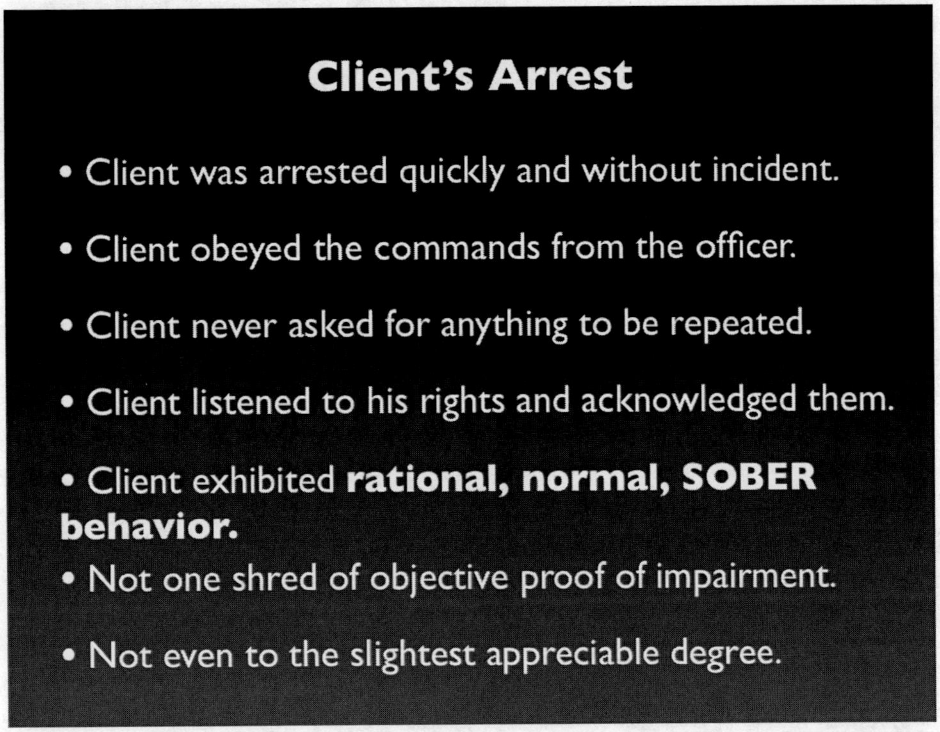

CLOSING ARGUMENTS

Fig. 7-32 Client's Arrest

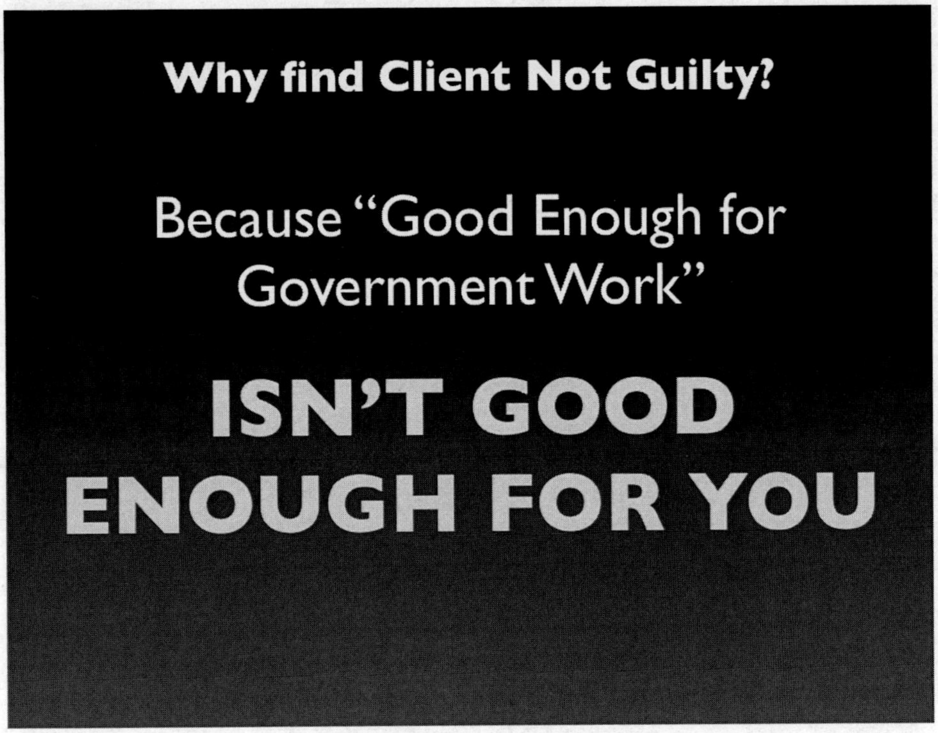

Fig. 7-33 Why Find Client Not Guilty

(This page intentionally left blank.)

CHAPTER 8

DEMONSTRATIVE EVIDENCE

DEMONSTRATIVE
EVIDENCE

I. INTRODUCTION

If it is true that a picture is worth a thousand words, and I for one believe that is true, then good demonstrative evidence is worth a hundred not guilty verdicts. In any type of trial, jurors often have a hard time conceptualizing things the attorneys take for granted. For example, anyone who has any trial experience can understand the concept of circumstantial evidence. Yet, for jurors, this concept is foreign. In most jurisdictions the judges use examples to get the meaning across. Often, those judge-given examples end up being the grounds for reversal or error.

In driving under the influence cases, the concepts are even more esoteric and harder to grasp. Jurors cannot automatically picture a blood alcohol curve. Typical breath exhalation profiles are foreign to them. Even the basic concept of the Walk-and-Turn is easier to comprehend when some physical manifestation is provided along with the verbal description.

I have heard, and firmly believe, that this is due in part to our becoming a visual rather than aural society. We tend to believe what we see, even when it is significantly weaker or open to more speculation, than what we hear, no matter how specific the latter may be over the former.

With that in mind, I have compiled a number of the better demonstrative evidence examples I have developed or seen over the years. It is no mere happenstance that many of the examples provided come from fellow attorneys. Perhaps no area of the drunk driving defense practice lends itself to free thought and creativity more than demonstrative evidence. There are a million different demonstrative tools for a creative practitioner to use. Very few of these ideas can actually be traced back to the original inventor. For example, the Dr. Scholl's pad idea [see §8:20] was first conveyed to me by Jim Nesci of Arizona. Yet when I mentioned it at a lecture in Ohio, Tim Huey, another good friend and fantastic lawyer, indicated he had come up with the idea. After several hours of fierce debate, the two agreed that it was a simultaneously obtained revelation.

So, with that in mind, I have tried to give credit where credit is due, to the person from whom I borrowed the concept. That is not to say that I have not expounded upon or specifically tailored these, just as I hope you will.

II. RISING ALCOHOL DEFENSE

§8:01 Blood Alcohol Curve

In many cases, the concept of rising alcohol plays a role. How do you explain this to a jury? You don't; you show it to them.

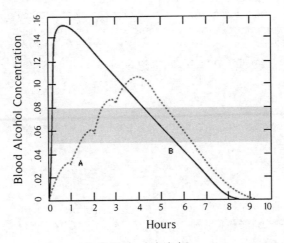

Fig. 8-01 Blood Alcohol Curve

This is a basic blood alcohol curve. This curve is especially useful because it represents two types of drinking. Line A represents the consumption of four mixed drinks (doubles) consumed one per hour. It shows BAC peaking once an hour with a light burnoff near the end of each hour. Line B is the same amount of alcohol slammed down at once with a peak in the first hour.

§8:02   Use at Trial

The prosecutor, in arguing against a rising alcohol case, will allege that your client is a B line individual, yet, there may be no evidence to suggest he or she is not an A line as you present.

This chart is also handy to show that if two tests are given a significant time apart, say 30 minutes, result in the same BAC, the peak BAC must have occurred in between and that therefore the client must have been rising.

Finally, if nothing else, the state's expert can be asked the following series of questions:

Q: You agree that when we consume alcohol, our BAC rises as the alcohol is absorbed?

A: Yes.

Q: And that will continue until we hit the peak alcohol level, which is based on the total amount of alcohol consumed and the time over which it was consumed?

A: Yes.

Q: That can be represented, generally speaking, in a chart or graph?

A: Yes.

Q: Like exhibit 1?

A: Yes

Q: The horizontal line is for time, the vertical for BAC?

A: Yes

Q: The convergence of the two is when Johnny started drinking?

A: Yes.

Q: What time was that?

A: I don't know?

Q: The downward slope you put in at around 1 hour later, what time was that?

A: Well, based on the literature, it would be about one hour after he stopped drinking.

Q: But since you just said you don't know the start time, doesn't that mean you don't know the time of the elimination either?

A: Yes.

Q: Well, can you put time of driving on this chart?

A: No.

Q: Can you put time of test on this chart?

A: No.

Q: So we do not know where on the curve the driving or testing occurred?

A: I am assuming the test was post absorptive given the time it took to get the defendant to the station.

Q: But according to your chart, one goes from absorbing to post absorption right here (point to the peak)?

A: Yes.

Q: Then Johnny could have been absorbing right up to the point of the minute before the test, so that the test caught his highest point?

A: That is possible.

That is all you need. If the state admits something is possible, then they have not proven the case beyond a reasonable doubt.

[§§8:03-8:09 Reserved]

III.   MEANING OF "AVERAGE," "NORMAL" AND "MOST PEOPLE"

§8:10   Standard Deviation

Throughout a trial, the terms "average," "normal," "most people," "within a normal range" or similar language is used. But in a scientific field, what exactly do they mean? The concepts are all based on the normal distribution curve. In a normal distribution, most of the data points are close to the middle or "average," and few are at the extremes. Plotting the data on a graph yields a bell shaped curve (an example of which is shown in Figure 8-02).

In general, when the prosecution expert says "most" people do this or that, the expert means 68% of people do this or that. Where does the 68% come from? In a normal distribution, 68% of the data is within plus or minus one standard deviation from the mean or average. See §8:11 for the mathematical formula for computing standard deviation.

Use the state's expert to get this information out. Ask about the research on partition ratios. This can be a way to start to get partition ratio evidence in without getting into its effect. Explain to the judge that you are not attacking the partition ratio but are merely using it as an example to explain the bell curve.

Get the expert to admit that a range of partition ratios is obtained from a sample of people, the mean is determined, and the formula for standard deviation is applied.

You may want to ask the expert the following.

Q: You indicated that the breath machine uses 2100 to 1 as the breath/blood partition ratio?

A: Yes

Q: Is that my client's ratio?

A: I don't know, that is an acceptable average.

Q: That means some people have a higher and some a lower true partition ratio?

A: Yes

Q: In fact, there is a formula for expressing percentages of people who fall outside the average, called standard deviation.

A: Yes

Q: Without going into the math (unless you want to) this is represented by a bell curve (show slide).

A: Okay.

Q: So when we go out, one standard deviation, we expect to capture 68% of the population.

A: Okay.

Q: But this range includes people with radically different blood breath ratios?

A: Yes.

Q: And if a person had a low ratio, then their real blood alcohol content would be extremely overstated by a breath test.

A: It could be.

Q: For example, at 1100 to 1 the breath result would overstate the blood by 200%?

A: True.

Q: And yet that person could be within this one deviation?

A: Maybe.

For example, on the graph below, the partition ratios measured in the sample population would be plotted on the horizontal or x-axis and the number of people in the sample with a particular partition ratio would be plotted on the vertical or y-axis.

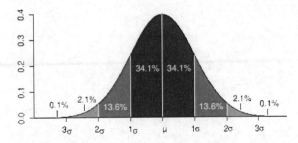

Fig. 8-02 Normal distribution showing one, two, and three standard deviations

In addition to the application to partition ratios illustrated above, this concept can also be applied to SFSTs, elimination, absorption, alcohol effects and so forth.

§8:11   Calculation Example

For those of you who are interested, here is an example of how to calculate standard deviation. We will show how to calculate the standard deviation of a population. Our example will use the ages of four young children: {5, 6, 8, 9}.

Step 1. Calculate the mean average, $\overline{x}$:

$$\overline{x} = \frac{1}{N}\sum_{i=1}^{N} x_i$$

We have $N = 4$ because there are four data points:

$$x_1 = 5$$
$$x_2 = 6$$
$$x_3 = 8$$
$$x_4 = 9$$

$$\overline{x} = \frac{1}{4}\sum_{i=1}^{4} x_i \quad \text{Replacing } N \text{ with 4}$$

$$\overline{x} = \frac{1}{4}(x_1 + x_2 + x_3 + x_4)$$

$$\overline{x} = \frac{1}{4}(5 + 6 + 8 + 9)$$

$$\overline{x} = 7 \quad \text{This is the mean.}$$

Step 2. Calculate the standard deviation σ:

$$\sigma = \sqrt{\frac{1}{N}\sum_{i=1}^{N}(x_i - \overline{x})^2}$$

$$\sigma = \sqrt{\frac{1}{4}\sum_{i=1}^{4}(x_i - \overline{x})^2} \quad \text{Replacing } N \text{ with 4}$$

$$\sigma = \sqrt{\frac{1}{4}\sum_{i=1}^{4}(x_i - 7)^2} \quad \text{Replacing } \overline{x} \text{ with 7}$$

$$\sigma = \sqrt{\frac{1}{4}[(x_1 - 7)^2 + (x_2 - 7)^2 + (x_3 - 7)^2 + (x_4 - 7)^2]}$$

$$\sigma = \sqrt{\frac{1}{4}[(5 - 7)^2 + (6 - 7)^2 + (8 - 7)^2 + (9 - 7)^2]}$$

$$\sigma = \sqrt{\frac{1}{4}((-2)^2 + (-1)^2 + 1^2 + 2^2)}$$

$$\sigma = \sqrt{\frac{1}{4}(4 + 1 + 1 + 4)}$$

$$\sigma = \sqrt{\frac{10}{4}}$$

$$\sigma = \sqrt{\frac{5}{2}} \approx 1.5811$$

So, the standard deviation is the square root of five halves, or approximately 1.5811.

§8:12   Use at Trial

One good way to drive this home is to perform the formula, or explain it and let the jurors do it, using their shoe sizes. Assuming a fairly normal jury, 68% of the jurors will have a shoe size that is within one size above or below (*i.e.*, one standard deviation) of the mean shoe size. That would mean that about two-thirds of the jury could fit into shoes within that range, and the others would have to suffer squished toes or flopping shoes. Ask the jurors: "So, which four of you want that? Does that even come close to proof beyond a reasonable doubt?"

[§§8:13-8:19 Reserved]

IV.   STANDARDIZED FIELD SOBRIETY TESTS

§8:20   Walk-and-Turn Demonstration

"The defendant was off the line on his first and fifth step, made an improper turn and missed heel to toe several times on the way back." Sounds terrible doesn't it? But how does it *look*? Jim Nesci of Arizona gets the credit for this one. Get 24 Dr. Scholl's insoles (or something similar) and paint *both* sides red with white out numbers 1 to 12. In other words, each pad should have the same number, 1-12, on each side, and there should be two sets. This will allow the officer to use one set out and one set back, *and* to use the correct insole as either left or right, depending on which way the officer puts it down. Think of the confusion that simple task will entail, *especially*, if you mix the insoles up a little bit.

Ladies and gentlemen, I asked the officer to perform a simple task of putting the insoles down as my client walked and he could not do it. Seems to me that this is much simpler than actually walking that line would be.

Unless your client was completely all over the place, the ensuing demonstration will not look all that bad.

§8:21   Horizontal Gaze Nystagmus Demonstration

Once you get the officer to admit that the angle of onset of nystagmus is the critical factor (lots of people have nystagmus or involuntary jerking of the eyes at maximum deviation especially when tired, etc.), then the following tool may be helpful.

Obtain a piece of foam core board or cardboard approximately 13 inches deep by 36 inches across. This will be more than wide enough for most people. If you want, have it made to your shoulder width for fun. Leave the top side blank, but on the underside, put a protractor. It should look like this:

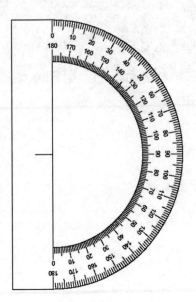

Fig. 8-03 Horizontal Gaze Nystagmus Demonstration

In the center of the board, punch a hole and insert some kind of dowel (a pencil will work) through the hole. Attach a string to the top and bottom of the pencil. Hold the board under your nose so the officer can only see the blank top, and ask him to move the string to 45 degrees. You then hold the string on top, which is attached to one on the bottom, to show the *true* angle.

So long as the length of one half of the board is longer than the depth, the officer will have a hard time. In fact, if the officer assumes that moving the string to the corner of the board creates a 45 degree angle, then at 36 inches (five inches more than the depth at the half), the officer will flag 45 degrees as about 35 degrees. Well if the angle at which your client exhibited nystagmus was in between 45 and 35, then the nystagmus is not a clue that your client was impaired.

§8:22 NHTSA SFST Slides

The following is yet another approach to SFSTs. These slides are reproductions of the actual Power Point presentation from the NHTSA SFST Student class. You can use them in trial to refresh the officer's recollection, and then again in closing.

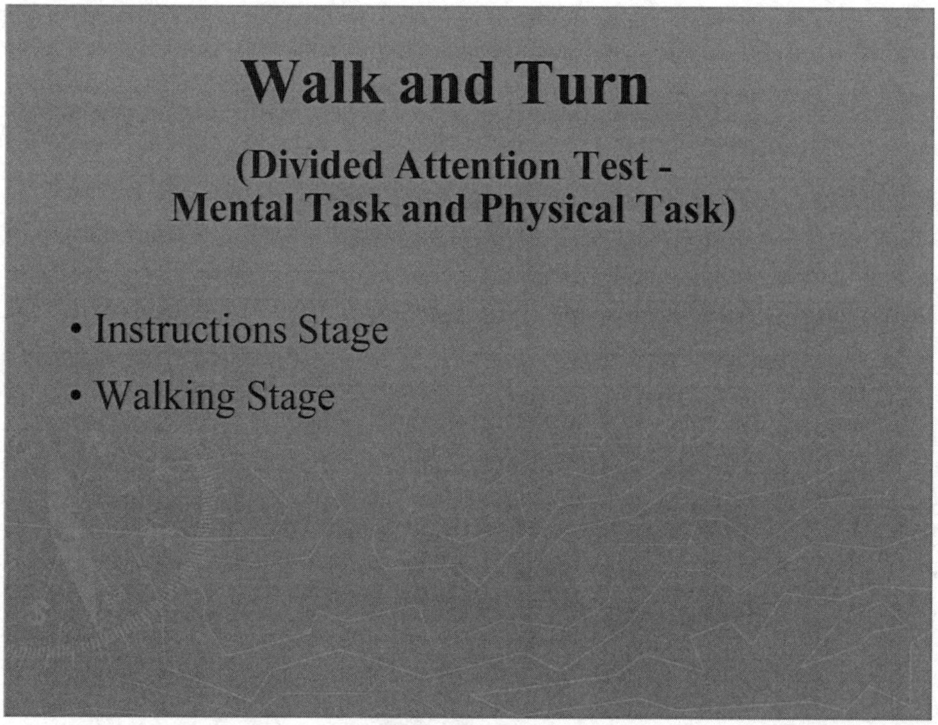

DEMONSTRATIVE EVIDENCE

Fig. 8-04 NHTSA SFST Slide: Walk & Turn #1

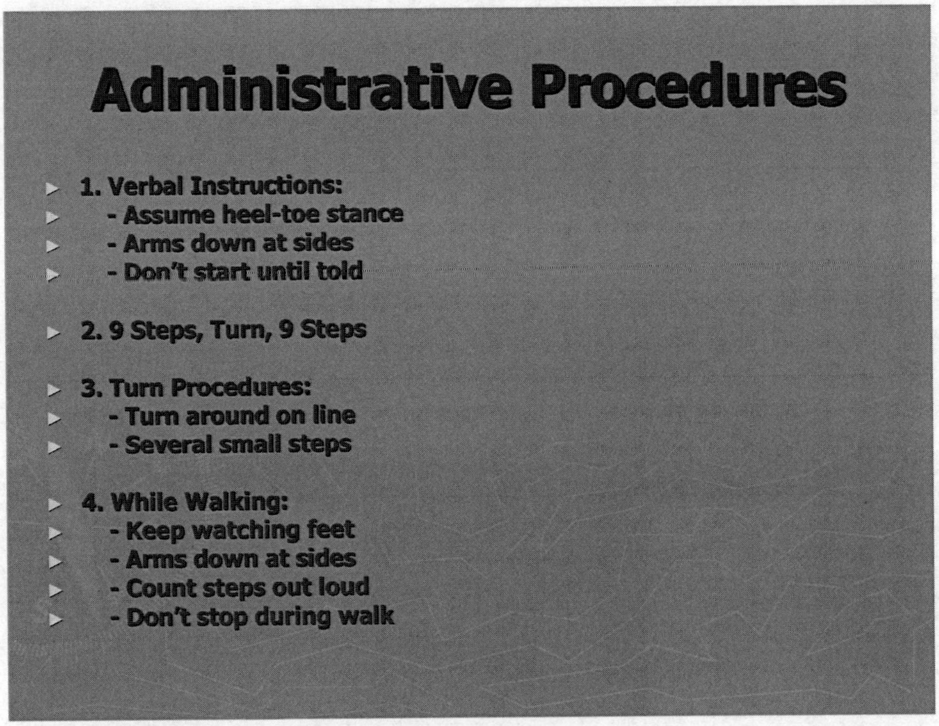

Administrative Procedures

▶ 1. Verbal Instructions:
▶   - Assume heel-toe stance
▶   - Arms down at sides
▶   - Don't start until told

▶ 2. 9 Steps, Turn, 9 Steps

▶ 3. Turn Procedures:
▶   - Turn around on line
▶   - Several small steps

▶ 4. While Walking:
▶   - Keep watching feet
▶   - Arms down at sides
▶   - Count steps out loud
▶   - Don't stop during walk

Fig. 8-05 NHTSA SFST Slide: Walk & Turn #2

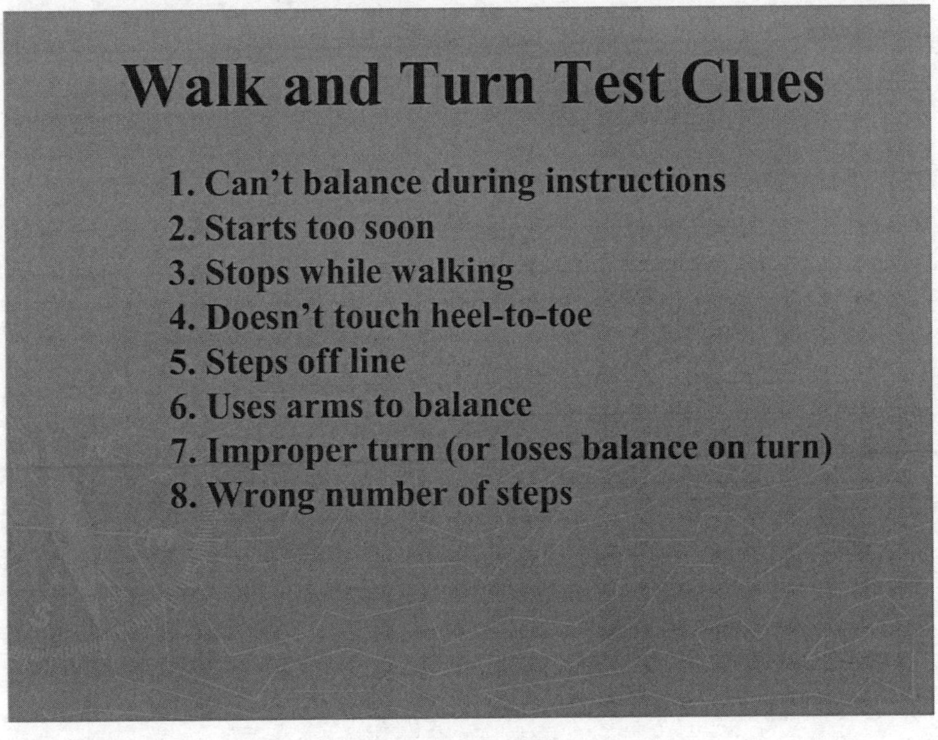

Walk and Turn Test Clues

1. Can't balance during instructions
2. Starts too soon
3. Stops while walking
4. Doesn't touch heel-to-toe
5. Steps off line
6. Uses arms to balance
7. Improper turn (or loses balance on turn)
8. Wrong number of steps

Fig. 8-06 NHTSA SFST Slide: Walk & Turn #3

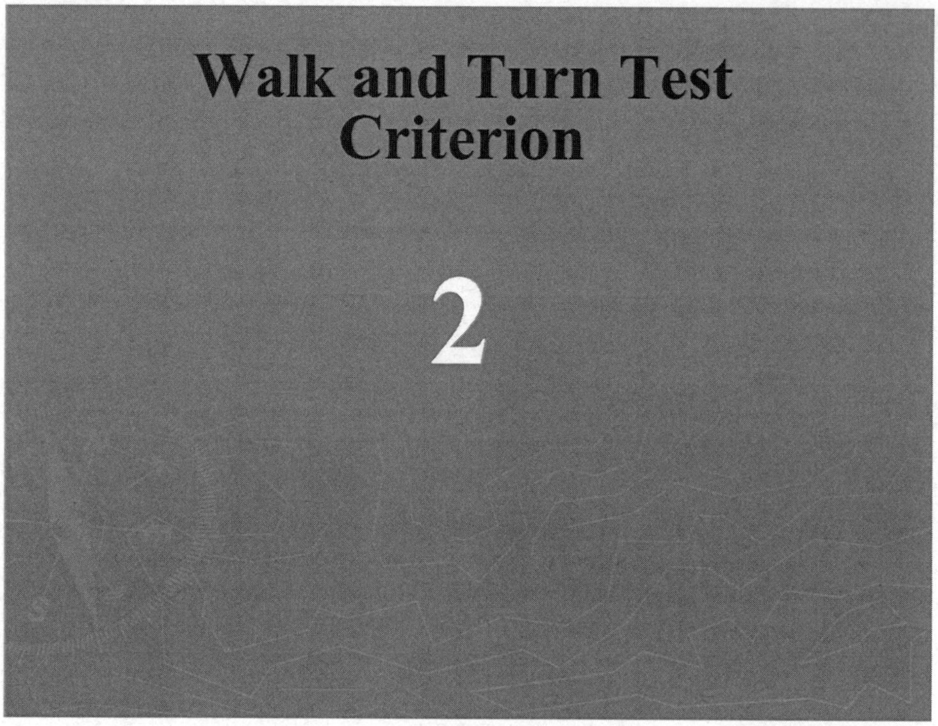

Fig. 8-07 NHTSA SFST Slide: Walk & Turn #4

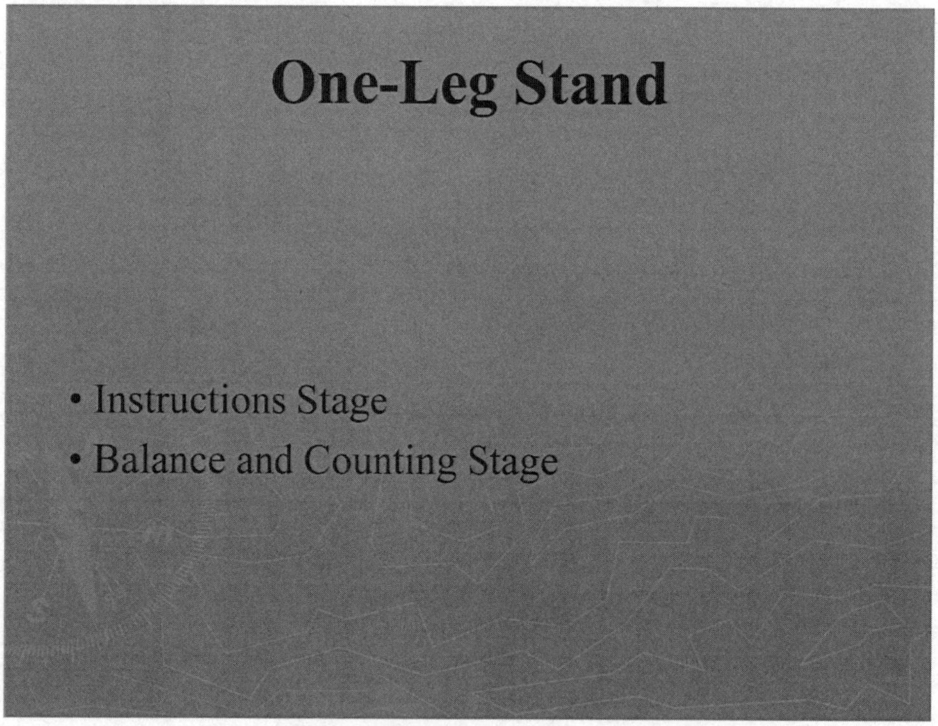

Fig. 8-08 NHTSA SFST Slide: One-Leg Stand-Slide #1

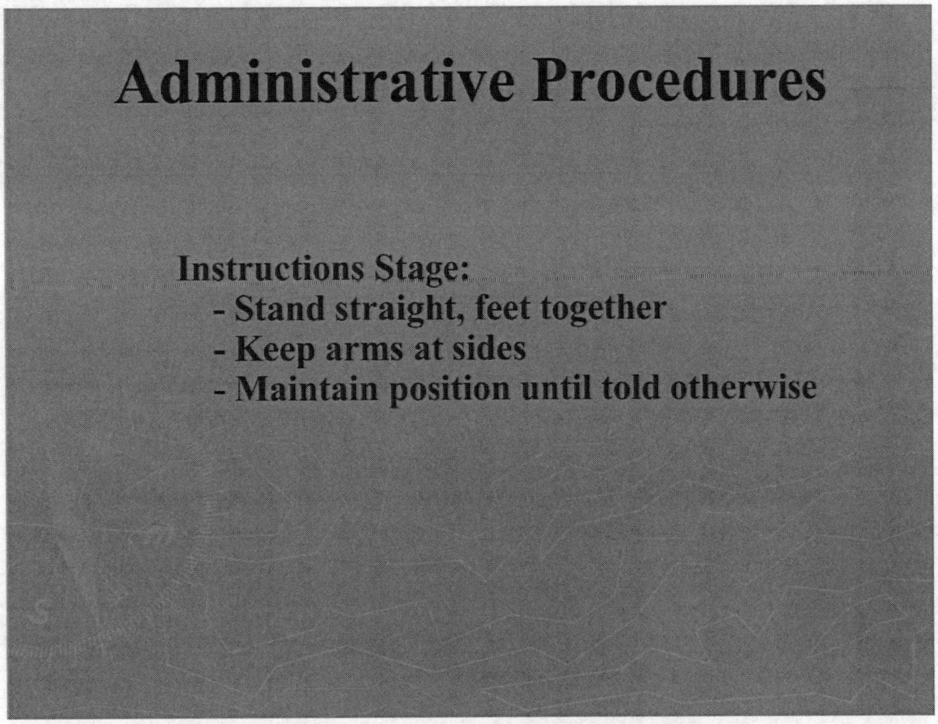

Fig. 8-09 NHTSA SFST Slide: One-Leg Stand-Slide #2

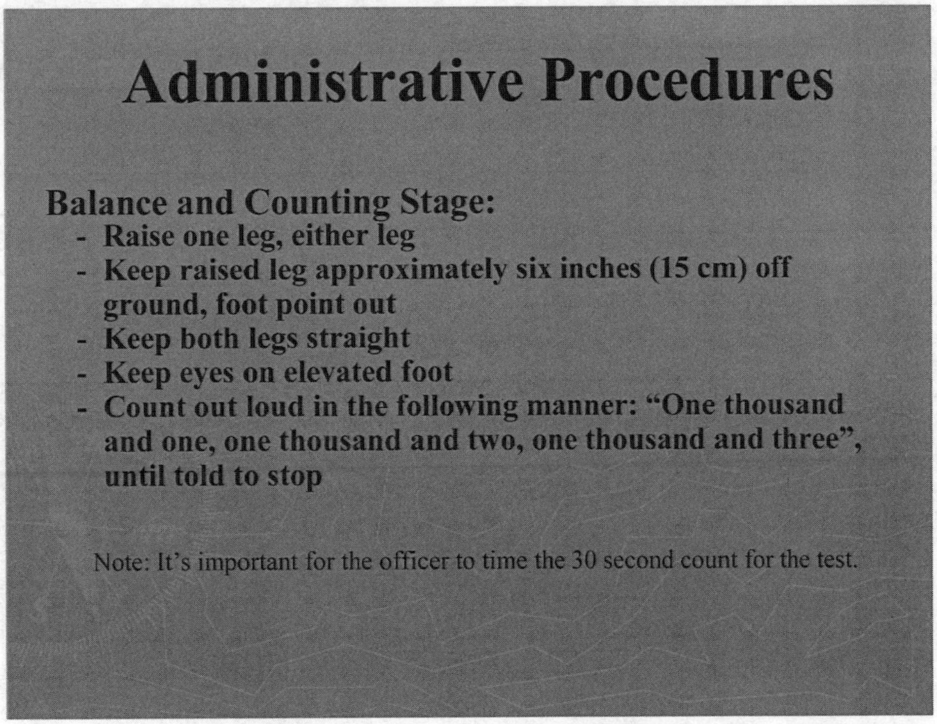

Fig. 8-10 NHTSA SFST Slide: One-Leg Stand-Slide #3

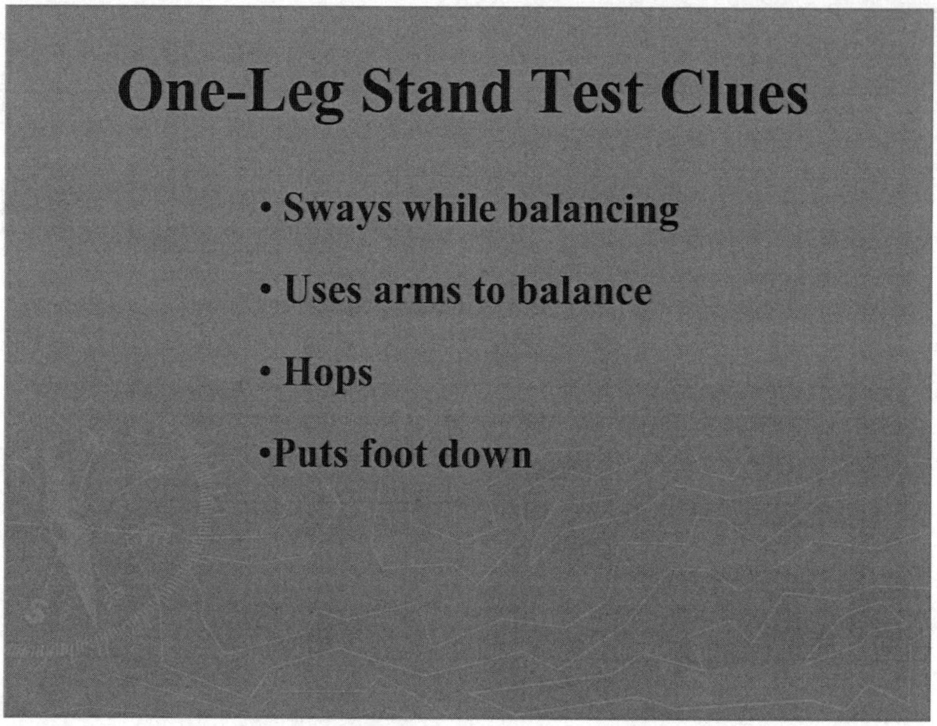

One-Leg Stand Test Clues

- Sways while balancing

- Uses arms to balance

- Hops

- Puts foot down

Fig. 8-11 NHTSA SFST Slide: One-Leg Stand-Slide #4

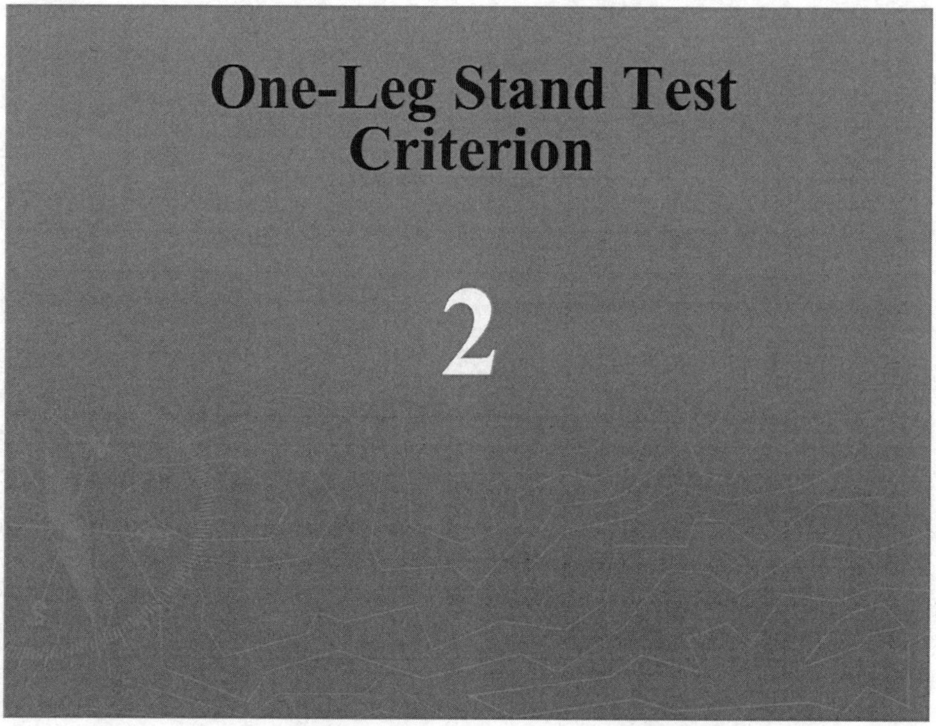

One-Leg Stand Test Criterion

2

Fig. 8-12 NHTSA SFST Slide: One-Leg Stand-Slide #5

§8:23   National College for DUI Defense Demonstration Boards

Suppose you want to show how the officer did a worse job in administering the SFSTs than your client did in performing them? The National College for DUI Defense developed boards for just such a demonstration. They list each instruction, each clue and leave room for notes to show what the officer added. Check out www.NCDD.com to see how they work.

§8:24   Scoring SFSTs

SFSTs can be scored just based on common sense. If you break down the performance on SFSTs into their individual components, you see a test with way more potential points than the officer will admit. But, every day people who have heard "totality of the circumstances" repeatedly from the officer will easily recognize that you are in fact providing the totality with the following charts.

You can use these charts during your cross of the officer. The points are how many tasks there are to each component. For example, nine steps in each direction is 18 steps. Since they must all be heel to toe, there are 18 times to lose a point. You put down what the officer says your client did wrong. If they stepped off the line twice then they get 16 points (18-2).

Then bring the chart back out in closing and do the math.

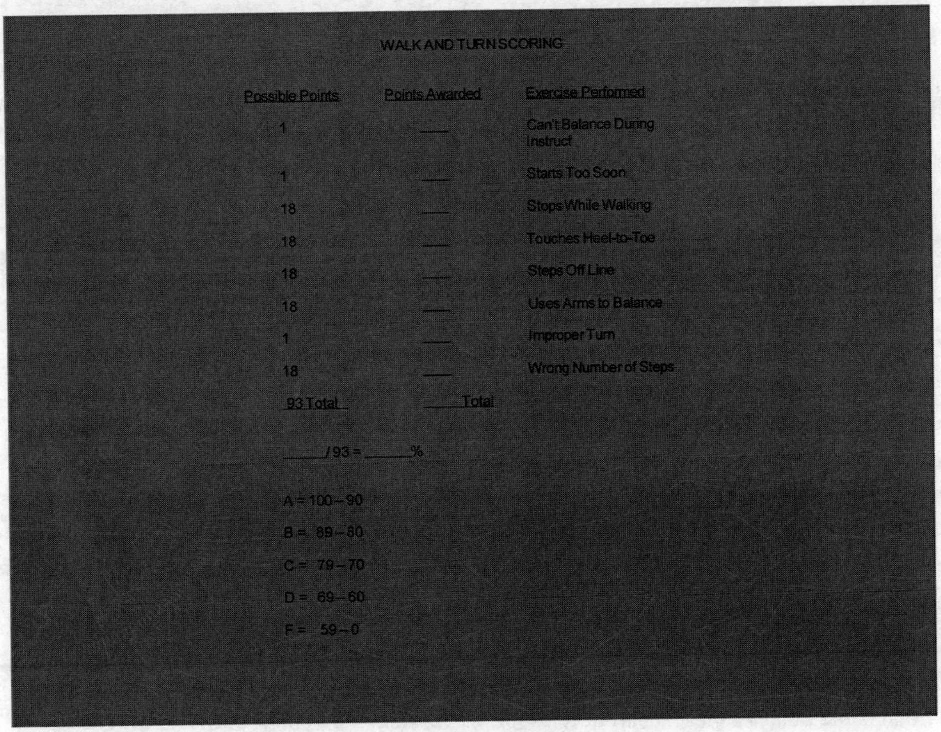

WALK AND TURN SCORING		
Possible Points	Points Awarded	Exercise Performed
1	___	Can't Balance During Instruct
1	___	Starts Too Soon
18	___	Stops While Walking
18	___	Touches Heel-to-Toe
18	___	Steps Off Line
18	___	Uses Arms to Balance
1	___	Improper Turn
18	___	Wrong Number of Steps
93 Total	___ Total	

___ / 93 = ___ %

A = 100—90
B = 89—80
C = 79—70
D = 69—60
F = 59—0

Fig. 8-13 Walk-and-Turn Scoring

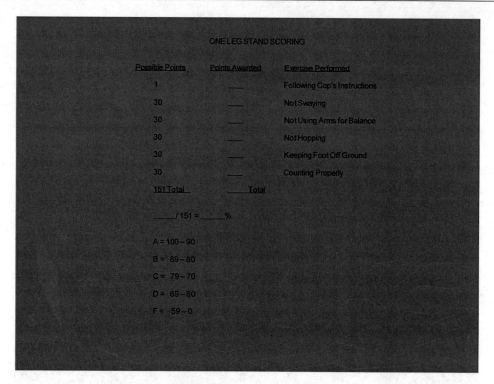

Fig. 8-14 One-Leg Stand Scoring

§8:25   Huser's Totality Charts

Every officer has certain phrases permanently engraved in his or her brain, one of which is "totality of the circumstances." Officers base every decision they make on this concept. But do we ever challenge it? As I see it, "totality" means all of it, good and bad. I bet the officer will agree. Could you just imagine the fun you would have if in cross-exam the officer told you that in making a decision based on the "totality of the circumstances" he or she used the bad stuff only? Since that won't happen, you have free reign to point out the good things your client did. But they must be relevant.

Troy Huser from Kansas, one of the all-around nice guys in this field, spent untold hours going through all of the SFST manuals for *all* of the "circumstances" an officer could use in his or her totality formula. The following chart is what he came up with.

Try to get a few answers from the officer *before* you unveil the chart. Or, use the "full, complete and accurate" line of questions talked about previously in Ch. 4 *Cross-Examination*.

Put up your chart and start questioning the officer going right down the line. Be straight forward and honest. Put a mark in one of the two columns. If the office is not sure, give it to him. There are so many impairment clues that will not be observed that giving the officer the benefit will make you look good and have no real effect. Or you can say that if the officer cannot recall or does not know, then the benefit of the doubt goes to the client.

N.H.T.S.A.
IMPAIRMENT CLUE CHART

Impairment Clue	Observed By Cop	Not Observed By Cop	Source: NHTSA 2000 [NHTSA 1995] {NHTSA 2002}
Initial Observations			
Slowed reactions			V-2, [V-2], {V-2}
Willingness to take risks			V-2, [V-2], {V-2}
Impaired vision			V-2, [V-2], {V-2}
Poor coordination			V-2, [V-2], {V-2}
Visual Cues of driving			
Turning with wide radius			V-4, [V-5 65%], {V-5}
Straddling center or lane marker			V-4, [V-5 65%], {V-5}
Appearing to be impaired			V-4, [V-5 60%], {V-5}
Eye Fixation			V-4, [V-5], {V-5}
Tightly gripping steering wheel			V-4, [V-5], {V-5}
Slouching in seat			V-4, [V-5], {V-5}
Gesturing erratically or obscenely			V-4, [V-5], {V-5}
Face close to the windshield			V-4, [V-5], {V-5}
Drinking in vehicle			V-4, [V-5], {V-5}
Drivers head protruding from vehicle			V-4, [V-5], {V-5}

Kapsack & Bair, LLP

1440 Broadway
Ste 902
Oakland, CA 94612
415-421-1021
Fax 415-421-8030

DEMONSTRATIVE EVIDENCE

DEMONSTRATIVE EVIDENCE

Impairment Clue	Observed By Cop	Not Observed By Cop	Source: NHTSA 2000 [NHTSA 1995] {NHTSA 2002}
Almost striking object or vehicle			V-4, [V-5 60%], {V-5}
Weaving			V-4, [V-5 60%], {V-5}
Driving on other than designated roadway			V-4, [V-5 55%], {V-5}
Swerving			V-5, [V-6 55%], {V-6}
Speed slower than 10 mph			V-5, [V-6 50%], {V-6}
Stopping in lane for no apparent reason			V-5, [V-6 50%], {V-6}
Following too closely			V-5, [V-6 50%], {V-6}
Drifting			V-5, [V-6 50%], {V-6}
Tires on center lane marker			V-5, [V-6 45%], {V-6}
Braking erratically			V-5, [V-6 45%], {V-6}
Drifting into opposing or oncoming traffic			V-6, [V-7 45%], {V-7}
Slow response to traffic signals			V-6, [V-7 40%], {V-7}
Signaling inconsistent with driving actions			V-6, [V-7 40%], {V-7}
Stopping inappropriately (other than in traffic lane)			V-6, [V-7 35%], {V-7}
Turning abruptly or illegally			V-6, [V-7 35%], {V-7}
Accelerating or decelerating rapidly			V-6, [V-7 30%], {V-7}
Headlights off			V-6, [V-7 30%], {V-7}
Stopping Sequence			
Attempt to flee			V-9, [V-10], {V-10}
No response			V-9, [V-10], {V-10}
Slow response			V-9, [V-10], {V-10}
Abrupt swerve			V-9, [V-10], {V-10}
Sudden Stop			V-9, [V-10], {V-10}
Striking the curb or object			V-9, [V-10], {V-10}

Impairment Clue	Observed By Cop	Not Observed By Cop	Source: NHTSA 2000 [NHTSA 1995] {NHTSA 2002}
Personal Contact			
Sight			
Bloodshot eyes			VI-3, [VI-3], {VI-3}
Soiled clothing			VI-3, [VI-3], {VI-3}
Fumbling fingers			VI-3, [VI-3], {VI-3}
Alcohol containers in vehicle			VI-3, [VI-3], {VI-3}
Drugs/Paraphernalia			VI-3, [VI-3], {VI-3}
Bruises/Bumps/Scratches			VI-3, [VI-3], {VI-3}
Unusual Actions			VI-3, [VI-3], {VI-3}
Hearing			
Slurred Speech			VI-3, [VI-3], {VI-3}
Admission of Drinking			VI-3, [VI-3], {VI-3}
Inconsistent Responses			VI-3, [VI-3], {VI-3}
Abusive Language			VI-3, [VI-3], {VI-3}
Unusual Statements			VI-3, [VI-3], {VI-3}
Smell			
Alcoholic Beverages			VI-3, [VI-3], {VI-3}
MJ			VI-3, [VI-3], {VI-3}
Breath cover ups, i.e. sprays			VI-3, [VI-3], {VI-3}
Unusual Odors			VI-3, [VI-3], {VI-3}
Pre-exit Interview			
Forgets to produce both documents			VI-4, [VI-4], {VI-4}
Produces documents other than requested			VI-4, [VI-4], {VI-4}
Fails to see items in wallet			VI-4, [VI-4], {VI-4}
Fumbles or drops wallet or document			VI-4, [VI-4], {VI-4}
Can't retrieve documents using fingertips			VI-4, [VI-4], {VI-4}

DEMONSTRATIVE EVIDENCE

Impairment Clue	Observed By Cop	Not Observed By Cop	Source: NHTSA 2000 [NHTSA 1995] {NHTSA 2002}
Exit Sequence			
Shows angry/unusual actions			VI-6, [VI-6], {VI-6}
Cannot follow instructions			VI-6, [VI-6], {VI-6}
Cannot open the door			VI-6, [VI-6], {VI-6}
Leaves vehicle in gear			VI-6, [VI-6], {VI-6}
"Climbs" out of vehicle			VI-6, [VI-6], {VI-6}
Leans on vehicle			VI-6, [VI-6], {VI-6}
Keeps hands on vehicle for balance			VI-6, [VI-6], {VI-6}
TOTALS			100-90 A 89-80 B 79-70 C 69-60 D

Fig. 8-15 Huser's Totality Charts

[§§8:26-8:29 Reserved]

V.   SLIDES FOR COMMON ISSUES AND CONCEPTS

§8:30   Introduction

The following slides are useful to make certain points with the jury in closing argument. Certain issues and concepts arise in virtually every case. Officers will misrepresent, misremember, or just fail to answer questions. Positive facts from your client will be overlooked, and negative facts magnified. While it is easy to talk about these situations, using some high-powered, and yes, sometimes inflammatory, slides can often drive your point home.

A word of caution: use of these slides *may* cause some jurors to be put off by your attacks. Use these only if they fit you, your case, and your jury. Most of the slides are self-explanatory.

§8:31   Witness Who Tells Only Bad Facts

What of a witness who only tells the jury the *bad* facts, for example, a police officer who only talks about what your client does poorly or incorrectly. He or she doesn't tell the jury what your client did right. He or she forgets what words your client slurred. He or she cannot remember all the correct responses. The witness is like the three monkeys.

DEMONSTRATIVE EVIDENCE

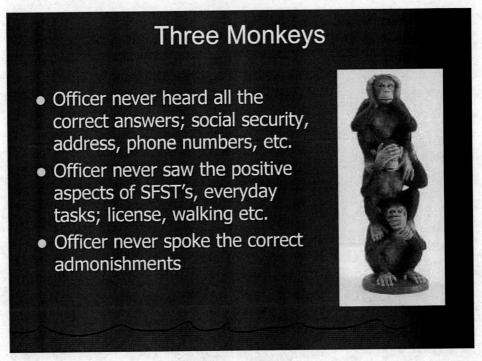

Fig. 8-16 Three Monkeys

§8:32   Objective Symptoms

How about the fact that the officer took objective symptoms (*e.g.*, red eyes from a late night or cold; slow responses in order to be accurate; shivering with cold) and inferred guilt from them rather than accepting the simple explanation your client provided?

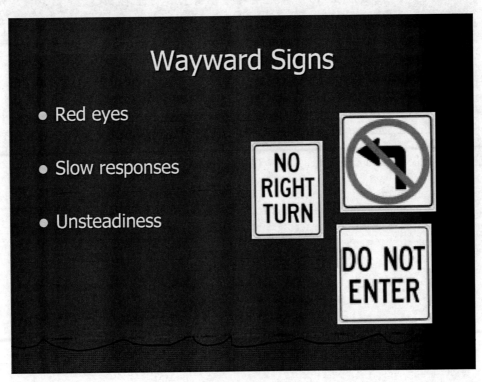

Fig. 8-17 Objective Symptoms

§8:33   Field Sobriety "Tests"

Use this slide when the FSTs were not administered according to the rules. When we were given tests there were rules. What rules were used here…none. Sounds more like a surprise quiz.

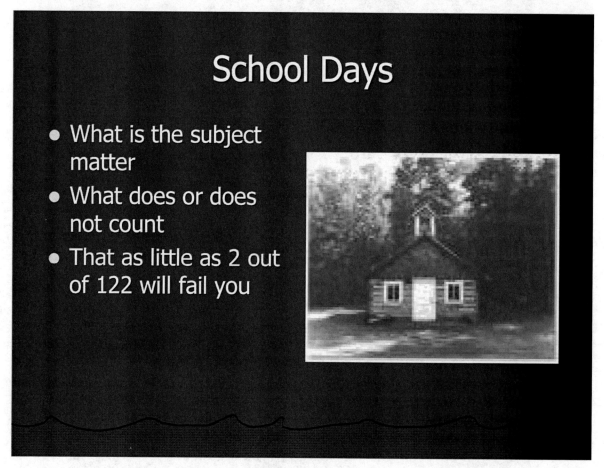

Fig. 8-18 School Days

§8:34   Precision and Accuracy

Precision and accuracy are two major aspects of any test, blood, breath, urine or even SFST. Accuracy, simply put, is the ability to hit the target. In alcohol testing that translates to the ability correctly analyze a known concentration within the acceptable margin of error. So that if we give any machine a .10 solution, it correctly states it is a .10.

Precision is the ability to consistently come within the same margin of error of the first reported value, regardless of the accuracy. In other words, if the value is 10 and we make four tests, obtaining a result of 6, 6.1, 5.9, 6, then we are precise, being within .1 of the average, but we are not accurate.

A truly viable scientific test must be both precise and accurate. So how do we show this to a jury?

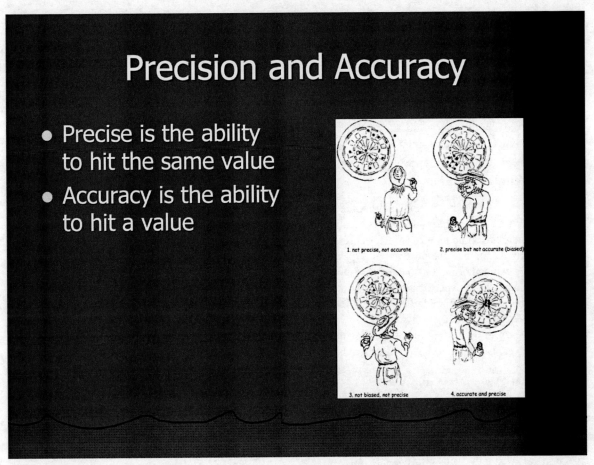

Fig. 8-19 Precision and Accuracy

For an additional demonstration, See Digital Access for the Power Point presentation "Precision and Accuracy."

[§§8:35-8:39 Reserved]

VI.   LOW BUDGET IDEAS

§8:40   Demonstrating Witness Unresponsiveness

So your client cannot afford much more than your fee. You are new and have no access to print shops, power point pros or major exhibits. There is still a lot of good demonstrative evidence you can use to drive home critical points in your trials. Let's start with the simple concept of the prosecution witnesses not answering you as well as they did the DA. Merely pointing this out to the jury is good, but a visual aid is better. Take a look at the following chart based on an idea from Gary Trichter of Texas. You can change the headers as you see fit.

I don't know	I can't remember	I'm not sure	I don't understand the question	Can you repeat the question
☒ ☒ ☒	☒ ☒	☒	☒ ☒ ☒	☒ ☒ ☒ ☒ ☒

Fig. 8-20 Witness Unresponsiveness

During your examination of the witness, place a pad of paper on an easel. Every time one of these answers comes up, put an x in the appropriate field. A couple of different results can happen. The witness may not care and you get a boatload of marks that can be tied into the softball analogy of closing arguments. See §7:61. Alternatively, the witness can become embarrassed and start to toss out answers just to save face. Well we all know what will happen then; the witness may very well open himself or herself up to a lot of impeachment.

Another way to use this chart is surreptitiously. Keep the scorecard at your table or in your hand, make the marks as outlined above. Then bring it out in large format in closing argument. The DA should object, and then you demand the reporter check your figures since the DA has basically accused you of perjury. If you want to have a little more fun, understate the number by one or two. That will get them.

§8:41   What's in a Beer

How often have we tried to explain that the expert is using *his* or *her* own definitions. Show it. If your client said he drank a couple of beers and the prosecution's expert states the client must have had more based on his test results, here are some pictures of beer glasses you may find useful. Unlike the standard bottle or can of beer which contains 12 ounces, the imperial pint glass contains 20 ounces and the half-yard glass contains 32 ounces. Alternatively, you can bring the actual glasses to court.

Start by asking the expert if he made a number of assumptions when it came to his/her testimony regarding the number of drinks consumed, the previous BAC and any other aspect of the trial. Then use this approach.

Q: So, expert, you say my client was not being truthful when he said he had two beers?
A: Well you cannot get to a .12 with just two beers
Q: What size beer?
A: I assumed 12 oz.
Q: Well, what if it were an imperial pint? [Show picture.]
A: I don't know
Q: What about a yard? Or a half yard? [Show picture.]
A: Well those would all change the equations.
Q: What alcohol level of beer did you assume?
A: Standard 5%.
Q: Who told you it was 5%?
A: No one, I just assumed it.
Q: Ever hear of Colt 45?
A: Yes.
Q: It's 7%
A: Okay.
Q: What about Pilsner Urquel 28?
A: Nope.
Q: It's 14%.
A: Wow.
Q: So now that would change the equation too?
A: Yes.
Q: So when you called my client a liar, you were wrong.
A: Based on those changes.
Q: Not based on those changes, just not based on your assumptions. Just like you assumption of 2100 to 1. If we change that then 2 beers could register a breath of .12 even if the true blood content was .06 based on a partition ratio of 1000 to 1 or so.
A: Yes.

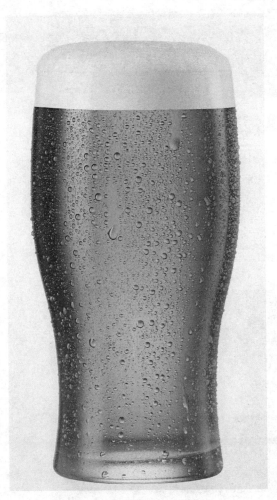

Fig. 8-21 Imperial Pint

Fig. 8-22 Half - Yard Glass

[§§8:42-8:49 Reserved]

VII.   MISCELLANEOUS DIAGRAMS AND PHOTOS

Thanks to Jeff Siffers of Oklahoma City for this entire section.

§8:50   Fuel Cell Diagrams

Some breath testing machines use fuel cell technology. This is a basic concept of how the fuel cell works. Alcohol interacts chemically with the electrode, creating a current that is measured by the machine. These are two charts to show this process.

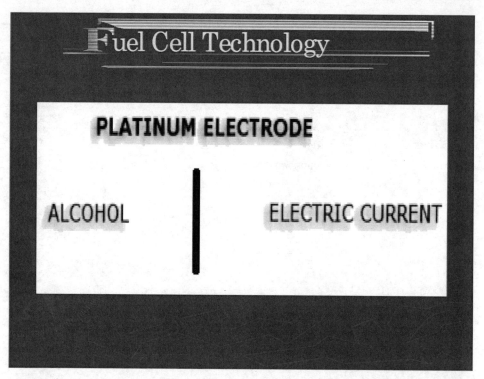

Fig. 8-23 Fuel Cell Technology #1

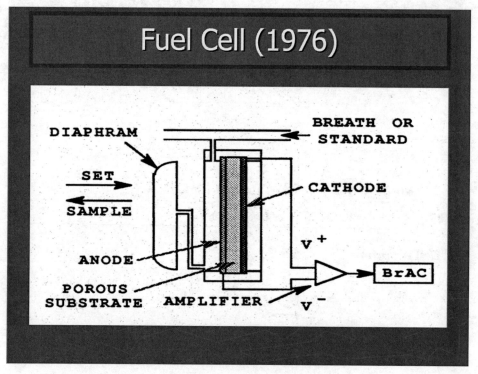

Fig. 8-24 Fuel Cell Technology #2

§8:51   Infrared Spectroscopy Diagrams

Some breath machines use infrared spectroscopy. Basically a light is shined through a chamber containing the breath and the light that is not absorbed is measured. The loss of light is then translated into a breath alcohol level.

Figure 8-25 shows how it works. Light from an infrared source (1) goes through a chamber (2) where the breath is introduced and out through a hole (3). The light is measured at a variety of frequencies (4) and analyzed and the BAC is measured (5) (6).

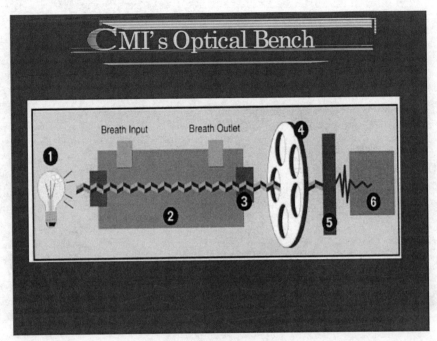

Fig. 8-25 CMI's Optical Bench

Figure 8-26 shows that all three types of alcohol—ethyl, methyl, and isopropyl will absorb some light.

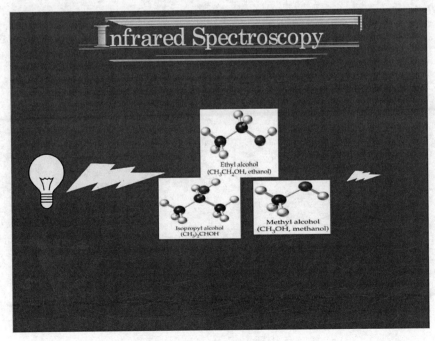

Fig. 8-26 Infrared Spectroscopy and Alcohol Absorption

§8:52　Intoxilyzer 5000 Photos

Figure 8-27 and Figure 8-28 show different views of the Intoxilyzer 5000. They can be used as general demonstrative evidence in any infrared case as a way to point out the parts of the machine to the jury.

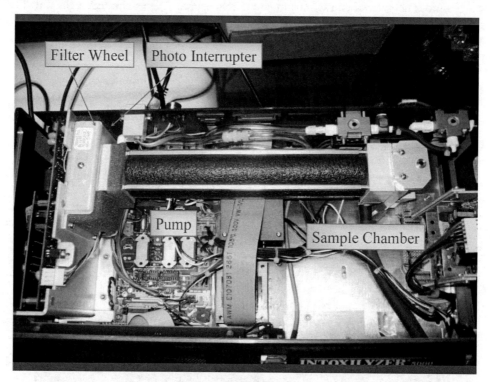

Fig. 8-27 Intoxilyzer 5000—View 1

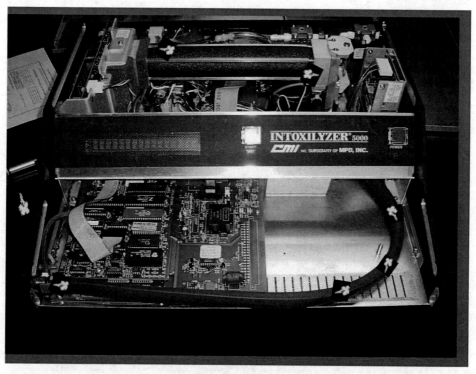

Fig. 8-28 Intoxilyzer 5000—View 2

§8:53   Filter Wheel Diagrams

Figure 8-29 is a mock-up of the filter wheel with the frequencies written in. The filter wheel in an IR machine is supposed to filter out other substances that could be mistaken for alcohol.

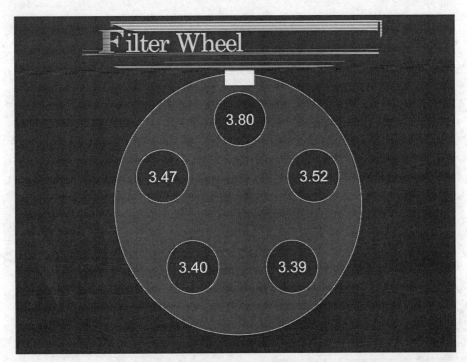

Fig. 8-29 Filter Wheel—5 Filters

Figure 8-30 is a filter wheel with three filters used in machines in some states. If the filter wheel used in your case had only three filters, you can contrast this figure with Figure 8-29 to show what safeguards have been omitted. The missing frequencies are for contaminants that look like alcohol but are not (toluene, acetone etc.).

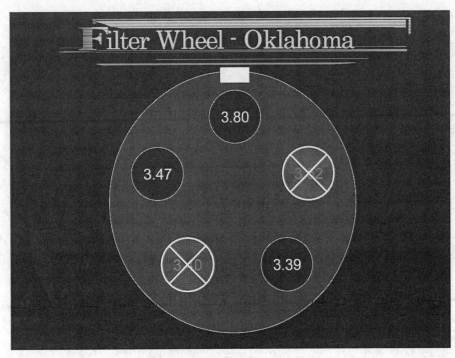

Fig. 8- 30 Filter Wheel—3 Filters

§8:54   Sample Chamber Diagrams

Figure 8-31 shows what happens in the sample chamber. A light that generates 6 or 4 hertz (depending on frequency) goes through an alcohol free chamber and the results are still 6 and 4.

Fig. 8- 31 Air Blank

Figure 8-32 shows what happens in the sample chamber when alcohol is introduced. At 3.47 frequency, 1hz of light is absorbed by the alcohol. (6-5.)

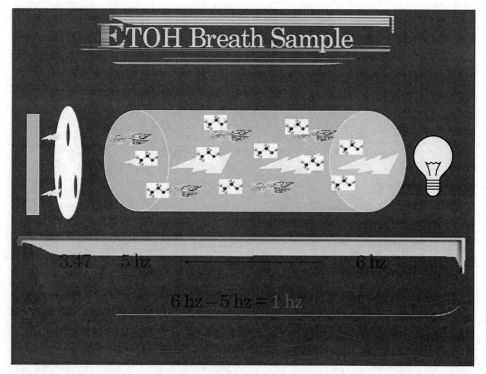

Fig. 8- 32 ETOH Breath Sample

Figure 8-33 shows what happens in the sample chamber when acetone (from paint thinner or other solvent inhaled at work), as well as alcohol, is in the breath. The acetone blocks some additional light.

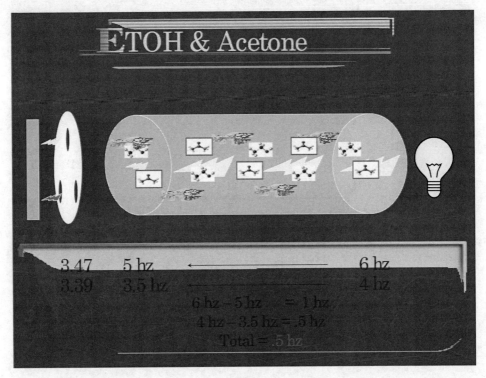

Fig. 8- 33 ETOH and Acetone

§8:55   Breath Machine Diagrams

Figure 8-34 is a diagram showing the main parts and operation of a breath machine that uses infrared spectroscopy only.

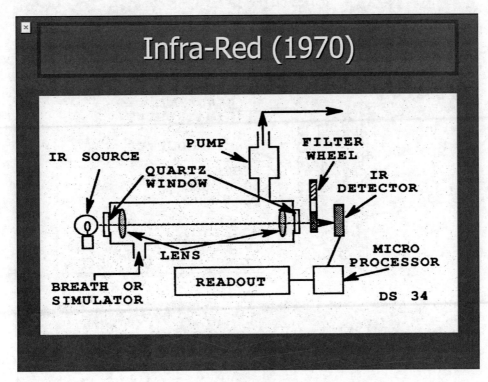

Fig. 8- 34 Diagram of Breath Machine Using IR Spectroscopy

Figure 8-35 is a diagram showing the main parts and operation of a breath machine that uses a combination of fuel cell and infrared spectroscopy.

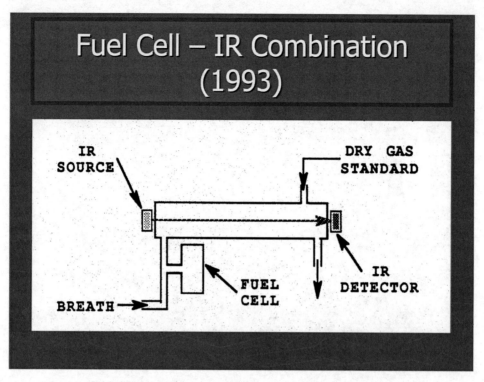

Fig. 8- 35 Diagram of Breath Machine Using Fuel Cell and IR Spectroscopy

If you are going to explain Henry's Law to the jury, then you may want to use Figure 8-36 to show what the liquid and the headspace gas are. You can then show how the gas gets into the breath machine.

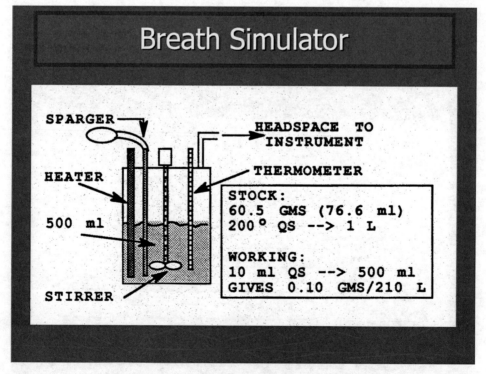

Fig. 8- 36 Breath Simulator

§8:56   Wavelength and Interference Diagrams

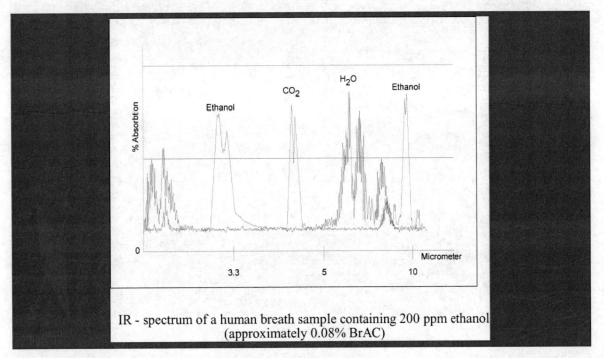

Fig. 8- 37 Wavelength Detection of Alcohol

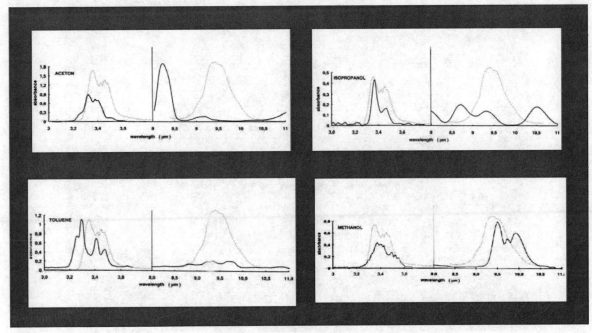

Fig. 8- 38 Interfering Substances Most Common in Human Breath

§8:57   Gas Chromatograph Photos

Figure 8-39 is the famous Hewlett Packard dual column gas chromatograph mentioned in the film *My Cousin Vinny*. It is the machine most commonly used to measure blood alcohol.

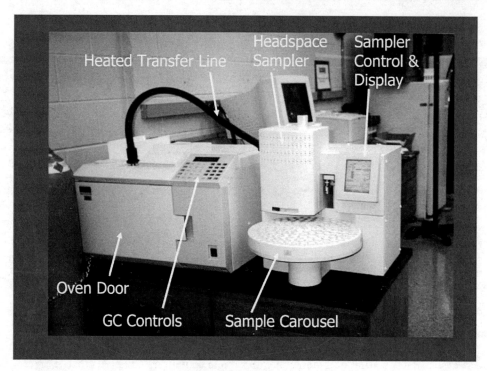

Fig. 8- 39 Dual Column Gas Chromatograph

The copper tubing is the guts of the GC. That is the column that is used to measure the alcohol content.

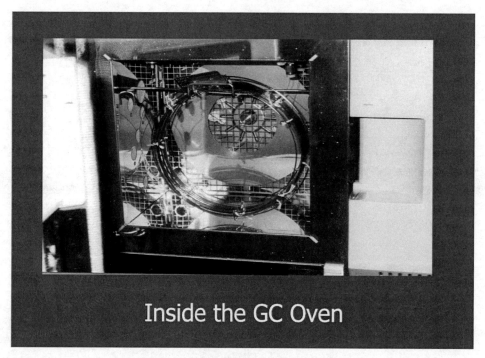

Fig. 8-40 Inside the GC Oven

[§§8:58-8:69 Reserved]

IX.   PERSPECTIVE: THINGS MAY NOT BE WHAT THEY SEEM

§8:70   Horse/Frog Sketch

One of the most difficult tasks we have as DUI defense attorneys is to overcome the prejudice against our clients. Mothers Against Drunk Driving, politicians and the media have convinced the American Public that alcohol and driving are automatically criminal. Of course, we know this is not the case, but we fight the uphill battle every day.

Here are two slides explaining perspective. First is the horse. Most people will see it with no problem.

Fig. 8-41 Drawing of Horse

But if you turn it slowly, you get:

Fig. 8-42 Drawing of Frog

A frog! This is used to demonstrate that what you see depends on where you stand. "The officer saw only the negative facts. The DA only talked about the negative facts. They only want you to see a horse. But if any of you see a frog, then you have a reasonable doubt and my client is not guilty."

§8:71   Dihydrogen Monoxide Power Point Presentation

One of the first tasks that the defense attorney must face is to show the jury that the presumptions they have been fed are not necessarily true. We can try to weed this out in voir dire, talk about it in opening and drive it home in closing, yet this is not always fruitful. Here is a Power Point production that drives the point home. It may be a bit long for some trials, but then again, it does make the point against listening to hype versus the evidence. See Digital Access for the complete Power Point presentation.

Fig. 8-43 Dihydrogen Monoxide: Slide 1

DEMONSTRATIVE EVIDENCE

Dihydrogen monoxide (DHMO) is colorless, odorless, tasteless, and kills uncounted thousands of people every year. Most of these deaths are caused by accidental inhalation of DHMO, but the dangers of dihydrogen monoxide do not end there. Prolonged exposure to its solid form causes severe tissue damage.

Symptoms of DHMO ingestion can include excessive sweating and urination, and possibly a bloated feeling, nausea, vomiting and body electrolyte imbalance. For those who have become dependent, DHMO withdrawal means certain death.

Fig. 8-44 Dihydrogen Monoxide: Slide 2

Dihydrogen monoxide:

- is also known as hydroxyl acid, and is the major component of acid rain
- contributes to the "greenhouse effect."
- may cause severe burns.
- contributes to the erosion of our natural landscape.
- accelerates corrosion and rusting of many metals.
- may cause electrical failures and decreased effectiveness of automobile brakes.
- has been found in excised tumors of terminal cancer patients.

Fig. 8-45 Dihydrogen Monoxide: Slide 3

DEMONSTRATIVE EVIDENCE

Contamination Is Reaching Epidemic Proportions!

Quantities of dihydrogen monoxide have been found in almost every stream, lake, and reservoir in America today. But the pollution is global, and the contaminant has even been found in Antarctic ice. DHMO has caused millions of dollars of property damage in the Midwest, and recently California.

Fig. 8-46 Dihydrogen Monoxide: Slide 4

Despite the danger, dihydrogen monoxide is often used:

- as an industrial solvent and coolant
- in nuclear power plants.
- in the production of Styrofoam.
- as a fire retardant.
- in many forms of cruel animal research.
- in the distribution of pesticides. Even after washing, produce remains contaminated by this chemical.
- as an additive in certain "junk-foods" and other food products.

Fig. 8-47 Dihydrogen Monoxide: Slide 5

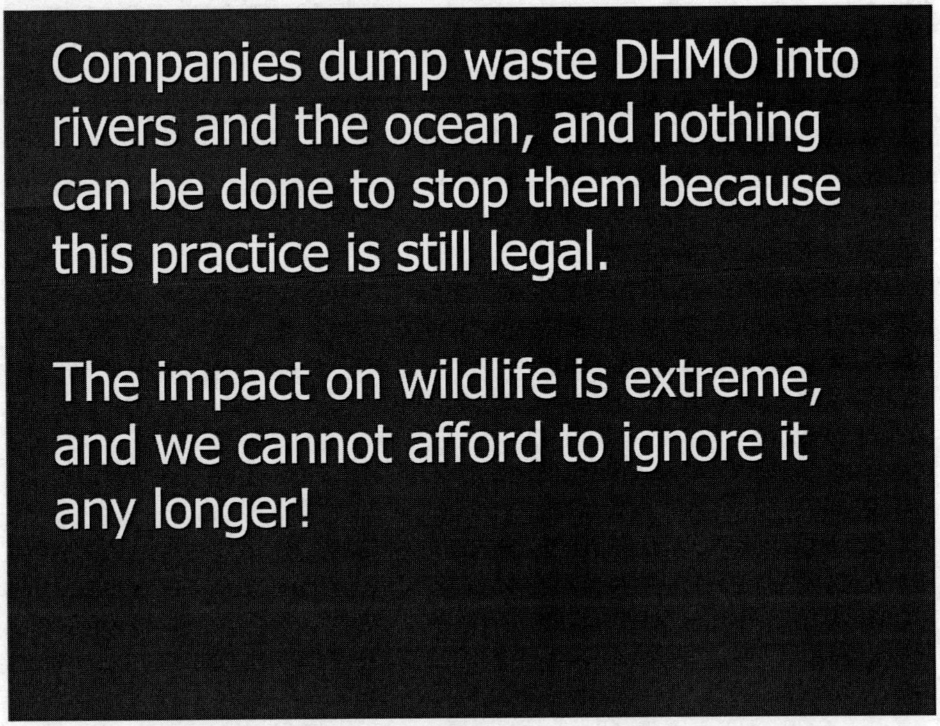

Companies dump waste DHMO into rivers and the ocean, and nothing can be done to stop them because this practice is still legal.

The impact on wildlife is extreme, and we cannot afford to ignore it any longer!

Fig. 8-48 Dihydrogen Monoxide: Slide 6

The Horror Must Be Stopped!

The American government has refused to ban the production, distribution, or use of this damaging chemical due to its "importance to the economic health of this nation." In fact, the navy and other military organizations are conducting experiments with DHMO, and designing multi-billion dollar devices to control and utilize it during warfare situations.

Hundreds of military research facilities receive tons of it through a highly sophisticated underground distribution network. Many store large quantities for later use.

Fig. 8-49 Dihydrogen Monoxide: Slide 7

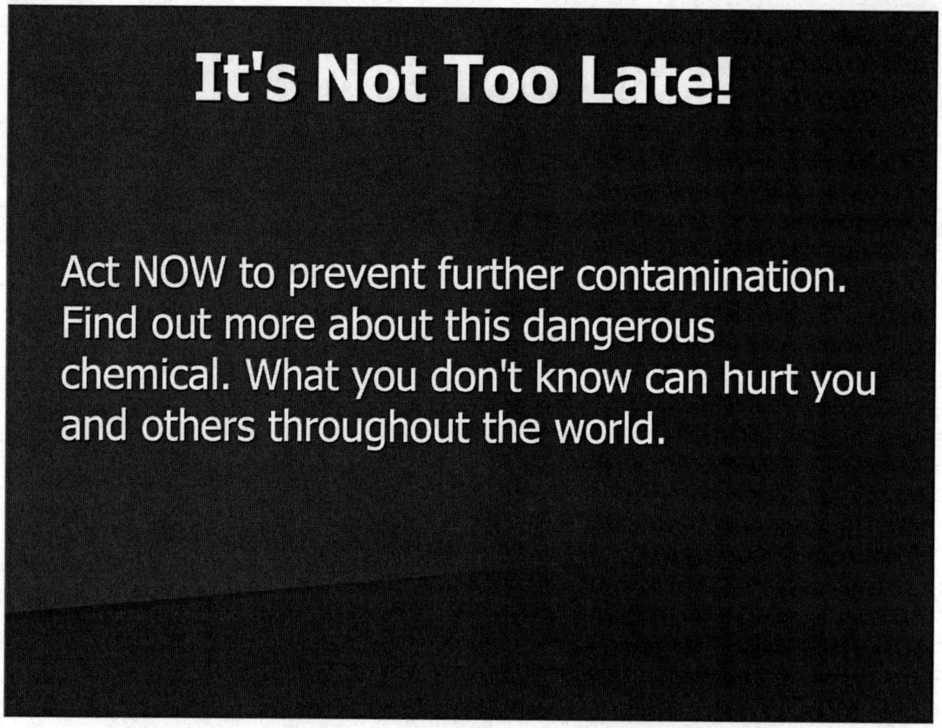

DEMONSTRATIVE EVIDENCE

It's Not Too Late!

Act NOW to prevent further contamination. Find out more about this dangerous chemical. What you don't know can hurt you and others throughout the world.

Fig. 8- 50 Dihydrogen Monoxide: Slide 8

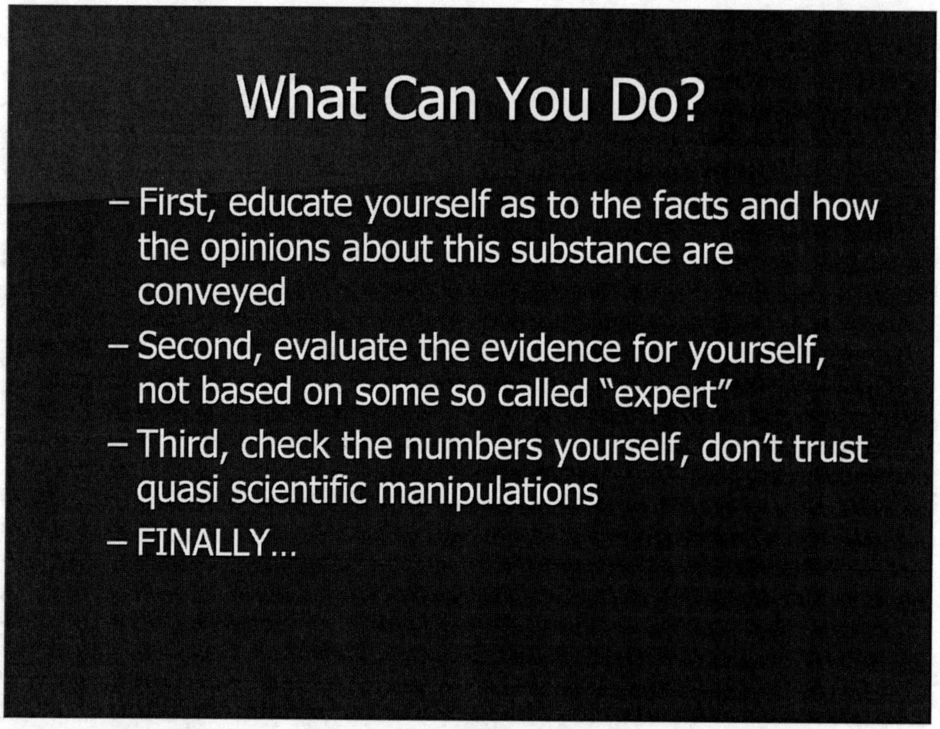

What Can You Do?

- First, educate yourself as to the facts and how the opinions about this substance are conveyed
- Second, evaluate the evidence for yourself, not based on some so called "expert"
- Third, check the numbers yourself, don't trust quasi scientific manipulations
- FINALLY...

Fig. 8- 51 Dihydrogen Monoxide: Slide 9

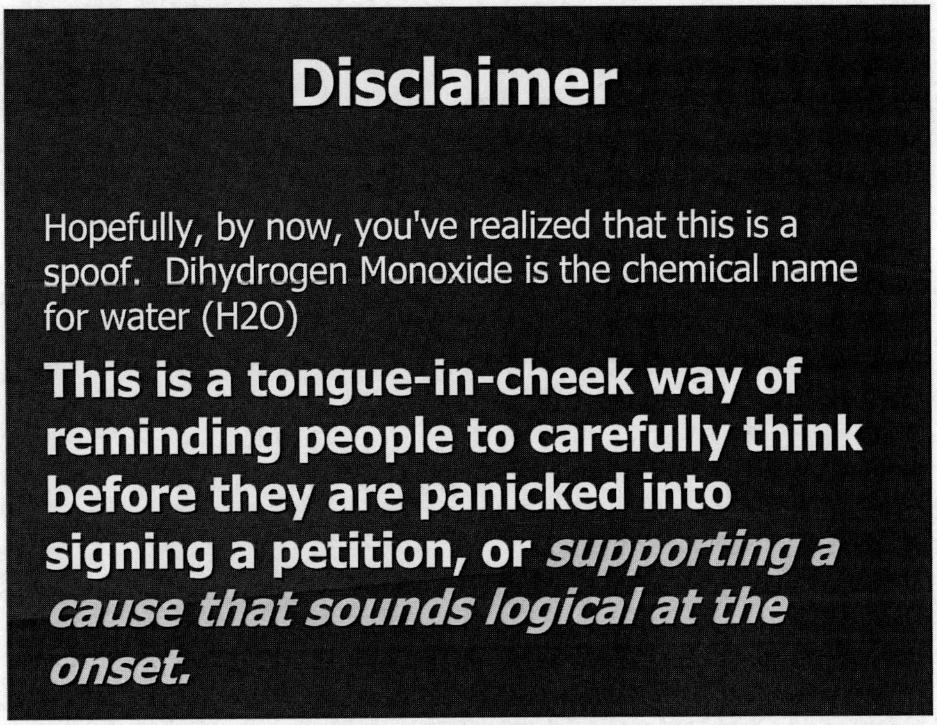

Disclaimer

Hopefully, by now, you've realized that this is a spoof. Dihydrogen Monoxide is the chemical name for water (H2O)

This is a tongue-in-cheek way of reminding people to carefully think before they are panicked into signing a petition, or *supporting a cause that sounds logical at the onset.*

Fig. 8- 52 Dihydrogen Monoxide: Slide 10

§8:72   The Beautiful House

See Digital Access for "The Beautiful House" presentation in PowerPoint format. See also §7:101 for a sample closing argument utilizing the Beautiful House theme.

BEAUTIFUL HOUSE FOR SALE

Owned by: Officer Smith

Agent: DA Jones

Buyer: Jury

Buyer's Agent: Bruce Kapsack

Fig. 8- 53 The Beautiful House: Slide 1

DEMONSTRATIVE EVIDENCE

Their Idea of the House

Fig. 8- 54 The Beautiful House: Slide 2

Closer Inspection

- Fine foundation
- Fully up to code
- No infestation

- Lots of cracks
- Variances
- Termite holes

Fig. 8- 55 The Beautiful House: Slide 3

FOUNDATION

- Working machine
- Calibration
- Sample
- Technique
- Assumptions
- Parameters

Fig. 8- 56 The Beautiful House: Slide 4

INSPECTION

- 13 not 15 minutes
- Not recently calibrated
- Officer not trained

Fig. 8- 57 The Beautiful House: Slide 5

DEMONSTRATIVE
EVIDENCE

RENOVATIONS

- Obtained permits
- Followed rules
- Full inspection
- Full disclosure

Fig. 8- 58 The Beautiful House: Slide 6

INSPECTION

- Did not use SFST
- Changed SFSTs
- Incorrect scoring

Fig. 8- 59 The Beautiful House: Slide 7

PESTS

- Certified no problems
- Bug-free
- Rodent-free

Fig. 8-60 The Beautiful House: Slide 8

INSPECTION

- Ant eggs
  - Driving
- Rodent Droppings
  - Officer problems
- Termite Holes
  - All the good stuff client did

Fig. 8-61 The Beautiful House: Slide 9

ROOF

- Putting it altogether

Fig. 8-62 The Beautiful House: Slide 10

INSPECTION

- Looks good from far away
- Leaks
- Old
- Needs replacing

Fig. 8-63 The Beautiful House: Slide 11

THE REAL HOUSE

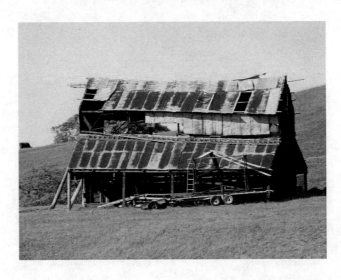

Fig. 8-64 The Beautiful House: Slide 12

(This page intentionally left blank.)

CHAPTER 9

DRIVING UNDER THE INFLUENCE OF DRUGS

(This page intentionally left blank.)

DRIVING UNDER THE
INFLUENCE OF DRUGS

I.   INTRODUCTION

§9:01   States Fall Into Two Camps

Driving under the Influence of Drugs (DUI-D) is the new frontier in impaired driving regulation. States are currently divided into two different schools of thought. The first group makes it illegal to drive with any measurable amount of certain drugs in the body, regardless of whether driving ability is impaired. These statutes are analogous to the *per se* DUI alcohol statutes.

The rationale for such broadly structured statutes is indefensible. As most people understand, an individual can have trace amounts of some drugs in the urine for days after use. Furthermore, an individual can have trace amounts of active narcotics in the blood that have no negative effect on the ability to drive a motor vehicle.

In these states with DUI-D *per se* statutes, little can be done in front of a jury unless you can attack the methodology of the blood or urine test. Attacks on the methodology of chemical tests are covered throughout this book. The information provided on discovery, openings, cross examination, and so forth can be used for a DUI-D case.

The other group of states define driving under the influence of drugs much the same as they do the common law crime of DUI alcohol (DUI-A)—some level of impairment of mental or physical abilities, or both, which affects the ability to drive a motor vehicle, is required.

§9:02   State Must Prove Impairment in Driving Ability

There is one concept that you must understand, and it is the central theme of this chapter: in states that do not have DUI-D *per se* statutes, a DUI-D case requires the state to prove impairment *in the ability to drive*. General impairment is irrelevant. Of course, before we even talk about impairment for a purpose, we need to understand what is meant by impairment.

Generally speaking, the government's witness will admit that the definition of impairment they use is similar to what the American Medical Association calls impairment: any deviation from the base line norm. Without getting in to the concept of how we know a client's particular base line norm, let's just use generalities and not specific numbers.

A number of drugs cause some form of impairment without impairing driving ability. Let's look at two extreme examples. First, if your client took a drug that has increased his pulse, raised his blood pressure, and dilated his pupils, you might start to worry. However, since it was merely a cup of coffee, there is no issue. As a matter of fact, as will be discussed later, this is a good jury voir dire point. Second, suppose the blood shows low levels of barbiturates. Sounds bad. But your client is epileptic and is required to take Phenobarbital to prevent seizures. So, once again the drug is impairing, in that it impairs the seizures, but it does not impair the driving.

Keep this concept in mind throughout this chapter.

§9:03   Drug Recognition Matrix

It is also critical that you understand the Drug Recognition Matrix. Here is a copy of it:

MAJOR INDICATORS	CNS DEPRESSANTS	CNS STIMULANTS	HALLUCINOGENS	PHENCYCLIDINE	NARCOTIC ANALGESIC	INHALANTS	CANNABIS
HGN	PRESENT	NONE	NONE	PRESENT	NONE	PRESENT	NONE
VERTICAL NYSTAGMUS	PRESENT *HIGH DOSES	NONE	NONE	PRESENT	NONE	PRESENT *HIGH DOSES	NONE
LACK OF CONVERGENCE	PRESENT	NONE	NONE	PRESENT	NONE	PRESENT	PRESENT*
PUPIL SIZE	NORMAL (1)	DILATED	DILATED	NORMAL	CONSTRICTED	NORMAL (4)	DILATED (6)
REACTION TO LIGHT	SLOW	SLOW	NORMAL (3)	NORMAL	LITTLE OR NONE VISIBLE	SLOW	NORMAL
PULSE RATE	DOWN (2)	UP	UP	UP	DOWN	UP	UP
BLOOD PRESSURE	DOWN	UP	UP	UP	DOWN	UP/DOWN (5)	UP
BODY TEMPERATURE	NORMAL	UP	UP	UP	DOWN	UP/DOWN/ NORMAL	NORMAL
MUSCLE TONE	FLACCID	RIGID	RIGID	RIGID	NORMAL TO FLACCID	FLACCID	NORMAL
GENERAL INDICATORS	UNCOORDINATED DISORIENTED SLUGGISH THICK, SLURRED SPEECH DRUNK-LIKE BEHAVIOR DROWSINESS DROOPY EYES FUMBLING GAIT ATAXIA *NOTE METHA-QUALONE, PULSE ELEVATED & BODY TREMORS ETOH & QUAALUDES ELEVATE PULSE SOMA & QUAALUDES DILATE PUPILS	RESTLESSNESS BODY TREMORS EXCITED EUPHORIC TALKATIVE EXAGGERATED REFLEXES ANXIETY GRINDING TEETH (BRUXISM) REDNESS TO NASAL AREA RUNNY NOSE LOSS OF APPETITE INSOMNIA INCREASED ALERTNESS DRY MOUTH IRRITABILITY	DAZED APPEARANCE BODY TREMORS SYNESTHESIA HALLUCINATIONS PARANOIA UNCOORDINATED NAUSEA DISORIENTED DIFFICULTY IN SPEECH PERSPIRING POOR PERCEPTION OF TIME & DISTANCE MEMORY LOSS DISORIENTATION FLASHBACKS *NOTE: LSD, PILORECTION MAY BE OBSERVED (GOOSE BUMPS, HAIR STANDING ON END)	PERSPIRING WARM TO THE TOUCH BLANK STARE VERY EARLY ANGLE OF HGN ONSET DIFFICULTY IN SPEECH INCOMPLETE VERBAL RESPONSES REPETITIVE SPEECH INCREASED PAIN THRESHOLD CYCLIC BEHAVIOR CONFUSED, AGITATED HALLUCINATIONS POSSIBLY VIOLENT & COMBATIVE CHEMICAL ODOR "MOON WALKING"	DROOPY EYELIDS- (PTOSIS) "ON THE NOD" DROWSINESS DEPRESSED REFLEXES LOW, RASPY, SLOW SPEECH DRY MOUTH FACIAL ITCHING EUPHORIA FRESH PUNCTURE MARKS NAUSEA TRACK MARKS *NOTE: TOLERANT USERS EXHIBIT RELATIVELY LITTLE PSYCHOMOTOR IMPAIRMENT (HIPPUS – RHYTHMIC PULSATING OF PUPILS AS THEY DILATE AND CONSTRICT).	RESIDUE OF SUBSTANCE AROUND NOSE & MOUTH ODOR OF SUBSTANCE POSSIBLE NAUSEA SLURRED SPEECH DISORIENTATION CONFUSION BLOODSHOT, WATERY EYES LACK OF MUSCLE CONTROL FLUSHED FACE NON-COMMUNI- ICATIVE INTENSE HEADACHES **NOTE: ANESTHETIC GASES CAUSE BELOW NORMAL BLOOD PRESSURE; VOLATILE SOLVENTS AND AEROSOLS CAUSE ABOVE NORMAL BLOOD PRESSURE.	MARKED REDDENING OF CONJUNCTIVA ODOR OF MARIJUANA MARIJUANA DEBRIS IN MOUTH BODY TREMORS EYELID TREMORS RELAXED INHIBITIONS INCREASED APPETITE IMPAIRED PERCEPTION OF TIME & DISTANCE DISORIENTATION POSSIBLE PARANOIA (REBOUND – PUPILS PULSATE IN SIZE, GROWING LARGER ON EXPANSION PULSATIONS)
DURATION OF EFFECTS	BARBITURATES: 1-16 HOURS TRANQUILIZERS: 4-8 HOURS METHAQUALONE: 4-8 HOURS	COCAINE: 5-90 MINUTES AMPHETAMINES: 4-8 HOURS METHAMPHETAMINES: 12 HOURS	DURATION VARIES WIDELY FROM ONE HALLUCINOGEN TO ANOTHER	ONSET: 1-5 MINUTES PEAK EFFECTS: 15-30 MINUTES EXHIBITS EFFECTS UP TO 4-6 HOURS	HEROIN: 4-6 HOURS METHADONE: UP TO 24 HOURS Others: vary	6-8 HOURS FOR MOST VOLATILE SOLVENTS – ANESTHETIC GASES AND AEROSOLS VERY SHORT DURATION	2-3 HOURS EXHIBITS EFFECTS – IMPAIRMENT MAY LAST UP TO 24 HOURS WITHOUT AWARENESS OF EFFECT.
USUAL METHODS OF ADMINISTRATION	ORAL INJECTED – OCCASIONALLY	INSUFFLATION (SNORTING) SMOKED INJECTED ORAL	ORAL INSUFFLATION SMOKED INJECTED TRANSDERMAL	SMOKED ORAL INSUFFLATION INJECTED EYE DROPS	INJECTED ORAL SMOKED INSUFFLATED	INSUFFLATED (HISTORICALLY, HAVE BEEN TAKEN ORALLY.)	SMOKED ORAL
OVERDOSE SIGNS	SHALLOW BREATHING COLD, CLAMMY SKIN PUPILS DILATED RAPID, WEAK PULSE COMA	AGITATION INCREASED BODY TEMP HALLUCINATIONS CONVULSIONS	LONG INTENSE TRIP	LONG INTENSE TRIP	SLOW, SHALLOW BREATHING CLAMMY SKIN – COMA CONVULSIONS	COMA	FATIGUE PARANOIA

FOOTNOTE: THESE INDICATORS ARE THE MOST CONSISTENT WITH THE CATEGORY.
NORMAL RANGES
KEEP IN MIND THAT THERE MAY BE VARIATIONS DUE TO INDIVIDUAL REACTION, DOSE TAKEN AND DRUG INTERACTIONS.
PULSE: 60-90 BEATS PER MINUTE
1. SOMA, QUAALUDES USUALLY DILATE PUPILS
2. QUAALUDES AND ETOH MAY ELEVATE PUPIL SIZE: 3.0MM-6.5MM
3. CERTAIN PSYCHADELIC AMPHETAMINES CAUSE SLOWING
4. NORMAL BUT MAY BE DILATED BLOOD PRESSURE: 120-140 SYSTOLIC
5. DOWN WITH ANESTHETIC GASES, BUT UP WITH VOLATILE SOLVENTS AND AEROSOLS 70 - 90 DIASTOLIC
6. PUPIL SIZE POSSIBLY NORMAL BODY TEMPERATURE: 98.6 +/- 1.0 DEGREE

DRIVING UNDER THE INFLUENCE OF DRUGS

[§§9:04-9:09 Reserved]

II.   DISCOVERY

§9:10   Understand Testing Procedures

Even more than a DUI-A case, a DUI-D case requires the defense attorney to have a solid working understanding of how blood or urine is collected, transported, stored, and analyzed. Before going further, refer to §§1:10 to 1:13 and appendix D for what you need and why you need it. When analyzing the reports from the lab as to what and how much of any chemicals were in your client's system, you cannot merely accept the summary report from the lab. You must see the actual printout of your client's run so you can see if (1) there is good separation between the various checked-for substances, (2) the graphs are sharp or have tailing in front or in back, and (3) the accuracy is really there.[1]

§9:11   Get a Retest

Second, it will usually be worthwhile to get a retest of the blood or urine. Unlike alcohol, where retesting is not usually productive, retesting for drugs can be. State crime labs are not nearly as accurate as private labs, and given the precision needed for drug results and the lack thereof in the state lab, varying results are likely. Furthermore, if the officer or the phlebotomist used the alcohol collection kit and not a drug collection kit, you may have procedural and evidential issues.

§9:12   Ask for Specifics

Finally, in discovery, be sure to ask the prosecution to produce *specific* studies, articles, or other resources upon which the expert will rely to support the opinion that the drug in question impaired your client's *driving* abilities. For example, some stimulants at low levels merely keep one from falling asleep, a condition which at 2 a.m. is *not* an impairment to driving.

[§§9:13-9:19 Reserved]

III.   JURY SELECTION

§9:20   Where the Case Will Be Won

More than any other case, DUI-D is won in voir dire. If the jury believes that the government is correct that any amount of the drug impairs driving ability, then you lose. If, on the other hand, you can show the jury that the government has to prove that your client's driving was impaired and that wasn't done, you win. As stated in Chapter 2, the best way to get people to agree with your position is if they believe it was already their own position.

§9:21   Sample Voir Dire

Potential jurors, you have been told that this case involves driving under the influence of drugs. In other words, Bob's ability to drive was impaired by some drug. Who here believes that using any drug automatically impairs your driving ability?

OK, thank you all for your honesty. Who here drinks coffee (or Coke, or tea or Red Bull, anything that has caffeine) in the morning? Who drank some before coming to court? So those of you who just said that consuming any drug and driving is illegal and who admitted to having coffee before coming here have just indicated that they committed a crime. Juror 4, you said any drug and admitted to coffee, how does that sound to you?

---

[1] It is not the function of this book to teach the basic Gas Chromatography Mass Spectrometry information one needs to truly understand how GCMS works. I would suggest that if you find yourself doing a fair amount of cases involving driving under the influence of drugs, you take a training class on how to read this information, get trained at a lab to do blood/urine analysis, take an entry-level college class locally, or do all three.

You are correct, it is confusing, so let me help you out and you tell me what you think. Coffee contains caffeine and that is a stimulant. Like you, I need it to wake up in the morning and quite frankly you don't want me driving without it; and I am sure we all know many people we would not want driving unless they have a cup first. But since coffee does contain a stimulant, and impairment will be defined as any deviation from normal, it could be criminal. What do you think now? How about juror 6?

That's the point, just because the caffeine impairs you doesn't mean it impairs your driving. So let me ask all of you: Does the mere fact that the drug is present in someone's system support a finding of guilty? Why or why not?

Let's take another example. Who here gets severe headaches? Do you take medicine? So the aspirin you take eases the pain. So you are admitting to being impaired, but it is not driving-related, just pain management. So who here thinks that not only must the government prove that the drug impairs driving, but they must also show a *negative* impairment? In other words, whatever the drug impaired, it had to affect driving skills. Juror 10, explain what you meant.

[§§9:22-9:29 Reserved]

IV.   DRUG RECOGNITION EVALUATOR PROGRAM

The following is a synopsis of the Drug Recognition Evaluator Program written by Anthony D. Palacios, a former drug recognition evaluator and drug recognition evaluator trainer. It explains the history and concept of the Drug Recognition Evaluator Program.

§9:30   Overview of the Drug Recognition Expert Program

In the early 1970's, personnel from the Los Angeles Police Department (LAPD) began developing the Drug Evaluation and Classification Program, better known as the Drug Recognition Expert Program. The purpose of this program was to assist officers in detecting drivers who were possibly impaired on intoxicants other than alcohol.

In 1979, the LAPD officially accepted the Drug Recognition Expert Program. The program consisted of a three-step process:
1.   Establish a driver is impaired and rule out alcohol as the sole cause of impairment.
2.   Rule out any medical issues as the cause of impairment.
3.   Determine what drug category or categories are the cause of impairment.

During the mid-1980's, the National Highway Traffic Safety Administration (NHTSA) sponsored two validation studies to determine the Drug Recognition Evaluator Program's effectiveness. In 1984, the John Hopkins Validation Study was conducted using four senior drug recognition evaluators from the LAPD. In 1985, the LAPD Field Validation Study was conducted using 28 drug recognition evaluators from the LAPD and the surrounding area. They examined persons arrested in Los Angeles on suspicion of drug influence. Both studies reported correct decisions over 90% of the time.

§9:31   Receiving Drug Recognition Evaluator Certification

In order to attend the drug recognition evaluator training program, an officer must first attend the NHTSA DUI Detection & Standardized Field Sobriety Testing student course and either the NHTSA Drugs That Impair Driving course (DTID) or the NHTSA Advanced Roadside Impaired Driving Enforcement course (ARIDE).

The drug recognition evaluator training program consists of three phases. Phase I consists of a two-day pre-school; Phase II consists of seven days of classroom instruction, which includes passing a comprehensive written examination; and Phase III consists of the field certification.

During the field certification, the drug recognition evaluator-in-training must complete a minimum of 12 evaluations, all of which are supervised and evaluated by a drug recognition evaluator instructor. Out of the 12 required evaluations, the drug recognition evaluator-in-training must be the evaluator in a minimum of six evaluations and identify at least three of the seven drug categories. Lastly, the drug recognition evaluator-in-training must pass a comprehensive final knowledge examination.

§9:32   Maintaining Drug Recognition Evaluator Certification

Drug Recognition Evaluators are required to renew their certification every two years. Prior to recertification, the drug recognition evaluator must attend a minimum of eight hours of training. The drug recognition evaluator is required to turn in an updated curriculum vitae and rolling log, and administer four evaluations. All four evaluations must be reviewed and approved by a drug recognition evaluator instructor, and one of the four evaluations must be witnessed by a drug recognition evaluator instructor.

§9:33   The 12-Step Drug Recognition Evaluator Evaluation

Step 1: Breath Alcohol Test: The first step is to rule out alcohol as the sole cause of the impairment. If a suspect's alcohol concentration is too high, a drug evaluation will not be conducted.

Step 2: Interview of the Arresting Officer: During this step, the drug recognition evaluator will speak with the arresting officer to determine what signs and symptoms of possible drug impairment the officer observed during the initial contact with the suspect.

Step 3: Preliminary Examination: During step three, the drug recognition evaluator asks the suspect a set of specific questions taken from a Drug Recognition Evaluator Face Sheet. During the questioning, the drug recognition evaluator is recording specific observations of the suspect. The purpose for this step is to help the drug recognition evaluator determine if the suspect may be impaired due to a medical condition. In addition to asking the specific questions from the Drug Recognition Evaluator Face Sheet, the drug recognition evaluator will check for equal pupil size, and equal tracking, and check the suspect's first pulse rate.

Step 4: Eye Examination: Step four consists of the Horizontal Gaze Nystagmus test, the Vertical Gaze Nystagmus test, and the Lack of Convergence test. During the HGN test, the drug recognition evaluator will attempt to obtain an angle of onset and then apply the angle in the Tharp's equation ($50 - \text{Angle} = \text{BAC}$).

Step 5: Divided Attention Tests: The fifth step consists of the Romberg Balance test, the Walk and Turn test, the One Leg Stand test, and the Finger to Nose test. During this step, the drug recognition evaluator is recording signs of psychophysical impairment.

Step 6: Vital Signs Examination: During the sixth step, the drug recognition evaluator will check the suspect's blood pressure and body temperature, utilizing drug recognition evaluator training-course-issued equipment. The drug recognition evaluator also is required to check the suspect's pulse for a second time.

Step 7: Dark Room Examination: During the seventh step, the drug recognition evaluator, utilizing the drug recognition evaluator training-course-issued pupillometer card and pen light, will estimate the suspect's pupil size in specific lighting situations (e.g., room light, near total darkness, and direct light). The drug recognition evaluator will also check for reaction to light, and check the suspect's mouth and nose for signs of drug ingestion.

Step 8: Muscle Tone Examination: The eighth step consists of the drug recognition evaluator checking the suspect's muscle tone in the left arm. The Drug Recognition Evaluator will record on the drug recognition evaluator Face Sheet whether the muscle tone is rigid, flaccid, or near normal.

Step 9: Check for Injection Sites and Third Pulse: During the ninth step, the drug recognition evaluator checks the suspect's arms, hands, and neck for signs of injection sites caused by hypodermic needles. The drug recognition evaluator also checks the suspect's pulse rate for the final time.

Step 10: Suspect's Statements and Other Observations: In the tenth step, the drug recognition evaluator will question the suspect based on the signs and symptoms observed and recorded during the nine previous steps discussed. By this point, the drug recognition evaluator should have at least a suspicion of which drug category or categories are present.

Step 11: Opinion of the Evaluator: The eleventh step requires the drug recognition evaluator to analyze all the signs and symptoms recorded on the Drug Recognition Evaluator Face Sheet during the entire evaluation and compare it to the Drug Symptomology Chart. The Drug Symptomology Chart, better known as the "Matrix," lists the major indicators and general indicators of each of the seven (7) drug categories, and is designed to assist the drug recognition evaluator in determining what drug category or categories are present.

Step 12: Toxicological Examination: In this final step, the drug recognition evaluator will request the suspect to submit to a chemical test or tests for the purposes of evidence collection to support the drug recognition evaluator's opinion.

Note: The 2005 drug recognition evaluator training curriculum revisions issued by the IACP Drug Recognition Evaluator Technical Advisory Panel (TAP) changed the drug recognition evaluator training curriculum to allow drug recognition evaluators to formulate an opinion in certain situations, even if the 12-step evaluation process was not fully completed. Examples of acceptable situations when a drug recognition evaluator may formulate an opinion when any steps are omitted include but are not limited to: injury to the suspect, uncooperativeness of a suspect, or equipment failure.

Prior to the 2005 revision, drug recognition evaluators were not allowed to formulate an opinion unless all 12 steps were conducted and completed.

[§§9:34-9:39 Reserved]

V.   CROSS-EXAMINATION OF THE DRUG RECOGNITION EVALUATOR

§9:40   The Nine Major Areas of Attack

Given the multitudes of drugs being used in today's society, it is impossible to present complete cross-examination for all drugs in all cases in this book. Instead, I will show the nine major areas on which to attack a drug recognition evaluator during cross-examination and use a few examples in each area to demonstrate the point.
But first, here are the nine areas ripe for cross-examination in a DUI-D case:
- Missing symptoms.
- Symptoms that were normal.
- Alternative explanations.
- Client's normals.
- Doctor cop.
- Just a cop.
- The unknown.
- Guessing game.
- Training comparisons.

Let's examine each of these.

§9:41   Missing Symptoms

This line of questioning focuses on the fact the client did not have all the expected signs or symptoms of the drug category the DRE has called in his or her expert opinion.

Example # 1:

Q: You were taught that elevated pulse is a sign of CNS Stimulant influence?
A: Yes.
Q: Mr. Smith did not have an elevated pulse?
A: No.

Example # 2:

Q: You were taught that lack of convergence is a major indicator of CNS Depressant influence?
A: Mr. Smith did not have lack of convergence.

Do not ask more than this. If you do so, then you are inviting the officer to explain WHY the symptom might be missing. Instead, save it for your closing.

§9:42   Symptoms That Are Normal

This line of questioning focuses on the fact the client had signs or symptoms that were normal, and therefore not consistent with the drug category in question.

Example # 1:

Q: You were taught the normal range of blood pressure in DRE training, weren't you?
A: Yes.
Q: That normal range is 120-140 Systolic?
A: Yes.
Q: 70-90 Diastolic?
A: Yes.
Q: What was Mr. Smith's systolic and diastolic blood pressure?
A: 128 over 80.
Q: 128 over 80 is within normal ranges?
A: Yes.
Q: Narcotic Analgesics lower the blood pressure?
A: Yes.

Example # 2:

Q: You were taught the normal range of pulse in DRE training?
A: Yes.
Q: The normal range is 60 to 90 beats per minute?
A: Yes.
Q: What was Mr. Smith's pulse?
A: 86.
Q: 86 is within normal range?
A: Yes.
Q: Cannabis elevates the pulse, doesn't it?
A: Yes.

§9:43   Alternative Explanations

Perhaps the most understandable technique for a jury, the alternative explanation line of inquiry accepts the symptoms as present, but focuses on everyday rationales for them. These alternative explanations can deal with sleep fatigue, stress, a traffic accident, medical conditions, etc.

Example # 1:

Q: An elevated pulse rate can be caused by things other than drugs?
A: Yes.
Q: Excitement may cause it?
A: Yes.
Q: Stress?

A: Yes.
Q: Being involved in a traffic accident can be stressful?
A: Yes.
Q: Being involved in a traffic accident may cause elevated pulse?
A: Yes.
Q: Fear can elevate pulse?
A: Yes.
Q: False accusations?
A: Yes.

Do not then sum it up, such as "Well, being accused and evaluated by you after this accident may have caused my client to be fearful and stressed, therefore elevating his pulse rate." A smart cop will say, "Not if he had nothing to worry about." Instead, point out to the jury that many of them probably had an elevated pulse rate when they were first called to sit in the jury box for the initial voir dire because of fear of answering questions and anxiety about what might happen.

Example # 2:

Q: Body tremors can be caused by things other than drugs?
A: Yes.
Q: Anxiety or stress may cause tremors?
A: Yes.
Q: Cold weather may make one shiver?
A: Yes.
Q: Nicotine withdrawals may cause it?
A: Yes.
Q: Even excessive amounts of caffeine may cause body tremors?
A: Yes.

Again, don't try to drive home the conclusion. Leave it out there or else be prepared to get slammed.

§9:44   Client's Normal

What is normal? What is average? Earlier in this book we discussed the use of Gausian Distribution (or bell curve) to show that "average" or "normal" accounts for very few people; and that in order to encompass the vast majority of folks, one needs to go out two or even three standard deviations. You can remind the jury of this during this part of the examination, by showing them that the officer has *no concept* of what normal or average really means.

Example # 1:

Q: You were taught the normal range for pulse in DRE training?
A: Yes.
Q: You agree that not all people fall in that normal range?
A: Yes.
Q: There are people with pulse rates above normal who are not on drugs?
A: Yes.
Q: People below normal who are not on drugs?
A: Yes.
Q: Do you know what the range of pulse rates is to capture one standard deviation from average, or about 68% of the population?
A: No.
Q: Do you know what the range is to capture about 95%, or two standard deviations?
A: No.
Q: What about to get to three deviations or 99% or so of the population?

DRIVING UNDER THE INFLUENCE OF DRUGS

A: No idea.

Q: A person's pulse changes over time?

A: Yes.

Q: You don't know what Mr. Smith's normal pulse rate is?

A: No.

Q: It could be in your so-called normal range?

A: Yes.

Q: But his "normal" could be outside the "normal range?"

A: Yes.

Q: In fact it could be higher or lower than your "normal range" and yet he could be one of the second deviation people, in other words, just part of the 95% of us, but not part of the 68%?

A: Huh?

§9:45   Doctor Cop/Just a Cop

This is best set up in opening or voir dire by asking a juror, especially someone who works in construction, if he uses a plumber to do the electrician's job or vice versa—for example, "Juror 5, if I told you I had a worker to do the plumbing but he was trained by an electrician, would that work for you? Why not?"

Example # 1:

Q: The instructors in this DRE school weren't doctors?

A: No.

Q: They weren't nurses either?

A: No.

Q: Pharmacologists?

A: No.

Q: Paramedics?

A: No.

Q: They were police officers?

A: Yes.

Example # 2:

Q: You're not a doctor?

A: No.

Q: A toxicologist?

A: No.

Q: A pharmacologist?

A: No.

Q: You don't have a degree in chemistry?

A: No.

Q: You're a police officer?

A: Yes.

You then combine these two lines of inquiry in summation to point out that *no one* would want to place what is essentially a medical diagnosis in the hands of someone who was taught how to take a pulse, measure pupil size, obtain blood pressure and evaluate outward symptoms by a cop at the police academy or even in a special class. Similarly, they wouldn't want a nurse to handle a hostage situation if he or she were trained by another nurse on how to do so in medical school. This is especially valuable if you are using a real doctor as your expert in the case.

§9:46   The Unknown

Also called "I can't say why," this attack challenges the DRE's expertise by requiring the officer to state he or she does not know how a sign or symptom is caused, but was told only that it should be there by the previously cop-trained cop.

Example # 1:

Q: You don't know how CNS stimulants dilate the pupils?
A: No.
Q: You don't know why?
A: No.
Q: So you don't know the difference between stimulant dilation and other forms of dilation?
A: No.

Example # 2:

Q: You don't know how cannabis causes the pupils to pulsate?
A: No.
Q: You can't tell the jury how or why?
A: No.
Q: You can't tell the difference between cannabis pulsation and strobe effect?
A: No.

Example # 3:

Q: You don't know how hallucinogens supposedly elevate the pulse?
A: No.
Q: You can't differentiate between that elevation and nervous elevation?
A: No.

§9:47   The Guessing Game

With the guessing game, the opinion is subjectively based and not objectively supported. Dilation, pulse rate, even blood pressure are important vital signs that require years of training to obtain and then years more to cross reference to determine a *possible* cause. Yet, officers use those three main tools to pick a drug. The jury needs to hear this. (This is predicated on discovery of the officer's record of DRE arrests, which the DRE is required to keep pursuant to his or her training in order to be evaluated and to be continually certified.)

Example # 1:

Q: Your opinion in a DRE case is subjective?
A: It is based on the information I obtained.
Q: You've made these beliefs in DRE cases in the past?
A: Yes.
Q: Sometimes toxicology didn't find the drug category you predicted?
A: Yes.
Q: In fact, sometimes toxicology didn't find any drug?
A: Yes.
Q: So, sometimes your opinion is not correct?
A: Yes.
Q: Sometimes you guessed wrong?
A: Yes.
Q: In fact when you first stopped my client, you thought he was under the influence of alcohol?

A: Possibly.
Q: You asked if he had been drinking?
A: Yes.
Q: But he tested *zero* for alcohol?
A: Yes.

Once more, don't ask follow-up because the officer will say that's why he went to drugs. Argue later to the jury that the cop thought alcohol and was *wrong*. He may be wrong here as well.

§9:48   Training Comparison

If you are confronted with a non-DRE trained officer, then you might want to consider running through how intense DRE training is to show the complete lack of experience the beat cop has. Another line of inquiry is the completeness of the training an officer receives in order to carry a gun versus what they get in order to be a DRE. Typically, weapons training is the toughest aspect of becoming a cop. Get the officer to describe how much training he needed to use that tool, which was taught by cops who use it, versus the training level for DRE, taught by non-professionals.

§9:49   Non-Specific Areas of Examination

Besides dealing with the specifics of the DRE protocol, or the specifics of your case, it may be worthwhile, either at the start or finish of your cross-examination, to show the jury that the officer really isn't much more than a parrot when it comes to understanding the science of the DRE regimen. In other words, the officer has no clue what this stuff is really based on. While many judges just accept DRE as a given, an open-minded judge may actually allow you to use this as a voir dire of the officer to preclude DRE testimony from even coming before the jury.

Q: You never read the actual data in the study beyond what's in the DRE manual?
A: No.
Q: You don't know how many people were tested in the study?
A: No.
Q: You don't know how many people were tested on the drug in question in your case?
A: No.
Q: You don't know in how many cases officers incorrectly indicated the drug in question in your case?
A: No.
Q: You don't know the protocols used in the research to define "correct calls" in the research?
A: No.
Q: You don't know specifically who (what scientist, if any) conducted the study?
A: No.
Q: You don't know what blood concentration positive subjects in the research were dosed to?
A: No.
Q: You don't know how many control subjects were involved in the research?
A: No.
Q: You don't know how many control subjects were falsely identified as positive?
A: No.
Q: You don't know how many control subjects were incorrectly classified as the drug class involved in your case?
A: No.
Q: In other words, you know nothing about the research subjects, the controls, false positives, correct guess rate, levels of dosage or any aspect of the methodology?
A: No, I don't.

[§§9:50-9:59 Reserved]

VI   MARIJUANA DUIS SPECIFICALLY

§9:60   Introduction

In many states, Washington included, marijuana has been decriminalized. As a result marijuana DUIs are on the rise. To be clear, it's always been a crime to drive while under the influence of marijuana, but now with many states having per se limits and additional penalties, more and more of our clients find themselves facing a marijuana DUI. I'll use the per se limit that is established in Washington State for the sake of illustration, 5.00 nanograms of THC per milliliter of blood.

Much has already been discussed in this volume about blood draws and ways to challenge them. This material focuses on the **pre-arrest** investigation portions of a marijuana DUI, as officers are mostly using the basic NHTSA curriculum and/or some things they've learned in ARIDE that are wholly inadequate as investigative tools.

Recall that every single DUI investigation is predicated on a three phase pre-arrest process. Each phase presents interesting issues for marijuana DUIs—and great areas of attack. However, note that these ideas are just starting points—especially considering that this area of law is still emerging. You can take the same arguments and use them as jumping off points to bigger and better arguments.

§9:61   Phase One—Vehicle in Motion

Before any of our clients can be given implied consent warnings or have blood drawn, or even find themselves arrested, they have to be stopped for a traffic infraction. This is a prime area of attack as it regards the question of marijuana impairment.

"But wait - impairment doesn't matter if my client's blood is above 5.00, right?"

Glad you asked. Of course it does! We get so locked down in BrAC numbers and THC measurements that we forget that before any of that happens, we need a valid arrest—based on **probable cause to believe a crime was committed**.

That means that when Trooper Friendly arrests your client, he needs reasonable grounds to believe one of two things:

1) Your client's blood has more than 5.00 ng of THC in it per milliliter. (**Note:** There is **no way** for any officer to know this—much like they can't know a person's BrAC without a PBT.)
2) Your client's **ability to drive was affected** by the marijuana.

So—the question is—can Trooper Friendly say **at the time of arrest** that he had grounds to believe your client's ability to drive was affected? And so we get back to the question of the observing your client's driving behavior.

The NHTSA manual tells you that 24 separate driving behaviors are statistically linked to a probability that a driver is impaired. **By alcohol.** Remember that every part of the basic NHTSA curriculum was designed and correlated to a BrAC—**not** THC levels or drugs of any kind. So if your officer has **not** been through ARIDE or a DRE training—his "NHTSA training" about marijuana is worthless. So then the ARIDE or DRE manuals must have a section about what a marijuana impaired driver will look like, right?

Here's what ARIDE has to say:

Subjects impaired by Cannabis may not be able to pay attention or may have a very brief attention span. The subjective effects can vary considerably, but they will exhibit divided attention impairment. The impact of these effects may be obvious in the classroom, but the consequences when driving can be fatal. ARIDE Manual—NHTSA 11/07—Session VI p21.

Yep. That's it. And if you boil it down to it's simplest statement it says "we have no idea what marijuana does to driving."

Maybe the DRE manual will help.

At recreational doses, effects may include relaxation, euphoria, relaxed inhibitions, sense of well-being, disorientation, altered time and distance perception, lack of concentration, impaired learning and memory, alterations in thought formation and expression, drowsiness, sedation, mood changes such as panic reactions and paranoia, and a more vivid sense of taste, sight, smell, and hearing. Because Cannabis impairs attention, divided attention tests are excellent tools for recognizing people who are under the influence of this category of drug. DRE Participant Manual—Session 21—p5.

Two important things we should learn from the DRE manual.
1) These are **possible** symptoms and **none talk about driving behavior**.
2) "A more vivid sense of sight and hearing"—this would seem to make drivers **more** vigilant!

NHTSA studied marijuana and driving—and released a huge report through the DOT in November 1993. DOT HS 808 078—Marijuana and Actual Driving Performance. In one section they studied THC impaired driving on normal highways. Here's their conclusion:

An important practical objective of this study was to determine whether degrees of driving impairment can be accurately predicted from either measured concentrations of THC in plasma or performance measured in potential roadside "sobriety" tests of tracking ability or hand and posture stability. These results, like many reported before, indicate that none of these measures accurately predicts change in actual driving performance under the influence of THC.

Interestingly, this study also found that THC seemed to impact driving more in the labs than in actual driving tests. Their driving group "complied with all instructions, even after high doses of THC. Changes in mood were often reported, but changes in personality were never observed. Most importantly, the subjects were always able to complete every ride without major interventions by the driving instructors and their safety was never compromised."
Most interestingly the study stated the following facts in the conclusion:
- Marijuana smoking which delivers THC up to a 300 µg/kg dose slightly impairs the ability to maintain a constant headway while following another car;
- A low THC dose (100 µg/kg) does not impair driving ability in urban traffic to the same extent as a blood alcohol concentration (BAC) of 0.04 g%;
- Drivers under the influence of marijuana tend to over-estimate the adverse effects of the drug on their driving quality and compensate when they can: e.g. by increasing effort to accomplish the task, increasing headway or slowing down, or a combination of these;
- Drivers under the influence of alcohol tend to under-estimate the adverse effects of the drug on their driving quality and do no invest compensatory effort;
- The maximum road tracking impairment after the highest THC dose (300 µg/kg) was within a range of effects produced by many commonly used medicinal drugs and less than that associated with a blood alcohol concentration (BAC) of 0.08 g% in previous studies employing the same test;
- It is not possible to conclude anything about a driver's impairment on the basis of his/her plasma concentrations of THC and THC-COOH determined in a single sample.

So—aside from the fact that NHTSA concluded that you cannot say anything about driving based on THC level, the study also told us that high doses of THC show a range of effects comparable with many common medicinal drugs and **less than a BrAC of 0.08**, which is what all those driving behaviors are correlated to. The conclusion most studies come to is that it's almost impossible to come to a conclusion about the effects of different drug levels on driving.
So how do we use this strategically?
We're building a probable cause argument, really. And if there's **nothing** about the driving that is indicative of marijuana impairment, then there's no reasonable articulable suspicion to even expand the scope of the stop. Is there?

§9:62   Phase Two—Personal Contact

In order to generate that reasonable articulable suspicion, officers do not just have to rely on driving. They can rely on their personal contact with the driver: the officer's observations of the driver's demeanor, physical characteristics, speech patterns, and more. We already know the NHTSA basic manual won't be able to help us, especially since the stopping sequence is also correlated to alcohol as are all of the physical observations in phase two.
So let's check in with ARIDE.

General Indicators include: marked reddening of the conjunctiva, odor of marijuana, marijuana debris in the mouth, body tremors, increased appetite, relaxed inhibitions, disoriented, possible paranoia, impaired perception of time and distance, eyelid tremors.

Now let's eliminate increased appetite and relaxed inhibitions as these aren't easily observable in a short period of time at roadside. But the important thing to remember is that these are signs of consumption not impairment. And for probable cause, the officer needs to believe the driver is impaired. The same exact indicators are seen in the DRE manual. But a great deal of additional information can be mined from the DRE Instructor manual.

People under the influence of Marijuana simply seem not to pay attention, or to have very brief attention spans. In particular, they do not divide their attention very successfully.

"Seem" is an awfully subjective word to be used before arresting someone, isn't it? Maybe it gets better. The next characteristic the DRE manual mentions in addition to those above is "possible green coating on the tongue" which many troopers profess to seeing.

However, immediately following that characteristic, the Instructor manual tells the instructor to "point out that there are **no known studies** that confirm marijuana causing a green coating on the tongue." So one of the characteristics officers use to arrest citizens is one that has no actual basis in fact? Great.

The rest of the characteristics are just as easily dealt with in Phase Two as evidence of consumption, not observable at roadside, or not backed up by scientific or practical evidence or studies. In other words - there's not a lot of there, there.

§9:63   Phase Three—Pre-Arrest Screening

Surely our officers have been trained in valid pre-arrest screening techniques for the detection of marijuana impairment. Especially through ARIDE and the DRE protocols. And yet, the tools they use are almost **useless** in relation to marijuana impairment (or even consumption, really).

Recall from your NHTSA manual that NHSTA statistically validated three specific standardized field sobriety tests for use in pre-arrest screening (I'll quickly remind you that the PBT can't check for THC). Those three are:

1.   Horizontal Gaze Nystagmus
2.   9 Step Walk and Turn
3.   One Leg Stand

These are the big three. We see them in almost every single DUI case we take. And say what you will about the science behind them—for alcohol DUIs—they're not bad (they're not great, but they're not bad).

So it would seem natural for an officer to think—"impairment is impairment—I should see the same things that I would in a subject impaired by alcohol. Let's run the subject through the SFSTs." And this is where the fun really starts.

The first thing officers will do is an HGN test. This test is quite effective in the detection of alcohol. But per the ARIDE and DRE manuals: **marijuana will not create HGN.** So if we're talking about marijuana, we should see zero of six clues on this. How does this help us? In a variety of ways.

If the officer sees any clues—they're **not** caused by marijuana. Maybe something else is going on—head injuries, medical issues, etc. And if the officer sees zero clues—well then the absence of a fact doesn't prove much. All we know is marijuana doesn't cause HGN. So the HGN is unhelpful as it relates to marijuana DUIs (also irrelevant, if we want to speak in legal terminology).

Now let's talk about the other things the officer **can** glean from the HGN test. For instance—pupil size can be observed. And marijuana can have an effect on pupil size. Or can it? According to both the ARIDE and DRE manuals—the pupils of someone who's consumed marijuana will be dilated. Or normal. Also unhelpful.

However, lack of convergence will be present with marijuana. So there is one thing we can see with marijuana: lack of convergence, which is also present with depressants, dissociative anesthetics, and inhalants and which again does not help. This brings us to a very useful item - the drug category matrix. This matrix is presented above in §9:02. It's a quick reference guide to many of the signs and symptoms that you may see with various drug categories.

Obviously, the symptoms list isn't exhaustive—but you can use it easily to start discriminating what drug category you might be dealing with. For instance, you can see some symptoms from one category and some from another—which you can argue rules out one or the other category. In other words, you can use the matrix to your advantage.

Now that we've removed the HGN from the calculations, we can move on to the remainder of the SFST battery: the Walk and Turn and the One Leg Stand. It should be noted that the instructions and grading of these tests do not change when marijuana intoxication is suspected (as it should be—if you alter the standardization, you compromise the validity of the tests).

However, recognize that the clues and grading were validated to **alcohol** not marijuana, which means the clues and grading are unhelpful and irrelevant to a marijuana case. Let's see if the DRE manual agrees with us.

Performance on the Romberg, Walk and Turn, One Leg Stand, and Finger to Nose tests will be impaired. Point out that, with subjects under the influence of Marijuana, poor performance on these tests will result principally from their inability to divide attention, and less so from impaired coordination or balance.

Wait. What? You mean all this time we've been talking about impaired coordination—and now they're telling us that if a subject on marijuana has difficulty on these tests, it's not as a result of impaired coordination? And now they're adding two tests—the Romberg and Finger to Nose.

The most important thing to understand from the manual, however, is that the clues and grading **simply don't apply** to marijuana. You can not draw a conclusion from them about marijuana intoxication and impairment, which makes them…wait for it…irrelevant.

So now let's briefly talk about the Romberg and Finger to Nose tests. They are: unstandardized tests; ungraded;. no method is available for interpreting the performance; there is no pass or fail line and no instructions. The two clues that both manuals tell us to look for on the Romberg are eyelid tremors and distorted perception of time.

And that's about it. That's the entirety of the pre-arrest marijuana screening information our officers have in order to attempt to make an arrest. That's how little information they really have about marijuana and impaired driving. But before we leave the topic—let's see how to put it all together.

§9:64　　Putting It All Together—A Probable Cause Argument

Recall that in order to show probable cause for a marijuana DUI arrest, an officer must have reasonable grounds to believe that your client is under the influence of (i.e. his ability to drive is affected by) marijuana.

Just swing down the list of observations:

- There's no driving that's indicative of marijuana impairment at all - since even at higher doses, the impairment is usually less than what you'd see at 0.08. (There are some studies that suggest driving **under** the speed limit is indicative of marijuana consumption—but is that impaired driving?)
- The physical observations made at roadside by the officer may be indicative of consumption **at best**. There are no physical observations that are indicative of **impairment** by marijuana (especially since marijuana doesn't affect coordination or balance—but only perhaps the ability to divide attention).
- The SFST (and non standardized test) battery in **no way** is correlated to marijuana consumption or impairment.

Sum that up and the best thing an arresting officer can really say is: "I guess he's impaired by marijuana—not sure why or how—but that's my best guess." And that's in no way reasonable grounds to believe a crime has been committed. Which means—no probable cause.

Using the manuals and the lack of quality studies and science to your advantage is a great way to challenge the prosecutor's case before your client ever gets to the hospital for that blood draw. Focusing on what sets marijuana apart from standard alcohol DUIs is where we can mine that material from.

Everything that we know about DUIs was correlated to and based on alcohol impairment, we don't yet have anything solid or accepted that is correlated to marijuana impairment. And that—is the most significant difference you need to know about.

DRIVING UNDER THE INFLUENCE OF DRUGS

(This page intentionally left blank.)

APPENDIX A

THE DISTRICT ATTORNEY'S MANUAL

APPENDIX A:
DA'S MANUAL

§A:357 "The People Get 'Two Bites at The Apple.' They Get to Argue to You Twice, But I Only Get One Chance."

§A:358 "The DA Didn't Disprove Our Case" or "Show My Client Was Lying; Therefore His Drinking Pattern Is to Be Believed, and Based Upon That Pattern, He Was Less Than .08 at the Time Of Driving."

§A:359 "And, Finally, Ladies and Gentleman, I Ask You to Remember That I Cannot Speak to You Again. Please Listen to the Prosecutor's Argument as I Will, Thinking of the Arguments That My Client and I Cannot Make."

(This page intentionally left blank.)

INTRODUCTION

It may be beneficial for practitioners to see what the typical prosecution theory of a driving under the influence trial would be. The following manual has been gleaned from a number of outlines used by prosecutor's offices in California over the last few years.

A DUI trial, like any other, needs a theme. One of the most employable prosecution themes is the "complete picture" theme. The idea is that a juror will need to look at all the facts, taken together, in order to arrive at the truth. This theme effectively rebuts the usual defense tactic of isolating certain facts, while ignoring others, and explaining those isolated pieces away.

Accordingly, it is important in a DUI trial to solicit from the People's witnesses ALL evidence, even evidence that is arguably exculpatory. By proceeding in this fashion, you accomplish three things:
*   First, you send your "complete picture" theme.
*   Second you take the wind out of defense sails by soliciting exculpatory evidence.
*   Third, you show the jurors that you are a "truth seeker."

I. PREPARING FOR TRIAL

A. Reviewing the Police Reports

1. In General

The prosecutor's initial case preparation involves a careful reading of all police reports prepared in connection with the arrest. Although various law enforcement agencies use different formats for driving under the influence reports, the following information should be contained in each report and should be studied by the prosecutor:

§A:01   Driving Pattern

Bad driving is not an element of the crime, but is evidence the jury may consider in determining whether the defendant was under the influence. See CALJIC 16.832. The defendant should not expect to receive bonus points or a gold star simply because he or she did not weave in the lane, or park up on or run into the curb, or hit the Botts dots. It is important to remember that a person is supposed to drive properly! It is the mistakes made while driving, no matter how small, that demonstrate impairment.

§A:02   Age

Older persons often receive jury sympathy, and any poor performance on coordination tests is not necessarily strong evidence of alcohol or drug impairment. Age (both old and very young) can affect a person's tolerance to the effects of alcohol. Youthful offenders often have a low tolerance to alcohol due to their inexperience with drinking. The prosecutor should explore these areas with the expert, prior to putting the expert on the stand, and be ready to present any favorable testimony regarding age and tolerance.

§A:03   Gender

If a female arrestee was violent and physical force was necessary to subdue her, claims of "brutality" should be anticipated. Also, assertions of sexual misconduct by a male arresting officer are occasionally made, especially if there is a long period of time between the stop and the booking.

§A:04   Race

Recently, assertions of racial bias have been on the rise, due in part to certain high profile cases that have received national media attention and have brought forth claims of police brutality and conspiracy. Officers would be well advised to tape-record any arrests where they suspect this claim will be raised, and also to take photos of the defendant before booking to show that no physical harm occurred.

§A:05　National Origin

Assertions of national origin bias are also common, particularly in refusal cases where English is not the defendant's primary language. Persons who do not speak English well (or at all) often base their defense on that fact. They can also claim that they did not understand the officer's directions on the FSTs, or that they did not understand the officer's explanation of the chemical tests and that is why they refused them. They may claim that their manner of speech (accent or difficulty dealing with English) gave the appearance of intoxication (confusion and seemingly slurred speech) to the officer. If an interpreter is used at the scene, and/or during the chemical tests admonition, any statements by the suspect can come in through the officer. *People v. Torres* (1989) 213 Cal. App. 3d 1248 holds that when a declarant makes an out of court statement through an interpreter, if that statement is otherwise admissible, the hearsay rule does not bar a percipient witness other than the interpreter from testifying to the content of the out of court statement, even though the witness testifies to the words uttered by the interpreter, not the declarant. [Note: the interpreter still needs to be called to testify as to his or her qualifications and that he or she accurately translated the questions and responses.]

§A:06　Height and Weight

Persons in good physical condition can be expected to perform better on the FSTs even when impaired, than persons in poor condition. For example, an obese person may have problems performing some tests even when sober. In addition, the defendant's weight is a very important factor used by the lab expert to compute the minimum amount of alcohol consumed by the defendant to reach the reported blood alcohol level. Therefore, it is necessary to ask the arresting officer, during direct examination, to estimate the defendant's weight at the time of the arrest. This is a permissible lay opinion (see Evidence Code section 801) to lay the foundation for the subsequent hypothetical question to the lab expert. If your officer copied the information from the defendant's driver's license, be sure to ask (in advance) if that information was consistent with his or her recollection of the defendant's size at the time of the arrest.

Although weight is very important to determine the number of drinks consumed, the height of the defendant has absolutely nothing to do with the blood alcohol level. With the weight, blood alcohol level, time of stop, time of test, and any statements by the defendant, the expert can form an opinion about the number of drinks that the defendant has consumed. This opinion often proves that the defendant either lied when he or she talked to the officer after the stop or when the defendant testified in court. Either way, it is a big plus for the prosecutor in argument.

§A:07　Medical Condition and/or Treatment

Always check to see if the police report reflects any medical condition or problems claimed by the defendant. Ask the officer if the defendant mentioned any medical problems or any physical/mental limitations that the officer may not have written in the report. IF the defendant attempts to explain on direct exam his or her poor performance of the FSTs, or other physical signs commonly attributed to alcohol or drug impairment at trial, the prosecutor will be able to show that the defendant never told this to the officer.

It is also important to determine whether the defendant received any medical treatment or if he or she was taken to a medical facility for any reason after the arrest. Most reports describe any medical treatment (or refusal of medical treatment) in the narrative portion of the report. If the defendant was seen by medical personnel, a copy of the medical report should be obtained before the trial. These reports may contain observations of signs of intoxication or lack thereof, and even the hospital's blood alcohol test result, both of which may be relevant in determining the strength of the People's case. This may also be valuable in cases involving drug intoxication where there are no chemical test results.

§A:08　Physical Oddities/Special Medical Problems

Physical disabilities or special medical problems are often used in trial to explain the defendant's poor coordination. An absence of such notations in the police reports tends to impeach the defendant who raises such a claim for the first time at trial. Be sure to check a medical/pharmacy reference book if the defendant claims he or she was taking a prescription medication, to determine what, if any, effects the medicine has—particularly if combined with alcohol! Prozac (depression), Zantac and Tagamet (ulcers), and Nyquil (colds) are the most common medications used to explain away blood alcohol levels by the defense. Remember that a person can be driving under the influence of a legal drug, as well as an illegal drug, and still be in violation of Vehicle Code Sections 23152(a).

Another common defense (in breath cases) is that the defendant was exposed to paint fumes. This can be easily refuted if your county lab uses an Intoximeter 3000 that will register "Interfering Substance" when chemicals contained in the paint are blown into it. See CALJIC 16.831.

§A:09   AKAs (Aliases)

Check for prior convictions under all names used by the defendant. See §A:10 "DMV Printouts."

§A:10   DMV Printouts

The DMV printout submitted on a DUI case can be particularly useful in finding other DUI cases the defendant might have pending. Check the printout to see if he or she has any Vehicle Code §14601.1(a) suspensions showing "J" service plus a reason of "Excessive Blood Alcohol." Check the date on any such suspension. It could be that the defendant was arrested recently for DUI, but the case is still pending in the system (i.e., CII, FBI, NCIC).

Also, be sure to familiarize yourself with the out-of-state DMV codes. You can get a list from the local DMV that shows DUI, wet reckless, or other alcohol and driving offenses. convictions. E.g., "17" is the code for a DUI conviction outside the state of California.

§A:11   Time Booked

Excessive or unexplained delays between the arrest and booking, especially where the defendant is female and the arresting officer is male, present potential problems. Be sure to ask your officer to check his or her shift log to see if the officer made other stops during the time the defendant was in custody. Also, delays between arrest and blood alcohol testing may pose problems for experts in their attempts to "relate back" the blood alcohol level to the time of driving. But remember, even if the time period between driving and the test is over three hours—a violation of Title 17—this goes to weight and not admissibility. See *People v. Perkins* (1981) 126 Cal.App.3d Supp. 12, 18-20.

§A:12   Destination and Origination

It is good practice to check the location from which the defendant claims he was coming, and his claimed destination. Many times the defendant's explanation of where he was going and what he was doing do not correspond to where he was seen driving, the direction of driving and/or the location at which the defendant was stopped by the officer. This information can also be useful when combined with the times given by the defendant as to any drinking pattern. Most officers are more than happy to drive a particular path described by the defendant and calculate the time it took, when necessary to impeach a defendant. A common claim of DUI defendants is that the officer was watching the bar where they were drinking, waiting for drivers they know have been drinking. While some jurors may find this offensive, it is no defense.

§A:13   Clothing Worn

Although generally not useful in the People's case-in-chief, have the officer review information in his or her report pertaining to manner of dress. This very common area of cross-examination involves testing the officer's memory of the events surrounding the arrest. However, the clothing may be highly relevant in a "switch" case (when the defense is that someone else in the car was driving) or occasionally, when someone claims the officer forced him to perform the FSTs in clothing or shoes that were inappropriate for the conditions (e.g., barefoot on hot pavement, high heels on an incline, etc.). Also, when a defendant wears a military uniform to court, it is good to point out to the jury that the defendant was not wearing a fancy military uniform on the date of the arrest.

§A:14   Vehicle Driven

Similarly, the officer should review the make, model, color, and year of the vehicle driven by the defendant to avoid impeachment. In addition, the defense frequently claims that the poor driving can be explained by the poor condition of the vehicle, especially if it is old. To counter such assertions, the prosecutor should look for indications that the vehicle was examined or driven by an officer. Also, be sure to request discovery if there are indications the defendant is going to produce some type of repair documents at trial that will show the car had some pre-existing defect.

[§§A:15–A:19 Reserved]

2. Statements Made by the Defendant

§A:20   Alcohol Consumption

Any statement made by the defendant indicating intoxication or that any alcohol was consumed can be extremely valuable in strengthening the People's case. Typically, the defendant will admit the consumption of some alcohol (usually "two beers"). This statement is useful for these reasons:
- It lets the jury know there was some alcohol involved, thereby corroborating the officer.
- It allows questions regarding the size of the drink container, i.e., pitchers, large cans, tall glasses.
- It also allows questions about the timing of the drinks (it is rarely credible when a defendant can precisely time a drinking pattern drink-for-drink).

The statement may later be used to discredit the defendant when the lab expert testifies that the defendant's blood alcohol level and weight prove that considerably more alcohol had been ingested. It proves that the defendant lied because it is not possible to reach the defendant's blood alcohol level based on the amount of alcohol the defendant claims to have consumed.

§A:21   Obscenities

Defendants often make other statements that are helpful to demonstrate intoxication. For example, the defendant's statements may have been laced with obscenities. While it is not necessary to dwell on the language, the officer should relate the specific language used by the defendant. Such evidence helps the jury to picture the defendant's behavior at the time of the offense, in contrast to the defendant's appearance and demeanor in court.

§A:22   Fatigue

Statements revealing when the defendant last slept and for how long can be important. Alcohol generally affects a tired person more quickly than one who is rested. These statements also alert the prosecutor to a potential "fatigue" defense to explain the defendant's impairment. (Be sure to review the "concurring cause" portion of CALJIC 16.831 [1981 Revision].) If, in an attempt to explain poor driving or poor FST performance, the defendant claims that he or she was tired, the prosecutor should make sure to ask why the defendant was drinking and why the defendant was driving, if he or she was so tired.

§A:23   Rising Blood Alcohol/Absorption

This is an extremely important area for preparation. Statements regarding what the defendant had eaten and when the defendant started and stopped drinking are relevant to the blood alcohol level for both the A count (driving under the influence) and the B count (driving with a blood alcohol over .08). Under count A (driving under the influence), the defendant's state of sobriety at the time of the driving is the issue, not his or her sobriety at the time of the subsequent chemical test. (But check with your local jury instructions and statutes for any that create an inference based in blood alcohol at the time of the test.)

The so-called "big gulp" or "absorption" defenses are common, especially if the defendant said to the officers that he or she had just stopped drinking before driving or had an open container in the vehicle. The theory is that the defendant consumed alcohol a very short time before being stopped and that the alcohol had not yet been "absorbed" into the bloodstream and therefore had not affected the driver's mental or physical abilities to drive. Stated another way, the argument is that the defendant was under the influence at the time of the chemical test, but was not yet under the influence when he or she was driving.

Similarly, the defense could argue that the alcohol level had not reached 0.08 percent while the defendant was driving (making him or her not guilty of the per se offense, even though the blood alcohol level at the time of the test was 0.08 percent or above).

§A:24   Investigatory Questions/Miranda

The defendant's answers to the officer's investigatory questions at the scene are admissible in the prosecutor's case-in-chief. Courts have consistently held that these questions are part of the officer's investigation of criminal activity and not the result of a custodial interrogation. *See Berkemer v. McCurty* (1984) 468 U.S. 420; *People v. Forster* (1994) 29 Cal.App.4th 1746.

As in any prosecution, if the defendant was advised of his or her *Miranda* rights and chose to remain silent, the recitation in trial of the warnings and the defendant's response would probably result in a mistrial under the theory that the jury would draw a negative inference from the defendant's choice to exercise the right to remain silent. *See Doyle v. Ohio* (1976) 426 U.S. 610). Caution the officer not to blurt this out. In addition to saving the case, it will also prevent an ethics violation allegation in a misconduct motion. If however, the defense questions the officer regarding the *Miranda* admonition, most courts will find that "the door has been opened," and the prosecutor would be allowed to question the officer on that area in redirect examination.

[§§A:25-A:29 Reserved]

3. Field Sobriety Tests

§A:30   Officer's Documentation

The police report will document the defendant's performance on a series of pre-demonstrated field sobriety tests. Frequently, the officer records the performance of certain tests, i.e., Walk-the-Line, Finger-to-Nose, and One-Leg Stand, on a diagram. Many officers now record the proceedings with either audio or video recorders. Poor performance on these tests is relevant evidence of intoxication.

> **PRACTICE TIP:**
> Object on relevance grounds to any attempt by the defense attorney to have your officer demonstrate the tests in court.

§A:31   Horizontal Gaze Nystagmus

Officers throughout the state have long used the "horizontal gaze nystagmus tests" (HGN) to assist them in determining the defendant's state of sobriety. Nystagmus (horizontal) is a bouncing movement of the eyes thought to be a clear indication of the ingestion of alcohol. It is typically observed by asking the subject to keep the head still while following a moving object with the eyes. The object is placed in the center of the subject's line of vision and is moved slowly to the left or right and the eyes are observed as they attempt to follow the object. The point at which the eyes cease a smooth pursuit of the object (beginning to "bounce" horizontally) is termed "onset" of the nystagmus. Some experts believe that the degree of this onset, calculated from the center of the line of vision (in degrees), correlates to the blood alcohol level.

Although the experience of law enforcement officers in using this test as an indication of alcohol impairment is impressive, it has been vigorously battled in the appellate courts of California. The most recent case to discuss horizontal gaze nystagmus is *People v. Joehnk* (1995) 35 Cal.App.4th 1488. In *Joehnk*, the 4th District Court of Appeals held that the arresting officer may use the evidence of the horizontal gaze nystagmus test as part of his opinion on the question of whether the defendant was under the influence of alcohol. Their ruling was based upon the fact that the prosecution called an expert in their case-in-chief to discuss the scientific reliability of HGN, and its acceptance within the scientific community.

§A:32   DUI Drugs

When the basis for the DUI arrest is that the defendant was under the influence of a controlled substance (or a combination of drugs and alcohol), you will most likely have a drug recognition expert (DRE). These officers are specially trained in recognizing the signs and symptoms of someone under the influence of a controlled substance. They follow a standardized 12-step analysis in making their determination of the person's condition, including testing done at the scene and at the station. The DRE program was developed in the late 1970s and early 1980s by the Los Angeles Police Department. Their officers continue to run training programs for other officers to become certified as DREs.

Not every drug DUI will have a DRE, but there are many officers who have vast experience in this area who have simply not received the specialized DRE training. These officers will still be able to qualify as experts in the area of drug recognition because of their "on the job" expertise.

Even if the officer has neither DRE training nor "on the job" expertise, the prosecution can still present an effective DUI case if there is a positive result for drugs in a chemical test. Remember, the officer arrested the defendant because the officer formed an opinion that the defendant was under the influence (generally of alcohol) for the purposes of driving. The fact that the officer believed the substance was alcohol should not matter.

The prosecutor can often use the testimony of the chemist or a narcotics officer to describe the effects of illegal drugs on the system. That testimony, in addition to the officer's opinion that the defendant was under the influence for the purpose of driving often results in a conviction. A DUI drug case should always be joined with a charge of Health & Safety Code §11550, which is proven by evidence that the defendant is under the influence or has recently used a controlled substance. Note that the definition for "under the influence" for purposes of §11550 is different than that of the DUI statute. See CALJIC 11.060: "If a controlled substance is appreciably affecting the nervous system, brain, muscles, or other parts of a person's body, or is creating in [him or her] any perceptible, abnormal, mental or physical condition, such a person is under the influence of a controlled substance."

§A:33   Refusals

In some cases the defendant, despite being advised of the potential consequences of such an act, refuses to provide a blood, breath or urine sample as required by law. Evidence of both the refusal and the Vehicle Code section 13353 advisement form used by the officer is admissible in this situation. The fact that someone would knowingly choose to accept a one-year license suspension rather than provide a sample for an objective chemical test is a strong indicator of a "consciousness of guilt" and should be vigorously argued as such to the jury. (See CALJIC 16.835.) Note that some defendants also refuse to do the FSTs. This too, is relevant evidence to bring before the jury.

§A:34   DMV Administrative Hearings

In almost every DUI case going to trial, the defendant has had an administrative hearing with the DMV to try to regain his license (especially in refusal cases). These proceedings are tape-recorded and provide a wealth of information about the possible defense being used, as well as for impeachment. They also give the prosecutor an idea of how the arresting officer will testify. If the defendant had an attorney at the time of the hearing, he or she will most likely already have the tapes. Many judges do not require the defense to give the prosecutor copies or transcripts of the tapes because they are impeachment evidence, so it will be necessary to obtain your own set of tapes from the DMV. However, if the prosecutor plans to use the tapes to impeach the defendant or a defense witness, the tapes will most likely have to be transcribed and a copy given to the defense.

§A:35   Scene Visits/Photos

After thoroughly reviewing the police reports, it is a good idea, if time permits, to drive by the location of the arrest and to take pictures of the relevant locations. A good photo of the location where the FSTs took place really stifles the defendant's claim he had to stand and balance on a 45 degree slope. It can also demonstrate how long/far the officer had to observe the bad driving if there was any.

[§§A:36-A:39 Reserved]

B. Interviewing Witnesses

§A:40 Police Officers

Most driving under the influence cases involve only police witnesses. In these cases, the officer should read the police report carefully before the witness interview, to refresh his or her memory regarding the incident. Never assume that the officer will bring the crime report to court, let alone read it. Any ambiguities or inconsistencies in the report should be discussed during an interview, and the officer should be made aware of the importance of accurate testimony.

The officer should be prepared to answer all the questions contained in §§A:100—A:120, Direct Examination of the Arresting Officer. Review with the officer his or her training and experience in investigating DUI cases. If a rigorous cross-examination of the officer is anticipated, the officer should be reminded that his or her professionalism during such cross-examination is crucial to the outcome of the case. Most importantly, the officer must be very familiar with the police report, as most defenses rest upon minor inconsistencies between the report and the testimony of the officer.

§A:41 Non-Police Witnesses

Non-police witnesses should also be interviewed before trial and may require some orientation to the court system and to procedures that will be used in the trial. These witnesses are usually victims of, or witnesses to, traffic accidents and are needed primarily to establish that the defendant was the driver of a vehicle involved in the accident. However, any observations made by non-police witnesses that demonstrate intoxication are quite persuasive, and all statements made by the defendant to such witnesses should be admissible.

[§§A:42-A:49 Reserved]

C. Preparing for the Introduction of the Blood Alcohol Results

§A:50 The Breath Test

Many DUI cases involve the breath test. This test requires the officer to fill out a form called a "Precautionary Checklist" to document the procedures followed and the defendant's performance on the test. It is imperative to review the form to make certain the officer filled it out correctly from top to bottom. The form should include at the top: the defendant's name, date and time, officer's name, and the serial number of the instrument used. All boxes preceding the procedural steps should be checked to corroborate the testimony that the steps were followed. The computer generated (on the newer machines) or graph paper printouts should be attached to the checklist, and should also contain the identifying information supplied by the officer at the time of the test. This information is typed directly into the machine by the officer.

The most vital step in the breath-testing procedure is the first step: a waiting period before the test during which the officer (or a combination of officers) observed the defendant to assure that he or she did not drink, burp, regurgitate, or vomit. The arrest report should contain the information regarding this observation period, but often does not. Title 17 requires a waiting period of fifteen minutes (California Administrative Code, Title 17, section 1219.3) although many police departments have a policy to observe the subject for twenty minutes. The purpose of the wait is to allow for the dissipation of any mouth alcohol that could accumulate as a result of burping, regurgitating or vomiting and be tested, resulting in an erroneously high reading.

The period during which the defendant is observed can include the time taken to investigate, to administer FSTs, to transport the defendant to the police station, and the time spent at the station before administering the chemical tests. The same officer need not have observed the defendant for the entire waiting period; however, all officers required to establish that the defendant did not burp, regurgitate, or vomit should be called to testify. Failure to observe the waiting period, however, goes to weight and not the admissibility of the blood alcohol results. See §A:11.

§A:51 The Blood Test

Blood tests seem to pose few problems at trial. Generally, absent a stipulation, the doctor or nurse who drew the blood must testify that he or she drew blood from the defendant by venipuncture, used a non-alcoholic sterilizing solution, and placed the blood in a tube and gave it to the officer. In a pinch, an experienced traffic officer can testify to his observations of the blood draw and that the sterilizing solution was betadine and did not smell of alcohol.

The doctor or nurse who drew the blood may be able to testify about preservative and anticoagulants in the blood vial. If not, the criminalist may be able to say that these substances were present, because the blood sample was not rotted or coagulated when it was analyzed some days later. The criminalist may also be able to examine the vial at trial if the presence of preservatives or anticoagulants is an issue. Such an examination should show that even months later, the sample has not spoiled or coagulated. Do not panic if a retest of the blood sample produces a blood alcohol result lower than the initial test result. The criminalist will testify that this is a common occurrence.

§A:52   The Urine Test

When a urine test is given, the sample for alcohol analysis must be taken from a second voiding of the defendant's bladder, not from the first. The delay between the two voids must be at least twenty minutes. California Administrative Code, Title 17, §1219.2(a). The sample for drug toxicology analysis may only be from the first voiding, and no waiting period or second voiding is required. If the defendant is a woman, a female officer will have observed the giving of the sample(s) and must testify to establish the chain of custody and the source of the sample, i.e., the defendant. Always make sure that the person who observed the test is subpoenaed to testify—do not assume this is the arresting officer.

§A:53   The Blood Alcohol Expert

The prosecutor should contact the criminalist or the crime lab before the trial begins to assure the expert's appearance at trial and to discuss any problems anticipated with respect to the introduction of the chemical test results. It is always helpful to the criminalist to provide him or her with a copy of the police reports so the criminalist can review the information relevant to his or her testimony. In a breath case, any criminalist involved with the laboratory's maintenance of the breath testing instruments may testify to lay the foundation for the admission of the breath results, even if he or she did not perform accuracy tests on the particular instrument used to test the defendant. In blood and urine cases, however, the criminalist who analyzed the particular sample to be introduced at trial must testify in order to lay the foundation for the admission of the blood alcohol result. See §§A:150-A:192.

[§§A:54-A:59 Reserved]

D.   Response to Discovery Motions

§A:60   Typical Defense Requests and Motions

For the majority of cases, prosecutors receive boilerplate discovery letters from the defense on DUI cases sometime after the defense has been provided with copies of the police reports. Typically, they are seeking the "lab packet," containing the lab results, any notes from the criminalist who did the work, and the maintenance records on the instrument used (in breath tests) that preceded and followed the test. Occasionally, they seek other information specific to the actual case at hand. In dealing with such motions, the following arguments may be of assistance.

§A:61   Maintenance History

The maintenance history of a particular instrument is completely irrelevant. "In general, the foundational prerequisites for admissibility of testing results are that: (1) the particular apparatus utilized was in proper working order; (2) the test used was properly administered; and (3) the operator was competent and qualified." *People v. Adams* (1976) 59 Cal. App. 3d 559, 561.

§A:62   Instructional Manuals

This may be a two-part request. First, the defense may request a manufacturer's manual. This is something that can be obtained from the manufacturer for a price. Any special manual prepared by the using agency is available only from that agency.

§A:63   Witness Rap Sheets

The defendant is entitled to information on felony convictions (or impeachable misdemeanors pursuant to *People v. Wheeler* (1992) 4 Ca.4th 284) suffered by potential prosecution witnesses. The rap sheet itself should not be turned over, particularly if it contains information about arrests or misdemeanor convictions that are not relevant.

[§§A:64-A:69 Reserved]

II.   JURY VOIR DIRE AND PROPOSED SAMPLE QUESTIONS

§A:70   Imposition of Judicial Voir Dire

The process of jury selection was radically changed with the passage of Proposition 115 on June 6, 1990, and its approval by courts in subsequent decisions. *See People v. Gilbert* (1992) 5 Cal.App.4th 1372 and *People v. Leung* (1992) 5 Cal.App.4th 482, cases in which Code of Civil Procedure §223 was found to be constitutional. Sections 190 through 236 of the Code of Civil Procedure now govern jury selection. Section 223, specifically, imposes the federal system of judicial voir dire of prospective jurors. This judicial voir dire replaces attorney questioning, except when a party makes a showing of good cause to allow attorney questioning. Good cause, however, is defined neither within the statute nor in the language of Proposition 115.

The provisions of Proposition 115 and its requirement of judicial voir dire have not been universally accepted or applied. Courts are not uniform in their implementation of judicial voir dire from county to county, or even within the same judicial district. Some judges adhere strictly to the requirement of judicial voir dire and will not ask any questions requested by the attorneys; other judges allow limited attorney voir dire for follow-up questions; and some have retained attorney voir dire. It is important for prosecutors to know their judges' preferences for voir dire, so that they are prepared to select a jury before they enter the courtroom.

§A:71   Scope of Voir Dire

Prosecutors must be aware that voir dire has also been severely limited in its scope. Prior law allowed voir dire to be used to aid in the exercise of preemptory challenges. *People v. Williams* (1981) 29 Cal. 3d 392, 402. Questions on relevant legal doctrines at issue in a case were also allowable. *Williams*; *People v. Balderas* (1985) 41 Cal.3d144. Current law (Code of Civil Procedure §223) now allows voir dire to aid only in the exercise of challenges for cause. The grounds for challenges for cause are set forth in Code of Civil Procedure §§227-229. Among those grounds are challenges for actual bias or implied bias.

§A:72   Bias

Bias is shown by the existence of a state of mind on the part of the juror that would render him or her unable to be impartial. "To find actual bias on the part of an individual juror, the court must find 'the existence of a state of mind' with reference to the case or the parties that would prevent the prospective juror from acting with entire impartiality and without prejudice to the substantial rights of either party." *People v. Sanchez* (1989) 208 Cal. App.3d 721. A juror who expresses an opinion that the type of case at issue would be too emotional and who, consequently, expresses a desire not to sit on such a case has not established an actual bias that will support a challenge for cause. *Sanchez*. However, a juror who admits to having firm opinions on issues involved in the case, if established as fact, can support a challenge for cause. *People v. Williams* (1988) 199 Cal.App. 3d 469.

§A:73   Voir Dire Questions

A prosecutor should be prepared to request some or all of the questions that follow as an aid in determining whether prospective jurors have an actual bias or an implied bias. The questions are designed to explore the backgrounds of the jurors for circumstances that might prejudice them either for or against the People in a driving under the influence case. These questions are suggestions only and the trial prosecutor should be prepared to formulate issue-specific questions for his or her case. Finally, although most judges prefer group questions versus individual questioning if the answer of a prospective juror raises doubt as to his or her impartiality, do not hesitate to request further follow-up questioning, so that you may develop the record for a challenge for cause.

The following outlines are examples of questions typically asked by the prosecutor in cases alleging driving under the influence, driving with blood alcohol level greater than .08, as well as refusal to submit to alcohol testing and "no driving" cases. Keep in mind these questions are examples that you may choose from, change to fit your style, or add to areas you see fit. Since Proposition 115, your voir dire time may be very limited (5 to 30 minutes) depending on the judge. Typically, the judge will cover basic areas with the prospective jurors. It is important to listen closely to each juror when he or she responds to both the judge's and the attorneys' questions. In evaluating the individual responses, use your common sense and follow up as appropriate.

Voir dire questioning is used to determine whether challenges for cause may be made, but it is also proper for gathering information to assist you in exercising your peremptory challenges so long as it is phrased in such a way as to meet the for cause determination mentioned previously. *People v. Williams*, 29 Cal3d 392, 402 (1981). In doing so, you should also educate the jury as to critical points in the prosecution and begin to develop your trial theme. Most importantly, you want to hear each juror speak.

Since your questioning time is limited, you will want the court to cover all the basics. Before the trial begins, submit a list of these areas to the court. If the court fails to inquire into a desired topic, request to approach the bench before the lawyers begin questioning and then ask the court to question on such topics.

These are the topics you want the court to cover:

- Occupation, marital status, number of children, city of residence, number of years in the area. (These facts should be contained in jury information sheets.)
- Previous jury experience.
- Jurors recognize/know any of the lawyers, parties, or witnesses.
- Friends or family in law enforcement or with any legal training or background.
- Any contacts with/feelings about police.

PRACTICE TIP:

Listen closely and do follow up in this area.

- Know anyone or personally been charged with a similar crime? If so, how were you treated by the system? Harbor any ill will? Have an axe to grind?
- General feelings about DUIs?
- Friends or family with connections with the liquor industry or businesses where liquor is sold?
- Do you understand that the charge is DUI, not drunk driving?

PRACTICE TIP:

This is a point you should re-emphasize in your questioning.

- Does everyone have a driver's license?
- Anyone been involved in a traffic accident where one of the drivers was apparently under the influence or affected by alcohol?
- Does anyone distrust scientific instruments?
- Have friends, family, or self been convicted of a crime, other than a minor traffic offense?
- How many drink socially? Anyone not drink?

PRACTICE TIP:

You want jurors who have some experience with alcohol.

- Would sitting as a juror create a hardship for anyone?
- Anyone have problems with vision or hearing?
- Anyone prefer not to sit on this type of case?
- Understand you cannot do experiments or visit the crime scene?
- Anyone have trouble sitting in judgment of another? (i.e., anyone have any religious or moral beliefs that would make it difficult to sit as a juror?)
- Will you follow the law?

PRACTICE TIP:

You also want the court to admonish the jury that during the trial, none of the attorneys or witnesses may interact with them. This makes the jurors understand why you will pass them in the hall without speaking.

Your voir dire will be limited so prioritize questions according to the facts of your case. If it is an accident case, look for people who feel DUIs cause harm. If it is refusal, look for people who feel you *must* cooperate with authority.

[§§A:74-A:79 Reserved]

III.   OPENING STATEMENT

A. The Prosecution's Position

§A:80   Strategy Checklist

- Opening statement is not the point in the trial where you are allowed to discuss the law in depth. However, give the jury a brief introduction to the two different counts and emphasize that although the counts are somewhat related and corroborate one another, for the most part, they are treated separately and different evidence will be presented to prove each charge.

PRACTICE TIP:

If you are calling witnesses out of order, alert the jury of that fact, and explain that one of the reasons why you get to give an opening statement is to give some order to the evidence to be presented.

- The evidence should be presented in a chronological fashion, so start at the beginning when the officer makes his/her first observations. Emphasize that this is when the People's evidence gathering commences.

PRACTICE TIP:

This is a good point to make because the defense may argue that the prosecution didn't disprove where the defendant says he/she was, or disprove how many drinks he/she said they had. First off, usually we can disprove the number of claimed drinks with the chemical test; and second, the defendant can say whatever he/she wants and the police officer will write it down. The police officer wasn't with the defendant—so what! It's not our burden to disprove these things; that doesn't mean they have to be believed either.

- Start building up your police officer's experience and training. Let the jury know his/her opinion was formed before any chemical tests were given.
- Start developing your complete picture theme. Be sure to give the defendant credit for any good things he did, like pulling over promptly and without hitting the curb, getting out his/her wallet without fumbling and so on. Emphasize how the officer didn't form an opinion until the officer gathered as much evidence as possible.
- If there are any weaknesses/problems with your case let the jurors know about them here. Better they hear it from you first.
- Begin educating the jury on the scientific evidence. You may want to use a picture of the Intoxilyzer and explain how it works. Also, you may want to explain the calculations that the criminalist will use to testify that the defendant was over .08 at the time of driving.
- On a breath case, emphasize how easy it is to operate a breath machine. Like a copy machine, once you start it up, it runs itself and in fact instructs the operator how to proceed step by step.

PRACTICE TIP:

This is to diffuse operator error inferences and arguments by defense. So when the defense starts getting into it with the operator on cross, the jury has already heard from you and the operator how automated the Intoxilyzer is.

§A:81   A and B Count

Opening argument is an opportunity to educate the jury on the law and the facts that support a conviction. Discuss the A and B count separately. Use charts to list the elements of the two counts. The charts should be provided with words large and dark enough for all jurors to read easily. The following is an example of a simple chart for each count.

Count A. 23152 (a) V.C.

1. Driving.
2. Under the influence of alcohol.

PRACTICE TIP:

It is very important to emphasize that defendant is charged with two separate counts. Make a separate chart defining "under the influence." See CALJIC 16.831.

Count B: 2315 (b) V.C.

1. Driving.
2. Blood alcohol level of .08% or more.

PRACTICE TIP:

Emphasize "no impairment required."

Prepare a chart listing the facts that support the above elements. These facts should include:
1. Quality of driving.
2. Symptoms of intoxication:
    a. Odor of alcohol.
    b. Bloodshot and water eyes.
    c. Slurred speech.
    d. Poor balance and coordination.
    e. Performance on FST.
3. Admission of drinking alcohol.
4. Officer's opinion—"Defendant driving under the influence."
5. Criminalist opinion—"Defendant driving under the influence."

[§§A:82-A:89 Reserved]

B. Preempting the Defense Arguments

§A:90   The A Count

The defense argument is that the symptoms and other facts listed on the chart are caused by something other than alcohol (e.g., mechanical or physical impairment).

In response, stress the cumulative weight of the evidence. Go through each symptom, discuss it, dwell on it, and concede that we could think of a cause other than alcohol for each symptom taken individually. Emphasize that we shouldn't base an opinion on any one thing taken separately, that you must take everything into account. And the one and only thing that each and every symptom can be caused by is alcohol. The one common denominator for every symptom is alcohol. Even the things that the defendant did correctly are consistent with being under the influence, since:

a. Alcohol affects everyone differently and every person will exhibit some symptoms but not all imaginable symptoms.
b. The defendant's BAC (.10) is such that he/she is impaired for the purpose of driving a motor vehicle but not to such a level that he/she will necessarily be "drunk."

The defense will have to discount the (a) count symptoms one at a time and you will have already emphasized over and over how the only fair judicious way to decide the (a) count is to take everything together—The Complete Picture.

§A:91   The B Count

As to the (b) count, use a chart emphasizing the following applicable points:
Breath Test Machine—Intoxilyzer 5000
1. Title 17 approved.
2. Licensed lab maintains machine.
3. Trained Operator.
4. Automated machine—practically runs itself.
5. Maintenance and calibration checks.
6. Safeguards:
    a. Mouth alcohol/negative slope detector built in.
    b. Calibration check within allowable limits and done for every test.
    c. Two sample by defendant within the allowable limits of .02 (self-authenticating results).
7. Machine fair:
    a. Correlation studies show breath tests 95% of the time underestimate true BAC by .01-.02.
8. Common sense:
    a. We've been able to put men on the moon for over 25 years; surely we can test a person's BA level with today's technology.
9. *Trombetta:*
    a. Defendant had a chance to preserve a sample of blood or urine if he/she disagreed with the breath result and he/she chose not to.
10. Inference by Law—taken within 3 hours of driving.

PRACTICE TIP:
Remember any noncompliance with Title 17 on any of these tests goes to weight and not admissibility.

11. Consistent with, corroborated by (a) count symptoms.

§A:92   Additional Points for Blood or Urine

1. Available for further testing by defendant.
2. Address chain of custody re: tampering allegations.

§A:93   Refusal

Argue the consciousness of guilt instruction and how a person who was not under the influence would demand all three tests and be righteously indignant.

[§§A:94-A:99 Reserved]

IV.   DIRECT EXAMINATION OF ARRESTING OFFICER AND OTHER PROSECUTION WITNESSES

A. Preparation for Examination of Arresting Officer

§A:100   Preparation Before Trial

Direct examination of the arresting officer is generally the key to a successful prosecution. The prosecutor must make sure that the officer comes across to the jury as both fair and accurate. By working questions precisely and advising the officer not to volunteer information while on the witness stand (to either the prosecutor or defense counsel), the testimony should meet these goals.

It is very important to review all the facts with the officer before trial, beginning with the first observations through the entire arrest sequence. The prosecutor should make certain that the officer can identify the defendant and discuss the facts of DUI evaluation information with the officer. If the officer prepares any exhibits, or has photographs or tapes, the prosecutor must show them to defense counsel before the trial begins, as part of the discovery. Some courts want exhibits to be pre-marked. If this is the case, the exhibits should be marked before the jury enters the courtroom.

The direct examination of the arresting officer should begin with laying a foundation by going over the officer's training and experience in investigating DUI offenses. These foundational questions, which ultimately lead to the officer's opinion that the defendant was under the influence, should cover the officer's background in observing driving, signs of intoxication and use of the field sobriety tests (FSTs). In refusal cases, in which no criminalist will testify about an alcohol test result, the officer's qualifications are especially important.

If the prosecutor discovers there are mistakes in the officer's report, he or she may want to bring them out in direct to draw out the sting. However, the mistakes may be so minor that they could be ignored. If the problems are raised, the jury may infer that the prosecution is not covering facts for the officer but rather is presenting all of the facts. For example, the officer could tell the jury that he or she had a long shift and mistakenly wrote the wrong date, instead of having a defense attorney question the officer's mental acuity.

§A:101   Checklist for Preparing Officer to Testify

Here is a list of things you should make sure to go over with the arresting officer prior to trial:
- Talk to the officer before trial and go over his/her reports and testimony with him/her.

PRACTICE TIP:

Try to get him/her to go by the scene before testifying and try to go there yourself. The defense will invariably make an issue out of something at the scene.

- Go over any problems or contradictions with him/her and prepare him/her to explain them.
- If the officer testifies to facts not found in his/her report, have him/her prepared to explain to the jury why they are not present. Most officers will tell you that the report is used to detail elements of the crime and to refresh their memory for trial.

PRACTICE TIP:

Good place here to let the jury know that the report is not a piece of evidence.

- Advise the officer to look at the jury while testifying.
- Have the officer prepare diagrams for trial.
- Prepare the officer for the facts you want him/her to demonstrate for the jury, for example, how the defendant was instructed to do FSTs.
- Show all diagrams and exhibits you plan to use in trial to defense counsel beforehand.

PRACTICE TIP:

Try and have all exhibits marked by the court clerk beforehand.

- Prepare the officer to give defendant credit for good things he/she did and to maintain a "Joe Friday, cop-just-doing-his job" demeanor.
- Have the officer read the report a couple of times to cut down the number of times while testifying that the officer will have to refresh his/her memory. However, remind the officer that it is okay not to remember everything and not to guess at an answer but ask to refer to his/her report.
- Remind the officer to readily admit that you went over the officer's testimony with him/her or that you talked before trial. The defense attorney will ask whether you two talked and he will do it in an insinuating tone of voice.

§A:102 Checklist for Questioning Officer at Trial

In addition to the facts of the case, a quick checklist follows of things you must be sure to cover each time you question an officer in a DUI case:

- Foundation (name/occupation/training/experience);
- Jurisdiction (county);
- Identification of the defendant as the driver;
- Officer's opinion that defendant was under the influence for purposes of driving; and
- Chemical test foundation if blood, breath or urine test, and test result if breath test, or Vehicle Code section 13353 form advisement for a refusal.

[§§A:103-A:109 Reserved]

B. Sample Direct Examination Questions for Arresting Officer

The sample questions are set forth below. Remember, not all questions apply to every case.

PRACTICE TIP:

Go over the questions with your officer beforehand. It will make his/her testimony go smoother and help avoid some embarrassing moments.

§A:110 General Background

Q: Good morning officer, please state your full name and spell your last name for the record.
Q: What is your occupation and assignment?
Q: What are your job duties?
A: (E.g., protect the peace, enforce traffic laws and the penal code, and assist citizens who need help.)
Q: How long have you been a police officer?
Q: Before becoming a police officer, did you attend an academy?
Q: In that academy, did you receive training regarding investigation of driving under the influence offenses?
Q: Please describe that training.

COMMENT:

Typically, the officer will merely name the classes and number of hours of training, and generically describe the content as something like "recognition of symptoms commonly associated with alcohol impairment." The officer should relate training in the signs or symptoms commonly exhibited by persons under the influence of alcohol. If this is a drug or combination of drugs and alcohol case, be sure to cover training in the signs of intoxication of the particular drug. Again the defendant's signs of intoxication should be included in what the officer has been trained to observe, e.g., bloodshot and/or watery eyes, odor of alcoholic beverage emanating from breath, slow or slurred speech, staggering gait, holding onto vehicle for support, and so forth.

The officer should describe training in administering and evaluating performance on FSTs, pre-demonstrated and pre-explained simple balance and coordination tests designed to detect the types of impairment caused by alcohol. Draw out specific symptoms he/she has trained to look for with follow up questions such as:

Q: Were you trained to look for things about a person's general appearance that might indicate alcohol consumption or impairment?

COMMENT:

The officer should describe things like bloodshot, watery eyes, odor of alcohol, slurred speech, and disheveled appearance.

Q: Were you trained to look for certain physical problems like balance or reflexes or motor control?
Q: Were you trained to administer field sobriety tests (FSTs)?

APPENDIX A: DA'S MANUAL

Q: What are FSTs? What are they used for?

COMMENT:

The officer should indicate that they are a tool to test a person's balance and coordination.

Q: Did you receive additional training in dui investigations after your initial academy training?

COMMENT:

Once again the officer will probably go through a list of classes and in service, roll call updates, and refresher courses. Flesh these out with questions like:

Q: When you first went out into the field, did you ride with experienced officers?
Q: Did you receive in-field DUI training from these experienced officers?
Q: Can you describe what type of training regarding dui investigation you have received?
Q: The refresher courses you've attended, where were they held and who taught them?

PRACTICE TIP:

If the officer has received any commendations or awards, or was a part of any special task force relating to DUIs, ask him/her about it.

Q: Approximately how many DUI investigations have you conducted or participated in?
Q: As a result of these _____ investigations, how many arrests were made for DUI?

COMMENT:

The number of arrests is usually 50%-70% of the number of investigations. This helps show the jury that the officer is fair and knows what he is doing.

PRACTICE TIP:

Occasionally an objection to this question is sustained. If that happens, simply ask the officer, "Do you arrest everyone you investigate for DUI?"

§A:111   The Stop

Q: Were you on duty as a _____ (police officer/sheriff/CHP) on _____ (date), at approximately _____ am/pm (time)?
Q: Were you in a marked police car?
Q: What was your assignment?
Q: Were you alone or with a partner?
Q: Were you in uniform?
Q: At approximately (time of observation), what was your location?
Q: Is that in the county of _____?
Q: Did a particular vehicle attract your attention?
Q: Describe the vehicle.
Q: Why did it attract your attention?

COMMENT:

The officer will relate a pattern of driving or a vehicle code violation.

Q: Have you prepared a diagram of the area where the driving took place?

COMMENT:

Have the diagram marked as People's One. If the stop was for an equipment violation or not due to bad driving, you probably don't want to use a diagram.

Q: Did you prepare this diagram for your testimony in court here today?
Q: Does the diagram fairly represent the locations depicted as they appeared on date of accident?
Q: Is the diagram to scale?
Q: Describe the diagram for us.
Q: With a black marker, note on the diagram with a "p" where your vehicle was when you first observed the other vehicle.

PRACTICE TIP:
Bring markers and chart paper to court with you. The court doesn't always have them.

Q: With a red marker please mark with a "d" where the other vehicle was when you first saw it.
Q: Now officer, please describe the driving you witnessed, and as you do, take the red marker and diagram the driving pattern of the defendant's vehicle.

COMMENT:
Develop the entire driving and parking sequence while filling in all the relevant details regarding: vehicle speeds; distance traveled; distance between vehicles; traffic conditions; road and weather conditions; type of area (residential vs. commercial); timing and manner of defendant's response including how far from curb vehicle stopped; describe the lighting of the area, especially where stopped.

The diagram should be offered into evidence with all the other exhibits at the conclusion of the People's case, just before resting.

Q: Identify where you stopped the vehicle.
Q: Why did you stop it?

COMMENT:
The officer may have suspected a DUI driver or it may have been only a Vehicle Code violation. You may want to have the officer cite any Vehicle Code section violated. Any suppression motion should have been handled pre-trial, but People v. Uribe (1993) 12 Cal.App.4th 1432, states that with any Vehicle Code violation, an officer may stop the vehicle and detain.

Q: How did the vehicle pull to the side of the road?

COMMENT:
Ask for greater detail if the driver had some difficulty pulling over.

§A:112   First Contact With Defendant

Q: Did you have any opinion as to the condition of the driver at this point?

COMMENT:
The answer should be no—a suspicion maybe, due to time of night and type of driving, but not an opinion.

Q: Did you make contact with the driver? How?
Q: Do you see the driver of that vehicle in court here today?
Q: Could you identify him/her for the jury please?

Your Honor, may the record reflect that the witness has identified the defendant.

Q: Was there anyone else in the car? (If yes) How many and where were they seated?

PRACTICE TIP:
If passengers were present and may testify, try and get officer to describe their conditions if they were drinking.

Q: Did you speak with the defendant/driver/Mr./Mrs._____ ?

PRACTICE TIP:

Your style and how the defendant appears will dictate how you refer to him or her. Typically a DUI defendant looks like an average citizen and you may not want to use the "defendant" moniker.

Q: While speaking with the defendant, did you notice anything unusual?

COMMENT:

Typically the officer's response will be that he/she smelled an odor of alcohol. Go through all the symptoms the officer noted at that first contact while defendant was in the car as well as typical symptoms that defendant didn't exhibit. If you don't, the defendant's attorney most assuredly will. Not all people exhibit all the possible symptoms. Alcohol affects everyone differently.

Q: Did you notice anything unusual about his/her eyes?

PRACTICE TIP:

Depending on the police department's DUI form, the officer just checks a box. For eyes, the descriptions are usually red, watery, bloodshot, or glassy. If the defense attorney makes a big deal out of the choice of words, emphasize through the officer that he/she uses the same pre-printed form for all DUI investigations and merely checks the appropriate box.

Q: How about his/her face?

COMMENT:

Flushed is usually the description.

Q: Did you notice anything unusual about defendant's speech?

COMMENT:

Slow, thick, slurred are the usual responses.

Q: Did you inform the defendant as to why you stopped him?
Q: What was the defendant's response (if any)?

COMMENT:

All statements elicited from the defendant up until the arrest are considered investigatory and are admissible under Berkemer v. McCarty 468 U.S. 420, 82 L.ED.2d 317, 104 Sup.Ct. 3138 (1984).

Q: Did you ask the defendant to provide you with a driver's license and registration?
Q: Did the defendant comply?

COMMENT:

If the defendant did comply this question may be skipped.

Q: Did you ask the defendant to step out of his/her vehicle and come to the side of the road?

COMMENT:

This is permitted by People v. Beal (1974) 44 Cal.App.3d 216, 220. Have the officer describe how the defendant got out of his/her car: e.g., stumbled when walking or getting out of the car; leaned on car for support; walked away from car; slow to respond to verbal commands.

Q: Was there anything unusual you noted about the defendant's appearance?

COMMENT:

The officer has probably already stated the following symptoms of alcohol intoxication. If not, have the officer relate what he observed: red/watery eyes; slurred speech; stupor/glazed look; alcohol on breath.

Q: Did you ask the defendant if he/she had been drinking?

COMMENT:

If the defense raises a Miranda objection, see below.

Q: What was the defendant's response?
Q: Did the defendant tell you how many drinks he/she had consumed?

COMMENT:

This is very important for the expert's testimony later in your case.

Q: Did you ask the defendant any other questions related to your investigation of whether or not the defendant was driving under the influence?

COMMENT:

This covers the standard investigative questions. Did the defendant feel the effects of the alcohol; how many total drinks were consumed; was the defendant under a doctor's care or taking any medication; what was the time of the last drink; what was the time of last meal; where was the defendant going to/coming from.

Officers normally ask the above questions before administering the FSTs. If the officer forgets during testimony, ask if he inquired into the above areas. These questions are permissible pursuant to *Berkemer v. McCarty*, (1984) 468 U.S. 420, 435-442; *People v. Carter* (1980) 108 Cal. App.3d 127.

Q: Did you record the defendant's weight on your report?

COMMENT:

This information is necessary for your expert to correctly calculate the defendant's blood alcohol level at the time of driving.

Q: What was the defendant's weight?

§A:113   FSTs

Q: What did you do next?

COMMENT:

The officer will indicate at this point, he had the defendant step out of his/her vehicle and walk to the side of the road to do FSTs. Administration of FSTs does not violate any constitutional protection. Whelen v. Municipal Court (1969) 274 Cal.App.2d 809; People v. Bennett (1938) 139 Cal.App.3d 767.

Videotape of a defendant's statements during FSTs are allowed. *See Pennsylvania v. Muniz* (1990) 496 U.S. 582, 602-603.

Q: What are field sobriety tests?
Q: Were you given training in how to conduct field sobriety tests?
Q: How many times have you had people perform FSTs for you?
Q: Where were you and the defendant standing when you asked the defendant to perform the FSTs?
Q: Did you explain the purpose of FSTs to the defendant?

COMMENT:

Commonly, officers will explain to suspects what FSTs are and give them some general instructions. It is important for the jury to hear this because often defendants will not follow directions.

Q: Why did you have defendant perform FSTs?

Q: Did you watch the defendant exit his/her vehicle?

Q: Did defendant have any difficulty? (If so….) Please describe (e.g., used door and side of car for assistance, stumbled, almost fell out, etc.).

Q: Did you direct defendant to a particular location to administer the FSTs?

Q: Did you observe defendant walk to that area?

Q: Did you notice anything unusual about how the defendant walked to that area? (If so…) Please describe (e.g., staggered, stumbled, used side of car for balance, etc.).

PRACTICE TIP:

There is usually a box in police reports for describing the manner of "walking," other than during the FSTs (which have their own boxes). This is the only "walking" the officer will observe, so you want it clear that the staggering or stumbling that is referred to occurred during this walking and is not the same as that which may or may not have occurred during the FSTs.

Q: Describe the area where you conducted the FSTs.

COMMENT:

The officer should address lighting and surface area.

Q: Mark on the diagram with an "x" where this area was in location to the vehicle(s).

PRACTICE TIP:

This may be important if defendant has a passenger he/she calls to testify regarding the performance on the FSTs.

Q: Describe for us how the defendant was standing.

PRACTICE TIP:

The officer may note some sway while standing not associated with an FST. This is where that observation typically comes in.

Q: Did you explain to the defendant why you were having him/her step over to the sidewalk?

PRACTICE TIP:

This may be important if defendant made some incriminating response.

Q: Prior to giving the FSTs did you ask the defendant some questions?

Q: Is that a standard set of questions that you ask all persons that you are investigating for DUI?

COMMENT:

Go through each and every question and response. Don't just select the ones that help your case. Remember, you are just laying out all the facts. You are fair. The most important responses are drinking pattern, any claimed car problems or physical defects, any admissions of feeling the effects of alcohol, and disorientation with regards to location and time.

Q: Did you also put in your report the defendant's height and weight? And what were those?

PRACTICE TIP:

You need the weight for the criminalist.

Q: Was the defendant cooperative?

Q: Did you form an opinion at this point as to whether or not the defendant was under the influence of alcohol?

COMMENT:

The answer should still be no, unless the defendant was falling down drunk. The idea being, the officer shouldn't jump to any conclusions, but be fair and wait until he has gathered all the evidence available.

Q: Did you then ask the defendant to perform some FSTs?

Q: Did you notice what kind of footwear the defendant had on?

COMMENT:

If it was boots or high heels, the officer will usually request that the defendant take them off.

Q: What was the first FST you asked him/her to perform?

COMMENT:

Typically it will be the MPA—modified position of attention.

Q: Did you demonstrate and instruct the defendant how to do this test before you asked him/her to do it?

Q: Could you please demonstrate for the jury exactly how you demonstrated for the defendant?

PRACTICE TIP:

You want the jury to see that the officer can do this by rote. This may become important later, when the defendant contends that the officer failed to instruct on certain parts of the test, as an excuse for his/her poor performance. Also, ask the officer how he physically held a flashlight, demonstrated the test, and took notes; and what became of those notes. A jury will wonder about these things.

Q: Did the defendant attempt the test before you finished instructing?

Q: Was the defendant told not to start the test before you finished instructing or told him/her to begin?

Q: Is ability to follow instructions one of the things you look for when administering these tests?

Q: Did the defendant attempt his/her FST?

Q: Could you describe his/her performance?

COMMENT:

Typically the defendant will have some sway on these tests. This is the point in questioning on each of the FSTs that you should go through and point out the bad and the good aspects of the defendant's performance, and then ask for the officer's evaluation of that performance. If you don't bring out the good things the defendant did, the defense attorney most assuredly will and you and your police officer will lose credibility with the jury. Plus, by doing this, you completely take the wind out of the defense attorney's sails.

PRACTICE TIP:

If the defense attorney asks the officer to demonstrate how the defendant performed, this is objectionable as the officer's acting ability is not in issue.

§A:114   Modified Position of Attention Test

Here is an example of how some specific follow-up questions and answers for the Modified Position of Attention Test could work.

Q: Officer, did the defendant put his/her feet together and his/her arms at his/her side as you instructed him/her to?

A: Yes.

Q: And officer, did he/she tilt his/her head back and close his/her eyes as you instructed him/her to?

A: Yes he/she did.

Q: And officer, did the defendant maintain that position for approximately 30 seconds as you had instructed him/her to?

A: [Yes or no, depending on performance.]
Q: Officer, you indicated the defendant had some sway on this test. could you elaborate?
A: He/she swayed two to three inches from side to side.

PRACTICE TIP:

On the two to three inches of sway, ask your officer beforehand if that is one and one-half inch from center or two to three inches from center, and ask what he used as a point of reference for center. You will typically find that the two to three inches is from center, and many times, the officer used a telephone or light pole behind the defendant as a point of reference. If so, bring all that out.

Q: Officer, overall how would you evaluate the defendant's performance on the particular test?
A: Well, in my opinion, it was unsatisfactory.
Q: And why is that?
A: I base that opinion on the sway. Overall the defendant didn't do too badly, except for the sway.

PRACTICE TIP:

Draw out of the officer, that this particular test is used primarily to see how much sway there is.

Q: Officer, based on the driving, the objective symptoms you observed, and the defendant's performance on this test, did you form an opinion regarding the defendant's condition?
A: No, I hadn't.
Q: Why not?
A: Because I base my opinion on everything and had yet to see how he performed on the other tests.
Q: Did you have the defendant perform another FST?
Q: What test was that?
Q: Did you demonstrate and instruct the defendant as to that test?
Q: Could you once again, officer, demonstrate that test for the jury as you did for the defendant on date?
Q: Did he/she appear to understand the instructions?
Q: Did he/she attempt to perform that test?

COMMENT:

Go through each FST with the police officer emphasizing the poor aspects of defendant's performance and conceding the things the defendant did properly.

§A:115   Post-FST Questions

Q: During the FSTs, did the defendant ever complain of physical defects or injuries?
Q: Did you observe any physical defects or injuries?
Q: (If yes) Did you take them into account in evaluating the defendant's performance?
Q: Did you form an opinion as to the defendant's condition?
Q: What was that opinion?
A: The defendant was under the influence for purposes of driving a motor vehicle.
Q: When did you form that opinion?
A: At the end of all of the testing.
Q: What did you base that opinion on?
A: Everything. The totality of the circumstances. Driving, symptoms, performance on FSTs, along with training and experience.
Q: Did you base that opinion on any one single factor?
A: No, on the totality of all observations.
Q: Do you take nervousness into account when evaluating FST performances?
A: Yes.
Q: What did you do next?
A: Placed the defendant under arrest.

PRACTICE TIP:

At this point, go through, in chronological order, what happened after the defendant was placed under arrest, including any spontaneous statements the defendant made on the ride to the station, the reading of the chemical admonition, the selection (or refusal) of a chemical test, and the administration of the test (if given). If the officer had the car moved for the defendant to a place where it wouldn't get towed, solicit that evidence, as well as what was the condition of any passengers and what became of them. Furthermore, if there were any back-up officers present, have the arresting officer downplay that officer's involvement in the arrest, since he/she wouldn't have generated a report, and typically won't remember much about arrest, and if called would be used by defense to contradict your arresting officer. Try to get in touch with any back-ups and question them beforehand, especially in refusals.

§A:116   Chemical Test Admonition

Q: Did you explain to the defendant the requirement to take a blood alcohol test?
Q: Did you tell the defendant he/she had a choice of tests?
Q: What choices were given to him/her?
Q: How did you give the defendant the choices?

COMMENT:

The officer should indicate that he read (or from memory) gave the defendant the admonition. If he read it, approach with a copy of the admonition and have him read it. If he gave the admonition from memory, have him explain to the jury how he gave it.

Q: Did the defendant appear to understand what he/she was being told?
Q: Did the defendant choose a test?
Q: What test did he/she choose?
Q: What did he/she say to indicate he/she wanted a _____ test?

§A:117   Refusal Admonition

Q: Officer, you indicated the defendant would not choose a chemical test. What exactly did he/she say to indicate this?
Q: Can you describe the tone of voice he/she used in refusing?
Q: Is there another admonition that you actually read to people refusing chemical tests?
A: Yes.
Q: Did you read that admonition for the defendant?
Q: Could you read the admonition for the jury please, as you read it to the defendant?

COMMENT:

The refusal admonition must be read in court to get in all the elements required in the jury instruction.

PRACTICE TIP:

Before trial, do a dry run with the officer. Sometimes the officer's reading in court is so disjointed that you may lose the refusal allegation because of the way it is read, i.e., it was not clear to the defendant.

Q: After reading the admonition, did the defendant indicate in any way that he did not understand what you had just read to him/her?
Q: Did he/she then indicate whether he/she would be willing to take a test?
Q: What was that response?
Q: Did anyone else advise the defendant of the requirement that he/she take a chemical test?
Q: What was the defendant's response to that second advisement?
Q: did the fact that a blood alcohol test was never taken of the defendant due to his/her refusal in any way affect the opinion you formed regarding his/her condition?

§A:118　Breath Test

General

Q: Where did you take the defendant to administer the breath test?

COMMENT:

Beforehand, ask the officer if he/she left the pac set/walkie talkie outside of the breath room. If he/she didn't don't ask about it in court. The reason to ask this is that the defense may try to suggest that electronic interference affected the machine.

Q: Who administered the breath test?

COMMENT:

If the officer did, then continue questions with him/her. If someone else administered the test, but the officer did the 15-minute observation period, go through the observation period questions with the officer. If the arresting officer did not administer the test but gave the Trombetta Advisement after the test, be sure to get that into evidence before he/she gets off the stand.

Q: What machine was used to administer the breath test?

Operator Training

Q: Have you received training in the operation of the Intoxilyzer 5000?
Q: Where did you receive this training?

COMMENT:

The next six questions are leading but should be allowed as foundation, if not, ask the operator to describe the training received.

Q: Did your training include the theory of operation of the Intoxilyzer 5000?
Q: Did your training include learning all about the mechanical and electrical components that make up the machine and how they function?

COMMENT:

The answers to the two preceding questions will be no. You want it made clear that the operators are not experts in how the machine functions. They are like key operators for copier machines.

Q: Did you receive any practical experience in operating the Intoxilyzer during your training?
Q: Could you briefly describe for the jury how you administer the breath test?

COMMENT:

Optional question. Good to ask if you have a picture of the Intoxilyzer.

Trombetta Advisement

COMMENT:

The next two questions are to be asked of the officer that gave the Trombetta Advisement (if one was given) that the machine does not retain a sample for retesting, but the defendant may choose to give a blood or urine sample for further testing. The failure to give such an advisement pursuant to VC §23157.5 (formerly §13353.5) does not affect the admissibility of the blood alcohol result. VC23157.5(d), *People v. Mills* (1985) 164 Cal.App.3d 652, 657; *People v. Lyon* (1985) 171 Cal.App.3d Supp. 20, 23.; *People v. Trombetta* (1985) 173 Cal.App.3d 1093, 1104; *People v. Alvarado* (1986) 181 Cal.App.3d Supp. 1, 4.

APPENDIX A: DA'S MANUAL

Q: Was the defendant made aware of his/her test results? or was the defendant made aware that his/her test results were over .08?

Q: Does the breath machine retain samples that can be retested?

Q: Was the defendant advised of that fact?

Q: What was the advisement he/she was given?

Q: Was the defendant advised that he/she could take a blood or urine test to preserve for testing?

PRACTICE TIP:

If advisement was not given, you may want to take the sting out of it now by asking the officer why it wasn't given if you think the defense may get into it. Or just prepare your officer to be ready to provide whatever reason he has for not giving it.

§A:119   Blood Tests

COMMENT:

The following are sample questions asked of the arresting officer who will also have watched the blood draw as well as the technician who actually drew the blood. If the technician is not available you can still get the blood and test results into evidence if the police officer can remember some details about the draw, or through a declaration from the technician pursuant to Evidence Code section 721.

PRACTICE TIP:

Have your police officer pick up the blood vial from the crime lab and bring it to court with him/her. Call the lab so they will have it ready at the front desk so the officer doesn't have to wait.

Q: Did you take the defendant to obtain a blood sample?

Q: Where?

Q: Did you observe the defendant sign any papers relating to the taking of the blood sample?

Q: Who else signed them?

Q: Was the blood taken in your presence?

Q: From what area of the defendant's body was the blood sample drawn?

Q: Who did the actual blood draw?

PRACTICE TIP:

The next 11 questions must be asked of the officer if the technician/nurse will not testify. The officer must have independent recollections of the draw, specifically that the solution applied to defendant's arm didn't have an alcohol smell and white powder was in the vial. If not and he's challenged on these points, a judge may keep the blood and results out of evidence for lack of evidence that the blood was drawn in a medically-approved manner (even though that lack should only go to weight and not admissibility.) If this happens, as to the white powder being present:

a. Get the blood technician/nurse/supervisor in to testify as to the technician's/nurse's training re: blood draws.

b. Get a criminalist from the crime lab to look at the condition of the blood and testify that the powder must have been present or the blood would have coagulated; and/or

c. Get a criminalist (preferably the one who prepared the vial) to testify how the vials are prepared.

As to the solution used:

a. Try to get the technician's/nurse's supervisor to testify to the solution that the technician/nurse is equipped with; and/or

b. Get a criminalist to testify as to how the testing results help indicate the absence of a contaminant or alcohol-type solution.

Q: Did the technician/nurse clean the defendant's arm with something?

Q: Do you know what solution was used?

Q: Did you smell the odor of alcohol from that solution?

APPENDIX A:
DA'S MANUAL

A: No.
Q: Did you observe the blood actually being drawn?
Q: Have you seen blood drawn before?
Q: Anything unusual about this blood draw?
Q: What did the technician/nurse do with the blood after it was drawn?
Q: Did you observe the vial, before the blood was placed into it or when it was empty?
Q: Did the empty vial contain anything?
A: Yes, a white powdery substance.
Q: Do you know what that white powdery substance was?

COMMENT:
The officer is not required to know what the substance is, so long as it was present.

Q: Did you make any identifying marks on the vial?

COMMENT:
End of questions required if technician/nurse will not testify.

Q: What time was it when the sample was taken?
Q: Were there any identifying marks of the defendant put on the vial?
A: Yes, a thumbprint and his name.
Q: After the sample was taken from the defendant, what happened to the vial?
A: It was put in an envelope and sealed.
Q: Did you mark the envelope in any manner?
Q: How did you mark it?

COMMENT:
Get the full description and have him/her look at it in court and point out the markings.

Q: What was done with the envelope?

COMMENT:
Booked into property, or taken by the technician/nurse.

Q: Did you bring that envelope to court with you today?
Q: To the court: Your Honor, I have in my hand an envelope labeled _____, which has been shown to defense counsel. May this be marked as people's ____ for identification? May I approach the witness?
Q: Officer, I'm showing you an envelope marked as people's ____. do you recognize it?
Q: How do you recognize it?

COMMENT:
He/she will identify it by the marking on the envelope and the vial inside.

Q: Where did you obtain this envelope before coming to court today?
Q: Is the envelope in the same condition as when you last saw it/or booked it into property?

COMMENT:
The answer will be no. Have the officer describe the different condition, usually new seals and additional markings from the crime lab.

§A:120   Urine Test

Q: Did you take the defendant somewhere to give him/her a urine test?
Q: As part of the procedures, was the defendant's bladder voided prior to giving a sample?

Q: Where did this occur?
Q: How do you know?
Q: After the initial voiding, how much time elapsed until the sample was obtained?
Q: Did you give the defendant a container for the sample?
Q: Where did you get this container?
Q: Was the container sealed when you got it?
Q: Did you break the seal?
Q: Did you notice anything inside the container? What?

COMMENT:

Check with officer before asking this question; there should have been a preservative, usually in the form of a crystal chip or powder, in the container.

Q: Did you watch the defendant urinate into the container?
Q: Why did you watch?
A: To ensure no dilution or substitution of the sample.
Q: After the defendant gave a sample, did you seal the container?
Q: Did you mark the container in some manner? How?
Q: What did you then do with the container?
A: Booked it into property.
Q: Did you bring that container with you to court today?
Q: To the Court: Your Honor, I have in my hand (describe the container or envelope if it was placed into an envelope.) which has been shown to the defense attorney. May this item _____ be marked as people's ___ for identification. May I approach the witness?
Q: Officer, I am showing you people's ___. Do you recognize it?
Q: How do you recognize it?
Q: Where did you obtain this item before coming to court today?

[§§A:121-A:129 Reserved]

C. Cross-Examination and Redirect Examination of Officer

§A:130 Cross-Examination of the Officer

Explain the expected areas of cross-examination to the officer in your witness interview. Many defense attorneys follow questions suggested in Erwin's Defense of Drunk Driving Cases (3rd ed. 1975). Relate how many areas raised on cross-examination can be dealt with on redirect by you.

§A:131 Demonstration of FSTs by Officer

If the defense asks the officer to demonstrate FSTs, you should object. If the court allows it, insist that the demonstration be performed in the manner demonstrated to the defendant at the time of arrest. Anything beyond that is clearly not relevant. If the defense asks the officer to perform FSTs the way the defendant did, object and state that the officer's acting ability, specifically the ability to act like a person under the influence, is not relevant.

§A:132 Was the Defendant 647(f) (Drunk in Public) or Other Arrestable Offense?

Whether the defendant was 647(f), is clearly not relevant. DUI does not require that the defendant be drunk. If defendant was "647(f)," do not object; let the officer answer the question.

§A:133 Redirect Examination

If the defense brings out that a person who is not DUI can also fail particular field sobriety tests, point out that is the reason why more than one FST is given.

If the defense has brought out that not all the facts testified to by an officer are contained in his/her police report, the officer should be given the opportunity to explain the purpose of writing reports, i.e., to record enough information so that he/she can recall the complete incident when he/she revises the report months later.

If the defense has brought out that the officer cannot remember anything about the arrests before or after this defendant, ask questions allowing the officer to explain how he/she has not reviewed the arrest reports of those persons which would refresh his/her recollection, as has been done in this case.

Conclude your redirect examination by asking:

Q: Officer, is there anything about any of your answers to the questions on cross-examination that affect your opinion as to the defendant's condition?

A: No my opinion still is that he/she was under the influence and unable to safely drive an automobile.

[§§A:134-A:139 Reserved]

D. Questions for Other Prosecution Witnesses

§A:140   Breath Machine Operator Questions

(In some jurisdictions this is the officer, in some there is a separate breath technician. These questions, or similar ones, should be what you would see in either case.)

Q: Are you familiar with the Intoxilyzer model 5000?

Q: What is an Intoxilyzer 5000?

Q: Is this instrument approved by the Federal Department of Transportation?

Q: Is this instrument approved for use by the state of California under Title 17 of the administrative code?

Q: What is Title 17?

Q: Please describe your training with the Intoxilyzer 5000.

Q: Please explain how an Intoxilyzer measures a breath sample for alcohol content.

Q: What steps are taken to insure that the Intoxilyzer is operated properly to produce acceptable results?

COMMENT:

Give criminalist the breath test checklist and breath test card.

Q: Showing you what is marked People's _____ for identification, is this an Intoxilyzer checklist?

Q: Referring to this checklist, what is the serial number of the instrument that was used?

Q: What is the purpose of the 15-minute waiting period prior to the subject giving a sample?

A: To insure against mouth alcohol.

PRACTICE TIP:

If there was some problem(s) with the observation period, ask about the other safeguards for mouth alcohol.

Q: What is the purpose of the air blanks?

Q: What is the purpose of the duplicate breath results?

Q: What is the purpose of the blank breath?

Q: What is the purpose of the simulator test/calibration check?

Q: Referring to the checklist, what was the actual result of the simulator solution as determined by the Intoxilyzer?

Q: Based on the checklist, what was the concentration of the simulator solution used?

Q: Do these results agree within the accepted range permitted by Title 17?

Q: Based upon the checklist, the print card, the activity log, and the accuracy records before you, do you have an opinion as to whether this Intoxilyzer was working properly at the time of the tests?

Q: What is that opinion?

Q: Referring to the checklist, what was the result of the first breath sample?

Q: Referring to the checklist, what was the result of the second breath sample?

Q: What is the acceptable range for a subject's duplicate breath tests?

Q: Are these within the acceptable range?
Q: [Optional] Do you know how many people a year are tested in Orange County with Intoxilyzer 5000 machines?
A: 7,000-10,000.

COMMENT:

This is a good question to ask when the integrity of the machine is being attacked.

§A:141   Blood Technician/Nurse Questions

Q: On _____, what was your occupation?
Q: By whom are you employed?
Q: Can you please give me your educational background?
Q: Are you licensed by the state?
Q: Can you please tell the jury what a blood alcohol kit is?
A: Each kit consists of an envelope, a vial containing a white powder and a label.
Q: Did you use a kit when you drew the defendant's blood?
A: Yes.
Q: Where did you get this kit?
A: It was in some approved storage area.
Q: Was it in a sealed condition when you got it?
A: Yes.
Q: Who has access to these kits?
Q: Was there a white powder in the vial?
A: Yes, it is zepherine chloride, a preservative.

COMMENT:

The technician probably is qualified only to testify to the presence of a white powder but not what the white powder is.

Q: To your knowledge, who prepares these kits?
A: The Orange County Crime Lab. The criminalists have access to records of kit preparation. The technician/nurse does not have access to these records.
Q: Do you remember the defendant?

COMMENT:

Usually the answer is no. It is not necessary for the technician/nurse to identify the defendant because the officer has already testified that he/she saw the defendant's blood go into the vial. The officer has also testified that he/she marked the vial and can identify it.

Q: Why don't you remember the defendant?
A: Because I draw so many samples every week.
Q: Then how do you know this is the defendant's blood vial?
A: By my initials/signature on the vial label and the envelope. The officer was present the entire time.
Q: Do you always follow the same steps every time?
A: Yes, I always follow the same steps in drawing the blood, marking the vial and envelope, etc.
Q: Do you always process defendants one at a time?
A: Yes, I never interrupt one withdrawal to begin another one or anything like that.
Q: What steps did you follow when you withdrew the defendant's blood?
A: I followed the steps on the envelope.

COMMENT:

Have the technician go through steps.

Q: Who was present?

A: Myself, the defendant and the officer.

Q: Did you take any precautions in order to prevent any contaminants from getting on the needle, on the defendant's arm or in the vial?

A: Yes, including swabbing the defendant's arm with a non-alcoholic solution.

Q: What time did you withdraw the blood?

Q: Did you place the defendant's fingerprints on the label?

Q: Were the vial and envelope marked and sealed?

Q: What happened next with the vial and envelope?

COMMENT:

The technician/nurse may have retained them and placed them in a locker at a later time, the technician/nurse may have given them to the officer, or the technician may have immediately deposited them in an appropriate receptacle.

Q: When and where did you see it before?

COMMENT:

Dates and times can be determined from labels on vial.

Q: Was the vial opened or sealed when you first observed it?

COMMENT:

If the answer is "opened," you may want to lay a foundation as to the "general laboratory procedure" in processing blood samples for forensic alcohol analysis.

Q: Was the blood alcohol kit prepared by your laboratory?

Q: Is the method of preparation of this kit included in your method approved by the state of California under Title 17?

Q: How are these kits prepared?

Q: What is the purpose of the white powder placed in the vial?

Q: Did this blood sample appear to be clotted or coagulated at the time of your analysis?

Q: How do you know it was/wasn't coagulated?

Q: What method did you use to determine the alcohol content of this blood sample?

Q: Is this method approved by the state of California under Title 17 for forensic alcohol analysis?

Q: Briefly explain this method.

Q: How do you insure the accuracy of this method in determining a blood alcohol level?

Q: Does your laboratory also participate in alcohol proficiency testing programs?

Q: Please describe these programs.

COMMENT:

This is where the state sends blood samples to the lab with known BA values for quality control testing.

Q: Did you analyze this blood sample for alcohol content?

Q: What was the alcohol level you determined?

COMMENT:

Place blood alcohol kit (vial and envelope) into evidence at this time.

[§§A:142-A:149 Reserved]

APPENDIX A:
DA'S MANUAL

V. EXAMINATION OF THE PROSECUTION'S ALCOHOL EXPERT

A. Introduction

§A:150 Goals for Direct Examination of Criminalist

Most often, the success of a DUI trial depends on the strength of the scientific evidence of impairment. Commonly the defense will rely upon challenging either (1) the reliability of the measurement of alcohol by the particular instrument; or (2) delayed absorption, also known as "last gulp," explained further below. The People's witness is usually a criminalist, employed by the Department of Justice or the county crime lab. Occasionally, the criminalist will use the title "Forensic Alcohol Supervisor," which indicates that he or she is licensed to test blood for alcohol content and testify to findings. It does not denote rank or supervisory status.

The expert is necessary to establish two important points for you:

- First, the blood/breath/urine testing instrument is accepted in the scientific community, was operating properly at the time of the test, and thus rendered a valid alcohol level result.
- Second, the significance of this alcohol level upon the ability to drive safely.

In sum, the direct examination of the criminalist should be uncomplicated, clean, and crisp. The more complicated scientific matters, such as how alcohol is absorbed, "burn-off," and the absorption of light by alcohol vapor in the Intoxilyzer should be deferred until redirect. The novice prosecutor should avoid getting fouled up with his or her own criminalist on direct. Jury confusion at this point is devastating.

EXCEPTION:

You may wish to allow the expert to explain during direct examination a highly unusual condition, such as a breath test from a person with one lung or other unusual medical conditions suffered by the defendant, or widely divergent Intoxilyzer readings (i.e., .08/.11/.10). These issues arise rarely. The criminalist will usually explain that they do not affect the reliability of the test.

§A:151 Blood Alcohol Not Exclusive Measurement of Impairment

You will also notice that we no longer rely upon blood alcohol as the exclusive measure of impairment. Presently, it is unlawful to drive with .08% by weight of blood or breath alcohol. Vehicle Code §23152(b); *People v. Bransford*, (1994) 8 Cal 4th 885, 35 Cal. Rptr 2d 613. This is significant because (1) the overwhelming majority of DUIs involve a breath test; and (2) it is no longer necessary to correlate the amount of breath alcohol to actual blood alcohol, thus making evidence of the "partition ration" inadmissible.

§A:152 Testing Methods

The two most prevalent testing methods in Northern California are the Intoxilyzer 5000 for breath testing and the gas chromatograph for the analysis of blood samples. The Intoxilyzer 5000, introduced around 1990, is a computerized version of the Omicron Intoxilyzer, which was used for about twenty years. The science is the same: the absorption of light at particular frequencies to detect the level of alcohol.

Officers like to use the Intoxilyzer because it is easy and they get immediate results. Arrestees like the breath test because it is non-invasive—no needles—and many people have trouble producing the second urine sample following the initial void. Urine testing is much less common.

The gas chromatograph uses the "headspace" air (between the cork and the liquid blood) to measure the blood alcohol level. It utilizes a slightly more complex scientific principle, although the lab report is usually a certain number (i.e., .105, .115).

[§§A:153-A:159 Reserved]

B. Breath Test Short-Form Direct Examination Questions

A model direct examination follows. It is designed to make the direct examination track your opening statement—specifically, that the Intoxilyzer has been used in excess of 20 years for breath testing, it was working fine, and the results are _____ breath alcohol, which impairs driving. On redirect you will have the opportunity to ask other questions to clear up the defense attempts at confusion. Examples include testimony that (1) there is no evidence that the instrument malfunctioned; (2) the instrument has safeguards, etc. Remember, at this point in the trial (direct examination of the criminalist), your focus is that the particular alcohol testing method is reliable.

§A:160   Intoxilyzer 5000

The following is the minimum number of questions necessary to establish the level of alcohol and its effect.

Q: What is your occupation?
Q: What is a criminalist?
Q: What are your qualifications to hold that position?
Q: Are you familiar with an instrument known as the Intoxilyzer 5000?

COMMENT:

Always refer to the Intoxilyzer as an instrument, not a machine. Machines are used to wash clothes, are not scientific, and break easily.

Q: Can you describe the Intoxilyzer 5000?
Q: Is it accepted within the scientific community as a method of detecting and measuring alcohol from a breath sample?
Q: Can you give us a simple explanation of how such an instrument works?

COMMENT:

This should be just that—that deep lung air is trapped in a chamber, a certain spectrum of light is passed through it which is absorbed by alcohol vapor, and a photometer detects how much light is absorbed. It is often compared to light or dark coffee—the more light absorbed, the higher the breath alcohol level.

Q: Was the instrument working properly on (date of test)?
Q: How do you know?

COMMENT:

The response should be that it was calibrated within 10 days before the test and within 10 days after the test. If this is a DOJ instrument, the calibration is done remotely by telephonic signal.

Q: Showing you people's exhibit ____ (the breath test record). Do you recognize such a record?
Q: Assuming it is the test record for the defendant, what results does it show?

COMMENT:

The answer you are looking for is the breath alcohol level at a particular date and time.

Q: Does it indicate the presence of any problems or abnormalities during the test?
Q: [Optional] Assuming the defendant had absorbed all the alcohol at the time of driving, what would his/her alcohol level be at the time of driving, say _____am/pm?

COMMENT:

You need not necessarily attempt to relate back the later test results to the time of driving. Instead, you could choose to rely upon the presumption in Vehicle Code §23152(b) that the defendant drove with that blood alcohol level if the test was conducted within three hours. The disadvantage of asking this question on direct is that it is probably where the defense will focus. The full absorption of alcohol must be part of your hypothetical or the criminalist will not be able to relate back reliably. Also, not all criminalists agree that the burn-off rate is .02 per hour. Instead of asking this question, you may choose to clear up the question on redirect.

Q: Are you familiar with the effect of alcohol upon the ability to drive safely?

COMMENT:

Notice the emphasis on the ability to drive safely. Anyone who is still conscious can drive a car.

Q: Would you explain your training and experience in this regard?
Q: Based upon your training and experience, do you have an opinion about at what alcohol level all persons are impaired and unable to drive safely?

COMMENT:

It is wise to do this now for two reasons. In the heat of battle, you may forget to do it later. Second, you will find out now—before the criminalist leaves—whether further foundational facts are necessary.

§A:161 Tips on Redirect

Almost surely the defense will endeavor to show that the test results are inaccurate because (1) the defendant burped or vomited during the waiting period; (2) there was mouth alcohol because of a cut inside the mouth (when an accident occurred); (3) the instrument was not calibrated correctly or the instrument had a long maintenance history; (4) radio interference; and (5) most commonly, that the absorption of alcohol was delayed, also known as "last gulp." The criminalist can testify that the Intoxilyzer 5000 has several built-in safeguards:

1. It can detect mouth alcohol vs. deep lung air;
2. It can tell if there was power interruption;
3. It can detect radio interference; and
4. Other chemicals that mimic alcohol in the Intoxilyzer, such as acetone, are lethal if present in detectable levels in breath air.

§A:162 Notes on Delayed Absorption

The defense theory is that the defendant had unabsorbed alcohol in his/her stomach while driving. Later, when tested at the jail, the additional alcohol absorbed and caused the test result to be higher than at the time of driving.

Remember: (1) The criminalist will testify that most alcohol is absorbed within 15 minutes of consumption; (2) the intoxication interrogation will usually reveal that the defendant claimed that he or she was drinking much earlier in the day. (It is the tendency of arrestees to deny drinking right before driving and to minimize their consumption.) This is inconsistent with the factual predicate for last gulp. This can be used for cross-examination of the defendant, as the last gulp usually relies upon heavy drinking right before driving.

This will also contradict the defendant's statement to the officer that he/she had a glass of wine with dinner, and that was all.

[§§A:163-A:169 Reserved]

C. Blood Draw Direct Examination

§A:170 Blood Alcohol Results

This examination format assumes that the blood is in evidence, that the officer authenticated the vial by his or her initials or other markings, and that the laboratory technician has testified to withdrawing the sample. Some counties dispense with the "blood tech," but in the absence of a stipulation it is hazardous to do so. First, it leaves an "empty chair" for several "Is it possible?" error questions, such as the type of swab and type of vial used. Second, it is difficult for the officer to testify that a non-alcoholic swab was used without relying upon hearsay. However, an experienced "blood tech" will have the officer initial the empty swab packet and place it in the small envelope with the blood sample.

Q: What is your occupation?

Q: What is a criminalist?

Q: What qualifications do you possess to hold such a position?

Q: Are you familiar with the analysis of blood to determine the blood alcohol level?

Q: Can you describe your training and experience in this regard?

Q: Showing you people's exhibit ___ (envelope with vile), do you recognize it?

COMMENT:

A competent criminalist will readily find his/her writing on the envelope and vial and will describe when he/she tested it.

A note on chain of evidence: Customarily, the officer does not transmit the sample to the lab; the officer usually places it in an evidence locker. However, depending on the customs of your court, it is seldom necessary to call the evidence technician as a witness. It is easier to rely upon the officer's testimony that the envelope was sealed when he/she relinquished it, and the criminalist's testimony that it was sealed when he/she received it. Also, the criminalist can usually testify to the method that blood alcohol samples are received and processed in the lab.

Q: What method did you use to test the blood?

Q: Is the gas chromatograph generally accepted within the scientific community as a method of determining the level of alcohol within blood?

Q: Was the instrument working properly on the date the blood was tested?

Q: How do you know?

A   It was calibrated before and after the "run."

Q: What were the results of your analysis?

Q: Are you familiar with the effect of alcohol consumption upon a person's ability to drive safely?

Q: Would you describe your training and experience in this regard?

Q: Do you have an opinion regarding the blood alcohol level at which all persons are under the influence of alcohol?

Q: What is that opinion?

COMMENT:

Move your exhibits into evidence.

No further questions.

§A:171   Redirect Examination

Each method of testing is vulnerable to mishandling. With blood, the defense may attempt to show one, or both of two things peculiar to blood alcohol testing: (1) If an alcohol-based swab is used, it is possible that the needle will absorb some as it penetrates the skin, thus raising the alcohol level; and/or (2) improperly preserved blood contains alcohol ferments, causing the alcohol level to skyrocket.

On redirect, you can establish: (1) the gas chromatograph distinguishes between isopropyl (rubbing) and ethyl (liquor) alcohol. Therefore, the use of an alcohol swab does not affect the reliability of the test; (2) a grey stopper is an industry standard, indicating that the vial contains a blood preservative to prevent fermentation. Also when alcohol ferments, the alcohol level goes way up—usually beyond lethal levels. Most criminalists agree that .50% and above is lethal. Therefore, these contents did not ferment.

[§§A:172-A:179 Reserved]

D. Urine Testing

§A:180 In General

Urine testing for blood alcohol content is less common than breath or blood testing. The direct examination is very similar to that for blood, except the officer has to lay the entire foundation (i.e., that the defendant urinated into the bottle in his/her presence).

CAUTION:

If you have a female defendant and a male officer, it is most likely that the void and sample were obtained by a female corrections officer. In the absence of a stipulation, this person is essential to your case.

§A:181 Points of Attack

Each method of testing is vulnerable to certain kinds of mishandling, and urine is no exception. In order for a urine test to be accurate, it must be preceded by a void at least twenty minutes prior to the actual sample. If there is no first void, it is not possible to offer an opinion about the blood alcohol level.

For that reason, the defense will often try to establish that the void was incomplete. To the point, the defendant testifies that he/she did not completely void all urine from his/her bladder. Testimony by the officer and cross-examination of the defendant on this point can become indelicate, but necessary: suffice it to say that there is no objective way to determine if the entire contents were voided.

Similar to blood, the defense may also contend that the urine was improperly preserved, causing fermentation.

PRACTICE TIP:

With female defendants, it is unlikely that the attending officer actually watched them urinate into the bottle. This can lead to "dipping" by defendants to dilute the urine. The criminalist can, however, determine if no urine is present and testify to this fact. In other words, the criminalist can, when appropriate testify that the sample is water. Mere dilution, however, is more problematic.

[§§A:182-A:189 Reserved]

E. General Questions and Blood Alcohol Calculation Questions

§A:190 Opinion Testimony by Experts

The criminalist from the crime lab can offer his/her opinion as an expert on the evidence as can the defense expert. Both will usually give their opinion as to whether or not the defendant is under the influence for purposes of driving. To give that opinion they will rely upon the driving, appearance and condition, FSTs, drinking pattern and chemical test. Note that the defense attorney will often describe the driving condition and appearance and FSTs inaccurately. Almost always there will be a new drinking pattern.

The opinion of your expert that defendant was over .08 at time of driving is important for your case. Always strongly argue the .08 inference by law.

§A:191 General-Interpretation Questions

Q: Have you conducted any research regarding the effect of alcohol on the human body, especially as it relates to the ability of a person to drive a motor vehicle?
Q: Did that research include correlation studies?
Q: What are correlation studies?

PRACTICE TIP:

Make sure to draw out details of correlation studies. How they corroborate amounts of alcohol consumed with blood alcohol levels; correlate blood breath and urine tests with each other; correlate blood alcohol levels with observable symptoms; test driving abilities at various blood alcohol levels, as well as correlating amounts of alcohol consumed with performances on FSTs.

PRACTICE TIP:

If you are trying a breath case, have the criminalist elaborate on the fact that in the correlation studies 95% of the breath results were the same as, or lower (by as much as .02), than the blood results.

Q: Have you personally conducted or been involved in any correlation studies?
Q: How many are you conducting or involved in now?
Q: Please describe one of the more recent correlation studies you have conducted, participated in or observed.
Q: What is peak?

COMMENT:

You want the distinction between absorption and peak made here. A defense expert will confuse the terms to help the rising defense.

Q: Is there an acceptable rate for how long it takes the average person to peak?

PRACTICE TIP:

Be sure and ask your criminalist for any articles or studies relating to a rising BA and the range of absorption periods specifically relating the variations on those times.

Q: How is alcohol eliminated from the body?
Q: What is elimination/burn-off? describe it please.
Q: Is there an accepted average burn-off rate?
A: Yes. .015 to .02 per/hour for men and .018 to .02 for women.
Q: Does the BA level include alcohol still in the stomach or intestines?
A: No.
Q: Does the BA level include alcohol that has been eliminated from the system?
A: No.
Q: So when you have a BA level, is that a measure of the alcohol you have in the blood and the other tissues it supplies?
A: Yes.
Q: Does alcohol affect everyone the same?
A: No.
Q: Is there such a thing as tolerance to alcohol?
A: Yes.
Q: What is tolerance?

PRACTICE TIP:

Tolerance will mask gross motor skill impairment, therefore a person with a high BA could have successfully completed part of the FSTs. Look for mental impairment on the FSTs because alcohol will affect a persons' mental ability before their physical ability.

Q: Does tolerance vary from person to person?
Q: What is an FST?
Q: What is your training and experience in regards to FSTs?
Q: Why are FSTs a useful tool in determining a person's ability to operate a vehicle safely?
Q: Can a person do well on all or most of the FSTs and still be under the influence for the purpose of operating a vehicle safely?
A: Yes
Q: Why is that?
Q: Based on your training and experience do you have an opinion as to when all persons are under the influence of alcohol and cannot operate their car safely?
Q: What is that opinion?

Q: Does your opinion include a person's tolerance to alcohol?
A: Yes.

PRACTICE TIP:

    Some criminalists still have an opinion of .10%, so if you have a .08 or .09 BA then you can deal with this problem in the following manner:

    a.   See if another criminalist is available to testify; or
    b.   Ask the criminalist when most people are under the influence instead of all.

Present a hypothetical of the driving symptoms and FST performances of your defendant to the criminalist and ask for his/her opinion as to that hypothetical person's fitness to safely operate a motor vehicle. Make sure you include in your hypothetical at least some of the things the defendant did well.

Q: Can you explain why?
Q: Do you base that opinion on any one thing?
Q: [Optional question] Would it change your opinion if [symptom] was caused by [excuse/other explanation by defense]?

COMMENT:

    You may use questions like this when defense has gotten into evidence through your police officer other explanations/excuses for certain symptoms.

Q: Can you think of any one thing other than alcohol that could cause the presence/occurrence of all of these symptoms?
A: No.
Q: Are these symptoms and FST performances consistent with (defendant's BA level)?

§A:192   Blood Alcohol (BA) Calculation Questions

    The defendant's blood alcohol "at the time of driving" is important and you must get into evidence a BA greater than .08 to survive an 1118.1 motion on the (b) count. Almost always the drinking pattern given to the police officer is untruthful in some respect, either in the number of drinks or time of drinking or both. Either way, it is not going to add up to a BA greater than .08. So first present the defendant's weight, time of driving and the time of the test. The calculation by the criminalist with this information will typically come out to a very low BA or .00. By doing this you've demonstrated that the facts from the defendant (at least as to the number of drinks) are not trustworthy, hence the only reliable unbiased evidence available to determine defendant's BA is the chemical test. With the chemical test certain assumptions need to be made and extrapolation calculations need to be done back to the time of driving.

    It is imperative that you go over these calculations with the criminalist before he/she testifies.

Q: Given the following facts (give the defendant's drinking pattern, start and stop times, and number of drinks, as well as the defendant's weight), what would you expect that person's BA to be at time of test?
Q: What would you expect that person's BA to be at time of driving?
Q: Can you calculate a person's BA at [time of driving] if given a chemical test result of that person at [the time of test]?

COMMENT:

    The criminalist will say yes, if certain assumptions are made, such as:

    a.   A drink is defined as a 1 oz. shot of 80 proof alcohol, a 12 oz. beer or an 8 oz. glass of wine, and
    b.   The burn-off rate used is .015, and
    c.   The defendant is post-peak when tested. (The criminalist can safely make this assumption if 1 hour has passed from drinking to test time.)

Q: [Hypothetical] A person is driving at (time of driving) and is tested at (time of test), what would you calculate that person's BA to be at the time of driving?

COMMENT:

If 1 hour hasn't passed from driving to testing, the criminalist can only give a range of BA levels because defendant could be rising. That's fine if the range is greater than .08. If it's not, then you will have to use the defendant's stopped drinking time—be careful.

Q: How much would one drink affect a person that weighed (defendant's weight)?

Q: how many drinks would a male/female who weighed (defendant's weight) have to have in his/her system to be a (defendant's BA at test time) or (driving time)?

Q: how many drinks would a male/female who weighed (defendant's weight) have to consume between (defendant's starting time if given) and (defendant's ending time if given) to be a (defendant's BA result) at the time of testing?

PRACTICE TIP:

The two preceding questions are optional. The first is a good one to use in a higher BA case, to demonstrate the number of drinks the defendant would have to have in his/her system to be a certain blood alcohol level. Example, in a case where defendant's BA is a .14, if defendant is a 160 pound man, he should have to have seven drinks (.02 per drink) in his system at the time of testing! Further, if you have reason to believe that the defendant's drinking pattern is credible (or one that the defense will stick with) but he/she lied about the number of drinks, use the second question. In doing so you will impress the jury not only with the number of drinks the defendant had in his/her system when tested but also the number of drinks he/she had throughout the course of the evening.

Example: Defendant (160 lb. male) drinks from 7:00 pm to 10:30 pm, and is tested at say 12:00 am with a BA result of .10. A .10 result means that the defendant has five drinks in his system (since one drink affects a 160 lb. male .02) when tested, but would have burned off approximately .08 since 7:00 pm (.015 to .02 X 5 hours), which would be the equivalent of four more drinks. With that information you can impress upon the jury that although the BA is only a .10 the defendant had at least nine beers/drinks and then got behind the wheel of a car (could this be a sign of poor judgment?). Furthermore, this calculation undoubtedly proves defendant's claim of two beers to be a lie.

Q: So, is there any possible way that a person could have had (the number of admitted drinks by defendant) between (times of drinking, if given) or have a result of (BA result) at (at time of testing?).

COMMENT:

This is repetitive of Step 1 but reinforces how defendant was untruthful about the number of drinks.

[§§A:193-A:199 Reserved]

VI.   COMMON DEFENSES FOR CHEMICAL TESTS

A. General

§A:200 Main Defense Approaches

The defense typically raises several defenses depending upon the chemical test in your case. Below is a list of the most popular defenses with suggested ways to handle them. As soon as you figure out which defense(s) are being used, then you can address them either:
- On direct of your criminalist, or
- On redirect of your criminalist, or
- On cross-examination of the defense expert.

There are four main approaches the defense attorney and their experts use to attack our test evidence and that we use to attack theirs:

- Qualification and bias of criminalist and defense expert.
- Blood alcohol result.
- The expert's opinion of the evidence.
- Hypothetical's as relate to this case (prolonged absorption, rising alcohol etc.).

§A:201 Qualification of Criminalist

The defense attorney will try to show his/her guy is more educated, more qualified and smarter than our guy. Most of defense experts you will come in contact with have lengthy qualifications but when you tear them apart they are not "as good as they sound." Find out all you can about the defense expert before he/she takes the stand.

Our experts are younger and have less job history so you will probably want to spend some time attacking the defense expert's qualifications.

[§§A:202-A:209 Reserved]

B. Breath Analysis Defense Issues

§A:210 Overview

Defense attorneys and their criminalists have a field day with breath tests. Here are the popular areas of attack and how to handle them. Remember your general questions cover the fact that the machine, the lab, the personnel, the testing and maintenance procedures are all approved by Title 17. Emphasize that many of the crime labs' testing procedures exceed Title 17 requirements. Discuss with your criminalist beforehand.

§A:211 Partition Ratio Generally

This is a ratio that expresses the conversion of the amount of alcohol in the breath to what it would be in the blood. Studies indicate that the average ratio among the general population is 2300 to 1; however Title 17 mandates a lower figure of 2100 to 1 be used. This ratio results in the breath tests coming in lower than blood tests by .01% on the average. This explains why correlation studies indicate the breath test is the same or lower than a corresponding blood test 95% of the time. Furthermore, 99.5% of the population falls between 1750 to 2800 to 1. If the defense alleges that the defendant has an unusually low partition ration (hence lower BA), draw all these facts out of your criminalist as well as the fact that a person can be tested for partition ratio (to argue when the defendant hasn't.)

> **NOTE:**
> _____
> *People v. Bransford* 15 Cal.App.4th 1626 (May 1993) held that partition ratio evidence is irrelevant, thus prosecutors can run 402 motions before trial and keep out even the mention of partition ratios at trial. Review of this case was granted in August, 1993, and as of November 1993, it was not citable. However, keep abreast of the developments in this area and argue the rational of the Bransford case to attempt and keep partition ratios from the jury. It's just another thing to confuse them.

The bottom line is, if the defense is asking the jury to consider that the defendant may have an unusually low partition ratio (where the defendant was not tested), point out that what the defense is really asking the jury to do is to speculate (guess), or consider evidence that has not been presented.

Although the defense has no obligation to present any evidence if they want the jury to consider this possibility they have the obligation to present evidence, particularly where the defendant could be tested. Essentially when the defense asks the jury to speculate they are asking the jury to disregard the law.

§A:212 Defendant's Individual Partition Ratio

Some criminalists will do a blood partition ratio on the defendant in their lab. You may want to run a *Kelly/ Frye* hearing outside the presence of the jury to keep the test out by showing that this procedure is not accepted as reliable within the scientific community and is not accurate because:

- The conditions and environment on the day of the DUI cannot be duplicated;

- The ratio at another day and time has no relevance to what it was on the day in question;
- Ratios calculated at low levels do not apply to the higher levels (and typically the defendant will be tested at a much lower level than on the day he/she was arrested);
- The ratio is ever-changing. No person's ratio remains the same;
- Whatever other reasons our criminalist(s) point out to you.

See People v. McDonald 206 Cal.App.3d 877; also make a 352 argument.

PRACTICE TIP:

If you run a *Kelly/Frye* motion have your criminalist sit in and take notes to:

1. Provide you with tips on areas to cross-examine on, and
2. So he/she can be prepared to testify to refute the defense.

If the defendant has been tested and the defense is allowed to put on evidence of the defendant's partition ratio test, cross-examine on the above mentioned areas as well as the specifics:

1. Calibration, maintenance, and record keeping of the breath machine used. Go through everything that our lab does with our machine, such as specifics about calibration checks, simulator solution preparation and changes, maintenance checks, safeguards against mouth alcohol, Title 17 licensing and testing procedures etc. You will find independent labs keep sloppy maintenance records, don't use the Intoxilyzer checklist, aren't licensed by Title 17, don't have printout result capabilities, have no built-in safeguards, and don't even come close to our machines for reliability.

2. Blood testing procedures. Naturally, to do a partition ratio study, a number of breath tests will be done and compared to simultaneously taken blood tests. Questions on specifics of the blood draws should be asked such as:
   a. Who prepared the kits and ensured the preservative and anticoagulants were present?
   b. Where are the blood samples?
   c. Who was the trained and licensed LVN or technician who drew the samples and where is he/she to testify?
   d. How can we be assured the blood was drawn in a medically-approved manner with a non-alcoholic swabbing solution?
   e. Was the blood drawn at the same time the breath samples were taken?
   f. What procedure was used to test the samples and was it approved by Title 17? Typically the enzymatic method of testing will be used so ask: "Isn't it true that that procedure is used by less than 5% of the labs across the county?"
   g. How many times was each sample tested to assure the accuracy of the testing?

PRACTICE TIP:

By the time you are though tearing apart the testing procedures, the jury is at the point where they not only distrust the test but the defense criminalist as well.

PRACTICE TIP:

A defense criminalist will always say a breath test is unreliable if done pre-peak (before equilibrium) of the absorption phase. Therefore, if the partition ratio test consists of only two or three tests, there is no way that defendant's absorption pattern could have been tracked and you can challenge the fact that we don't know what stage of absorption the defendant was in when tested. Hence the partition ratio testing is unreliable.

§A:213   Mouth Alcohol

The defense may try and say the breath sample or samples were contaminated with mouth alcohol. The reasons this is a bogus claim are because:

1. The 15-minute waiting period and questioning of the defendant guarantees that no mouth alcohol is present and any that was previously present will have dissipated. Title 17 mandates 15 minutes, which was followed, so argue it.

2. The results themselves are a safeguard evidencing that no mouth alcohol was present, since they are within .02 of one another. If mouth alcohol was present, it would have been expelled in one of the blows and the readings would have a much greater disparity than the allowable .02 variance and the machine would shut itself down.
3. The Intoxilyzer has a built in negative slope detector that senses mouth alcohol and will shut the machine down.
4. Dubowski, a recognized expert, says mouth alcohol is always gone in 9 minutes.

§A:214   Maintenance of Instrument

Have the criminalist explain how the maintenance done by the crime lab exceeds the Title 17 requirements.

§A:215   Radio Frequency Interference

1. The machine has an RFI detector.
2. If the defense asserts that the RFI detector was not working:
    a. It is only a problem if the officer brought his/her radio into the breath room and if it is transmitting, or if there is a power surge—unlikely!

PRACTICE TIP:

Ask the officer on direct if he/she left his/her pac set outside of the room. Most are trained to do so.

    b. Interference from a radio is typically de minimis, and if it was detectable it would cause random test results that would be detected.
3. The fact the tests were within .02 of one another indicates there was no problem.

§A:216   Acetone and Solvent Interferences

The defense may claim some substances mimic alcohol and fool the instrument. This just doesn't happen. The instrument is set up to detect and invalidate where there is a foreign substance. The old Intoxilyzer 4011A0 could be fooled and this is why diabetics used to have a defense. This is no longer true with the Intoxilyzer 5000.

§A:217   Arterial vs. Venous Blood

The breath machine tests arterial blood, which has higher concentration of alcohol than venous blood for blood draws, especially during the absorption phase.

The only real noticeable difference when arterial blood can be drastically higher than venous is very early in the absorption phase, because alcohol makes its way into the arteries before the veins. By the time the defendant is tested he/she is well into or past peak absorption where, if anything the defendant will be falling at that time.

The arterial and venous blood will be the same or so close the difference is unremarkable. The venous always catches up to the arterial, and after all what's so wrong with testing the arterial BA level? Aren't the arteries pumping oxygen and the alcohol to the brain? And doesn't the brain control all the functions of the body?

§A:218   Temperature

A person with a fever could blow a higher test, but it would take a 2 degree Fahrenheit in body temperature to affect a test by .01.

§A:219   Hematocrit

Measure of blood made up of cells. The variation is not more than .01% difference.

§A:220   Mother Solution for Calibration Checks

The crime lab mixes up 25 liters of the original solution and uses it for 4 or 5 months. The solution is rechecked constantly and the Intoxilyzer also checks it every time it is used. Bogus defense.

APPENDIX A:
DA'S MANUAL

§A:221   Low Calibration Checks Readings

Pursuant to Title 17, the acceptable range for the calibration check is .01 difference from the known value. One low calibration check does not make a .07. However, if the defense subpoenas the activity maintenance logs and can show a pattern of the machine consistently reading low, they can argue the test is really closer to being .01 less than the reading, however:

1. This cuts both ways if we can show it is consistently reading high.
2. Remember the breath machines underestimate the true BA, so it's a wash.
3. The machine truncates the third digit; you can get the other digits into evidence if available through your criminalist.

§A:222   Simulator Solution Temperature

Title 17 mandates the temperature of the solution be above 33.8 degrees and below 34.2 degrees. Outside these ranges will cause some difference in the calibration check result but doesn't necessarily affect the breath results. Any non-compliance with Title 17 goes to weight and not admissible.

[§§A:223-A:229 Reserved]

C.   Blood Analysis Defense Issues

§A:230   Lack of Preservative/Anticoagulant

Have criminalist shake/smell/observe the blood tube. Preservative anticoagulant is a powder mixture put in all at once. Free flowing blood has anticoagulant in it, thus it is also preserved. No bacteria can grow to produce alcohol or destroy alcohol, and no clotting has taken place to alter the blood alcohol result on the gas chromatograph.

§A:231   Micro Clots

Since blood samples are mixed/homogenized prior to testing, micro clots don't make a micro difference.

§A:232   Bacterial Growth

Doesn't happen.

§A:233   Contamination of Sample From Arm Swab

Typically a non-alcoholic solution is used to swab the arm. Our approved arm swabs contain so little alcohol it won't register. Injected straight, it is only a .02% and it is used diluted. Common sense dictates that it is nearly impossible to get any of this solution into the needle when you think about the procedure used.

§A:234   Switched Samples

Samples are done in duplicate by two criminalist who both check LR numbers. If the results don't agree within .01% the test is repeated.

§A:235   Instrument Calibration

Runs contain two quality control samples, one calibrator checks sample, at least two linearity samples, one blank and a separation sample. All ranges will cause some difference in the calibration check result but don't necessarily affect the breath results. Any non-compliance with Title 17 goes to weight and not admissibility.

§A:236   Hematocrit (Blood Cell Count)

Normal healthy variation in hematocrit can change blood alcohol level less than .01%; this is a smoke screen.

§A:237 Drug/Alcohol Interactions

Most drugs are made more potent by alcohol, especially tranquilizers and antidepressants. Stimulants give you an alert drunk, i.e., a little less drowsy, but still slower to react.

§A:238 Aspirin/Tagamet

Drugs that affect the stomach lining may speed the absorption of alcohol so that more alcohol is absorbed sooner. The blood alcohol level will be a little higher than otherwise, but it is a real blood alcohol level.

§A:239 Venous vs. Arterial Blood

Hitting an artery is a cardinal sin for blood technicians. One would have to be purposefully trying to do this. A criminalist may be able to tell by color of blood.

[§§A:240-A:249 Reserved]

D. Urine Analysis Defense Issues

§A:250 1.3:1 Ratio (Blood to Urine)

Variation in the blood to urine ratio does occur but is between 1.1 and 1.5 to 1. This is only in properly-collected second samples. The ratio has a strong tendency to be 1.3 to 1 during elimination and when the BAC is above a .04%. Strange ratios occur below .04 or during absorption.

§A:251 Void Studies

Wide variations in ratios are commonly found in studies that analyze the void (first) urine samples. The authors commonly state that for this reason urine is a poor substitute for blood alcohol analysis UNLESS THERE IS A VOID. This is irrelevant to second samples, those taken after a void. Flannagan, Morgan, Payne, Forjentes, etc. all did studies using voids (i.e., first time samples).

§A:252 Residual Urine

It is physiologically impossible to completely void the bladder. However, the amount of urine left in a cooperative healthy subject is insignificant to the BA result of the second sample.

§A:253 Special Note

Urine is the poorest choice for an alcohol test. To be valid:
- The urine sample must be obtained during the elimination phase of alcohol ingestion.
- The BAC must be above a .04%.
- The urine sample must be from a second voiding of the defendant's bladder 20 to 30 minutes after a first void.

[§§A:254-A:259 Reserved]

E. Widmark Calculations Defense Issues

§A:260 Time to Peak Alcohol Level

Peak alcohol level varies according to the amount of food in the stomach and also sometimes the type of drink. On an empty stomach, the peak may be reached within 15 to 45 minutes, averaging 30 minutes, and sometimes taking up to 60 minutes, especially with strong drinks straight. On a full stomach the rate is 15 minutes to 90 minutes, with an average of 60 minutes, sometimes up to 120 minutes. The curves are lower and broader than empty stomach curves. Time to peak is different than time to total absorption. Absorption phase is up to peak. Elimination is after peak. Defense experts will stretch out the time it takes to reach peak to help the rising BA defense.

§A:261 Burn-Off Rate

Burn-off rate varies between .010% per hour to .030% per hour. The average is between .015% and .020% hour. Calculations may be done using whatever factor you wish. Using .015 to .018 gives the benefit to the defendant.

§A:262 Widmark's Factor

Widmark's factor varies for men from .60 to .73; for woman it is between .44 and .66. Averages are .68 for men, .55 to .60 for women. This relates to the percentage of the body that will attract alcohol (alcohol is attracted to any tissue or other part of the body containing water). Lower numbers are for fatter people. Higher numbers are for trim, athletic people.

SPECIAL NOTE:
Many defense criminalists will use ranges rather than averages and go on possibilities rather than probabilities to create doubt as to accuracy.

[§§A:263-A:269 Reserved]

VII. CROSS-EXAMINATION OF DEFENSE WITNESSES

A. Cross-Examination of Defense Expert

§A:270 Breath Questions

Always inquire about Dubowski before you start to question defense expert if it hasn't come up on direct.

Q: In forming your opinions about people who are under the influence for purpose of driving, have you read and relied upon the work of Dr. Kurt M. Dubowski?
Q: Isn't it true that Dr. Dubowski is an acknowledged expert in the area of chemical testing for alcohol?
Q: Are you familiar with his published work?

Mouth Alcohol

Q: Hasn't the vast majority of scientific literature reported that 15 minutes is more than long enough for any source of mouth alcohol including food, candy, dentures, dental work, breath sprays and medical inhalers to be eliminated?
Q: Doesn't Dr. Dubowski state in "recent developments in alcohol analysis" that he found mouth alcohol always gone in 9 minutes, and in 6 minutes if the person rinsed the mouth after drinking alcohol?

Acetone

Q: Doesn't Dr. Dubowski state that, even at the maximum breath acetone concentrations possible in diabetics and dieters, there is no significant effect on breath testing instruments?

Radio Frequency Interference

Q: Doesn't Dr. Dubowski in state that RFI is a "spurious allegation?"
Q: Isn't it true that Dubowski said he doesn't like the conversion of breath to blood concept of the breath test, but that the instrument itself is not a problem? That the result should be straight breath alcohol conversion, as the law now is in California?

§A:271 Questions if Defense Says FSTs Are Not Valid

Q: Isn't it true that FSTs are intended to allow the officer to observe the ability of the person to mentally follow instructions as well as physically carry them out?

Q: To your knowledge do most police agencies use FSTs?

Q: Is it your opinion then that police agencies are wrong to use FSTs and are just wasting their time in giving them?

Q: Are you assuming that something other than alcohol consumption caused the poor driving observed by the officer on date of arrest?

Q: Are you making that assumption because it favors the defendant?

Q: You were not present at (time of arrest) on (date of arrest) were you?

Q: So you don't know what caused the defendant to drive the way he did?

Q: You are simply assuming that it wasn't caused by alcohol consumption aren't you?

§A:272 Questions Defense Expert Says It Takes Two Hours for Absorption

Q: Isn't it true that the average rate of total absorption of alcohol into the blood is 45 minutes plus or minus 15 minutes?

Q: Do you have any personal knowledge or evidence to prove that this defendant did not have an average absorption rate on (date of arrest)?

§A:273 Questions to Show Bias of Defense Expert

Q: Do you consider yourself any unbiased witness in this case?

Q: Are you being paid for your preparation and testimony?

Q: How much?

Q: Do you consider yourself a professional witness?

Q: How much of your income is from misdemeanor DUI cases?

Q: How many times have you testified in DUI cases in the last year?

Q: What is your total income in the last year as a result of being called as a defense witness?

Q: Isn't it a fact that you are concerned that if this defendant is convicted it may reduce the number of times you are called as a defense witness in the future?

Q: How many times have you testified as an expert for the defense in DUI cases it the past two years?

Another way to go about doing this:

Q: How many times have you testified as an expert for the prosecution in the past two years? (If the expert says he/she has at all, ask for specifics like court, DA presiding judge, case…. The expert won't be able to give any.)

Q: Isn't it true that in each and every one of those (number of cases) that you testified where there was a chemical test, your opinion was that the defendant was under .08 at the time of driving?…

Q: And that regardless whether the defendant took a blood, breath, or urine test?

Q: And in fact, you've testified that a person with a test result of .28 was less than a .08 at the time of driving. Isn't that true?

[§§A:274-A:279 Reserved]

B. Cross-Examination of Defendant/Defense Witnesses

§A:280 Strategy

Like cross-examination of any witness you should try not to be chained to a script of questions but rather have areas you want to cover. You will be at your best if you relax, listen closely, and follow up on things that don't make sense. Don't just go over the defendant's story again with him/her. The defendant has practiced that story over and over and having him/her reiterate it again only reinforces it. Jump around on areas of questioning to keep the defendant off guard. Try and recognize when you are not getting anywhere or are getting hurt and move on. Try to end on a high note. Save an area you know you'll score some points on to the end.

§A:281   Driving Patterns

1. If there is a pattern of weaving, have the defendant mark the driving pattern on the same diagram used by the officer. (Have the defendant use a different colored maker than the officer used.)
2. Pin the defendant down on whether the officer accurately described the driving pattern. If not, how is it different?
3. Ask the defendant if the description by the officer represents the defendant's normal driving pattern.
4. If the defendant offers an excuse for poor driving, ask whether the defendant offered that excuse to the officer at the time of the stop. Ask this question only if he/she didn't, and, officer has testified this excuse was not offered.

§A:282   Activities Prior to Arrest

1. Pin the defendant down in detail as to all activities, including food and drink consumption, work activities, rest, etc., during the entire day prior to the arrest.
2. Find out everyone who saw the defendant prior to arrest and after drinking had concluded. Find out if these people know the defendant; if not, find out whether any effort was made to find them. If they are not called as witnesses, mention this in argument.
3. If the defendant offers any medical excuse, ask whether the arresting officer was so advised. Find out whether medical treatment continues and from whom; if medical testimony is not offered or something other than alcohol is used to explain; first go into detail as to every way in which it was different, then, at the end, ask if it isn't possible if these differences might be in part associated with the consumption of alcohol.

§A:283   Symptoms That Alcohol and Over Consumption Usually Produce in Defendant

Inquire whether the defendant has had sufficient experience with alcohol to know what personal symptoms it produces, particularly when an excessive amount has been consumed. If such symptoms are admitted, then go down the list of all symptoms the officer observed and ask if each is a symptom in the personal experience of the defendant after an excessive amount of alcohol has been consumed. Usually the defendant will concur; then you have developed some good opportunities for argument.

The "Have you stopped beating your wife?" question of DUIs is "Would you consider yourself a light or heavy drinker?" The defendant will invariably state he/she is a light drinker and then you can:

1. Confront him/her with the number of drinks you've calculated he/she had that evening; and/or
2. Use this statement to follow up with questions about how he/she would feel the effects right away or have low tolerance because they are a light or inexperienced drinker.

§A:284   The Obvious

Don't be afraid to comment on or question the obvious. When the defendant keeps looking over to his/her attorney before answering, ask, "Do you need to talk to him/her before you answer my questions? He wasn't there that night was he?"

If the defendant volunteers something gratuitous like "I go to church all the time," ask why the defendant felt the need to volunteer that to the jury. Or if the defendant starts sweating or looking down when you start questioning, you don't have to be confrontational or even comment on these things if they are very obvious or you don't feel comfortable. Develop your own style and be yourself.

§A:285   New Drinking Pattern

The defendant will have changed his/her drinking pattern to take advantage of the rising BA defense. If the defendant hasn't taken the position that the cop was lying or mistaken about the old drinking pattern, confront the defendant with the fact that he/she lied to get out of trouble.

§A:286   Drinking Companion Questions

Q: You distinctly remember at this time that the defendant had one drink when you first arrived and one drink about an hour later?

Q: You distinctly remember at this time that you had only one drink during the course of the evening?

COMMENT:

At this time the jury should have been left with the impression that the witness enjoys total recall. If there were other persons present in addition to the witness and the defendant, have the witness describe exactly how much and what they had to drink. Memory is likely to fade quickly and this will seem odd if you have previously established that recollection of the number of drinks the defendant had was a product of the witness' own recall as opposed to a suggestion of the defendant or someone else. Inquire as to how many times the witness has been with the defendant on similar occasions and then test recall as to drinks consumed on those occasions. Ask the witness to describe what the defendant was wearing; if the witness remembers the number of drinks, such things as attire should also be remembered.

Toward the end of your examination, ask if the witness knew what defendant's condition was at the time of the arrest. This is an especially good question if the witness and defendant parted company a few hours before the stop.

To establish through the defense witness that the defendant was under the influence (if the witness has stated an opinion that the defendant was not drunk) the following approach is suggested. The first thing to do is define the terms. When a witness testifies the defendant was not drunk, it is a negative statement; the witness is not saying the defendant was sober. You're not interested in whether defendant was "drunk" or intoxicated. Generally, the answer includes inference to slurred speech, staggering, swaying, inability to stand, etc. Once you have established this description from the witness, then work down the scale of intoxication. Often you can get a witness to say that the defendant was "having a good time." Use the term "loose" or "relaxed." Most people rationalize drinking alcohol by indicating that it is a relaxant; i.e., it makes them feel relaxed and loose. Also ask the witness to compare the defendant's nondrinking personality (i.e., in court) with the defendant's drinking personality (i.e., in the bar). In the event you cannot get the witness to say that the defendant was "relaxed," then you should turn to the question of whether the witness has seen the defendant drunk before.

Q: Then I take it that what you are saying is that the defendant was not falling down drunk?

COMMENT:

Keep in mind during the cross-examination of the defense witness (or the defendant), that the witness may honestly believe that the defendant was not intoxicated. This belief is based on the witness' concept of someone who is too intoxicated to drive, which usually is a person bouncing off the walls. Therefore, do not conclude with a mere negative statement that the defendant was not intoxicated. Make the witness convey to the jury a picture of someone who is too intoxicated to drive. You will find that more often than not the witness' concept of the driver who is under the influence is about the standards set by law.

If the witness admits never having seen the defendant intoxicated, then start questioning the basis of the witness/ opinion. For example:

Q: You have never seen the defendant under the influence?
Q: Do you base your opinion that the defendant was not drunk on comparison with intoxicated persons you have seen?
Q: Would that be the person with the slurred speech, staggering gait, etc.?
Q: You say you have never seen the defendant intoxicated, have you seen the defendant drink an alcoholic beverage before?
Q: You do agree that there are degrees of intoxication ranging from "under the influence" to "dead drunk"?
Q: You do agree that a person can feel the effects of alcohol without being drunk?
Q: When you say you have never seen the defendant intoxicated, don't you mean that you have never seen the defendant intoxicated to the point of inability to walk, talk, etc.?
Q: When asked to search your memory concerning the defendant's state of sobriety on the day of arrest, didn't you think back and remember the defendant was not drunk?
Q: You weren't searching your mind to determine whether the defendant may have been feeling the effects of alcohol, were you?

§A:287   Questions for Bartender

Q: How long after you began working did the defendant arrive?
Q: Between the time you began working and the time of the defendant's arrival, were there any other customers in the bar?
Q: How many customers arrived and departed during that period of time?
Q: How many customers were present at the bar at the time of the defendant's arrival?
Q: When the defendant arrived was he in the presence of other persons?
Q: Please identify them.
Q: What did the defendant do after he arrived at the bar?
Q: What was the defendant wearing?
Q: Had you seen the defendant in the bar on other occasions?
Q: On how many occasions had you seen the defendant in the bar?
Q: After arriving in the bar, did the defendant order a drink?
Q: What did the defendant order?
Q: Did you supply the defendant with a drink?
Q: At the time you provided the drink were there any other persons present in the bar?
Q: Please identify the other persons.
Q: What were they drinking?
Q: What were they wearing?
Q: How many bar stool customers do you have to tend to?
Q: How many cocktail waitresses work in the bar?
Q: Do you stock your own supplies, get your own ice?
Q: Do you have to ring up purchases on a cash register?
Q: You've testified that the defendant was not drunk. You've seen a drunk before, haven't you?
Q: Describe the symptoms of someone you believe to be drunk.
Q: Before serving someone do you make it a point to check their state of sobriety?
Q: Are you aware the law doesn't allow you to serve an alcoholic beverage to a drunk?
Q: Isn't it a fact that you would lose your license if you served alcohol to a drunk?
Q: Isn't it a fact that when you are checking a person's state of sobriety you are looking only for the drunk and not the person who is loose, relaxed or a little bit tipsy?

COMMENT:

The above set of questions is asked for the purpose of making three points on final argument.

1. The bartender's recollection of this particular customer on the day in questions is highly questionable.
2. Even assuming the bartender does remember the defendant, the bartender's opinion of the defendant's sobriety is of little value because all the bartender ever really looks for is a person who is drunk to the point that more alcohol should not be served, as opposed to a person who is under the influence.
3. The bartender could not say the defendant was drunk because to do so would be admitting to a violation of the law.

Again, the key word is reasonable and the latter portion of the circumstantial evidence instruction should be emphasized to make it clear that all unreasonable interpretations must be rejected. In addition, the "two reasonable interpretations" argument applies to the totality of the evidence, not to any one fact. Taken as a whole (the totality of the circumstances) there is but one reasonable inference to be drawn.

Finally, the "two reasonable interpretations" issue should be separated from credibility determinations. A witness should not be believed just because he or she might be telling the truth. If that were the state of the law, we would not need juries to determine who is telling the truth!

[§§A:288-A:299 Reserved]

VIII. CLOSING ARGUMENT

A. Introduction

§A:300 Preparation

Closing argument is your opportunity to persuade the jury that the evidence in your case establishes guilt. It is the time to bring the facts together with the law to show the jury that defendant was driving under the influence.

The key to good argument is preparation. Start by reviewing the charges. Read the jury instructions and know the elements of the law. Next, review the facts. Organize the important facts in a logical fashion. Focus on those facts that establish guilt. Be specific. Do not assume that the jury heard the evidence the way you intended it.

Once you have reviewed the facts and the law, outline your argument.

§A:301 Moral Behavior and Physical Appearance

As a prosecutor you have an ethical duty to see that justice is done. Always take the moral high ground. Scrupulously avoid any impropriety in argument. Do not mention defendant's failure to testify. Never discuss post-arrest silence. Avoid stating any personal opinion or belief. Finally, do not refer to any facts that were not admitted.

Your physical appearance also sends a message to the jury. Stand straight and tall, make eye contact, and address the jury directly. Speak clearly. Do not pace or move nervously about the courtroom. Finally, keep your argument short. Most people lose patience after 20 minutes.

[§§A:302-A:309 Reserved]

B. First Argument

§A:310 Outline

Your first argument should cover three things:
- Explain the charges.
- Discuss the facts.
- Argue for conviction.

§A:311 Explain the Charges

Start by explaining the charges to the jury. Review the jury instructions and prepare a chart of the elements before you argue (CALJIC 16.830, 16.830.1, 16.831). Use these charts during your argument to explain the law. This gives the jurors a framework for making their decision. Keep it simple:
1. Driving Under the Influence:
   a. Driving;
   b. Under the influence.
2. Driving with Blood Alcohol .08 or Greater:
   a. Driving;
   b. With blood alcohol of .08 or greater.

Do not assume that the jurors know the law! Help them with their job by giving them this framework to determine guilt.

§A:312 Discuss the Facts

Facts are the motivators that win cases. Use the facts to paint a picture of an intoxicated driver. Get to the point. Review the important facts that establish driving under the influence. Emphasize the facts that help you; do not focus on the weaknesses in your case. Prepare charts that outline the facts. Most cases can be divided into the following areas:

1. Driving

Point out unusual driving. Remind the jury of any weaving, speeding, crossing lines, collisions, or other vehicle code violations. Discuss each fact separately, and emphasize these driving errors.

2. Physical Appearance

Describe defendant's appearance. Specifically, note the odor of alcohol; red, bloodshot, watery eyes; slurred speech; poor balance and coordination. Repeat the particular phrases used by witnesses during trial. For instance, if the officer said that "the defendant appeared disoriented" remind the jury of that.

3. Statements

Repeat defendant's statements that support your case. Emphasize his statements about drinking: how much he had to drink, what he was drinking, where he was drinking, and how long he was at the bar. If defendant was untruthful, emphasize those statements to the jury—for example "only two beers."

4. Field Sobriety Tests

List the field sobriety tests and review defendant's performance. Point out the mistakes: put foot down, swayed side to side, and failed to follow instructions. Help the jury understand field sobriety tests by explaining that they are simply balance and coordination tests to help indicate whether defendant was under the influence.

Explain that field sobriety tests and driving both require divided attention. If the defendant is so impaired that he cannot perform these simple balance tests, surely he cannot safely drive a car.

If the Preliminary Alcohol Screening results were admitted to show presence of alcohol, remind the jury of that fact.

5. Officer's Opinion

Remind the jury of the officer's opinion that defendant was under the influence. Explain that the officer is trained in the investigation of DUI cases. Emphasize his experience. Point out that the officer's opinion was based on all of the circumstances: erratic driving, physical appearance of defendant, and performance on the field sobriety tests.

6. Blood Alcohol Tests Results/Criminalist

Write the blood alcohol test results so the jury can see them. If the accuracy of the test is an issue, remind the jury that the testing method is approved by the State of California. Remind the jury that the criminalist is trained and licensed, and that he also gave an opinion that defendant was under the influence. If the defendant refused to take test, argue that his refusal shows he was conscious of his guilt, and that he did not want to provide a sample that would incriminate him. (CALJIC 16.835)

§A:313   Ask Jury to Convict

Remind the jury to consider all facts. All facts taken together establish guilt. End your argument with a planned statement asking the jury to convict.

[§§A:314-A:319 Reserved]

C. Defense Argument and Rebuttal

§A:320   Defense Argument

Most defense arguments will focus on a weakness in one part of your case. These arguments ask the jury to ignore other factors. In reaching a verdict, jurors should consider all of the facts. Point this out. Take notes of the points raised by the defense during argument. Summarize these points so that you can answer them in a logical manner. Most judges allow a wide range in closing argument. Objections should be made sparingly, if at all. You should object if defense argues facts not in evidence or misstates the law.

§A:321   Rebuttal Argument

Your rebuttal argument is limited to responding to points raised in the defense argument. Rebut these points by returning to the specific facts that support your case. Reconcile any factual conflicts raised by the defense. Answer questions and resolve any confusion that the defense has raised. Do not leave the jury with unanswered questions. Correct misstatements of the law. If the defense has incorrectly stated the law, explain the law to the jury. Finally, ask the jury to convict. Plan your closing sentence to request that the jury convict.

[§§A:322-A:329 Reserved]

D. Checklists for Closing Argument

§A:330   What to Do

- Review the charges.
- Review the facts.
- Outline your argument.
- Be logical and organized.
- Prepare charts.
- Use exhibits.
- Practice your argument.
- Make eye contact.
- Speak clearly and directly.
- Stand straight.
- Take the moral high ground.
- Get to the point.
- Keep it short.

§A:331   What to Avoid

- Do not state personal beliefs.
- Do not argue facts not in evidence.
- Do not pace or shift nervously.
- Do not make reference to the defendant's failure to testify.
- Make no mention of post-arrest silence.
- Do not argue to emotions or passions.
- Avoid discussing weaknesses in your case.

[§§A:332-A:339 Reserved]

E. Common Defenses/Responses

Here are some common defense arguments and responses to them.

§A:340   "My Client Only Made a Few Mistakes on the Field Sobriety Tests."

Driving is a matter of inches. It only takes a slight mistake to cause a fatal accident. There is not room for mistakes.

§A:341 "There Was No Accident."

The law does not require an accident—it seeks to prevent accidents. The law requires only that defendant be under the influence. Poor driving is only one of the factors that lead to the conclusion that the defendant was under the influence.

§A:342 "My Client Wasn't Driving."

If defendant wasn't driving, who was? Cars don't drive by themselves. Who was driving? *If* defendant testifies at trial that another person was driving, ask the jury why he didn't tell this to the officer on the night of the arrest?

§A:343 "The Officer Made a Mistake in the Investigation."

Defendant seeks to shift the blame to the officer by focusing on errors in the investigation. Identify this argument for what it is—an attempt to shift the blame. Even if the officer did make a mistake, defendant was still driving under the influence. Focus the guilt back on defendant by refocusing on the facts.

§A:344 "The Officer Is Biased and Just Wants to Win This Case."

Let the jury know that the officer was doing his job, keeping the streets safe by investigating driving under the influence. The officer has nothing to gain in this case. The officer will be back on the street tonight, protecting our streets.

§A:345 "The Chemical Test Results Are Incorrect."

The testing instrument is approved by the Federal Department of Transportation and regulated by the California Department of Public Health for the analysis of breath, blood, and urine samples for legal purposes; the instrument was properly operated when the defendant took the test; and the instrument was maintained properly under the law to assure accuracy.

In addition, the defense argument is asking the jury to speculate that something may have gone wrong. The jury may not speculate, and the sole evidence should point to a properly operated and maintained instrument.

The jury should again be urged to view all of the evidence together, the "totality of the circumstances." It may be appropriate to argue that the alcohol result is merely "the icing on the cake"—that all of the other evidence supports the alcohol result, and that not too many years ago juries made decision based solely upon the objective signs of intoxication and impairment, i.e., that a chemical test result is a piece of evidence meant to corroborate the conclusion that the impairment was due to alcohol.

§A:346 "My Client Had a Rising Blood Alcohol."

This type of argument should be overcome with help from your criminalist. You will need to review the specific facts regarding the time of driving, time of the test, and the alcohol burn-off rate. Have your criminalist help you prepare a chart to explain to the jury.

§A:347 "The People Did Not Call a Certain Witness, so You Don't Have All of the Evidence."

Defendant can call witnesses, and could have subpoenaed the witness. Furthermore, one credible witness is sufficient to prove any fact (CALJIC 2.11).

§A:348 "The Evidence Leaves a Reasonable Doubt."

In responding to reasonable doubt arguments, emphasize "reasonable." Ask the jury to be reasonable, and to use their common sense. Remind the jury to consider all facts together. When all facts are considered, it is clear that defendant is guilty.

Intoxicated persons should be prohibited from driving even if they do not cause an accident. Furthermore, the manner of driving is only one of many factors which may be considered in evaluating whether the driver was under the influence; it is the condition of the drive, not the driving itself, which is important. See CALJIC 16.832.

§A:349 "There Really Was No Bad Driving in This Case."

Bad driving is not an element of the offense; the jury need only find that the defendant drove. Consider the risk the officer runs in permitting a person whose driving is even slightly erratic to continue in the hope that worse driving will occur. Driving under the influence enforcement is most effective when the officers act quickly, before the "bad driving." The argument based upon CALJIC 16.832 indicated in the preceding paragraph is also applicable.

§A:350 "The Officer Is Mistaken, or Has Lied."

Compare the points of view. The officer was sober. The defendant admits to drinking (if applicable) and was found to have a blood alcohol level of ___% (or refused to take a test which would have shown exactly how much he had to drink). Use all portions of the credibility jury instruction to assist in contrasting the officer's and the defendant's believability. The scientific evidence corroborates the officer's observations, not the defendant's story.

§A:351 Arguments Based on Sympathy, Including Those With Racial Overtones

If there is a chemical result, the instrument can be characterized as a truly unbiased witness. It does not distinguish between persons except as to their blood alcohol levels. If the defense asserts that a conviction will cause the defendant to lose his or her job, to be deported, to be separated from his or her family in order to go to jail, or to suffer any consequences, an objection should be made immediately and discussion should be had at the bench with respect to the clear impropriety of the defense argument. The prosecutor should request that the court admonish the jury to disregard counsel's remarks and to reiterate the instructions regarding sympathy and penalty or punishment.

§A:352 "A Critical Fact Is Missing From the Arrest Report and the Officer Is Now Embellishing on the Report to Make the Case Seem Stronger."

Use the whole picture, reiterate the extent of the evidence of against the defendant.

§A:353 "My Client Was Honest With You. He Didn't Come in Here and Tell You That he Hadn't Had Anything to Drink. He Had Two Beers, and That Was All" (the "Two Beers" Defense.)

The admission to the officer or during trial to having consumed any alcohol confirms the officer's detection of alcohol on the defendant's breath. The admission itself, in view of the other evidence indicates a consciousness of guilt, and few people would be willing to—or perhaps even able to—reveal the total amount of alcohol consumed under these circumstances. Few count their drinks, and it is especially difficult to do so after two or three. Finally, a few people act the way the defendant was acting after only two beers; those who do, have a low tolerance for alcohol and are under the influence almost regardless of the amount of alcohol consumed.

If there is a blood alcohol reading, it will corroborate the observations of the officer and impeach the defendant's claim. If the defendant refuses to take a chemical test, the defendant clearly had something to hide, because the test would have shown the actual amount consumed.

§A:354 "My Client Explained to You Why He Refused to Take the Chemical Test."

These explanations vary from case to case and should be discussed in advance with an experienced prosecutor. Occasionally the defendant will assert that the officer did not offer the chemical tests (or refused to let the defendant take one.) The issue then becomes one of credibility, and it may be helpful to call an additional witness in rebuttal that also was present when the defendant refused. It is the practice of many police departments to have a sergeant re-advise the defendant regarding the chemical tests, providing at least two witnesses to the refusal.

§A:355   "Only a Minute Sample of Breath Was Actually Analyzed. You Can't Even See the Alcohol in Such a Small Amount. Can You Convict a Person of a Crime Based Upon Such a Tiny Amount of Alcohol?"

This is truly a bogus argument, yet it may have some appeal to a few jurors if not refuted. If the "minute sample" is a point raised by the defense during the cross-examination of the criminalist, questions such as the following should be asked in redirect examination: "Would you be any more confident of a result if a quart or a liter of breath was analyzed? Why not?" The responses to these questions proved the best basis for the argument against the "minute sample" appeal. Gas chromatography (or whatever scientific principle was utilized in the test in question) does not depend upon whether the naked eye could detect the alcohol; it was approved by the Department of Health because it is an instrument of analysis.

§A:356   "Because My Client Performed Well on the Field Sobriety Tests, He Should Be Acquitted Because That Performance Raised a Reasonable Doubt."

This argument (or any argument concentrating on only one factor) views each factor in a vacuum. Good performance on a field sobriety test does not reasonably explain the totality of the evidence.

§A:357   "The People Get 'Two Bites at the Apple.' They Get to Argue to You Twice, but I Only Get Once Chance."

This or similar comments are almost always made at some point during the defense argument. *It* is seldom persuasive as to any issue in the trial and may not deserve comment during the prosecutor's rebuttal. If, however, a response seems to be called for, it might be simply explained that legal rules of procedure dictate the order of the arguments, and that the People are given the opportunity to refute any arguments made by the defense because the People have the burden of proof.

§A:358   "The DA Didn't Disprove Our Case" or "Show My Client Was Lying; Therefore His Drinking Pattern Is to Be Believed, and Based Upon That Pattern, He Was Less Than .08 at the Time of Driving."

Emphasize that only on TV is an attorney skillful enough to get the defendant to break down on the stand and admit he is lying, and just because you didn't prove he was lying does not mean he is to be believed. The defendant can come into court and say anything he wants about what happened before he was stopped by the police. It's not our burden to disprove that, it is up to the jury to use their common sense and consider the source of the new drinking pattern that just happens to put him under .08 when driving. Did we think for a minute he'd come up with one that put him over? No, the only unbiased, reliable evidence as to his BA is the machine that tested his blood/breath/urine.

EXAMPLE:

We could give the Pope a glass of wine, and Charles Manson water, and the Intoxilyzer would pick out right away which one of those two people had consumed alcohol.

§A:359   "And, Finally, Ladies and Gentleman, I Ask You to Remember That I Cannot Speak to You Again. Please Listen to the Prosecutor's Argument as I Will, Thinking of the Arguments That My Client and I Cannot Make."

This is another one of those rare arguments which probably deserves an objection. The defense is asking the jury to be advocates on behalf of the defendant, urging the jurors to formulate arguments for one of the parties prior to deliberations. This is clearly contrary to the jury instruction admonishing the jurors to keep an open mind and not be advocates for either side. See CALJIC 16.000, Section XVI.

NOTE:

The most valuable resource available to you is your fellow deputies. Don't hesitate to go through the phone list and call any of the deputies in the office and ask about any legal or practical questions you may have.

APPENDIX B

THE DEPOSITION OF MARCELLINE BURNS

INTRODUCTION

In 1998 when Hudson and I formed Kapsack & Bair, the first project we undertook was getting Dr. Burns, the preeminent authority on SFSTs, on the record. We used DMV procedures to notice her deposition and paid her to be there.

Before the deposition, she spent an hour informally discussing SFSTs and her research with us. Once we went on the record, we spent a lot of time to get the two points we wanted:
- SFSTs do not measure driving ability; and
- SFSTs do not show a specific blood alcohol level.

Additionally, Dr. Burns told us SFSTs must be administered correctly and scored according to the NHTSA standards to obtain a valid result.

Months later, Dr. Burns came to a seminar in San Francisco and reiterated these points on videotape, which Troy McKinney of Houston, Texas keeps.

The following deposition was taken on Friday April 17, 1998.

```
 1
 2
 3
 4  IN RE:                        )
 5                                )
    EXAMINATION UNDER OATH        )
 6                                )
                                  )
 7         OF                     )
                                  ) Pages 1 - 62
 8                                )
    MARCELLINE BURNS              )
 9                                )
                                  )
10
11
12
13
14
15
16
17  EXAMINATION UNDER OATH OF MARCELLINE BURNS, Ph.D.
18                    TAKEN ON
19           FRIDAY, APRIL 17, 1998
20
21
22
23
24  REPORTED BY:  LORI RAYE
25           CSR NO. 7052
                                              Page 1
```

```
 1                I N D E X
 2
 3              WITNESS
         MARCELLINE BURNS, Ph.D.
 4
 5
 6  EXAMINATION                        PAGE
 7  BY MR. KAPSACK ....................    4
 8
 9
10
11              EXHIBITS
12
13  NO.          DESCRIPTION          PAGE
14
15  1    Curriculum Vitae of Marcelline    5
         Burns, Ph.D.
16
17
18
19
20
21
22
23
24
25
                                              Page 3
```

```
 1
 2      Examination Under Oath of MARCELLINE BURNS,
 3  Ph.D., taken at 12400 Wilshire Boulevard,
 4  Suite 1300, Los Angeles, California, on Friday,
 5  April 17, 1998, at 12:15 p.m., before Lori Raye,
 6  CSR No. 7052, pursuant to notice.
 7
 8
 9
10  APPEARANCES:
11
12
13  FOR ROBERT SONN:
14
15
    KAPSACK & BAIR, LLP
16  BY:  BRUCE KAPSACK, ESQ.
         HUDSON BAIR, ESQ.
17  353 Sacramento Street
    Suite 1500
18  San Francisco, California  94111
    (415) 421-1021
19
20
21
22
23
24
25
                                              Page 2
```

```
 1 LOS ANGELES, CALIFORNIA, FRIDAY, APRIL 17, 1998
 2          12:20 p.m.
 3
 4
 5      MARCELLINE BURNS, Ph.D.,
 6   HAVING BEEN FIRST DULY SWORN, WAS
 7   EXAMINED AND TESTIFIED AS FOLLOWS:
 8
 9          EXAMINATION
10
11 BY MR. KAPSACK:
12   Q.   Could you please state your name and
13 spell your last name for the record.
14   A.   My name is Marcelline Burns,
15 B-u-r-n-s.
16   Q.   And it's Dr. Burns; correct?
17   A.   Correct.
18   Q.   Have you had your deposition or
19 examination under oath taken in the past,
20 Dr. Burns?
21   A.   I have.
22   Q.   On more than a couple of occasions?
23   A.   Yes.
24   Q.   So you're familiar with the rules of
25 depositions?
                                              Page 4
```

1   A.   I am.
2   Q.   Is there any need for me to go over
3 them with you?
4   A.   No.
5   Q.   Obviously, at the end of this, you'll
6 receive a copy of the transcript. If you need to
7 make any changes, you'll have an opportunity to do
8 so.
9   A.   Okay.
10 Q.   I have here what will be marked as
11 Exhibit 1, a copy of your CV that you gave me
12 today.
13   Is this an accurate and up-to-date
14 copy of your CV?
15 A.   It is.
16 Q.   I'm not going to go into it in any
17 depth.
18   (THE DOCUMENT REFERRED TO WAS MARKED
19 BY THE REPORTER AS EXHIBIT 1 FOR IDENTIFICATION AND
20 IS ATTACHED HERETO)
21 BY MR. KAPSACK:
22 Q.   We're here today to discuss
23 standardized field sobriety tests.
24   Are you familiar with that subject?
25 A.   I am.

Page 5

1   Q.   Could you tell us briefly how it is
2 that you know about standardized field sobriety
3 tests, outside of maybe saying it's something that
4 your father knew and his father before him knew.
5   A.   Well, I'm one of the founders of and
6 the current director of the Southern California
7 Research Institute. That's a nonprofit research
8 group. We're funded by grants and contracts.
9   I don't know how much you know about
10 that process, but contracts are issued when the
11 government agency identifies an area of research
12 that they think needs to be done, and they issue a
13 request for proposal. Any research group that
14 believes they are competent to do that work can
15 respond with a cost proposal and technical
16 proposal.
17   In 1975, the National Highway Traffic
18 Safety Administration, NHTSA, realized that the --
19 this is my understanding of what led to the request
20 for proposals. They recognized that the average
21 blood alcohol concentration of arrests nationwide
22 was .17 percent BAC.
23   The prevailing statute was
24 .10 percent. There may have been one or two that
25 still had a high one, but most of the states had

Page 6

1 gone to .10. If the average arrest is .17, that
2 means that a lot of people who probably ought to go
3 to jail are not doing so because the officer is
4 either not detecting the driving pattern that leads
5 him to stop the vehicle, or once he stops a
6 vehicle, he's not recognizing the presence of
7 alcohol.
8   The National Highway Safety
9 Administration actually funded several research
10 contracts, but the RFP that we responded to was
11 specifically to develop a battery of tests that
12 police officers could use at roadside that would
13 help them to make the correct decision so that it
14 is a competitive bidding process.
15   Our bid, both the technical proposal
16 which outlines how to expect to do it, what your
17 expertise is, so forth, and our cost proposal won
18 that award, and we began that research in 1975.
19 The final report was submitted in 1977, and it was
20 in that report that we recommended the three tests,
21 Horizontal Gaze Nystagmus, Walk-and-Turn and
22 One-Leg Stand.
23   Based on that recommendation, they
24 subsequently issued a second contract to us to do a
25 second study with just those three tests, and that

Page 7

1 one was completed in 1981. So that's how I got
2 into this area.
3   Q.   Okay. Your background information
4 regarding your ability to get into this area, your
5 expertise, et cetera, is covered in your CV;
6 correct?
7   A.   Yes and no.
8   Q.   Okay.
9   A.   At that time, I had several years'
10 background in studying the effects of alcohol and
11 other drugs. I didn't have any background in
12 roadside tests, nor do I think anybody in this
13 country did at that time. It's not a research
14 topic that has gotten a lot of attention worldwide.
15 Q.   Okay. I forgot to ask this in the
16 beginning, so I'll ask it now.
17   Have you testified in court previously
18 regarding standardized field sobriety tests?
19 A.   Yes.
20 Q.   Can you give us a ballpark figure as
21 to the number of times?
22 A.   No, not really. Not an accurate one.
23 A lot of times, but I have no idea how many.
24 Q.   More than ten?
25 A.   Yes.

Page 8

1 Q. More than 100?

2 A. Well, if you include hearings as being

3 testimony, it probably would not be more than 100.

4 I don't know. I have no idea.

5 Q. The times that you have testified

6 either at trials or hearings, have you been

7 admitted as an expert --

8 A. Yes.

9 Q. -- regarding standardized field

10 sobriety tests?

11 A. Yes.

12 Q. Subsequent to your study, were the

13 three standardized field sobriety tests adopted by

14 NHTSA?

15 A. I don't know that NHTSA uses the word

16 "adopted." What they did is they took the

17 findings that we reported to them. They also took

18 our data, our actual data set, and one of their

19 staff, a man named Schweitz, did some additional

20 analysis. Ultimately, they produced a training

21 manual and began to sponsor training.

22   Now, I've told you about all I know

23 about that because I don't work for NHTSA, except

24 as a researcher. So I'm not really privy to all

25 those processes.

Page 9

1 Q. Going back to 1975, shortly after you

2 get the go-ahead and the funding to start the

3 research in this area, did you start with the idea

4 that there were these three tests, Horizontal Gaze

5 Nystagmus, Walk-and-Turn and One-Leg Stand, that

6 you were going to evaluate, or did you look at a

7 broader base of tests that were currently being

8 used or talked about in the field?

9 A. Neither.

10 Q. Okay.

11 A. Any research project -- well, that's a

12 pretty broad statement. I began a project with the

13 literature reviewed to find out what the state of

14 knowledge was concerning that topic at that time.

15 That was the first thing I did.

16   The second thing I did was went around

17 various places in the United States and rode with

18 DUI teams, special enforcement teams to actually

19 determine what it was that they were doing.

20   Then finally, we compiled a fairly

21 long list of tests. I think there were on the

22 order of 15 to 20 that we thought might work. We

23 did some pilot testing with them. It soon became

24 evident that given the constraints at roadside, the

25 time, variability and circumstances, the weather,

Page 10

1 the wide-ranging skills of the people you're

2 dealing with, all of those things, plus you're

3 dealing with the fact of what the squad cars don't

4 have -- they already have too much, and we couldn't

5 suggest adding apparatus on the basis of both cost

6 and just practicality.

7   We had to think about officer safety,

8 what they could do, and all those things eliminated

9 most of the potential tests. We ended with six

10 that we believed had some merit, and then conducted

11 the first laboratory study with those.

12 Q. Regarding the initial list of   15

13 tests, you eliminated some of those based on a

14 variety of reasons.

15   Were there any tests at that time that

16 were being given by officers which, although they

17 may have been given in that particular jurisdiction

18 for a long time, really had no basis in science, no

19 viability? In other words, they really didn't

20 relate to what the officers were investigating?

21 A. I'm not sure I know how to answer

22 that.

23   What officers were doing in 1975

24 was -- there was a lot of variability between

25 agencies, even between officers and even between

Page 11

1 one arrest and the next. "Standardized" was not a

2 word that had entered law enforcement in 1975. I

3 think they were doing the best they could.

4   I've been puzzled about this for a

5 long time, that since the automobile was introduced

6 around the turn of the century, it was recognized

7 that alcohol and driving weren't going to combine

8 very well, if you look at the literature. Why had

9 there been nothing done? The first statute with a

10 number, which happened to be .15, was enacted in

11 Indiana fairly early on. I don't remember the

12 exact date. I have to look it up. So I was really

13 puzzled about why nobody thought about how the

14 officers were going to enforce these statutes.

15   If you think about it, if you're

16 talking about .15, you're talking about a visibly,

17 obviously intoxicated person. Probably they didn't

18 need a lot of help at that point. But when it

19 switched from thinking about drunk drivers to

20 thinking about impaired drivers, which is what the

21 scientific literature was moving toward, then it

22 became clear that officers need some help in being

23 able to recognize the signs and symptoms associated

24 with impairment by alcohol.

25   I forgot why I got onto that long

Page 12

1 exposition, but that's kind of the history of --
2   Q.   My question was, during your initial
3 ride-alongs and stuff, did you see that there were
4 certain tests that really were sort of folklorish,
5 and wonder whether or not they had any basis to aid
6 the officer in the decision you just talked about?
7   For instance, before we started the
8 deposition, I mentioned there was one place where
9 they said they had stopped people and made them
10 recite the alphabet backwards, and that had
11 absolutely no connection.
12   Did you discover, in either some of
13 the tests that you didn't include in your group of
14 15, or later on, that there were certain tests
15 where people or officers or the community thought,
16 hey, this is a good test to give somebody as an
17 indication, but it turns out it really wasn't a
18 good test?
19   A.   Well, certainly, I observed tests that
20 didn't make the cut. Where those tests — you
21 characterized them as folklorish. I don't know
22 where they came from. Since there had been no
23 research in this area, since there had not been a
24 big emphasis on alcohol enforcement, I don't know,
25 but I would suspect they just developed what they

Page 13

1 found to help them. Because at that point, there
2 was no research on the validity and reliability of
3 these things. But yes, there were tests being used
4 in 1975 which did not make it into the first
5 experiment.
6   Q.   Okay. Now, after your initial reading
7 of the literature and some of your ride-alongs,
8 you've culled down to a group of 15. Then you said
9 shortly after moving it into the lab, some of those
10 were cut out for economic reasons or just
11 practicality reasons, like you said, the officer
12 not having the time or equipment, or not being safe
13 to conduct some of these tests on the side of the
14 road, which is the environment the officer finds
15 himself in; correct?
16   A.   Not quite. Those issues are all
17 constraints at roadside. But the reason some of
18 those tests were eliminated in pilot studies could
19 be one of several. Either they weren't sensitive
20 to alcohol, they didn't discriminate between above
21 and below .10, or they were not suitable for
22 certain ages or certain conditions. There were a
23 variety of reasons why they just wouldn't work.
24   Q.   Didn't make the grade?
25   A.   Didn't make the grade.

Page 14

1   Q.   Let me back up a little bit.
2   Obviously, you didn't jump from a huge
3 number, from 15 to 3. It must have been different
4 stages along the way.
5   About how long did that process take?
6   A.   You're talking about almost 25 years
7 ago. I don't know.
8   Q.   Okay. I understand.
9   A.   The research began in '75. A final
10 report was issued in June of '77. I did all the
11 traveling, the literature review and the pilot test
12 before we actually began the experiment. So I
13 would guess it was probably three or four months,
14 but I don't recall.
15   Q.   So obviously, it wasn't a hasty,
16 overnight decision. It went through the stages you
17 just described, the initial reading and observation
18 by yourself, and then some pilot studies?
19   A.   Yes. And when you perform research
20 for the federal government for agencies, they don't
21 just give you the money and walk away and say "Let
22 me know when you get finished." There is an
23 overview process. So you're making monthly
24 progress reports to them, and they're part of the
25 decision process and part of the evolvement of what

Page 15

1 you actually do.
2   So if I had said, just arbitrarily,
3 "Well, I don't like these, and I like these," I
4 would have been called on that. So it's a rigorous
5 process.
6   Q.   Thank you. That was exactly the
7 question I was trying to get to and I didn't hit it
8 quite right, but your answer did.
9   So you didn't say, "I don't like this
10 test, I'm not going to bother with it"; if a test
11 appeared to be a test that was going to make the
12 grade, it stayed in whether you liked it or not,
13 and if it appeared it wasn't going to make the
14 grade, it got dumped by the wayside whether you
15 liked it or not; correct?
16   A.   That's very accurate. Whether I liked
17 it or didn't like it, I don't remember having any
18 strong feelings one way or the other. But in
19 research, numbers are what make the decisions, not
20 your subjective evaluations.
21   Q.   To state the obvious, because that's
22 part of the reason why we're here, this was all
23 done in what is considered scientifically
24 acceptable means; correct, all these testings?
25   A.   That's correct.

Page 16

1   Q.   As you said before, you weren't
2 just -- let me back up.
3   We're saying "you." You weren't alone
4 in this project, were you?
5   A.   No, I was the project director on the
6 first experiment. My colleague, Herbert Moskowitz,
7 was also involved in that one.
8   Q.   So we're using the plural "you," so to
9 speak.
10   A.   Right.
11   Q.   You weren't given the money and cut
12 loose, and the feds said, "Give us a report in two
13 years"; they were watching you, expecting regular
14 reports back?
15   A.   That's correct. Part of your
16 contractual agreement is that you report your
17 progress on a monthly basis.
18   Q.   This may be hard for you to recall,
19 and if you don't recall that's fine.
20   At any time during this process, did
21 the agency or department, whoever was overseeing
22 you for the federal government, besides accepting
23 reports or anything else, ever come in and say
24 "Wait a minute," or "Look at this," or direct you
25 in any way, or were you pretty much allowed to

Page 17

1 focus on what you felt was scientifically correct?
2   A.   I don't recall any instance of them
3 taking exception to anything that we reported and
4 saying "We don't agree with this," or "Take another
5 look," no. We're very good research people, so
6 that's not something that happens to us.
7   Q.   Plus it must have been a little bit
8 hard for anybody, since you're the first ones going
9 down the path, to say "You're not going the right
10 way"?
11   A.   That's true and not true. There was
12 another large-scale project going on in Finland
13 slightly before this. I didn't know about it early
14 on, and so I don't know if NHTSA knew about it.
15 But in fact, there had been a pretty good and
16 rather extensive study that was done differently
17 than what we did because they did it
18 retrospectively by looking at records. But
19 interestingly enough, they came to the same
20 conclusions independently.
21   Q.   So you're at this project for a couple
22 years, and your file report -- I don't know what
23 the right word is. I don't want to say culls or
24 whittles, but you develop the position that the
25 three best tests are the tests that you mentioned

Page 18

1 before, Horizontal Gaze Nystagmus, Walk-and-Turn
2 and One-Leg Stand?
3   A.   That's correct, based on the
4 statistical analysis of that first experiment.
5   Q.   Again, it's not based on any whim or
6 anything; this is what the numbers show?
7   A.   Absolutely.
8   Q.   So you give the final blue ribbon
9 report, all typed on the right-size pages with the
10 right margins that the federal government always
11 wants, tape instead of staples so no one cuts their
12 fingers, and you give it to NHTSA?
13   A.   That's correct.
14   Q.   And now, NHTSA, it's my understanding,
15 put it together in a training manual; correct?
16   A.   Not yet. There's another process.
17   Q.   Okay. Go ahead. What happens next?
18   A.   Well, understand that the first
19 experiment we were examining -- not we. Police
20 officers were examining subjects who had zero
21 to .15 BAC in a double-blind designed experiment
22 with six tests. We had come out of the pilot
23 experiment with six tests that we believed might
24 work at roadside.
25   Q.   Let me interrupt for a minute.

Page 19

1   Could you please tell us what the
2 other three tests were? I'm assuming that three of
3 them are the ones that we've been talking about,
4 and there were three more?
5   A.   Correct. I'll probably have to look
6 at my report.
7   One of them was the Paper-and-Pencil
8 test. We wanted very much to find something to use
9 when the person says, "But I have a bad leg --" or
10 whatever -- "and can't do balance tests." So we
11 had Paper-and-Pencil actually, a couple. We had
12 one and an alternate. Neither one of them proved
13 workable. All of the other tests had some level of
14 accuracy.
15   What we did was take the best ones.
16 Let me -- one of them was the Finger-to-Nose. I'll
17 tell you what the other one was. Finger Count, I
18 think. Correct, Finger Count. So there were the
19 three tests that we finally recommended for the
20 test battery, Finger-to-Nose, Finger Count and
21 Paper-and-Pencil test.
22   Q.   Just so we're clear, given that it was
23 20-some-odd years ago, you had to refresh your
24 recollection.
25   Could you tell us what you looked at?

Page 20

1   A.   I looked at the final report for the
2 research contract.
3   Q.   Okay. So you come out of the pilot
4 program with these six tests?
5   A.   Correct.
6   Q.   You send a report regarding that to
7 NHTSA; is that correct?
8   A.   I'm sure the results of the pilot were
9 reported in a progress report. I no longer have
10 that. Based on the pilot work, we then said, "We
11 propose to do the experiment with these six tests,"
12 and then proceeded to do so.
13   Q.   Is this still under NHTSA? Is this
14 who you're still answering to for the federal
15 government?
16   A.   I don't know what that question
17 means. I don't answer to the federal government.
18   MR. BAIR: Are they the agency that employed
19 you to conduct the study, NHTSA?
20   THE WITNESS: We were under contract to them,
21 yes.
22 BY MR. KAPSACK:
23   Q.   And it hasn't changed to a different
24 organization? This is --
25   A.   During this research?   Page 21

1 you were going to use as experiments.
2   Can you tell us what you mean by
3 "experiment"? This isn't like a chemistry thing.
4   A.   I can describe exactly what we did.
5   Q.   Sure.
6   A.   We recruited the human subjects for
7 the study. The qualifications for this particular
8 study were that they had to be licensed drivers and
9 they had to be willing to drink alcohol. Other
10 than that -- because we wanted to recruit a
11 cross-section of the driving population such that
12 police officers were going to encounter at
13 roadside.
14   By random procedures, we assigned
15 them, unknown to them, to various alcohol
16 conditions. There were more people at zero -- even
17 though they drank a beverage, who were at zero
18 because otherwise, we would have created the
19 expectation to the officer that every other one or
20 every third one is going to be under the influence,
21 and we didn't want to do that. So an officer on a
22 given day might see six people on the road who had
23 had no alcohol. The actual range of BAC's was zero
24 to .15.
25   We recruited ten police officers from   Page 23

1   Q.   Right.
2   A.   No, it was always NHTSA.
3   Q.   I wanted to make sure we were clear on
4 that, and the CIA didn't come in and say "We're
5 taking over this project."
6   A.   No.
7   Q.   So in the report, you suggest to NHTSA
8 that you be allowed to use these six tests to take
9 into the field or into the laboratory?
10   A.   Yes. Although I don't have those
11 progress reports, I'm sure what happened was at the
12 end of the pilot study, in our progress report, we
13 reported the findings on the pilot studies,
14 reported the six that we expected to examine and
15 experiment, and undoubtedly detailed how we were
16 going to conduct the experiment.
17   Q.   Then I would take it that you got the
18 official go-ahead.
19   A.   I'm sure we did.
20   Q.   Because you went ahead?
21   A.   We went ahead.
22   Q.   Okay. So now you go ahead with these
23 six tests?
24   A.   Right.
25   Q.   And you said that these are the ones   Page 22

1 law enforcement agencies in and around Los Angeles,
2 and brought them in for one session which was about
3 four hours long, and we trained them on how we
4 wanted them to administer these six tests. In
5 other words, "You do it this way; not creative, not
6 inventive; you do it this way." But it was a short
7 training, and given that police officers had not
8 had any experience with standardized testing
9 methods, I feel fairly confident saying they hadn't
10 developed any particular confidence themselves in
11 what they were doing.
12   Nonetheless, we brought them in two at
13 the time on weekend days. We brought in, as I
14 recall, about 15 to 20 people for drinking
15 sessions. The officers didn't see the people
16 during the drinking period. They were segregated.
17 They had no contact with them until they reached
18 their peak BAC, measured via breath instrument, and
19 they were introduced into the room. At that point,
20 the officer could ask questions.
21   We had one of our staff in the room as
22 well to observe everything that was going on. He
23 could ask them the kinds of things he asked them at
24 roadside, then administered the test, and then he
25 had to record a decision whether he believed that   Page 24

1 person was above or below .10, which was the
2 statute in California at that time, and whether in
3 the real world, this person would be subject to
4 arrest.
5   Q.   And again, obviously, this was not the
6 type of thing that was done in one weekend or two,
7 but must have stretched out over some time?
8   A.   It did. I don't recall exactly how
9 long. As I said, because it completely took over
10 our facility to have all these people in our
11 facility, we did it on weekends, Saturdays and
12 Sundays. We had two police officers per day, and
13 as I recall, about 15 to 20 subjects, and we ran a
14 total of 238. So it took a while.
15   Q.   Again, you've already mentioned
16 double-blind and the fact that the officers did not
17 see the drinking, so you followed appropriate
18 scientific measures for the experiment.
19   A.   We did.
20   Q.   Again, out of everybody who was
21 working on the experiment throughout any of these
22 tests, the standard field sobriety tests or the six
23 that you were evaluating, nobody did it based on
24 any whim, it was all based on pure numbers?
25   A.   Correct.

Page 25

1   Q.   Did you drop any of the six along the
2 way, or did you wait for the entire experiment to
3 be finished to look at the data?
4   A.   All of the subjects had at least five
5 tests. At this time, I don't remember how we
6 administered the Paper-and-Pencil test, whether it
7 was just people who had some problem with balance.
8 I suspect we administered it to everybody, but I
9 truthfully don't recall without looking it up. But
10 everybody had the complete set of tests.
11   Q.   Then this experimental portion comes
12 to an end, and I guess that's where your hard work
13 really starts is you sit down and look at the data
14 and analyze the data; right?
15   A.   Correct. It's not the hard part.
16 It's the fun part.
17   Q.   Personally, I would have thought the
18 fun part would have been going to hit the drinks.
19   A.   That's the difference between
20 attorneys and research people. We like math.
21   Q.   The only math most attorneys like is
22 33 and 40 percent.
23   A.   I've found that out.
24   Q.   So you crunch the numbers, and you
25 make a determination that you should -- well, let

Page 26

1 me ask you.
2   What happens next, do you determine
3 that three of these are not valid or more valid or
4 what? Where do you go next?
5   A.   Well, once the data is collected, then
6 we do the statistical analysis, and you probably
7 don't want to know about this, but we did things
8 like step-wise linear regression where you put some
9 in and take some out to see which works best.
10   I did canonical correlation, which
11 shows you how you best separate above and below,
12 which tests do that best. I did discriminant
13 function. All of these are very sophisticated and
14 are done by computer. You don't crunch them on
15 your calculator. They're very sophisticated
16 statistical methods for what we needed to do, which
17 is not just the best test but the best
18 combination.
19   It's fairly complex, because one might
20 be the best test, and two might be the second best
21 test, but if one and two are measuring the same
22 kind of thing, you might actually have a better
23 test by taking one and then the third one. So you
24 need to configure the battery as a whole, that best
25 discriminates the above and below .10.

Page 27

1   In fact, what the analysis showed us
2 is that balance is a good measure, walking is a
3 good measure, but if you've already measured
4 balance, you don't gain much by measuring it
5 again. So although Romberg, which was one of our
6 alternates, is a very good test, an excellent test,
7 if you're going to use the One-Leg Stand, you don't
8 really gain enough by doing another balance test to
9 include it. It doesn't mean it's a bad test. It's
10 a good test. But you have not gained anything by
11 adding -- you have not harmed anything, but you've
12 taken up more time.
13   Q.   Right. It's repetitive?
14   A.   It's repetitive. So the final
15 configuration were the three best tests in total
16 for making this discrimination.
17   Q.   Okay. You described the three other
18 tests, and we'll skip the Paper-and-Pencil test
19 because we don't remember it too well, and I've
20 never even heard of it before today.
21   You described the Finger-to-Nose test
22 or Touch-the-Nose test.
23   Was that repetitive of one of the
24 other tests, or was it found not to be an accurate
25 test, or was there just a better configuration as

Page 28

1 to why it was left behind, so to speak?
2   A. It was a sensitive test, as I recall,
3 but it just wasn't quite as good as the ones we
4 recommended. The analysis didn't show it to
5 improve the overall correlation with BAC, either.
6   Q. And the other one was Finger Count?
7   A. Right. Same answer.
8   Q. Same thing, okay.
9   Getting back to something you said,
10 when the officers first came in and you trained
11 them, this was the first time they had really
12 experienced a standardized format.
13   Is that important?
14   A. The standardized?
15   Q. Standardization, is that an important
16 factor?
17   A. Yes, it is.
18   Q. How important? Is it critical, fatal,
19 sort of important?
20   A. Well, if the tests are going to have
21 meaning as objective measures, they have to be
22 administered in a standardized way.
23   If Officer A — let's use
24 Walk-and-Turn, for example.
25   If officer A uses 10 steps down and 12

Page 29

1 steps back, there's nothing inherently wrong with
2 that, and it may give him a good idea whether he's
3 looking at an impairment or not, but it's not the
4 standardized instructions. Therefore, the scoring
5 and the observations don't relate to any of the
6 research data or any of the accumulated data over
7 the years. So it's not that the officer hasn't
8 gained any information; he doesn't have the same
9 base to refer it to if he changes it.
10   Q. So it's almost as if he's creating a
11 new test because he doesn't have the scientific
12 data to back it up on?
13   A. Well, he's just not doing it in a
14 standardized way. "Standardized" means everybody
15 is going to do it the same way every time. So if
16 it's used in Seattle or Miami, it's going to be
17 used in the same way and it's going to be subject
18 to the same interpretation and it's going to have
19 the same meaning when you get into court with it.
20   Q. When you say "meaning," you mean as
21 far as reliability or accuracy?
22   A. I mean both.
23   Q. I think I understand.
24   So if it's given according to the
25 standardized criteria, then the conclusions that

Page 30

1 come from it or the data that's collected from that
2 individual can be related to the data that you've
3 compiled over the years because the officer who
4 gave it in that particular case did it the way it's
5 always been done in the experimental situations
6 correct?
7   A. In the experimental situation and in
8 the field situation, because now we have
9 accumulated a lot of years of experience.
10   Q. Okay. Is there any way that you can
11 adjust for deviation from the standard? For
12 instance, let's just say, speaking generally, that
13 there's a test that the standardized format
14 requires the officer to do five things or asks the
15 individual to do five things, but the officer only
16 does four of those so the officer actually gave
17 80 percent standardization.
18   Can you correlate that back to the
19 data? Can you say, "Since the officer was only
20 80 percent standardized, I should adjust the final
21 result," or does it mean the final result really
22 has no backing?
23   A. Neither of the above.
24   Q. Okay.
25   A. I would not try to adjust it by any

Page 31

1 percentage. But whether or not it has any meaning
2 kind of depends on what the deviation was. Let me
3 give you an example.
4   I once saw an officer taken to task,
5 and that's all I'll say about that because he used
6 the word "pivot" for the Walk-and-Turn. In other
7 words, he said, "You take nine heel-toe steps,
8 counting out loud, leave your arms to the side,
9 watch your step, and when you get to the ninth
10 step, pivot on that step and return in the same
11 manner." The argument being that's not the right
12 word, and you should tell him to turn around by
13 taking small steps. I don't think that makes much
14 difference.
15   There are things that make a
16 difference; there are things that don't make a
17 difference. And I really think you'd have to
18 evaluate it. Some of the things that people get
19 upset about don't make much difference. I mean,
20 use a little common sense. The word "pivot," in my
21 mind, is not a world-shaking error. There are
22 other things that are more distressing.
23   If you don't give the instructions
24 properly, you don't tell them to leave their arms
25 at their side, count their steps out loud, take

Page 32

1 nine steps, et cetera, those are critical because
2 the nature of the task requires them to assume the
3 stance on the line, to stand in that position while
4 they're given instructions, and the ability to
5 understand and follow the instructions is part of
6 the test.
7   ~~So if they don't do that, that's~~
8 ~~important. And then whether or not the results~~
9 ~~have as much meaning as you would like them to~~
10 ~~becomes problematic.~~
11   Q.   Let me see if I can bring this to a
12 level that at least I understand.
13   For instance, nine steps is the
14 standard on a Walk-and-Turn; correct?
15   A.   Correct.
16   Q.   If the officer tells the person to
17 take only seven steps instead of nine, but the
18 person falls off the line each and every time, it's
19 not really important that he only had him do seven?
20   A.   That's correct.
21   Q.   But on the other hand, if the officer
22 says "I want you to take 35 steps," and after 13 or
23 14 the guy steps off the line, that kind of
24 deviation may mean that the officer's conclusion
25 that the person is under the influence or over a

Page 33

1 certain level could be wrong because he's gone to
2 the point that it could be fatigue or something
3 else?
4   A.   I think you got the meaning of it. I
5 frequently hear, for example, a lot of argument in
6 court about whether or not the stimulus for HGN was
7 held exactly 12 inches in front of the person. We
8 wrote into the instructions a distance as being a
9 comfortable focal distance so that the person is
10 not trying to focus too near and gets sick and
11 throws up, or is so far you're not sure.
12   You know, whether it's 11 and a half
13 or 13, I don't really care. But you have to give
14 an instruction. In other words, hold the stimulus
15 approximately 12 inches in front, up a little bit
16 so you can see their eyes. You have to take these
17 things in context.
18   MR. BAIR: But sort of also within reason?
19   THE WITNESS: That's correct. The
20 instructions, as they're written, are written for a
21 reason. You know, having them assume the position
22 on the line while they listen to the instructions,
23 that's an important component of the test. How the
24 stimulus is held and how it's moved, those are all
25 part of the test. But a slight deviation of the

Page 34

1 focal distance is not going to undermine the
2 results.
3 BY MR. KAPSACK:
4   Q.   Okay. These instructions that you
5 talk about are the instructions that eventually
6 found their way into the NHTSA manual?
7   A.   Correct.
8   Q.   Did you get an opportunity -- and I
9 know we're jumping around a little bit, but did you
10 get an opportunity to review the NHTSA manual
11 before it was put into mass publication to make
12 sure they didn't change any of the things you had
13 told them along the way?
14   A.   Again, yes and no. The first manual
15 was sent to me, and I reviewed it, and there was at
16 least one thing in the manual which I thought was
17 an error and advised them of it. It was
18 subsequently changed. But there have been
19 subsequent editions, and I'm not sure that I have
20 reviewed all of those, certainly not prior to their
21 release. I may have eventually obtained a copy of
22 all of them, but I didn't review them.
23   MR. BAIR: But, really, the conclusions from
24 your first study, more or less, have remained the
25 same? All of your additional studies have only

Page 35

1 served to compound those conclusions or to
2 reinforce those conclusions?
3   THE WITNESS: There have been no substantive
4 changes in the tests or the -- NHTSA developed the
5 scoring; I didn't. There have been some slight
6 changes. NHTSA made some slight changes in
7 instructions that differ from what we did. Again,
8 I don't think they're substantive, and I don't
9 think they matter.
10   MR. BAIR: Have you done any tests regarding
11 the effectiveness of, like, the Hand-Pat test as a
12 method of testing the sobriety of the driver?
13   THE WITNESS: Unless the Hand-Pat was part of
14 that original series that we pilot tested, the
15 answer is no. I don't remember if it was in that,
16 but we didn't use it in either of the main
17 experiments.
18   MR. BAIR: So over the years, I guess, like
19 law enforcement has developed certain kinds of
20 tests, have you added any of them in and tested
21 their efficacy, or have you continued to stick with
22 the three that you originally determined to be the
23 most accurate?
24   THE WITNESS: Standardized field sobriety
25 testing, which includes the three tests we're

Page 36

1 talking about here, has not changed.
2   Let me add that the drug recognition
3 expert policeman uses five tests, and they include
4 the Finger-to-Nose and the Romberg with a time
5 estimation. There are very good reasons for doing
6 that when you're looking for drugs because those
7 two tests give you information with regard to drug
8 symptoms that the others don't. But the
9 standardized field sobriety tests have not
10 changed.
11 BY MR. KAPSACK:
12   Q.   I guess part of the question that I
13 was picking up is, has there been any time that
14 somebody said, "Hey, the officers in Alabama have
15 just started doing this test, and they say it works
16 really well"?
17   Have you had that kind of information
18 come to you and had a chance to evaluate that? Has
19 anybody said, "There's a new test that officers are
20 using," and you say, "Let's put it in the lab and
21 see if it works"?
22   A.   No. First of all, I see a lot of road
23 tests used by officers because I see arrest
24 reports. But you have to understand when you're
25 nonprofit research, you only do what somebody pays

Page 37

1 you to do. You don't have the luxury of doing
2 anything else.
3   Q.   I assume that you keep up to date in
4 this field, keep abreast of any other studies that
5 are going on regarding —
6   A.   Field sobriety tests?
7   Q.   Yes.
8   A.   To my knowledge, there are not any
9 others going on.
10   Q.   Well, that was the follow-up
11 question.
12   A.   To my knowledge. It's possible that
13 somebody somewhere is doing something, but I have
14 no information about that.
15   Q.   Obviously, some little sheriff's
16 office somewhere could be doing their own
17 experiment. But if it was a major type of thing,
18 you would know about it?
19   A.   Yes, I would. Let me add, there has
20 been a revalidation or validation study for
21 the .08. That was done by a research group called
22 National Public Services Research Institute in
23 Landover, Maryland. It was done two or three years
24 ago. Essentially, they said, "Guess what? These
25 are the best tests."

Page 38

1   Q.   I know the answer, but we have to get
2 it down for the reporter.
3   When you say "Guess what? These are
4 the best tests," you mean the same three we've been
5 talking about?
6   A.   Correct.
7   Q.   Now, these standardized tests were
8 developed as an aid for officers to make an initial
9 determination in the field as to initially whether
10 or not the person had a blood alcohol level that
11 was over .1; correct? That was the initial —
12   A.   That's correct, .1 or above.
13   Q.   These tests, in and of themselves,
14 don't state whether the person is able to drive the
15 vehicle. In other words, these tests show there is
16 a likelihood that someone is over .1, and since the
17 medical community is pretty much in agreement that
18 over .1 means you're not capable of operating a
19 motor vehicle reasonably under the law, at least,
20 the tests can therefore be used for that, but
21 directly, the tests don't show the ability or
22 inability to operate a motor vehicle; correct?
23   A.   Correct. What you're asking is, are
24 these tests of driving? They are not. If they
25 were tests of driving, they would be field driving

Page 39

1 tests. I can elaborate on the reasons and
2 everything behind that if you want, but they are
3 not tests of driving. They are tests of sobriety.
4 There's a whole series of literature that tests
5 alcohol and driving schools.
6   Q.   That's the missing link, so to speak.
7 The sobriety tests will tell you the probable level
8 of alcohol, or at least the probable minimal level
9 of alcohol, and then you go to the literature or
10 the expert or the doctor to say what effect that
11 level of alcohol will have on a person's mental and
12 physical abilities regarding driving?
13   A.   Well, the research over the years is
14 what led the legislators to choose the levels that
15 they did. And as the research accumulates, those
16 levels keep coming down. The officer is not
17 charged with making a decision about driving skills
18 at roadside. He couldn't. There's no way you can
19 judge somebody in five minutes at roadside that you
20 never saw before to make a decision about their
21 driving skills.
22   What he is charged with doing is
23 making a judgment about their sobriety or presence
24 of alcohol or impairment by alcohol, if you will.
25   Q.   To fill in the blanks a little bit, I

Page 40

1 believe we left off historically with your taking
2 the original six through the experimental stages,
3 and coming down with three.
4   A.   Correct.
5   Q.   And do you recall about when that was?
6   A.   That report was submitted in June of
7 1977.
8   MR. BAIR: That was the '77 report?
9   THE WITNESS: Correct.
10   MR. BAIR: And you did a report in '81?
11   THE WITNESS: That was the follow-up contract
12 that studied only the three.
13 BY MR. KAPSACK:
14   Q.   So '77 comes, you've been submitting
15 progress reports to NHTSA all along, but now you
16 start with the ride-alongs and the reading, culling
17 it down to 15, taking the 15 down to six, and the
18 six to the experiment. Now you say, "These three
19 are the three best, as far as we're concerned, that
20 we recommend should be the standardized battery,"
21 NHTSA takes that and agrees with you?
22   A.   I don't know if we used the word
23 "recommend." What you do in the final report is
24 you report everything you did. Everything. Who
25 the subjects were, how you did the experiment, your

Page 41

1 data analysis. Then you reach some conclusions
2 based on that set of work. Those conclusions were
3 that those three tests were the best at
4 discriminating between above and below .10.
5   Q.   So now four years goes by.
6   A.   Couple years. A year and a half, two
7 years.
8   Q.   Okay. I'm not going to ask you what
9 NHTSA did, because you don't work for them so you
10 don't know. But they turn around and say "We're
11 soliciting proposals again," or something along
12 those lines?
13   A.   Yes.
14   Q.   This time, it's for a follow-up study?
15   A.   What the second study was to do was to
16 do further research with the three tests to
17 standardize them. In other words, to standardize
18 them and develop the scoring and the administration
19 procedures so that they would be as sensitive as
20 you can make them. In other words, we have
21 identified the best tests. Now let's make it the
22 very best test battery we can make it.
23   Q.   Some fine-tuning?
24   A.   Some fine-tuning.
25   Q.   Same type of thing, you submit your

Page 42

1 proposal and you get it?
2   A.   Correct.
3   Q.   You get the contract?
4   A.   Correct.
5   Q.   This was in what year, if you recall?
6   A.   Well, the final report was in '81,
7 which leads me to believe it would have been '79.
8 I don't recall the exact date of the initiation,
9 but it was, again, a two-and-a-half to three-year
10 project.
11   Q.   So you spent about a year and a half,
12 two years analyzing data again, fine-tuning —
13   A.   We ran a whole other experiment.
14   Q.   You ran a whole other experiment?
15 Okay. Same type of experiment you described
16 before?
17   A.   Very similar, except now we only use
18 three tests, not six, but the design was similar.
19 We brought ten police officers in, trained them how
20 to do it in a standardized way, recruited
21 subjects. Everything was double-blind.
22   One thing we did differently between
23 the two and the one is that in the second study, we
24 brought about 100 of the subjects back for a second
25 session. The reason for that was to examine the

Page 43

1 reliability of the tests. "Reliability" being used
2 here in the statistical sense. It's very similar,
3 but has a very specific meaning.
4   If you bring the subjects back,
5 produce the same BAC, have them examined again with
6 the same tests, sometimes by the same officer,
7 that's one kind of check. Sometimes by a different
8 officer. Do you get the same results?
9   And you have to have two
10 administrations of the test battery to the same
11 person in order to do that. So that was an
12 addition.
13   Also, we did a small field study. Not
14 a good field study, not big enough. There were a
15 lot of things that we didn't like about it, and
16 reported that we didn't like it because there
17 weren't funds to do it. That was the second.
18   Q.   So you submit that report, or the
19 report of all this in '81?
20   A.   Correct.
21   Q.   And you fine-tune the standardization?
22   A.   Correct.
23   Q.   And supplement your findings with the
24 additional data?
25   A.   This time we had 297 subjects.

Page 44

1   Q.   And that's 18 years ago.
2   What's the next?
3   A.   Well, the next step is NHTSA's step,
4   and I'm not really the person to tell you exactly
5   what and how and why they did it, except as an
6   outsider, to say that training began sometime
7   thereafter of law enforcement nationwide.
8   Q.   I take it throughout this you're still
9   involved in it to a certain degree.
10   When is the next time you get a
11 contract or do a study, or anything along those
12 lines?
13 A.   Well, the next time I actually worked
14 for NHTSA that involved these tests was with a
15 study of the Drug Recognition Program, of which
16 these tests are a component, and that was in 1985.
17 That's the only work I directly did for NHTSA,
18 except to appear as an expert.
19 Q.   Getting back to the tests themselves,
20 why three? Is there any significance to why —
21 you've already told us you found that some of them
22 were repetitive and things like that.
23   Can the officer make a reliable
24 decision based on one test, or does he need all
25 three?   Page 45

1   A.   Okay. One of the reasons for three,
2   coming at it from one direction, is officers don't
3   have all night to do all the tests in the world out
4   there. There is a limit as to the amount of time
5   they can invest in any one stop. So the
6   redundancy -- I can't justify the redundancy. If
7   you're not getting more information, why do more
8   tests?
9   Coming at it from the other direction,
10 although Horizontal Gaze Nystagmus is almost as
11 good alone a predictor as all three tests, it's
12 kind of a maximum of testing, whether roadside or
13 educational or psychological or medical testing,
14 that if it's an important decision, you don't want
15 to base it, unless you have to, unless
16 circumstances force you to -- but you would prefer
17 to have evidence from more than one test.
18   If you had very disparate results —
19 let's take another field. If you went to your
20 physician and he had one test that said you have
21 diabetes and another that said you have heart
22 disease and another that said you have cancer, I
23 think he would be a little puzzled. He would like
24 to see all his markers, blood tests, EKG's,
25 pointing in one direction to give him some
                                              Page 46

1   confidence in his diagnosis.
2   So instead of saying, "Horizontal Gaze
3   Nystagmus is a pretty good test and predictor;
4   we'll just go with that," you really need more
5   evidence, in my view. And I think that's a pretty
6   widely held view.
7   So there were three, but as I said
8   before, we found adding to that of those six that
9   we identified didn't really improve predictions, so
10 we didn't have four or five.
11 Q.   And you don't have only one for the
12 reasons you just stated, because you want a second
13 opinion, you want a little backup there?
14 A.   Well, there's always a risk if you
15 rely on a single marker. Now, sometimes an officer
16 may have to. The circumstances may be such that
17 the only thing he can do is look at their eyes.
18 But let's suppose you have somebody who has a real
19 problem with balance because of some medical
20 condition, or you have somebody who has really
21 strange eyes for some reason that I don't know.
22 But if that's the only test you have, you really
23 don't have any basis for a decision.
24 Q.   Now, initially when you did the
25 experiments on these, they were done in the   Page 47

1   facilities where you have a somewhat controlled
2   environment?
3   A.   Absolutely.
4   Q.   The overwhelming percentage, if not
5   100 percent of the time these tests are given on
6   the side of the road, how much of a factor does
7   that play?
8   A.   That plays a factor that works --
9   well, there's a number of factors working here, and
10 it works both ways. Certainly, in the controlled
11 environment where there was no consequence to an
12 officer's error, that had to affect the data. If
13 you look at the data, you can see it did.
14   One of the things that I'm often
15 challenged on is in the first experiment, they made
16 a lot of false alarms. That is, they said this
17 person is above .10 when, in fact, they weren't.
18 If you look at the data as I did, you discover that
19 their criterion was really .08. In other words,
20 they were saying arrest at the point they saw
21 significant impairment. That was .08, not .10.
22   Their sergeants are not going to be
23 upset and the lieutenant is not going to be upset
24 if they make an error, and this person is not going
25 back on the road driving impaired. So you can't
                                              Page 48

1 recreate all the same variables in the laboratory
2 that you have at roadside, which is one of the
3 reasons I wanted to do a field study.
4   Q.   And conversely, in the laboratory, you
5 don't have some of the distractions that you would
6 have on the roadside?
7   A.   That's true.
8   Q.   For instance, I would assume you kept
9 the laboratory fairly well lit. It's not the kind
10 of nighttime stop that officers get involved in.
11   A.   True. Another important variable is
12 that those officers had just been trained, with one
13 exception, and that was in the second study. None
14 of them had heard of Horizontal Gaze Nystagmus
15 before. It takes a period of learning to believe
16 what you really see for officers who are trained in
17 nystagmus. So my concern, my interest was in
18 finding what officers who had used the test battery
19 for a period of time were capable.
20   (DISCUSSION HELD OFF THE RECORD)
21 BY MR. KAPSACK:
22   Q.   There also must be a period of
23 institutional learning for which most police
24 departments are notoriously slow. When you talk
25 about confidence, the officers had to have

Page 49

1 confidence when they came to you individually. I'm
2 sure the first few times you told the officers,
3 "You're going to take a stimulus and move it in
4 front of their eyes," they must have looked at you
5 like you were crazy.
6   A.   I'm sure they did.
7   Q.   But then when they went back to their
8 departments and they said, "No, it really works,"
9 I'm sure the rest of the officers looked at them
10 like they were crazy, too.
11   A.   There is a period of accepting.
12 Police officers are notorious for not accepting
13 newfangled ideas, so to speak.
14   Q.   When these tests are done on the side
15 of the road, is there a set standard or a given
16 margin that the officer should use regarding
17 mistakes or failures in the field sobriety tests
18 that he should attribute to the environment, if you
19 understand me?
20   A.   I understand you. I'm trying to think
21 if there's any such thing.
22   The only thing that's required for
23 nystagmus is that the suspect be able to see the
24 stimulus and the officer be able to see his eyes.
25 It doesn't matter if the wind is blowing or it's

Page 50

1 raining, you know. Those things just don't
2 matter.
3   Walk-and-Turn, preferably, is done on
4 a flat, dry surface. If it cannot be, then I think
5 the officer is going to have to take that into
6 account. But to my knowledge, there are no
7 particular guidelines that -- there's been no
8 research that says that if the pavement slopes X
9 number of degrees, that cannot been done. But I
10 don't think it would be possible to do it.
11   Again, I think it's a matter of common
12 sense, but it has not been a matter of research.
13   MR. BAIR: Footwear would make a significant
14 impact on a study with regard to the
15 Walk-and-Turn.
16   THE WITNESS: It can, and I think it depends
17 on the individual. Depending on where it is and
18 the circumstances, officers very often give
19 somebody who is wearing high heels or boots with
20 heels the option of taking them off.
21 BY MR. KAPSACK:
22   Q.   I would assume that Walk-and-Turn
23 would be hard in a six-inch spike heel.
24   A.   Unless you do every day, then it's a
25 piece of cake.

Page 51

1   MR. BAIR: Tennis shoes may be difficult,
2 then.
3 BY MR. KAPSACK:
4   Q.   Have you ever been asked by NHTSA, or
5 has there ever been a proposal that was requested
6 regarding any of the other tests that have come and
7 gone, such as, I believe the Hand-Pat was
8 mentioned, or a written alphabet or anything like
9 that that you know of that you've been involved in?
10   A.   I've never been asked to do any
11 research with those. It's possible -- I don't
12 remember the report from the more recent study for
13 the .08. They did use some other tests, but I
14 don't remember now what they were.
15   MR. BAIR: I think I just would like to get
16 down specifically what those three tests are. If
17 you could, tell us the walk out nine steps, walk
18 back, exactly what those tests are so that we have
19 a record of exactly what those tests are that your
20 group came to the conclusion were accurate.
21   THE WITNESS: Well, HGN, which is a jerking
22 movement of the eyeballs, is administered by having
23 the individual stand with their arms at their side,
24 holding his or her head still, and the officer or
25 person administering the test holds the stimulus

Page 52

1 approximately 12 inches in front of their face,
2 elevated slightly so they'll open their eyes.
3 Because the point is, you have to see their eyes.
4 Then he or she moves the stimulus -- how shall I
5 describe it? -- back and forth in front of the
6 eyes laterally and observes that individual's
7 eyes.
8   First of all, the determination is
9 made whether the eyes can track the stimulus
10 smoothly, or whether they jerk as they move. I'm
11 tempted to use my hands because I teach it. So
12 lack of smooth pursuit is one sign. That's worth
13 one point in each eye.
14   The second sign is the distinct
15 jerking at maximum deviation. In other words, when
16 the eyes have been moved as far as they can go to
17 the side, and then held there for about four
18 seconds, is there a distinct jerking, not just a
19 little tremor? Because that can occur because it's
20 an uncomfortable position. There needs to be a
21 distinct jerking that persists.
22   And then finally, the person who is
23 administering the test looks for the angle of gaze
24 when there's the first onset of jerking. In other
25 words, has the individual deviated his eyes 40

Page 53

1 degrees, 45 degrees or 30 degrees? Because it's
2 the relationship between that and the BAC.
3   MR. BAIR: Each one of those is worth one
4 point in each eye?
5   THE WITNESS: That's correct. So a maximum of
6 six, and four points is a basis for taking them
7 in.
8   The Walk-and-Turn test is just what it
9 sounds like, a test of the individual's ability to
10 walk and execute a turn and return. They're told
11 to put the left foot on the line, put the right
12 foot in front of it and stand in that position
13 while the officer gives the rest of the
14 instructions.
15   He then instructs and demonstrates by
16 showing what heel-to-toe is. He tells the
17 individuals, "I want you to take nine heel-to-toe
18 steps along the line. Watch your feet at all
19 times, leave your arms at your side, and count your
20 steps aloud. When you get to the ninth step, turn
21 around, take small steps turning around and come
22 back along the line in the same way with nine
23 heel-to-toe steps. Do you understand?"
24   And if the individual says "I don't
25 understand," then the officer repeats the

Page 54

1 instructions. And there are eight -- I believe
2 there are eight errors that can be scored. Two
3 errors are reason to arrest.
4 BY MR. KAPSACK:
5   Q. Let me interrupt you for a second
6 here. We talked about this a little bit earlier.
7   You said they should take little
8 steps, and we talked about how the officer has to
9 use common sense.
10   A. He demonstrates that, by the way.
11   Q. Right.
12   I have seen this where the officer has
13 prescribed that it must be a specific number of
14 steps.
15   A. To turn around?
16   Q. To turn around. I have seen and heard
17 them say "You must pivot on your foot using three
18 steps to turn around."
19   A. I'm not aware of the source of that.
20   Q. This is part of the problem, little
21 bits that have been added and taken away that have
22 occurred in some places.
23   A. Let me say that I don't think that
24 would do any harm unless he scored an error for
25 failure to take three steps. If he wants them to

Page 55

1 take three steps, I don't think that's a big deal.
2 But he has no basis to score against them for
3 taking four because that's not part of the
4 standardized testing.
5   Q. That gets back to your testimony
6 before, because that's what gives it its
7 reliability.
8   A. That's what gives it its predictive
9 power.
10   Q. Predictive power?
11   A. "Reliability" means something
12 different to me.
13   Q. I like that, "predictive power."
14   A. Yeah. What you're trying to do is
15 predict accurately whether this person is going to
16 have a breath test that shows above or below .10.
17   Q. If I, as an officer, score something
18 as an error that's not considered an error under
19 the standardized rules, then my power of
20 predictability is not very good.
21   MR. BAIR: Or has been diminished.
22 BY MR. KAPSACK:
23   Q. Could be getting worse, because we've
24 never studied that aspect.
25   A. Could be. Sometimes officers tell me

Page 56

1 with misguided pride that they've made the test a
2 little more difficult, or changed it. I don't like
3 to discourage hard-working police officers, but I
4 have to say to them, "That's very interesting, and
5 it may be that your test is better, but we don't
6 know that. So please don't do it."
7   MR. BAIR: Maybe they're getting down to .06,
8 which may be the next test.
9   THE WITNESS: If the American Medical
10 Association and MADD has its way, we're going to
11 .05.
12 BY MR. KAPSACK:
13   Q.   The third test I think is where we
14 were.
15   A.   Third is the One-Leg Stand, and the
16 suspect is told to stand with their feet together,
17 to lift one leg, either one, approximately six
18 inches off the ground, point the toe, watch their
19 toe, their foot at all times, and to count.
20   Now, this is a place where NHTSA has
21 made a change. Our instructions were -- I don't
22 think it's a significant change, but just so you're
23 aware of it, originally we said you count 1,001,
24 1,002, 1,003, until you reach 1,030.
25   We wanted to be sure they held that

Page 57

1 stance for 30 seconds because it turns out that
2 people at .10 very often can hold it to 20 or 25
3 seconds. It's only when the attention begins to
4 waiver that the balance gets messed up. So it's
5 critical to hold it for 30 seconds, and that was
6 the point of the counting.
7   NHTSA has just within the last couple
8 years changed that instruction so that they're now
9 told "Count 1,001, 1,002, 1,003, until I tell you
10 to stop." And the officer now times it for 30
11 seconds and then records the count. In other
12 words, if a person was at 25, they write down 25.
13 And that's what they do.
14   Q.   You had been giving us points before.
15   Do you recall the points on this one?
16   A.   I believe it's two.
17   Q.   Again, getting back to one of the
18 broader themes, the person is supposed to hold
19 their foot six inches off the ground, but the six
20 inches isn't the key here?
21   A.   No.
22   Q.   It's holding it off the ground?
23   A.   Correct.
24   Q.   The officer should not be out there
25 measuring whether it's five and a half or eight

Page 58

1 inches?
2   A.   No. You have to give them some
3 instruction. I mean, there's a difference between
4 six inches and straight out. But if it's five and
5 a half inches or seven inches, it's not going to
6 make a difference in the test. I suppose there's
7 some point like a fulcrum at which it's easier to
8 balance, perhaps. I don't know. But the
9 instructions are six inches, approximately six
10 inches off the ground.
11   Q.   In all these tests, again, common
12 sense plays an important role. For instance, you
13 know, for any of these tests, I would guess,
14 standing on one leg came to my mind immediately if
15 it's being done in a place where the highway goes
16 in a mountain gap, and you've got 25-mile-an-hour
17 winds. It's probably not the best place to give
18 the test, and that's going to have some effect.
19   A.   It might be difficult, but, you know,
20 the field tests we did in Colorado, one of the
21 things we were interested in was, are these tests
22 valid in Colorado mountains where it snows and
23 blows and does all kinds of unpleasant things? And
24 we didn't find any significant effect of the
25 weather, except that officers tended to make a

Page 59

1 mistake by letting people go who should have been
2 arrested if they didn't have on adequate clothing.
3 In other words, if it was cold and they didn't have
4 a jacket, they tended to make an error by releasing
5 them.
6   Q.   By assuming some of the mistakes were
7 as a result of being cold?
8   A.   Either that, or they just felt sorry
9 for them.
10   MR. BAIR: Didn't complete the tests?
11   THE WITNESS: Just didn't keep them -- that's
12 the only thing I can assume. If officers make an
13 error, it's far more likely to be a release than an
14 arrest. They don't arrest very many incorrectly,
15 but they release enough incorrectly that, as road
16 users, we should worry.
17   MR. KAPSACK: I'd like to take a five-minute
18 break.
19   (BRIEF RECESS)
20   MR. KAPSACK: That's all we have. Thank you.
21
22
23
24
25

Page 60

<table>
<tr><td>

1   DECLARATION

2

3

4

5   I hereby declare that I am the deponent in the

6 within matter; that I have read the foregoing

7 examination under oath and know the contents

8 thereof. And I declare that the same is true of my

9 knowledge, except as to the matters which are

10 therein stated upon my information or belief, and

11 as to those matters, I believe it to be true

12   I declare under the penalties of perjury of

13 the State of California that the foregoing is true

14 and correct.

15   Executed on the _____ day of _____

16 19 , at _____ .

17

18

19

20   *

21   ——————W I T N E S S—————

22

23

24

25

                                        Page 61

</td><td>

1

2   I, Lori Raye, A Certified Shorthand Reporter

3 for the State of California, do hereby certify:

4   That prior to being examined, MARCELLINE

5 BURNS, Ph.D., the witness named in the foregoing

6 examination under oath was by me duly sworn to

7 testify the truth, the whole truth and nothing but

8 the truth pursuant to Section No. 2093 of the Code

9 of Civil Procedure;

10   That said examination under oath was taken

11 before me, at the time and place therein set forth,

12 and was taken down by me stenographically and

13 thereafter transcribed;

14   I further certify that I am neither counsel

15 for, nor related to, any party to said action, nor

16 in anywise interested in the outcome thereof.

17   In witness whereof, I have hereunto

18 subscribed my name this 5th day of May 1998.

19

20

21

22   ——————————————
         LORI RAYE

23   CSR No. 7052

24

25

                                        Page 62

</td></tr>
</table>

(This page intentionally left blank.)

APPENDIX C

ARREST VIDEO ANALYSIS FORM

Client's Name: _____ Date of Offense: _____

Phase I: Vehicle in Motion

Video start time: _____ Video end time: _____

Stop location: _____ Accident: Y / N

Less safe charge: _____

Where does officer begin to follow client? _____

Start time: _____ Place: _____

Initial observations: _____

Stop time: _____

Observation of stop: _____

_____

Phase II: Personal Contact

First statement by officer: _____

_____

First statement to officer by client: _____

_____

Production of driver's license and insurance: _____

_____

_____

Exit of vehicle: _____

_____

Speech: _____ Attitude: _____

Swaying: Y / N   Balance: _____

Phase III: Pre-arrest Screening

I. Horizontal Gaze Nystagmus

For officer safety, the officer should keep his or her weapon pointed away from the suspect.

Any lights flashing: Y / N   Where? _____

What direction is suspect placed in relation to flashing lights or lights on the scene? _____

_____

Instructional Phase:

"I am going to check your eyes."

"Keep your head still and follow this stimulus with your eyes only."

"Keep following the stimulus with your eyes until I tell you to stop."

Eyeglasses removed: Y / N

Position the stimulus approximately 12-15 inches from the suspect's nose: Y / N

Position the stimulus slightly above eye level: Y / N

Eyes checked for equal pupil size: Y / N

Resting nystagmus checked: Y / N

Equal tracking (time of test): _____   Are eyes tracking stimulus together? Y / N

Stimulus moved side to side: Y / N   45-degree angle: Y / N   Client swaying: Y / N

Stimulus stopped and held at maximum deviation for minimum of four seconds: Y / N

Length of actual time: _____

Head held still: Y / N

Vertical gaze nystagmus checked: Y / N

Instructional Phase:

"Keep your head still and follow this stimulus with your eyes only."

"Keep following the stimulus with your eyes until I tell you to stop."

Stimulus held 12" to 15" from nose: Y / N

Stimulus held slightly above eye level: Y / N

Head held still: Y / N   Client swaying: Y / N

Stimulus held for minimum of four seconds: Y / N

Length of actual time: _____

II. Walk and Turn

Start time: _____   Stop time: _____

Instructional Phase for Initial Positioning:

"Place your left foot on the line."   Demonstrated by officer: Y / N

"Place your right foot on the line ahead of the left foot, with the heel of the right foot against the toe of left foot."

Demonstrated by officer: Y / N

"Place your arms down at your sides."   Demonstrated by officer: Y / N

"Maintain this position until I have completed the instructions. Do not start until told to do so."

"Do you understand the instructions so far?"

Cannot keep balance (feet must break apart): Y / N   Starts too soon: Y / N

Instructional Phase for Walking Stage:

"When I tell you to start, take nine heel-to-toe steps, turn, and take nine heel-to-toe steps back."

"When you turn, keep the front foot on the line, and turn by taking a series of small steps with the other foot, like this."

Demonstrated by officer: Y / N

"While you are walking, keep your arms at your sides, watch your feet at all times, and count your steps out loud."

"Once you start walking, don't stop until you have completed the test."

"Do you understand the instructions?"

"Begin, and count your first step from the heel-to-toe position as 'One.'"

First Nine Steps	Second Nine Steps

First Nine Steps

Stops while walking: Y / N

Misses heel to toe: 1 2 3 4 5 6 7 8 9

Raises arms: _____

Steps off line: _____

Actual steps taken: _____

Incorrect # of steps: _____

Second Nine Steps

Stops while walking: Y / N

Misses heel to toe: 1 2 3 4 5 6 7 8 9

Raises arms: _____

Steps off line: _____

Actual steps taken: _____

Incorrect # of steps: _____

Misc Factors:

If wearing heels 2 inches or more: was suspect given opportunity to remove shoes prior to exam? Y / N

Surface Area:

Dry: Y / N   Hard: Y / N   Level: Y / N   Nonslippery: Y / N   A safety concern: Y / N

Well lit: Y / N   Distracting conditions: Y / N   Lots of traffic: Y / N

III. One Leg Stand

Instructional Phase:

"Please stand with your feet together and your arms down at the sides, like this."

Officer demonstrates: Y / N

"Do not start to perform this test until I tell you to do so. Do you understand the instructions so far?"

Officer confirms understanding with subject: Y / N

Demonstration and Instructions for the Balance and Counting Stage:

"When I tell you to start, raise one leg, either leg, with the foot approximately six inches off the ground, keeping your raised foot parallel to the ground. You must keep both legs straight, arms at your side. While holding that position, count out loud in the following manner: 'One thousand and one, one thousand and two, one thousand and three,' until told to stop."

Demonstrated by officer (for officer safety, officer does not look at his foot) counting "One thousand and one, one thousand and two, one thousand and three, etc.": Y / N

"Keep your arms at your sides at all times and keep watching the raised foot. Do you understand?"

Officer should acknowledge understanding by subject.

"Go ahead and perform the test."

Officer should always time the 30 seconds and observe the subject from a safe distance. If the subject places a foot down, the officer should give instructions to "Pick the foot up again and continue counting from the point at which the foot touched the ground." Always terminate the test at 30 seconds.

Officer gives correct instructions: Y / N

Type of footwear worn: _____

Can you see the feet in the video? Y / N

Start time: _____   Finish time: _____

Uses arms to balance: Y / N   Client holds position: Y / N   Balance maintained: Y / N

Swaying: Y / N   Hopping: Y / N   Puts foot down: Y / N

Counting: _____   Speech: _____

Balance: _____   Slurs while counting: _____

Doesn't count: _____   Miscounts: _____

Other: _____

Comments: _____

Alcosensor taken? Y / N   Digital readout on video? Y / N   Audio: Y / N

OTHER NON-STANDARD FIELD EVALUATIONS PERFORMED: _____

_____

RHOMBERG: _____

FINGER DEXTERITY: _____

ABCs: _____

Time defendant placed under arrest: _____

Nature of immediate conversation: _____

_____

Any custodial issues? _____

Implied consent read? _____

Appropriate card for age? _____

BAC: _____   Time of first test: _____   Time of second BAC: _____

REFUSAL: Y / N   Or: Insufficient Sample? _____

Time first: _____   Time second: _____

INDEPENDENT TEST REQUESTED OR SPOKEN ABOUT? _____

_____

ANY LAPSES IN VIDEO? _____

_____

ANY AUDIO PROBLEMS WITH VIDEO? _____

_____

DOES THE VIDEO HAVE POOR VISUAL QUALITY? _____

ARE THERE OTHER OFFICERS, EMS, OR OTHER WITNESSES IN THE VIDEO? _____

_____

COMMENTS: _____

_____

_____

_____

_____

_____

_____

_____

APPENDIX D

COMPREHENSIVE DISCOVERY REQUEST TO LABORATORY IN BLOOD CASE

By Justin J. McShane[1]

CAUTION:

The comprehensive blood discovery request provided here is a formidable weapon to be used only by those skilled enough to appreciate it. In using the request, an untrained attorney, even a well-intentioned one, can make some truly bad law that many generations in the criminal defense community could be stuck with for a long time.

I have provided the form only for use in litigation and only by those who are prepared to prove it up. My goal is to provide well-trained attorneys the first opportunity to litigate these matters as they are the mostly likely to achieve success. For commentary on the form including instructions for proper use, see Ch. 1, §§1:10 et seq. In particular, please read §§1:11 and 1:11.1 before you consider using this form.

DOCUMENTATION REQUIRED FOR INDEPENDENT EXTERNAL SCIENTIFIC VALIDATION FOR REPORTED AND ALLEGED TEST RESULTS INVOLVING BLOOD TESTS FOR ETOH NOT MADE BY ENZYMATIC PROCESS

Please provide,

The Following Items Concern General Matters:
1. A copy of any accreditation certificates for the laboratory that were in effect at the time of the analysis.
2. The laboratory's overall policies as to testing and calibration.
3. The laboratory's overall protocols as to testing and calibration.
4. The policy that applies to the section of the laboratory where this particular testing or calibration event occurred.
5. The procedure that applies to the section of the laboratory where this particular testing or calibration event occurred.

---

[1] Justin J. McShane, Esquire is a Harrisburg, Pennsylvania based attorney who specializes in using forensic science for the benefit of citizens accused of crimes. He is a board certified trial attorney by the National Board of Trial Advocacy as well as board certified as a DUI Specialist by the National College for DUI Defense. He is a Fellow with the American Institute of Chemists (AIC). He is a member of numerous scientific organizations including the American Chemical Society (ACS), American Institute of Chemists (AIC), American Academy of Forensic Science (AAFS), American College of Forensic Examiners, Society for Analytical Chemists (SACP), National Fire Protection Association (NFPA), The Chromatography Forum of Delaware Valley, American Society for Testing and Materials (ASTM), American Association for Clinical Chemistry (AACC), National Conference of Standards Laboratories International (NCSLI International), Association of Analytical Communities (AOAC International), American Society for Mass Spectrometry (ASMS), Society for Applied Spectroscopy (SAS), and the American Society for Quality (ASQ). He is a published author. He is a frequently invited guest lecturer at national, state, and local seminars that are attended by lawyers, judges, scientists and policy-makers. He has twice been invited to lecture at the ACS National meeting and has been accepted to present AAFS. He is the Chairman/CEO of The McShane Firm, LLC, a six attorney criminal defense and DUI law firm. He maintains two blogs: www.TheTruthAboutForensicScience.com and www.PADUIBlog.com.

The Following Items Concern Pre-analytical Matters

6. Validation studies (both internal and external) that proves the validation of the method and protocols used.

7. The policy that applies to the assay performed in this particular test or calibration event that covers the calibration or the achieving of a calibration curve.

8. The procedure that applies to the assay performed in this particular test or calibration event that covers the calibration or the achieving of a calibration curve.

9. The instructions that apply to the assay performed in this particular test or calibration event that covers the calibration or the achieving of a calibration curve.

10. The calibration curves and all chromatograms generated on the batch on the machine on which the sample in this case was tested.

11. The identification and source of all internal standards, standards standard mixtures (separation matrix), verifiers, blanks, and controls that were run within the batch in which the sample in this case was run.

12. All records reflecting internal testing or quality control testing of all solutions, reagents, or standard mixtures used as, as part of, or in relation to internal standards, controls, standard mixtures, or standards in the batch in which the sample in this case was run.

13. All refrigeration logs, reports, or other documents in whatever form, for all refrigerated compartments in which this sample, other unknowns within the run, internal standards, controls, standard mixtures, standards, and reagents used in or in relation to the analysis in this case were stored or kept at any time.

14. All proficiency testing results for the section of the laboratory testing the sample in this case as well as for the person who conducted the testing in this case – since the last date of accreditation inspection preceding the test, and for any such testing since the testing in this case. This specifically includes the summary report of expected results for the proficiency testing (and the manufacturer's information sheet) against which the proficiency test results are judged.

15. Quarterly balance quality control records on any balance instrument related to the calibration of the alcohol standard solution or the preparation of knowns or unknowns used in the blood alcohol testing of the samples in this case. The records reflecting the calibration of weights on any balance or instrument related to this case as well as the control charts kept.

The Following Items Concern Analytical Matters:

16. The instructions that apply to the assay that was used in this particular testing or calibration event occurred.

17. The employee training record, curriculum vitae, and resume for any person listed on chain of custody documents in this case or who performed the analysis.

18. Identify the make, model, and brand/manufacturer of the instruments and other supporting instruments (i.e. balance, pipette, etc.) used during the analysis and/or preparation of the samples in this case and the variables used in its installation and operation.

19. The policy concerning the sample selection criteria used in this particular case.

20. The procedure concerning the sample selection criteria used in this particular case.

21. The instructions concerning the sample selection criteria used in this particular case.

22. The source and type of all consumables used in collection, preparation, and analysis of the samples run in the batch.

23. If a Gas or Liquid Chromatograph is used, the reporting of t0 time according to the method.

The Following Items Concern Reporting Matters:

24. The particular records for this testing or calibration event.

25. The quality control policy and protocol for the laboratory, the section, and the assay performed.

26. The quality assurance policy and protocol for the laboratory, the section, and the assay performed.

27. The full reporting and the underlying validation of the valuation of the uncertainty measurement (UM) in the ultimate reported result.

28. If a Mass Spectrometer is used, then the following additional materials should be provided:

28.1 If a spectral library is used to examine spectra and elucidate spectra, the source of the library spectra.

28.2 The hit list, and the hit histogram for the spectra examined and reported.

28.3 All "tune" reports ran within one year if a MS detector was used.

APPENDIX E

FRAMING TECHNIQUES

USING SCIENTIFIC TECHNIQUES EMPLOYED BY HIGHLY PAID POLITICAL CONSULTANTS TO WIN OVI CASES

CLEVE M. JOHNSON
ATTORNEY AT LAW

495 South High Street, Suite 400; Columbus, Ohio 43215-5058
(614) 299-8235 Fax (614) 358-6633

(This page intentionally left blank.)

Trials are framing-battles.
—Dr. Sunwolf. Practical Jury Dynamics p.113 §6-3(c) Matthew Bender

USING TECHNIQUES EMPLOYED BY KARL ROVE AND FRANK LUNTZ AGAINST THE PROSECUTION.

Suppose you represent a rich man's son who led a rather wild and irresponsible youth. He avoided combat during the Vietnam war because he had a rich and well-connected father who got him into the Alabama National Guard even though he was not from Alabama. Unlike today, the guard then was often a haven from the draft for the sons of the rich and privileged. Because many were trying to do the same thing, it was harder to get into the National Guard then than it is now. By the way, after he enlisted in the guard the son went AWOL.

Your job is to convince people that your client would make a stronger and more responsible wartime leader than a Vietnam combat veteran who was awarded a Bronze Star, a Silver Star, and three Purple Hearts. Can doing this be any harder than winning a drunk driving case, even one with a test?

We all know the aforementioned political feat can be accomplished. People like Rove and Luntz have by and large been beating the Democrats for years using these techniques and the Democrats have been mostly clueless as to how this was being done. The prosecution has unwittingly been using similar techniques against the defense in drunk driving cases to the same effect.

These techniques are so powerful that they cause large numbers of people to regularly vote against their economic interests. What scientists have found is that people vote their identity, not their interests. For example, union members were predominantly strong supporters of Ronald Reagan even though he shut down the air traffic controller's union. We think we cannot get judges to vote against their perceived political interests. This may not be true.

Even if you think you know how Rove did this, you are probably wrong unless you are familiar with recent principles of cognitive science. A superficial analysis like, "they win by scaring people to death", misses the more subtle and refined techniques that are being employed. This outline will attempt to show how to use the techniques developed by the most adept and well paid persuaders in the world in a drunk driving case.

If we do this right, it will work and the other side will not understand what is happening, just like the Democrats have been largely oblivious to why they have been losing.

UNNOTICED PSYCHOLOGICAL EFFECTS OF STANDARD PROSECUTION ARGUMENTS.

Juries are being instructed to decide cases using a preponderance or even lower standard.

By trial and error, prosecutors have stumbled upon arguments that employ a technique psychologists call framing. The net effect is that prosecutors have reduced the burden of proof to a preponderance and made requiring proof beyond a reasonable doubt seem contrary to common sense. In some cases, the burden has been reduced further to less than a preponderance. The precise nature of how this is done is described below.

Unfortunately, the defense by and large has not stumbled upon a response that utilizes equally effective tactics. Instead, it has unwittingly attempted to fight the battle on the prosecution's terms. This, in turn, requires the defense to have an exceptional case in order to win.

THE SUBTLETIES OF FRAMING.

It is not choosing from a list of magic words.

Suppose a husband, wife and a mother-in-law are in a room. The couple's son comes in, points over to a corner and yells "snake." The mother-in-law is alarmed and jumps up on her chair. The husband enjoys this because the mother-in-law has been on his nerves all day. There is no snake. The child was playing a prank. The child and the husband start laughing until they figure out that the women are mad at them.

The wife scolds her son for lying. The husband argues that no harm was done. He says this was just a harmless prank and that the women should lighten up a bit and enjoy the fun. He says they are just upset because they were scared and they should not be scolding the boy for lying.

The wife replies: "This is like the boy who cried wolf. Someday there could be a real snake around." The husband reconsiders and agrees with the wife. He also tells the son that it was wrong to lie.

APPENDIX E: FRAMING TECHNIQUES

The framing involved:

The wife's argument carries the day because the husband now looks at the situation in a different way. He can see that if the boy gets in the habit of doing things like this regularly he could get a reputation such that no one would believe him in the case of a genuine emergency. There could be a snake there some day.

The husband does not reject the truth behind the analogy of the boy who cried wolf because he learned it at an early age from his mother whom he respected and the story is engrained cultural wisdom. Thus, by framing the issue this way, the only issue left is: does the analogy apply to the current situation? That is an easier issue for the wife to win on than the issue of whether the prank was just harmless fun.

When the husband was looking at the situation as just some harmless fun at the expense of his mother-in-law, there was no perceived danger or negative consequences to the boy. The husband and wife could argue back and forth all day about whether a little harmless fun would hurt anything with both the husband and the wife sticking to their respective positions. Nobody was hurt. Laughing is good for you. You are just a poor sport. By reframing the issue, the wife changed the situation from one of harmless fun to one of a son whose behavior was on a path that could lead to danger down the road.

The phrase "the boy who cried wolf" brings to mind the perspective on such statements set forth in the Aesop's fable of the same name. The story has to do with how lying can have consequences. It shows how it can be dangerous to get the reputation as a liar. The way of looking at things analogized to by reference to the story is what is meant by the term *frame*. A frame can be thought of as a sort of shorthand analogy. It says to the target of the frame: "This new situation you are trying to evaluate should be interpreted the same way as this past situation to which it is being analogized."

The frame contains a meaning different than that of the individual words. If you looked up the meanings of each word in the phrase "the boy who cried wolf" you would not come up with the words liar, reputation, consequences, or danger. A fluent speaker of English from another culture also would not get the non-dictionary meaning if he had not heard the story. Something more than the meaning of the words is conveyed by the phrase.

Suppose that when the husband told the wife to "lighten up" the wife had said: "This is reminiscent of the son who loudly issued a predatory canine alert." Note that in terms of the ordinary dictionary meaning of the words, this phrase is very similar to the phrase "the boy who cried wolf." If the husband was smart and thought about it for a bit, he might link the "canine alert" phrase to the phrase "the boy who cried wolf," but initially he probably wouldn't know what the wife was talking about. If the conversation continued and there was no time for reflection, the underlying reference of the canine alert phrase to the moral of the fable would probably be lost.

Invoking the frame of the fable with the phrase "the boy who cried wolf" takes no time to decipher and the meaning conveyed by the words is instantly recognized. The actual meanings conveyed by the words is quite different than the dictionary definitions of the words themselves. Political consultants use such techniques to inject race into a political race where an overt reference to race would have negative consequences for the candidate. As will be shown, a similar phenomenon arises in court.

There is also nothing magical about the words "the boy who cried wolf" in and of themselves. The wife could use all of these words in arguing with the husband to no effect. The words are important only because they invoke the frame. For example, suppose the wife says:

This *boy* bears your family name of *Wolf*. I almost *cried* because of *the* asinine remark he made. *Who* is going to discipline him if you do not.

Note that this reply contains the same words but does not invoke the same meaning. It is not the individual words that are important, it is the frame. It is the perspective the analogy brings to mind that is important. Even though all of the same words are there, the words no longer convey the meaning that allowing your son to lie about such things may be dangerous for him someday.

It is not a matter of using magic words. One must understand the frames those words invoke. The people you are trying to persuade do not have to understand that they are rejecting someone else's frame and adopting yours. In fact, it is better if they do not. You, however, have to understand in order to select the right fame, get your frame adopted and block your opponent's frame.

WHY JUDGES AND JURIES IGNORE THE CONSTITUTION AND LAWS FAVORING THE DEFENSE.

It is because we argue the law instead of concentrating on the actual factors that persuade decision makers.

or

FRAMES TRUMP FACTS

FRAMES TRUMP LOGIC

FRAMES TRUMP THE LAW

The side that is successful in framing the issue is the side that wins. We are taught that the way to win cases is by formulating the best logical argument or citing the best precedent. This is a misperception.

George Bush may very well have won the debates, but only spin doctors and their ilk would claim he did this by the strength of his intellect or by be being better versed on the facts and more logical than John Kerry or Al Gore. People with formal training in debate generally thought he lost. The people that coached him understood something more important than logic. They understood how people actually make up their minds.

People ignore logical arguments and decide cases based upon the frames they are using. If the logical arguments or even the facts do not fit with the frames, people will ignore the facts and ignore logic and go with the frames. As George Lakoff puts it: Frames trump facts.

Have you ever had the experience of proving a fact with very strong evidence only to have the judge/jury ignore it? Have you ever thought, how could it even be possible for the judge/jury to not get that? What probably happened was that you proved the fact but did not activate the right frame. This is perhaps the most counterintuitive principle of framing and it bears repetition. *If the facts do not fit the frames, people ignore the facts and make the decision the frame dictates.* As George Lakoff puts it: "Frames trump facts." This has nothing to do with being smart or stupid, it is how our brains work.

An illustration of this point appears in *To Kill A Mockingbird* where the defense lawyer was logically, factually, and legally correct and he still lost. The frames used by the jurors were stronger than logic or the law.

Entire books have been written explaining the subject of framing (see references at the end). They are well worth reviewing. My purpose here is not to duplicate what has been done, but rather to apply these concepts to criminal law in the context of a drunk driving case. To my knowledge, this has not been done before.

We think people make decisions based upon the law or based upon their religion. Such belief systems are at best no better than a secondary basis for the decision. The existence of terms such as "religious hypocrisy" and "result driven decisions" demonstrate that there is another higher belief system at work.

There are not many Buddhists or Michigan fans among people born and raised in Columbus, Ohio. While this seems obvious, it is so obvious that we miss the significance of it. How you were raised and/or your life experiences by and large govern what you believe. This is more basic than religion or the law. Most people generally choose religion based on how they were raised. They do not sit down and do a rational and logical analysis of all the various religions and choose the logically best one. If a law seems idiotic, it is generally ignored. The frames (life experiences/beliefs about the world) trump religion and the law. The law generally works because it is consistent with the belief systems people were raised with. If it is not, the law is not respected.

The way people's brains work is not going to change no matter how much we complain about result driven decisions. We cannot change the way the brain works. What we can do is understand and use the way the brain works to our advantage. Framing is a technique that causes the brain to look at the same issue in a different way.

An illustration of this is in the movie *Wag the Dog*. The William Macy character wants to kill the Robert DeNiro character because he thinks they are acting at cross purposes. The DeNiro character calmly convinces him not to kill him by showing him that they have common interests and that he just was not looking at things the right way.

If you make an argument based upon the law but ignore the frames employed by the judge or jury, any success you have will be a coincidence. You will have succeeded because you coincidentally activated the right frames in the decision maker, not because you made a good legal argument.

HOW TO WIN USING FRAMING.

You have to pick the right frame and get the decision maker to think of the issue in terms of your frame rather than the prosecution's. Generally the side that wins is the side that picks the frame. There are two ways to pick the right frame. One is on purpose, the other is by accident. The thought is that on purpose will work better. Later I will have some specific ideas on how to pick frames on purpose in a drunk driving case.

Although I am again grossly oversimplifying things here, the term "frame" is a term scientists use. It is generally a way of looking at the world. You may think of it as a set of preconceived ideas, life experiences, or beliefs about the world. Frames are used to compare new experiences to experiences one has had in the past. The past experiences are used as a guide or frame to interpret the new experience. Unconsciously, the decision maker asks himself what past analogy will help him decide what to do in this new situation (or case).

Some scientists believe that people think of the world almost exclusively in terms of analogy. Words themselves are largely analogies, even mathematical terms. The number seven, for instance, was learned by analogizing the written number to seven objects.

Framing is about picking the "analogy" that favors your side and preventing the prosecution from using an "analogy" that favors them. All of us have similar and competing frames in our brains. The trick is reaching into people's brains and picking the frame that favors your side.

Here are examples of competing frames:

Global warming (implies rising oceans, flooded coastal cities, drought, etc.).
vs.
Climate change (implies normal historical fluctuation, not an area of concern).

Estate tax (implies making a fairer distribution of wealth
applicable only to people who have way too much money in the first place).
vs.
Death tax (implies taxing misery, lacking in compassion, potentially
applicable to everyone, the government is trying to take my inheritance away).

Logging in the national forests (implies campaign contributors feeding at the public trough by
getting discounts on public resources and destroying parks and wilderness belonging to all of us).
vs.
Healthy forests initiative (implies clearing out dead wood that
would provide fuel for forest fires, thereby preserving our parks and wilderness).

The battle is generally over which frame is to be adopted. The result flowing from the frame is more or less determined once the frame is adopted. Many frames are not nearly as controversial as those above. They can be suggested and employed without any conscious recognition on the part of the subject that a framing battle is even being waged. Sometimes suggestion and repetition is all that it takes to get your frame adopted. The hard part is finding the appropriate frame in the first place.

The aforementioned terms did not arise by accident. A lot of time, effort, and money was involved in developing them. Supplanting the original term by the new term is a major victory for those involved. Getting the press to use your frame is a major victory for political operatives. Getting your opponent to use it is even better. It is a major mistake to use the other side's frames. Notice how often this unwittingly happens in the real world. Lawyers unwittingly do it all the time in court.

MAKE SURE YOU FRAME FOR THE ACTUAL BELIEF, NOT A RATIONALIZATION.

Suppose your case depends on persuading a judge/juror that evolution is true. The judge/juror tells you that she does not believe in evolution because she is religious and believing in evolution is inconsistent with a belief in God. You respond with the following frame. Is God smart enough to have created evolution? You think that this is a masterpiece of framing because the person has to answer yes to the question and that in turn means they have to concede your point. The problem is that it doesn't work. It doesn't change the judge or juror's mind. Why?

The problem is that the stated reason for the belief wasn't the real reason for the belief. The real reason is probably something like this: I was raised to believe that the idea of evolution is evil and that people who believe in it are evil. The people in this life who I respect think evolution is evil. Now perhaps this person has been educated to the extent that he starts to think that he needs to appear to be more rational. Thus she rationalizes that evolution is inconsistent with a belief in God. Maybe it is simpler than this. Maybe she just agrees that evolution is inconsistent with religion because it supports a preexisting belief. If evolution being godless isn't the reason for the underlying belief in the first place, then refuting that reason will not change the underlying belief.

You have to make sure you understand the real reason for the belief. This is by and large the problem with arguing the law. As a general rule, the law just supports preexisting moral or common sense beliefs. Making a good legal argument doesn't change the underlying moral/common sense belief or frame. Unless you can reframe your position as the moral/common sense one as well as the legal one, you will generally lose even if the law is on your side.

How does this work in a drunk driving case? Fortunately, we don't have to convince fact finders that drunk driving is a good thing. Unfortunately, the real frame at work here may be just about as difficult. That frame is that everyone is guilty. This frame is probably more entrenched in judges than it is in juries.

We all know the rationale. It goes like this. If the defendant was innocent, he would have taken the test and passed, absent this, he is guilty. Drunk driving is a serious offense. Convicting guilty drunk drivers is the right thing to do morally, from a common sense standpoint, and politically. Unless you can change the fact finder's mind about this proposition, at least under the particular circumstances of your case, you will generally lose.

This belief depends on a couple of tacit premises that aren't necessarily true. 1. The machine is always right. 2. A defendant always knows when he is guilty and can have no reason other than consciousness of guilt for refusing the test. It would appear that these are the issues to win on. There may be others. Suggestions are welcomed.

THE SIGNIFICANCE OF THE "STRICT FATHER" "NURTURANT PARENT" DICHOTOMY.

According to George Lakoff, a major difference in how people look at the world (i.e. the frames they use) depends upon whether they have a "strict father" or a "nurturant parent" morality. Lakoff finds this dichotomy especially important in the political world. It would seem that it would be significant in the legal context as well.

Strict father morality

In general the strict father morality places a strict father at the head of the household. The strict father is to be obeyed. There is no discussion. The wife is the helper of the husband but cannot be the head of the family because she is not as strong as the strict father. The father is the moral authority and he knows right from wrong. The father has to be strong to protect the family. Children are not consulted. Their duty is to obey.

People with a strict father background generally believe that there is an absolute right and wrong, that the world is a dangerous place and that it takes discipline to succeed. They believe that children are born evil in the sense that they lack self-control and only seek pleasure. Children need strict discipline to succeed in life. Individual responsibility is important. Capitalism separates those with discipline from those who lack it. Thus, those who succeed financially are the disciplined people. They are better people and they deserve what they obtain. The exception to this is people who do not play by the rules, for example rich criminals.

Welfare and social programs are immoral because they reward lack of discipline and keep people dependent. Those who do not believe in strict discipline for their children are immoral because they do not prepare their children for the harsh competitive world they will have to face. Once a child becomes an adult, the child becomes his own moral authority and the strict father should not meddle in the child's affairs.

People use this model to apply to situations outside the family. The nation metaphorically is a family with the president as the strict father. The strict father God is the Old Testament strike-you-down-with-a-bolt-of-lightening God. He is the ultimate strict father. Lakoff says if you understand a John Wayne movie, you understand the strict father morality.

Nurturant parent morality

Empathy predominates in the nurturant parent model. The husband and wife are a team rather than a hierarchy. Cooperation and understanding are the model. Both want to nurture and protect the family from danger. Children are taught by example and through discussion. Responsibility is important but discipline is less central. Behavior is more likely to be shaped through positive rewards rather than punishment.

If you empathize with your child you want to protect the child not just from crime and terrorism, but also from poor health, disease, and environmental hazards. You also want your child to be happy and fulfilled and try to teach the child to be this kind of person. To be happy, the child has to be free and prosperous. Fairness is a central value as well because the child cannot be happy if he or she is treated unfairly. Two way communication is also valued. You want the child to live in a good community and environment so values that strengthen the community and the environment are also favored. Lakoff says if you understand the Cosby show, you understand nurturant parent morality. The nurturant God is the New Testament forgiving and turn-the-other-cheek God.

Many people are bi-conceptual. They may follow a strict father model at home when raising their children but are nurturant at work with regard to other union members. Similarly, a person may be nurturant at home but use a strict father model while working as a teacher. Most people have elements of both models in their backgrounds.

What the morality model means in court

People will look at the same facts very differently depending on whether they have a strict father or a nurturant parent morality. Counterintuitive effects also flow from the morality system one believes in. For example, people vote their identity not their interests. To be more specific, Ronald Reagan was clearly the strict father candidate. Many union members with a strict father identity voted for him even though economically he was no friend to labor (e.g. breaking the air traffic controller's union).

While it is not hard to tell which model is generally conservative and which is liberal, it is more problematic to determine which model is better for the drunk driving jury. The initial thought would be that the absolute right and wrong harsh justice model would seem to be horrible for the defense. On the other hand, the nurturant parent model could trigger a strong protective reaction as well (keeping us safe from drunk drivers). What this may mean is what we essentially knew already, namely, everyone is against us and our clients.

People with strict father morality will look at life through very different frames than people with nurturant morality. This may place a limit on what is possible in reframing any issue or group of issues. Gay marriage is anathema to those of a strict father background. The strict father is not a mommy and there are not two strict fathers. What does this mean if you have a gay defendant? It is unlikely that you can exclude all strict father types from the jury. There are many such issues. This is not a simple area to figure out. I am still trying to think this through.

It would be a mistake to think that the lesson of framing is just to choose a judge or jury with nurturant values on the theory that they are presumably less hostile. There are not enough preemptory challenges to accomplish this and you often cannot pick your judge. People with a strict father upbringing have nurturant frames even though the strict frames predominate and people with a nurturant upbringing have strict father frames even though the nurturant frames predominate. The trick is to find the frames that favor your client which are possessed by even those with a strict father morality and activate those frames.

THE MOST COMMON FRAMING MISTAKE.

George Lakoff has a maxim that "Negating a frame evokes the frame." That is the meaning of the title of his book, *Don't Think Of An Elephant*. Telling people not to think of an elephant makes them think of one. To take another example, when Richard Nixon said "I am not a crook", most people thought he was a crook. This is a catch 22 situation for lawyers who think they must rebut the other side's point. By rebutting the point, you strengthen the point. There is a solution to this dilemma; however, traditionally we have been doing rebuttal the wrong way.

Suppose you want to call an officer a liar but are afraid that the jury will hold this against you. The aforementioned principle can be used to do this and not get punished. For example: "I am not saying the officer is a liar, but I think you are entitled to an explanation of why many of the statements in his report are contradicted by the video recording." You have denied calling the officer a liar while simultaneously suggesting to the jury that they should reach that conclusion "on their own." Negating a frame invokes the frame.

What we want to do is to get the judge or jury to use our frames. We may even be able to get the prosecutor to use them. If the prosecutor uses your frame, even in an attempt to rebut it, this is a victory. Likewise, you should not use the prosecutors' frames even to rebut their arguments. Substitute your own frames, do not use theirs.

Bad frames for drunk driving defendants—If the defendant was innocent he would have taken the test and passed. Common sense tells us that police rarely arrest innocent or sober people. The officer was trained and knows an intoxicated person when he sees one. This is a simple case. Do not let some slick defense attorney make you start doubting your common sense. Drunk drivers endanger the public. Voting for the prosecution will keep you safe. The only reason to vote not guilty is sympathy for the defendant. The defendant does not deserve sympathy. Drinking to excess is irresponsible. Irresponsible people deserve to suffer the consequences of their actions. Irresponsible people need discipline. Conviction and punishment will provide discipline. Common sense tells us that an innocent person will protest. If the defendant does not testify, that means he is guilty.

Good frames for drunk driving defendants—Everyone is entitled to a fair trial (jurors who do not have this frame are entitled to a challenge for cause). It is not fair to assume people are guilty without proof. There are two sides to every story. I would not want to convict an innocent person. The government frequently makes mistakes. We should give people the benefit of the doubt. Even police officers can make mistakes. It never hurts to check someone else's work. If you say something bad about someone, you should be prepared to prove it.

Frames normally used against the defendant that can be used against the state— People who do not tell the whole story cannot be trusted. People do not hide unimportant things. If a person is hiding something, there is more to the matter than meets the eye.

HOW THE PROSECUTION FRAMES US:

Prosecution's opening/closing:

Most prosecution arguments seem to be a variation on the following theme. The prosecutor starts out by listing in story form the various indications of alcohol that the officer noted. *Ladies and gentlemen, on the night in question, the defendant was stopped for speeding, when the officer came up to the vehicle he noticed a strong odor of alcohol, bloodshot eyes, etc.* The enumeration of alcohol related indicia is followed up with a claim that these are the facts and it is unlikely that all these signs of intoxication are a coincidence. It is submitted that the defendant is either guilty or the most unlucky person in the world.

A variation on this is: If it looks like a duck (drunk), quacks like a duck, and walks like a duck, it's a duck. Note that the original phrase used by the red-baiting Senator Joseph McCarthy was "It's *probably* a duck." The word "probably" is omitted by prosecutors who have some idea of what they are doing. This omission is extremely significant because the word "probably" connotes a preponderance argument. A mere preponderance is supposed to be insufficient in a criminal case. In reality, it usually carries the day because we do not understand what is being done to us.

The unstated but devastating prosecution argument:

This is a simple case, things are as they appear.

I am just giving you the facts (facts are true—I am giving you the truth, not excuses and possibilities). Common sense (i.e. the assumptions—frames you walked in with) tells you the defendant is guilty.

The prosecution is fair and unbiased with no motive to lie or slant things (because they are just giving you the facts).

Everyone should use common sense. Common sense tells us that people charged with crimes are probably guilty. Since it is ok to use your common sense, it is likewise ok to assume guilt without proof.

Urging jurors to use their common sense is a hidden way of urging them to assume guilt without proof. Arguing to the contrary puts defense counsel in the position of urging jurors to reject common sense.

These frames unconstitutionally reduce the burden of proof to a preponderance or worse and tell the jury to vote their prejudices against drunk drivers.

How the "some evidence" standard is substituted for proof beyond a reasonable doubt:

In Ohio a defendant is guilty if alcohol has "any noticeable effect" on him. A smart prosecutor can use this to argue: Ladies and gentlemen, ask yourself this: Out of all the factors I have listed, was there at least one noticeable effect of alcohol? If your answer to this question is yes, then you must vote guilty.

The unstated switch in burdens:

This is the worst possible frame for the defense. What it says is that if there is any evidence of intoxication at all a guilty verdict is required. The burden has been reduced from a preponderance to the mere requirement of having to produce some evidence. Such a low burden is insufficient even in a civil case. Through framing, it is being substituted for proof beyond a reasonable doubt without anybody understanding what is happening.

WHY THE DEFENDANT STARTS OUT PRE-FRAMED AS GUILTY AND THE PROSECUTION AS CREDIBLE.

The prosecution's opening has the effect of putting the focus on the defendant. The normal prosecution opening is essentially this: "This is a case about a driver who was drunk and we have evidence to prove it." The jury starts out thinking that people accused of this are rarely innocent. The prosecutor does not have to say this. The frame is set by specifying the charge. The prosecutor has credibility because she is just summarizing what the officer says. Officers are generally thought of as credible because they are perceived as having no motive to lie or shade their testimony.

It is pretty close to worthless for the defendant to get up and deny guilt. It will not be believed. Defense attorneys have next to no credibility and are perceived (pre-framed) as people who will say anything for money to get their clients off. As a result, if defense counsel tries to make any positive statement, it is unlikely that it will be believed. Even the attempt to do this may prompt jurors to think about how they are being lied to and how the defense attorney is insulting their intelligence by thinking they will believe whatever claims of innocence he is trying to set forth. How does one avoid this trap?

Asking the jury to keep an open mind is equally worthless. This is another meaningless platitude. The jury's attitude is "we will listen to the defendant, but this stuff the prosecutor says sounds pretty bad and unless you can convince us it is not true, we will convict him after we finish listening." You do not want the jury to go back and talk about the defendant and the signs of intoxication the prosecutor listed. You want them talking about whether there is a problem with the state's evidence (reasonable doubt). You must shift the focus of the case immediately. But how does a defense attorney do this if anything he says in this regard will not be believed?

HOW WE FALL INTO THEIR TRAP.

The standard losing defense strategy:

The defense then gets up and does a pretty good job of rebutting each and every one of the prosecutor's list of alcohol indications.

Defense counsel sits down thinking, "I have explained everything on the prosecutor's list and none of those things necessarily proves the client guilty. If the jury will just follow the law and believe in reasonable doubt we should have a good case."

The mistake:

The defense is making the worst mistake possible. It is using the prosecution frame and not substituting its own frame.

HOW THEY FINISH US OFF IN REBUTTAL.

The jury is then told that the defense attorney is a good lawyer, and sure enough he was able to come up with an excuse for everything. The facts are the facts. Do not be misled by smoke and mirrors in the hands of an experienced defense lawyer. All these bad facts cannot be a coincidence.

The deadly unstated argument:

Common sense tells you people who make excuses are guilty. Criminal defense attorneys are untrustworthy. Prosecutors and police are trustworthy, because they give facts, not excuses.

Note also that the smoke and mirrors/tricky defense attorney line of argument is probably objectionable, but there is a better way to handle this problem than objecting. Do not waste time arguing with the judge only to have him uphold the prosecution while the prosecutor's points sink in to the juror's brains. Even if the judge does tell the jury that it was wrong for the prosecutor to imply that defense lawyers are tricky, this just reinforces the tricky frame it does not change it. It also makes the defense look weak, like it is running home to mama instead of standing up to a fight. This too is not a plus with jurors. Instead, immediately show the jury that the prosecutor has been misleading them (see below).

PERSUADING JURORS WHO THINK THE DEFENSE LIES

Getting the jury to arrive at your position on their own is possible and it is more effective than trying to sell the defense position.

For years I have heard good trial lawyers say that you should let the jury discover your arguments on their own rather than telling them what you want them to do. This always seemed to make sense in the abstract, but it also seemed impractical. The jury does not get it when I tell them about it directly—how will it work better if I make things more vague so that they can "discover" our position on their own? There are some simple techniques for solving this dilemma.

Switching the juror's suspicions from you to the prosecutor

If someone you think is untrustworthy tries to tell you something, you are going to be suspicious of him and question everything he says. This in turn will distract you from any point they are trying to make because you will constantly be thinking about the motives of the speaker rather than concentrating on the speaker's message. People also often do not like people who try to lecture them or sell them on a particular course of action. Since they start out thinking the defendant is guilty and you try to tell them the opposite, they perceive you as trying to fool them. This insults their intelligence. This is the starting position occupied by defense attorneys. It makes persuasion difficult. Note also that prosecutors and police do not have to contend with this impediment because they are not perceived as suspicious at the outset. What we have to do is to switch this so that jurors are not suspicious of the defense but are suspicious of the prosecution and police. It can be done.

Techniques for getting the jury to discover your position on their own

If jurors are skeptical, and distracted when defense attorneys try to tell them things, then do not tell them things. You can achieve the same end by asking rhetorical questions. If you ask questions, the jurors do not feel like you are trying to force them to come to the conclusions you want. They are also not necessarily suspicious in the same way they are when you argue for a position.

The questions should, of course, be framed in such a way that the only answers that make any sense are answers favoring your case.

You get the same information across without encountering the need to break through the skepticism and distraction that arguing for the point would trigger. The jurors' minds go to the same place but without the resistance and distraction. If the jurors' think about the question and come up with the answer you intended, they choose to adopt your position on their own rather than giving in to your arguments. They were not "sold" on your position (i.e. manipulated or taken for chumps), but rather they made up their own minds.

Jurors who start out pro-prosecution may be insulted by any attempt you make to get them to adopt a defense position. The unconscious assumption presumably would be that the prosecution position is the correct position and any attempt you make to divert them to your position must, of necessity, involve deceit or trickery. People do not like or cooperate with people whom they think are trying to deceive or trick them. You do not insult them by asking them questions and inviting them to make up their own minds (assuming the question is one you would ask an intelligent adult—we are not speaking to children). After the prosecutor finishes his opening/closing, start out with something like this:

PERSUASION TECHNIQUES THAT ARE NOT HAMSTRUNG BY THE LOW CREDIBILITY OF DEFENSE ATTORNEYS.

Diverting the focus of the case away from your client.

- What did the prosecutor leave out?
- Why did he leave it out?
- What does this say about reasonable doubt?

These should be the first words of the defense attorney's opening and closing. This technique also introduces a bit of mystery into the case and makes it more interesting. Was something really left out? What was left out? Could the prosecution possibly be misleading us? By contrast, the prosecutor's theme is pretty dull. Dull, however, can favor the state. There are no surprises here. We all know this guy was drunk. The defense is wasting your valuable time with a trial. Things are as they appear. You should punish the defendant for wasting your time and trying to mislead you.

On the other hand, everyone likes a mystery. Jurors expect this from TV. Furthermore, mystery is inconsistent with "everything is routine", you know what to do, convict the defendant. If there really is some mystery, maybe things are not as they seem. Maybe the defendant is not guilty.

You do not need to tell them your theme (problems with the evidence/reasonable doubt)—at least not in so many words. You just ask the right questions and devote enough time to the topic and they will discover it for themselves. They will not believe it if you tell it to them anyhow, but they will like it much better if they decide it for themselves. You definitely want to *suggest* the theme, but there is a difference between suggesting and telling.

These questions also make the prosecution the focus of the inquiry, not your client. Do you want the jurors to go back and talk about whether the symptoms the prosecutor listed show the defendant was guilty, or do you want them to go back and discuss whether the prosecutor tried to hide things from them?

MAKING YOUR REBUTTAL A SWORD INSTEAD OF A SHIELD.

The three questions set forth above become a sword if you follow them up with examples. I would repeat the questions a second time. Repetition is essential to, but not the essence of, getting your frames adopted. Note also that these questions follow some other time honored rules of rhetoric. They break the issue into three parts and they rhyme:

- What did the prosecutor leave out?
- Why did he leave it out?
- What does this say about reasonable doubt?

One thing the prosecutor did not mention is that the defendant walked normally during normal activities. The officer indicated/will indicate that people who are under the influence frequently have trouble walking. Did the prosecutor just forget to tell you about this or is it possible that they did not want you to think about the fact that the defendant was walking normally? Were they afraid that this might create a reasonable doubt in your mind?

Another thing the prosecutor did not mention is that the officer left this out of his report. If the officer is just fair and unbiased, if he is just giving you the facts, why did he leave this out of his report? Can you really rely on reports or witnesses that only give you one side of the story?

Ladies and gentlemen, use your common sense. It is just not possible for the defendant to have been under the influence when he forgot to signal, but normal a few seconds later when he walked around the side of the car. If alcohol was the problem, it should have been present in his legs as well as his arms. What this shows you is that the failure to signal was caused by something other than alcohol.

Repeat the above sequences for each other fact favoring the defense that the prosecution omitted.

Example of officer cross on walking normally:

Officer, can you point to any part of the video where [?] had any trouble walking normally during normal activities?

There also was nothing in your report indicating that [?] had any trouble walking normally during normal activities, true?

You agree then that [?] did not have any trouble walking normally during normal activities, correct?

People who have had too much to drink can have a problem walking normally during normal activities, true?

People who have not had too much to drink usually walk normally during normal activities, true?

So walking abnormally is consistent with intoxication and walking normally is consistent with sobriety, true?

Did you only put things in your report that are consistent with intoxication and you leave out things that are consistent with sobriety?

Is that the way you were trained? Did they tell you at the academy to leave things out of your report that might indicate that [?] was sober?

How many other things that were consistent with being innocent did you leave out of your report?

It is harder to remember them if you do not write them down at the time, true?

That is why you write reports so you do not forget, true?

So when you do not put the things consistent with innocence in your report, you make it easier to forget these things, true?

So both your report and your testimony are biased towards guilt, true?

HOW TO REBUT WITHOUT REPEATING PROSECUTION FRAMES OR MAKING EXCUSES THAT WILL NOT BE BELIEVED.

With regard to the prosecution's points: The prosecution mentioned that the defendant had bloodshot eyes. They did not say anything about the fact that he has allergies. Do you think that they left the allergies part out because it was unimportant or could they have left it out because they did not want you to think there was a reasonable doubt about whether the bloodshot eyes were a sign of intoxication?

Again, repeat this sequence for each other prosecution point.

Defense Frame/comment:

The prosecution/officer is biased.

The prosecution is hiding things. People who hide things cannot be trusted.

There are a number of things in this case that are inconsistent with intoxication.

The things the defendant did right show that the things he did wrong were not caused by alcohol.

Karl Rove is fond of saying that if you are explaining you are losing. This technique shifts the defense to the offensive from the very first sentence. You are no longer giving a list of excuses. You can still rebut each and every allegation of the prosecution's case, but you frame it as something the prosecutor left out. They are no longer excuses but rather examples of things the prosecution tried to slip past the jury. People do not like those who try to mislead or hide things from them.

If you are lucky, the prosecutor may be so worried about appearing biased on rebuttal that they start telling both sides of the argument and weaken their case. This has some similarity to what is called a "strategic initiative." You not only achieve your short term purpose of rebutting the prosecution, but you also achieve a broader objective of damaging their ability to argue in general.

Parenthetically, I should mention an excellent technique suggested by Larry Denny, an outstanding DUI lawyer from Dayton, Ohio. Whenever you have to sit down and let a prosecutor follow you, give the prosecutor assignments. List five questions for the prosecutor to answer. If nothing else, it breaks their rhythm. If they fail to respond, it looks like they are being evasive. If they do respond, Rove's maxim kicks in. If you are explaining, you are losing. Lakoff's maxim also applies, negating the frame evokes the frame. Getting the prosecution to talk about your issues rather than theirs is a plus.

Defense opening/closing (continued):

The prosecution listed five things that they claim shows [?] was under the influence. They argue that it cannot be a coincidence that these five things are here. What they did not do is list the 55 clues to intoxication from the officer's manual that were not present in this case. If someone flips a coin and get heads five times, that might make one think that this could not be a coincidence and that the coin must be weighted to come up heads. Based on that information, you might think heads would be a good bet.

If you later find out that the coin was actually flipped 60 times and that only 5 of them came up heads, that theory about the coin being weighted to come up heads does not look so good. That, in a nutshell, is the problem with the prosecutor's case. They have five heads out of 60 and they are trying to convince you that you should vote heads. The prosecution argues that all the clues do not need to be present. That is true, they do not have to get 60 heads in a row to make heads a good bet.

It is also true, however, that if they are going to have proof beyond a reasonable doubt, they should have more than five out of 60 before they ask you to vote heads. What we are asking you is: have they given you a good reason to vote heads when 55 out of 60 tosses have come up tails?

Now the judge will tell you that you are supposed to use that standard of judgment that you would use in your most important affairs. For example, the standard you would use in making decisions about your pension or about your house. Would you bet your pension or your house that the coin would come up heads if heads had come up only 5 out of 60 tosses?

Has the prosecution presented proof beyond a reasonable doubt that rules out everything but alcohol as a cause of the weaving? Think back to the house buying example that we talked about earlier.

You are buying a house. You hire an independent inspector. The inspector sees a bug that looks like a termite. The realtor quickly steps on it and says it is a flying ant. Do you make the seller have the house inspected for termites, or do you take the realtor's word for it? Do you have to prove that the bug they squashed was a termite or do they have to rule it out? In our most important affairs we say they have to rule it out. It is no different here. The government has to rule out everything but alcohol as a cause. We do not have to prove anything else was a cause.

[Apologies to Felipe Plascencia who created the house buying analogy.]

Note also that this is a shortened version of the analogy given on voir dire (see below). One should repeat the key elements of the analogy to reinforce the frame but at the same time one should try to avoid tedious repetition. The ultimate goal is to get the jurors to know your frame from just a few words, like "the boy who cried wolf." That way you can make your point with just a few words.

If your opponent does not have a competing frame established, he will have to go into a long winded explanation to rebut your frame. This in turn may give the appearance that they are losing the point. People tend to think that short simple answers are the best and that long winded ones are obfuscation. While this is often not true, it is a common perception. It is said that this is especially true for the short attention span generation. The politician's maxim that "perception *is* reality" is frequently true in court as well.

VOIR DIRE

It is crucial to set the frames as soon as possible and repeat them as many times as possible. *Voir dire* is the place to start. I put *voir dire* last in this outline only because I wanted to first show the trial frames so that what needs to be accomplished in voir dire would make more sense in that context.

Jurors come to the courtroom thinking the defendant is probably guilty, that the officer is a better judge of this than they are and that if the defendant is innocent he should be able to prove it. They think the majority should rule and that if most people think the defendant is guilty, they will go along with it. The frames are already set. The prosecutor does not have to do much.

The defense is not going to change these attitudes. The trick is to get them to think about the problem from a different perspective rather than to attempt to change entrenched views. That is what framing is all about.

THE LAW IS ON OUR SIDE, BUT IT IS IGNORED.

If we could just get the jurors to believe and follow the basic constitutional requirements listed below, we would be in pretty good shape.

The defendant is innocent until proven guilty.

The prosecution should have the burden to prove the defendant is guilty

The defendant is innocent unless there is proof beyond a reasonable doubt of guilt.

Remaining silent is not proof of guilt.

WHY JURORS IGNORE THE CONSTITUTION.

The problem is that the constitutional requirements enumerated above are psychologically untrue to most people. A judge may be able to bully jurors into agreeing with the enumerated statements or jurors may say they believe them because they know this is what is expected of them. The problem is that common sense (the frames accumulated through life) tells them they are not true.

People reject the law when it seems to defy their common sense. Jurors do not abandon common sense when they enter the jury room. They do not think differently because a judge pretends to tell them to favor the defense. We are no different.

When we see some celebrity being led away in handcuffs, our first thought is not "There goes an innocent person." We think they are guilty. Thus, psychologically, we do not believe people are innocent until proven guilty. Likewise, we do not think the celebrity is innocent just because it is possible to doubt his or her guilt.

Common sense tells us that if someone is innocent, they will protest their innocence and they should be able to explain why. If they do not, they are probably guilty. Thus, if someone is silent, psychologically, we do not believe he is innocent and we do not require proof of guilt. Defense lawyers are in a difficult position if success depends upon denying common sense.

HOW TO GET JURORS TO FOLLOW THE LAW WHEN THEIR COMMON SENSE TELLS THEM NOT TO.

Dealing with the negative frames the jurors walked in with:

Concepts like innocent until proven guilty have been used so much that they are essentially meaningless clichés that go in one ear and out the other. People have a vague idea that the law wants them to treat people that way, but they do not believe it is true. They think they have to pay lip service to such technicalities in order to be politically correct, but they do not really believe it.

The key to getting jurors to follow the law is the right to a fair trial. Even if they do not agree with the rights enumerated above, most people in this country believe that everyone should receive a fair trial. Those who do not are subject to challenge for cause.

The trick is to convince them that the defendant cannot receive a fair trial if the constitutional requirements enumerated above are not followed. Similarly you want to show them that they do not have to abandon their common sense in order to give your client the legal protections the law requires. Instead, we have to show them that these protections make a great deal of sense once you understand the reason why they are there.

By and large, juries are not going to follow the law unless it makes sense to them and they understand why it is important—in other words, unless they understand why it is important to follow the law.

If we do not show them clearly and concisely why the constitutional protections are necessary, the core constitutional protections seem like they are merely some pretentious intellectual's idea of political correctness that some pompous slick lawyer is trying to impose on them. They know how to deal with such people they will then give lip service to the defense attorney's questions, ignore what he asks them to do, and go with their common sense which tells them that police do not arrest innocent people very often.

Suppose the weather is bad and there is a back door to a movie theater which will let patrons take a shortcut to the parking lot. Which of these two signs do you think will be more effective at keeping patrons from going out the door?

Do not exit.

or

Danger high voltage electrical repairs in progress, do not exit.

If just telling people to follow the law worked, everyone would go the speed limit. Here are some questions that might help the jury to understand why the legal protections contained in the Constitution are absolutely essential rather than clichés written by lawyers with base motives or who lack common sense.

In a minute I am going to ask you how many of you think my client is probably guilty.

Some of you may be afraid that you will give the wrong answer. At this point, some of you may be thinking that he represents the defendant. He does not want to hear that many of us think the defendant is guilty. I know people are supposed to be innocent until they are proven guilty. Even though I think it's likely that the defendant is guilty, I probably better not raise my hand. Is there anyone here who was *not* having those kind of thoughts?

Let me tell you now, it is OK to tell me if you think the defendant is guilty. It is a natural reaction. When we see people led away in handcuffs on the news, our first thought is not "I bet that person is innocent."

The only wrong answer you can give is an answer that is not true. Even white lies are not allowed in court. Now something you say may mean that you are not the right person to be on this jury. That does not mean that you gave a bad answer. It probably means you gave a good, that is a truthful, answer.

When you hear about some celebrity being arrested for drunk driving, is there anyone here whose first thought is "I bet that person is innocent"?

With all this in mind, how many of you think the defendant is probably guilty. [make record of numbers—question carefully anyone who claims **not** to think the defendant is guilty—they are probably lying or do not understand]

[Comment—Hopefully you will get a lot of hands. Showing that the jury is overwhelmingly pro conviction should help with a judge that wants to cut off *voir dire*.]

How many of you think the defendant is entitled to a fair trial?

You see the problem? Just because a police officer has arrested someone, we think they are guilty. How can someone get a fair trial when we start out thinking that way?

This is a difficult problem. We think the defendant is guilty and we think he is entitled to a fair trial. How can anyone ever get a fair trial if the jury starts out thinking he is guilty?

The founding fathers were pretty smart people. Here is the answer they came up with to solve this problem.

Juries must start out biased in favor of the defendant; they have to treat the defendant as innocent unless he is proven guilty.

Juries cannot assume guilt in any way. The government has the burden to prove its case.

The proof must be so strong that a reasonable person cannot doubt it?

The defendant does not have to testify.

Some of you may think this sounds too technical. You may think, I am just going to use my common sense rather than follow these legal technicalities. Think about what this means. Common sense tells us that the defendant is guilty from the start. Think of the celebrity being led away in handcuffs. If you just go with common sense assumptions and do not require proof you are really just saying that I am going to just assume the defendant is guilty rather than following the law. We all agreed that this is not fair.

I tell you what; we will come back to these things.

When prosecutors tell jurors to use their common sense, whether they know it or not, they are telling jurors to assume guilt without proof from the fact that the person has been arrested and charged. If the defense tries to get jurors to say that such people are innocent, it may be interpreted as some slick lawyer trying to get them to deny their common sense because the law expects it of them. If the law wants them to deny their common sense, then the law must be wrong as must the lawyer who is trying to get them to do that. We do not want to start the case out that way.

This approach also shows that the defense is not trying to get them to reject their common sense. It shows them that they have to do more than just use their common sense in court. They have to require strong proof.

You are telling them that they will not be embarrassed if they do not give the politically correct answer and that in fact they might be embarrassed if they do because the defense attorney knows the difference and will not accept a politically correct answer unchallenged.

By the way, the term "politically correct" did not originate by accident. It is a frame intentionally devised by conservative political theorists to become a sort of shorthand (i.e. frame) for attempts by the hated liberal activists to tell the average person how they are supposed to think.

Notice also that by devising that term, the conservative strategists are in essence saying "reject what the liberals tell you"; however, it is not perceived as such. It is perceived, if at all, as liberation from liberal dogma when it is in reality just dogma of a different kind. I bring such things up not to take political shots, but rather to show how sophisticated, subtle, and intelligent this method and its strategists are. The moral is that if you are thought of by jurors as someone who is trying to get them to be politically correct, you will be disliked and the jury will respond accordingly.

DEALING WITH UNNOTICED EFFECTS OF PROSECUTION *VOIR DIRE.*

The strongest prosecution frame:

We can counteract the prosecution's strongest voir dire frame by using it as a device to show the jury why the presumption of innocence is necessary.

My experience is that, in many ways, the prosecution voir dire is usually rather dull and ineffective at setting frames. Where do you work? Do you know anyone in the courtroom, etc.? If the jurors already come predisposed to vote guilty, the prosecution does not have to be all that effective at voir dire. It is sufficient to just weed out the obvious exceptions to the general predisposition.

There is; however, one very effective frame that prosecutors usually seem to set. How many times have you heard the prosecutor ask the jury if they can be fair both to the defendant and to the state.

What is really going on when the prosecutor asks jurors if they can be fair to both sides? It is not merely hypocritical and self-serving; there is more to it than that.

The prosecution is setting the following frame: I am fair, unbiased and impartial. I will give you just the facts. I am trustworthy. I will not give you just one side of the case like that tricky defense lawyer (who does not even ask you to be fair).

Whether they know it or not, the prosecution is asking the jury to do the exact opposite of being fair. They are asking the jury to give the state an extreme unfair advantage.

The jury starts out thinking that the police do not charge innocent people very often. They are suspicious of defense evidence because the defendant has a motive to lie. If he does not give evidence they are suspicious of that because they think an innocent person would defend himself. The state also has more resources than the defendant. It can double team him with police officers and prosecutors, it can afford to pay its lawyers to go as far as it takes and it has access to experts and investigators that many defendants cannot afford. The state starts out with an extreme advantage. If you treat both parties the same in this situation, it is like hiring an impartial and fair referee to oversee a game between a little league team and the World Series champions. This is not fair. It is the opposite of fair.

By asking the jury to be fair, the prosecutor is also trying to sit up there on the bench with the judge. This is so because the judge has normally already asked the jury if it can be fair. The judge is usually perceived as having no interest in the outcome and therefore as unbiased and trustworthy. The judge may also be the ultimate strict father. This would have great weight for those of that background (unless the judge gives signs of being one of those hated, and largely nonexistent, liberal activist judges that have been intentionally framed as such for the last forty years or so).

As defense attorneys, we know that generally prosecutors do not want fairness, they want to win, but it puts us in a difficult position. While we may think the prosecution is being hypocritical, nobody would believe us. How can you object to the prosecutor asking the jury to be fair anyhow. Even if you did, it would be worse, to go crying to the judge and let him take the default position of sustaining the prosecutor.

Here is the problem. One meaning of the concept of fairness involves equality. Equality is a part of fairness from a common sense standpoint. If you do not treat two people the same, you are being unfair to one of them. *If you allow this meaning of fairness to stand, you destroy innocent until proven guilty, burden of proof, and proof beyond a reasonable doubt.*

Notice how this works. *The prosecution's request is ostensibly proper and something that every objective person should agree with. At the same time that request very effectively motivates the jury to do the exact opposite of its ostensible meaning. It does so in such a way that even very smart people do not consciously realize it.* Well-crafted advertisements and political commercials frequently do this. In the wrong hands, framing can be (and has been) quite Orwellian and Machiavellian.

I have tried in this writing to avoid such tendencies. My goal is only to try to restore what the law already requires. Theoretically to do otherwise might be unethical; however, few would understand how or why. The politician's ploy of plausible deniability would almost always be present in any ethics inquiry. For example, would a prosecutor ever be disciplined for asking the jury to be fair even if he understood what he was doing and the opposite was his true intention? Furthermore, if we can actually get the fact finders to just do what the law already requires, this should be more than sufficient.

HOW TO OVERCOME THE STRONGEST PROSECUTION FRAMES:

Keeping "the presumption of innocence" from being a meaningless platitude that jurors give lip service to and then ignore.

To deal with the prosecution frame of being fair to both sides, you have to show the jury that treating both sides equally is not fair. The defense starts out at an extreme disadvantage. Treating both sides equally in a drunk driving case is like matching the world heavyweight champion against a twelve year old. Even if the referee very scrupulously treats the heavyweight and the twelve year old the same, it is not a fair fight. By exposing this problem you may also show the jury that what the prosecutor was asking them to do was unfair. First, make it clear what the prosecutor's request implies.

Ladies and gentlemen, earlier you told the prosecutor that you would be fair to both sides. Did you mean by that that you would treat both sides equally and not prefer one side to the other? [Maybe make a record of hands?]

When we see someone on the news being led away in handcuffs or hear of the latest celebrity being arrested of drunk driving, we do not think: There goes an innocent person. *Common sense* tells us that the person is probably guilty. We think that most people arrested for drunk driving are probably guilty. Does anyone disagree? [Make a record of hands in case judge wants to cut off the following questions (statements)]

Matching the defendant against the government is not a fair fight from the start.

The state can afford to pay lawyers to fight as long as it takes. They can make sure their lawyers are well trained.

If they need an investigator to help prepare the case or to testify, they can afford it.

If they need to consult or call an expert, they have the money.

They can afford tests and machines that the defendant does not have access to.

They can double team the defendant with police officers if they want to. They can put two police officers on the case so that it is two against one in terms of the prosecution testimony versus the defense.

They can double team the defendant with lawyers if they want.

They can afford to go to the legislature to lobby and have the law changed in their favor.

Who is stronger here, the defendant or the State. Is it even a close contest? Does anyone think this is a fair fight?

Damon Runyon once said: "The race may not always be to the swift nor the battle to the strong, but that's the way to bet."

Maybe if Bill Gates was on trial, he could afford to even up some of these advantages and make things more of a fair fight. My client is not Bill Gates.

Here is something that is interesting though. Even Bill Gates, with all his money and connections would have a disadvantage fighting the government in this situation. It would be a disadvantage that money cannot cure.

From the minute someone is charged with a crime, *common sense* tells us that that person has a motive to lie. If the person says something that that makes them sound not guilty, we are suspicious that he is making it up to get off. Even Bill Gates would have this problem. Does anyone disagree?

So we all agree that someone who has been charged with a crime has a motive to lie. On the other hand, the police officer that arrested the person normally does not have a motive to lie. Does anyone disagree with that statement?

So if the defendant denies his guilt or tries to explain, we are going to be suspicious of him but not suspicious of the officer who testifies against him. Does anyone disagree with that statement?

So we start out thinking the defendant is guilty and we do not believe him when he says he is not. The question I have is how can anyone receive a fair trial when we start out thinking that way? Does anyone have any ideas?

Now in our everyday lives, we think that if we were accused of something we did not do, we would just explain and people would believe us because we are honest people. How many of you think this?

What if you had to explain this to strangers who do not know you and do not know you are an honest person?

Do you think the strangers would be suspicious of you because you would have a motive to lie?

Even if you brought in your friends to tell the jury that you are an honest person, they will be suspicious of your friends because they will think that they may be shading their testimony to help a friend. Even if you are honest, do you think a group of strangers will believe it?

So the government double-teams you with police. They double-team you with lawyers. They place you in a situation where most people think you are guilty from the start. They put you in a position where people are suspicious of anything you say or do and anything your friends and acquaintances say or do. They have almost unlimited funds and resources to prosecute you but you have limited funds. Then you are expected to show that you are innocent. Even Bill Gates would have most of these problems. Jesus himself did not do well when he was put on trial. Ladies and gentlemen, my client does not have the resources of Bill Gates. He is not Jesus. What hope is there for him to get a fair trial? Does anyone see a way?

Now my client does the best he can, but he is just not in the same league as the State of Ohio. Matching the defendant against the State is truly David vs. Goliath, but without the sling shot. It is a heavyweight in a boxing match against a twelve year old. This is not a fair fight. The government starts out with almost overwhelming advantages. Treating both sides the same is no more fair than treating the heavyweight and the twelve year old the same. Does anyone disagree?

If you go back and just ask yourselves which side do I think is correct, that is not a fair question. The deck is stacked against the defendant from the start. To get your vote, you are asking the twelve year old to prevail against the heavyweight. So what should you do?

Smarter people than I have realized that treating the government the same as the defendant does not result in a fair fight. Experience has taught us over the years that if you do not build some protections into the system, you are going to end up convicting innocent people. To protect against this, some safeguards have been built into the law.

The government has given David a slingshot. It still may not be a fair fight, but it is better than before.

You all know one solution the law has come up with. The defendant is innocent until proven guilty. It is only fair to make it harder for the prosecution to prove its case. Treating both sides equally in a mismatched contest is not fair. The law says you have to start out biased in favor of the defendant. You are not allowed to treat both sides equally. You have to start out on the defendant's side and you cannot change unless you are given the strongest proof known to the law.

What do you think about this?

Does anyone think that this is unfair to the prosecution?

How many of you are willing to take back your answer to the prosecutor? Are you now willing to tell the prosecutor that you will not treat both sides equally? Will you tell him that you will start out on the defendant's side and that you will not change your mind unless you are given the strongest proof known to the law?

If you had to vote right now, how many would vote guilty, how many not guilty. How many feel they couldn't vote because they need more information.

Needing more information is another way of saying that the case has not been proven. If you start out on the defendant's side and you do not have any proof at all, has the defendant been proven guilty beyond a reasonable doubt?

If you start out on the defendant's side and you have some proof but you would like more, has the defendant been proven guilty beyond a reasonable doubt?

What should you do where there is a lack of proof?

How many of you think you should not reach any decision if you need more information?

How many of you think it would be unfair to the prosecution to vote not guilty or even to reach any decision if you need more information?

How you can inadvertently insult the jury:

The prosecution asks jurors if they will use their common sense. By contrast, the defense tries to get jurors to say they believe the defendant is innocent. The defense has essentially come to the fight pre-framed as the bad side. You are essentially insulting the juror's intelligence if you try to get them to say your client is innocent.

How stupid does he think I am if he wants me to think his client is innocent? The police do not arrest a lot of innocent people. The jurors end up thinking either that you are stupid (and they figure lawyers probably are not) or that you think they are. This, in turn, is perceived as a tacit insult. They know how to get back at people who insult them. They can show you who is smarter.

By explaining why the presumption of innocence is necessary, hopefully you can get jurors to see that it is not a lawyer trick or insult but rather an absolute necessity if there is to be a fair trial.

KEEPING "BEYOND A REASONABLE DOUBT" FROM BEING A MEANINGLESS PLATITUDE THAT JURORS GIVE LIP SERVICE TO AND THEN IGNORE.

The *government has to **rule out** every reasonable doub*t in this case. You all have heard this before. This is another idea the law has come up with to help the defendant have a fighting chance. The government is required to produce proof so strong that no reasonable person can doubt it. It is not just a question of which side do you think is right. The question is: is there even one doubt about the government's case? If so, is that doubt reasonable. If there is a reasonable doubt raised about some issue, the defendant does not have to prove it is true; the government has to prove it is not true.

Comment: the "rule out" frame fits nicely with the scientific concept that you cannot prove a negative. You want the jury going back asking if the prosecution *ruled out* whether the defendant was weaving because he was falling asleep, not whether they believe the defense's excuse that sleep caused the defendant to weave. The "ruled out" frame reinforces the burden of proof legal requirement.

Notice also how you are giving them your frame and telling them they have heard it before. This way your frame does not depend upon your credibility but rather upon common knowledge that is unlikely to be questioned. They may not, of course, have heard the "rule out" frame in the context of reasonable doubt before, but the distinction will probably be missed. Such a tactic might verge on the Orwellian or Machiavellian if it were not also true and an accurate reflection of the law.

Let me give you an example. How many people here either have bought a house or plan to buy a house some day?

The judge will tell you later that you are supposed to exercise the same degree of caution in this case that you would exercise in your most important affairs.

How many of you think what you do here should be treated at least as seriously as buying a house.

Suppose you are buying a house. You hire an independent inspector to go through the house with you. The inspector sees a bug that sort of looks like a termite. He is not sure because he is not an exterminator but he is suspicious. He recommends that you have an exterminator and a structural engineer to look at the house. Neither you nor the inspector can prove that there is a termite problem at this point but you are worried because termites can cause very expensive damage to houses. The inspector shows the bug to the realtor and he says it is a flying ant and steps on it quickly. Is that good enough for you or would you have wanted an exterminator or an entomologist to look at the bug. Do you make them have the house inspected for termites, or do you take the realtor's word for it. Do you have to prove that the bug they squashed was a termite or do they have to prove to you that the house is free of termites? What do you think Mrs. X. Does anyone disagree? [Again apologies to Felipe Plascencia.]

Suppose the realtor lists a number of factors supporting their side:
*   The house is in a good neighborhood.
*   It is painted a nice color.
*   There are the right numbers of rooms.
*   It has a nice lawn.
*   The carpet is new.
*   The furnace is new.
*   The price is good.
*   It is in a convenient location to your work.

The realtor says all these good things cannot just be a coincidence; this must be a good house to buy. The realtor says you cannot prove that there is even one termite in this house. The realtor says the seller cannot wait any longer for a decision, you have to decide based on the information you have now. What do you do? Do you buy the house?

In this case you are the buyer; the police officer is the seller; the prosecutor is the realtor; and I am the inspector. The question is: do you make us prove that there is a problem with the case or do you make the prosecution rule out every potential problem? What do you think Mr. X? Do you have to prove that there are termites or do they have to *rule it out*?

Comment: Upon first hearing this example, most lawyers smile in a sort of embarrassed manner about the perceived slickness of taking the defendant out of the picture and putting the state in the position of the seller. If you really think about it though, this shows how brainwashed we are. The state *does* have the burden and the jury *is* supposed to be skeptical. The state's case *is* on trial. The defendant is allowed to be out of the picture. That is what not having to testify means. This is a fair analogy. We have to stop thinking about the case as the defendant being on trial and start thinking of it as the state's case being on trial. That is the way it is supposed to be. We have to think this way and we have to figure out how to get juries, and maybe someday even judges, to think this way.

MAKING IT HARD TO PROVE ALCOHOL
CAUSED THE BAD DRIVING.

A closing technique to reinforce the "rule it out" frame set on voir dire:

Ladies and gentlemen, the judge is going to tell you that alcohol has to be the cause of the bad driving rather than something else. How do you tell this? You list the possible causes and then you determine if the government has ruled them all out except for alcohol. If there are some causes other than alcohol that have not been ruled out, then they have not proven that alcohol was the cause. They have to rule everything else out.

For example, weaving could be caused by alcohol, but it also could be caused by play in the steering wheel. It would be a simple matter for the officer to rule this out. He could have simply just jiggled the wheel back and forth a bit to see if there is any play in it. He could have asked the defendant if there were any mechanical problems with the car. The question you have to ask yourselves is: *did the government rule out causes other than alcohol or are they just asking you to make assumptions without proof?*

The weaving also could have been caused by a lack of sleep. The defendant could have been drifting off to sleep when the officer saw him. How could the officer rule out sleep as a possible cause? He could have done a very simple investigation. He could have asked the defendant how much sleep he got the night before. He could have asked how many hours he had been up straight. He could have just asked if he was tired when he was driving. It was late at night. These would be obvious questions to ask for anyone who did not have his mind made up from the start. The officer did not ask any of these questions. Again, the question you have to ask yourselves is *did the government rule out causes other than alcohol or are they just asking you to make assumptions without proof?*

Now you might think at this point: if the defendant was sleepy, he should have got up on the witness stand and told us so. This gets back to what we were talking about earlier. If he did this, you would be suspicious of him because he has a motive to lie. You might not believe him. It is very hard to prove something like that when the deck is stacked against you. If instead we just question the other side's proof, at least nobody is going to accuse us of lying. That is why the government is required to rule out sleep as a factor. The question is not what could the defendant have proven but rather did the government rule out all reasonable doubt?

Here is another thing you might want to consider. If someone is under the influence, they are not under the influence one minute and sober five minutes later. Therefore if alcohol is affecting the performance of one task, it should also affect performance of all tasks of similar or greater difficulty.

On the other hand, someone can be drifting off to sleep one minute and be much more alert five minutes later when he has been stopped by the police. If alcohol caused the defendant to weave, why didn't it cause him to park crooked? Why didn't it cause him to fumble with his wallet when he was getting his driver's license out? Why didn't it cause him to walk abnormally when he got out of the cruiser? Drifting off to sleep and then being jolted awake could account for the change in behavior. Alcohol cannot. The officer told you that the defendant's alcohol level could not change that quickly. Not only have they failed to rule sleep out as a cause, their own witness makes a pretty good case for sleep rather than alcohol being the cause.

Comment:

If you do not give the jury a method to determine if alcohol affected the driving, the thought process will probably be something like this: Alcohol can cause a driver to weave. The defendant clearly consumed alcohol. It must have had some effect. The defendant didn't convince us that sleep was the cause of the weaving. It looks like he is guilty. The "rule it out" frame gets the jury to consider the issue in terms of reasonable doubt rather than in terms of what probably happened or what was proven (i.e. a preponderance standard). Showing facts inconsistent with intoxication shows evidence that has not been ruled out. How you frame the issue determines the level of difficulty involved in winning the point. You probably will not convince them that sleep was the cause, but you may convince them that the government did not rule it out.

FRAMING SO YOU CAN WIN WITH ONLY ONE JUROR ON YOUR SIDE:

[Credit here should go to Tim Huey who relayed this technique to me.]

Mr. Juror, can two people have an honest disagreement or do you believe that if two people disagree about something one of them must be being unreasonable?

Reasonable people can disagree. Does anyone here think that statement is untrue?

Ladies and gentlemen: When you go back and begin your deliberations, you may find that there is a disagreement among you about which way to vote. You may think at this point that it is your job to decide whose opinion is right and whose is wrong.

If you do this, you are asking the wrong question. The question you need to ask is this: Is there an honest disagreement or are the people who want to vote "not guilty" being unreasonable. If you think the people who want to vote not guilty are being reasonable, then even though you disagree with their opinion, there is reasonable doubt in the case. Does everyone understand this?

Can all of you agree to vote not guilty in such a case even if you think your fellow juror is wrong and you have the opposite opinion?

Will each of you promise to consider carefully whether anyone who wants to vote not guilty is being unreasonable rather than just considering whether or not you agree with them?

Will you promise not to vote guilty unless you can honestly tell the other juror to his or her face that you think he is an unreasonable person?

"Proof beyond a reasonable doubt is proof of such character that **an ordinary person** would be willing to rely and act upon it in the most important of his own affairs."

The law says the standard is the "ordinary person." It does not even have to be one of your fellow jurors. If you think your wife, your minister, your sister-in-law, or someone else you know would have reasonable doubts about the defendant's guilt and you think they are reasonable people, you have to vote not guilty.

The question is not do you think the defendant is guilty or even does the majority think the defendant is guilty. The question you have to decide is could a reasonable person doubt that the defendant is guilty. Can you all agree to decide the case this way?

Mr. X, let's say you go back and everyone but Mrs. Y thinks the defendant is guilty. You disagree with Mrs. Y, but it is an honest disagreement. You do not think she is being unreasonable. Would you be willing to stand up for Mrs. Y and remind everyone else on the jury that they have to vote not guilty even if they disagree with Mrs. Y unless they think she is being unreasonable?

The framing involved:

This technique should not be reserved for cases where it is thought the jury might be hung. It should be used every single time. This series of questions is a good example of how getting a juror to accept your frame is what usually decides the case. My theory is that if we use frames the right way, the prosecutors and judges will not even realize what we are doing (the Democrats have not understood how the Republicans have been using framing against them for 30 years).

Prosecution Frame: Our job is to decide who is right, the majority of us who favor conviction or those few holdouts who favor innocence. If the jurors think this way, a hung jury is the best you can hope for. We have been taught from a young age that the majority is right and the majority controls. We do not want the jury going back and arguing about whether the majority should control. If that is the frame that is going to be used, we know what the answer is going to be (unless you have an unusually strong defense case).

Defense Frame: Our job is to decide if there is just an honest disagreement or if the people who favor acquittal are being unreasonable. This frame can turn a hung jury into a defense jury or maybe even 11 to 1 pro-prosecution into a not guilty verdict.

The case is probably going to be decided by which of these two frames the jury uses. Using the right frame shifts the focus from the issue of who is right, the majority favoring conviction or the few holdouts; to the issue of, are the people who disagree with me unreasonable people. That is where the focus should be under the law and it is easier to win on that issue.

It is unlikely that we will change the juror's minds about the truth of the prosecution frame (majority rules). Trying to persuade people that their frame is wrong is the mistake we usually make. That is very hard and it usually does not work. Instead we have to change the issue (frame) to one we can win. They can still think that they are right about the prosecution frame. They can still think the majority is right, but yet still vote not guilty.

Note that the concepts of "common sense" and "this is a simple case" tells jurors that the job is to figure out who is right and go with the what the majority wants. That is why I say that common sense and simplicity are the enemies of proof beyond a reasonable doubt.

There is also the side benefit that framing the issue this way essentially puts pro prosecution jurors in the position of having to assert that their fellow juror or jurors are unreasonable and to argue this to their face before the other jurors. This may in turn cause resentment in the holdouts. In response they may dig in their heels and hang the jury rather than yield to the peer pressure to go along with the majority.

I think I would use these questions on voir dire and reinforce them in closing. Repetition is one factor in getting your frames adopted. Getting your frame out there first before the other side's frame is adopted is probably the most important factor. Thus you do it on *voir dire*. If you are good and/or lucky, by doing this you can get the other side to use your frames. The Republicans have been successful at getting Democrats to use their frames for years. For example, Democrats frequently will unwittingly use the words "climate change" instead of "global warming."

USING VENUE AS A STEALTH WEAPON TO ATTACK THE TEST AND TO ILLUSTRATE THE PROOF REQUIREMENT.

At the end of the case, the judge is going to tell you that the prosecution has to prove that if there was a crime, it happened in the City of Columbus. Suppose the prosecution just forgets to prove this. Can you just use your common sense and assume that since a Columbus police officer testified, it must have happened in Columbus?

If yes, how is this different than assuming that because he was arrested, the defendant is probably guilty?

Is it because you think the location is a really safe assumption?

What if a fellow juror thinks that assuming the defendant is guilty because he was arrested is a really safe assumption?

Could you just assume that if the driving did not happen in Columbus, the defendant would have shown this?

Suppose you thought the defendant was dangerously drunk. I stand up at the end of the case and say only two sentences. The state did not prove an offense occurred in Columbus. I ask you to vote not guilty. Could you vote not guilty?

Is there anything wrong with this? [burden of proof]

What if you think I know the judge said there has to be proof, but I cannot see any harm in assuming this happened in Columbus, and I am going to just use my common sense and vote guilty. Anyone disagree with that statement?

What if I could show you a way, would you agree to require proof of every single thing?

Suppose the defendant was slightly outside the Columbus City limits and was actually in Gahanna but the officer did not know it. Suppose also that Gahanna as well as Columbus has charged him with drunk driving. The judge says this case is about what happened in Columbus and he is not going to let any evidence in about Gahanna. If you ignore the location requirement, he could be punished twice for the same thing. This would not be fair. Did anyone think of this when they thought it was too technical to require proof of location?

In Ohio, prosecutors never prove the testing instrument is accurate; people just assume this. While we cannot attack testing machines in general, we can attack the particular machine for accuracy.

Suppose you breathe into a breath machine and it says you have had too much to drink. You know that you have not had too much to drink. Who do you think people will believe, you or the machine?

Does anyone think that people will believe you over the machine?

Machines make mistakes. Even machines designed by rocket scientists malfunction. Does anyone disagree with this?

What protection does a person have from a charge based upon a mistaken machine?

Should the government have to prove the machine is accurate? [Who disagrees?]

Can't you just assume the machine is accurate?

How is this different than just assuming the offense occurred in the City of Columbus?

How many of you think that it should be up to the defendant to prove that the machine is wrong?

How would we do that? Do you think the government is going to turn their machine over to us and let us do experiments with it to see if it is working properly?

The government has an advantage. The government had an agent there representing its interests. The defendant did not have anyone there that night to check the testing process and make sure that it was fair. The moment is past. It is **too late to double check the defendant's result.** The government can afford to spend a lot of money on alcohol testing. We cannot. How can we overcome all the advantages that the government has?

How can the defendant get a fair trial when the government has all these advantages?

When the government has all the advantages, is it fair to make the defendant prove the machine was wrong?

[*In closing you could argue:*] Ladies and gentlemen, they have had this machine since 1992 and they have not checked it once to see if it can tell the difference between air from the lungs and air from the stomach. They checked other things on the machine, but this is like blowing the horn to see if the tires are ok. They have not proven this machine is accurate and you cannot assume this without proof. We cannot assume that the operation occurred in the City of Columbus without proof. Likewise we should not assume that a machine that has not been checked at least since 1992 is accurate.

DEALING WITH JURORS WHO WANT TO ENFORCE THEIR
ANTI-DRUNK DRIVING VIEWS RATHER THAN FOLLOW THE LAW.

How many of you think it is wrong to get behind the wheel of a car with any alcohol at all in your system? Scale of 1-5?

Is there anyone who thinks there is nothing wrong with getting behind wheel with alcohol in his or her system?

How many think that if the defendant drove after drinking, he did something wrong and he deserves to be convicted and punished? Scale of 1-5?

What if the judge tells you that it is not illegal to drink and drive and that it does not matter how much alcohol you had as long as it does not affect your driving. Would anyone have a problem following that law?

What if you are back in the jury room and someone says, I do not care if there was any proof that alcohol affected the defendant's driving, he had no business getting behind the wheel of the car with alcohol in his system and I am voting guilty. The question I have for you is: would you be willing to tell the judge that one of your fellow jurors is refusing to follow the law?

By the way, you do not need to have anyone's permission to write a note to the judge. You do not even have to tell anyone. You just slip a note to the bailiff and she will get it to the judge. Juror X, would you be willing to tell the judge if one of your fellow jurors refuses to follow the law?

Suppose you get back to the jury room and it becomes clear to you that under the law the defendant is technically not guilty but you think the defendant deserves to be convicted. What would you do? Let me give you an example. Suppose you are convinced that the defendant drove under the influence. You think it is not right for him to escape punishment. Suppose you are also convinced that the government failed to prove that this happened in the City of Columbus. Would you vote to convict him anyway, or would you vote not guilty on a technicality?

What do you think about writing the judge a note yourself and telling him that morally you do not think you can follow the law. This would seem to be a better choice than violating your oath and your promise to follow the law. Would you be willing to do this rather than imposing your personal moral views in place of the law?

Frames at work:

Frame: As long as I do what is right, it does not matter if I follow the law. Doing the right thing is more important. They cannot do anything to me if I decide to follow my conscience. Opposing frame. It is wrong to swear falsely under oath and to break a promise. I could be doing something wrong by violating the law. I also might get caught. Somebody might write a note to the judge. This would be embarrassing and I might get in trouble with the judge. Not following the law could have consequences.

DEALING WITH THE COMMON SENSE BELIEF THAT
A DEFENDANT WHO DOES NOT TESTIFY IS GUILTY.

Earlier we talked about the fact that we are suspicious of the defendant from the moment charges are filed because that gives him a motive to lie. We also noted that the prosecution does not have the same problem.

So we start out believing the officer and not believing the defendant. We have these beliefs even though there has been no proof.

If you are going to be suspicious of anything the defendant says because he has a motive to lie, do you blame him for not saying anything?

If a jury is usually not going to believe a defendant over a police officer, maybe it makes sense to not try to fight on those terms. As a practical matter, making the defendant's case through the officer's statements is the only realistic way to approach these cases.

This is a very difficult situation to be in. We are suspicious of anything he says if he testifies. If he disagrees with the officer, you will probably think he is lying. If he does not testify we think he must be hiding something and is therefore guilty. Both choices are bad. Just by being charged, he has been put in a position where either decision he makes is going to be viewed negatively. Is it fair to place someone in this position?

Can you blame him for deciding that if he decides to rely just on pointing out flaws with the government's case? That way at least nobody can accuse him of lying. What do you think Mr. X.?

Whichever way he decides you are going to be suspicious of him. Does anyone disagree?

Suppose you are back in the jury room and one of your fellow jurors says that if the defendant is innocent he would have testified. What would you do?

Would you be willing to remind him that legally that does not matter and that he cannot decide the case based on that?

Suppose he says he does not care about such technicalities and he is voting guilty because an innocent person would have taken the stand. Would you be willing to write a note to the judge and tell him that one of the jurors is refusing to follow the law?

MAKING REFUSAL A SIGN OF SOBRIETY RATHER THAN OF GUILT.

The point of framing is that how you frame the question determines the answer. You should have a pretty good idea whether you have framed things properly because the answer you want should be the obvious conclusion from the frame you choose.

If you ask jurors how many of them believe that people refuse to take the test because they are guilty, they will generally agree. Some cannot think of any other reason why someone would refuse the test. You are not going to change their minds about this. Just by using the words, you reinforce the prosecutor's frame. You do not, however, want them going back to the jury room discussing the question of whether refusing the test means the defendant is guilty.

You might have more success framing the issue this way:

If you need legal advice, is it better to get that advice from a lawyer or from a police officer?

Suppose you are trying to decide whether to take a breath test. You have heard one thing from lawyers in the past but now the police officer is trying to tell you something different. Is it a sign of intoxication if you decide to take the lawyer's advice over that of a police officer?

If you think a police officer has misread the situation and accused you of things you did not do, would that make you question the officer's judgment and advice?

Is it a sign of intoxication to reject the advice of an officer who seems to be using bad judgment?

You set this frame in voir dire and try to repeat it on cross and closing. That way hopefully they are discussing the question of whether taking a lawyer's advice over that of a police officer means makes sense rather than discussing whether refusing means you are intoxicated.

AVOIDING A STRICT FATHER FOREMAN

Earlier the strict father/nurturant parent dichotomy was downplayed as not being as important in court as it is in politics. The rationale was that it is likely that both groups start out biased against DUI defendants. As such, eliminating those believing in strict father morality is not the formula for success. Even if it were, doing so is probably a practical impossibility since there are likely more believers in strict father morality than there are preemptory challenges.

The strict father/nurturant parent dichotomy is important in jury dynamics. The defense does not want a strict father as the foreperson of the jury. Strict fathers are most aligned with the prosecution. They believe the leader decides what is right and it is the job of everyone else to fall in line and support the leader. There is less tolerance for discussion, dissent and minority positions.

One of the major strategies discussed earlier was that of persuading one juror that there is a reasonable doubt and then getting the other jurors to agree that they would vote not guilty despite their personal views as long as they believed the dissident juror was a reasonable person. To achieve this goal, there needs to be an atmosphere in the jury room that favors free discussion and dissent. This is less likely to happen with a strict father foreperson in control.

Picture the strict father on his first day back to work after jury duty:

Coworker: How did it go on jury duty?

Foreman: Real good! I was on a DUI jury. I was the foreman.

Coworker: Did you convict him:

Foreman: We sure did. I ran a tight ship. I wasn't going to let any slick-talking lawyer pull the wool over my jury's eyes like they did in that OJ case. We got a guilty verdict in just under an hour. There were a few bleeding hearts on the jury but they were weak and our side won. We showed them how stupid it was to waste everyone's time discussing their irrational liberal views just to turn loose some dangerous drunk driver so he can go out and do it again.

This is not who you want setting the tone of discussion on your jury. Professor Sunwolf (see references below) has some excellent techniques for avoiding this scenario and they are well worth study. While her book does not discuss jury dynamics in terms of the strict father/nurturant parent dichotomy, it is readily apparent which techniques to use to foster open discussion and tolerance of dissent.

Even though nurturant types are also predisposed against DUI defendants, that does not mean that they want to deny their fellow jurors an equal voice in deliberations. They are also less likely to ridicule people with views different than their own.

Those with a strict father upbringing are more likely to want to be in charge. Hence, they are more likely to nominate themselves for foreperson. Nurturant types are often less inclined towards conflict and less likely to oppose them. Voir dire questions suggested by Dr. Sunwolf which might be appropriate in this regard are as follows:

"[I]s it possible that the best possible leader for a jury might be someone who would never volunteer for the job?" *Supra*, 179.

"[H]ow would you go about making sure a leader helped the group, without also hurting the group by dominating? " *Supra*, 184.

"What are your feelings about a result that says we don't all feel the same? " *Supra*, 189.

"What are your thoughts about how the jury should treat those who disagree with the majority?" *Supra*, 190.

"What is your opinion about what sort of tactics are improper when trying to get others to change their votes? " *Supra*, 190.

"What are your thoughts about how jurors should react when one juror is openly showing anger or disgust for another juror? Can that poison the process? What would you do? " *Supra*, 190.

Defense counsel might pick a nurturant type and nominate her for foreperson: Ms. Juror, suppose your fellow jurors think you have an understanding and tolerant personality and because of that, they choose you as foreperson. If you are chosen, could you be fair to everyone and make sure that all voices are heard. If women predominate, maybe ask how many think the jury foreperson should be a man.

As Racehorse Haynes says, if they don't pick her as foreperson after that, who is she going to be mad at, them or you? If you do find someone who is an obvious strict father choice for foreman, you might try making him promise to listen to all and not cut anyone off and to not ridicule anyone for their opinion. Then follow this up with a suggestion to jurors that they write a note to the judge if this doesn't happen. The implication is that bullying has consequences.

DEALING WITH JUDGES WHO MAKE BIASED JURORS SAY THEY CAN BE FAIR

A while ago you told the judge that you could set aside your belief that it is wrong to drive if you have had anything at all to drink. I want to ask you some questions about that. Do you understand?

When you said you could set the belief aside, did you mean that you could put the belief out of your head, that you could not think of it?

Mr. Y, for the next few minutes, I don't want you to think of an elephant. Can you do that, can you go the next few minutes without thinking of an elephant?

Now you know what I mean by elephant. I mean the animals with the long grey trunk, big heavy legs, big floppy ears, and a short tail. Most of us saw them at the zoo as children.

I bet you haven't been able to keep the idea of an elephant out of your head since I mentioned the word. Am I correct?

Suppose you have an itch somewhere. If the judge tells you to just put that idea out of you head, does the itch go away? Can you keep the idea of an itch from coming into your head?

We often can't control the ideas that come into our heads, true?

Do you want to reconsider your answer to the judge about being able to set aside your belief that it is wrong to drive if you have had anything at all to drink?

Did you mean that you would ignore your common sense and do what the judge said instead?

Now I am going to ask you a question like your mother probably used to ask you. Suppose the judge told you to jump off the top of this building, would you do it?

So you are going to use a little common sense first before you decide whether you will follow the judge's instructions. Do you agree.

Let's take a less drastic example. Suppose the judge told you that you had to come back here tomorrow with your head shaved. Would you do that?

So your decision to disregard what the judge tells you isn't limited only to life threatening situations.

Would it be fair to say that you are only going to do what the judge tells you to if it make common sense to you?

Do you want to reconsider your answer to the judge about being able to set aside your belief that it is wrong to drive if you have had anything at all to drink?

When you told the judge you could set aside your belief, did you mean that you would ignore your moral beliefs and do what the judge said instead?

Suppose the judge told you that it was your duty to do something that you thought was immoral. Would you do what you thought was right or would you do what the judge said?

Does your common sense/moral belief tell you that it is wrong to drive if you have had anything at all to drink?

Ms. Juror, suppose you get back in the jury room. You thought you could ignore your belief that it is wrong to have anything to drink and drive. You thought you could do what the judge wanted you to do. The more you think about it, however, you have to admit to yourself, that this belief is too strong to ignore. Would you be willing to write a note to the judge and tell her that you can't be fair in this case?

Comment: If the judge is paying attention, this last question tells the judge that there may be consequences to making an unfair juror say he will be fair. It may not just be the defendant who suffers as a result of bullying jurors into agreement. The judge may have to go through the whole trial only to have to declare a mistrial and start over again. What is the safe thing for the judge to do? Excuse the juror or let her serve?

If the judge doesn't seem to get it, maybe it would be a good idea to approach her in a side bar *after* the note idea has been planted and suggest that leaving this juror on might be a waste of everyone's time. Judges generally hate retrials more than the "wrong" side winning.

Consider asking the judge to allow questioning of the jurors after instructions. The worst that happens is you get no for an answer. On the other hand, if it is allowed, doubts may be raised about the fitness of the jury to deliberate. "Judge, when you were reading the instructions, I was watching the jurors. Some of them had expressions that would indicate that they did not fully understand what you were telling them. We think due process requires that the jurors be questioned to make sure they did, in fact, understand your instructions."

AREN'T THESE TACTICS WE HAVE USED FOR YEARS?

Yes and no. Many of the techniques described here are not new. It would be a mistake to conclude that therefore one technique is as good as another or that nothing new is being done. The new part is sorting through the techniques we have been using, selecting the ones that set the right frames, rejecting the ones that do not, and devising new ones that set the frames we need. The prosecutor's arguments are not new. We can, however, gain a new understanding of how the brain interprets those arguments and learn effective ways to counteract them.

WHO MADE CLEVE JOHNSON AN EXPERT ON TRIAL PRACTICE?

I do not claim to be Jerry Spence. While I have an undergraduate degree in psychology and philosophy, I also do not claim to be an academic. The underlying ideas set forth here were derived from the references below, especially George Lakoff and Drew Westen. While Karl Rove and the late Lee Atwater used these tactics for years, they have not publically written about their methodology. Thus, there are no references to them below.

What I am trying to do is to extrapolate these techniques and apply them to drunk driving cases. While academics originally discovered this information, it is being successfully used by the rich and powerful. That is probably a good indication that there is something there. I am trying to get the word out that this is available and hopefully find collaborators to help refine these techniques so that we can jointly succeed.

Understanding how this works is hard and I could use some help. The biggest problem in this respect is finding people who get it and understand that there is something here worth pursuing. If you do, please contact me. I am probably wrong about some of my theories about how to apply framing to drunk driving cases. My hope is that together these mistakes can be corrected and even better ways of employing these psychological concepts can be devised.

TECHNICAL NOTE

I have used the term defendant throughout. This was done for the sake of convenience and simplicity. In court the standard humanization technique of using the defendant's name would be employed instead of using the term defendant.

SOURCES/REFERENCES (IN ORDER OF PERCEIVED VALUE TO THE READER)

Lakoff, George. *Don't Think of an Elephant*

Lakoff, George. *Whose Freedom?*

Westen, Drew. *The Political Brain: The Role of Emotion in Deciding the Fate of the Nation*

Lakoff, George. *A Cognitive Scientist Looks at Daubert*

Framing Blog (highly political) http://frameshopisopen.com/

Frank, Thomas. *What's the Matter with Kansas? How Conservatives Won the Heart of America*

Lakoff, George. *Moral Politics How Liberals and Conservatives Think*

W. B. Gallie, *Essentially Contested Concepts*, 56 Proceedings of the Aristotelian Society 167 (1956).

Dr. Sunwolf. *Practical Jury Dynamics* p.113 §6-3(c) Matthew Bender

APPENDIX E:
FRAMING TECHNIQUES

APPENDIX F

IMPORTANT ARTICLES, BOOKS AND OTHER WRITINGS FOR DUI DEFENSE

It is the opinion of this author, that in order to provide quality DUI Defense work, one should read and maintain a strong library. The following is information to which I turn on a regular basis:

- *Absorption, Distribution and Elimination of Alcohol: Highway Safety Aspects*, Kurt Dubowski.

- *Accuracy and Precision of Breath Alcohol Measurements for Subjects in the Absorptive Phase*, G. Simpson.

- *Common Legal Challenges and Responses in Forensic Breath Alcohol Determination*, R. Gulberg.

- *How Breathalyzers Work*, Craig Freudenrich.

- *Measuring Ethanol in Blood and Breath for Legal Purposes: Variability Between Laboratories and Between Breath Test Instruments*, A.W. Jones.

- *Medicolegal Aspects of Alcohol*, James Garriott, Lawyers and Judges Publishing.

- *National Highway Traffic Safety Association Standardized Field Sobriety Test Manuals* (Both Instructor and Student).

In addition, you should acquire and review the operating manual for whatever breath machines are used in your jurisdiction.

(This page intentionally left blank.)

INDEX

INDEX

- AS -

- CR -

- FI -

- PR -

- UR -

V

Vehicle Driven By Arrestee
Police reports, §A:14
Voir Dire. *See also* **Jury Selection**
Bias
exposing, §§2:01, 2:01.2, 2A:25
Bias, showing of, §A:72
District Attorney Manual, §§A:70–A:72
How to collaborate with jury panel
get jurors to agree to be unfair and partial, §2A:22
get jurors to describe good driving, §2A:27
get jurors to doubt breath/blood testing accuracy, §2A:28
get jurors to internalize presumption of innocence, §2A:21
get jurors to internalize proof beyond a reasonable doubt, §2A:23
get jurors to reveal biases, §2A:25
get jurors to reveal themselves, §2A:29
get jurors to understand meaning of beyond a reasonable doubt, §2A:24
get jurors to understand why the defendant is not testifying, §2A:26
How to out-perform the state during
be memorable, §2A:11
enlist client's help, §2A:13
know state's mistakes, §2A:10
listen to your gut, §2A:14
make a mini closing, §2A:12
tell a story, §2A:14
Judicial voir dire, imposition of, §A:70
Prosecution experts, §4:71
Purpose of, §§2:01, 2A
Mini-opening statement, §2:02.2
Opening or voir dire, §5:91
Outline, §§2A:40, 2A:41
Sample voir dire,
drug case jury selection, §9:21
Scope of, §§2:02, A:71
Slides and scorecard
how to use, §2:80
sample slides, §2:81
Staircase metaphor, §2:57
Time limits, §§2:02, 2A:20
Voir Dire Questions. *See also* **Jury Selection**
Alcohol-related, §2:56
Blood analysis, §2:46
Bodily functions, §2:54
Constitutional issues, §2:47
Defendant, relationship to, §2:41
District Attorney Manual, §A:73
Eliciting the key words, §2:01.1

Expert opinion, §2:45
Finding leaders, §2:03
How to use, §2:40
Intoxicated persons' physical characteristics, §2:49
Intoxication-related, §2:53
Law enforcement, relationship to, §2:41
Memory, §2:50
Nervousness, §2:52
Odor of alcohol, §2:51
Offense of DUI, §2:55
Police officers, §2:42
Pre-rehabilitation, §2:04
Punishment-related, §2:43
Sample questions, §§2:41–2:56
Scientific evidence, §2:44
Staircase metaphor, §2:57
Uncovering juror personality types, §2:03
Witnesses, relationship to, §2:41

W

Walk and Turn Test
Demonstration, §8:20
Field test expert, examination of, §5:26
Wavelength and Interference Diagrams
Demonstrative evidence, §8:56
Weight of Arrestee
Police reports, §A:06
Widmark Calculations
District Attorney Manual, §§A:260–A:261
Witnesses and Testimony
Arresting officer. *See* **Arresting Officer**
Client's testimony. *See* **Client's Testimony**
Closing arguments, §7:61
Compulsory process, §1:20
Confrontation Clause, §§4:130–4:132
Cross-examination. *See* **Cross-Examination**
Defense witnesses. *See* **Defendant/Defense Witnesses**
District Attorney Manual
arresting officer. *See* **Arresting Officer**
defendant/defense witnesses, §§A:280–A:287
interviewing witnesses, §§A:40, A:41
prosecution's alcohol expert. *See* **Prosecution Experts**
prosecution witnesses. *See* **Prosecution Witnesses**
Examination of witnesses
arresting officer. *See* **Arresting Officer**
closing argument, tailoring your examination to, §7:34
cross-examination. *See* **Cross-Examination**

(This page intentionally left blank.)